Comparative Politics
Structures and Choices

Second Edition

Lowell Barrington, Marquette University

WADSWORTH
CENGAGE Learning·

Australia • Brazil • Japan • Korea • Mexico • Singapore • Spain • United Kingdom • United States

WADSWORTH
CENGAGE Learning·

Comparative Politics, Second Edition

Lowell Barrington

Senior Publisher: Suzanne Jeans

Executive Editor: Carolyn Merrill

Acquisitions Editor: Anita Devine

Development Editor: Jennifer Jacobson, Ohlinger Publishing Services

Assistant Editor: Laura Ross

Editorial Assistant: Scott Greenan

Marketing Manager: Lydia LeStar

Marketing Program Manager: Caitlin Green

Art Director: Linda May

Manufacturing Planner: Fola Orekoya

Rights Acquisition Specialist: Jennifer Meyer Dare

Production Service: Cenveo Publisher Services

Cover Designer: Rokusek Design

Cover Image: Carlos Castilla/© Shutterstock

Compositor: Cenveo Publisher Services

For product information and technology assistance, contact us at **Cengage Learning Customer & Sales Support, 1-800-354-9706**

For permission to use material from this text or product, submit all requests online at **www.cengage.com/permissions.**

Further permissions questions can be emailed to **permissionrequest@cengage.com**.

Library of Congress Control Number: 2011942386

International Edition:

ISBN-13: 978-1-111-34196-1

ISBN-10: 1-111-34196-6

Cengage Learning International Offices

Asia
www.cengageasia.com
tel: (65) 6410 1200

India
www.cengage.co.in
tel: (91) 11 4364 1111

Australia/New Zealand
www.cengage.com.au
tel: (61) 3 9685 4111

Latin America
www.cengage.com.mx
tel: (52) 55 1500 6000

Brazil
www.cengage.com.br
tel: (55) 11 3665 9900

UK/Europe/Middle East/Africa
www.cengage.co.uk
tel: (44) 0 1264 332 424

Represented in Canada by Nelson Education, Ltd.
www.nelson.com
tel: (416) 752 9100/(800) 668 0671

Cengage Learning is a leading provider of customized learning solutions with office locations around the globe, including Singapore, the United Kingdom, Australia, Mexico, Brazil, and Japan. Locate your local office at: **www.cengage.com/global**

For product information and free companion resources: **www.cengage.com/international** Visit your local office: **www.cengage.com/global**

Printed in the United States of America
1 2 3 4 5 6 7 14 13 12 11

Dedication

This book is for my parents, Byron and Barbara, who
first taught me about the importance of politics. As
I grew up, our evening meal was a time not only for
food but also for discussions about science, economics,
and current events that fueled my desire to better
understand political structures and choices.

Brief Contents

Contents

CHAPTER 3

Ideas as Structure: Political Culture and Ideology   63

Every four years, Americans have the opportunity to go to the polls to select the next president of the United States. The act of choosing the government's most important leader in a free and fair setting is something some Americans take for granted. In other parts of the world, many individuals long for such a chance. In the last decade, large numbers of people have taken to the streets, sometimes with tragic results, to demand the right. For much of 2011, the world watched as protests in the Middle East and North Africa challenged the rule of long-established dictators.

"The Barrington text is a new standard for teaching comparative politics. It combines clear concept conceptualization with outstanding application. It is fundamentally comparative and reinforces the importance of comparative study and new knowledge creation by political scientists."

Jennifer E. Horan, University of North Carolina Wilmington

So much of the world is different from the United States that an introduction to the field of comparative politics is enormously valuable for American students. When students complete an introductory comparative politics course, they should have a better understanding of many of the world's largest and most important countries. The journey toward understanding politics outside the American context should also provide them with a comprehensive introduction to central concepts, important theoretical perspectives, and research methods for studying other parts of the world.

There are two traditional approaches to introductory comparative politics. The first is to spend most of the semester discussing countries, often covering one country a week, and attempting to bring in important broad themes along the way. This often becomes primarily a fact-based exercise, leaving students without a framework to use in comparing countries. The second approach is to spend the first half of the semester on important themes, followed by a study of specific countries. Although providing a conceptual and theoretical framework is important, early in the course students may not see the relevancy of the concepts, and they long for country-specific examples to apply to the concepts and theories being discussed. For professors and students alike, both approaches can be frustrating.

"The Barrington text solves the age-old problem of teaching Comparative Politics. It blends thoughtful teaching of core concepts with specific illustrations from several countries. Students can apply the concepts even as times change but still feel they are leaving the reading with concrete examples."

Jennifer Haydel, Montgomery College

Thematic Material is Linked with Country-Specific Information

The second edition of *Comparative Politics: Structures and Choices* is designed to address the typical shortcomings of introductory comparative politics textbooks by providing students with a framework for understanding major political outcomes and clearly linking thematic material with country-specific information. This framework organizes theories and concepts associated with economic, cultural, identity, and political structures and brings to light the key role that leadership and decision making play in major political outcomes. In each chapter, the presentation of major concepts is immediately followed by an overview of how these topics play out in a set of countries. This "Topic in Countries" or "TIC" section of the chapter, described in detail below, shows students how economic, social, and political structures and individuals' political choices drive political outcomes in some of the world's most important countries. Students are encouraged to consider how existing structures both constrain political decision makers and provide them with opportunities. This portion of the chapter also introduces important comparative politics theories and immediately links them to one of the emphasized countries.

"The integration of theory and country examples is the most fruitful way to teach the general introduction to CP and is a major reason I adopted [the Barrington text]."

Erik Herron, University of Kansas

The central goal of revising the second edition has been to maximize students' ability to process and integrate thematic material and country-specific information. A new approach to the Topic in Countries sections allows students to understand how the various thematic components in each chapter relate to one another before turning to the way those topics play out in the TIC cases. The new Spotlight on . . . boxes incorporate coverage of three additional countries. Likewise, the Countries-at-a-Glance reference, "What to Look for" feature, at the opening of each TIC section, and the TIC Wrap-Ups and Country Summaries at the end of each TIC section reinforce the connection between the book's thematic framework and the information it presents about real-world cases. The new Research in Context feature highlights contemporary comparative politics research and provides an additional link between the theories and concepts presented in the chapters and the way they affect the lives of ordinary citizens.

A comparative politics textbook must reflect the most current political events. The second edition of the book includes a variety of updates, both in the TIC sections and with numerous references to recent events, including those in the Middle East and North Africa. A new author blog, at http://structuresandchoices.blogspot.com, provides timely connections of real-life events to topics covered in the textbook. In addition to the necessary updates to the content, one of the most significant content changes in the second edition is the elimination of what had been Chapter 2 in the first edition and the movement of its content to other chapters. Chapter 1, for example, now includes an introduction of key concepts related to society, the nation, and the state.

Pedagogical Features

Chapter-opening pedagogy. Each chapter opens with a chapter outline, learning objectives, and a dynamic vignette that draws students into the material.

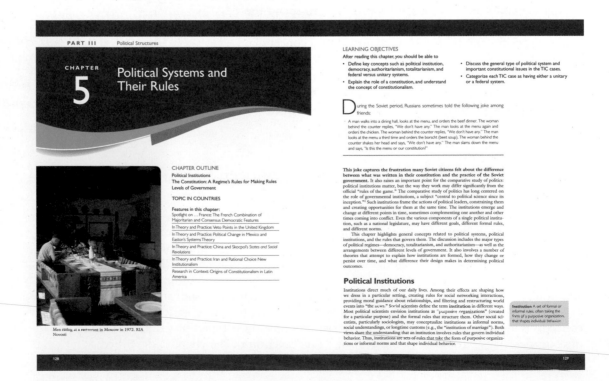

NEW!

Countries-at-a-Glance. This helpful reference, featured in the front of the book, includes the following information for each of the nine Topic in Countries cases and the three Spotlight on . . . countries: a map, basic economic statistics, key cultural themes, identity divisions, regime type, legislatures and executives, unelected components of government, interest groups and social movements, political parties and elections, and leadership.

Marginal Glossary. Terms are carefully defined and placed near where they appear in the text.

Think and Discuss. Ready-made questions for students to consider and discuss are provided in the Think and Discuss boxes.

Did You Know? Brief features give readers interesting facts related to the topic being covered at that point in the book.

"The 'Did You Know?' boxes are nice breaks in the narrative. Students like those."

Jennifer Haydel, Montgomery College

Topic in Countries Sections Show How Structures and Choices Drive Political Outcomes

The Topic in Countries (TIC) sections tie together concepts, theories, and country-specific information seamlessly. An important set of concepts is introduced and then applied to each of nine countries: the United Kingdom, Germany, Mexico, Brazil, Russia, China, India, Nigeria, and Iran. TIC sections appear in all chapters other than Chapter 1 and the epilogue.

"I like the diversity of TIC cases."

David Price, author of the Instructor's Manual, Santa Fe College

The nine TIC cases are among the most important countries in the world for American students to understand. They allow students to see how the major comparative politics concepts and theories play out in different types of countries. The nine countries have different histories of economic development, varying roles for the government in the economy, distinct political cultures, and differing identity-related challenges. They also represent a variety of regime types, from consolidated democracies (the United Kingdom, Germany, and India) and established but not yet consolidated democracies (Mexico, Brazil, and Nigeria) to semi-authoritarian and authoritarian systems (Russia, China, and Iran). They provide examples of different executive and legislative arrangements; contrasting roles for and issues facing the judiciary, bureaucracy, and military; differing approaches to interest groups; diverse

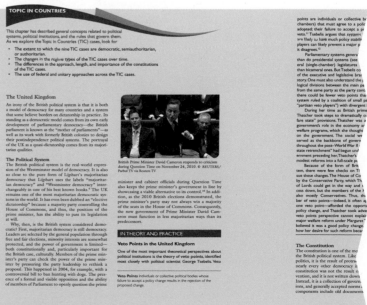

electoral and political party systems; and chief executives with interesting and distinct backgrounds and leadership approaches.

The second edition organizes and refines the TIC sections for greater student learning. Unlike the first edition, it collects the information on each country in the TIC sections in one place. With this change, the second edition maintains the application of concepts and theories to the real-world cases, while facilitating student command of the country-specific information. The restructuring of the TIC sections reduces redundancy of country-specific content. Furthermore, the text is streamlined and is more reader-friendly. In addition, the redesigned layout of the second edition allows the Topic in Countries sections to be clearly distinguished from the thematic portions of the chapters.

France, South Africa, and Iraq Appear Prominently in the Book in Spotlight on ... Boxes

"In Chapter 1, the Spotlight on France helps students understand how various territories can be part of the same state, even though scattered around the world. . . . It is a really well selected and useful example."

Anca Turcu, Iowa State University

Spotlight on ... FRANCE

The Territorial Aspects of the French State

When one thinks of the territory of an internationally recognized state, the image is often a single, continuous body of land. For many of the world's states, however, this image is inaccurate. That is the case with well-known states, such as France. The territory of France can be thought of as three

NEW!

Spotlight on ... Boxes. In addition to the nine countries covered in the TIC sections of each chapter, France, South Africa, and Iraq appear prominently in Spotlight on . . . boxes. These countries are well suited to shorter, more focused linkages to particular key concepts. France is one of the world's best-known democracies. Its important features include its use of semi-presidentialism within a mature democratic system. South Africa provides an excellent example of democratic transition, identity politics issues, and the importance of leadership. It is also a budding economic powerhouse in Africa (South Africa is the S in the BRICS acronym, which represents the world's most important emerging market economies). Iraq is a crucial case of democratic establishment in the MENA (Middle East and North Africa) region. It also provides a key example of the role of external influences on political development.

Each of the Spotlight on . . . countries appears in at least three chapters. These boxes complement the country-specific information in the TIC sections and the use of the United States as a common example in the thematic section of the chapters.

NEW!

What to Look for and TIC Wrap-Up. At the start of each Topic in Countries section, a bulleted introduction has been added to help the reader identify information to look for in the subsequent presentation of country-specific material. Each of the TIC sections concludes with a brief TIC Wrap-Up to highlight themes across the cases.

TOPIC IN COUNTRIES

The Topic in Countries (TIC) cases illustrate the concepts related to economic structure introduced in the preceding sections of this chapter. As you read through the following TIC sections, be sure to look for

- The class structures of the TIC cases, particularly the relative size of the middle class to the working class and lower class.
- The overall level of economic development of each of the TIC cases.
- The role of the state in each country's development process.
- The extent to which the economies of the TIC cases are globalized.
- The evolution of government involvement in the economy in the TIC cases.

TIC Wrap-Up

The class structures, development patterns and levels, roles of government in the economy, exposure to globalization, and political importance of these economic structural features are similar and different across the nine TIC countries (see the Country Summary). The

"I love the 'What to Look for' at the beginning and the 'Wrap-Up' sections at the end—very useful!"

Jody Baumgartner, East Carolina University

NEW!

Country Summary. At the end of each TIC section, a Country Summary table succinctly organizes and provides a review of the TIC information just covered. In addition, these tables include content for France, Iraq, and South Africa to further inform students about the Spotlight on . . . countries. The Country Summary tables provide an additional way for students to organize the country-specific information, using the range of structural and choice categories introduced in the book.

COUNTRY SUMMARY

TIC Country	Judiciary	Bureaucracy	Military
United Kingdom	Common law approach; parliamentary supremacy concept limits judicial power; new UK Supreme Court in place since 2009	Decrease in size but increase in autonomy under Thatcher; importance of permanent secretary position; ITAP feature on bureaucratic autonomy theory	One of the world's most powerful militaries; strong civilian control; military is professionalized and has an external focus, except for its use in Northern Ireland
Germany	Federal Constitutional Court with judicial review authority; organized according to German brand of federalism	More decentralized today than in past; comparatively small in size at the federal level	Dominant role historically; much smaller role since World War II; compulsory military service ended in 2011
India	Historically served as a check on legislators; tensions between the Supreme Court and legislative branch over the power to amend the constitution	Indian Administrative Service (IAS) serves as the select group at the top of a huge public sector; growing problem of brain drain to private sector	Second largest military in the world (after China); possesses nuclear weapons; typically follows political leaders rather than intervening in politics
Mexico	Civil law tradition; subservience to other branches of government; more independent since 1990s, but not fully	Developed more as a political machine than a merit-based civil service; largely unsuccessful at professionalizing the	Significant in revolutionary periods; civilian control during PRI period; ITAP feature on new professionalism theory and use of military to fight growing

In Theory and Practice. Embedded within the TIC sections, In Theory and Practice (ITAP) coverage delves deeper to inspire students to critically think about and discuss the central topics of each chapter. Consistent with the book's overall approach, important comparative politics theories are introduced in a way that unites thematic and country-specific information. Each ITAP box provides a brief overview of a key comparative politics theory and then discusses its application to one of the TIC cases.

IN THEORY AND PRACTICE

The United Kingdom and Party Government Theory

Political scientists have long tried to explain and predict patterns in legislative behavior, developing a number of theories, including George Tsebelis's theory of the importance of veto points discussed in the previous chapter, to help understand legislative outcomes. One such argument,

> *"The In Theory and Practice [features] continue to impress me as good ways to drive home the abstract concept of 'theory' with the concrete concept of 'evidence' in a comparative perspective."*
>
> Ryan Carlin, Georgia State University

NEW!

Research in Context. The American Political Science Association has urged political scientists in recent years to make their research more policy relevant. Each Research in Context feature summarizes a recent important comparative politics research article relating to that chapter's topics. The feature includes research questions and hypotheses, major theories examined, and the resulting findings. The second part of the feature focuses on the real-world importance and application of the research. Most chapters include a Research in Context feature.

Research in Context

One of this textbook's central themes is that causal factors that shape major political outcomes can be understood as different types of structures and choices. Comparativists sometimes employ this framework in their own research. One example is comparativist Francesco Stolfi's recent research project on budget reform in Italy.[61] Stolfi sought to understand major changes to the "formulation, approval, and implementation stages of Italy's budget process in the 1990s."[62] He compared structural arguments with those emphasizing the ideas and actions of individual political leaders and concluded that ideas played roles in the various

> *"[P]resenting some of the most recent research . . . will help [students] see what the field actually does—and help generate discussions."*
>
> Jeremy Youde, University of Minnesota Duluth

Research in Context plays an important role in student learning. First, it provides a consistent reminder across the book of the many methods and options for conducting political science research presented in the first chapter. Second, it links the recent political science research methodology to chapter topics. Last, it emphasizes real-world importance at a crucial time in the history of political science.

Supplements

A tightly integrated set of instructional materials accompanies *Comparative Politics: Structures and Choices,* Second Edition:
PowerLecture DVD with JoinIn™ and ExamView®
ISBN-10: 1111342288 | ISBN-13: 9781111342289

This DVD provides access to interactive PowerPoint® lectures, the Test Bank, and the Instructor's Manual. Interactive, book-specific PowerPoint® lectures make it easy for you to assemble, edit, publish, and present custom lectures for your course. The slides provide outlines specific to every chapter of the textbook and include tables, statistical charts, graphs, and photos from the book as well as from outside sources. In addition, they are completely customizable for a powerful and personalized presentation. The test bank in Microsoft® Word and ExamView® computerized testing offers a large array of well-crafted multiple-choice and essay questions, along with answers and page references.

The Instructor's Manual includes learning objectives, chapter outlines, discussion questions, suggestions for class activities and projects, tips on integrating media into your class (including step-by-step instructions on how to create your own podcasts), suggested readings, and Web resources. A section specifically designed for teaching assistants and adjuncts helps instructors get started teaching right away. JoinIn™ offers book-specific "clicker" questions that test and track student comprehension of key concepts. Save the data from students' responses all semester, track their progress, and show them how political science works by incorporating this exciting new tool into your classroom. It is available for college and university adopters only.

Web Tutor Toolbox on WebCT

ISBN-10: 0534274889 | ISBN-13: 9780534274887
WebTutor Toolbox is a Web-based teaching and learning tool that integrates with your school's learning management system. It offers access to the ExamView® test bank and online study tools including learning objectives, flashcards, Web links, and practice quizzes.

Web Tutor Toolbox on Blackboard

ISBN-10: 0534274897 | ISBN-13: 9780534274894
WebTutor Toolbox is a Web-based teaching and learning tool that integrates with your school's learning management system. It offers access to the ExamView® test bank and online study tools including learning objectives, flashcards, Web links, and practice quizzes.

Companion Web Site

ISBN-10: 1111298874 | ISBN-13: 9781111298876
Students will find open access to learning objectives, tutorial quizzes, chapter glossaries, flashcards, and crossword puzzles, all correlated by chapter. Instructors also have access to the Instructor's Manual and PowerPoint® slides. Access the book's companion site at www.cengage.com/politicalscience/barrington/comparative politicsstructuresandchoices2e.

CourseReader: Comparative Politics

ISBN-10: 1111477604 | ISBN-13: 9781111477608
CourseReader 0-30: Comparative Politics Printed Access Card
ISBN-10: 1111477620 | ISBN-13: 9781111477622
CourseReader 0-30: Comparative Politics Instant Access Code
ISBN-10: 1111477612 | ISBN-13: 9781111477615
CourseReader 0-30: Comparative Politics SSO
ISBN-10: 1111680507 | ISBN-13: 9781111680503
CourseReader 0-60: Comparative Politics Printed Access Card
ISBN-10: 1111680493 | ISBN-13: 9781111680497
CourseReader 0-60: Comparative Politics Instant Access Code
ISBN-10: 1111680485 | ISBN-13: 9781111680480
CourseReader 0-60: Comparative Politics SSO
ISBN-10: 1111680531 | ISBN-13: 9781111680534
CourseReader Unlimited: Comparative Politics Printed Access Card
ISBN-10: 1111680523 | ISBN-13: 9781111680527
CourseReader Unlimited: Comparative Politics Instant Access Code
ISBN-10: 1111680515 | ISBN-13: 9781111680510
CourseReader Unlimited: Comparative Politics SSO

CourseReader: Comparative Politics is a fully customizable online reader that provides access to hundreds of readings and audio and video selections from multiple disciplines. This easy-to-use solution allows you to select exactly the content you need for your courses. It is loaded with convenient pedagogical features like highlighting, printing, note-taking, and audio downloads. It gives you the freedom to assign individualized content at an affordable price. CourseReader: Comparative Politics is the perfect complement to any class.

Acknowledgements

A large number of people played crucial roles in the development of this book during the production of the second edition. Fitting her title, the most important was the book's developmental editor, Jennifer Jacobson. Jen helped solidify the approach of the second edition, oversaw reviews of the manuscript, provided editorial guidance, and, perhaps most challenging, pushed me to stay on schedule. Serving as a developmental editor is a rather thankless job, except to this author, from whom no amount of thanks to Jen can do justice to how valuable she has been.

The staff at and working for Cengage Learning/Wadsworth, from the editorial team and those involved in marketing to those who were involved with the production process, put significant effort into this text. This started at the top, with the executive editor, Carolyn Merrill, and the sponsoring editor, Anita Devine. Carolyn was very helpful and reassuring during the initial period following Cengage's purchase of Houghton Mifflin's College Division and helped keep me on task at key moments during the production of the second edition. Anita took over as sponsoring editor during the early stages of editing and was nothing but supportive throughout the rest of the second edition's development. Josh Allen deftly managed the production phase of this project, which included the work of Linda May, Jennifer Meyer Dare, Laura Ross, Sybil Sosin, Alexa Orr of the Bill Smith Group, Melissa Tomaselli of PreMediaGlobal, and Sangeetha Vijay of Cenveo Publisher Services. Thanks also to David Price of Santa Fe College for his work on the Instructor's Manual and to John Occhipinti of Canisius College for his work on the Test Bank.

A large number of reviewers provided suggestions, criticism, and encouragement. The book would not be anything close to what it is without their input. Reviewers involved in the second edition include Caroline Beer, University of Vermont; Rachel Bowen, The Ohio State University at Mansfield; Ryan Carlin, Georgia State University; Matt Evans, Penn State Altoona; Erik Herron, University of Kansas; Jennifer Horan, University of North Carolina Wilmington; J. James Kim, California State Polytechnic University, Pomona; Asbed Kotchikian, Bentley University; Paulette Kurzer, University of Arizona; Lisa Laverty, Eastern Michigan University; Mariely Lopez-Santana, George Mason University; John Occhipinti, Canisius College; Glenn Perry, Indiana State University; Meredith-Joy Petersheim, Winthrop University; David Price, Santa Fe College; Aaron Rodrigues, Cuesta College; Dietmar Schirmer, University of Florida; Curtis Simon, Mt. San Antonio College; Tressa Tabares, American River College; Greg Weeks, University of North Carolina at Charlotte; John Willerton, University of Arizona; Jeremy Youde, University of Minnesota Duluth; Andris Zimelis, University of Illinois at Chicago.

Reviewers involved in the first edition include Nozar Alaolmolki, Hiram College; Valentine J. Belfiglio, Texas Woman's University; Prosper Bernard, College of Staten Island; Terry Clark, Creighton University; Jane Leftwich Curry, Santa Clara University; Eliot Dickinson, Western Oregon University; Richard Farkas, DePaul University; Julie George, Queens College, City University of New York; Anke Grosskopf, Long Island University—C.W. Post Campus; Jennifer Horan, University of North Carolina Wilmington; Zachary T. Irwin, Pennsylvania State University—Erie; F. David Levenbach, Arkansas State University; Stephen P. Mumme, Colorado State University; John Occhipinti, Canisius College; Ronald M. Schneider, Queens College, City University of New York; Michael Shepherd, Har-Ber High School, Springdale, Arkansas; and Carole Wilson, University of Texas, Dallas.

Four scholars made significant contributions to the first edition, particularly in the discussion of four of the countries highlighted in the book: Mike Bosia (who wrote on France), Kate Bruhn (Brazil), Sue Giaimo (Germany), and Dean McHenry (India). Their expertise and their valuable comments and suggestions made the first edition a much better book than it would have been without them. Although much of the text has been revised and updated, some of the text they contributed has been carried over to the second edition.

At Marquette University, many of my colleagues in the Department of Political Science read drafts of chapters and provided helpful feedback. They included Julia Azari, Janet Boles, Jeff Drope, Michael Fleet, Rich Friman, Ryan Hanley, Larry LeBlanc, John McAdams, Barry McCormick, Duane Swank, Christopher Wolfe, and McGee Young. A number of graduate research assistants—including Katherine Arnold, Brooke Chichakly, Craig Frizzell, Yuliya Humphrey, Ivana Ivanovic, John LeJeune, Anne Mozena, Lauren Reeves, Craig Shockley, Kate Springsteen, Natalie Worlow, and Lilia Yakova—also played important roles throughout the development of the first and second editions.

Above all, my family was more than understanding about the long hours of writing, revising, and polishing during the process of completing the second edition. For my wife, Therese, and our children, Alex, Colin, Tristan, and Quinn, the words "Dad is working on his book" became an all-too-common phrase. I am deeply grateful for their patience and support.

My final thanks go to the professors and students who are using the second edition as part of their comparative politics course. I hope students find it both helpful and interesting. I have tried to create a book that provides students not only with information about particular countries but also, and more important, with a framework for understanding major political outcomes. When they have finished the book, they will have a deeper understanding of many of the world's most important countries. They will also have improved their ability to analyze and discuss political outcomes, not only this semester but also long after their introductory comparative politics course is done.

About the Author

Lowell Barrington is Associate Professor, Assistant Chair, and Director of Graduate Studies in the Department of Political Science at Marquette University. He received his Ph.D. in Political Science from the University of Michigan in 1995. His teaching and research interests include ethnicity and nationalism, democratization, postcommunist politics, and political science research methodology. He has held political office at the local level twice, serving as a village trustee and a school board member.

Countries-at-a-Glance

United Kingdom

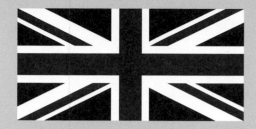

Economic Traits

- Economically developed country
- Sizable middle class
- GDP/per capita-PPP (2012 est.): $36,700*
- Highly globalized economy, with the exception of trade

Political Culture

- More individualistic than much of continental Europe; less individualistic than the United States
- Combination of noblesse oblige and working-class deference

Identity Traits

- Population: Approx. 62 million
- Ethnic groups: English, Northern Irish, Scottish, Welsh, numerous immigrant minorities
- Language(s): Primarily English
- Religion(s): Majority Christian (Church of England, Roman Catholic), many nonpracticing; large number of atheists and agnostics; small but growing Muslim population

Political System

- Democracy

Federal or Unitary?

- Unitary; but important powers have been granted to Northern Ireland, Scotland, and Wales through devolution

Presidential or Parliamentary System?

- Parliamentary, with weak monarch as head of state

---

*Source: Based on estimates in the International Monetary Fund World Economic Outlook Database, April 2011. This statistic is an update of the estimate for 2011 presented in Chapter 2 of the book.

Chief Executive(s)

- Head of government: Prime minister
  - David Cameron, since May 2010
  - Leader of Conservative Party-led coalition government in the House of Commons
- Head of state: Monarch
  - Queen Elizabeth II, since 1952

National Legislature

- House of Commons
  - The lower house
  - Has significant powers
  - Next election held no later than May 2015
- House of Lords
  - The upper house
  - Has limited powers

Judiciary

- The Supreme Court of the United Kingdom
  - The UK's new high court
  - Replaced the Law Lords of the House of Lords in 2009
- No official (and very limited in practice) constitutional review authority

Interest Group System

- Mix of corporatist and pluralist approaches

National Legislative Electoral System

- First past the post (FPTP), single-member district system

Political Party System

- Two-and-a-half party system

Major Political Parties

- Conservative Party
- Labour Party
- Liberal Democratic Party

Other Important Features

- "Unwritten" constitution
- Magna Carta limited powers of the Crown in 1215
- History of evolutionary rather than revolutionary political change

Germany

Economic Traits
- Economically developed country
- Sizable middle class
- GDP/per capita-PPP (2012 est.): $38,800[†]
- Moderately globalized economy

Political Culture
- More collectivistic than the United Kingdom
- Policy implementation reflects attachment to the Catholic social doctrine of subsidiarity
- Reluctance to participate in overt displays of nationalism due to Nazi past

Identity Traits
- Population: Approx. 82 million
- Ethnic groups: Germans, numerous immigrant minorities, particularly ethnic Turks
- Language(s): Primarily German, though many immigrants speak Turkish
- Religion(s): Majority Christian (Protestant, Roman Catholic), many nonpracticing; large number of atheists and agnostics; sizable Muslim population

Political System
- Democracy

Federal or Unitary?
- Federal
- Territory divided into sixteen *Länder*

Presidential or Parliamentary System?
- Parliamentary

Chief Executive(s)
- Head of government: Chancellor
  - Angela Merkel, since November 2005
  - Leader of a coalition in the *Bundestag* involving the CDU/CSU and the FDP

- Head of state: President
  - Christian Wulff, since July 2010
  - Next election 2015
  - Few significant powers

National Legislature
- *Bundestag* (Federal Assembly)
  - The lower house
  - Next election tentatively scheduled for September 2013
- *Bundesrat* (Federal Council)
  - The upper house
  - Weaker than the *Bundestag* on federal matters, but has absolute veto power over bills directly affecting the *Länder*

Judiciary
- *Bundesverfassungsgericht* (Federal Constitutional Court, highest court ruling on constitutional matters)
- *Bundesgerichtshof* (Federal Court of Justice, highest court of appeals)
- Lower levels of the court system overseen by the *Länder*

Interest Group System
- Corporatist

National Legislative Electoral System
- Combination of proportional representation (PR) and first past the post (FPTP) district system

Political Party System
- Multiparty system

Major Political Parties
- Christian Democratic Union (CDU)/Christian Social Union (CSU)
- Social Democratic Party (SPD)
- Free Democratic Party (FDP)
- The Left (*Die Linke*)
- Alliance '90/The Greens (*Bündnis 90/Die Grünen*)

Other Important Features
- Significant regional identities
- Federal system based more on the shared powers approach than the reserved powers approach, the latter being the approach to federalism in the United States
- Important legacies remain from the post-World War II split of the country into the German Democratic Republic (East Germany) and Federal Republic of Germany (West Germany)

[†]Source: Based on estimates in the International Monetary Fund World Economic Outlook Database, April 2011. This statistic is an update of the estimate for 2011 presented in Chapter 2 of the book.

India

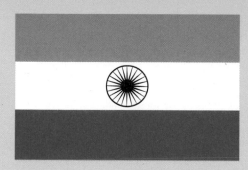

Economic Traits
- Lesser-developed country/emerging market/BRICS case
- Visible middle class, but significant inequality
- GDP/per capita-PPP (2012 est.): $3,900‡
- Moderately globalized economy

Political Culture
- Heterogeneous, but more individualistic than most other Asian political cultures
- Shared features include an overarching identity based on the idea of unity in diversity

Identity Traits
- Population: Approx. 1.2 billion
- Ethnic groups: Significant ethnic diversity, largest groups are Indo-Aryan (across the north and northwest of the country) and Dravidian (across the southeast)
- Language: Significant linguistic diversity (estimates of more than four hundred languages in regular use), mostly Indo-Aryan and Dravidian languages; widespread English
- Religion: Mostly Hindu, sizable numbers of Muslims and Christians

Political System
- Democracy

Federal or Unitary?
- Federal, but with a stronger central government than in most federal systems
- Territory divided into twenty-eight federal territorial units (called "states") and seven union territories, including the National Capital Territory of Delhi, home to India's capital city of New Delhi

Presidential or Parliamentary System?
- Parliamentary

---

‡Source: Based on estimates in the International Monetary Fund World Economic Outlook Database, April 2011. This statistic is an update of the estimate for 2011 presented in Chapter 2 of the book.

Chief Executive
- Head of government: Prime Minister
  - (Manmohan Singh ["Dr. Singh"], since May 2004; head of the Council of Ministers)
- Head of state: President
  - (Pratibha Patil, since July 2007; theoretically strong powers, but defers to the prime minister in practice)

National Legislature
- *Lok Sabha* (House of the People)
  - The lower house
  - Next election scheduled for May 2014
- *Rajya Sabha* (Council of States): The upper house

Judiciary
- Supreme Court
  - Highest court ruling on constitutional matters
  - Highest appeals court
- High Courts
  - The level below the Supreme Court
  - Rule on cases in individual federal territorial units or groups of units

Interest Group System
- Pluralist

National Legislative Electoral System
- Members of the *Lok Sabha* are elected through a first past the post (FPTP), single-member district system
- In addition to the twelve members selected by the president, legislatures of the federal units elect members of the *Rajya Sabha*, with one-third of the seats standing for election every two years

Political Party System
- Multiparty

Major Political Parties
- Indian National Congress: INC or Congress Party, leading party of the United Progressive Alliance in the *Lok Sabha*
- Bharatiya Janata Party: BJP, leading party of the National Democratic Alliance in the *Lok Sabha*
- Communist Party of India (Marxist): CPI[M], leading party of the Left Front party group in the *Lok Sabha*
- Samajwadi Party: SP; based almost entirely in the province of Uttar Pradesh, India's most populous region

Other Important Features
- India's colonial past and its current focus on enhancing its economic prospects through globalization encourage English language acquisition
- Sessions of the *Lok Sabha* are routinely disrupted by protests on the floor of the chamber

Mexico

Economic Traits
- Lesser-developed country/emerging market
- Visible middle class, but significant inequality
- GDP/per capita-PPP (2012 est.): $15,800[§]
- Moderately globalized economy

Political Culture
- Relatively collectivistic, especially compared to countries like the United States
- General deference to social authority coupled with admiration of revolutionary spirit

Identity Traits
- Population: Approx. 115 million
- Ethnic groups: Majority mestizo (mix of indigenous populations and European settlers); significant numbers consider themselves indigenous; some Europeans
- Language: Population is nearly universally Spanish speaking, with the exception of a small portion of the indigenous population
- Religion: Majority Christian (mostly Roman Catholic); small but growing Protestant population

Political System
- Democracy

Federal or Unitary?
- Federal
- Territory divided into thirty-one *estados* and one federal district (Mexico City)

Presidential or Parliamentary System?
- Presidential

Chief Executive
- Head of government: President
  - Felipe de Jesús Calderón Hinojosa (Felipe Calderón), since December 2006; cannot run for reelection
  - Next election in 2012
- Head of state: President

National Legislature
- *Cámara de Diputados* (Chamber of Deputies)
  - The lower house
  - Next election scheduled for the summer of 2012
- *Senado* (Senate)
  - The upper house
  - Next election scheduled for the summer of 2012
- Constitutional amendment under consideration to allow legislators to seek reelection (currently they cannot run for reelection)

Judiciary
- *Suprema Corte de Justicia de la Nación* (SCJN, Supreme Court of Justice of the Nation)
  - Highest court ruling on constitutional matters
  - Rulings apply to specific cases rather than establishing broad constitutional precedent
  - Also the highest appeals court

Interest Group System
- Corporatist (previously run through the Institutional Revolutionary Party)

National Legislative Electoral System
- Three hundred of the five hundred members of the Chamber of Deputies are elected by a first past the post (FPTP) system, and the remaining two hundred by proportional representation (PR)
- Senate elections involve a combination of electoral approaches that take into account the performance of candidates from particular parties within the *estados* and nationally

Political Party System
- Multiparty

Major Political Parties
- National Action Party (PAN)
- Party of the Democratic Revolution (PRD)
- Institutional Revolutionary Party (PRI)

Other Important Features
- The PRI dominated the political system from the late 1920s until the late 1990s
- Considered an established democracy only since 2000

[§]Source: Based on estimates in the International Monetary Fund World Economic Outlook Database, April 2011. This statistic is an update of the estimate for 2011 presented in Chapter 2 of the book.

Brazil

Economic Traits

- Lesser-developed country/emerging market/BRICS case
- Visible middle class, but very high levels of inequality
- GDP/per capita-PPP (2012 est.): $12,300[**]
- Minimally globalized economy

Political Culture

- Heterogeneous political culture, broadly supportive of hierarchal authority and security over freedom; low levels of interpersonal trust and political system legitimacy
- Prevailing *jeito* (the Brazilian tendency to circumvent rules)
- High levels of corruption

Identity Traits

- Population: Approx. 195 million
- Ethnic groups: Ethnically diverse, with significant intermixing among the descendants of indigenous groups, Portuguese and other European immigrants, and African slaves; racial categories are more important than ethnic ones, with the census identifying different racial groups (white, brown [mixed race], black, and others [mainly Asians and native groups])
- Language: Nearly universally Portuguese, with the exception of some members of the indigenous population
- Religion: Majority Christian (mostly Roman Catholic); small but growing Protestant population

Political System

- Democracy

Federal or Unitary?

- Federal
- Territory divided into twenty-six *estados* and one federal district (Brasília)

**Source: Based on estimates in the International Monetary Fund World Economic Outlook Database, April 2011. This statistic is an update of the estimate for 2011 presented in Chapter 2 of the book.

Presidential or Parliamentary System?

- Presidential

Chief Executive

- Head of government: President
  - Dilma Rousseff, since January 2011
  - Next election in October 2014
- Head of state: President

National Legislature

- *Câmara dos Deputados* (Chamber of Deputies)
  - The lower house
  - Next election scheduled for October 2014
- *Senado Federal* (Federal Senate)
  - The upper house
  - Elected in staggered elections, with one-third to be elected next in 2014 and the other two-thirds to be elected next in 2018

Judiciary

- *Supremo Tribunal Federal* (Supreme Federal Court)
  - Highest court ruling on constitutional matters
  - Hears criminal cases against top government officials
- *Superior Tribunal de Justiça* (Superior Court of Justice): Highest appeals court on nonconstitutional matters

Interest Group System

- Corporatist

National Legislative Electoral System

- Proportional Representation (PR) system for the Chamber of Deputies
- First past the post (FPTP) system for the Federal Senate, with senators chosen from each *estado* in Brazil's federal system

Political Party System

- Multiparty

Major Political Parties

- Workers' Party (PT)
- Brazilian Democratic Movement Party (PMDB)
- Brazilian Social Democratic Party (PSDB)
- Liberal Front Party (PFL)
- A large number of moderately sized parties

Other Important Features

- In 2010, twenty-two different parties won seats in the Chamber of Deputies, and fifteen parties won seats in the Senate
- Corruption well above the average of Latin American countries
- History of military involvement in politics

Nigeria

Economic Traits
- Lesser-developed country
- Small middle class and significant inequality
- GDP/per capita-PPP (2012 est.): $2,700[††]
- Moderately globalized economy, mostly focused on the energy sector

Political Culture
- Differences among three main ethnic groups, overall relatively collectivistic, emphasizes deference to traditional social authorities
- Difficulties establishing attachment to an overarching Nigerian identity due to deep ethnic divisions reinforced by region and religion

Identity Traits
- Population: Approx. 160 million
- Ethnic groups: Hausa-Fulani, Ibo, Yoruba, a large number of smaller groups
- Language: Three main languages: Hausa, Ibo, and Yoruba; huge number of additional languages used by small portions of the population; widespread use of English, particularly among the elite
- Religion: Approximately half Muslim; 40% Christian; approx. 10% traditional indigenous religions

Political System
- Democracy, though many comparativists are concerned about the fragile nature of the democratic system because of widespread corruption

Federal or Unitary?
- Federal
- Territory divided into thirty-six federal regions (called "states" in Nigeria) and a federal capital territory, Abuja

---

††Source: Based on estimates in the International Monetary Fund World Economic Outlook Database, April 2011. This statistic is an update of the estimate for 2011 presented in Chapter 2 of the book.

Presidential or Parliamentary System?
- Presidential

Chief Executive
- Head of government: President
  - Goodluck Jonathan, assumed the presidency in May 2010; reelected in April 2011
  - Next election in April 2015
- Head of state: President

National Legislature
- House of Representatives
  - The lower house
  - Next election scheduled for April 2015
- Senate
  - The upper house
  - Next election scheduled for April 2015

Judiciary
- Supreme Court
  - Highest court ruling on constitutional matters
  - Highest appeals court
- Court of Appeal
  - Hears appeals from the top courts of the thirty-six federal regions
  - Its decisions can be appealed to the Supreme Court

Interest Group System
- Weak pluralist system, with corruption a central feature of interest group activities

National Legislative Electoral System
- House of Representatives uses a first past the post (FPTP), single-member district system
- Senate elections also use a first past the post (FPTP) format, with one senator selected from each of three senatorial districts within each of the thirty-six regions and an additional senator elected from the federal capital territory

Political Party System
- Multiparty, but possibly an emerging one party dominant system under the PDP

Major Political Parties
- Peoples Democratic Party (PDP)
- Congress for Progressive Change (CPC)
- All Nigeria Peoples Party (ANPP)
- Action Congress (AC)

Other Important Features
- Often used as an example of the resource curse
- Estimated that more than five hundred languages are used in the country
- Long periods of military rule since independence in 1960

Russia

Economic Traits
- Country in transition/emerging market/BRICS case
- Small, growing middle class
- GDP/per capita-PPP (2012 est.): $17,900[‡‡]
- Moderately globalized economy

Political Culture
- Collectivistic, with emphasis on collective care of the individual rather than individual sacrificing for the collective
- Security and order more important than personal freedom
- Disagreements over central components of national identity

Identity Traits
- Population: Approx. 142 million
- Ethnic groups: Russian; a large number of small minority groups, particularly in outlying areas of the country
- Language(s): Primarily Russian, some minority groups also use their native languages
- Religion(s): Large number of atheists and agnostics, many in the population call themselves Christian (mostly Russian Orthodox), sizable Muslim population in some regions

Political System
- Semiauthoritarian

Federal or Unitary?
- Federal, but increasing centralization of power since 2000
- Territory divided into eighty-three regions

Presidential or Parliamentary System?
- Semi-presidential system with a strong president

Chief Executive(s)
- Head of government: Prime minister
  - Vladimir Putin, since May 2008
  - Chairman of the United Russia Party, which controls a majority of seats in the Duma; may seek the presidency in 2012
- Head of state: President
  - Dmitry Medvedev, since May 2008
  - Next election scheduled for March 2012

[‡‡]Source: Based on estimates in the International Monetary Fund World Economic Outlook Database, April 2011. This statistic is an update of the estimate for 2011 presented in Chapter 2 of the book.

National Legislature
- *Gosudarstvennaya Duma* (State Duma, or simply "the Duma")
  - The lower house; recent election in December 2011
  - Next election scheduled for December 2015
- *Soviet Federatsii* (Federation Council)
  - The upper house
  - Has limited powers, especially compared to the Duma and the executive

Judiciary
- *Konstitutsionnyi Sud Rossiiskoi Federatsii* (Constitutional Court of the Russian Federation): has constitutional review authority
- *Verkhovnyi Sud Rossiiskoi Federatsii* (Supreme Court of the Russian Federation): The highest appellate court

Interest Group System
- Mix of corporatist and pluralist approaches

National Legislative Electoral System
- Proportional representation (PR) system for the Duma
- The governments of Russia's eighty-three regions each select two representatives to the Federation Council

Political Party System
- One-party dominant system (under United Russia)

Major Political Parties
- United Russia
- Smaller parties include the Communist Party of the Russian Federation, the Liberal Democratic Party, and Fair Russia

Other Important Features
- Long history of undemocratic governments
- Brief attempts at democracy in 1917 and from late 1991 to the early 2000s
- Energy-based economy; economic successes and challenges since 2000 directly related to world energy prices (with high energy prices fueling Russian economic growth)
- Consolidation of smaller territories has resulted in a reduction in regions from the original eighty-nine to eighty-three; further reductions are possible over the next several years

China

Economic Traits
- Lesser-developed country/emerging market/BRICS case
- Growing middle class
- GDP/per capita-PPP (2012 est.): $9,200[§§]
- Moderately globalized economy

Political Culture
- Traditional emphasis on Confucianism, along with government efforts during the Communist era, stressed order over freedom and collectivism over individualism
- Capitalist economic development over the last three decades has weakened some Confucianism-based cultural components

Identity Traits
- Population: Approx. 1.3 billion
- Ethnic groups
  - Han Chinese (more than 90%)
  - Numerous ethnic minorities, particularly in outlying regions of the country
- Languages
  - Majority of the population speaks a dialect or sublanguage of Chinese, including Mandarin, Wu, Min, and Cantonese
  - Some ethnic minority groups speak non-Chinese languages
- Religions
  - Significant religious diversity
  - Religions include Buddhism, Taoism, Christianity, Islam, traditional religions based on Confucianism, and combinations of more than one religion
  - A large portion of the population is atheist or agnostic

Political System
- Authoritarian

Federal or Unitary?
- Unitary, although regional and local officials often have notable autonomy over policy implementation

Presidential or Parliamentary System?
- Semi-presidential (but nondemocratic) system

Chief Executive(s)
- Head of government: Premier
  - Wen Jiabao, since March 2003; reelected in 2008
  - Heads the State Council
  - Officially elected by the National People's Congress (NPC)
  - Next scheduled election is in 2013; Wen cannot seek the office again
- Head of state: President
  - Hu Jintao, since March 2003; reelected in 2008
  - Officially elected by the NPC
  - Next scheduled election is in 2013; Hu cannot seek the office again
  - Hu is considered China's Paramount Leader
  - Hu is also general secretary of the Chinese Communist Party (CCP); his term as CCP general secretary ends in 2012
  - Since 2004, Hu has also held the powerful positions of chairman of the Central Military Commission of both the state and the CCP

National Legislature
- The National People's Congress (NPC)
  - Three-thousand-member legislature meets once per year
  - The eleventh NPC has been in place since 2008; next NPC to be selected in 2013
- Standing Committee of the NPC
  - Smaller set of NPC members
  - Meets more regularly than the NPC and has the authority to enact most types of legislation

Judiciary
- Supreme People's Court (SPC, or Supreme Court)
  - Highest court of appeal for criminal cases
  - Over two hundred justices hear cases in smaller tribunals
  - In 2006, three special criminal tribunals were established to approve all death sentences in China

Interest Group System
- Corporatist, with politically relevant interest groups used and closely watched by the CCP

National Legislative Electoral System
- Members of the NPC are indirectly elected
  - They are officially selected by the provincial People's Congresses
  - The CCP actively controls the selection process
- Members of the NPC Standing Committee are selected by the NPC

Political Party System
- One-party system

Major Political Party
- Chinese Communist Party (CCP)

Other Important Features
- World's oldest continuous civilization (more than four thousand years old)
- Communist China's great revolutionary leader, Mao Zedong, died in September 1976
- Elements of capitalism appear as a result of CCP-led economic reform beginning in the late 1970s

---

[§§]Source: Based on estimates in the International Monetary Fund World Economic Outlook Database, April 2011. This statistic is an update of the estimate for 2011 presented in Chapter 2 of the book.

Iran

Economic Traits
- Lesser-developed country
- Visible middle class, concentrated in large cities
- GDP/per capita-PPP (2012 est.): $11,100***
- Minimally globalized economy

Political Culture
- Relatively collectivistic, but less so than other Middle Eastern countries
- Political values more supportive of democracy than those of many neighboring countries
- Difficult to ascertain political system legitimacy

Identity Traits
- Population: Approx. 76 million; estimates differ significantly depending on source
- Ethnic groups: Approximately half Persian; one-quarter Azeri (concentrated in areas bordering Azerbaijan); sizable Kurdish minority
- Language: More than half speak Persian; a little more than one-quarter speak Azeri or another Turkic language
- Religion: Almost entirely Muslim; 90% Shiite and 10% Sunni

Political System
- Authoritarian theocracy; some comparativists consider it a semiauthoritarian system because of its elected president and legislature

Federal or Unitary?
- Unitary, but divided into thirty provinces

Presidential or Parliamentary System?
- Presidential, with a dual executive approach (Supreme Leader and president)

Chief Executive
- Head of government: President
  - Mahmoud Ahmadinejad, since August 2005; reelected in 2009
  - Next election scheduled for mid-2013
  - Less powerful than the Supreme Leader
- Head of state: Supreme Leader
  - Ayatollah Ali Khamenei
  - Has held the position since 1989, following the death of Ayatollah Ruhollah Khomeini
- Guardian Council, Expediency Council, and Assembly of Experts also perform important executive functions

National Legislature
- *Majles-e-Shora-ye Eslami* (or simply *Majles* [sometimes spelled *Majlis*], Islamic Consultative Assembly)
  - The sole national legislative chamber in Iran
  - Next election scheduled for the spring of 2012

Judiciary
- Supreme Court
  - Highest appeals court
  - Does not review cases against clergy, which are handled by a separate judicial body, the Special Clerical Court
- Guardian Council, Expediency Council, and the Supreme Leader play a role in reviewing laws passed by the *Majles*
- Head of the Judiciary (appointed by the Supreme Leader to a five-year term) has significant powers, appointing half of the members of the Guardian Council and all members of the Supreme Court

Interest Group System
- Mixed system with elements of pluralist, corporatist, and state-run interest group systems

National Legislative Electoral System
- Members of the *Majles* are selected through modified majority system, with a threshold requirement for candidates to avoid a runoff; small number of seats are reserved for religious minorities; many single-member districts; the district that includes Tehran has thirty representatives and its voters can vote for up to thirty candidates

Political Party System
- Loosely constructed electoral alliances that give supporters lists of preferred candidates take precedence over many small and constantly changing political parties and organizations

Broad Ideological Blocs
- Hard-liners (sometimes called conservatives or principlists)
- Pragmatic conservatives
- Moderates

Other Important Features
- Often labeled the Islamic Republic of Iran
- Iran's theocratic system has been in place since 1979
- Guardian Council uses its power to review candidates for the *Majles* in order to prevent candidates who support reform of Iran's theocratic system from running
- The Iran-Iraq War (1980–1988) took a large toll on both countries

***Source: Based on estimates in the International Monetary Fund World Economic Outlook Database, April 2011. This statistic is an update of the estimate for 2011 presented in Chapter 2 of the book.

France

Economic Traits
- Economically developed country
- Large middle class, politically relevant agricultural sector
- GDP/per capita-PPP (2012 est.): $35,800[†††]
- Moderately globalized economy

Political Culture
- More collectivistic than the United Kingdom
- Strong emphasis on *laïcité*, a form of secularism stressing religion as a private matter

Identity Traits
- Population: Approx. 66 million
- Ethnic groups: French, immigrant minorities
- Language(s): Primarily French, with weaker use of French among residents of outlying regions such as Brittany and Alsace, as well as among recent immigrants
- Religion(s): Slim Christian majority (mostly Roman Catholic), though many are nonpracticing; large number of atheists and agnostics; small Muslim population

Political System
- Democracy

Federal or Unitary?
- Unitary
- Territory divided into twenty-six *régions*, including four overseas territories
- The *régions* are further divided into 101 total *départements*

Presidential or Parliamentary System?
- Semi-presidential system, with a strong president

†††Source: Based on estimates in the International Monetary Fund World Economic Outlook Database, April 2011. This statistic is an update of the estimate for 2011 presented in Chapter 2 of the book.

Chief Executive(s)
- Head of government: Prime minister
  - François Fillon, since May 2007
  - Leader of Union for a Popular Movement majority government in the National Assembly
- Head of state: President
  - Nicolas Sarkozy, since May 2007
  - Next election in the spring of 2012

National Legislature
- *Assemblée Nationale* (National Assembly)
  - The lower house
  - Next election tentatively scheduled for June 2012
- *Sénat* (Senate)
  - The upper house
  - Only slightly less powerful than the lower house

Judiciary
- *Conseil Constitutionnel* (Constitutional Council): Highest court ruling on constitutional matters
- *Cour de Cassation* (Court of Cassation): Highest appeals court, except in cases of administrative law
- *Conseil d'État* (Council of State)
  - Highest administrative law court, ruling on cases brought against government agencies
  - Also assists the executive with legal advice

Interest Group System
- Mix of corporatist and pluralist approaches

National Legislative Electoral System
- Modified majority (25% to avoid a runoff), single-member district system for the National Assembly
- Senate selected by representatives of France's *départements*

Political Party System
- Multiparty, but considered a multiparty bipolar system, with a large number of parties organized into two groups, one on the political Left and one on the Right

Major Political Parties
- Union for a Popular Movement (UMP)
- Socialist Party (PS)
- A large number of smaller parties

Other Important Features
- Continued emphasis on the Republican tradition of the French Revolution and the concepts of *liberté*, *égalité*, *fraternité*, particularly emphasized since the Third Republic (1870–1940)
- Mayor of Paris is one of the most powerful positions in the French political system

Iraq

Economic Traits
- Lesser-developed country
- Limited middle class due to oil extraction focus and flight by the middle class to other countries during the U.S.-led war against Iraq
- 2011 GDP/per capita-PPP: $4,300***

Political Culture
- Collectivism over individualism, connected to ethno-religious group identity
- Political culture affected by repeated experiences of dictatorship, war, and occupation
- Official commitment to democracy, but depth of attachment unclear

Identity Traits
- Population: Approx. 32 million
- Ethnic Groups
  - Arabs (Shiite and Sunni)
  - Kurds, mostly concentrated in the north of the country
  - Small numbers of ethnic Turkmen and Assyrian populations, also in the north
- Languages
  - Arabic is the official language
  - Kurdish is official language of the Kurdish regions
  - Other small language groups include Turkmen and Assyrian
- Religions
  - Vast majority of population is Muslim
  - Shiites are 60–65% of population, while Sunnis are 30–35%
  - Small Christian population

Political System
- Democracy, established but still fragile

Federal or Unitary?
- Federal
- Divided into eighteen governorates

Presidential or Parliamentary System?
- Parliamentary

***

*** Source: Based on estimates in the International Monetary Fund World Economic Outlook Database, April 2011. This statistic is an update of the estimate for 2011 presented in Chapter 2 of the book.

Chief Executive(s)
- Head of government:
  - Prime Minister (Nouri al-Maliki, since May 2006; selected to his second term in December 2010)
- Head of state:
  - President (Jalal Talabani, since April 2005; reelected by the Council of Representatives in November 2010)

National Legislature
- Council of Representatives
  - 325 seats, of which 8 are reserved for minorities
  - Next election to be held in 2014
- Federation Council
  - Not yet established
  - Once established, it will be the upper house

Judiciary
- Higher Judicial Council
  - Oversees the federal court system and nominates the chief justice of the Supreme Court
  - Has led efforts to improve training of judges
- Federal Supreme Court
  - Highest appeals court
  - Has authority to rule on constitutionality of laws
- Other lower-level courts

Interest Group System
- Slow development of interest groups
- Islamist movements appeared during the U.S.-led occupation, but less influential today
- Civil society groups have begun to emerge, but many are hesitant to criticize government officials

National Legislative Electoral System
- Open-list PR for Council of Representatives
- At least 25% of members of parliament must be women

Political Party System
- Multiparty system

Major Political Parties
- State of Law Coalition
- Iraqi National Movement (INM)
- National Iraqi Alliance (INA)
- Kurdistan Alliance

Other Important Features
- U.S.-led occupation following the ouster of Saddam Hussein
- Economy heavily dependent on energy revenue
- Sunni population has demanded more representation after initially withdrawing from Iraq's developing democratic arrangements
- Growing acceptance of the political institutional arrangements despite difficulties creating a government following the 2010 elections

South Africa

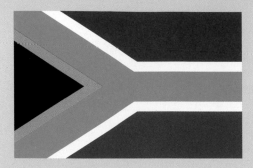

Economic Traits
- Lesser-developed country/emerging market/BRICS case
- Widening divide between rich and poor
- Minimally globalized economy, but globalization ranking is higher than Brazil, India, and Iran
- GDP/per capita-PPP (2012 est.): $11,300‡‡‡

Political Culture
- Respect for traditional social structures
- Relatively strong sense of legitimacy of the democratic system, but corruption remains an issue
- Race-based ideological positions and Afrikaner nationalism weakened with end of apartheid system

Identity Traits
- Population: Approx. 52 million
- Ethnic Groups
  - Great ethnic diversity
  - Official racial categories include Black African, Caucasian, Colored, and Indian/Asian
- Languages
  - Eleven official languages
  - Most popular are IsiZulu (around one-quarter of the total population) and IsiXhosa (18%)
  - The white population mostly speaks Afrikaans (13% of the total population) and English (8%)
- Religions
  - Predominantly Christian (approx. 80%)
  - Also traditional religious practices and a small Muslim population

Political System
- Democracy

Federal or Unitary?
- Unitary
- Divided into nine provinces

Presidential or Parliamentary System?
- Parliamentary, with the chief executive holding the title of president

‡‡‡Source: Based on estimates in the International Monetary Fund World Economic Outlook Database, April 2011. This statistic is an update of the estimate for 2011 presented in Chapter 2 of the book.

Chief Executive(s)
- Head of government: President (Jacob Zuma, since May 2009)
  - Elected by the members of the National Assembly
  - Next election in 2014, following the seating of the National Assembly members elected in 2014
- Head of state: President

National Legislature
- National Assembly
  - Lower house
  - Next elections scheduled for 2014
- National Council of Provinces
  - Upper house
  - Ninety members, ten from each of the nine provinces
  - Next elections scheduled for 2014

Judiciary
- Constitutional Court
  - Final court of appeal on all constitutional questions
  - Can overturn acts of the government on constitutional grounds
- Supreme Court of Appeals
  - Final court of appeal on nonconstitutional questions
  - Only hears appeals cases from lower courts
- High Courts
  - The top courts at the regional level
  - Thirteen courts spread across the nine regions
- Lower-level courts include regional courts, magistrates' courts, and a large number of specialty courts that hear cases on particular topics only

Interest Group System
- Corporatist approach
- Significant civil society helped end apartheid

National Legislative Electoral System
- National Assembly
  - Half of the seats come from closed-list PR races in nine regions
  - Remaining seats come from PR based on results of national vote
- Council of Provinces: Elected by the members of the provincial assemblies
- President: Indirectly elected (selected by the National Assembly)

Political Party System
- One-party dominant

Major Political Parties
- African National Congress (ANC)
- Democratic Alliance (DA)
- Congress of the People (COPE)

Other Important Features
- Apartheid system legalized racial segregation and discrimination until it was dismantled in 1990
- Class and other identity divisions have continued in the postapartheid era

CHAPTER

1

The Comparative Study of Politics

CHAPTER OUTLINE

Features in this chapter:

Wael Ghonim (center, smiling), a key leader of the uprisings that ousted former Egyptian President Hosni Mubarak.
© KHALED EL FIQI/epa/Corbis

LEARNING OBJECTIVES

After reading this chapter, you should be able to

- Define key terms covered in the chapter, such as politics, power, the state, nation, science, hypothesis, and variable.
- Discuss the basic steps involved in the scientific research method, including the use of hypotheses and theories.
- Summarize the comparative method and the alternative approaches within it.
- Describe the basic difference between structures and choices.
- Summarize the defining features of the economic, cultural, identity, and political structures of the Topic in Countries (TIC) cases.

According to an old saying, "One person can change the world." In the arena of politics, this seems to be quite a stretch. After all, even presidents of the United States cannot pass legislation or force countries to agree on solutions to pressing global problems. However, one person can sometimes be the spark for many others to get involved and take action. Such is the story of Wael Ghonim.

Ghonim, a Google marketing executive from Egypt, played an important role in spreading the word about the initial protests in Egypt. He was arrested by the government of then-President Hosni Mubarak. Twelve days later he was freed, largely because of growing domestic and international pressure in support of his release. In an interview shown on Egypt's Dream 2 television station, Ghonim praised the courage of the protesters and wept as he was shown video of protesters who died in the uprising during the time he had been detained.[1] He later spoke in Tahrir Square, the central location of the protests, encouraging the protesters and telling them and the pro-Mubarak forces, "We will not give up."[2] Many analysts credited him with reenergizing the anti-Mubarak movement when its momentum appeared to be fading and with symbolizing the important role of social networking media in "Revolution 2.0."[3] Observers and Egyptian citizens alike also praised his humble responses to claims that he was the hero of the uprising.

The protests and consequent resignation of Mubarak did not happen because of one person alone. "Changing the world" of Egyptian politics required hundreds of thousands of ordinary Egyptians in Cairo, Alexandria, and other cities to risk everything to force a dictator from power. Yet, Wael Ghonim's role in the uprising reminds us that one person can indeed make a tremendous difference by understanding when a major change becomes politically possible, acting on this understanding, and inspiring others to work together to achieve the desired outcome. Whatever form the Egyptian political system takes in the years ahead, the protests that ended Mubarak's rule underscore the importance of people—leaders and ordinary citizens alike—who understand their social, economic, and political structures and decide to try to change them.

Comparative politics involves the systematic study of events like the protests that led to Hosni Mubarak's resignation in Egypt, along with other, less sensational events, to gain a better understanding of the forces that drive key political outcomes around the world. The forces include both underlying conditions and institutional arrangements in a country and the role of individuals like Wael Ghonim. The political outcomes studied in comparative politics include everything from elections, constitutional reforms, and policy changes to mass protests, coups, and civil wars. As a result, comparative politics is demanding. Political scientists Mark Lichbach and Alan Zuckerman point out that this field of political science "asserts an ambitious scope of inquiry. No political phenomenon is foreign to it; no level of analysis is irrelevant, and no time period is beyond its reach."[4]

Comparative politics scholars, called **comparativists**, are required to understand the structures that shape political decisions, the process of making those decisions, and the leaders who oversee the process in a variety of settings. However, comparative politics is not as complex as it might first appear. Comparativists compare and contrast the domestic politics of a country or countries with the domestic politics of another country or countries. Generally, they do not focus on foreign policy or international relations, though they certainly consider the role that trends and events outside a country can have on politics within it. They only occasionally concentrate on local politics. They commonly know well only one country or a small set of countries in the same part of the world. Comparativists in the United States frequently, but not always, exclude the American case from their investigations. Instead, in the United States, American politics has the status of its own field in political science (studied and taught by scholars called "Americanists").

Getting Started with Key Concepts: Politics and Power

Like the natural sciences (chemistry, biology, etc.), the social sciences rely on a set of central concepts that most scholars generally accept. Political science is no exception, and agreement on central concepts and their definitions is particularly important in comparative politics. These central concepts are introduced and defined in this chapter. We begin with two of the most interesting political science concepts: politics and power. Then we move on to other central concepts such as society, norms, state, regime, and government.

Politics: Who Gets What, When, and How

If politics is the main arena of the political scientist, what does this arena look like? The term *politics* is used in many ways in everyday language, often with a negative implication of self-interest, backstabbing, and trickery, such as in the phrase "office politics." This characterization is not completely unfair; politics often involves such intrigue. But one need not think of politics only as a negative endeavor. Despite the common joke that the word comes from *poly* (meaning many) and *ticks* (blood-sucking insects), politics is an essential activity for any sizable group of people. As Aristotle put it in *The Politics*, "Man is a political animal." Without cooperation and the ability to enforce the rules established to govern behavior, large groups would be subject to chaos and to the will of the strongest to a much greater extent than happens in modern societies.

In light of this discussion, what does the word **politics** mean to political scientists? The concept of politics has two aspects. The first is a relatively hopeful and positive view of politics: that it is a set of activities that help organize individuals, systematically resolve disputes, and maintain order in society. These actions include passing and enforcing laws governing individual behavior, mobilizing and channeling mass participation, and socializing individuals to support the political system and the values on which it is based. Activities and institutional arrangements designed to

Comparative Politics The field of political science that engages in the systematic study of political outcomes through the comparison of different cases.

Comparativists Scholars who investigate and compare domestic politics of countries around the world.

"Did You Know?" The real origin of *politics* is the Greek word *polis*, meaning "city."

Politics The set of activities that organizes individuals, resolves disputes, and maintains order in society through the creation and enforcement of rules and policies. Such decisions involve winners and losers; as a result, politics can also be thought of as the process of deciding "who gets what, when, and how" in a particular society.

Policy An official decision on how to organize people, resolve disputes, or address other collective problems.

prevent and resolve disputes require decisions to be made. In politics, such decisions are known as **policy**. The individuals and decision-making mechanisms that generate this policy are known as the government.

The other side of politics is less upbeat. In exchange for the order that government provides, individuals surrender a certain degree of their freedom. They surrender a certain amount of wealth as well because governmental policies generally cost money. Consequently, the government's ability to extract resources from society and redistribute them through its policy decisions is one of the keys to a successful, stable political system. Because politics generates policies that extract and distribute resources as well as policies that address grievances and settle disagreements, politics involves winners and losers. The winners get something from a governmental decision, and the losers do not—or at least not as much as they give. As political scientist Harold Lasswell described it in the early twentieth century, politics concerns "who gets what, when, and how."[5] Politics touches nearly everything in a person's life.

Think and Discuss

In this chapter, you are presented with two ideas about politics. The first is more positive: an activity that helps organize individuals, systematically resolve disputes, and maintain order in society. The second looks at politics as a process that decides "who gets what" and thus produces winners and losers. It is less encouraging. Which of the two ideas of politics better captures the essence of the concept? Why?

Power: How People Get What They Want

Power Defined by political scientists both as influence—A getting B to do something even if B does not want to do it—and as the capabilities that allow A to get B to do what A wants.

When and how people get what they want depends to a large extent on their **power**, their influence over others and the capabilities that make such influence possible. The products of politics—such as governmental policies—come from decisions made by individuals. These individuals have certain powers, including the official ability to make policy decisions, but other individuals and groups also influence them in these decisions.

Power as Influence

Power as Influence The conceptualization of power as the ability of A to get B to do what A wants, even if B does not want to do it.

Power involves influence: getting people to do what you want them to do. The concept of **power as influence** includes the idea that one person in a power relationship can overcome the resistance of another. Unfortunately, defining power as influence over others creates problems in practice. Seeking to understand power relationships in a particular country, a political scientist who views power as influence would try to observe influence as it occurs. But it is not always easy to observe one person's influence over another. Influence can manifest itself in numerous ways, some of which are much easier to see than others. Though scholars have written about various levels of influence (or "faces of power"), there is a general consensus that influence can range from being aboveboard and understood by all involved to being unspoken and not understood by everyone. The more complex and interesting power relationships get, the more difficult it is to identify and understand them.

Power as Capabilities

Power as Capabilities The conceptualization of power focusing on characteristics that would give a person the ability to influence important outcomes.

The difficulties of measuring and observing power as influence have led scholars to discuss and study power in a different way: **power as capabilities**. Rather than looking for an actual instance of one person influencing another as it is taking place, the political scientist instead looks at the abilities a person might possess that allow him or her to get another person to do what he or she wants the person to do. In other words, thinking about power as capabilities allows political scientists to look for more tangible, easier to measure indicators of power.

Thinking about power as capabilities assumes that a scholar can identify tangible and easily measured indicators of power. In the realm of politics, many characteristics that would provide the potential for influence are obvious: official positions in government, money, control of armed forces, and so on. However, some capabilities are harder to observe than others. This is particularly true of noncoercive capabilities, a topic of the next section.

Coercive versus Noncoercive Power

When someone gets another person to do something that the second person would rather not do, why does the second person do it? Broadly speaking, power has two foundations. The first is coercion. With **coercive power**, a person is obeyed because of the rewards and/or punishments at his or her disposal. For example, a boss has the ability to reward or punish an employee with a promotion or a raise or with a cut in pay or termination of employment.

Rewards and punishments are plentiful in politics. Government leaders pass laws that prohibit certain actions and prescribe punishments for those who break the laws. In authoritarian and totalitarian political systems, officials can punish people who threaten their rule, even people who have not broken a formal law. Rewards are a key part of the idea of "who gets what" from the government. Many government programs redistribute money. Such financial rewards can lead individuals to behave in ways government officials desire, but, in democracies at least, this is not a one-way power relationship.

Citizens also hold some power in their ability to reward and punish government officials. The coercive power of ordinary citizens is most conspicuous at election time. As a result, government officials' decisions often take into account the possibility that voters will hold them accountable in future elections.

Noncoercive power rests on a different foundation, one that does not involve rewards and punishments. In this case, power results from a sense of **legitimacy**. Legitimacy is the belief in the right of an individual, a political system, or the state to rule. The belief in a right to rule does not mean that all government decisions are supported. A person does not have to agree with the specific policies that the U.S. Congress produces, for example, to believe that Congress has the right to make these rules.

A system that is legitimate will be able to produce and enforce policies more effectively than one that lacks legitimacy. Rulers of totalitarian, authoritarian, and democratic systems generally all strive to establish legitimacy. Securing it makes their lives easier. But how can a scholar observe legitimacy? How can he or she determine who believes in a system's legitimacy and who follows its rules due to fear of punishment or hope for reward? Surveys can provide a sense of the extent to which people believe in the system's right to rule in democracies, but valid survey data are hard to collect in nondemocratic countries. When a nondemocratic system collapses due to large-scale violent protests, it is reasonable to conclude that the system lacked both legitimacy and effective coercive capacity. What about a stable nondemocratic system that is repressive but whose leaders work hard to develop legitimacy by stressing impressive economic performance or socializing the population to accept an official ideology? Identifying whether people obey because of legitimacy or because of fear is one of a political scientist's more difficult tasks.

Authority is a concept closely related to legitimacy. Some political scientists use the term *authority* interchangeably with *power*, but most think of authority as power based on legitimacy. In other words, *authority* is another term for noncoercive power.

In a famous 1918 speech, sociologist Max Weber (pronounced "Vay-ber") linked the concepts of politics and power, stating that politics "means striving to share power or striving to influence the distribution of power."[6] Weber is also well known for outlining three types of authority throughout history. The first is **traditional authority**. Monarchies often hold this form of authority, deriving their legitimacy from their subjects' belief that a particular family deserves the throne, or that the monarch has a "divine right to rule." In the latter case, ordinary people believe that the monarch has been chosen by God to lead. For example, with the help of the Russian Orthodox Church, Russian tsars presented themselves as a link between God and the general

Coercive Power Getting what one wants by using rewards and punishments.

Noncoercive Power Getting what one wants because of legitimacy.

Legitimacy The belief by those obeying commands that those making the commands have the right to rule.

Authority Power exercised through legitimacy rather than through coercion, though some political scientists use the term interchangeably with *power*.

Traditional Authority A type of authority based the leader's family's claim to the throne and/ or the belief that God has granted the leader the right to rule.

Hugo Chavez has relied heavily on charismatic authority to maintain his position as president of Venezuela. © Reuters

Charismatic Authority A form of authority based on the general population's personal attachment to a particular leader.

Legal Authority A form of authority based on an established set of rules that govern how leaders are chosen and how they make policy decisions.

Society A large group of people connected through interactions and common traits, such as proximity.

Norms Unwritten rules or expectations of behavior that help govern society.

population. In such a setting, one can certainly understand why the masses follow the political system's rules. To disobey would be to disobey God. Such an approach to claiming authority works better in some settings than in others. Authority is related to other features of society, such as its political culture (the central topic of Chapter 3).

Weber's second type of authority is **charismatic authority**. The leader's legitimacy, and perhaps that of the system as a whole, comes from the leader's ability to inspire people or to get them to like or feel attached to him or her. The weakness of this form of legitimacy is that it is closely tied to an individual leader. If the leader dies or somehow loses mass support, the entire political system may be in trouble.

Weber's final form of authority is **legal authority**. Here, legitimacy is based on an established constitution—a political system's set of rules for making new rules—to which the political leaders adhere. It can also involve selecting leaders through elections. People who vote for a losing candidate may not like the person who wins, but the process of selecting the leaders through an election adds to the legitimacy of the policies that the government produces.

Think and Discuss

If power is central to understanding politics, and politics is about "who gets what," can the underprivileged in society ever get a fair deal from the government? Why?

Society and Norms

While politics and the use of power in politics are at the center of what political scientists study, politics takes place within society. *Society* may be one of the most used and yet most difficult to define social science terms. This is partly due to its hidden quality: One can point to governmental institutions, but it is harder to see society.

Society

Society refers to a large collective of people who are connected in some meaningful way. This connection includes members' interactions and common traits that provide a sense of identity. Physical proximity (physical closeness) is usually one of the binding traits. Members of a particular society generally do not live in different parts of the world. Exceptions include groups with common interests, such as those linked together via the Internet. Linkage via the Internet serves as proximity, allowing members to interact more with each other than with their neighbors. The interactions among members of a particular society create a degree of affiliation and interdependence that does not exist with those who are not part of this society.

Though based on the Latin word *societas*, meaning "friendly relations with others," the term *society* is often used to refer to the population of a country, a group that is too large for all members to know one another and whose members do not always behave toward each other in a friendly way. The larger a society, the more subgroups exist within it, and the more complex it is. This complexity has historically led groups of individuals to organize themselves politically, forming governments to establish official rules regarding the behavior of the society's members.

Norms

Government rules are not the only rules in a society. Unwritten rules or expectations of behavior, called **norms**, can develop through the interactions of individuals. For example, a large number of government-created rules regulate driving a car. Driving is also regulated by norms that emerge over time, such as flashing headlights to warn approaching drivers about a police speed trap, waving to a driver who lets one enter a lane of traffic, or speeding up to prevent a driver from entering one's lane. Both norms and written rules often correspond closely to the underlying values of the society. In addition, other organizations in society—for example, families, religions, private educational institutions, and businesses—produce official rules meant to influence society members' behavior. As discussed in the next section, official rules produced by the state generally take precedence over both norms and the official rules of other social organizations.

The State

The state is one of the most important concepts in all parts of political science. Many key concepts in political science, including those already discussed in this chapter, relate to the state. Society, for example, can provide a framework for understanding the state by allowing one to think about state-society relations. The state is also often where comparativists look first when trying to uncover and explain interesting political patterns. Area studies specialists, comparativists who specialize in a particular area of the world, tend to know one or more states very well.

What political scientists mean by "the state" is different from its meaning in everyday language in the United States. People use the word *state* to mean a territorial division within the United States: New York, Texas, Wisconsin, and so on. The American politics field of political science also often uses the term *state* in this way. Comparativists, on the other hand, typically refer to such internal territorial divisions as regions, provinces, or territories.

In addition, as you will see by the end of this section, the term is frustrating because it is complex. The definition of *state* encompasses a large number of attributes, and scholars and politicians also place states around the world into a variety of categories: democratic states, developing states, rogue states, states in transition, and so on. It requires effort to keep track of both the different components of the state and the different types of states.

With that in mind, how should one define the term **state**? A state is something like a combination of what, in everyday language, Americans call a country and what they call a government. The state is the basic unit of political organization in the world and the focal point of political power. Its leaders govern a population in a designated territory or area through a set of ruling institutions. Therefore, political scientists generally consider a state to include a permanent population, a given territory, governing institutions, sovereignty, and international recognition.

Territory

When a specific state is mentioned, most people think of its territory. It is hard to explain the connection of people to territory, but denying the connection's importance is impossible. In many countries, a sports team includes the name of its home city as a way of increasing fan loyalty. The players are no longer just a team; they are *our* team. This link between territory and identity is not lost on political elites. People are willing to give up certain freedoms in the name of defending the territory of the state from external and internal threats. The government body that coordinates activities to prevent terrorism in the United States could have been called many things, such as the Terrorism Prevention Department. Instead, it is the Department of *Homeland* Security.

The history of warfare is full of disputes over territory. Some states have small, easily defensible borders; others have long borders contested by many neighbors. The peaceful acceptance of the border between the United States and Canada is not typical. International recognition is crucial to a state, but border agreements with neighbors may be even more important to the state's stability. Border agreements do not guarantee peace, but they greatly reduce the odds of combat with neighboring states.

State The basic unit of political organization in the world, combining a permanent population, a defined territory, governing institutions, sovereignty over its territory, and international recognition.

"Did You Know?" More than twice as many Azeris live in Iran as in Azerbaijan, the group's internationally recognized state.

"Did You Know?" Vatican City has the smallest population of an internationally recognized state, with fewer than one thousand residents.

Spotlight on ... FRANCE

The Territorial Aspects of the French State

When one thinks of the territory of an internationally recognized state, the image is often a single, continuous body of land. For many of the world's states, however, this image is inaccurate. That is the case with well-known states, such as France. The territory of France can be thought of as three geographic units. First, there is metropolitan France—the area in Europe that most people think of as France. At more than 540,000 square kilometers, it is the largest country in Western Europe. It is often called "the hexagon" because it has six distinct sides created largely by natural borders that include the Mediterranean and the Alps in the south and the Rhine and the English Channel in the north. In addition to this core of France, the country's territory includes the Overseas Departments of Guadeloupe and Martinique in the Caribbean, French Guyana in South America, and the island of Réunion in the Indian Ocean, each fully integrated into the French Republic. Finally, New Caledonia and Tahiti in the South Pacific and Saint Pierre and Miquelon off Canada's northeast coast, with different degrees of self-government, are part of the French Republic. All together, the French Republic spans nearly 675,000 square kilometers with around 65 million inhabitants. Approximately 60 million of them live within the hexagon.

Population

Citizenship A designation of official membership that a state confers to most of its permanent population, carrying rights and responsibilities not afforded noncitizens.

Dual Citizenship The status of a person who holds official citizenship in more than one state.

Stateless A designation for those who lack citizenship in any state.

China and India have over a billion people living within their borders, but very small states, like Barbados and Maldives, may also have sizable populations. The vast majority of residents of most states hold a special designation that marks them as "official members of the state."[7] This designation is called **citizenship** (also traditionally called nationality), and those who hold it are known as citizens. An individual is generally a citizen of a single state. Some people, however, hold citizenship in two or more states. This situation, deemed **dual citizenship**, used to be rare but has become increasingly common. Citizenship carries with it not just special rights, but also duties, such as military service, that represent loyalty to the state. Persons with dual citizenship, therefore, can have dual loyalties as well, something that the governments of most states find troubling.

It is also possible for an individual to lack citizenship in any state, a condition known as being **stateless**. Statelessness can result from the collapse of an existing state (for example, the Soviet Union in 1991), from conflicts that generate refugees who leave the state and are not welcomed back, or from governments that pass policies stripping certain groups of their citizenship. In 2010, the United Nations High Commissioner for Refugees (UNHCR) estimated a population of around 12 million stateless people in the world. Although this may not sound like a lot of people in a world of nearly 7 billion, it is equivalent to the total population of New York City and Chicago.

It is also not unusual for individuals to live outside the country in which they hold citizenship. While the bulk of the population of most existing states consists of citizens of those states, a number of other people may live in a state for long periods of time, even their entire lives, without being citizens of that state. Labels for such individuals are many. Those living in a country legally may be called permanent residents, resident aliens, or guest workers. Those who live there unlawfully are known as illegal aliens or illegal immigrants. Around the world, the question of what to do with illegal immigrants has become particularly controversial. All immigrants are potential targets of persecution, and immigration has become a potent political issue in developed and developing countries alike.

Institutions

A state's ruling institutions are the heart of its political organization. Social scientists disagree about the nature of institutions: economists think of institutions as sets of rules; sociologists highlight the importance of unwritten norms; and political scientists see institutions as organizational arrangements.[8] As is common in political science texts, this book places a greater emphasis on the nature of organizational arrangements, including the composition and official roles of legislatures, executives, and judiciaries. Such general patterns of institutional arrangements define the main types of political systems—democracy, authoritarianism, and totalitarianism—as well as categories within these broad types such as majoritarian versus consensus democracy (see Chapter 5).

A state's institutions form its political structure, and later chapters of this book focus on a variety of institutional arrangements in detail. The arrangement of institutions in a state can have profound implications for policy creation, tensions between groups in society, and the state's stability. The state's institutions are, therefore, part of the overall structure that influences individuals' political actions but are also themselves the result of past choices.

Sovereignty

Sovereignty is an important part of what makes a state different from other levels of political organization such as local governments or international organizations. Within the international political system, sovereignty is a legal principle that gives the state ultimate control over affairs within its territory. The term is also used to refer to the state's actual control over its territory. As a result, there can be a difference between having sovereignty in principle and having it in practice.

Not all states have full control over every aspect of their political business at all times. States may choose to surrender a degree of sovereignty to international organizations or other entities. They may lose control of part or all of their territory to rebel groups or foreign powers. After the first Gulf War in 1991, for example, the United States, the United Kingdom, and France established "no fly zones" that prevented the Iraqi government from using its military as it desired in two large areas of the country. Finally, issues seen as international problems, such as the environment, raise questions about the limits of state sovereignty. Does Brazil's government, for example, have the right to pursue economic development strategies that destroy large areas of the Brazilian rain forest?

Think and Discuss

The issue of the environment causes problems for the concept of state sovereignty. What other issues create questions about whether states have the right to control their own affairs?

Many noted scholars have emphasized the idea of being "in control of its own affairs" in their conceptualizations of the state. Some consider Max Weber's 1918 lecture, "Politics as a Vocation," to be the most important talk ever given by a social scientist. Its ideas about the state and power—remember the discussion of Weber's three types of authority earlier in this chapter—influence how scholars think about these terms to this day. In his speech, Weber put forth the idea of the state as "a human community that (successfully) claims the monopoly of the legitimate use of physical force within a given territory."[9] Thus, Weber tied his idea of the state to the concept of power. Later in the speech, he called the modern state "a compulsory association which organizes domination."[10]

International Recognition

At least in the short run, states can exist without sovereignty as long as they do not also lose **international recognition**. International recognition is the external acceptance, sanctioning, and legal endorsement of a state's sovereignty by other states in

New American citizens take their oath of citizenship at Monticello, the historic home of Thomas Jefferson in Charlottesville, Virginia, on July 4, 2008.
© AP Photo/Steve Helber

Sovereignty The legal right of a state to conduct its own affairs within its territory; also the actual ability to control the territory.

International Recognition The international community's acceptance of a state's right to sovereignty.

the international state system. This recognition can be granted before sovereignty has been achieved, and it can continue after sovereignty has, in reality, been lost. The European and U.S. governments, for example, recognized the independence of several republics of Yugoslavia, Slovenia, Croatia, and eventually Bosnia before the governments of these republics had wrested complete control over their territory from the Yugoslav military.

After the U.S.-led coalition invaded Iraq in 2003—and even after the return of power to the new Iraqi government in 2004 and elections for a provisional parliament in 2005—the United States and its allies largely controlled the affairs of the Iraqi state. Yet, even with its lack of actual sovereignty, the international community continued to recognize Iraq's status as a state. Thus, international recognition is best thought of as the recognition of the right of a state to be sovereign rather than the recognition of actual sovereignty.

When a territory is recognized as a state, it gains more than just a vote in the United Nations General Assembly. International recognition gives those in control of the territory a greater ability, within reason, to use force to maintain order without fear of international intervention. It also increases the likelihood that the new state will gain legitimacy among its own people, making the use of force to maintain order less necessary. Finally, international recognition allows the state to enter into binding agreements with other states, improving its ability to trade, address problems with causes beyond its own borders, and defend itself.

Regimes, Governments, and Leaders

If asked what influences political outcomes in a particular country, many people would initially point to the leaders of that country. If pushed, some might also consider the particular governing institutions, while still others would take into account the broad features of the political system, such as the extent to which the country is a democracy or an authoritarian system. Although this book also highlights the importance of social and economic structures, leaders and the political structures in which they operate are crucial components in any country's political setting.

Regime

Regime The political system of a state.

When most people use the word **regime**, they often are referring to the particular leaders of a state. For political scientists, the word *regime* means a set of rules that determine the way decisions are made. In comparative politics, a regime is best thought of as the particular political system in a state under which the government operates. The regime includes the official set of rules for making government policy (the rules for deciding "who gets what"), known as the constitution. It also includes the extent to which the government deviates from the process spelled out in the constitution when it actually makes decisions.

As a system of rules, regimes organize political activities. They provide political structure, which helps shape political behavior. This is not to imply that the regimes themselves fully control the actions of political participants. Rather, they are like a complex web of roads on which citizens and leaders can drive. Political leaders may choose to turn the country in a particular direction, but the options that the political system provides influence the exact route that turn can initiate.

In addition to broad categories of regime type, such as democracy, authoritarianism, and totalitarianism (see Chapter 5), political scientists also study more distinctive types of political systems. One such regime type is **theocracy**, a political system in which religious leaders control political decisions and religious law provides the basis for policy decisions. The Taliban, who controlled Afghanistan prior to the U.S.-led military action after the attacks of September 11, 2001, represented an extreme form of theocracy. A less extreme case—but one important to the study of comparative politics—is Iran. Though not all of the political outcomes in Iran are as extreme as they are sometimes portrayed, Iran is a good example of theocracy in practice. The

Theocracy A political system in which religious leaders hold the main government positions and religious law is the basis of policy decisions.

position of Supreme Leader in Iran (currently Ayatollah Ali Hoseini-Khamenei) and a certain number of other positions in the government must be held by scholars of Islamic jurisprudence.

Government

The term **government** has two meanings in political science. The first is broad: the ruling institutions and the people who occupy positions of power in a state. Governments are the instruments of state sovereignty. They comprise the individuals and decision-making mechanisms that generate policy. They make decisions about how the state conducts its affairs within its borders and in its relations with other states. The more narrow meaning of the term *government* refers to a political system's chief executive and cabinet officials, particularly in parliamentary systems. For example, the phrase "the Cameron government" typically refers only to United Kingdom Prime Minister David Cameron and his ministers, while someone using the phrase "the British government" is likely referring to all the institutions and officials who govern the United Kingdom. In either meaning, the individuals who make up the government can be changed by elections, by the overthrow of a leader, and by other means. Such changes in the government's makeup need not lead to a change in the overall way the political system is organized or the general set of rules that instruct how policy decisions are made and enforced.

Leaders

To understand political outcomes, one must consider both the underlying setting of political decisions and the decisions themselves. Political decisions are made by individuals acting alone or, often, in groups. Particularly in democracies, ordinary citizens make and act upon many decisions that can influence political outcomes. Yet, the most important choices are made by political leaders. They also have the ability to enforce political decisions, including through the exercise of authority when the political system is seen as legitimate.

The Nation

Within the broader society, some or all of the people share an identity that unites and binds them together. This is called their **national identity**, and the group that shares the identity is a **nation**. National identity is arguably the most important group identity in the world today. When reinforced by existing state boundaries, a strong national identity can generate tensions with neighboring states. When national identity and state boundaries do not coincide, conflict is even more likely—either between two states or between a state and a portion of its population seeking to control its own territory.

In everyday language, people use the word *nation* to mean country. They commonly talk about the "nation of France" or the "nation of Estonia." Even some political scientists—especially Americanists, who tend to refer to the United States as a nation—use the term in this way in their general discussion of countries. However, this is not how people use the word *nation* in other parts of the world, and it is not how it is used among comparativists. Instead, for comparativists, *nation* refers to a large group of people who recognize themselves as members of a group and are united by shared cultural features, especially myths and symbols but often other traits such as language. The members need not speak a single language, though unilingualism makes group unity easier.

So far, this description depicts many groups in society. A religious group in a particular country, for example, can have a large number of self-aware members united by their religion—a shared cultural feature. Yet, this is not enough to make them a nation. Therefore, while size, awareness, and unifying cultural features are necessary components of a nation, these qualities alone do not distinguish between nations and certain other large social groups. The most important feature distinguishing nations from other large groups in society is a particular belief: members of the nation believe in the group's

Government In its broad meaning, the set of individuals who produce policy decisions on behalf of the state, including the roles those individuals play and the institutions in which they function; in its narrow meaning, the leading policy-making officials such as a prime minister and cabinet at a given time in a particular country.

"Did You Know?" From June 1945 to June 2001, Italy formed new governments, in the narrow meaning of the term, nearly sixty times. Even with some individuals serving as prime minister more than once, Italy had twenty-five different prime ministers during those fifty-six years. By comparison, the United States had eleven different presidents in the same period.

National Identity A nation's self-awareness and sense of unity.

Nation A large, self-aware segment of society united by shared cultural features and possessing a belief in the right of political control over a particular territory.

A Kurdish family stands together near a tent after fleeing to the mountains in Khalifan in northern Iraq. © Patrick Barth/Getty Images

right to exert political control over a certain territory. In other words, nations have a "territorial referent,"[11] and this makes them different from other collective identities such as ethnic groups. Nations believe that they deserve to control their own affairs within a given territory.

The members of the nation often consider this territory to be the national "homeland." The land could coincide with the territory of an existing state. This is particularly common when the state's territorial boundaries were established prior to the emergence of a strong sense of national identity across that territory. Sometimes, nations exist without their own states—as do, for example, the Kurds and Palestinians. In these cases, members of the nation may pursue political control of a territory within an existing state or even several states. Many Kurds believe in their right to control Kurdistan, a territory encompassing parts of Iraq, Turkey, Syria, and Iran. The cause of Kurdish nationalism has been thwarted not only by opposition from elements of the international community, including the four states that contain parts of Kurdistan, but also by disputes between leaders of the Kurdish communities in these four states.

Civic versus Ethnic Nations

Though ethnic groups and nations are distinct concepts, comparativists who study national identity do not ignore ethnicity. In some parts of the world, ethnic identity provides the cultural common ground for national identity, and the nation's membership boundaries coincide with membership boundaries of a specific ethnic group. The ethnic group's criteria for membership become the criteria for national membership as well.[12] (Ethnicity is also a socially and politically important form of identity in its own right, and it is discussed in detail in Chapter 4.)

A nation whose membership is based on a common ethnic identity is called an **ethnic nation**. Ethnic nations are most common in Asia and Eastern Europe. Members of the Estonian nation, for example, are considered Estonian not because they live in, or even are citizens of, Estonia. Rather, they are members of the Estonian nation because they are ethnically Estonian and believe in Estonians' right to control the state of Estonia.

Many other nations, especially in North America, South America, and Africa, are multiethnic. Their membership boundaries are based primarily on an adherence to a set of political values and on citizenship in an existing state, rather than on a specific ethnic identity. As a result, this kind of nation is called a political nation or, more commonly, a **civic nation**. In civic nations, the overarching cultural features may favor one ethnic group over another. For example, often a single national language is used in schools and by government, which privileges those who speak it, but membership in the nation is open to people of different ethnic backgrounds.

These two types of nations are best thought of as ideal types. An **ideal type** is a pure form of a concept that may never be realized in practice. Many social scientists consider Americans, for example, to be as close to the ideal civic nation as any nation in the world. How closely Americans approach this ideal of civic national identity is a matter of debate. In the development of American national identity, membership has historically been open to a variety of ethnic groups and has centered on U.S. citizenship and acceptance of a general set of values about personal liberty and political equality. That said, the unifying cultural features chosen by those with the power to shape American identity—for example, competency in English—have privileged some ethnic groups over others.

Ethnic Nation A nation whose national identity is based on its ethnic identity.

Civic Nation A nation whose members are united by multiethnic cultural features and citizenship in the state rather than by shared ethnic identity.

Ideal Type A pure form of a concept that may never be realized in practice.

Think and Discuss

To what extent are Americans really a civic, as opposed to an ethnic, nation? Do Americans have enough of a unified sense of identity to be considered a nation at all?

Nationalism

Nationalism is the process of pursuing a set of rights for a nation, including at least the right of territorial self-determination. This pursuit of territorial control need not be successful, nor must the leader of a nationalist movement—called a **nationalist**—strive for complete independence and the establishment of an internationally recognized state. The quest for **territorial autonomy** within an existing state is consistent with nationalism. When a group has territorial autonomy, it controls much of the daily happenings of a particular area of the country, but it surrenders authority over some matters (e.g., national defense) to the country's central government. An independent national state is the ultimate goal of most nationalists. The term **nation-state** highlights this goal: an independent state existing for a single nation.

In seeking this perceived right to territorial control, nationalists must tell a convincing story about two boundaries. The first is the identity boundary, which marks the membership limits for the nation. This requires explaining who belongs to the nation. Second, nationalists must delineate the territorial boundaries of the national homeland. In other words, they must address what territory the nation should control. Appeals to these two corresponding boundaries make nationalism a powerful force in modern politics; nationalism unites the passions of belonging to a group with the feeling of connection to a territory. Belonging to a group and connecting to the land are arguably among the most powerful emotional triggers in humans. Nationalism combines them, and nationalists exploit them.

The response to the "Who belongs to the nation?" question generally takes either a more ethnic or a more civic form. It is thus possible to talk about ethnic nationalism—also commonly called ethno-nationalism—and civic nationalism. These different strains of nationalism are based on different views of the membership boundaries of the nation.

Answering the "Who belongs to the nation?" question also typically involves highlighting the differences between those who belong to the nation and those who do not. Thus, nationalists may portray the "other" as physically different, culturally inferior, and less intelligent as well as a threat to the nation. This representation of the other as a threat is a common theme in ethno-nationalist conflicts, even before such conflicts turn violent.

Nationalists also have to demarcate the territory that they are pursuing and justify control of it. They may emphasize historical ties to a region, demographic dominance of it, or some other aspect illustrating the nation's connection to the territory. These traits are presented as evidence that the territory is the nation's homeland. Problems arise when the territory that one nation perceives to be its homeland is claimed in a similar way by another national group. The existence of **overlapping homelands** is one of the key causes of conflict in the world. For example, the overlapping homelands predicament drives, in part at least, the conflict between Israelis and Palestinians. It is most common in cases of ethnic nationalism in which two ethnic groups have lived in the same area for a long period of time and have developed distinct national identities.

Think and Discuss

Although nationalism is often portrayed in a negative light, a core principle of national identity—control over one's own political affairs—is also a core principle of democracy. Are nationalism and democracy complementary or contrasting pursuits?

Political Science as a Science

Political scientists study important political outcomes: election results, democratization, major policy reforms, and more. They collect and analyze data, describe and categorize the data, and use theories to explain causal relationships within the data and predict future political outcomes. They also sometimes prescribe policies to address social problems based on their research. Political science has become increasingly

Nationalism The pursuit of a set of rights for a nation, including the right of political control over a certain territory.

Nationalist A leader of a movement based on nationalism.

Territorial Autonomy A group's control of much of what happens in a particular region that is not officially independent.

Nation-state An independent state that exists for a single nation, it is the ultimate goal of most nationalists.

"Did You Know?" Estimates vary considerably, but it is reasonable to conclude that several thousand distinct ethnic groups exist in the world. As a result, though the concept of self-determination sounds good in theory, recognizing each ethnic group as an ethnic nation that deserves control over its own territorial homeland would lead to an explosion in the number of states in the world. Imagine the United Nations General Assembly with three thousand members!

Overlapping Homelands A situation in which two or more nations lay claim to the same territory as part or all of their homeland.

concerned with making its research "policy relevant"—that is, useful to political leaders and to the people in charge of administering public policy. Most of the chapters of this book end with a "Research in Context" feature that provides an overview of a recent comparative politics research article related to the topic of the chapter. Within each of these features, a section titled "So What?" discusses the relevance of the research for policy makers and ordinary American citizens.

The rest of this chapter is devoted to a discussion of how comparativists and other political scientists examine causal relationships in a systematic manner. The discussion includes the principles of scientific research, the extent to which political science is a science, and how comparative political research is conducted. The chapter also introduces the notion of structure versus choice, a framework for sorting out the many causal arguments about political outcomes you will encounter in your comparative politics course.

Scientific Research and Scientific Knowledge

Political science is one of the few academic disciplines that includes the word *science* in its name. But political science faces difficulties that some of the natural sciences do not. Before considering how scientific political science can be, it is helpful to discuss the goals and methods of scientific inquiry.

The term **science** refers to a particular form of systematic study to better understand events and processes. As the basis for such understanding, science pursues knowledge that is reliable and general in that it can be applied to help comprehend a variety of settings. Science seeks regularities or patterns in nature, including in human behavior. It aims to discover how factors relate to one another and to use that understanding to predict future relations between those factors. Discoveries come from analyzing empirical data (observations) and utilizing a generally accepted methodology to allow others to replicate findings. Unlike philosophy, science focuses on questions about how things are rather than how things ought to be.

Causality

Causality is a central consideration in any discussion of science. A causal relationship involves two or more **variables**. Variables are objects or phenomena whose existence or value can vary, such as gross domestic product per capita, type of economic system, or whether a political system is a democracy. Such variables include the outcome (the result or effect) that a researcher seeks to understand. This type of variable is called a **dependent variable** because its value or existence is dependent on the presence and/or values of other variables. The elements that the researcher examines as possible causes of the presence and/or value of the dependent variable are called **independent variables**. They are given this label because their magnitude or occurrence does not depend on the value or presence of other variables examined in the study.

Think and Discuss

Name a type of major political outcome that you think would make an interesting dependent variable.

Theories as Causal Stories

Observations alone may not provide definitive evidence about causality. In such cases, making causal claims requires more than data collection and analysis. It requires a **theory** to provide the "causal story" behind the patterns in the data. Furnishing the underpinnings of hypotheses, theories are the backbone of scientific inquiry. A theoretical framework that claims that two or more variables are causally related transforms observations of what happened into an explanation of why it happened. For example, the next chapter of this book contains an overview of dependency theory, a theory that provides a causal story for why so many economically developing countries struggle to become more prosperous and more democratic.

Science A form of systematic study undertaken to better understand nature and human behavior that relies on empirical data, employs a generally accepted methodology to allow others to replicate findings, and focuses on questions about how things are rather than how things ought to be.

Causality A relationship between two or more variables in which changes in the presence or value of one produces a change in the presence or value of another.

Variable An item whose existence or value can change.

Dependent Variable The outcome that investigators seek to explain.

Independent Variable Something investigators use to explain an outcome, whose value or existence is not affected by the rest of the factors they examine.

Theory A set of propositions about how and why phenomena relate to one another in a variety of settings.

Thus, it is generally not the data themselves but rather new or existing theories that allow political scientists to make causal claims. Political scientists often test existing theories or develop new ones by collecting and examining data. Such data include everything from direct observations, historical documents, and economic statistics to interviews with government officials and responses to survey questions. Data that are consistent with a theory support that theory, but they cannot prove that the theory is correct. Data that are inconsistent with a theory, however, do call it into question. One cannot have confidence in a theory that offers an explanation for something that appears not to have taken place.

At other times, political scientists are not testing a theory but rather are seeking to understand an important political outcome in a given country. In such instances, theories help them make sense of what happened. Throughout this book are boxes labeled "In Theory and Practice." Each lays out a key theory related to a topic of the chapter. Some of the boxes stress how the country supports or challenges the theory, while others focus on how the theory can help us understand that country.

The Scientific Method

What does the practice of scientific inquiry look like? How does one discover general and reliable knowledge? What does it mean to study a topic scientifically? Most political scientists believe that engaging in scientific study does not depend on the subject of the study. Though studying politics scientifically may be more difficult than studying other topics, it can be done. How scientific an endeavor is depends on the method of the research. Scientific research involves a generally accepted process of collecting, analyzing, and interpreting data.

Research Questions

The research process begins with the identification of a **research question** (see Figure 1.1). This question generally entails some puzzle that the researcher finds interesting and that does not have an obvious answer; if it did, there would be little reason to engage in its systematic study. The question is also usually a "why" question, such as "Why do some countries become democracies and others do not?"

In the early stages of research on a topic, it is necessary first to establish the basic patterns in the variables under study. In these initial stages, the research questions might ask who, what, when, where, or how. For example, early studies of democracy by political scientists asked "What are the identifiable features of a democracy?"; "When did democracy emerge?"; and so forth. Several of the "Research in Context" features highlight such descriptive, pattern-establishing efforts. Once the general

Research Question A puzzle that does not have an obvious answer and forms the basis for a research project.

A Diagram of the Research Process

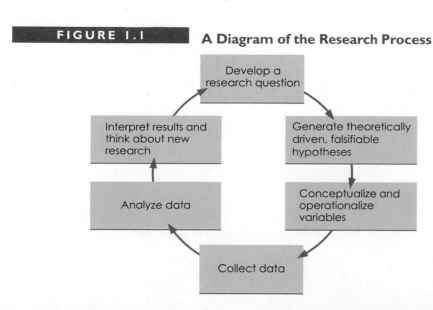

patterns have been established, researchers turn to understanding the reasons for the patterns. Understanding requires answers to "why" questions.

Hypotheses

The next step is to develop a **hypothesis**. This is a tentative statement representing an answer to the research question (see Figure 1.2). A hypothesis is tentative because it is based on existing theories or logic and needs to be tested.

Here, theories serve as "hypothesis generators." Through their general causal story about how certain phenomena are related to one another, theories also provide more specific, testable claims. A theory about how historical, economic, and other differences between regions within a country affect political attitudes, for example, could be used to generate a hypothesis about regional divisions in a specific country (such as Ukraine) and their impact on particular attitudes (such as support for independence from Russia).

The hypothesis must be **falsifiable**. This does not mean the researcher must find that the hypothesis is false. Rather, it means that a possibility must exist that the statement is false. In other words, the hypothesis cannot be a statement that is true by definition. For example, the statement that large countries have more territory to defend than small countries is not falsifiable. It is true by definition. Such a claim is called a **tautology**.

The researcher then tests the hypothesis or hypotheses. If the data are not supportive of the research hypothesis, the researcher rejects the hypothesis. If the data are consistent with a particular hypothesis, the researcher can claim that the research findings provide support for that hypothesis. Analysis of the data cannot prove a hypothesis to be true.

Conceptualizing and Operationalizing Variables

Once a hypothesis has been developed, a researcher should clearly define the key terms in the study and how they will be measured. In a study of democratization, for example, a researcher not only should define democracy but also should make clear the observed criteria that will be used in the study to decide how democratic a particular country is. These two processes are called **conceptualization** and **operationalization.** Conceptualization is the way that a researcher thinks about a particular concept (e.g., what democracy means), including which aspects are most important to consider when studying it. Operationalization is the establishment of a particular measurement scheme for that concept, allowing the researcher to observe and categorize data about the concept.

Collecting and Analyzing Data about Variables

The next steps in the scientific method are to collect and analyze data. Political scientists seeking to collect data involving people usually require the approval of a board that reviews their proposed research and looks for ethical concerns. The analysis must also conform to certain accepted standards. Statistical analysis, for example, involves procedures that are generally understood by those who use it. A researcher

Hypothesis A tentative statement by a researcher about the expected relationship between what the researcher is seeking to understand and what the researcher is examining as a potential cause or causes.

Falsifiable A trait of a good hypothesis, the term means that the hypothesis is not a statement that is true by definition.

Tautology A statement that is true by definition.

Conceptualization The way that a researcher thinks about a particular concept, including which aspects are most important to consider when studying it.

Operationalization The establishment of a particular measurement scheme for a concept, allowing one to observe and categorize data about it.

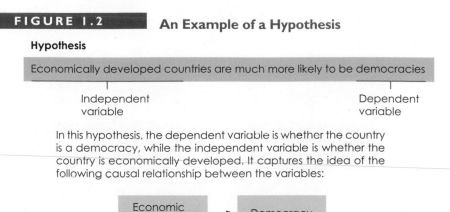

FIGURE 1.2   **An Example of a Hypothesis**

Hypothesis

Economically developed countries are much more likely to be democracies

Independent variable   Dependent variable

In this hypothesis, the dependent variable is whether the country is a democracy, while the independent variable is whether the country is economically developed. It captures the idea of the following causal relationship between the variables:

Economic development → Democracy

also adheres to particular scientific norms in presenting the findings of the research, though the exact norms may differ from discipline to discipline. This openness and use of accepted norms relates to the idea of "transmissibility" of scientific knowledge. If other scholars cannot determine how a colleague arrived at a particular finding, that finding will be received with skepticism.

How Scientific Is Political Science?

Political science, like other social sciences, is limited in its ability to produce generalizable causal claims because its subject matter involves people. People are more complex, less predictable, and more unruly than chemicals in a laboratory. Some political scientists challenge the idea that definitive causal statements can be made about something as complex and multifaceted as politics. They emphasize the difficulties of measuring important concepts in practice and contend that the most central concepts, such as power, tend to be the most difficult to measure and observe. As a result, they argue that measurement difficulties are not simply research challenges but strike at the heart of the ability of political scientists to study their subject in a scientific manner.

Fotini Christia, a professor at MIT, collects data by interviewing a local warlord in Afghanistan.
© Fotini Christia

The complexity of politics, difficulty in measuring key concepts, and challenges to controlling for rival explanations lead some political science scholars to reject causality as central to their study of politics. Instead, they tend to focus on "degrees of association" between two or more variables. They examine how certain variables appear to be correlated with one another but do not generate claims about the strength or direction of causality.

Still others contend that political scientists find it more difficult to be objective than other researchers in the social and natural sciences. Because politics is, among other things, about how resources get extracted from and distributed across society, it is not surprising for political scientists to have strong beliefs about how the subjects they study ought to be in addition to how they actually are. Caring about how to confront social problems is what attracts many to politics and its study.

Although it is important to keep these concerns in mind, political science is not condemned to be unscientific. Political scientists can and do employ research strategies to make their work as scientific as possible. To do so requires an understanding of the goals of scientific inquiry and of the scientific method, as well as the limitations involved when studying politics and the options available to scholars to address these limitations. It also means acknowledging the importance of theory in causal explanations.

Methods of Comparing to Understand Politics

Comparativists face three vital questions when designing a research project: (1) what level of analysis to employ, (2) how many cases to examine, and (3) what form of data to collect and study.

Levels of Analysis

The term **level of analysis** relates to where one looks for the answer to the research question. Researchers in all disciplines must determine the level of analysis when designing their research. In political science, a number of possibilities exist. Some political scientists collect data on individuals, including their attitudes or their decision-making strategies. Many political scientists examine groups within a particular

Level of Analysis A choice from a continuum of options—from the individual to the international system—concerning where a researcher will look for data.

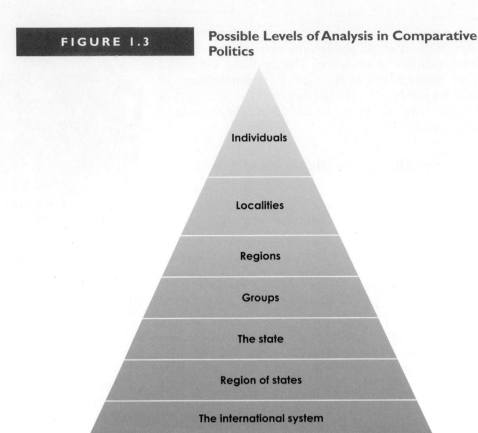

FIGURE 1.3   Possible Levels of Analysis in Comparative Politics

society or compare such groups in more than one society, searching for differences in their collective political behavior and trying to explain the differences. Others study localities or regions within one or more states, making comparisons and seeking to understand variation among them. Still others examine aspects of the political system, looking at the political institutions, their rules, and their outputs. Others prefer to examine and compare regions of states, systems, or societies. A researcher might ask, for example, why the depth of integration—the interconnections among countries—is greater in Europe at the present time than in any other region. Still other political scientists, particularly those who study international relations, compare the international community as a whole at different points in time. Figure 1.3 summarizes the levels of analysis options in political science.

Number of Cases

Political science research can be divided into two categories, **quantitative studies** and **qualitative studies**, based on the number of cases. In comparative politics, a case is often a country. It is important to remember, however, that cases can come from any of the levels of analysis in Figure 1.3. Quantitative studies are sometimes called "large N" research, with *N* referring to the number of cases. Quantitative studies allow statistical analysis of the data. Qualitative studies involve a small number of cases ("small N" research). The specific research question can drive the decision to engage in qualitative or quantitative research. Some research questions are better answered with a large number of cases, others with a small number of cases.

Case Studies

The smallest number of cases examined in a political science research study is one. A research project that looks at only one case is called a **case study** or, sometimes, a **single case study**. The two terms can be used interchangeably. In a case study, the advantages and disadvantages of small N research are most apparent. A case study

Quantitative Studies Studies that involve a large number of cases, allowing the researcher to use statistical techniques to analyze the data.

Qualitative Studies Studies that involve a small number of cases and do not allow the researcher to use statistical techniques to analyze the data.

Case Study A research project looking at only one case; also called a **single case study**.

allows a deep understanding of the events in question in that case. It provides an opportunity for "thick description." Arguably, it can also allow what one might call "thick explanation,"[13] if the in-depth study allows the researcher to see the causal mechanism in progress.

Being able to see the causal process in action can give case studies powerful **internal validity.** Internal validity refers to how sound the claims of a causal relationship are based on the researcher's data. Internal validity does not mean the finding would hold in all cases, but rather that the researcher appeared to get it right in this particular study.

On the other hand, in a case study researchers cannot control for certain variables while looking at the effects of others in the way that they can in, for example, an experiment involving a number of subjects. That is, with only one case, it is impossible to examine the effects of a particular variable while holding the others constant. All variables that might theoretically affect the dependent variable are in play at the same time. Judging the relative effects of multiple variables in only one case places a great burden on the researcher. This burden includes the problem of objectivity, which can be difficult when one gets too close to the subject of the study. The researcher may pay more attention to institutions or individuals he or she likes personally. The ability to be objective is a challenge for all researchers, especially those who work on only a single case.

Another limit of a case study relates to the ability of the researcher to generalize from the findings. How can one know if the findings of the case would hold in other cases if one does not examine any other cases? This means that case studies are, in general, weak on **external validity.** External validity is the sense that a researcher's claims about a causal relationship would apply to cases the researcher did not examine. The greater the sense that the findings apply to a large number of cases, the greater the external validity. Consequently, the more cases that a researcher examines, the more confident that researcher can be that strong patterns found in the data would hold in other cases as well. The fewer cases the researcher examines, the less confident he or she can be that the findings apply generally.

Because it is difficult to generalize from a single case, case studies are also limited in helping researchers test existing theories about political outcomes. If the theory leads to an unqualified hypothesis, such as "All democracies are the result of high levels of economic development," a case study could allow a researcher to call the theory into question. India, for example, can do great damage to a theory that claims that high levels of economic development are necessary for the development of democracy. However, political science theories are rarely absolute. The more common form of theory is a probabilistic theory, leading to a hypothesis such as "Democracies are more likely in countries with high levels of economic development." A single case can do minimal damage to a probabilistic theory.

This does not mean case studies are unhelpful to scholars interested in political science theories. First, looking at a single case might help a researcher generate a new theory that could be examined in other cases. The case study is not a test of the theory because the case was used to develop the theory. It can add a degree of validity to the theory, however, by showing that it works in at least one case.

Second, political scientists occasionally conduct what is known as a **deviant case study.** This approach examines a case that seems to be an outlier, that does not fit into a broader pattern. For example, comparativists interested in democratization often study India as a deviant case because it violates so many of their general understandings about conditions that facilitate the development of a stable democracy. By understanding why a case like India differs so greatly, a researcher may gain insight into other cases. Deviant case studies can lead researchers to consider different explanations that they might have ignored if they had also ignored the deviant case.

The flip side of the deviant case approach is the **critical case study.** A researcher employing a critical case approach seeks a case that provides a particularly powerful example of the research question in practice, such as one that offers a tough test of the study's key theories and hypothesis. Danish social scientist Bent Flyvbjerg, a specialist in case study methodology, claims that the goal is to find a case that leads one to "a generalization of the sort, 'If it is valid for *this* case, it is valid for all (or many) cases.'"[14]

Internal Validity The soundness of the researcher's claims based on the data.

External Validity The extent to which the findings of a study would hold up if data from cases not examined in the study were analyzed.

Deviant Case Study A project that examines a research question in a case that exhibits characteristics very different from a generally known pattern.

Critical Case Study A type of case study in which the case is selected because it provides a tough test of the central hypothesis or hypotheses in the researcher's study.

Finally, a single case study can be valuable because the case itself is important to understand. In addition to testing theories, comparativists are expected to have a handle on the domestic politics of one or more countries and to use that knowledge to help those in charge of making government policy. For instance, a U.S. Department of State official may be much less interested in the generalizability of a particular political science theory than in a deep and convincing explanation of recent political events in a country like Russia, China, or Iran.

Quantitative Statistical Analysis

At the opposite extreme from the case study is quantitative, large N research. This form of data analysis involves examination of a large number of cases—usually no fewer than fifty; typically well over one thousand—with the help of such software programs as SPSS or STATA. The cases may be events, or they may be individuals. Quantitative analysis of data from surveys of mass attitudes is relatively common in political science.

An important advantage of large N studies is that the analysis can incorporate an element of control similar to that in experiments and absent in case studies. The more cases, the more easily a statistical software program can control for the effects of one variable while estimating the effects of another. This control can help prevent researchers from mistakenly believing that two variables are causally related when they are not. Take the example of party identification in the United States. Republicans sometimes point out that those who identify themselves as Republicans tend to be more educated than self-identified Democrats. Before one makes a causal claim about this correlation ("Better education leads to identification with the Republican Party"), one must control for other factors, such as income. Income correlates both with Republican Party identification and with education. Having many cases allows one to control for income when looking at the impact of education. Doing so weakens greatly the case that more education leads to becoming a Republican.

In addition, large N research possesses a great advantage for generalizability. Sometimes statistical analysis can be performed on the entire group of cases one wants to understand. More often the analysis is performed on a sample of that group. Assuming proper sampling techniques, the larger the number of cases in the sample, the more confident the researcher can be that the sample reflects patterns in the larger group. Thus, the external validity of large N studies is one of their important strengths.

Large N research also has limitations. The most basic disadvantage is that information about each case is limited. Large N studies lack the depth of knowledge about each case that is the hallmark of case study research. As a result, there is no opportunity to see the causal relationship in practice, as can sometimes occur in case studies. Quantitative research is typically dependent on theory to turn findings of correlation into causal claims.

The Comparative Method

A final approach seeks to combine the best of case study and large N statistical analysis. Although many comparativists rely on case studies or large N research, this alternative approach, called the **comparative method**, is widely accepted as the cornerstone of comparative politics research.

By examining a smaller number of cases, typically between three and ten, the comparative method seeks to bring in some of the rich detail of the case study. At the same time, by examining more than one case, the approach attempts to provide a degree of generalizability and the ability to control for rival explanations. Along with combining the best of the case study and large N approaches, the comparative method incorporates the weaknesses of the other two approaches as well. The comparative method cannot incorporate statistical control; there are not enough cases. It also cannot provide the depth of understanding of each case that a single case study can. Researchers engaged in comparative studies hope that the strengths outweigh the weaknesses, but they also search for other ways to address the limitations.

Comparative Method A research design that seeks to understand the causes of a dependent variable by examining a small number of carefully selected cases.

One important way to address the inability to use statistical control involves the introduction of something similar to statistical control through the careful selection of cases. Two main forms of this technique are the **most similar approach** and the **most different approach**. A comparativist's resources and existing knowledge of particular countries, as well as the substantive problem that he or she wants to address, affects which of these approaches the comparativist chooses.

The most similar approach examines cases that are, at first glance, very much alike. A most similar study might include the cases of Canada, the United States, the United Kingdom, Australia, and New Zealand. They share a number of key features as Western cultures with predominantly English-speaking populations, high levels of economic development, large middle classes, and sizable native and/or ethnic minority populations. Despite their similarities, they pose a puzzle for the researcher: the dependent variable—for example, percentage of the national budget spent on the military—differs noticeably across them.

The similar characteristics allow the researcher to rule out a number of possible explanations for why the dependent variable's values differ across the cases. The shared features (e.g., level of economic development) are essentially constant across the cases, while the dependent variable is varying. There is no correlation between a constant and a fluctuating variable, so no causal relationship can exist between them. By controlling for these mutual characteristics, the researcher can look for other factors that vary along with the dependent variable. These additional independent variables would be chosen based on existing theories. In Table 1.1, the first independent variable appears not to be related to the dependent variable, while the second independent variable appears to be negatively related to it.

The most similar approach has strengths and weaknesses. Its major strength is that the findings would seem to apply to countries with very different values of the dependent variable. The main weakness is that the approach limits the researcher's ability to generalize from the findings to countries that are different from the ones examined in the study. Because the countries studied are similar in so many ways, the results might only apply to the type of country examined in the study.

The most different approach is the opposite, both in the types of countries and the pattern of the dependent variable. A most different comparative study might include the countries of Germany, Russia, Costa Rica, Argentina, Thailand, and Israel. Although these countries appear to have little in common, they pose a puzzle, as the dependent variable in the study, perhaps something like portion of the government budget spent on retirement programs, is essentially constant across them. Because so many features of the countries are dissimilar, the researcher is able to rule out a number of possible explanations for the values of the dependent variable. In this case, many possible independent variables are varying, while the dependent variable is not, again producing a lack of correlation and, therefore, of a causal relationship between the variables and the dependent variable.

The task for the researcher in the most different study is to find one or more independent variables that have similar values in the otherwise diverse cases. Again, the researcher would turn to existing theories for guidance about which variables to

Most Similar Approach A form of the comparative method examining cases that are very much alike, but in which the dependent variable varies.

Most Different Approach A form of the comparative method examining cases that are very different from one another, but in which the dependent variable is similar.

TABLE 1.1		An Example of a Most Similar Approach Comparative Study	
Case	**Dependent Variable**	**Independent Variable$_1$**	**Independent Variable$_2$**
1	Low	High	High
2	High	Medium	Low
3	High	High	Low
4	Medium	Low	Medium
5	Low	Medium	High

TABLE 1.2	An Example of a Most Different Approach Comparative Study		
Case	**Dependent Variable**	**Independent Variable$_1$**	**Independent Variable$_2$**
1	High	High	High
2	High	High	Low
3	High	High	Low
4	High	High	Medium
5	High	High	High

observe. In the example in Table 1.2, the first independent variable appears to have a strong positive relationship with the dependent variable, while the second independent variable seems to have no relationship at all.

The major strength of the most different approach is it allows the researcher to generalize the findings to a wide range of countries. If the results apply to this diverse group of countries, why would one expect them not to hold in other cases? The drawback is that the findings apply at best only to countries with roughly the same value of the dependent variable as those in the study. The researcher is unable to generalize to cases in which the particular dependent variable looks quite different.

A Framework for Understanding Political Outcomes: Structure versus Choice

The study of comparative political science is a little less difficult when you are armed with a general framework to help make sense of the various concepts, theories, and discussions of politics in other parts of the world. This section introduces structure versus choice as such a framework. The structure versus choice framework combines traditional ideas of political science with emerging new approaches.

Examining Structures

Structural Approach A broad approach to studying politics that seeks to explain political outcomes by looking at the effects of the underlying economic, social, or political-institutional setting in a country or set of countries.

The **structural approach** has been prevalent in political science for decades and remains popular today. It examines underlying economic, social, and political structures in an effort to understand the political outcomes that interest the researcher. Thus, the many variants of the structural approach share one feature: they focus on the broader setting in which individuals make political decisions rather than on the individuals or the decisions themselves.

Some scholars view politics as best understood through the use of structural approaches. They believe that efforts to understand political outcomes by looking at decision making are incomplete at best and terribly misleading at worst. Greater attention to structures (even at the expense of examining the decision-making process) provides a better way of answering the most important questions in the comparative study of politics. Put bluntly, to structural theorists, it matters little who is making a specific decision, and the decision-making process itself is fundamentally uninteresting.

Structures can be domestic or global. Even among scholars who focus on domestic structures, some emphasize the impact of economic development on political outcomes, and others look at the collective identities in a particular society to understand that society's politics. This book puts forward four categories of structure—economic, cultural, identity, and political-institutional—and illustrates their influence on political outcomes.

Examining Choices

A second approach involves looking at leaders and political decisions. This route has evolved into a focus on the process of decision making among elites and masses. Thus, the **choice approach** includes the role of individual leaders, ideas of leadership, and perspectives on political decision making. Decision-making theories often center on how rational individuals' political choices are.

Choice-based explanations of political outcomes bring together two somewhat distinct ideas. One is that the identity of the particular political decision makers makes a big difference; political scientists must be aware of the individuals involved in the political process under investigation. Arguing that familiarity with the person making a political decision is crucial to understanding the resultant political outcome, however, can cause a problem. If each individual is unique, how can a researcher develop and test theories useful in analyzing events at different points in time and in varying settings around the world?

The answer is that most scholars taking the choice approach anchor themselves to the level of the individual but do not stop there. Their ultimate goal is to understand political action in a general sense. They do this by focusing on the second half of the choice approach's dual nature: the process of individual decision making. Although applicable to specific cases of decision making, theories that focus on the decision-making process include general assumptions. A common one is that humans act rationally to maximize their personal satisfaction. Thus, explanations of specific political events—democratization in a particular country, for example—might highlight the role of individual action, but theorizing about democratization moves scholars into the more generalizable realm of decision making. How others decide to act and the need to make similar decisions over time also influence political decisions. Choice arguments can be extended to explain decisions over time, such as voting, and decisions involving other individuals, such as whether to join a political organization. As Chapters 8–10 discuss in detail, these are common topics for arguments that assume rational action.

> **Choice Approach** A broad approach to studying politics that seeks to explain political outcomes by looking at the effects of individual political actors and gaining an understanding of their decision-making process.

Structures, Choices, and Levels of Analysis

Whether one leans in the structure or choice direction has implications for decisions such as which level of analysis to employ. For those taking a choice approach, the level of analysis is often the individual. The choice scholar may prefer to interview particular political leaders, organize focus groups with small numbers of participants, or collect survey data involving large numbers of respondents. For those taking a structural approach, the level of analysis is generally the state; the political system; society; a collection of states, systems, or societies; or the international community. The structure scholar might turn to data on economic development or assess the extent to which different ethnic groups in a country speak different languages and have different religious faiths.

Those who make structural arguments generally contend that individuals are not autonomous from the structures in which they reside. This view, of course, limits the ability of structural approaches to help understand the political decisions of a single person. Using structural theories to explain a specific individual's actions invites an **ecological fallacy**: an error in explanation due to the assumption that observations that apply to groups also apply to the individuals who make up the groups. This assumption is flawed for two reasons: Rarely does the average value of a group apply to every member of that group, and group dynamics do not always translate well to the individual level. For example, just because a researcher discovers that members of the middle class tend to be more supportive of immigration than members of the working class, the researcher could not say with certainty how two specific individuals, one middle class and one working class, feel about immigration.

> **Ecological Fallacy** An error resulting from assuming that general trends or observations of groups correspond to particular events or actions of specific individuals.

Structures and Choices: Contradictory or Complementary?

Consolidating the different political science traditions into two broad categories helps make sense of the array of causal factors examined in political science. This book is far from the first work to employ the structure versus choice framework, which is widely used in such disciplines as sociology and anthropology. Political scientists, particularly those studying democratization, have also frequently utilized the structure-choice dichotomy. Mark Lichbach has stated that "interests, identity, and institutions contend for theoretical primacy in comparative politics."[15] To Lichbach, institutions include not only political structures but also underlying socioeconomic ones. His "identity" translates into this textbook's focus on identity-based and cultural structures, while his "interests" are a main part of what this book discusses as decisions or choices. Though Lichbach uses slightly different terminology from that in this book, his basic point that these theoretical perspectives are seen as rivals battling for supremacy is persuasive.

By the time you reach the end of this book, you may come to believe that this battle is misguided. In its pure form, structural determinism—the perspective in which underlying structures are seen as ultimately driving all important political outcomes—is incompatible with an argument centering only on individual leadership and choice. But comparativists need not, and often do not, operate at such extremes. Rival theoretical approaches can often be placed on a continuum with a gray area in the middle. Within this gray area, theories initially seen as contradictory can complement one another. They might even be used together to form a less elegant, but often more honest, explanation of events. However, before one can bring them together, one must first discuss the issues and theories connected to particular structural and choice variables in their more pure form and treat them as distinct from one another.

Linking Concepts and Cases through Topic in Countries Sections

Comparativists have many levels of analysis from which to choose. The state level, which most people would describe as comparing countries, is the most common. Comparative politics scholars are expected to know well the political, economic, and social situations in a number of countries, typically including one or more of the world's largest and most influential countries.

The Purpose of the Topic in Countries Sections

Comparative politics students face similar expectations. Although an introduction to comparative politics should expose students to the field's key concepts, theories, and approaches, it should also provide them with knowledge about many of the world's most important countries. As a result, while the next three sections of this book introduce you to important themes concerning major economic structures, cultural and identity structures, and key political structures in which laws and government policies are generated and implemented and political elites are linked to the general public, these chapters also contain "Topic in Countries" (TIC) sections. The TIC sections show how the major concepts introduced in the chapters play out in nine of the world's most important countries: the United Kingdom, Germany, Mexico, Brazil, Russia, China, India, Nigeria, and Iran.

The TIC sections cover the same nine countries each time, helping you develop a familiarity with these important countries. The sections are complemented by a number of "Spotlight on . . ." boxes, which examine a particular concept in one of three countries, France, Iraq, and South Africa, which are not included in the set of TIC cases. A "Country Summary" organizes the information presented in each TIC section in a succinct table that appears at the end of the TIC section. These tables include the three "Spotlight on . . ." countries to augment their coverage. Thematic and country-specific information is also integrated in the "In Theory and Practice" features, each of which introduces an important theory that comparativists employ and immediately links that theory to one of the TIC cases.

The Topic in Countries Cases

The nine TIC cases are some of the largest, most populous, and most powerful countries in the world. None of their populations is homogeneous; each contains politically important identity divisions. These are the only features that they all share. In many other ways, the nine countries can be grouped into contrasting categories, which means that they provide valuable examples about how the sets of causal factors—structural and choice-based—examined in this book can generate different political outcomes.

Only two of the nine TIC cases, the United Kingdom and Germany, are considered to be clear examples of economically developed countries (EDCs), a label described in more detail in Chapter 2. Their gross domestic products (GDPs) per capita are much higher than those of the other seven TIC cases, and both have large middle classes. Several of the other countries are labeled "emerging markets," though Mexico, Brazil, China, and India are also often considered lesser developed countries (LDCs). One other, Russia, is often labeled a "country in transition" (CIT) because of the combination of a transition from its previous Communist system, some traits that look like those of an EDC, and other traits that resemble an LDC. The two other TIC cases, Nigeria and Iran, are LDCs that, due either to a very low level of economic development (Nigeria) or to a reluctance to open its economy to outside investment (Iran), do not fall into the emerging market category.

The political cultures of the nine TIC cases differ significantly as well. As discussed in Chapter 3, the political cultures tend to emphasize collectivism over individualism, though this is less true of the United Kingdom and, somewhat, of India. Levels of interpersonal trust, belief in the legitimacy of the political system, and attachment to an overarching political community vary greatly across the cases. In many of the countries, especially Mexico, Brazil, Russia, China, and Nigeria, corruption is a serious problem.

Although identity is a politically relevant factor in all of the TIC cases, the specific issues differ from case to case. In Brazil, racial categories are more important than ethnic ones, and caste divisions in India remain socially powerful even if officially discredited by the Indian government. In China, the ethnic minority groups are small in percentage terms, but China's population size means that they are large in absolute terms, and the minorities also tend to be regionally concentrated. The concentration of minority groups in border areas is also a concern for the governments of Russia and Iran. In other cases, including Nigeria, the extent to which ethnic identity is complemented by other identity categories like religion deepens its political influence. In the United Kingdom and Germany, the immigrant population receives significant attention from the government—and from the rest of the population.

Several of the countries are considered democracies, including the United Kingdom, Germany, Mexico, Brazil, India, and, to a lesser extent, Nigeria. Three of them—the United Kingdom, Germany, and India—are consolidated democracies (a concept discussed in Chapter 11), and the other three are established democracies. The remaining three TIC countries are not democracies, ranging from highly authoritarian China to Russia and Iran, which have some democratic features but fall far short of democratic standards in many ways. Russia's political system has succumbed to creeping authoritarianism over the previous decade, and Iran's theocratic regime greatly restricts political competition.

How the governing institutions are organized in the TIC cases also varies. As discussed in Chapter 6, the United Kingdom, Germany, and India are parliamentary systems, with the head of government (the prime minister in the United Kingdom and India, the chancellor in Germany) responsible to the legislative branch rather than acting as a check upon it. Mexico, Brazil, and Nigeria use a presidential system, which separates executive and legislative power. The Iranian institutional arrangement also has features of a presidential system, but its theocracy gives great power to key unelected officials, which limits the influence of the Iranian president. China and Russia have "semipresidential" systems with both a president and a prime minister, but the less-than-democratic nature of both systems makes it hard to generalize about the impact of their semipresidential arrangements. (Other countries, like France, employ the semipresidential system within the context of a functioning democracy.)

As discussed in detail in Chapter 7, the political influence of the main unelected components of government—the judiciary, bureaucracy, and military—differs across the TIC countries. Many of the countries have high courts that can rule on the constitutionality of government acts, but historically the high courts in Mexico, Brazil, Russia, China, and Nigeria have struggled to maintain their independence from the executive branch. The bureaucracies in a number of the countries have expanded their authority, but in the United Kingdom and others the size of the bureaucracy has been curtailed in the recent past. Some militaries are strongly under the control of the civilian government, with the United Kingdom and Germany serving as the models among the TIC cases of civilian control, but others have had, or continue to have, a strong governing role in the political system.

The patterns of mass political participation differ significantly across the nine TIC countries. Voting rates differ, along with the extent to which members of the general population engage in unconventional forms of participation, including violent protests and terrorism. Interest groups, which can help link the general population to the government, are organized differently as well. As highlighted in Chapter 8, some countries (Germany, for example) employ a system of corporatism, where select interest groups are brought directly into the policy process. Others rely on the pluralist approach familiar to Americans, in which interest group compete against each other, lobbying the government during the policy-making process.

With a mix of consolidated and relatively new democracies alongside several non-democracies, it is perhaps no surprise that elections differ greatly. In most of China, elections are a formality. In countries like Russia and Iran, elections are far from the "free and fair" democratic ideal. In addition, as detailed in Chapter 9, the electoral rules vary significantly. Some of the TIC cases, such as the United Kingdom, India, and Nigeria, elect representatives from districts through a "first past the post" (FPTP) system, which is commonly used in the United States as well. Others, including Brazil and Russia in their lower house elections, use a system of proportional representation (PR) in which the percentage of votes for a political party is translated into the percentage of seats it receives in the legislature. Still others, including Germany and Mexico in their lower house elections, combine the FPTP and PR approaches.

Finally, as presented in Chapter 10, the traits of the leaders and the extent to which political decisions are based on careful, rational calculations are different from country to country, and even from time to time within the same country. In the United Kingdom, for example, Tony Blair, who served as British prime minister from May 1997 to June 2007, was known for his effective use of rhetoric and his ability to mobilize the population in support of his policies. His successor, Gordon Brown, was seen as someone who understood the details of government policy but had a difficult time effectively presenting his case to the British public. Consequently, by the start of 2010, Brown's popularity had plummeted with new elections looming. Those elections brought down Gordon Brown's government, leading him to resign as prime minister and as leader of the Labour Party.

CONCLUSION

The discipline of political science provides researchers, students, and politicians with a better understanding of politics and its impact on society. The field of comparative politics captures the complexities, divisions, and satisfactions of this discipline. Your comparative politics course will enhance your appreciation of the importance of politics, while improving your ability to assess political systems and understand political outcomes outside the United States. You will learn about concepts—such as politics and power, introduced in this chapter—that comparativists use in their work. These concepts can be challenging, so it is important to have a solid understanding of them and to use them in a consistent manner.

This introduction has aimed to provide an overview of the scientific study of politics and the approaches to studying comparative politics. This included a discussion of the research process, from developing a research question and generating hypotheses to developing new research questions based on the research. It also introduced you to different data collection methods and the issues surrounding the number of cases comparativists examine. You read about the comparative method, an approach to comparative politics research that seeks the depth of understanding of a case study and the control and generalizability of large N research.

Finally, you were introduced to the idea of structure versus choice as a framework for understanding comparative politics. This framework is used throughout the book. Chapter 2, for example, deals entirely with the topic of economic structure, and it is followed by a series of chapters addressing cultural, social, and political structures. You will be able to use this framework in other political science and social science courses, and in your daily observations of the political world around you.

KEY TERMS

Authority, p. 5
Case study, p. 18
Causality, p. 14
Charismatic authority, p. 6
Choice approach, p. 23
Citizenship, p. 8
Civic nation, p. 12
Coercive power, p. 5
Comparative method, p. 20
Comparative politics, p. 3
Comparativists, p. 3
Conceptualization, p. 16
Critical case study, p. 19
Dependent variable, p. 14
Deviant case study, p. 19
Dual citizenship, p. 8
Ecological fallacy, p. 23
Ethnic nation, p. 12
External validity, p. 19
Falsifiable, p. 16
Government, p. 11

Hypothesis, p. 16
Ideal type, p. 12
Independent variable, p. 14
Internal validity, p. 19
International recognition, p. 9
Legal authority, p. 6
Legitimacy, p. 5
Level of analysis, p. 17
Most different approach, p. 21
Most similar approach, p. 21
Nation, p. 11
National identity, p. 11
Nationalism, p. 13
Nationalist, p. 13
Nation-state, p. 13
Noncoercive power, p. 5
Norms, p. 6
Operationalization, p. 16
Overlapping homelands, p. 13
Politics, p. 3
Policy, p. 4

Power, p. 4
Power as capabilities, p. 4
Power as influence, p. 4
Qualitative studies, p. 18
Quantitative studies, p. 18
Regime, p. 10
Research question, p. 15
Science, p. 14
Single case study, p. 18
Society, p. 6
Sovereignty, p. 9
State, p. 7
Stateless, p. 8
Structural approach, p. 22
Tautology, p. 16
Territorial autonomy, p. 13
Theocracy, p. 10
Theory, p. 14
Traditional authority, p. 5
Variable, p. 14

CHAPTER 2

Economic Class, Development, Systems, and Globalization

Nigerian women dry cassava near an oil refinery in the
Niger Delta region. © George Steinmetz/Corbis

CHAPTER OUTLINE

Class and Class Structure
Economic Development
The Economic System: Government Involvement
   in the Economy
Economic Globalization

TOPIC IN COUNTRIES

Features in this chapter:

Spotlight on . . . France: Class Structure and Inequality

In Theory and Practice: Globalization, Weak State versus
Strong State Theories and the Case of Mexico's Adoption
of NAFTA

In Theory and Practice: Dependency Theory and Its
Application to Nigeria

In Theory and Practice: Modernization Theory and Its
Application to China

Research in Context: Poverty Policies in Chile and Mexico
following Pro-Market Economic Reforms

LEARNING OBJECTIVES

After reading this chapter, you should be able to

- Define key terms such as class, economic development, and globalization.

- Describe the social and cultural changes that accompany economic development.

- Discuss globalization, its role in economic development, and whether it helps or hurts the poor around the world.

- Describe the class structures, level of economic development, role of the government in the economy, and degree of globalization in the Topic in Countries cases.

- Explain the arguments that globalization (1) strengthens states, (2) weakens states, or (3) has mixed effects.

Reivu Umukoro is a mother of four who lives near the oil facility in Utorogu, a community in Nigeria's Niger Delta region. This seventy-thousand-square-kilometer region produces most of Nigeria's oil. The only benefit Umukoro has received from living in this oil-rich territory is the ability to dry recently harvested cassava (the most important food product in southern Nigeria) in the fires produced by the oil facility as it discharges unused natural gas.[1] Meanwhile, her nearby town lacks electricity and clean drinking water.

Umukoro's story is not unique. The suffering of citizens of postcolonial Nigeria comes partly from their government's failure to translate oil revenues into a diversified economy with a vibrant middle class. Nigeria's economic setting also matters in seeking to understand the country's political outcomes and those of other countries like it.

Reivu Umukoro's story reflects the importance of underlying economic conditions to the study of comparative politics. Many comparativists view economic structure, such as the level of economic development in a country, as the primary factor that shapes newly created political systems, fosters changes in these systems over time, and affects the policies they generate. Such scholars consider it impossible to understand politics in isolation from economics. Thus, economic structure is the first major type of structure examined in this book. Subsequent chapters address the important structures of political culture, identity, and political institutions.

The relationship between economics and politics is not unidirectional. Politics also shapes elements of economics. The interplay between economics and politics is considered an important part of political science, known as **political economy**. In addition to studying economic effects on politics and political effects on economics, political economists examine more complex relationships. This chapter centers on the extent to which economic structure influences politics. In other words, it mostly looks at only one part—the effect of economic structure on political outcomes—of the complex relationship between economics and politics that political economists study in depth.

Political Economy The part of political science that focuses on the connections between economics and politics.

The study of economic structural effects on political outcomes has four broad themes: class, economic development, economic systems, and globalization. Each deserves its own detailed discussion, but these four topics are also related to one another. Developed economies have different class structures from lesser developed ones, economies that are more interconnected with other economies often develop at a faster rate, and governments intervene in the economy to foster economic development and reduce poverty.

Class and Class Structure

Class is a crucial concept in the study of economic structure. Scholars define and use the term *class* differently. Many who research political behavior measure class by an individual's wealth and/or income. Scholars who study economic development are much more likely to think of class in terms of occupation, status, property ownership, and the resulting relationship with people who have other occupations, status levels, or ownership circumstances. Sociologist Max Weber brought class and status together by emphasizing an individual's present lifestyle and future life chances. Most would agree that ownership of property improves one's life chances, but Weber believed it was far from the only factor. Weber's ideas influence how the term *class* is used in this textbook: to refer to a large group of individuals with comparable social and economic attributes and, as a result, broadly similar lifestyles and future life chances.

Karl Marx also had a profound impact on the way many social scientists understand class and class conflict. Part historian and part forecaster, Marx believed that economics provides the "substructure"—think of a house's foundation—for everything else in society. Marx viewed class as being about *how* money was made rather than about *how much* money was made. For Marx, the **mode of production** is the cornerstone of any understanding of society and government.[2] The mode of production is an economy's structure based on the methods of production, patterns of property ownership, and relations between workers and owners. Accordingly, different modes of production correspond to different patterns of control over the **means of production**, the individual factories and businesses that produce goods and the machines and inputs used to produce them. Marx argued that the wealth capitalism generates and the subsequent inequality in wealth between classes are keys to understanding economics, social relations, and politics.

Marx emphasized two main classes in capitalist society: the **bourgeoisie**, who own the means of production, and the **proletariat**, who use the means of production in their work but do not own them. Relations between classes flow from this ownership disparity. According to Marx, the bourgeoisie exploit the proletariat by paying workers far less than the value of their work. This difference, called surplus value, is an important component of the profits that the bourgeoisie receive from capitalist production. Though Marx saw class relations as real, he also believed that power relationships and other causal processes may be hidden. Marx, and Marxists after him, rejected the idea that if something cannot be observed and measured it cannot be important to understanding patterns of behavior.

Among comparativists the terms **working class** and **middle class** have generally replaced proletariat and bourgeoisie. Some divide the middle class into the **old middle class** (similar to the small business owners who made up a portion of Marx's bourgeoisie) and the **new middle class** (service sector, white-collar, and civil service jobs). This new middle class has grown dramatically in many countries. By the 1950s, members of the new middle class made up a larger portion of the American workforce than did manual laborers. A few decades later, they became a majority of the workforce in many developed countries.

As other scholars considered the complexities of class in more detail, they added additional categories, in some cases creating as many as ten different class categories. Two of the additional categories—the **upper class** (those with the greatest wealth and status in a country) and the **underclass** (the poorest in the country with few prospects for improvement in their fate)—are particularly important to consider. Members of the upper class have high levels of status, connections with others in the upper class, and opulent lifestyles, while the underclass comprises people with the fewest life chances (generally the least educated) and worst lifestyles (low income, small living space or homeless, poor health). Certain ethnic or racial groups may be disproportionately found in the underclass. African Americans in the United States, for example, are three times more likely than white Americans to fall into the category of underclass.[3]

Class A large group of people with similar economic attributes that shape their lifestyles and life chances.

Mode of Production The type of economic system based on methods of production, patterns of property ownership, and relations between workers and owners.

Means of Production The individual businesses, factories, and other entities that produce goods, as well as the machines and other inputs used to produce them.

Bourgeoisie A term used by political economy scholars such as Karl Marx to refer to the individuals who own the means of production.

Proletariat A term used by political economy scholars like Karl Marx to refer to the individuals who use the means of production in their work but do not own them.

Working Class Includes individuals in a variety of occupations, such as manual laborers, who have historically generated relatively low levels of income.

Middle Class Includes individuals in a variety of occupations who generate moderate levels of income, including small business owners and service sector employees.

Old Middle Class Small business owners.

New Middle Class Service workers, white-collar managers, and civil servants.

Upper Class The wealthiest and most powerful members of society.

Underclass The poorest individuals in society who have few chances for improving their lives.

Measuring Class and Poverty

In comparative politics, some debates over class boil down to disagreements about measurement. How to measure poverty and determine who falls into the underclass category is a matter of particular contention. Typical measures used today calculate the number of people and portion of the population living on less than $1, $1.25, $2, or $2.50 per day of income. Though this measurement makes sense in many developing countries, it does not take into account the cost of living, so others have suggested looking at people who earn a certain percentage of the country's **median income**. Median income is the income level that half of the population falls below and half of the population falls above. It can be stated in terms of either individuals or households. In the United States, for example, median household income in 2007 was estimated at $52,163; by 2009 it had declined to $50,221.[4]

Child labor is common in countries with a large underclass. Here, a young girl helps her family pick cotton in China's Xinjiang province. © Chien-min Chung/Getty Images

Class Structure

The particular arrangement of the population into different classes is known as a country's **class structure**. Class structure clearly relates to level of economic equality.[5] Countries with high levels of wealth concentration tend to have little to no middle class. Class structure can also give strong hints at the degree of industrialization a country has experienced. In a postindustrial, economically developed country, the majority of the population falls into the middle class. On the contrary, a sizable middle class is highly unusual in a country that has not experienced significant industrialization.

Median Income The amount of income above that earned by those in the bottom half of the population and below that earned by those in the upper half of the population.

Class Structure The pattern of how the population of a particular country falls into different class categories; relates to level of economic equality.

Think and Discuss

If class structure is related to inequality, how can some countries, including the United States, have such a large middle class and yet such high levels of wealth concentration?

Spotlight on . . . FRANCE

Class Structure and Inequality

Karl Marx recognized three social groups in France—capitalists, workers, and peasants—but considered only workers and capitalists to be distinct classes. For Marx, peasants were no more than a "sack of potatoes" because they could not understand their collective interests.[6] Marx plainly underestimated the importance of French peasants, failing to anticipate that they would become a key constituency of the French democratic system.

Although French workers have played a significant role in political life, not all of them share the same interests. By the nineteenth century, the French working class was divided between urban artisans—for example, skilled workers in small businesses and factories producing specialty goods such as bread and luxury items like fine porcelain—and unskilled workers in industrial and mining operations, many in the industrialized north. Even the peasants were divided. Those in the Provence region practiced smaller scale farming because of dispersed land ownership. In the west of France, large concentrations of land allowed for mechanization and single-crop production.

Despite occupational differences and recent increases in wealth concentration related to globalization, wealth disparities in today's France are among the lowest in the world. Since the end of World War II, many elites have come to value prestige and status over financial gain, ending the influence and power of private money held by the traditional center of French wealth, the so-called "200 families."[7] The government has instituted a variety of programs to reallocate wealth, increase purchasing power, and expand economic opportunities for the working class. One view of France's political economy regards the resulting economy—uniting an intrusive bureaucracy, powerful unions, and generous government subsidies—as stagnant and unfriendly to innovation. Another view is that these efforts have produced free university education, universal health care, a thirty-five-hour workweek, and at least five weeks of paid vacation every year.

Class Consciousness and Its Decline

Class Consciousness The sense of belonging to and solidarity with a particular class, as well as the recognition of this class's relationship with other classes.

The extent to which people are aware of, or attached to, their identity as members of a particular class varies. This awareness, **class consciousness**, emerges as individuals become aware of their location in a particular class, develop a sense of solidarity with other members of this class, and come to deem important the relationship, usually thought of as conflicting, between their class and other classes.[8] The greater the degree of class consciousness, the more important class is as a factor shaping political outcomes.

At the time of Marx's most influential writings, class divisions were fairly clear-cut, and class consciousness, particularly among the lower class, was emerging. After 1850, Marx became more pessimistic about the possibility that working class consciousness would lead to a worldwide workers' revolution. One could argue that this pessimism was premature, given the large number of Communist states that emerged during the twentieth century. On the other hand, since World War II, class distinctions and class consciousness have declined throughout the world.

One reason for the decline of class as a force in politics is the blurring of the line between the middle class and the working class. As Russell Dalton puts it, increased pay for certain manual labor occupations has led to the "embourgeoisement" of the working class, and the growth of the service sector, often with relatively low-paying jobs, has brought a "proletarianization" of the middle class.[9] This does not mean that appeals to class—often derided in the United States as "class warfare"—have no effect on political outcomes. It simply means that class is one part of an individual's identity and may not be the primary identity component.

Think and Discuss

In the United States, to what extent is a person's class determined at birth by the class of the family? To what extent is class the result of effort? How representative is the United States on this point compared with other countries around the world?

Economic Development

The second broad topic in the study of economic structure is development. Development underscores the way in which economics and politics are linked. Though one can separate the economic components of development from the political components, political scientists often use the term *development* to refer to both processes occurring at the same time—for example, the establishment of democracy in Mexico at the same time its economy was continuing to develop and its culture was undergoing change. This chapter focuses primarily on economic development and its consequences; Chapter 11 centers on a major topic of political development: democratization.

Economic development involves changes in the structure of the economic system, including economic diversification, and increases in overall prosperity due to these changes. One way to summarize a country's economic system is to look at the kinds of goods it produces. Most economies develop by creating new products, using technology to increase production of existing products, and finding ways to improve worker productivity. Some economies change more quickly than others, but a general pattern—moving from agrarian economies based on labor-intensive agriculture to industrial economies based on products made in factories and then to postindustrial service economies—is common. Moving from an agricultural economy to an industrialized one has economic consequences that, in turn, affect politics. It is no accident that the poorest countries in the world are those that have failed to industrialize and, at best, rely on the export of raw materials and agricultural products.

Economic Growth

Structural changes to the economy affect economic growth and prosperity. **Economic growth** refers to the increase in a state's economic production over a particular period of time. The standard way to measure economic growth is to look at annual changes in a country's **gross domestic product (GDP)**. GDP is the sum value of the goods and services in a country's economy. When researchers (academic or governmental) examine GDP over time, they often measure it in **constant dollars**. This technique controls for the additional value of goods and services resulting from inflation.

Economists and political scientists used to measure a state's overall wealth by looking at its gross national product (GNP). More recently, the emphasis has shifted to the GDP. GNP is the value of all the goods and services that citizens of a country produce, whether they live inside the country or abroad; GDP is the sum of all goods and services produced within the borders of a country, whether by citizens or not. Why use GDP instead of GNP? Countries increasingly find themselves with a large number of noncitizens (permanent residents, guest workers, etc.). As the number of such noncitizen residents increases, excluding these individuals from the calculations of gross product becomes harder and harder to justify.

Although GDP is a measure of economic activity, it measures neither tasks such as housework nor illegal economic activity such as the sale of stolen goods. Some analysts estimate that goods and services produced or distributed illegally, what political economists call the **informal economy**, make up more than $15 trillion globally! A World Bank–sponsored publication describes the informal economy as including "unreported income from the production of legal goods and services, either from monetary or barter transactions—hence all economic activities which would generally be taxable were they reported to the state (tax) authorities."[10] It commonly includes goods and services provided by domestic workers and street vendors, and also illegal exchanges such as prostitution and black market trade. Because of the elusive nature of the activities involved in the informal economy, and because different scholars have different definitions of what it entails,[11] comparativists struggle to measure it accurately. As a result, estimates of the value of goods and services made up by the informal economy vary, though some believe it comprises over 40 percent of the total value of economic activity across Africa and Latin America.[12]

Economic Prosperity

Prosperity refers to the overall wealth and standard of living of a country. One could use GDP alone to get a sense of a country's prosperity, but GDP tells little about how the average person in that country is doing. A country might have a GDP five times the size of its neighbor, but if it has ten times the number of people, it is hard to call it more prosperous. One approach to solving this problem is to take population size into account. Thus, overall prosperity of a country is often measured in terms of **GDP per capita**. This is the GDP of the country divided by the number of people in the country.

Economic Development Changes over time in an economy that enhance its productive capacity and improve society's prosperity.

Economic Growth One way of thinking about economic development, it looks at annual changes in a country's GDP.

Gross Domestic Product (GDP) The sum value of the goods and services in a country's economy.

Constant Dollars Technique that controls for increased value due to inflation.

Informal Economy The portion of a country's economic activity from illegal undertakings as well as unreported legal economic activities.

Prosperity The overall wealth and standard of living of a country; it is usually measured by GDP per capita or similar statistics.

GDP Per Capita The gross domestic product of a state divided by the number of people in that state.

Using GDP per capita to gauge a country's prosperity is better than using GDP alone, but it can still be misleading. A second "correction" to GDP takes into account the cost of living, adjusting for how much one can purchase with the same amount of money in different countries. This adjustment to GDP is known as **purchasing power parity (PPP)**. It can make a big difference in per capita GDP estimates. Luxembourg has the highest per capita GDP in the world. According to the International Monetary Fund's World Economic Outlook database, its unadjusted GDP per capita was estimated to be more than $108,000 in 2011. But goods and services in Luxembourg are so expensive that the PPP correction took this number down to around $82,500.[13] On the other hand, the purchasing power parity correction for Vietnam nearly tripled its 2011 GDP per capita figure from $1,272 to $3,339.

Even when correcting for purchasing power, using GDP per capita to gauge prosperity tells an incomplete story. The United Arab Emirates, for example, has a relatively high GDP per capita-PPP (around $37,500 in 2011), but its income and wealth are among the most concentrated in the world. In such cases, the country may appear prosperous, but most of the people do not share in the prosperity. Thus, political economists also look at income and/or wealth inequality. These statistics are typically estimated by considering the percentage of income or wealth controlled by the wealthiest 1 percent, 10 percent, 20 percent, and so on, as well as the bottom 40 percent or 20 percent of the population. Wealth and income inequality relate to a country's class structure. The more concentrated wealth is in a country, the less likely that it has a sizable middle class.

Whether one focuses on wealth or income inequality depends in part on how reliable the two types of statistics are in a particular case. Many statistics that address economic well-being use income (wages, interest earnings, etc.) rather than wealth (the total value of an individual's assets) because valid indicators of wealth are harder to observe. Assessments of inequality can differ significantly, however, depending on whether the measure of prosperity is income-based or wealth-based. Since wealthier individuals use their higher incomes to accumulate assets (such as property) over time and often inherit portions of their wealth from family members, the use of income-based statistics tends to underestimate the gap between the wealthiest and least wealthy in a particular population.

Alternatives to GDP-Based Statistics?

Increasingly, scholars and analysts who study economic development are questioning whether gross domestic product–based statistics are the best way to measure economic development and prosperity. Many argue that focusing on GDP places too great an emphasis on economic growth and pays too little attention to other quality of life issues. As a result, some are emphasizing a number of rival statistics to replace—or at least exist alongside—GDP, GDP per capita, and GDP per capita-PPP. One of the best known, the **Human Development Index (HDI)**, was created in 1990. The HDI scores countries not only on GDP but also on the population's education levels and overall health.[15] It is used widely by organizations like the United Nations.

Types of Countries Based on Economic Development

Comparativists use the label **economically developed countries (EDCs)** for the most economically prosperous states. There are several labels for the countries that do not fall into the EDC category (see Table 2.1 on page 35). The broadest label is **lesser developed countries (LDCs)**. At the opposite ends of the spectrum within the LDC category are two subsets: the **least developed of the lesser developed countries (LLDCs)**

TABLE 2.1	Categories and Labels of Development

Economically Developed Countries	Lesser Developed Countries
Other Labels • The North • Developed Countries • More Developed Countries • Industrialized Countries • Postindustrial Countries • Rich Countries **Subcategories** • Countries in Transition (CITs)	**Other Labels** • The South • Developing Countries • Underdeveloped Countries • Less Industrialized Countries • Poor Countries **Subcategories** • Least Developed of the Lesser Countries (LLDCs) • Newly Industrialized Countries (NICs) • Countries in Transition (CITs) • Emerging Market Countries

and the **newly industrialized countries (NICs)**. LLDCs are the poorest, least economically developed countries in the world. The NICs, found especially in Asia and Latin America, are countries whose economic development statistics have improved greatly over the last several decades but that still retain enough traits of LDCs to keep them from being broadly considered as EDCs. According to some scholars, countries such as South Korea and Taiwan used to be appropriately labeled NICs, but today are more accurately considered as EDCs.

The differences in overall prosperity between LDCs and EDCs correspond to other differences as well. EDCs generally have a different class structure than LDCs, with sizable middle classes in EDCs and small (though perhaps emerging) middle classes in LDCs. EDCs also have more diverse economies, while LDCs tend to concentrate their economic activity in agriculture and extraction of raw materials. Countries relying on raw materials, even raw materials like oil that can generate a lot of money, face a problem. **Finished products**, products that are manufactured from raw materials, cost more money than the raw materials that go into them. It takes a lot of raw material sales to afford the purchase of finished products. Even as oil rose above $100 per barrel in early 2011, paying for many of today's high-tech consumer goods still required the sale of a lot of oil.

Some countries' development patterns are unique enough to necessitate additional labels. The Eastern European and Eurasian postcommunist states, for example, are often called **countries in transition (CITs)**. On some economic statistics—such as per capita GDP—they resemble LDCs, but in other ways (such as urbanization and education), they look more like EDCs. In addition, a number of them are now members of the European Union, making the LDC label even more problematic. Thus, though sometimes considered an additional subset of the LDC category, the CITs are often thought of as justifying their own development category.

Many NICs and CITs have attracted a great deal of investment from foreign countries in recent years. The perception of international investors is that, while somewhat risky, these countries have the potential to offer a significant return on their investment. As a result, countries as diverse as Brazil, China, Egypt, India, Indonesia, Mexico, Poland, and Russia also share the label of **emerging markets**. Five of the largest of these emerging market examples (which also happen to be four of this book's TIC cases and one of its Spotlight on cases)—Brazil, Russia, India, China, and South Africa—are the focus of so much attention by companies looking to invest abroad that the first letter of each of their names forms a commonly used acronym: **BRICS**. The BRICS cases have seen impressive economic growth over the last decade, and the sizes (and even greater prospective sizes) of their domestic markets make them particularly attractive.

Newly Industrialized Countries (NICs) The more economically developed LDCs, found particularly in Asia and Latin America.

"Did You Know?" In 2011, the sum of the estimated GDP figures for all the countries in the world, known as the gross world product (GWP), was $65.4 trillion. Of this, the vast majority came from EDCs, with more than $15 trillion from the United States alone.

Finished Products Goods produced from raw materials, which are much more expensive than the raw materials that go into them.

Countries in Transition (CITs) Another term for the postcommunist states.

Emerging Markets The LDCs and CITs that are most desirable to foreign investors.

BRICS Acronym for five of the most important emerging market countries: Brazil, Russia, India, China, and South Africa.

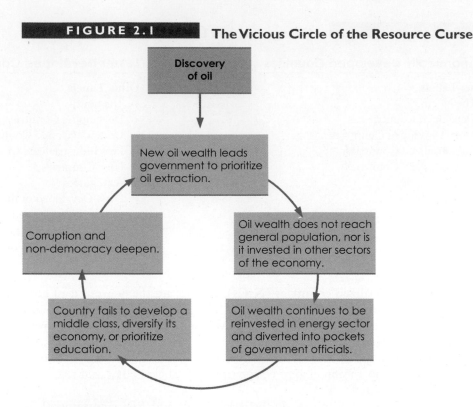

FIGURE 2.1   The Vicious Circle of the Resource Curse

Discovery of oil

New oil wealth leads government to prioritize oil extraction.

Oil wealth does not reach general population, nor is it invested in other sectors of the economy.

Corruption and non-democracy deepen.

Oil wealth continues to be reinvested in energy sector and diverted into pockets of government officials.

Country fails to develop a middle class, diversify its economy, or prioritize education.

The Resource Curse

Resource Curse The tendency for developing countries with an exportable commodity to focus on the extraction of that resource at the expense of broader economic development; associated with government corruption and failure to develop a middle class.

For countries with a large amount of a sought-after raw material, the incentive to focus on the extraction and export of that commodity is great, even if it discourages economic diversity. As a result, the wealth from these exports may not generate comprehensive economic development. Political economists refer to this situation as the **resource curse**. The resource curse can be thought of a vicious circle (see Figure 2.1). The discovery of oil or a similar resource such as diamonds, for example, leads a government to place priority on its extraction. Because the extraction can be achieved with low-skilled or foreign workers, the economy does not develop a vibrant middle class. The wealth generated by exports of the resource is not invested into other sectors of the economy but rather feeds government corruption. Extraction of the resource commands even greater attention from leaders, who are increasingly dependent on the resource to prop up the country's economy—and to line their own pockets.

"Did You Know?"
In 2010, according to *Forbes* magazine, the assets of the world's three wealthiest people equaled $153.5 billion.[16] Based on 2010 estimates by the International Monetary Fund, this amount exceeded the *combined* gross domestic products of 130 of the countries in the world.[17]

A number of countries, including large ones like Nigeria, have fallen victim to the resource curse. On the other hand, not all developing countries with natural resources end up being cursed. In sub-Saharan Africa, both Botswana and Namibia have largely avoided many of the problems associated with the resource curse. Some political economists who have examined these two cases in detail claim that they point to the importance of leadership. Strong, pragmatic leaders who are willing to tackle corruption can overcome the pressures that push other countries down the resource curse path. Thus, the resource curse concept shows that while a country's economic structure can provide the incentives for its leader to rule in undemocratic ways, participate in corruption, and fail to diversify the economy, the choices that such a leader makes are at least as important to the country's major political outcomes as is its economic structure.

The Economic System: Government Involvement in the Economy

As discussed in the previous section, one can categorize countries based on how economically developed they are, and economic development can play an important role in major political outcomes. Countries' economic systems can also be categorized by the extent to which government plays an active role in the economy. The extent to which the government has a presence in a country's economy can also shape important political outcomes. Scholars have generally identified three broad types of economic systems: capitalist, socialist, and mixed. Attempts to reform the economy, at least in any significant way, typically involve moving away from one of these types and toward another.

Free-Market Capitalism

Capitalism is an economic system based on three fundamental ideas: the belief in private ownership of property and business, the principle that economic activity should take place within the **market**, and the view that economic decisions should be made by individual companies and consumers. A market is a system of economic exchange in which those supplying goods and services and those seeking to purchase such goods and services find each other and come to agreement about the terms of the transaction. If one side is unhappy with the terms and an agreement cannot be reached, no transaction will occur. **Market forces** such as supply and demand determine many of the terms of economic exchanges, the most important of which is the asking price for goods or services. In the pure (ideal type) capitalist system, often referred to as **free-market capitalism**, the state plays little or no role in economic activity. Pure capitalism rejects state involvement in setting workplace standards (including minimum wages), coordinating retirement benefits through a social security system, and equalizing sharp divisions in income or wealth.

In practice, countries used as examples of the capitalist system do interfere in their economies. Interference often takes the form of protection from formation of a **monopoly** (when an individual company controls all or nearly all of the market for a particular good or service). Governments also develop regulations to protect consumers and the environment, create government-controlled retirement systems, and establish at least limited workers' rights regarding wages and working conditions. But governments of countries labeled as capitalist engage in economic intervention much less than do governments of other countries.

Although Americans often view the United States as the model of free-market capitalism, other countries—Singapore, for example—have even less government involvement in the economy than does the United States. Still, among wealthy, postindustrial countries, the United States has one of the most free-market approaches. It became the wealthiest country in the history of the world partly because of its strong tradition of entrepreneurial activity and innovation. Yet, it is also a country with a relatively large gap between rich and poor, and a sizable portion of the population has lacked basic health insurance coverage.

Socialism

At the opposite extreme from the ideal type of free-market capitalism is **socialism**, often called the central planning approach. Socialism involves government ownership of the means of production. The state owns the physical capital, and the workers are thus employed by the state. In addition, the government makes most of the decisions about production and distribution. Government officials decide what products the country's various factories manufacture, how many of each item are produced, and at what prices the products are sold. Although some of the small decisions may be made at the level of the firm, more fundamental decisions about targets for production are made by government bureaucrats.

In the United States, the word *socialism* is often used in political debates to condemn an opponent's support of a new government program. Residents of Russia who lived during the Soviet period would likely have been amused by the use of the term in the United States during arguments over proposals for health care reform in 2009 and 2010: nothing in American health care reform comes close to the role the socialist

---

Capitalism An economic system based on private ownership of property with business and economic activity taking place within the market.

Market A system of economic exchange in which suppliers and purchasers find each other and agree to the terms of the transaction.

Market Forces Forces, such as supply and demand, that drive the terms of transaction in capitalism.

Free-Market Capitalism Another name for the capitalist ideal, with minimal government regulation of the economy and little social welfare spending.

Monopoly Control of all or nearly all the market for a given good or service by a single company.

Socialism An economic approach that emphasizes government ownership of the means of production and government control of economic decisions such as the supply and prices of particular products; also known as central planning.

government played in people's daily lives in the Soviet Union prior to its breakup in 1991.

Soviet government officials created economic plans and determined the terms of economic transactions from the supply of products to setting prices. Heavy industry production was privileged at the expense of the production of consumer goods. Artificial prices were set for certain goods, with consumer goods generally expensive and of poor quality, and the prices of food and energy were kept low for political gain.

However, Soviet central planners could not force consumers to buy the products they supplied at the quality and prices they offered. When the demands of consumers were not met through the state-run economy, a **black market** economy emerged. In a black market economy, products and services are bought and sold illegally. The black market began to play a greater role in the Soviet economy under Mikhail Gorbachev in the late 1980s, when the Soviet Union introduced limited market economic features. The confusion, corruption, and distributional difficulties in this era of partial reforms allowed people with political connections, those who participated in the growing organized crime sector, and those who were particularly creative and daring to make sizable amounts of money selling products illegally.

The Soviets also had a difficult time getting workers to work hard, especially prior to Gorbachev's reforms. With little monetary incentive for hard work, Soviet workers developed a poor work ethic: "We pretend to work, and they pretend to pay us," they said. Absenteeism and overly long lunch breaks became the norm.

As a result of these problems, the "Soviet experiment"[18] and other real-world socialist systems showed that lack of economic efficiency is an inherent problem of central planning systems. Centrally planned systems also lack the entrepreneurial spirit and innovation found in capitalist systems. The result in the Soviet Union was slower economic growth than in the capitalist West, especially as the world economy became more technology-dependent. The Soviet Union became the world's leading steel producer just when no one cared about that anymore, when it was becoming much more important to be the world's leading producer of consumer electronics.

On the other hand, the socialist systems that emerged in the twentieth century tended to produce less inequality than capitalist systems. They were also, arguably, better able to direct economic resources to address pressing national needs. Early in Soviet history, such efforts included the rapid development of the country's energy infrastructure and industrial sector. Finally, they avoided the ups and downs of the business cycle commonly found during the same period in the West. Though economic growth had come to a standstill by the middle 1980s, the Soviet and Eastern European economies did not collapse until economic and political reforms were unleashed by Gorbachev.

Mixed Systems

Some approaches, often lumped together under the heading of **mixed economies**, fall between the ideal types of capitalism and socialism. Because they are not outright socialist systems employing central planning, political scientists and economists usually discuss them and the more free-market approach as "varieties of capitalism." The varieties are often associated with particular countries. Economist Lester Thurow provides a useful starting point for discussing them by highlighting differences among the more free-market approach of the United States, the welfare-state system of Europe, and the leadership role of the state in Japan.[19] Employing Thurow's three-part categorization, political scientist David Coates has called free-market capitalism "market-led capitalism" and has described two categories of mixed systems as labor-led and state-led.[20]

Labor-led capitalism, also known as a social democratic system, accepts many of the general principles of capitalism, including private ownership and the belief that most economic activity should be based on market principles of supply and demand. It deviates significantly from the free-market ideal type in the level of acceptable government intervention in the economic structure, allowing for extensive government

Black Market A market in which goods and services are bought and sold illegally.

Mixed Economies Economies with elements of capitalist and socialist practices.

Labor-Led Capitalism Approach that involves a substantial role for government in the regulation of the economy and the establishment of social welfare programs; also known as a social democratic system.

intervention and even government ownership of particularly important large industries. Social democrats believe that governments have a responsibility to regulate economic activity—heavily, if necessary—to protect consumers, laborers, and the environment. As a result, individual rights and personal responsibility are balanced by collective benefits and the responsibility of society to protect vulnerable individuals.

This approach is consistent with the concept of a **welfare state**, in which government provides numerous welfare benefits and services. In most countries, social welfare is protected through a combination of government policies, private interests, and individual responsibility. The more numerous and expensive the welfare provisions enacted by the government, the more substantial that country's welfare state. Countries in northern Europe, Sweden in particular, are most associated with social democracy and welfare state systems.

A system of **state-led capitalism** accepts the principle of private ownership and, to a lesser extent, individual decision making. However, it also emphasizes the good of the group over the individual and is associated with a more conservative, nationalistic culture.[21] The approach allows for significant government intervention in the economy in the form of guiding investment into growing sectors of the economy and phasing out unprofitable businesses and economic sectors. The governments of Japan and South Korea, for example, have used their power to control credit and to grant licenses to favor certain sectors of the economy and specific companies within particular sectors.[22] There are fewer social welfare protections than in labor-led economies, but often more than in market-led ones.

State-led capitalism can also involve **mercantilism**. A mercantilist (or protectionist) approach to capitalism accepts the free-market principle within the domestic sphere, but it rejects the idea of free-market competition internationally. Instead, mercantilism supports government involvement in the economy to protect domestic economic interests, particularly employment, through subsidies to particular businesses and tariffs and quotas on imports. This protection encourages the purchase of domestic products, but it also increases the cost of products for consumers.

In addition to the labor-led and state-led mixed systems, political economists have identified a relatively new mixed system, which they call **state capitalism**. Particularly in many former Communist countries of Eastern Europe and Eurasia, the state neither heavily regulates the economy nor creates large social welfare systems. Rather, it participates in the economy alongside private businesses through full or partial ownership of large individual companies.

Compared with social democratic capitalism, state capitalism involves a greater role for state ownership of economic entities but less of a role in regulation and social welfare protection. Thus, it functions more like a free-market economy than social welfare capitalist economies do, but with the state as a major economic player in the market. This approach has been increasingly evident in Russia, where the privatization of state-run enterprises led many businesses to come under private control, but the most lucrative of them—for example, large oil companies—to remain under or return to state control.

Economic Globalization

The opening chapter in this book introduced the idea that structures can be domestic or global. This distinction is particularly pertinent due to the increasing influence of forces outside a country's borders on internal decision making. People are more interconnected than ever before with those in neighboring countries and with those on the other side of the world. National governments are also increasingly influenced by international organizations (e.g., the European Union) and nonstate economic actors (e.g., McDonald's, Nike, or Microsoft). Social scientists have dubbed this process of expanding international interconnections **globalization**.

Most economists agree that globalization improves overall global economic efficiency. How individuals benefit from globalization is less clear. Some countries benefit

Welfare State An approach in which a broad set of government programs provide significant welfare benefits and services.

State-Led Capitalism A system in which the government intervenes in the economy to guide economic activities in an effort to foster economic growth.

Mercantilism A form of capitalism that accepts the general principal of free-market economics but allows significant government involvement in the economy in order to protect domestic economic interests; also known as protectionism.

State Capitalism A system in which the government neither engages in economic planning nor oversees an extensive welfare state, but owns certain individual enterprises, typically in lucrative industries such as energy.

Globalization The process of increasing connections in the areas of economics, communications, technology, and politics.

more than others, and even within a particular country globalization can have positive and negative effects. The wealthiest members of developing countries, for example, often benefit more from globalization than does the rest of the population. At the same time, countries whose economies were more integrated with others had higher economic growth rates in the 1990s. As a result, the chief economist of the World Bank, Nicholas Stern, proclaimed in 2001 that "globalization often has been a very powerful force for poverty reduction," adding that "too many countries and people have been left out."[23] In other words, although globalization has the potential to reduce poverty, the potential remains unrealized in many countries.

Most measures of the extent of economic globalization use multiple indicators. Two of the most common are trade as a portion of GDP and **foreign direct investment (FDI)**. Trade includes both **imports** (goods and services produced outside a country that are brought into the country for consumption) and **exports** (goods and services produced inside a country that are sent outside its borders for consumption). FDI is investment from outside a country into a particular economic entity with the goal of establishing a lasting presence. Because FDI is intended to develop a long-term presence, portfolio investments (such as in stocks of companies) are not considered FDI. The International Monetary Fund (IMF) requires ownership of 10 percent or more of a company before investment in that company is considered FDI.

Although globalization is anchored by deepening economic ties between countries, scholars generally agree that it involves other aspects. The A.T. Kearney/ Foreign Policy Globalization Index ranks seventy-two countries on fourteen components in four categories: economics, personal connections/communications, technology, and political ties. In this chapter, the discussion of globalization focuses on the way economic interconnectedness can shape the domestic economic and political landscape of countries around the world. Other chapters examine globalization's cultural and political manifestations.

Foreign Direct Investment (FDI) Investment from outside a country into a particular economic entity that is designed to develop a lasting presence.

Imports Products and services made outside the borders of a state that are brought inside for consumption.

Exports Products and services produced inside the borders of a state that are sent outside for consumption.

TOPIC IN COUNTRIES

The Topic in Countries (TIC) cases illustrate the concepts related to economic structure introduced in the preceding sections of this chapter. As you read through the following TIC sections, be sure to look for

- The class structures of the TIC cases, particularly the relative size of the middle class to the working class and lower class.
- The overall level of economic development of each of the TIC cases.
- The role of the state in each country's development process.
- The extent to which the economies of the TIC cases are globalized.
- The evolution of government involvement in the economy in the TIC cases.

The United Kingdom

Early industrialization and a large and generally poor urban population fostered sharp class divisions earlier in British history. Like other European countries, the British government put in a place a mixed capitalist system following World War II, though one that was less labor-led than others in Western Europe. Today, the United Kingdom (UK) is one of the more economically developed countries in the world. Its GDP-related statistics put it just behind Germany and make it the second most prosperous of the TIC cases. Although it is interconnected with other countries in a number of ways, its economy is less globalized than one might expect.

Class

Class no longer drives political behavior in the UK the way it did in the past, but it remains important to understanding British political outcomes. Despite the country's large middle class, a sizable portion of the people would identify themselves as working class—certainly a greater portion than would embrace that label in the United States. As in other economically developed countries, the UK's upper class is small but economically and politically powerful. The top 1 percent controls a smaller portion of wealth than the top 1 percent does in the United States, but some observers contend that the British upper class has had even greater advantages in education and personal connections.

From the earliest days of industrialization, economic inequality has been prevalent in British society, and it remains a problem. At present, the UK's population is economically more equal than that of the United States, but the gap between the poorest and the wealthiest remains substantial. As in many countries, gaps in income correlate with race, ethnicity, and immigrant status.

Economic Development

Urbanization in England followed the development of improved agricultural practices. For example, the seed drill, which allowed seeds to planted into the soil rather than spread across it, and crop rotation allowed farmers with large landholdings to be much more productive than those with small amounts of land. These developments were aided by the Enclosure Acts, a series of edicts in the 1700s and 1800s that allowed large landowners to consolidate their holdings and drive small farmers off the land. The poorer farmers had no choice but to move to the increasingly swelling cities.

The rise of industrial factories, which increased productivity through labor specialization and machinery, contributed to sharp class distinctions. Although British workers failed to act on Marx's vision of a violent revolution, economic development had important effects on the British political system. British political development tended to be evolutionary rather than revolutionary, but the cumulative changes over time were considerable.

Today, the UK has a highly developed economy. Its comparatively high cost of living, however, means that it is punished by purchasing power parity (PPP) corrections to GDP-related statistics. Consequently, its estimated GDP per capita in 2011 was around $38,200, but the per capita-PPP figure was just under $36,000, or more than $12,000 less than that of the United States.[24]

Government's Role in the Economy

The UK never developed the kind of full-blown, labor-led economic system found in other parts of Europe. However, the emergence of a politically powerful working class played an important role in its decision to join much of Western Europe in adopting the **postwar settlement** after World War II, a compromise that ensured a largely capitalist economic system, but with significant social welfare protections.[25] Even the Conservative

Party, the major political party on the right of the British political spectrum, accepted the significant social welfare protections, at least until the reforms instituted by then-Prime Minister Margaret Thatcher beginning in the late 1970s.

When Tony Blair's Labour Party came to power in 1997, it did not set out to undo completely the Conservatives' reduction of British government involvement in the economy. Blair called his party "New Labour," indicating that it was open to the idea that government should not own major industries and should limit its regulation of economic activity, while still finding ways to protect the social welfare of the British population. The extent to which Blair succeeded in this balancing act is open to debate, but the involvement of government in the British economy remains low by international standards. An annual ranking of economic freedom by the Heritage Foundation and the *Wall Street Journal* places the UK at number 11 in the world, the highest ranking of the TIC cases (and only three places below the United States).[26]

Globalization

British citizens benefit from globalization in many ways, but some are apprehensive about its potential negative effects. Many imported products are less expensive for British consumers—in some cases, much less expensive—than if they had been produced in the UK. Yet, the large number of British multinational corporations is a source of concern. Some fear that the UK's exposure to the global economy pushes down wages at home since companies can threaten to outsource jobs or move to another country, and workers who have lost their jobs to outsourcing have difficulties finding work and often earn less when they eventually do.

Is the UK really as globalized as British citizens believe that it is? How does it compare with the other TIC cases? Combining the A.T. Kearney/Foreign Policy Globalization Index's four components, the UK scores in the upper fifth of the seventy-two countries in the most recent A.T. Kearney/Foreign Policy rankings available (see Table 2.2). Its overall ranking of 12, however, is somewhat misleading. Although its technological and political rankings are high (9 and 6, respectively), its economic ranking is 18. In the economic measure trade, the UK ranks number 53 out of 72.

How can a member of the European Union (EU) be so sheltered from global trade? It is always important to consider how a variable is measured. In the globalization index, trade is measured by dividing the value of exports by the country's overall GDP. Including imports in the

---

Postwar Settlement The compromise in Western Europe after World War II between those who wanted a socialist system and those who desired one that was more free market.

measure might increase the ranking of the UK's openness to global trade, but probably only somewhat. Also, the UK trades openly with other EU members, but EU rules do not easily allow non-EU countries to penetrate EU markets. Thus, using trade as a measure, the UK's economy is more regionalized (connected to other European economies) than it is globalized. Finally, countries with sizable economies may have a large total value of imports and exports but a comparatively low value as a portion of the overall economy. Think about your own life. How many of your daily activities involve goods and services from abroad or destined for export? As you ponder this, consider that the A.T. Kearney/Foreign Policy Globalization Index score for the trade dimension places the United States at 71 out of the 72 countries examined, ahead of only Algeria.

Germany

Like the UK, Germany has a large middle class, but German levels of inequality and poverty are much lower as a result of Germany's generous welfare state, progressive taxation, and wage compression achieved through agreements between industrial unions and employers' associations.[27] Germany's economy industrialized later and more rapidly than the British economy, which profoundly influenced Germany's political development. Its post–World War II economic approach, the "social market economy," included strong social welfare protections. Its development strategy focused on high-quality products, which allowed it to trade effectively with other countries even as it has struggled to attract foreign direct investment.

Class

Today's class structure of unified Germany, with its sizable middle class, grew out of the class structure of West Germany after the 1950s. The Communist East German state (1949–89) had a dichotomous class structure of a large working class and a small elite of Communist Party members. Since unification, Germany's eastern region has experienced greater levels of economic hardship than the western part of the country, with regional inequality increasing during the 1990s. Privatization of state industries in the east, coupled with the decision to equalize wages in the two regions as much as possible, led to massive deindustrialization and unemployment in Germany's east.[28] East German enterprises, less efficient than their western counterparts to begin with, were unable to survive with higher wage costs resulting from the wage parity efforts. The worst of the economic shakeout of the 1990s has now passed. Yet, with unemployment in the east remaining stubbornly high, Germany is a country that continues to have different class structures between its east and its west.

Economic Development

In the mid-nineteenth century, the German economy lagged behind the economies of the UK. and the United States, spurring the German economic and political elites to pursue a course of rapid industrial catch-up. The strategy was successful, and by the end of the nineteenth century, Germany had become a major economic power pursuing an expansionist foreign policy. Rapid industrialization created a large working class, which fragmented into a reformist Social Democratic Party and a radical Communist Party. Class polarization survived into the

TABLE 2.2			Topic in Countries Cases, A.T. Kearney/Foreign Policy Globalization Rankings (of 72 Countries Ranked)				
Country	Overall	Economic— Total	Economic— Trade	Econonmic— FDI	Personal— Total	Technological— Total	Political— Total
United Kingdom	12	18	53	12	21	9	6
Germany	22	45	36	50	34	16	19
Mexico	49	50	49	43	45	41	37
Nigeria	57	39	34	37	58	65	45
Russia	62	49	54	38	60	46	52
China	66	43	44	35	67	56	65
Brazil	67	69	70	58	71	39	42
India	71	66	62	67	59	63	69
Iran	72	65	55	72	72	54	70

Source: The Globalization Index 2007: Globalization Index Rankings, *Foreign Policy*, no. 163 (November/December 2007), http://www.foreignpolicy.com/articles/2007/10/11/the_globalization_index_2007.

Weimar Republic—the failed experiment with democracy between the two world wars—and contributed to the rise of the Nazi dictatorship.

Following World War II, reconstruction became the new pattern of economic development in the Federal Republic (West Germany). Out of the rubble of the war, the "economic miracle" of the 1950s and 1960s transformed the Federal Republic into a prosperous country. Growth rates in the 1950s exceeded 8 percent per year and averaged 4.4 percent from 1960 through 1973.[29] These impressive growth rates were matched by low inflation, essentially full employment, and large trade surpluses. All classes took part in the prosperity, which helped legitimize the new democratic republic. The economic miracle ended when the oil-producing countries withheld supplies during the 1970s and oil prices rose drastically.

The German Democratic Republic (East Germany) also enjoyed strong growth in the 1960s and 1970s. Its economy was propped up by the combination of cheap oil from the Soviet Union, West German loans, and the shelter of the Communist trading bloc. However, economic problems set in by the mid-1970s. Although the Communist system did not officially have unemployment, state enterprises generated underemployment, basic goods were in short supply, and living standards stagnated.[30]

Economically, the first two decades of unification have been difficult. Economic growth has been anemic, averaging a meager 1.5 percent between 1990 and 2000,[31] though it picked up in 2006 and stood above 3 percent in 2010. Germany's 2011 GDP per capita was around $41,200, while its GDP per capita-PPP was a little more than $37,200. Unemployment in 2004 stood at 8.4 percent in the west and 18.3 percent in the east.[32] The overall unemployment rate was well above 9 percent. It began to drop by 2007 and was around 7 percent by early 2011. At the same time, a shrinking pool of workers were financing a burgeoning number of pensioners and unemployed, placing the welfare state under enormous financial strain. Using the welfare state to hide unemployment has led to "welfare without work" that politicians have painstakingly tried to address.[33]

Government's Role in the Economy

In the three broad categories of economic systems—free market, mixed, and socialist—Germany is best placed in the mixed category, though this is somewhat misleading. Germany's **social market economy (SME)** is a distinctive variety of capitalism with a comprehensive conservative corporatist welfare state (corporatism is discussed in Chapter 8). Unlike many of the mixed systems of Western Europe, conservative social forces created the German SME, and its institutions and practices reflect traditional values.[34]

This variety of capitalism and welfare state thus differs from the labor-led social democratic welfare state, of which unions and social democratic parties were the key architects, and free-market capitalism and its residual welfare state aimed at categories of the population deemed the "deserving poor." The SME preserves private property and generally views the market as the best way to allocate resources and generate economic growth. As a result, Germany ranks relatively high on the Heritage/WSJ Economic Freedom Index, at number 22 in the world and as the second highest TIC case.

The core values underpinning the German welfare state and the broader SME are decidedly conservative. First, the principle of solidarity envisions a community that cares for its less fortunate members. But this community has class, status, and occupational hierarchies that are reflected in the design of social insurance programs, which means that some categories of employees enjoy more generous benefits than others. On the whole, however, the German welfare state is distinguished by the comprehensiveness of benefits such as national health insurance, by universal child allowances, and by relatively generous social assistance (welfare).

Second, the "subsidiarity" principle (see the discussion of German political culture in Chapter 3) requires that individuals look first to the family for social assistance; then to natural social groups like unions, employers, or churches; and finally to the government as a provider of last resort. Rather than directly providing social programs, the state acts as the guarantor of social welfare by setting out the broad goals and parameters of the welfare state in framework legislation and then granting wide latitude to corporatist groups to implement the laws and deliver welfare state services under the principle of self-governance. At the same time, the state possesses the authority to sanction these actors, and in some cases to intervene directly if they refuse to fulfill the law.

Finally, the welfare state embodies a strong dose of social Catholicism that champions human dignity, work, and a traditional family structure. Thus, the social market economy institutionalizes worker consultation in industry ("codetermination"), while the welfare state promotes traditional gender roles by allotting generous family allowances, well beyond those of countries like the United States, and leave time to allow women to stay at home and care for children.[35]

Globalization

Post–World War II Germany's economic success owes much to its strategy of "diversified quality production,"

Social Market Economy (SME) The economic approach that developed in Germany, which united corporatism and welfare state protections with traditional social values.

the export of high-quality, high-valued-added goods that required a skilled workforce and that underwrote high wages, a generous welfare state, and extensive vocational training.[36] Regional integration through the EU has also had important effects on German economic performance. Germany was a founding member of the institutions in 1950 that later evolved into the EU. Unlike the UK, Germany has participated in the single European currency, the euro, since 2002, which replaced its former national currency, the Deutsche Mark.

The A.T. Kearney/Foreign Policy Globalization Index ranks Germany 22 in its latest survey. Germany's noneconomic globalization rankings are high, including on political integration, especially in the category of participation in international organizations like the United Nations (where it ranks fifth). Its economic dimension ranking (45 out of 72), however, put it well below the UK. Within the economic category, Germany ranked 36 on trade and 50 on foreign direct investment (FDI). Its trade ranking is higher than that of the UK, but much of Germany's trade is with other EU member states. It lags well behind the UK on FDI. The low level of FDI has sparked much soul-searching among political and business elites, who worry that Germany's regulatory climate and high production costs from its diversified quality production approach continue to discourage beneficial foreign investment.

India

India's class structure resembles that of other developing countries, but it also shares a key feature with its fellow TIC cases Russia and China. All three have shifted toward liberal economies over the last few decades, and inequality has increased since this liberalization. On the other hand, liberalization has fostered significant higher economic growth rates. India's acceptance of a greater role for the market has been balanced by concerns about domestic economic entities, such as farmers, which have limited the openness of the Indian economy to foreign investment.

Class

India's economic hierarchy corresponds roughly to the country's complex social hierarchy of mostly Hindu-based castes and tribes (see Chapter 4) and "backward classes" identified by the government for affirmative action purposes. Commentators point to the growing disparity in the income of the richest and poorest, but solutions to the hardships of those suffering from economic deprivation can be addressed in democratic India's political system. Unlike in many other countries, the poor in India are more likely to vote than the rich.

At the very top of the class structure is a small group of extremely affluent businesspeople. In 2009,

Forbes.com estimated that India had more than fifty billionaires, two of whom, Mukesh Ambani and Lakshmi Mittal, were identified as among the eight richest people in the world.[37] Showing the importance of manufacturing in the Indian economy, Ambani's and Mittal's fortunes came from the petrochemicals and steel industries, respectively. Key politicians and bureaucrats might be included in this leading class as well, due to the power they can wield over the economic fortunes of both the rich and the poor.

The significant growth of the Indian economy has produced an enlarged middle class, estimated by some at over 300 million. It includes individuals in both the public and private sectors. Much of the population, however, falls into the lower classes. The poorest in India, members of the underclass, number in the hundreds of millions; according to the United Nations Development Program, an estimated 320 million people in India live on $1 per day or less.[38] They and those whose income is only slightly higher live mostly, but not exclusively, in rural areas and engage in many different economic activities in order to survive.[39] Their lives are in stark contrast to the lives of the growing middle class. Many farmers are so deeply in debt that they see no future, and suicides are widespread.

Economic Development

Along with China, India has one of the oldest civilizations on earth. Urban settlement and small-scale trade in the Indus River Valley can be traced back as far as 2500 B.C. Over the next three thousand years, portions of the territory of present-day India became united, were torn apart again, and fell under outside control (such as Mongol rule from the twelfth through fourteenth centuries). Still, during the centuries prior to British colonial rule, India had one of the world's largest economies, second only to China's. During the 1700s and 1800s, however, countries such as England, France, and the United States began to emerge as the world's economic powers. India's development was directed to the benefit of the British, who controlled India from the mid-1800s until 1947.

India turned to economic planning, relying on Soviet-style five-year plans, in the postindependence period. Growth rates varied. During the first postindependence economic plan (1951–56), the average was 3.6 percent. During the fourth plan (1969–74), growth barely averaged 2 percent. During the seventh plan (1985–90), growth rates rose to just over 6 percent.

In 1991, India began the transition from a planned to a liberal economy. In the early stages of the liberalization period, growth continued to average 6 percent. Since then, though, growth rates have risen dramatically to between 7 and 9 percent per year, and estimates placed economic growth in 2010 at near 10 percent. These recent changes have led many to believe that an economic "takeoff," similar to that which began three decades ago in China, is well underway in India.

Estimated at nearly $1.6 trillion in 2011, India's GDP places it as the eleventh largest economy in the world. Unlike in many developing countries, the economy has a strong service sector (making up slightly more than half of the economy), with another 30 percent in industry and 20 percent in agriculture. India's 2011 GDP per capita and GDP per capita-PPP figures differ markedly: $1,300 and $3,500, respectively.

Government's Role in the Economy

When India gained its independence from British control, its leaders leaned toward a socialist model of development with significant government planning and state ownership of entire sectors of the economy. This trend continued through the 1970s, although large portions of the economy—generating significant portions of India's GDP—remained under the control of the private sector. The private sector was especially focused on the production of consumer goods (typically a weak point in fully planned economies), although even the consumer goods market was well regulated by the government.

At the start of the 1990s, the economic liberalization policies stimulated intense debate about the speed of privatization, the sectors in which privatization should take place, the degree of openness to foreign capital, the sectors of the economy that should be out of bounds to foreign capital, and the subsidies that should be removed or added. The creation of special economic zones to lure private business gave rise to a great deal of debate between those championing the rights of farmers whose land was to be acquired and those championing the transition to an industrialized economy.

How government should balance such competing views is an issue that India has still failed to resolve. Rankings such as the Heritage/WSJ Economic Freedom Index—in which India comes in at number 124 globally—highlight the extent to which the government of India remains active in managing the economy. Yet, most of India's political leaders are committed to continuing the country's move away from its pre-1991 attempts at socialist planning.

Globalization

India's reforms in 1991 encouraged connections with the world economy. India has advantages over some of its rivals. In contrast to Russia and China, for example, English is deeply embedded in India. A vibrant English-language press exists, education at English-medium schools is in great demand, and English is the language of instruction in most universities. The presence of a workforce relatively fluent in English facilitates economically developed countries' outsourcing of information technology work to India. Call centers that handle customer service for a variety of American companies are located at many sites in India.

Although these examples signify the aspiration of a part of the Indian business class to involve itself more in the international economy, that involvement remains limited. India's A.T. Kearney/Foreign Policy Globalization Index ranking stands at 71, ahead of only Iran. It ranks 66 in economic integration, with comparatively low ranks on both trade (62) and FDI (67). FDI had been rising sharply, but fell from nearly $27 billion in 2009 to around $21 billion in 2010.

Given the size of India's economy and the features that could be expected to attract foreign investors, what explains India's modest FDI rates? Elements of the political Left remain deeply suspicious of moves to open the economy more fully. When land has been sought for both national and international industries, local political leaders have kindled peasant opposition to their loss of land. Selling public corporations to international firms has also elicited strong opposition from labor unions, though once again such opposition has often been solicited by politicians rather than being genuine grassroots protests. Thus, India's open political system has allowed politicians to voice the concerns of people who fear the consequences of globalization, placing constraints on other political leaders' efforts to become more fully a part of a globalized world.

Mexico

The Mexican economy has continued to develop in recent years, producing a visible middle class. Mexico has also retained many features of a developing economy. There is significant inequality, and prosperity is hampered by newer problems such as drug violence and older ones such as corruption. Mexico's economic connections with other countries have been regional more than global, with the North American Free Trade Agreement (NAFTA) tying the Mexican economy more closely to that of the United States.

Class

Though less so than countries like the UK and Germany, Mexico has a notable middle class, particularly in the industrial north. Estimates of the portion of the population in the middle class vary, but are often above 25 percent. The Mexican middle class has traditionally been politically passive, tolerating political corruption in exchange for economic well-being. Over the last decade, however, the middle class has occasionally flexed its political muscle. In Mexico City in August 2008, for example, more than a hundred thousand people—many from the middle class—protested against increasing drug-related violence and President Felipe Calderón's ineffective response to it.

Doctors wearing red-stained coats protest drug-related violence in the northern border city of Ciudad Juarez, Mexico, on December 13, 2010. Eleven doctors in the city were kidnapped in 2010 alone. AP Photo/Raymundo Ruiz

Having a noticeable middle class does not mean that Mexican society is economically equal. The country contains a small number of wealthy individuals and a large number who fall into the working class and underclass. A decade ago, World Bank Chief Economist François Bourguignon claimed that "extreme poverty in Mexico today affects 20 percent of the population."[40] He stated that reduction of inequality and increased economic growth were needed to make a significant dent in Mexico's poverty problem. The picture has changed little since Bourguignon's report.

Economic Development
Mexico is an excellent example of the way in which economic development can foster political development. Mexico experienced significant economic growth in 1770–99, 1895–1909, and 1933–81. Especially high and sustained growth rates from the 1940s and 1970s fed and were fed by trends such as urbanization and improvements in education. Each of these periods of economic development changed the social fabric of the country, and economic downturns that caused the population to perceive threats to economic well-being triggered attempts at political change.

Many consider Mexico to be an emerging market and even an NIC, but it remains an LDC in many ways. Its per capita GDP for 2011 was nearly $9,500, while its GDP per capita-PPP figure was over $14,800. This is slightly above Brazil's and slightly below Russia's, but still less than one-third that of the United States. Mexico produces a great deal of energy. Much of its oil reserves—the fourth largest in the Western Hemisphere—are exported to the United States, and it has benefited from high oil prices over the last few years. Yet, it desperately needs to modernize and reform its domestic energy market.[41] Despite directing government assistance to its poorest states, Mexico's north remains notably more prosperous than its south.

Government's Role in the Economy
The Mexican state became heavily involved in the economy in the twentieth century. This was partly because of Mexico's late start in industrialization and also because its "party authoritarian" system (see Chapter 5) under the Institutional Revolutionary Party (PRI) tied the working class to the ruling party.[42] In the years leading to the establishment of democracy, privatization was pursued more aggressively and regulation of foreign investment into Mexico curtailed. Still, debate swirled around economic policies such as NAFTA and questions about the stability of the Mexican currency. In early 1995, newly inaugurated President Ernesto Zedillo took measures to prop up the peso, the value of which had fallen 40 percent. His fiscal and monetary policy included steep spending cuts and drew on a U.S. credit package to help stabilize the peso.

Today, Mexico's economy has, by many accounts, a moderate level of governmental involvement. The Heritage/WSJ Economic Freedom Index places Mexico at number 41 globally. This puts it in the top quarter of the 179 countries ranked and makes it the third highest ranked of the TIC cases. Although its ranking is quite a bit lower than those of Germany and, especially, the UK, it is well above the rest of the TIC cases. (The fourth ranked TIC case, Nigeria, stands at number 106 globally.) Looking ahead in the near term, those who support the relatively high levels of economic freedom in Mexico should be particularly concerned about the explosion of drug violence in the country in 2009 and 2010. Getting serious about dramatically reducing such violence will require the Mexican government to penetrate more forcefully into all parts of society, including the economy.[43]

Globalization
Mexico's economic interconnectedness has been more regional than global. **The North American Free Trade Agreement (NAFTA)** with the United States and Canada is Mexico's most important trade agreement, but far from its only regional one. It also participates in trade arrangements with other Latin American countries. NAFTA was launched at the beginning of 1994. Predictions of its effects on Mexico were extreme, and the results have been moderate in comparison. Mexico has not experienced the kind of economic growth that NAFTA advocates had expected, but its trade and foreign investment numbers have improved markedly.[44]

Because Mexico's economic development was low and its trade barriers were high prior to NAFTA, the

North American Free Trade Agreement (NAFTA) A trade agreement involving Canada, Mexico, and the United States launched at the beginning of 1994.

agreement did not turn Mexico into a highly globalized economy. Mexico's A.T. Kearney/Foreign Policy Globalization Index ranking stands at 49, with component rankings ranging from 50 (economic) to 37 (political). Mexico's relatively low trade ranking (49) again points to the danger of assuming that a country's participation in trade agreements is a sign of high levels of economic interconnectedness. However, NAFTA remains an important topic in Mexican politics and among scholars studying the effects of regional and global economic connections. The In Theory and Practice feature focuses on the question of whether globalization makes states weaker or stronger, looking in particular at the case of Mexico and NAFTA.

IN THEORY AND PRACTICE

Globalization, Weak State versus Strong State Theories, and the Case of Mexico's Adoption of NAFTA

Over the last few decades, a number of political economy scholars have tackled the question of globalization's political effects. A central issue is the impact of economic interconnections and openness on the size and power of national governments.

Weak State Theories

One set of globalization theories, known as **weak state theories**, emphasize the state's deterioration in the face of globalization. Comparative politics scholars have been more reluctant than antiglobalization activists to propose that globalization weakens states. Yet a number of scholarly works over the last couple of decades, such as former Harvard economist David Korten's book, *When Corporations Rule the World*, can be placed in the weak state camp.[45] Korten argues that globalization encourages a **race to the bottom**. Developing countries, seeking to attract multinational corporations, compete with one another to lure companies to move production facilities to their country. This competition encourages poorer working conditions and lower wages, reduced government oversight of economic activities, and weaker environmental standards. Standards continue to decline in this race to the bottom, cheered on by multinationals hoping to make as much money as possible.[46] Weak state theory proponents point to the presence of sweatshops in developing countries and persistent government corruption in LDCs as evidence of the effects of the global race to the bottom, though much of their evidence is anecdotal.[47]

Strong State Theories

In contrast, **strong state theories** suggest that increased economic interconnections do not weaken states but rather require a large state apparatus. One group of strong state theorists postulates that globalization leads to greater domestic fear of economic displacement. Such fear generates demands for government policies to protect workers from the consequences of economic upheaval, such as by providing unemployment compensation, worker training, and insurance benefits. The government's efforts to compensate for the effects—or presumed effects—of globalization lead to increases in spending, including on social welfare programs.

A second strain of strong state theories focuses on the need for regulation and rule of law as capital becomes more mobile. Investors want to know that their investments are going to be secure and that contracts are going to be obeyed. To varying degrees, this emphasis on rule of law can lead to a more transparent relationship between governments, corporations, and investors, and this transparency allows for greater scrutiny of rules and practices. Though transparency does not rule out government corruption, making the climate appealing to investors does require rules that are understood and enforced, which in turn require a strong and functioning government.

Mexico and NAFTA

When NAFTA was debated in the United States in the early 1990s, Mexico was often demonized as the source of a looming "sucking sound" of American jobs being pulled to the south.[48] Arguments against NAFTA were similar to those of race to the bottom theorists: Mexican workers would work for lower wages, Mexico has minimal environmental standards, and large American companies will force standards even lower by promising to move factories across the border. Did Mexico engage in a race to the bottom after NAFTA? The evidence is mixed. Some problems associated with a race to the bottom, such as corruption and environmental concerns, existed long before NAFTA but have certainly not been solved by it. Environmental conditions have improved in some areas and worsened in others.

A straightforward answer to the question of NAFTA's effects is also complicated by economic problems that coincided with the launch of the trade agreement. A large amount of investment flowed into Mexico in advance of NAFTA's commencement; however, by the end of 1994, the amount of investment leaving the country was reaching a crisis level.[49] In part because of this, the peso fell dramatically

---

Weak State Theories A set of theories that argue that globalization limits the ability of governments to tax, spend, and regulate.

Race to the Bottom A component of weak state theories that contends that states lower standards and reduce regulations to attract or maintain the presence of large corporations.

Strong State Theories A set of theories that argue that even with increasing globalization, governments have maintained and even enhanced their ability to tax, spend, and regulate.

against the dollar. The resulting economic downturn caused real (inflation-adjusted) wages in the country to decline 20 percent. Real GDP declined more than 6 percent in 1995. Thus, NAFTA critics who point to problems such as minimal gains in real wages in the country are correct, but largely because the baseline dropped so much in 1994 and 1995. Since 1996, gains in real wages have been sizable,[50] challenging the idea that NAFTA fueled a sustained race to the bottom in Mexico.

Brazil

Economic inequality is one of Brazil's defining features; it is severe even by developing country standards. Nevertheless, the growth of the industrial and service sectors has fed an emerging middle class. Brazil has been attractive to foreign investors, although its prevalent corruption and heavy-handed bureaucracy continue to limit the globalization of Brazil's economy.

Class

Poverty and inequality are blatant in Brazil. The poorest 10 percent of the Brazilian population captures less than 1 percent of national income, while the richest 10 percent captures nearly 45 percent.[51] Nearly one-third of the population lives below the poverty line; one-fourth lives on less than $2 per day. As a result, Brazil ranks among the five most unequal countries on earth. The inequality is a legacy of colonialism and slavery. Class and race are still strongly associated: white Brazilians and newer Asian immigrants have generally higher levels of education and income than black Brazilians and indigenous peoples. Inequality tends to perpetuate itself. Children of the poor have less access to education, health care, and good nutrition, decreasing future income and life expectancy.

Despite these features, Brazil's middle class has grown in recent years. Its size is hard to estimate and fluctuates along with periods of economic crisis or stability, but in good times, it may constitute as much as 30 percent of the population. Manual workers in the formal sector of the economy earn almost as much as the lower ranking members of the middle class.

Where the social system breaks down is among those who work in the informal sector. Nearly 10 percent of Brazilians declare that they are unemployed, but as much as 40 percent of the population works in the informal economy. These workers get no health care, no pension, and no stable income. They frequently work in dangerous conditions, and they earn very little money, often at or below the poverty line. Despite the large class differences, class has typically not shaped voter choices outside of the unionized workers who support the Workers' Party (Partido dos Trabalhadores, PT).

Economic Development

Brazil's early economic development revolved around the export of agricultural products and minerals. Following a brief period of trade in timber, the sugar plantation economy emerged in the late sixteenth century. Brazil industrialized by following a strategy very similar to that of Mexico in the 1930–80 period. The policy, known as **import substitution industrialization (ISI)**, involved government protection of domestic industries from foreign competition and subsidies of key inputs such as energy and steel.

As in Mexico, the result was a prolonged period of rapid economic growth. Between 1945 and 1973, Brazil's GDP growth rate was well above the world average. By the end of the 1970s, however, Brazil's economy slowed down. The debt crisis that erupted across Latin America in the early 1980s put an end to Brazil's rapid economic growth.

Brazil still exports many primary products; by 2004, it had become the world's third largest exporter of agricultural products. It also constructs finished products for export. The share of manufactured goods in Brazil's exports to the United States rose from 48 percent in the early 1980s to nearly 70 percent by the late 1990s. Domestically, agriculture accounts for only 8 percent of Brazilian GDP, compared with 38 percent for industry and 54 percent for services. As of 2011, Brazil's per capita GDP was estimated to be more than $11,200, while its GDP per capita-PPP was only slightly higher at $11,800.

Government's Role in the Economy

The government's role in economic development has long been the most salient policy problem in Brazil. The First Republic's (1889–1930) proclamation of goals—order and progress—saw progress principally in economic terms. Yet, beyond the idea that some level of order is a prerequisite to the achievement of progress, Brazilian governments have disagreed about how best to develop the economy. Much of Brazil's historical political instability can be attributed at least in part to pendulum swings between governments that emphasized equality and redistribution and governments (often the product of military coups) that emphasized economic growth, privileging the property rights of the ruling class in order to stimulate investment.

The emergence of the so-called Washington Consensus, which favors the free-market model of capitalism, has tended to resolve this conflict in favor of

Import Substitution Industrialization (ISI) A development strategy emphasizing subsidies of key domestic industries and other protectionist trade policies; used by countries such as Mexico and Brazil, particularly from World War II through the 1970s.

economic growth over equality, particularly in countries such as Brazil where the management of a massive public debt tied the state to international lending agencies such as the IMF. These agencies typically require adoption of market-oriented policies as a condition for emergency loans. Within this context, substantial redistribution becomes more difficult. Even a leftist president like Luiz Inácio "Lula" da Silva (2003–2011) found himself constrained by the terms of deals with the IMF to keep state spending low and to cut subsidies to the poor.

The goal of economic growth has also faced significant challenges, including from government regulatory practices that make starting a business in Brazil more difficult than in many other developing countries. Such practices, along with the prevalence of corruption across Brazilian society, led to Brazil's receiving a global ranking of 113 on the Heritage/WSJ Economic Freedom Index. This places it in the bottom half of the global rankings but in the middle of the TIC cases.

Globalization

As in much of the rest of the world, the 1980s and 1990s saw Brazil embarking on a project of economic reform that limited state involvement in the economy, lowered protectionist barriers, and opened the economy to free trade and globalization. As in Mexico, many of these connections are more regional than truly global. Unlike in Mexico, however, Brazilian trade is highly diversified in terms of its regional export partners. By the mid-1990s, only 20 percent of Brazilian exports were destined for the United States, compared with over 80 percent of Mexico's exports, but an additional 24 percent of Brazilian exports went to other Latin American countries, primarily its Southern Common Market (Mercosur) partners: Argentina, Paraguay, Uruguay, and Venezuela.

Nevertheless, Brazil ranks well below Mexico and most other countries in the A.T. Kearney/Foreign Policy Globalization Index. At number 67 overall, Brazil scores higher than just five countries, including India and Iran. Brazil's highest ranking (39) is on technological connectivity, and its lowest (71) is on personal contact (telephone, travel, and remittances), ahead of only Iran. One would expect this ranking to have improved over the last several years; Brazil's telecommunication system was privatized in the late 1990s, and the government has increased expenditures on its airports and harbors. On economic integration, Brazil ranked 69 of 72. As one of the BRICS countries, Brazil does attract some foreign direct investment, though this is driven more by Brazil's large population and abundant natural resources than by government policy or the ease of starting up new businesses. In terms of trade openness, Brazil's number 70 ranking is the lowest of the TIC cases.

Nigeria

Despite the income that its oil reserves generate, Nigeria is the poorest of the TIC cases. It has great potential but chronic poverty, and it is often named as an example of the resource curse and of the extent to which LDCs remain dependent on EDCs.

Class

Nigeria is a country with extreme inequality. Economists Benjamin Senauer and Linda Goetz estimate the Nigerian middle class at considerably less than 5 percent of the country's population.[52] The vast majority of the population falls into the working class and underclass. Poverty in Nigeria is not regionally concentrated; the poor live in all parts of the country and in both rural and urban areas. During the 1990s, more than 70 percent of Nigerians lived on less than $1 per day, and more than 90 percent lived on less than $2 per day, leading many individuals to search for or grow their own food and exchange goods through barter. Even taking into account the cost of living in Nigeria, these are stunning levels of poverty for a country with Nigeria's oil wealth.

Although the government has pledged to address poverty at different times over the last couple of decades, economic growth in Nigeria has failed to benefit those in poverty.[53] One of the major difficulties, in addition to government corruption, is the country's high population growth rate. In 1975, the population was around 65 million; thirty years later it had more than doubled. Current estimates put the population at more than 150 million in 2010, nearly 170 million by 2015, and pushing 200 million only a decade later.[54]

Economic Development

At the time of its independence in 1960, Nigeria appeared to have greater economic potential than most postcolonial states. By African standards, it had a solid infrastructure, did not need to import food, and had a moderately diverse economy. The discovery of oil in the 1950s seemed to be a reason for even more optimism. Instead, Nigeria's economic development since independence has been uneven. The country allowed oil to dominate its export sector, making it vulnerable to fluctuations in global prices, and it did not use its oil wealth to improve its long-term development prospects. With the 1970s oil boom came urbanization and other changes that normally accompany development. The government mandated universal primary education, a goal that was difficult to meet but did help increase literacy in the country dramatically. Still, as recently as 2010, an estimated 40 million people in the country remained illiterate.

After rising significantly during the 1970s, GDP per capita-PPP declined in the early 1980s and again in the early 1990s. From 1994 to 2008, it began a fairly steady rise, finally reaching $1,000 in 2003. By 2011, Nigeria's GDP per capita-PPP had improved to more than $2,500. Per capita GDP without the PPP correction stood at just $1,450. Despite the impressive growth in its overall GDP over the last fifteen years, Nigeria remains one of the poorest countries in the world.

In recent decades, changes in Nigeria's GDP have correlated with global oil prices. This correlation is not surprising, as oil provides up to 95 percent of the country's export revenue and 80 percent of total government income.[55] Thus, the dramatic rise in global oil prices from 2004 through 2008 had a positive effect on Nigeria's economy. The government could have used the increased revenue to pay down its debt, to invest in education to improve the country's human capital, and to bring much needed diversity of production into the economy. Given that Nigeria typically spends such windfalls on short-term fixes and allows corrupt government officials to waste the money, the early sign are not encouraging.

IN THEORY AND PRACTICE

Dependency Theory and Its Application to Nigeria

Dependency theory is one of two main theories that seek to explain differences in capitalist development and its social and political consequences across countries. The other theory, modernization theory, is introduced in the In Theory and Practice box on China. Although **dependency theory** first developed among Latin American scholars, and proponents were labeled *dependencistas* or *dependistas*, it quickly spread across the globe.[56] Dependency theory explains the gap between LDCs and EDCs as a function of the international capitalist system and of the efforts of capitalists in the EDCs and their political allies in both EDCs and LDCs. It holds that the blatant and direct control of LDCs as colonies in the past has been replaced by less transparent conditions of dependency in the present. Dependency theorists contend that EDCs, international organizations, and multinational companies employ a series of strategies to impede LDC development, including

- Developing trade relationships with LDCs that encourage them to specialize in a small number of raw material exports.
- Encouraging LDCs to amass mounting debt, which prevents effective long-term economic planning.
- Controlling new economic development in LDCs.
- Supporting repressive political regimes that maintain these conditions.

Thus, dependency theory has two implications for the economic and political systems in a dependent country: the country stays underdeveloped economically, and it stays corrupt and authoritarian politically.

The Nigerian case supports dependency theory proponents' claims. Nigeria's dependence on natural resource exports, the failure of its oil wealth to trickle down to the general population, and the tendency to be dominated by corrupt, authoritarian leaders since independence are features that dependency theorists blame on the global capitalist economy. Clearly, Nigeria and many other countries in Africa provide more evidence in support of dependency theory than do the NICs in Asia.

At the same time, some changes in Nigeria are consistent with the assumptions of modernization theory. Urbanization has increased, education has improved, and consolidated democracy has become conceivable. Lingering corruption and the failure of the growing economy to reach ordinary citizens remain the largest arguments against modernization theory and in favor of dependency theory. Until Nigeria's class structure begins to resemble that of an NIC, dependency theorists will continue to single out Nigeria to support the theory.

Government's Role in the Economy

Like Brazil, Nigeria's military and civilian political leaders have taken different approaches to the role of government in the economy. Following independence from British rule, Nigeria increasingly fell under the spell of the resource curse, and the government focused its attention on the energy extraction sector. With the decline in oil prices in the 1980s, international financial institutions pressured Nigeria to engage in structural adjustments to its economy, including significantly curtailing government spending. These reforms were followed by a subsequent round of IMF-inspired changes in the first decade of the twenty-first century. The Nigerian government encouraged outside investment in the country, got serious about reforming the banking system, and even privatized some of the government-run components of the energy sector.

These changes took Nigeria more in the direction of a free-market economy, but it remains far from the ideal of the free-market economic model. Nigeria is the fourth-ranked TIC case in the Heritage/WSJ Economic Freedom Index, but it comes in at 106 (of 179 countries) in the global standings. While Nigeria's economic system is far from the free-market ideal, its people largely accept the free-market model. Surveys conducted as part of the Pew Global Attitudes Project in 2002 and 2007 showed nearly 80 percent of Nigerians agreeing that "Most people are better off in a free market economy." As one might expect, the global economic recession that began in 2008 reduced such support, and in 2009, only 66 percent of Nigerian survey respondents held pro-market views.[57]

Dependency Theory The view that LDCs have become economically dependent on the EDCs through the system of international capitalism.

Globalization

Globalization has affected Nigeria more than many other developing countries. Nigeria's A.T. Kearney/Foreign Policy Globalization Index ranking for economics is 39 of the 72 countries, higher than all but one of the eight other TIC cases. Largely fueled by investment in its oil sector, Nigeria's FDI ranking stands at 37, similar to such other cases as Russia, China, and Mexico. This oil-based interconnectedness with other countries has not spilled over to other areas of globalization. The country's overall ranking is 57, pulled down in part by its number 58 ranking in personal contacts and its number 65 ranking in technological connectivity.

Nigeria also shows that the relationship between globalization and domestic unrest in a country can be a two-way street. The renewed threat of worker strikes in the oil sector, along with local groups' threats to blow up oil installations and kidnap oil company officials or family members, some of which were acted on, helped drive world oil prices up over $50 per barrel in late 2004, $70 per barrel in early 2006, and $140 per barrel in mid-2008. On the other hand, the agreement between the government and the rebel groups of the Niger Delta region in 2009 played at least a small part in oil price declines that year. Thus, while political scientists often focus on ways in which economic globalization can influence politics in

a developing country, Nigeria shows how a single country's political instability can have significant implications for the global economy.

Russia

Economic reform in the late Soviet and early post-Soviet periods hurt a large portion of the population but also set the stage for the emergence of a small middle class and a new and more politically influential upper class. The small number of hyper-wealthy individuals led to talk in the 1990s about the economic domination of "oligarchs." Since 2000, the Russian government has become more active in the economy, with a strong presence in important parts such as the energy sector, thus reestablishing itself as the country's major economic player. Although there has been some foreign investment, Russia's failure to develop a strong commitment to the rule of law has hurt its ability to attract significant, and much needed, investment in its economy.

Class

During the economic stagnation of the late 1970s and early 1980s, a social contract emerged between the Soviet government and the people: Don't speak out about being unhappy, and you won't have to work too hard; life will not be great, but it will be okay. This and other Soviet policies created a large lower class, not starving but not much better off than Americans living in poverty. Especially if one takes into account prestige and standard of living, there was also an upper class: the Communist Party elite.

When market economic elements were introduced in the late Soviet and early post-Soviet periods, the ensuing economic collapse hurt many people. Severe inflation meant that workers' and pensioners' life savings disappeared. Meanwhile, a new upper class of "new Russians" (*novye russkie*) emerged. Many in this new class had held important state or party positions. A few were true entrepreneurs, but most had ties to the old system's privileges, and sometimes ties to or participation in organized crime. During privatization, these connections gave them an advantage. A small number of individuals came to dominate segments of the economy and shape political developments in the 1990s under then-President Boris Yeltsin.

In the late 1990s and early 2000s, a small middle class also emerged, primarily concentrated in larger cities and composed of younger residents. Though older and rural people remained poor, the general prosperity of the early 2000s did trickle down to them, partly in the form of government programs designed to rein in discontent. Then-President Vladimir Putin also successfully took on a number of the wealthiest individuals in Russia, mostly in an effort to limit their economic and political power as

Henry Okah, a senior figure in MEND (Movement for the Emancipation of the Niger Delta), leaves a court in Johannesburg, South Africa on October 14, 2010. Okah, who was living in South Africa, was charged with conspiracy to commit a terrorist act in connection with a bombing that killed ten people in Nigeria. © REUTERS/Siphiwe Sibeko

he worked to deepen his own hold on the Russian political system. Even though many of people understood the political motivations, a large portion of Russian population supported Putin's actions.

Economic Development

Prior to the collapse of the tsarist system in 1917, Russia was underdeveloped. Heavily agrarian and generally poor, the country had just begun capitalist development. The Soviets' socialist system emphasized heavy industry over the production of consumer goods. The result was uneven but rapid economic development before and after World War II. Even though World War II set back Soviet development significantly, by the 1960s and 1970s, many in the West were concerned about Soviet economic advances.

In the 1970s and early 1980s, however, economic growth slowed and worker productivity declined. When Mikhail Gorbachev took office, he instituted small reforms, and then launched his *perestroika* (restructuring) reforms in 1987. These reforms introduced some market principles, but still protected many inefficient state-run industries. Along with other Gorbachev reforms, perestroika sped up the process of Soviet economic collapse. By the end of 1991, the Soviet Union was gone.

The Russian economy has been uneven since 1991, though statistics like GDP point to dramatic growth in recent years. From 1992 through 1994, real GDP declined more than 10 percent annually. The following three years brought signs of hope, but the economy again took a sharp downturn in 1998. For much of the 1990s, GDP per capita-PPP hovered between $6,000 and $7,000. Conditions have improved markedly, and in the last decade, Russia's growth has been impressive. By 2011, GDP per capita-PPP figure were estimated at over $16,700 (around $12,000 without the PPP adjustment).

Russia's economic collapse in 1998 continues to serve as a reminder of the fragility of its economy. Much of Russia's post-1998 economic success resulted from the high global price of oil. Like other countries that depend heavily on a single source of revenue, Russia cannot assume that such oil profits will last forever. As the Russian economy grew, inequality rose dramatically. Thus, the Russian economy resembles an LDC more than an EDC, with a substantial gap between rich and poor and dependence on the world price of a single commodity.

Government's Role in the Economy

After 1991, the Russian government initially focused on removing the state from the economy through privatization. Later, the state reentered the domestic economy as a major player. More than Soviet leader Mikhail Gorbachev had done, President Boris Yeltsin introduced elements of capitalism into the Russian economy. The Russian government privatized most state-owned enterprises during the 1990s but maintained some large state-owned companies. A handful of incredibly wealthy individuals dominated the economy and used their political weight to guide Yeltsin's policy decisions, leading a number of analysts to label the 1990s economic system **oligarchic capitalism**.[58]

After Vladimir Putin became president, Russia moved away from oligarchic capitalism into an era of state capitalism, becoming the model of the state capitalist ideal type. The system is much more capitalist than socialist, but it is a Russian brand of capitalism, with political connections and state power visible beneath the façade of free-market liberalism. Entrepreneurs are encouraged to create new, profitable entities, but they are often forced to compete with enterprises connected to or run by the state or forced to work with state bureaucrats, making themselves vulnerable to political shakedowns.[59] As a result, Russian scores poorly on the Heritage/WSJ Economic Freedom Index, barely missing being labeled a repressed economy and ranking 143rd in the world.

Globalization

Russia's economic ups and downs last two decades were driven in part by its increasing connections to the global economy, but it has not become the important player in international trade and finance that some had anticipated. Russia faces two significant problems. First, much of Russian industry is inefficient, producing products with little appeal in the West. Russia exports energy, but Russian finished products are in low demand. The second problem is corruption and the lack of the rule of law in which government would hold itself accountable for illegality of actions and businesses would honor the terms of contracts (for more on the concept of rule of law, see Chapter 5).

Russia's A.T. Kearney/Foreign Policy Globalization Index ranking places it 62 out of 72 countries. Its economic ranking is 49, its technology ranking 42, and its political ranking 52. Its personal contact ranking is 60—higher than China, Brazil, and Iran, but lower than Nigeria and India. Within the economic dimension, Russia's trade ranking is 54. Befitting its BRICS status, its FDI ranking stands at a noticeably higher 38.

China

Like Russia and India, China has seen a dramatic increase in economic inequality following pro-market reforms. It has also had some of the most impressive annual economic growth rates. The combination of market-based

---

Oligarchic Capitalism A term used by analysts to describe the Russian economic system of the 1990s, which they believed benefited a small number of economically and politically powerful individuals.

economic principles, significant foreign direct investment, and targeted, government-led development strategies has fueled its growth. Although underlying problems in the Chinese economy exist, it is now the second largest economy in the world, behind only the United States.

Class

Inequality in China is greater today than at any time since Communist Party rule began in 1949. The divide between rural areas and larger cities is especially sharp. Rural incomes did rise in the late 1970s and early 1980s, but these increases were quickly outpaced in large cities, and the gap grew larger as rural income stagnated by the middle of the 1990s.[60] Since more than half of China's population lives in the countryside, the Chinese government ignores rural poverty at its peril.

With capitalist development comes a middle class, and China is no exception. Its middle class is small (perhaps as little as 5 percent of the population), but continues to grow. China's actions to reincorporate former territories have made the middle class more visible and potentially destabilizing. Hong Kong, which rejoined China in 1997, brought millions of new residents, many of them middle class. Hong Kong's middle class might favor democracy, but it is less clear that the rest of China's middle class is as supportive. As political scientist An Chen argues, the Chinese middle class is used to political submission. It has little economic autonomy from the state that it can translate into political power, as the middle class tends to do in Western countries, and many middle-class Chinese have become wealthy via links to corrupt government officials.[61]

Economic Development

Until recently, China's history was marked by slow economic development as a result of climatic constraints (e.g., the small portion of land that is suitable for agriculture), a large population that grew dramatically in the nineteenth and twentieth centuries, and efforts to control its vast territory with a centralized and heavily bureaucratized political system. Its potential was also held down by key political decisions during the Communist period, such as the Great Leap Forward and Cultural Revolution (see Chapter 10). Over the last several decades, however, Chinese economic growth has been sizable. Reforms following the death of Mao Zedong in 1976 introduced capitalist practices to an economy previously dominated by state planners. The state's control over economic activities declined during the 1980s and 1990s, although it actively oversaw economic progress and protected Chinese companies from external competition. The result has been average economic growth of around 9.5 percent per year since the late 1970s.

Today, China's economy continues to grow at an impressive rate. At less than $4,800, its 2011 per capita GDP figure looks low. However, China's GDP figures improve significantly with the PPP adjustment. China's GDP per

A man and a woman wear masks to guard against air pollution in Beijing. China's economic development has generated high GDP growth rates but also problems such as severe pollution in large cities.
© Lou Linwei/Alamy

capita-PPP for 2011 was over $8,300, much higher than the TIC cases of India and Nigeria, but still behind Iran, Russia, Brazil, and Mexico. China's economy is currently just under three-quarters the size of the U.S. economy if one takes PPP into account, but it is unlikely to overtake the United States in the near future without the PPP adjustment. Because of the size of its population, the possibility of catching up with EDCs in per capita GDP is decades away, even taking PPP into account. In addition, many of China's visible and highly positive macroeconomic numbers hide serious economic and financial problems, including unemployment, underemployment, low tax revenue, bad debt in state-owned banks, and conflicts between the Chinese government and Western companies that invest in China.[62]

IN THEORY AND PRACTICE

Modernization Theory and Its Application to China

Modernization theory is based on a belief that Western Europe and the United States are models for economic and political development.[63] Like Marx, modernization theorists suggest that economic development follows stages of growth, but their stages are notably different from Marx's. In modernization theory, capitalist democracy represents the pinnacle of development. Popular especially in the 1950s and early 1960s, modernization theory reemerged with the collapse of Communist rule at the end of the cold war in the 1980s.

Modernization Theory The view that a country's move from underdevelopment to modernization can be understood from and modeled after development in the West.

Modernization theory predicts that a number of social, cultural, and political changes take place along with economic development. These include **urbanization**. Bigger cities allow factories to be situated near a large number of workers. Development is also associated with increases in education and literacy rates. To develop economically, a country needs **physical capital** and **human capital**. Physical capital comprises the machines and factories workers use to produce goods and provide services; a factory needs up-to-date and well-functioning machinery. Human capital is no less important. Workers must be competent and possess relevant skills. Governments invest in human capital through their support of education.

Modernization theory also proposes that economic development is related to cultural changes. As people become more prosperous, gain education, and live in larger cities, underlying values, such as the relative importance of freedom versus order, change. Finally, modernization theorists argue that economic development fosters democratization, largely due to the creation of a large middle class that values political equality.

Proponents of modernization theory point to the economic success of many Asian countries and the political liberalization that has often accompanied it. China is a rapidly growing LDC. Whether the other aspects of development that modernization theory highlights, especially establishment of democracy, will eventually come to China is uncertain. China may democratize in the near future for several reasons. First and foremost is the track record of political liberalization in countries that reach the levels of economic development that China is approaching. Second, this growth has fueled continually rising expectations among China's people, which have already resulted in disappointment in the countryside and could do the same in the large cities if China experiences a sustained economic slowdown. Third, the Chinese Communist Party has almost completely abandoned Marxist ideology and continues to scale back state-run economic activity. This does not guarantee democracy; nondemocratic capitalist countries lack a strong government ideology. However, the less the government controls society, the more the door to democracy opens.

On the other hand, unlike in many other cases of democratization, the Chinese middle class appears unlikely to push for democracy. For many middle-class Chinese, the costs of political instability outweigh the potential benefits of increased political rights, and connections between the middle class and the state remain strong. Chinese leaders also witnessed the collapse not only of Soviet Communist Party control but also of the Soviet Union itself under the weight of forces released by Gorbachev's political reforms. Chinese Communist officials may envision greater democracy in the future, but even if modernization speeds up this process, the lesson of the Soviet Union makes a democratic China unlikely any time soon.

Government's Role in the Economy

After Mao Zedong's death in 1976, Deng Xiaoping emerged as China's leader. He emphasized the importance of finding economic approaches that worked over theory and ideology, and his consolidation of power in 1978 set the stage for a dramatic shift in Chinese economic policy. A 1981 statement by the party's Central Committee strongly denounced Mao's Cultural Revolution. The question was no longer whether there would be important economic reform but rather how considerable it would be. It turned out to be very considerable.

Deng's decision to institute radical economic reform was of monumental consequence and risk. By abandoning the economic principles of Marxist-Leninist Maoism, Deng was basing the legitimacy of Chinese Communist Party rule largely on economic performance. Chinese agricultural and industrial production soared in the 1980s, but the downsides of market-based economic growth—inflation, unemployment, inequality, and, perhaps most important, rising expectations—created new challenges.

As a result of Deng's policies and their impact on China's economic development, the country became a symbol of the **Asian economic model**, a combination of mercantilism, other state-led development measures, and a less-than-democratic approach to governing. The model, which was often viewed as the means for LDCs to become EDCs, began to unravel in the 1990s. Not only did growing prosperity lead to pressures to democratize, but the Asian economic crisis of the late 1990s also called into question the economic components of the approach taken by countries like China. Still, China has retained state intervention in the economy even as it continues to further liberalize its formerly socialist economy. This is reflected in its Heritage/WSJ Economic Freedom Index ranking of 140, only slightly ahead of Russia.

Globalization

Repeatedly being informed of the large trade deficit that the United States has with China and seeing "Made in China" on scores of products, many Americans view China as the poster child of globalization. They would be surprised to learn that the A.T. Kearney/Foreign

---

Urbanization A dramatic increase in the portion of a country's population that lives in large cities.

Physical Capital The means of production used in an enterprise.

Human Capital The skills and other productive characteristics of workers.

Asian Economic Model A combination of state-led development measures and authoritarian political practices; commonly found in Asia from the 1970s through the 1990s.

Policy Globalization Index places China at 66 of the 72 countries ranked. As was the case with some other TIC cases, China's economic ranking differs from its personal, technological, and political rankings. China's economic ranking of 43 is much higher than its ranking in the other three categories (67, 56, and 65). Its FDI ranking within the economic category is 35, the second highest of the nine TIC cases.

Despite its desire for FDI and the large increases in imports since it became a member of the World Trade Organization in 2003, China remains less open to global connections than many countries. China's long commitment to mercantilist policies—fed by nationalism and the country's historical experience of foreign penetration—has prevented closer ties with the global economy. One of the most important questions for the international community is whether China will accept norms, agreements, and procedural disciplines from the outside when it fails to accept these practices internally.[64] Domestically, the country has liberalized economically without dramatic political liberalization. Internationally, it is hard to imagine how China can avoid political integration as it continues to pursue additional economic integration.[65]

Iran

The Iranian economy remains isolated from much of the rest of the world. Despite actions over the last several years to reduce the government's role in the economy, the legacies of state intervention from the early-post-revolution period have limited the country's economic growth. Its GDP-based statistics place it in the middle of the pack of the TIC cases. The younger members of Iran's urban middle class have displayed their unhappiness with the current government and have the potential to play an influential role in Iran's political future.

Class

The prosperity of the late 1960s and early 1970s brought industrialization and an emerging middle class to Iran. Expansion of the government bureaucracy under the shah helped to develop a sizable middle class. By the middle 1970s, however, the economic bubble had burst. Few ordinary Iranians were seeing the newly generated wealth trickle down to them. Thus, although the Islamic Revolution of 1979 was clearly political and religious, it was also about transferring some of the country's prosperity to ordinary citizens.

The post-revolution economic system has prevented that transfer and has limited further expansion of the middle class, although it is still noticeable in the larger cities. Members of the middle class, particularly of the young, educated, urban middle-class, have been among the strongest supporters of reform. Although the reformist former president, Mohammed Khatami, had broad support from across the electorate, his support among members of the middle class was much greater than his support among the other classes.

Iranian President Mahmoud Ahmadinejad was elected in 2005 partly because he expressed concern about Iran's less economically fortunate. Highlighting the extent to which Iran's oil wealth had not reached the working class, Ahmadinejad used populist rhetoric to appeal to Iran's working class and underclass, whose members display considerable class consciousness. Ahmadinejad again appealed to the poorer segments of the population during the presidential campaign in 2009, and their support played an important role in his reelection.

Economic Development

Throughout much of its history, and despite its challenging climate, Iran was agricultural. During the twentieth century, it experienced rapid development fueled by revenues from the sale of oil. Profits from oil exports led Iran's economy to grow sharply in the early 1970s. As often happens in countries at Iran's level of development that suddenly experience an infusion of wealth, the population's expectations rose alongside the prospering economy. These expectations have, for the most part, gone unmet.

The reasons for this disappointment are both internal and external. Poor relations with the United States have limited Iran's economic potential since the Islamic Revolution. An even larger factor, however, was the war with Iraq during much of the 1980s. This conflict created economic displacement and focused the government on military production and procurement. Another problem is the heavy dependence on the sale of oil that continued after the revolution. Petroleum exports make up more than 80 percent of Iran's export revenue and up to half of government revenue. When world oil prices declined in the middle 1980s, late 1990s, and late 2000s, Iran's economy suffered.

Another challenge is the population explosion and increase in urbanization that have affected Iran's post-revolution development prospects. Urbanization normally accompanies economic development, but the Iranian government's initial opposition to birth control and encouragement of population increase also drove Iran's demographic patterns. Although population growth slowed in the middle to late 1980s, the Iranian baby boom of the early 1980s continues to have consequences. With a large percentage of the population recently entering the workforce, the government's ability to provide jobs continues to be tested.

Even more frustrating for Iran's youth, educational opportunities have not emerged. Only around 10 percent of the country's high school students are admitted to universities; many of the best and brightest have left the country to pursue educational opportunities in the West, causing a "brain drain" that further threatens long-term economic development.[66] Some of those who remain have sought to engage the system through participation in periodic political rallies and protests.

Positive economic statistics hide many of these problems. With the rebound in world oil prices, economic growth was strong in the early part of the 2000s, averaging almost 6 percent annual real growth from 2002 to 2008. GDP per capita-PPP has risen as well, from just under $6,000 in 2000 to over $9,500 in 2008 and $11,300 in 2011. Without the PPP adjustment, Iran's GDP per capita figure was around $4,500 in 2011, again showing the importance of considering a country's cost of living when judging its relative prosperity. Significant wealth and income gaps remain.

Government's Role in the Economy

Both before and after the Islamic Revolution, Iranian governments stressed improving the country's economy and ordinary citizens' lives. Following the 1979 revolution, the government's efforts included nationalization of many industries and banks. The Iranian government also proposed three successive development plans from 1989 to 2005. Iran's economic development plans reflected tensions over how best to use the country's oil money. Like other oil-rich countries with significant poverty, some in Iran have favored a dramatic short-term redistribution of wealth, while others have supported a longer-term strategy based on investment and diversification of the economy.

After 2005, the government initially implemented some of the populist policies on which President Ahmadinejad had campaigned. The result was a dramatic increase in government spending. By 2010, however, the government began to get more serious about economic reform that would include reduced government subsidies and control over prices. The Iranian national legislature passed a major subsidy reform program in January 2010, although the plan calls for significant social welfare spending to counteract higher food and energy prices. At the same time that the Iranian government looks to reduce its role in regulating prices, other parts of the economy may require increased government investment. Ironically, given Iran's image as an oil state, one of the most pressing needs is renewed investment in the energy sector.

Iran's government has learned what many other governments have also found out over the years: although a good idea economically, reducing the state's presence in the economy is not always politically popular. Consequently, the process of economic reform remains slow. Although it is not the ideal type of a socialist economy, Iran remains closer to the socialist variant, with some elements of the state capitalist approach. If the momentum that had developed by the beginning of 2010 continues to push Iran to implement further reforms over the next several years, the mixed economy label may eventually become more appropriate. For now, as Table 2.3 indicates, its Heritage/WSJ Economic Freedom Index ranking is 168, the lowest of the TIC cases (and one of the lowest rankings in the world). This low ranking points to the Iranian state's heavy-handed approach to its economic system.

Globalization

The Islamic Revolution isolated Iran from the West. Though the government of former President Khatami, a moderate reformer, sought greater openness, even then the process was slow. Despite Khatami's efforts at reform, Islamic conservatives who dominate key positions in Iran's political system feared dependence on and cultural

TABLE 2.3	Heritage/WSJ Economic Freedom Index Rankings for the Nine TIC Cases
Country	**Heritage/WSJ Economic Freedom Ranking**
United Kingdom	11
Germany	23
Mexico	41
Nigeria	106
Brazil	113
India	124
China	140
Russia	143
Iran	168

contamination from the West. Their suspicious nature made closer connections with the United States impossible. For its part, the United States maintained sanctions on Iran during Khatami's two terms as president.

Iran's overall A.T. Kearney/Foreign Policy Globalization Index ranking places it last among the 72 countries examined, just below India. Only its technology ranking (54) is not near the very bottom, thanks to a 52 position in the category of Internet users. Its economic, political, and personal rankings are 65, 70, and 72, respectively. The Law on the Attraction and Protection of Foreign Investment passed in 2002 has done little to increase FDI. The FDI component of the economic dimension garners a number 72 ranking. Iran's oil exports help give it a ranking of 55 on trade.

TIC Wrap-Up

The class structures, development patterns and levels, roles of government in the economy, exposure to globalization, and political importance of these economic structural features are similar and different across the nine TIC countries (see the Country Summary). The TIC cases fall roughly into three groups: (1) the UK and Germany; (2) Mexico, Brazil, Nigeria, and Iran; and (3) Russia, China, and India.

Having developed economically long ago and the two most economically developed of the TIC cases, both the UK and Germany have large middle classes. The UK is less economically equal than Germany, however, due to the Germans' greater commitment to level the economic playing field by means of government policies. The UK and Germany are both EDCs, but their development paths differed both in time and approach. As the birthplace of the Industrial Revolution, the UK urbanized earlier, maintained a larger portion of its population in cities, and limited the role of the state in economic development more than did other major European countries. Germany developed with the help of significant state involvement, and its development took place over a much shorter period of time. There has been a general move toward the free-market approach to government involvement in the economy across the TIC cases. In some countries, such as the UK, this change has meant a move from a mixed economy toward a system with even less government intervention. The economies of the UK and Germany are less globalized than the economies of many lesser developed countries. As members of the EU,

their regional interconnections are ample, but their ties to non-EU members are less substantial, and a large portion of their economies are domestically oriented.

The class structures of Mexico, Brazil, Iran, and Nigeria are more typical of LDCs. All have large working classes and underclasses, and inequality is significant. Compared to Nigeria, Mexico, Brazil, and Iran have more noticeable and more politically relevant middle classes. Historically, Mexico and Brazil depended on agriculture and natural resource extraction, but their economies have moved toward the manufacture of finished products in recent decades. This has made them attractive to foreign investors and has led them to be considered as NICs or as emerging market countries. While Brazil's exports go to a variety of countries, Mexico's are directed largely at the United States. Nigeria and Iran have retained more traditional LDC features. Both generate a large portion of their export revenue from oil, and both have fallen victim to the resource curse, but Iran has been much less open to attracting FDI to bolster its oil industry than has Nigeria.

Russia, China, and India share a legacy of a socialist approach to economic development for the latter half of the twentieth century and a rejection of that approach in favor of economic liberalization from the 1990s to the present. During the period of state control of the economy, all three saw significant economic development, though annual growth rates were lower than they have been over the last decade. Class divisions were also minimized during the socialist planning period. Their move toward capitalist economic systems over the last couple of decades has generated significant wealth. It has also produced economic inequality at levels unseen in the previous period. Compared to the other two cases, Russian economic growth in the postcommunist period was much stronger in the 2000s than in the 1990s, but global oil prices affected annual growth rates in both decades. Russia, China, and India have Jekyll and Hyde relationships with globalization. Increased economic ties to other countries over the previous decade have aided economic expansion. FDI into their countries, on the other hand, has been hampered by corruption and domestic concerns about the economic, social, and political consequences of increased links to external forces.

Below is the first Country Summary, which organizes the information about the nine countries presented in the TIC section above. This table also amplifies coverage of the three Spotlight on countries.

COUNTRY SUMMARY

TIC Country	Class Structure and Inequality	Economic Development	Government's Role in Economy	Globalization
United Kingdom	Sizable middle class; working-class identity still visible	EDC; 2011 GDP per capita–PPP: $36,000	Post–World War II settlement led to social welfare protections within a largely capitalist framework	Attracts FDI; smaller portion of economy related to trade than some other TIC cases
Germany	Large middle class; low levels of inequality compared to other TIC cases	EDC; 2011 GDP per capita–PPP: $37,200	Social market form of capitalism; significant welfare state	Trades with other EU members; low level of FDI worries government officials
India	Emerging middle class, but significant poverty and inequality	LDC/emerging market / BRICS case; 2011 GDP per capita–PPP: $3,500	More involvement before 1991 than today; visible intervention remains, but liberalization efforts continue	Potential for much more globalized economy; FDI and trade as a portion of the economy remain low
Mexico	Visible and politically relevant middle class; inequality remains a problem	NIC/emerging market; 2011 GDP per capita–PPP: $14,800	Moderate government involvement; drug violence may prompt more regulation	Importance of regional economic connections; NAFTA; ITAP feature on globalization and weak state versus strong state theories
Brazil	Severe inequality; growing middle class, but exact size is difficult to estimate	NIC/emerging market/ BRICS case; 2011 GDP per capita–PPP: $11,800	Traditional heavy presence in the economy continues despite liberalization efforts; regulatory practices limit new business development	Emerging market (BRICS) status means some FDI; lowest trade ranking of TIC cases
Nigeria	Worst poverty of TIC cases; poverty present across all regions of the country; very small middle class	LDC/LLDC; 2011 GDP per capita–PPP: $2,500; ITAP feature on dependency theory	Liberalization efforts encouraged by IMF; support for free-market approach among the Nigerian people; those most benefiting from corruption support continued government involvement	FDI related to the oil sector; second highest globalization ranking of TIC cases
Russia	High levels of poverty; large lower class and underclass	CIT/BRICS case; 2011 GDP per capita–PPP: $16,700	Postcommunist liberalization bred oligarchic capitalism; under Putin, state became more active as owner of key businesses rather than planner or regulator; model of state capitalism today	FDI related to the energy sector; heavy reliance on oil export revenue means economic successes and downturns tied to global oil prices

TIC Country	Class Structure and Inequality	Economic Development	Government's Role in Economy	Globalization
China	Large lower class and underclass; new upper class; growing inequality	LDC/NIC/emerging market/BRICS case; 2011 GDP per capita–PPP: $8,300; ITAP feature on modernization theory	Significant liberalization replaced socialist planning system; state-led development efforts (Asian economic model) helped generate high rates of economic growth	Significant FDI; tradition of merchantilist policies limits openness to global economy
Iran	Significant wealth and income gaps; politically important middle class	LDC; 2011 GDP per capita–PPP: $11,300	Slow process of economic reform; state remains highly involved in economic planning and regulation; lowest economic freedom ranking of TIC cases	Government suspicion of interconnections with other countries limits globalization effects; least globalized of TIC cases

Spotlight on . . . Country

	Class Structure and Inequality	Economic Development	Government's Role in Economy	Globalization
France	Large middle class; increasing inequality, but still low in comparative terms	EDC; 2011 GDP per capita–PPP: $34,950	Large role for the state in directing economic development and overseeing welfare state programs	Relative low trade rankings because of size of economy and focus on intra-EU trade; significant FDI
Iraq	Significant poverty; many in the middle class fled during the war; focus on oil extraction limits middle class development	LDC; 2011 GDP per capita–PPP: $4,000	Evolving post-occupation economic system; government likely to remain involved in energy sector	War and U.S.-led occupation limited trade and FDI; some increases in FDI in 2009 and 2010 focused on energy sector
South Africa	Significant wealth and income gaps; widening divide between rich and poor, including within the black population	LDC/NIC/emerging market/BRICS case; 2011 GDP per capita–PPP: $10,880	Moderate role for the state in the economy; government under increasing pressure to address high unemployment rate (estimated at nearly 25 percent in 2011)	Relatively low levels of trade and FDI; economic globalization ranking higher than Iran, India, and Brazil

Research in Context

The penultimate section of this chapter contains the book's first "Research in Context" feature. This feature, coming prior to the conclusion of this and every subsequent chapter in the book, provides an overview of recent research in comparative politics related to the topic of the chapter. Summarizing how the research study addresses some of the topics discussed in Chapter 1—the study's research question, the case(s) examined, the type of data employed, etc.—the discussion of this research project then addresses why political leaders, as well as ordinary citizens, should care about the research.

Poverty Policies in Chile and Mexico following Pro-Market Economic Reforms

The 2009 issue of the *International Political Science Review* contains an article by Judith A. Teichman titled "Competing Visions of Democracy and Development in the Era of Neoliberalism in Mexico and Chile." Teichman studied Chile and Mexico to better understand the way that governments that engage in free-market economic reforms choose among policy options to address poverty. As discussed earlier in the chapter, in the 1980s, the International Monetary Fund (IMF) encouraged Mexico to adopt **neoliberalism**, an approach that emphasizes a reduced role of the government in the economy to foster economic growth. Teichman argues that this decision had consequences for future policy decisions. Specifically, in both Mexico and Chile, nongovernmental organizations (NGOs) pressured the government to adopt broad, community-focused antipoverty programs, but the governments instead focused on conditional cash transfer programs, which provide targeted payments to individuals who meet specific criteria.

> **Neoliberalism** A pro-market economic approach that emphasizes reductions in the role of government to encourage economic growth.

Teichman's research question centers on why the two countries, which had different economic and political experiences, took similar approaches to antipoverty policies. She collected data, including a large number of interviews with international organization officials, Mexican and Chilean government officials, and leaders of local NGOs.

In her article, Teichman argues that because the leaders of Mexico and Chile had accepted many of the underlying principles of neoliberal economics, they assumed "that market-led economic growth will eliminate most poverty" and believed that antipoverty programs should target individuals rather than communities.[67] Local organizations, however, held a view that Teichman labels the "community development perspective," which criticizes the conditional cash transfer programs for being based on a one-size-fits-all approach and for failing to focus money on community building initiatives. In both countries, the governments resisted significant opposition from local NGOs. Based on her interview data, Teichman argues that the commitment of the government to a pro-market orientation meant excluding groups that called for actions contrary to that commitment from the policy-making process.

So What?

Assuming the accuracy of Teichman's interpretation of the Mexican and Chilean antipoverty approaches, what is the real-world relevance of this research? American policy makers have been emphasizing a neoliberal, pro-market economic approach for decades. Teichman contends that in countries like Chile and Mexico this emphasis has "produced neither equitable prosperity nor widespread poverty reduction"[68]—a point, though, that some who study Latin America would challenge. In addition, she argues that the extent to which the governments of these two countries are willing to ignore the advice of prominent local organizations should give one pause. Her research may signal the need to encourage greater local NGO involvement in antipoverty policy development and implementation. Finally, the idea that addressing poverty may take more than conditional cash transfers to individuals has relevance for the United States. Local communities that develop economically tend to have fewer poor individuals, and American antipoverty efforts might benefit from a careful consideration of how better to target economic development at the local level.

Although this chapter centers on the impact of economic structure on major political outcomes, Teichman's study also helps illustrate how governments can work to alter different components of their economic structure. Hoping to decrease poverty and develop their economies, Mexico and Chile heeded the advice of organizations like the IMF, altered their economic systems in a capitalist direction, and made themselves more open to globalization. According to Teichman, some of these efforts succeeded, but ultimately the governments failed to dramatically reduce poverty. Thus, Teichman's study touches on all four components of economic structure—class structure, development, economic system, and globalization—and demonstrates the difficulty of changing well-established economic structures.

CONCLUSION

This chapter deals with central concepts and some key comparative politics theories regarding the potential influence of economic structure on political outcomes. Economic structure approaches have been prominent in comparative politics for decades. They draw on intellectual work from the last three centuries by scholars such as Adam Smith and Karl Marx, and they continue to be relevant as the world becomes increasingly economically, culturally, and politically globalized.

This chapter also presents key economic structural features of the nine countries examined in detail throughout this textbook. These cases provide different examples of class structure, patterns of economic development, government role in the economy, and degrees of economic interconnections with other countries. Their study also generates common themes about economic setting and its political consequences.

For many comparativists, an examination of economic structure is the starting point for understanding political outcomes. This does not mean that the economic structural approach is beyond criticism. Critics argue that events of the late twentieth century demonstrate that Karl Marx got it wrong, that economic factors have at most indirect effects on politics, that scholars' economic arguments about politics reflect the scholars' normative position, and that focusing on economics leads comparativists to miss other important factors such as culture, identity, political institutions, and political decision making.

Such criticisms have some validity, but ignoring economics is no better than focusing on it exclusively. Economics plays an important role in structuring political outcomes in countries at different levels of economic development and with different types of political systems. These effects are both direct and indirect. For example, class structure and economic development directly influence the likelihood that a country will become a stable democracy. At the same time, economic structural conditions help shape other structural features that, in turn, affect a political outcome like democratization. These include political culture and identity, the topics of the next two chapters.

KEY TERMS

Asian economic model, p. 54

Black market, p. 38

Bourgeoisie, p. 30

BRICS, p. 35

Capitalism, p. 37

Class, p. 30

Class consciousness, p. 32

Class structure, p. 31

Constant dollars, p. 33

Countries in transition (CITs), p. 35

Dependency theory, p. 50

Economically developed countries (EDCs), p. 34

Economic development, p.33

Economic growth, p. 33

Emerging markets, p. 36

Exports, p. 40

Finished products, p. 35

Foreign direct investment (FDI), p. 40

Free-market capitalism, p. 37

GDP per capita, p. 33

Globalization, p. 39

Gross domestic product (GDP), p. 33

Human capital, p. 54

Human Development Index (HDI), p. 34

Imports, p. 40

Import substitution industrialization (ISI), p. 48

Informal economy, p. 33

Labor-led capitalism, p. 38

Least developed of the lesser developed countries (LLDCs), p. 34

Lesser developed countries (LDCs), p. 34

Market, p. 37

Market forces, p. 37

Means of production, p. 30

Median income, p. 31

Mercantilism, p. 39

Middle class, p. 30

Mixed economies, p. 38

Mode of production, p. 30

Modernization theory, p. 53

CHAPTER OUTLINE

Political Culture

The Sources of Political Culture

Political Ideologies: From Values and Systems of
   Meaning to Blueprints

TOPIC IN COUNTRIES

Features in this chapter:

Spotlight on … France: The Features of French Political
Culture

In Theory and Practice: The United Kingdom and Almond
and Verba's Civic Culture Theory

In Theory and Practice: China and Ronald Inglehart's
Postmaterialism Theory

In Theory and Practice: Iran and Benjamin Barber's
"Jihad versus McWorld" Framework

Research in Context: Migration from Mexico and Political
Culture in Mexico

Alexis de Tocqueville, a nineteenth century French scholar
best known today for his work on American political culture.
© The Art Gallery Collection/Alamy

LEARNING OBJECTIVES

After reading this chapter, you should be able to

- Define *culture* and *political culture*.
- Discuss how socialization, major events, and long-term processes can shape political culture over time.
- Describe the meaning of *ideology*, and distinguish among several major ideological perspectives.
- Compare and contrast the features and the development of the political cultures of the TIC cases.
- Explain the findings from the Research in Context feature in this chapter.

In 1831, Alexis de Tocqueville, a French aristocrat in his mid twenties, came to the United States. He spent less than one year in the country, but he traveled extensively—from New York to Green Bay, from New Orleans to Washington, D.C.—fighting health problems that would plague him throughout his life. In 1834, two years after he returned to France, Tocqueville published the first volume of his two-volume work, *Democracy in America*. The book presented Tocqueville's views of American society and its relationship with the American political system. It remains a classic in the study of political culture. Although Tocqueville paid relatively little attention to political institutions, he wove together his observations about the United States with theories about how values form and how they influence political life. The book won numerous prizes after its publication, and it became even more popular as time went on.

Democracy in America also represents the potential dangers of a single-minded focus on political culture, including the tendency to make broad generalizations from a limited set of observations and to see and interpret a society through the filter of one's own values. Among his many claims, Tocqueville stated that Americans pay little attention to philosophy, have a deep belief in human self-improvement, are "more addicted to practical science than theoretical science,"[1] and constantly form new organizations. Although one could claim that such statements have a certain degree of validity 180 years later, they are generalizations that held true, and continue to hold true, about some but not all Americans.

As the arguments in Chapter 2 highlight, economics can strongly influence many political outcomes. But how much people expect from government and how much government they are willing to tolerate often come from something deeper than their pocketbooks. Tocqueville's study of American life in the 1800s served as an early discussion of how values and beliefs can affect political outcomes. These embedded beliefs and values act as a lens through which group members see the world and judge what they see. This lens is the group's culture. The portion of that lens that is used to see and judge political events, and that consequently helps structure political behaviors, is the group's political culture.

Political culture is not reserved for individuals who are actively involved in political events; everyone shares in a political culture. Individual values and beliefs are the products of past and present life experiences, the social institutions that guide individuals through childhood and continue to mold them as adults, and the actions and stances of political institutions and leaders. The values and beliefs of many people combine to form a collective culture. This chapter provides an overview of how political culture develops, how it changes and is maintained, and how it can affect political behavior and other political outcomes. The chapter also examines ideology, the extension of political culture's underlying values into a political blueprint for society and its governance.

Although this chapter is primarily about political culture rather than culture in general, it is necessary to first discuss broader ideas of culture. Within the social sciences, **culture** is generally defined in two distinct but related ways. The first way is as the **underlying values** in a society that shape behavior by attaching a sense of good or bad to an action. For example, a person who deeply values stability and order is less likely to engage in political protests designed to destabilize the government than is a person who deeply values freedom and individual self-expression. Note that values are not the same thing as attitudes, which are closer to the surface of an individual's hierarchy of views and positions and more susceptible to day-to-day fluctuations. Values are deeper and less vulnerable to sudden changes. They are, in other words, "sticky."

> **Culture** Defined in two distinct but related ways: (1) as a particular group's underlying values, and (2) as a system of meaning that shapes the way members of groups make sense of the people and events they encounter.

Other social scientists conceptualize culture as a **system of meaning**. In this view, culture is a frame that shapes how people understand someone or something with which they come into contact (good or bad, like us or different from us, etc.). As political scientist Marc Howard Ross puts it, culture "frames the context in which politics occurs."[2] The idea of culture as a system of meaning makes clear that both experiences and how individuals interpret those experiences shape culture.

Both views of culture reflect culture as a collective concept. It takes a group to have a culture. An individual can have deep beliefs and a particular way of interpreting events, but an individual cannot have a culture.

This idea of the collective values and systems of meaning of a group does not mean that everyone in the group holds the same values or interprets the world in the same way. Generally speaking, when consensus exists, then **cultural homogeneity** exists across the group. On the other hand, when a wide range of beliefs are present, a high degree of **cultural heterogeneity** is present.

> **Cultural Homogeneity** The case when members of a group are relatively unified in their beliefs and system of meaning.
>
> **Cultural Heterogeneity** The case when a wide range of beliefs exists within a group.

One source of cultural heterogeneity is the presence of multiple identity groups, each of which may itself be culturally homogeneous. Members of an ethnic group often share similar beliefs, but these beliefs differ greatly from those held by members of other ethnic groups. This type of overall cultural heterogeneity—with sharp cultural differences corresponding to social group boundaries—is more threatening to social stability than when various sets of beliefs are more randomly spread across the population.

Political Culture

Political culture is the underlying set of values and beliefs about politics and the system of meaning for interpreting politics held by a given population. Political scientists examine a number of values and beliefs that are components of political culture and look at how these values and beliefs interact. This chapter highlights five sets of values and beliefs to provide a framework for understanding political culture. They are summarized in Table 3.1.

> **Political Culture** A given population's underlying set of values and beliefs about politics and system of meaning for interpreting politics.

Components of Political Culture

The first set of values that political scientists emphasize concerns social relations and authority. These beliefs address whether the masses accept the authority of a social elite and, consequently, whether social relations are vertical or horizontal.

TABLE 3.1	The Five Major Components of Political Culture
Component	**Questions**
1. Beliefs about Authority	1A. Are social elites accepted as legitimate? 1B. Are social relations vertical or horizontal?
2. Group versus Individual	2A. Is the collective more important than the individual? 2B. Is equality more important than personal freedom?
3. Liberty versus Security	3. Do people value freedom from state action, even if it means less stability and less security?
4. Political System Legitimacy	4A. Does the existing political regime have the right to rule? 4B. Can political leaders generally be trusted?
5. The Political Community	5A. With what political unit does the population identify most readily? 5B. Does the population as a whole have a strong attachment to an overarching national identity?

Vertical Social Relations Social relations in societies that emphasize an authority hierarchy.

Horizontal Social Relations Social relations that highlight equality among members of society to help shape political and social decisions.

Individualistic Political Cultures Political cultures that discourage government involvement in society.

Collectivistic Political Cultures Political cultures that support government action aimed at benefiting large numbers of people.

Vertical social relations occur in hierarchical societies, with those at the top (including political leaders) having the right to impose their decisions upon those at the bottom. **Horizontal social relations**, on the other hand, emphasize equality and a role for many members of society to help shape political and social decisions.

The second set of values concerns group welfare versus the interests of the individual. Is society individualistic, or is the fate of the collective more important than that of individuals? **Individualistic political cultures** discourage governments from implementing policies that protect groups or that level the economic playing field in society. **Collectivistic political cultures** tend to coincide with government programs aimed at benefiting large numbers of people.

The third set of values concerns the potential trade-off between liberty and security. Do people accept a strong state that uses rules governing individual behavior to penetrate into society to maintain order? Or do they value freedom from state action, with the state leaving most decisions to individuals, even if doing so means less stability and security? Different answers to these questions shape governmental institutions and policies in a particular country. Where freedom is more important than order and security, there will be a strong emphasis on "negative rights"—freedoms from government action or, put another way, things government cannot do to citizens of the state. If security and order are more important than freedom, the state may be highly intrusive in the name of maintaining order.

The fourth set of beliefs centers on the legitimacy of the political system and its leaders. Do individuals accept the existing political regime as having the right to rule? Can political leaders generally be trusted, or must society carefully monitor the activities of government?

The final set of beliefs centers on what political scientist David Easton called the "political community." With what political unit does the population identify most readily? Does the population as a whole have a strong attachment to an overarching national identity? Other identities within a country can be more powerful than national identity. People's loyalties may lie with other parts of their identities, such as race, ethnic group, or region of residence.

Think and Discuss

Look at the five components of political culture presented in Table 3.1. Which of the five is the most important, and why?

Different Forms of Political Culture

A comparativist seeking to understand the political culture in a state must first characterize that culture. Looking at the particular combination of the five sets of values that seems to be dominant—as well as how dominant that particular combination is—allows one to characterize the structure of a group's political culture. Several of the five general features of political culture are complementary, such as individualism (the individual is the focus) over collectivism (society as a whole has more meaning than the individual), a belief in liberty at the expense of order, and a general suspicion of government institutions. At the same time, the five components can be combined in many different ways. A society that views social relations as horizontal, for example, can have either individualistic or collectivistic values.

Different combinations of the five main sets of political cultural values and different degrees of homogeneity of the political culture add up to different political cultural structures, each with its own array of implications for politics. Just as a combination of the various components of political culture may be unique to a society, so too may it be unique to a particular point in time. Political cultures are usually slow to change. Later in this chapter, circumstances that cause the political culture of a society to undergo a radical shift in a fairly short amount of time are discussed.

It is also necessary to distinguish between mass and elite political culture. Elites and members of the general public sometimes value different things. Political scientists typically use the term *political culture* to refer to the values and/or systems of meaning in the general population. Some focus on political culture at the elite level, including the extent to which it matches mass political culture. In studies of democracy, for example, it is not unusual for comparativists to pay more attention to the commitment to democracy of elites rather than of the general population. Without such a commitment among the ruling elite, democracy is difficult to establish. Without a commitment to democracy among the general population, however, maintaining a democracy over the long term becomes a challenge.

Spotlight on ... FRANCE

The Features of French Political Culture

French political culture has long been divided by the competing legacies of the French Revolution of the 1790s.[3] Supporters of the republican approach follow the motto of that revolution—*Liberté, Egalité, Fraternité*—while their opponents have historically emphasized what are considered the more established attributes of French society, including traditional social relationships, religion, and the country's history prior to the revolution. Like the Napoleonic empire of the early nineteenth century, the current French political system, the Fifth Republic, represents an attempt to consolidate the social advances of republican political culture while appropriating the symbols of authority, status, and order important to the revolution's opponents. The Fifth Republic weakened the legislature (the National Assembly), but French republicans still consider it to be the institution that represents the citizens and embodies the general will or sovereignty of the French Republic. At the same time, the president in the Fifth Republic is meant to embody the nation and to have the chief responsibility for the security of the state, the social order, and the preservation of the principles spelled out in the constitution. Consequently, most French presidents are above the law while they hold office. During his two terms (1995–2007), for example, Jacques Chirac refused to be questioned by investigators looking into corruption scandals that emerged from his years as mayor of Paris.

Broadly speaking, therefore, the French political system today reflects an attempt to compromise on the core values of authority, equality, liberty, and security. To a large extent, the endeavor has been successful. The ideals of the French Revolution resonate across the political spectrum. French citizens value liberty, as it enables the organized expression of political dissent and partisan debate. Fraternité (brotherhood) includes the principle of solidarity, which emphasizes the collective obligation of all citizens to each other. They also value equality: the only legitimate forms of social hierarchy are those based on individual training and merit.

The potential for contradiction in a culture forged by compromise has been most evident in the arena of the French political community. In recent years, for example, the government banned students in public schools from wearing religious emblems, such as Muslim head scarves, Jewish yarmulkes, or Catholic crucifixes. The republicans live by the principle of *laïcité*, a form of secularism in which religion is considered a private matter, the expression of which has no place in a public institution. But in a nod to traditional social groups, the Fifth Republic also strongly supports private religious education, with extensive state funding for Catholic and Jewish schools.

This debate over religious expression also illustrates the power of reason in French political culture. As the home of the Enlightenment—an eighteenth-century movement that transformed social life through the power of philosophical learning and debate—France considers itself the country that thinks more than any other. In France, philosophers and intellectuals are celebrities, the television network news broadcasts take place during prime time, and a significant portion of other prime-time broadcasts consists of issue-oriented or philosophical talk shows, history telecasts, and arts programs. In the debate over religious symbolism in schools, deputies in the National Assembly from the mainstream Right and Left argued that religion was in conflict with reason and that schools should be free of religious thought and places where students could explore all realms of knowledge.

The Sources of Political Culture

In addition to studying the impact of political culture on important political outcomes, political scientists also study how political culture is maintained and how it can change over time. Those who focus on the factors that shape political culture generally emphasize defining events, repeated experiences, and socialization.

Events, Experiences, and Socialization

Because political culture is sticky, life experiences of the individuals whose values and systems of meaning compose a particular culture do not change that culture easily. To make a difference, events must be either dramatic or sustained over a period of time. **Defining events** can shock society and overwhelm the tendency of political culture to resist change. When people feel threatened, for example, their desire for security will often lead them to support preventive action by government even if it restricts their freedom.[4] The terrorist attacks on September 11, 2001, for example, shocked the American people. Many Americans' values and systems of meaning shifted, and as a result, the collective political culture was transformed as well.

Ongoing or **repeated experiences** may affect political culture, particularly if they continue for years or decades. Chapter 2 discussed how economic development can have cultural consequences. But just as economic development is a protracted process, its impact on culture is gradual as well. In West Germany after World War II, decades of economic success accompanied the reestablishment of democracy. This economic boom eventually undid many of the negative beliefs about democracy that had emerged when the implementation of the Weimar democratic system after World War I was followed by an economic depression. Negative experiences can also shape values and beliefs. The Great Depression greatly affected Americans and many others

Defining Events One factor that can shape political culture; such events are dramatic, providing a shock to the existing political culture.

Repeated Experiences Events that recur or are sustained over time that can shape political culture.

around the world, altering their views about the role of government in the economy and the necessity of a social safety net.

Political culture is also shaped through **socialization**, the process of transmitting values and systems of meaning, usually from one generation to the next. This process takes place within the major social institutions that are responsible for laying down beliefs about right and wrong. The most important institution in this regard is the family. Though the correlation is not perfect, a strong predictor of the political beliefs of young adults is the beliefs of their parents. Other important institutions in the socialization process include places of worship, the workplace, the media, the educational system, and the government.

Sometimes socialization is more subtle than telling children what is right and wrong. Schools are a powerful venue for socialization through what they do and do not emphasize. One of the most important socialization tasks of schools is to teach the society's history. Events in the past are filtered through the institutions of socialization in the present. Although it is difficult to make up or fully ignore significant historical events, it is possible to highlight some events more than others, to underscore those events' positive or negative implications, and to explore history through the viewpoint of one particular class, race, or gender. History can be molded and shaped to suit the interests of the powerful. Recent years have seen a movement toward including the perspectives of more marginalized peoples in the study of history, but determining how to present history largely remains the prerogative of the victor.

Taken together, events and socialization are the starting point for a model of political culture and its consequences. This model is captured in Figure 3.1. Note that the model includes both the direct effects of events on political culture and the filtering of events through the socialization process before they shape political culture. The theories discussed in this chapter's "In Theory and Practice" boxes focus on parts of this model, providing causal stories about why political culture develops and/or influences political behavior.

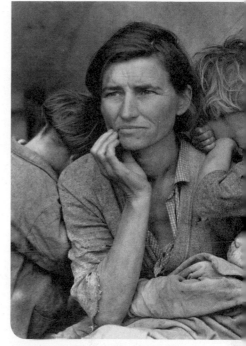

Migrant Mother, a photograph of Florence Owens Thompson and her three children during the Great Depression, by renowned photographer Dorothea Lange.
© Dorothea Lange/Corbis

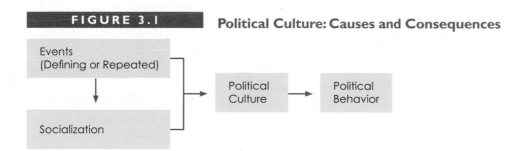

FIGURE 3.1   Political Culture: Causes and Consequences

Events (Defining or Repeated) →

Socialization →

Political Culture → Political Behavior

> **Socialization** The process of transmitting components of a political culture to the next generation through social institutions, such as families, churches, and schools.

Globalization, Socialization, and Political Culture

In addition to the important domestic institutions that foster socialization, cultures are increasingly shaped by globalization. The machinery of globalization expands the range of international connections and makes individuals more aware of their shrinking world. Chapter 2 highlighted the economic aspects of globalization. Globalization occurs in many arenas, some of which are noneconomic, such as culture.

Globalization's impact on culture is undeniable. When two cultures meet, one or both are bound to change. Globalization is an avenue for socialization, with the Internet, Western films, and advertisements by multinational corporations tending to encourage consumerism, capitalism, and attachment to technology. Globalization also magnifies the importance of events outside a country. In a globalizing world, incidents such as the Gulf of Mexico oil spill in 2010 influence more than just individuals who are directly affected. They can shape values on a global scale. Finally, globalization serves as a transmission belt for culture by encouraging increased migration across political borders. Migrants bring their values with them. Although the political culture of a particular group of immigrants may transform over time due to the influence of their new setting, so too may the new setting be affected by their beliefs.

Political Ideologies: From Values and Systems of Meaning to Blueprints

One of the central parts of political culture is the set of values about how and how much society ought to be governed. These values include the role of government in the economy and other aspects of government penetration into society. When these values are spelled out as part of a plan to improve society, they become political ideologies. A **political ideology** is a set of guiding principles about the proper design and functioning of politics and society. It is both normative and prescriptive, combining a sense of what ought to be with a blueprint for putting it in place. The statement "wealth should be more evenly distributed through a highly progressive system of taxation" is an ideological position. Although American political economist Francis Fukuyama proclaimed that the collapse of Communism meant the end of ideological struggles and thus "the end of history,"[5] most social scientists believe that, to paraphrase Mark Twain, the reports of the death of ideology as a political force have been greatly exaggerated.

Political Ideology A set of beliefs or guiding principles about the proper functioning of politics and society.

Given that values about government and society are at the core of both political culture and ideology, the five components of political culture discussed in the previous section can be helpful in making sense of different ideological blueprints. Various combinations of political cultural components can yield distinct ideological categories. For example, ideological prescriptions that require a strong role for the central government would be opposed by a group that values social equality over deference to a dominant elite, prefers personal freedom to economic equality, places liberty above security and order, is suspicious of political leaders, and has a strong attachment to a regional identity at the expense of the overarching political community.

One can use the concept of ideology to distinguish between types of regimes or to differentiate groups within a political system, including political parties. In the case of regimes, discussions of political systems during the cold war emphasized differences between Western-style democracy and the systems of the Communist states. Political systems may have official ideologies; Communist systems were known for their clear sets of guiding principles, even if countries like China have largely abandoned those principles today.

In other systems, including many democracies, the ruling government may not lay out an ideology so explicitly. Yet, ideology can still be significant in such systems. As discussed in detail in Chapters 8 and 9, most democratic political parties link elites and the general population through "programmatic" appeals. In other words, the parties lay out their specific policy positions in pursuit of support at election time. These policy preferences are presented within a broader ideological framework. Although most voters in the United States could not recite in detail the specific policy positions of the Democratic and Republican parties on most issues, many could accurately summarize the basic ideological differences between the two parties. Because political parties in democratic political systems typically provide voters with an ideologically distinct choice, one could argue that ideology is even more important in democracies than in one-party systems.

Think and Discuss
To what extent does the United States have an official ideology?

Ideological Positions on Economics

The topic of government's role in society is a common way to differentiate between ideological positions, and the role of government in society is closely connected to economics. Political scientists understand that the state's ability to penetrate into society to extract economic resources is crucial for effective governing. But individuals—whether politicians or members of the general public—frequently disagree on the proper extent to which government should infringe on personal freedoms or engage in the redistribution of income and wealth. As a result, economic issues like the redistribution of wealth and income provide a useful starting point for thinking about different ideological perspectives.

Ideologies related to the role of government in redistributing income or wealth can be loosely placed on a left to right spectrum. Figure 3.2 presents such a spectrum. To the left of center on the spectrum is what is known in the United States as liberal approaches to politics. This is not how this term is used in other parts of the world, including Europe, where liberals are often political moderates, advocating generally limited government while maintaining social welfare protections. Therefore, labeling the left of center position as a **progressive ideology** is more appropriate for comparative politics. This position supports an active role for government in society and defends policies such as a strongly progressive taxation system that assists in the redistribution of income in society.

Social democratic ideology traditionally went a step further, supporting the nationalization of major industries in the economy but stopping short of the overthrow of capitalism. Today, social democratic parties in Europe have generally abandoned calls for nationalization, centering their efforts on maintaining elements of the **welfare state**, a system of significant intervention in the economy and guarantees of economic and social assistance such as health care and retirement benefits. Due to demographic patterns—aging populations in which more people collect retirement benefits—and the collapse of Communist systems in Eastern Europe and the former Soviet Union, the welfare state has been under attack in Europe since the late 1970s. In the United States, the ideological position of most politicians who run as Democrats can be labeled as either progressive or social democratic.

Even further to the left would be **Marxist ideology**. As introduced in Chapter 2, Marxism focuses on control of the means of production and the use of the political system by the economically powerful to maintain their dominant position at the expense of the working class. Marxist ideologies advocate gaining control of the government in the name of the working class, collective ownership of property, and other aggressive actions to reduce exploitation and economic inequality. With the collapse of most of the world's Marxist regimes since the 1980s, these ideologies have taken a more significant hit than have their counterparts on the ideological left.

To the right of center on the spectrum is **conservative ideology**. In the realm of economics, conservatives advocate smaller government, stronger property rights, less regulation of the economy, and decreased emphasis on income redistribution. Further to the right are **libertarian ideology** and **reactionary ideology**. Libertarians emphasize a minimal role for government in all aspects of people's lives. They strongly oppose government policies designed to remake society, including efforts at income and wealth redistribution. Most politicians who run as Republicans in the United States hold conservative or libertarian ideological positions and support a free-market capitalist approach more than do Democrats, with little role for government in redistributing wealth and income. Reactionary ideologies advocate

Progressive Ideology An ideology that supports an active role for government in income redistribution through use of taxes and government programs.

Social Democratic Ideology An ideology that traditionally supported nationalization of industry but today focuses more on maintaining welfare state protections.

Welfare State A system that guarantees economic and social assistance, such as health care and retirement benefits, from the government.

Marxist Ideology An ideology that supports control of the government on behalf of the working class and the elimination of significant income differences.

Conservative Ideology An ideology that advocates minimal regulation of the economy and decreased emphasis on income redistribution.

Libertarian Ideology An ideology that seeks even more limited government in all facets of society than that promoted by conservatives.

Reactionary Ideology An ideology that advocates a return to traditional social arrangements, including those that economically privilege one group over another.

| FIGURE 3.2 | **A Left-Right Ideological Spectrum Regarding Wealth Distribution** |

| Marxist | Social Democratic | Progressive | Moderate | Conservative | Libertarian | Reactionary |

the return to traditional society, including the undoing of reforms meant to empower the lower classes.

In the spectrum's middle falls **moderate ideology**. It includes positions that fall between the ideologies to its left and right. For example, moderates may support a system of taxation that is more progressive than that desired by the ideological Right, while rejecting more aggressive policies of economic regulation and income redistribution supported by the Left. In the United States, those who support moderate ideological positions often support both Republican and Democratic candidates, as neither party has strongly laid claim to the moderate range of the ideological spectrum.

Moderate Ideology An ideology that advocates positions that fall between progressive and conservative approaches.

Think and Discuss

The Left-Right ideological spectrum regarding income redistribution presented in this chapter lists the following ideological positions: Marxist, social democratic, progressive, moderate, conservative, libertarian, and reactionary. What portion of the American population do you believe falls into each of these categories? What does this tell you about American politics?

Noneconomic Ideologies

Ideologies do not focus exclusively on economics. Another major ideological division is social, often referred to in the United States as the "values question." On the topic of social values, the ideological Left advocates greater tolerance of unconventional lifestyles, while the Right favors more traditional ways of life. On this ideological dimension, the Left is often highly opposed to government action, since such action often seeks to suppress nontraditional values. Meanwhile, in battles over social values, many on the Right favor government intervention. They see government as responsible for protecting traditional norms and social institutions such as marriage. Thus, a cultural conservative may have a very different idea about the role of government than an economic conservative. Libertarians tend to be more consistent in both realms, being highly suspicious of any government action taken in the name of the greater good.

Ideologies can also differ in relation to identity. The Left advocates tolerance of minority groups, multicultural education, and special privileges for groups that have faced discrimination in the past: women, homosexuals, and ethnic, racial, religious, and linguistic minorities. The Right emphasizes the value of an overarching identity to unite diverse peoples, considering affirmative action programs to be a form of discrimination, although it often supports other government initiatives, such as facilitating cultural unification by giving one language official status. The extreme Right's fascist or ethno-nationalist ideologies advocate the elimination of cultural diversity through forced assimilation, expulsion of minority identity groups, or genocide.

Ideologies based on narrow interpretations of religion have gained prominence in recent years. Although not the only religion-based ideology, **Islamism** has received much attention. Islamism is, in general, anti-West and anti-modernization. It is fueled by opposition to Western influence and presence in Muslim countries in the form of military troops and governments perceived to be puppets of the West. Advocating the use of Islamic law and protection from the cultural influences of Western-led globalization, Islamists gained control of governments in Afghanistan—where they were subsequently forced from power—and, in a milder form, Iran. In its extreme form, Islamist ideology has been a potent tool for the mobilization of Islamic terrorists. Like other religion-based ideologies, including Christian fundamentalism and Hindu nationalism, however, Islamism also takes much less radical forms, including serving as a guiding principle of relatively moderate political parties that seek power through peaceful means.

Islamism An ideology advocating Islamic law as the basis of government structure and policies and as a way to immunize Muslim countries from the corrupting cultural influences of Western-led globalization.

TOPIC IN COUNTRIES

The following sections of the chapter examine how the concepts related to political culture and its sources and the concepts related to ideology play out in the Topic in Countries cases. Each country section provides an overview of that country's political culture, along with discussions of socialization, experiences, and events and ideology. As you read these sections, be sure to look for

- An overview of each country's political culture, using the five component framework presented earlier in the chapter.
- The main sources of socialization in each country.
- The role of repeated experiences or defining events.
- Examples of ideology across the country as a whole and associated with major political parties in each of the TIC cases.

The United Kingdom

As it developed over time, British political culture combined the political elite's openness to government programs (and eventually political power) for the lower classes with the lower classes' deference to elite authority. The result was stability and a tradition of evolutionary progression toward greater democracy. Socialization and significant events in the United Kingdom (UK) have driven political culture toward its present form. The important events in recent decades include acts of violence, including those of relatively brief duration such as terrorist bombings. Democracies push certain ideologies both to unify the population and to distinguish among competing political parties. The UK is no exception, though ideology is less central there than in many other countries.

Political Culture

Consistent with the stereotype of the British as being overly concerned about proper etiquette, British political culture places a great deal of emphasis on status and the authority of elites. This holds particularly true among the working class, which over the years has generally respected the authority of economic and political elites. This belief in the authority of political elites is known as **working-class deference**, and it has had a number of important consequences. It is part of the reason for the general lack of violent class-based uprisings, for the maintenance of the monarchy even as its power was whittled away, and for the relative success of the UK's Conservative Party among working-class voters.

Working-class deference is only half the story. In the past, and arguably still today, the upper class also held an important value about its relationship with the lower classes. Elites saw their economic and social privileges not only as advantages but also as responsibilities to look out for society's less fortunate. This value, known as **noblesse oblige**, has combined with working-class

deference to promote British political stability. It also played a role in the process of decolonization. Compared with other European powers, the British surrendered control over their colonies more slowly, more cooperatively, and with more of an attempt to give the colonies a chance to survive as politically stable democracies.

When discussing individualism versus collectivism in British political culture, it is natural to compare it to the cultures of both United States and continental Europe. In such comparisons, American political culture is typically described as more individualistic and more suspicious of authority than British political culture.[6] At the same time, British political culture is seen as less collectivistic than that of the rest of Western Europe. British philosophers (e.g., John Locke) and some British politicians (e.g., Margaret Thatcher) have emphasized individual liberty and restraints on government control.[7] But the American experiences of separation from British control and settlement of the frontier had no counterpart for the British. It is likely that these events contributed to the development of a stronger American individualism.

Geert Hofstede, a Dutch professor of business and organizational anthropology, produced a well-known comparative study of culture initially based on surveys of IBM employees around the world in the 1970s. He was criticized for using these data, and one should not assume that IBM workers have the same values as the rest of a country's population. But comparing workers for the same company in different countries can be informative, and Hofstede has updated his index with more

---

Working-Class Deference The belief by the lower classes, present throughout English and British history, that the British elite have the authority to rule over them.

Noblesse Oblige The belief among the British social, economic, and political elite that their position implies an obligation to enhance the quality of life for those less fortunate than themselves.

recent and diverse data over the years. He focuses on five dimensions of culture, one of which is individualism.[8] His score for the British on this component is high (89), behind only Australia (90) and the United States (91).[9] The average for European countries that Hofstede examined is under 60, indicating that the British may be much more like the residents of their former colonies than like their continental European neighbors on questions of individual versus collective orientation.

The British have participated in a number of wars, but these wars were rarely the result of foreign invasion. Therefore, concerns about security are less central in British culture than in the cultures of most other countries. Hofstede also looks at order and security (which he calls "uncertainty avoidance"). The British score of 30 is relatively low on this component compared with a European average of almost 70. It is also noticeably lower than the U.S. score of 46.

Even so, the British have a tradition of secrecy in matters related to national security that was codified in the country's Official Secrets Act as early as 1911.[10] The idea of a trade-off between freedom and security became more prevalent in the minds of the British public with the terrorist campaigns of the Irish Republican Army (IRA) in the second half of the twentieth century. Just as concerns about IRA terrorism were diminishing, Islamic terrorists attacked the British public transportation system on July 7, 2005. Because of significant differences in damage and loss of life compared to the September 11, 2001, attacks in the United States, the "7/7" events in the United Kingdom were less of a shock to British political culture than the 9/11 attacks were to American political culture.

The tradition of deference and the tendency for changes to the political system to be evolutionary rather than revolutionary—to be slow and progressive rather than huge and rapid—have combined to create generally high levels of political system legitimacy in the UK. But, as discussed in Chapter 1, system legitimacy does not necessarily translate into support for specific leaders or policies. British political culture is marked by a concurrent faith in institutions of government and belief in the individual's right to protest specific government actions. In the summer of 2010, for example, Prime Minister Gordon Brown was ousted as voters turned against him and his ruling Labour Party. The British people still believed in the political system's right to rule, but they had enough of the person in charge of that system.

The question of attachment to the political community is complex in the case of the UK. The presence of sharp ethnic divisions, reinforced by territorial boundaries, has made attachment to the overarching British national identity tenuous at times. In recent decades, ethnic politics have rekindled the nationalism of the past, and the central government has made concessions to the Scots, the Northern Irish, and the Welsh that have increased their

control over their own political affairs. The government has also struggled to address growing tensions between immigrants and traditional Britons.

At the same time, the people of the UK show a stronger commitment to the national political community than do citizens of many other countries. As citizens of an island country, the UK's ethnic groups have more in common with one another than with other Europeans. The European integration process has also brought the ethnic groups of the UK together more than it has divided them. The decision by the British government to opt out of the European Union's European Monetary Union (EMU) program and not to adopt the euro as the official currency had as much to do with the identity-based emotion connected to abandoning the British pound as it did with rational economic calculations about the costs and benefits of EMU participation.

IN THEORY AND PRACTICE

The United Kingdom and Almond and Verba's Civic Culture Theory

In 1963, Gabriel Almond and Sidney Verba published one of the more influential and controversial books in comparative politics, *The Civic Culture*.[11] They argued that the cultural form of a society influences prospects for successful democracy and based their argument on assumptions common to other political culture theories: that culture can be observed; that it is, to a great extent, fixed in a particular setting; and that it influences political outcomes. The authors examined five countries: the United States, the UK, West Germany, Italy, and Mexico.

In their work, Almond and Verba identified three main political cultures—participatory, subject, and parochial—based largely on an examination of survey data from the countries. The three types of culture differ on the extent to which people follow politics and believe in being active citizens. Participants believe that their participation can influence political outcomes, subjects are interested in politics but feel disconnected from the political system, and parochials have little knowledge of the political system and thus no desire to participate. Almond and Verba stated that no country possesses a pure form of one of the three cultures. Rather, each involves a relatively unique mix, the composition of which has substantial political implications.

For Almond and Verba, predominantly subject cultures, like those in Italy and Mexico, have fewer prospects for democratic success than participatory cultures such as that in the United States. Ultimately, however, they argued that the British mix of participatory and subject cultures provides the greatest degree of democratic stability. At the time that they were writing, British history seemed to bear out their characterization of the UK's culture and its political consequences. Shortly after the book was published, however, the UK was nearly torn apart by the troubles in Northern Ireland, violent crime increased, and the long-standing deference to authority seemed less solid than before.

This shift points to the potential problem of using a snapshot in time (in this case, surveys from 1959–60) to capture a country's culture and make predictions. The Almond and Verba study was also criticized for the design of the survey questions, and some critics contended surveys of individuals cannot capture culture. Still other detractors deemed the theory to be ethnocentric and more prescriptive than objective and empirical.

Nonetheless, Almond and Verba's **civic culture theory** is an important example of a cultural theory that explains a political outcome (democratic stability) on the basis of a country's type of culture. Their characterization of the balance between deference and participation remains a useful summary of British political culture. That the British political system survived numerous challenges supports the vision of a stable British political system flowing from a well-balanced political culture.

Sources of Political Culture: Socialization, Experiences, and Events

Throughout British history, government socialization efforts have been less effective than those of other major social institutions. Like other monarchies in Europe, the English Crown attempted to foster traditional authority based on the concept of a divine right to rule. Its efforts were only partially successful. English elites challenged the principle of an absolute monarchy based on divine power earlier than elites elsewhere in Europe (e.g., by forcing the monarch to accept the Magna Carta in 1215). As a result, the number of people who composed the political elite was larger in England than elsewhere.

Today, the socialization process in the UK is carried out by institutions such as the family, the media, and the educational system. The structure of the educational system especially contributes to the degree of elitism in British political culture. Which secondary school an individual attends affects the person's social standing and prospects for economic well-being more than in a country like the United States. The elite private schools (called "public schools" in the UK) lead to entry into top universities and the best jobs after college graduation.[12] As mentioned in the discussion of freedom versus security, the subway bombings in the UK in July 2005 were events dramatic enough to reshape political culture, even though they failed to produce the devastation of the 9/11 attacks in the United States. Traditions about limits on government involvement in personal liberties and community affairs were challenged by calls for tightening restrictions on groups and individuals suspected to be engaged in or supportive of terrorism. The British case demonstrates that, in the immediate aftermath, short-lived single events such as terrorist attacks can affect political culture noticeably. It also provides evidence, however, that in the absence of repetition of such events, the previous core values may reemerge over time. In the end, British political culture changed, but not as dramatically as it appeared to directly following the event.

Ideology

The theme of moderation carries over to British ideology. Many of the best-known political and economic philosophers of the last several centuries have been British. The country was the home to John Locke, Adam Smith, David Hume, and John Stuart Mill and, some argue, was the birthplace of modern nationalism.[13] Nevertheless, the British tradition of evolutionary political change and the post–World War II settlement in the arena of economics created little space for sharp ideological divides. Extremist political parties have had little success, and zealous leaders of the mainstream parties have been unable to implement their visions for remaking society.

In the 1980s, Margaret Thatcher had some success in openly injecting conservative ideology and libertarian rhetoric into British political dialogue. Ultimately, she had to compromise on a number of social and economic policies, and many of her efforts did not last beyond her term in office. Tony Blair's designation of a New Labour Party, moving away from social democracy toward more a moderate ideological position, made him, for most of his term in office, one of the more popular and powerful prime ministers of the last century. While Blair's successor, Gordon Brown, put the Labour Party more squarely on the political left, he maintained many of Blair's more moderate approaches. David Cameron seized on Labour's move to the left. Though far from the only reason for the Conservatives' success in the 2010 elections, Cameron staked claim to the political middle ground. Borrowing a term from U.S. President George H. W. Bush, Cameron announced himself to be a supporter of "compassionate conservatism," stating that he would stand "for compassion and aspiration in equal measure."[14]

Germany

Compared to its British counterpart, German political culture was less supportive of democracy—valuing traditional social relations along with order and stability—until it was dramatically remade after World War II. One of the lasting legacies of the war was the division between

---

Civic Culture Theory A theory that each society has a distinctive mix of participatory, deferential, and subject political cultures, and that the mix influences political outcomes such as the likelihood of successful democracy.

the east and west of the country. Though the two Germanys have been reunified for more than two decades, the cultural divide remains. At the same time, some shared features are apparent. While emphasizing collectivism, for example, German political culture accepts a strong role for social organizations and the family at the expense of heavy-handed government policies. Ideological debates in Germany are muted by the acceptance of the social market economy by leaders on both sides of the political spectrum.

Political Culture

The Second Reich, which created a single German nation-state in 1871, glorified traditional social relations and authority. These values reflected the country's feudal structure and the dominance of the Prussian aristocracy in the military, bureaucracy, judiciary, and educational system. Socialists, who promoted a classless society along Marxist lines, challenged this hierarchical social structure, but they were disenfranchised by the regime. The value of hierarchical deference reached its apex in the Nazi regime with the leadership principle, or *Führerprinzip*, which required the absolute obedience and devotion of the population to Adolf Hitler. Deferential and authoritarian values eroded during the democratic regime in the Federal Republic (West Germany) after World War II, while the East German Communist regime promoted the values of a classless society.

German culture largely values collectivism over individualism. The liberal tradition associated with individual rights in the economy and society has been historically weak: a revolution advocating political liberalism was crushed in 1848, and today's Free Democratic Party representing liberalism remains small, mustering less than 10 percent of the vote. As discussed in detail in Chapter 8, German society is highly organized along corporatist lines, with peak associations representing major sectors of the economy, society, and the professions.

Dating from the medieval guild tradition, collectivist organizations and values were also legitimated by the Social Catholic doctrine of the nineteenth century. Social Catholicism promotes the idea of **subsidiarity**, which holds that major responsibilities for social provision should remain at the lowest level of social organization possible: first the family, then the group, and finally the state. This has had an impact on German approaches to social welfare. The state plays a limited role in the welfare state in Germany, substantially delegating administration of social welfare programs to churches, labor unions, and employers' associations.

More oppressive versions of group identity have existed in German history. During the Nazi regime, individuals were expected to subsume their will into the greater good of the German nation. In Communist East Germany, the regime discouraged individual effort and

thinking and instead promoted its vision of society based on Marxism-Leninism.

Security, both national and economic, has taken precedence over liberty for much of Germany's history. The lack of natural borders, frequent wars with its neighbors, and late political unification caused many Germans in the nineteenth and early twentieth centuries to value the security of the nation ahead of individual liberty. Liberty was all but crushed under subsequent Nazi and East German Communist totalitarianism, but the Federal Republic did enshrine individual rights in the constitution. Partly because of two periods of hyperinflation and the Great Depression in the twentieth century, Germans also value economic security and stability. They continue to support a generous welfare state safety net, a hallmark of the Federal Republic.

System legitimacy under the Weimar democratic system (1919–33) rested on its performance. The humiliation of the Versailles Treaty following Germany's defeat in World War I, plus the economic woes of the Great Depression, turned many Germans against the fragile democracy. In the initial years of the Federal Republic, the population also judged the regime on its performance. Fortunately, the "economic miracle" of the 1950s and 1960s delivered spectacular prosperity, which helped legitimize democratic rule. The passing of the Nazi generation also helped cement democratic values. Today, the democratic institutions of the Federal Republic enjoy broad public support that has endured despite difficult economic performance and high unemployment in the last two decades.[15] By contrast, the legitimacy of Communist East Germany's regime faltered as a result of the economic downturn, leading to the street demonstrations that brought down the regime in 1989.[16]

Equating the political community to the nation came later in Germany than in other parts of Europe. It was forged in 1871 by elites among a scattering of principalities. The Nazi regime defined the political community, the *Volk*, as comprising ethnic Germans. The country's partition into West and East Germany after 1949 bifurcated this national identity, although the official line in West Germany was that the country remained a single nation-state.

The reunification of Germany in 1990 fulfilled the vision of a single German nation-state. However, in reaction to the Nazi past, many Germans are suspicious of nationalism. Instead, elite and popular opinion tends to subscribe to a European Germany, firmly embedded in the institutions of the European Union. Regional identities and attachment to territorial units of the German federal system have also remained strong, particularly in the case of Bavaria.

Subsidiarity An idea from Social Catholicism that individuals have a right to make decisions for themselves and that, as much as possible, families and small social organizations should provide economic protection and distribute social goods to individuals.

Sources of Political Culture: Socialization, Experiences, and Events

Along with the family, the educational system and the media have been the most important agents of political socialization in Germany. The educational system reinforces the hierarchical class structure from early on, with students deciding at age ten or eleven whether to pursue the university track or the vocational track. Most working-class children pursue vocational education rather than attend a university. The totalitarian regimes of the Nazis and the GDR (post–World War II East Germany) relied on a mass-based party and its associated organizations, or front groups, throughout society to reshape political culture. They also effectively used the media. Following World War II, the occupying powers in West Germany imposed tight controls on the media as well, though in this case the media and the educational system were used to push pro-democratic messages in an effort to weaken the existing authoritarian political culture.

While Germany's political culture—particularly its strong collectivist strand and hierarchical social relations—has its origins in the country's feudal past, major events in the twentieth century also imprinted the cultural land-

scape. Germany's defeat in two world wars, the hardships of the Great Depression, the horrors of the Nazi period, the Communist regime in East Germany, and the reunification of the country in 1990 have shaped German political culture. The traumatic events of the Nazi dictatorship and World War II left particularly deep marks. In addition to their skepticism of nationalist appeals, most Germans now champion individual civil liberties and the rule of law and support a limited foreign policy aimed at peacekeeping missions instead of expansionist military excursions.

Ideology

Perhaps as a response to Germany's negative experiences with ideologically driven governments in the twentieth century, the country's largest political parties differ less on ideology than in the past. Germany's social market economy (SME), introduced in the previous chapter, reconciles conservatives and progressives to a particular type of state intervention in the economy and society.[17] The SME predates World War II and was successfully resurrected in postwar West Germany. However, it has been slower to take root in the former East Germany, whose people lived for more than four decades under the Marxist ideology of central state ownership and planning.

Holding that the market is the best way to allocate resources and generate wealth but not to distribute such wealth, the state sets out general guidelines of market activity. The major groups in the economy and society—such as employers' associations, labor unions, and banks—regulate their activities in line with these parameters. The SME also requires the state to protect and compensate losers in the market with generous welfare state programs. Although the state mandates these programs, they are administered by major social groups such as churches and trade unions.

India

Perhaps partly due to the British colonial legacy, India's political culture is more individualistic than those of many other Asia countries. Indian culture also views personal connections as more important than official rules and values social status. The diversity of the country's culture makes an overarching socialization process difficult. Instead, the family and localized institutions guide political cultural maintenance. Events surrounding independence, specifically violence during the partition process that separated Pakistan from India, have created lasting memories reinforced by each new wave of communal violence. While the market-based economic reforms of the 1990s represented a significant deviation from the country's previous ideological commitments, the major parties in India have come to accept the idea of market-led economic growth.

Political Culture

Recognizing the complexity of Indian values and systems of meaning is a starting point for discussing their political

Germans protest at the Berlin Wall shortly before the collapse of the Communist system in East Germany. © Caro/Alamy

role. Mohandas Gandhi (called Mahatma, an honorific title denoting wisdom and selflessness), for example, emphasized the practice of nonviolence, but his assassination, and those of Prime Ministers Indira Gandhi and Rajiv Gandhi, provided a dissonant view of the values underlying Indian political behavior. Popular deference to the wealthy, such as the Ambani family, which controls Reliance Industries, India's largest private sector enterprise, indicates that capitalism is culturally accepted, but popular deference to leaders of the Communist Party of India (Marxist), such as Jyoti Basu, suggests that it is not.

Nevertheless, India's cultural heterogeneity does not mean that the country lacks widely disbursed common attributes. Indian analyst Pavan Varma suggests that such components include a high level of tolerance for inconvenience and hardship, a low level of social trust, a desire to achieve ends regardless of the means, "materialistic pragmatism," "natural amorality," and an "excessive love for the perks of power."[18] Focusing on beliefs about authority and social hierarchy, he continues, "As the legatees of a centuries-old system of hierarchy, Indians have a special weakness for status; power is coveted for the status it guarantees; the state is the highest repository of both status and power; and politics is the highest-yielding path to the resources of the state."[19]

Indian sociologist Dipankar Gupta suggests that Hindu fundamentalism is unlikely to arise because Hinduism is more individual than congregation-based: "As fundamentalism does not allow for any differences among the faithful, it will find it very difficult to take root in Hindu India."[20] Commenting on trust and legitimacy, Gupta contends that, within Hinduism, "trust is more often placed on individuals and rarely ever on institutions."[21] In addition, he claims that "While democracy and elections give the impression of representation" in India, "governance at all levels is oiled by connections."[22] Echoing these claims, Geert Hofstede's analysis of Indian political culture ranks it well above the global norm on the power distance dimension, indicating an acceptance of high levels of social inequality. He also points to the Indian people's individualism and tolerance of "unstructured ideas and situations."[23]

Encompassing the individualism inherent in Indian political culture is the notion of a political community based on the concept of unity in diversity. This concept seems to have been contradicted by certain political leaders who have emphasized divisions within the population to mobilize their political supporters. Nonetheless, it became a basic part of India's political culture and was reinforced by the partition in 1947.

In summary, in the midst of the contradictory attributes and great overall complexity, Indian political culture has identifiable features: accepting an underlying hierarchical system that values power and status, appreciating the utility of personal connections more than institutional rules,

valuing the achievement of ends over adherence to rules guiding means, tolerating inconvenience, and accepting the notion of unity in diversity. These traits have combined to help maintain democracy, despite economic hardship, identity divisions, and social and political corruption.

Sources of Political Culture: Socialization, Experiences, and Events

India's political culture rest upon long-standing aspects of society and experiences at the time of and subsequent to independence. The components include the caste system, discussed in detail in Chapter 4, which has long characterized social relations; the religious division between Hinduism and Islam; the various ethnic groups in the country; and substantial regional variation. Each has contributed to the complexity of Indian political culture. Within this complexity, however, patterns of socialization are identifiable. The family remains a powerful vehicle for transmitting values, while the national educational system continues to impress the unity in diversity theme on schoolchildren and college students alike.

Events have also shaped aspects of India's political culture and political behavior in important ways. The most dramatic event was the country's birth in 1947 and the horror of the partition, which helped reinforce a certain level of cultural unity. Wars with Pakistan and China, along with the assassinations of Mohandas Gandhi, Indira Gandhi, and Rajiv Gandhi were shared experiences that had opposing impacts on facets of the political culture. On the one hand, they fostered a sense of unity among most Indians. On the other hand, the anti-Muslim and anti-Sikh riots that accompanied some of these events worked in the opposite direction. The destruction of the Babri Mosque at Ayodhya in 1992 by a segment of the Hindu population challenged the unity in diversity aspect of India's political culture but seemed in accord with other components of India's composite political culture, such as those involving the desire for power and belief in the importance of ends over means.

Ideology

The ideologies that have arisen in the Indian polity have often seemed incongruent with aspects of India's fragmented political culture. This may be part of the reason for ideology's limited impact in India. The period following independence was marked by socialist ideas. Although the economy included some elements of capitalism, the state was to be the leader in economic development. According to Pavan Varma, "The socialist era, although not entirely unproductive, was antithetical to the genius of the Indian people."[24]

Today, disputes between the major political parties do not center on grand economic ideologies. In 1991, the Congress Party formally shifted from pursuing state-led development to supporting market-based economic policy, although it did retain its commitment to secularism. In 1998, the Bharatiya Janata Party (BJP), with a similar view on the role of the state in the economy but with a communal orientation embodied in an ideology called *Hindutva*, defeated the Congress Party and dominated the Lok Sabha, the lower house of the Indian parliament, until 2004. The Congress Party's return to power after 2004 altered the ideological approach to national identity, but little changed in the area of economics.

Mexico

Mexico's political culture displays a tension between respect for institutions of authority and admiration for revolutionary figures. The Mexican Revolution (1910–1920) helped establish a connection between the government and the masses, at least until the end of the twentieth century. By 2000, the year in which the Institutional Revolutionary Party (PRI) ended its domination of the presidency, it was clear that many aspects of traditional Mexican political culture were breaking down. Corruption, on the other hand, has only increased, and ongoing episodes of drug-related violence have fueled a new suspicion of the government's ability to maintain social order. Mexico's long period without democracy in the twentieth century centered more on pragmatic considerations than on ideological commitment. The establishment of democracy has allowed ideological divisions to become more apparent.

Political Culture

The Mexican political culture rests on an interesting tension regarding beliefs about authority and social relations. In many ways, it is a highly authoritarian culture, acquiescent to elite rule and emphasizing social hierarchy that includes patriarchy. These values were solidified during colonial rule by Spanish culture, strong state control, and the Catholic Church's domination of social institutions. (The Catholic Church owned a sizable portion of the land in Mexico by the end of the colonial period.) At the same time, Mexico has had a number of uprisings—against the Spanish, during the Mexican Revolution, and more recently in the region of Chiapas. These uprisings were as much social as political, with many of the great revolutionary leaders championing landownership for the impoverished peasantry.

The combination of deference to social authority and admiration of revolutionary spirit would appear, at first glance, to be incongruent. Yet, it helps explain the dominance of the PRI for much of the twentieth century. As the heirs to the revolutionary victors and as a party officially representing those in society who had rebelled, PRI leaders could play the "revolution card" when it suited their purposes. Nevertheless, the system that the PRI created was authoritarian and hierarchical, which complemented deeply established social values.

Looking at the component of collective versus individual orientation, Mexican political culture is much less individualistic than that of its neighbor to the north. The family is a particularly important social institution, and extended family relations are typically closer than in the United States. In Geert Hofstede's examination of various components of political culture in a number of countries, Mexico's individualism score of 30 is stark in comparison to the U.S. score of more than 90.[25]

The PRI's name, combining the concepts of revolution and institution, reflects the dichotomy in Mexican culture between an embrace of freedom and a focus on security. Until recently, Mexicans have leaned much more toward order and security than toward freedom and liberty. In Hofstede's study, Mexico's uncertainty avoidance index score of 82 was its highest score for all components (the U.S. score was under 50), representing the desire for order and stability.[26] The events of the last several decades—in which democracy, even if it means some instability, has been increasingly valued—appear to have signaled a shift in this balance. Survey results in the late 1990s and early 2000s indicated some attachment to values associated with democracy. Some of this new appreciation of democracy, however, has been shaken by the noticeable increase of drug violence since 2009.

While perhaps hard for Americans to believe, the PRI-dominant regime had, for many decades, a great deal of system legitimacy. Individual party leaders may not have been popular, but the connection to the 1910 revolution and years of impressive economic growth fed a belief that the PRI was the only game in town. This began to change as time wore on, and a cultural shift led an increasing number of people to consider the potential for a more democratic system.

In addition to the drug-related violence, corruption remains the Achilles's heel of the new democracy's legitimacy. Vicente Fox's victory in the 2000 presidential election was, in part, a condemnation of PRI corruption over the previous decades. Yet, surveys in 2002 indicated that while a majority of Mexicans felt that Fox's election would lessen corruption in the office of the president, less than one-third thought corruption had declined in the previous year, a small percentage thought Fox would be able to reduce overall corruption a great deal, and most felt that other social institutions like the Catholic Church had a better chance of attacking corruption than did the government.[27] If the Mexican people perceive that National Action Party (PAN) leaders like Fox and his successor, Felipe Calderón, have been unable to address corruption effectively, it is not only a threat to the PAN's future electoral prospects, but it could also undercut Mexicans' belief in democracy.

Mexico has faced challenges in the political community component of its culture but has been relatively successful in addressing them. Building attachment to Mexican national identity has been a long endeavor. At the time of independence in the early 1820s, the Mexican population was sharply divided along ethnic and class lines. The colonial period—during which Spanish men greatly outnumbered Spanish women—resulted in a large *mestizo* (part native, part European) portion of the population. At the same time, a significant number of "unmixed" indigenous and European inhabitants remained, as well as a sizable black population descended from slaves in some parts of the country.

The Mexican Revolution did little to end these divisions, even reinforcing them in the short run. Thus, along with economic development, a major task of the government that emerged from the revolution, led by the political coalition that would eventually become the PRI, was to develop a sense of attachment to an overarching political community. Through a combination of effort and favorable conditions—the presence of a single, dominant religion and the near universal use of the Spanish language—the PRI by and large succeeded in building an attachment to Mexican identity and the Mexican state.

Sources of Political Culture: Socialization, Experiences, and Events

As is typical of authoritarian political systems, the PRI tried to socialize the people not only to be loyal to the political system but also to accept their position as subjects rather than to believe in the value of participation. Government control of the history presented in Mexican schools helped cultivate traditional political and social values. At least until the Second Vatican Council, the Catholic Church in Mexico complemented these efforts. The Church and the country's educational system remain powerful socializing institutions today, though one should not discount the importance of socialization within the family. Family bonds are generally stronger in Mexico than in the United States.

A feeling of solidarity between Mexicans and their political system facilitated the long period of one-party rule in the twentieth century. The 1910 revolution and the ideals articulated around that time helped establish this connection. The Mexican Revolution remains a dominant event in the shaping of Mexican culture and thus provides an example of the lingering effect that a single event can have on a political culture.

In the long run, however, the elections in 1997, in which the PRI lost its majority in the national legislature, and the 2000 presidential election, when it lost the presidency, have the potential to be at least as defining. The elections signaled a shift in mass values and presented a new view of Mexican political culture, one based upon growing frustration with corruption and inequality. By demonstrating to the Mexican people that they could peacefully change their political system, the elections also affirmed and encouraged such values. Survey data from 1997 and 2000 indicate a substantial shift in values like tolerance in a more pro-democratic direction.[28]

Ideology

The development of a democratic system has also opened the door to an increasingly ideological political scene, a marked change from the previous era. As the overseer of an authoritarian rather than a totalitarian political system, the PRI was less ideological than the ruling parties in the Communist systems of Eastern Europe and the Soviet Union. Authoritarian leaders are generally more pragmatic than totalitarian ones (see Chapter 5); their main goal is to preserve authoritarian rule rather than to remake society. The PRI used the rhetoric of revolution when it was beneficial, but it reached out to all groups in society and sought to make them dependent on the party while discouraging them from being politically active. This is not the stuff of highly ideological systems. This pragmatic approach worked for a long time. Business leaders, for example, were reluctant to pressure the government for change because the PRI had fairly effectively bought them off.

With democratization and the emergence of rival political parties with genuine opportunities to win elections, ideological disputes resurfaced. Mexico demonstrates how electoral competition in a democracy can make ideological divisions within the population more visible. The extent to which Mexico should base economic development on free markets and free trade is a point of contention. This ideological divide between the major parties is certainly larger than in the United States though less pronounced than in other Latin American countries, including Brazil.

Brazil

Even more than in Mexico, the population of Brazil remains unconvinced about the political system's legitimacy and has a relatively weak commitment to an overarching political community. As in India, regional differences in Brazil contribute to significant heterogeneity within its political culture. In addition, Brazil never experienced the kind of foundational event that might have brought about shared values across social groups. Instead, events have affected different groups in different ways, contributing to the development of Brazil's diverse political culture. In Brazil, the theme of diversity carries over to discussions of ideology, with notable ideological differences between parties of the Left and the Right.

Political Culture

Brazilian political culture is heterogeneous, the result of its multiethnic and multicultural population as well as of unresolved economic and social inequalities that render some ethnic groups more marginalized and others more privileged. The life of a black agricultural worker in

Brazil's impoverished northwest bears little resemblance to the life of a white banker in São Paulo whose children attend private schools, shop at upscale malls, and vacation abroad in the summer. That said, one can broadly identify general political and cultural traits.

Brazilian political culture remains highly, though decreasingly, authoritarian. Despite its deep inequalities, Brazil never produced a major social revolution to counteract the hierarchical and authoritarian culture imported from Portugal. Independence was won without a shot being fired or a peasant being mobilized. Brazil is the only Latin American state to have established a successful monarchy, one that died in a palace coup rather than via mass protests.

Rebellions in Brazil mostly took the form of evasions and escapes rather than direct confrontations with power, perhaps because its vast and largely empty territory provided an easier route to political autonomy than did bloody fighting. An example of the effectiveness of the strategy of evading rather than fighting is the *quilombo* communities founded by escaped African slaves and other socially marginalized people during the 1600s. One of the largest communities, Palmares, contained at its height some thirty thousand individuals and lasted nearly a hundred years. Many such communities exist to this day, with residents speaking a mixture of African languages and Portuguese.

Another form of evasion of power is the *jeito* (pronounced zhī-to), a nearly untranslatable Brazilian word suggesting a way of getting around formal rules.[29] Brazilians are proud of their ingenuity in circumventing their state's bureaucratic rules, but the jeito can apply to nearly any social or economic interaction. Rules are obeyed in form but not in substance. One does not attempt to overturn an unjust law; one simply sidesteps it. Despite its subversive potential, the jeito provides little real equality. While cleverness is appreciated, connections and money matter more. Some people are better placed to exercise the jeito than others, and they are free to extract "gifts" from those they help. When Brazilian president Lula da Silva's party was caught taking kickbacks to finance political campaigns, his overall reaction was to shrug and argue that everyone does it.

The jeito is also more individualistic than collective. Benefits are won not for groups, but for individuals with the clout to get around the system. Accordingly, Brazilian political culture is somewhat more individualistic than the norm in Latin America, with a score of 38 on Hofstede's index as compared with the average Latin American score of 21.[30] Nevertheless, as in Mexico, the family remains the most important social unit and tempers tendencies toward individualism.

Brazilians strongly prefer security over freedom, a preference incorporated into the country's flag: across the blue globe in the flag's center is a white band with the words "Order and Progress." This design was adopted for the

Brazilian republic in 1889 and thus precedes the current violence and drug trafficking that might motivate modern Brazilians to prioritize security. Brazil's highest score on Hofstede's cultural index is 76 for uncertainty avoidance.[31]

However, most Brazilians do not believe that their political system can deliver security. The legitimacy of Brazilian democracy is unusually low. Survey results repeatedly show less than a majority of the population viewing democracy as preferable to any other form of government. Brazilians tend to like the president more than the Congress, and the Congress more than the political parties, which win approval from fewer than one-third of Brazilians. More generally, Brazilians have the lowest level of interpersonal trust of any of the Latin American countries. In one major survey, only 6 percent of Brazilians thought that you "can trust most people," well below the Latin American average of 17 percent.[32]

Along with these low levels of trust, Brazilians also feel a low level of attachment to political community. To the extent that political communities exist, they are based on regional identities. Brazil's historical tradition of federalism grants a lot of power to regional leaders. Political careers are made first at the regional level, often through governorships, and then projected onto the national stage. Powerful political dynasties use their control of regions to manipulate the selection of national political candidates, especially for the legislature.

Sources of Political Culture: Socialization, Experiences, and Events

Twentieth-century Brazilian politics contained an assortment of fragile democracies, military coups, and unstable strongmen. Political party systems sometimes appeared and disappeared within a single generation. Ironically, given the Brazilian republic's original goal of order and progress, it achieved relatively little of either. Within this political turmoil, socialization fell to traditional social forces such as the family and religious institutions.

The most prominent repeated experience shaping contemporary Brazilian political culture, at least among older Brazilians, was the encounter with military dictatorship from 1964 to 1985. Under the dictatorship, Brazil had a prolonged period of political stability accompanied by considerable economic growth. The price was repression and human rights abuses by the military junta, and the result was a revalorization of democracy, particularly by the political Left, which had previously expressed skepticism that democracy could offer any hope of significant social change. In the process of bringing about a democratic transition, Brazilian society became mobilized to a degree never before experienced. New independent

---

Jeito A key component of Brazilian political culture emphasizing and valuing the ability to get around social and political rules.

unions, social movements, and political parties formed to challenge the regime, culminating in a national campaign of *Diretas Ja*—direct elections now—that forced the military to relinquish power and schedule a new constitutional assembly.

Nearly one-third of the Brazilian population—over 62 million people—is under the age of eighteen.[33] These young people do not remember the military dictatorship. Their formative experiences include repeated economic crises and corruption scandals touching every presidency in post-transition Brazil. One president was impeached and forced from office.

Ideology

The Brazilian political spectrum is fairly wide, certainly as compared with countries such as the United States, where voters and parties are clustered in the center, but also as compared with other Latin American countries. On a scale of 0 to 10, where 0 is "very Left" and 10 is "very Right," Brazilian citizens average a score of 5.1 according to late 2000s survey data.[34] This apparently moderate ranking conceals wide disparities. More than one-quarter (28 percent) of Brazilians consider themselves Leftist, while almost one-third (31 percent) consider themselves Rightist. Thus, around 60 percent of Brazilians place themselves outside the political center. In continental Latin America, only El Salvador, Nicaragua, and Venezuela have higher percentages of noncentrists. The first two have endured civil wars in the last twenty years, and the third is locked in an ongoing conflict that has produced two attempted coups.

This ideological diversity is reflected in the party system: Brazil has nearly four times as many political parties as Mexico, ranging from Communist parties on the left to conservative and religious parties on the right. As in the United States, evangelical politicians wield considerable influence. However, in contrast to the United States, Brazilian evangelical politicians often hold progressive economic positions along with socially conservative ones. A prominent example is Rosinha Garotinho, ex-governor of the state of Rio de Janeiro, who opposed gay unions but belonged to the Brazilian Socialist Party. Garotinho is a helpful reminder that cultural and ideological patterns in other countries may look quite different from those in the United States.

Nigeria

Like other states with developing economies and fragile democratic systems, traditional values and systems of meaning are conspicuous in Nigeria. At the same time, Nigeria, like other TIC cases such as India and Brazil, has a large degree of political cultural heterogeneity, driven to a great extent by the ethnic, religious, and regional diversity of its people. Of Nigeria's many experiences with the potential to affect its political culture, some have helped to foster unified values, while others have highlighted deep divisions between different social groups. In Nigeria, ideological divides are more connected to cultural and identity divisions, such as the dispute over the implementation of Islamic law (Sharia) in Muslim-majority regions of the country.

Political Culture

An examination of political culture in Nigeria is complicated by its diverse population and by the importance of religion in society. The country's cultural fissures along religious and ethnic lines lead to a heterogeneous political culture. One Nigerian scholar states clearly the effect: unlike much of the Western world, "Nigeria does not have a 'national culture.'"[35]

On average, however, Nigerians respect authority and accept vertical social relations. The British colonial rulers encouraged the continuation of the precolonial tendency to accept authority and unequal social relations. British rulers needed a stable social hierarchy with which to work, and in places where one did not exist they created it. In rural areas, social position remains very important. A sense of horizontal social relations is lacking, as is acceptance of the idea that an individual can be socially mobile and move beyond the standing inherited at birth.

Given the deep social divisions in Nigeria, it is not surprising that these views differ to an extent among different ethnic groups. The Hausa-Fulani (Muslims concentrated across Nigeria's north) have traditionally valued social hierarchy more than the Ibo (who live mostly in the southeast) and the Yoruba (who live in the southwest). The Yoruba, whose region of Nigeria is highly urbanized and industrial, are also somewhat more inclined to believe in the possibility of social advancement than the Hausa-Fulani.

On the whole, precolonial Nigerian political culture emphasized collectivism over individualism. The Ibo have traditionally been more individualistic than the other peoples within the borders of Nigeria. The British never set out to develop a spirit of individualism, and thus the overall collectivism and the division between Ibos and others changed little during the colonial period. In the postcolonial period, collectivist values have been encouraged by religious and ethnic elites, the official representatives of the religious or ethnic collectives, who sought loyalty from the masses. Because the ethnic divisions in the country have remained sharp since independence, the willingness of Nigerians to make individual sacrifices for the group depends greatly on whether the sacrifices benefit "our" group or "their" group.[36]

In the arena of freedom versus security, Nigeria's experiences with democracy have given the population little reason to believe that freedom brings prosperity or that freedom can coexist with stability. The unrest that has accompanied independence has severely impeded Nigeria's ability to develop both economically and politically. Unstable politics and economic hardship among the vast majority of the population have reinforced traditional values of order and security.

This is not to say freedom has no value to Nigerians. Geert Hofstede's political culture studies do not include Nigeria. However, Ronald Inglehart's World Values Survey project includes a survival versus self-expression dimension, which is similar to Hofstede's uncertainty avoidance index. According to Inglehart's analysis, Nigerians fall in the middle of this index. They are less focused on security and order than Russians and slightly less than the Chinese, but they are more concerned with stability and order than Mexicans and much more so than the British.[37]

It is hard for political system legitimacy to exist in settings where the legitimacy of the state itself is weak. In the early Nigerian postindependence period, the state's right to exist was in dispute. Only after a violent civil war and the redesign of the Nigerian federal system did the desire to break apart the country begin to erode. Even as the legitimacy of the state increased, the legitimacy of the postcolonial political system continued to face hurdles. Two significant attempts at postindependence democracy failed due to deep social divisions, poor institutional design, and corruption. Between the democratic periods, the military ruled through a highly authoritarian and highly corrupt system.

Despite the acute social cleavages, Nigerians do share certain beliefs regarding government accountability and a strong dislike of corruption. Accusations of corruption and mismanagement of resources, therefore, hurt both the military and democratic governments. Since the reinstitution of democracy in 1999, Nigeria has struggled to unify its population and purge the vestiges of corruption from within its government. But there is much to overcome. The latest attempt to establish a working democracy has been a struggle. While Nigerians were strongly supportive of democracy in 1999, backing has declined since, especially after the disputed 2007 elections. That year's electoral fraud deepened beliefs that Nigeria's government had fallen victim to the corruption it had pledged to tackle.

Long before the arrival of European colonizers, which ultimately led to the creation of the present boundaries of the country, the main groups of Nigeria were culturally distinct, with different economic, religious, and political traditions. Thus, no overarching attachment to a political community existed beyond the local affiliations of the population in a region. British rule did little to change this. Even British attempts to leave Nigeria with a functioning democracy did as much to reinforce divisions as they did to overcome them, and loyalty to one's ethnic group dominated loyalty to the Nigerian nation.

Sources of Political Culture: Socialization, Experiences, and Events

Consistent with the idea that Nigerians respect authority and accept vertical social relations is a strong belief that children should obey their parents. As a result, socialization within the family is more likely to shape children's behavior than it is in many other countries. Once more, however, this varies from group to group. Ibo children tend to be encouraged to be more individualistic and independent than children of Hausa-Fulani families.

Socialization also takes place in Nigeria's government-controlled educational system and in the powerful social and political organizations that emerged during the anticolonial struggle. Often, these political organizations and government agencies socialize members and clients into the practice of bribery. Those who give and take bribes advance; those who do not are left out. Unlike other components of Nigerian political culture, however, corruption is not part of traditional Nigerian culture. Rather, it was learned over the last two centuries and became one of the few cultural features of the overarching Nigerian political culture.

Some shared events and experiences counter the tendency for Nigeria's ethnic diversity to produce cultural heterogeneity. These include the colonial period, the Nigerian civil war (1967–70), multiple periods of military rule, and Nigeria's attempts at democracy in the postcolonial period. Memories of colonial rule and the repressive military regimes that dominated much of Nigeria's postcolonial history have affected the population in all parts of the country.

Periods of military rule were fraught with dishonesty and uncertainty, and many Nigerians came to believe that the elite use the rich resources of the country, including its significant petroleum reserves, to increase their personal fortunes, while the country as a whole grapples with rampant social and civil problems. Encounters with military rule have weakened the legitimacy of nondemocratic political systems, but they also have fed the desire for stability and security, which can affect the legitimacy of Nigeria's democratic system as well.

Ongoing events that continue to affect Nigerian political culture include the latest chapter of democracy (since 1999), including the death in office of the Nigerian president in 2010 and repeated instances of Christian-Muslim violence. The current democratic regime has given Nigerians hope, but it has also reinforced the idea that corruption will be hard to eradicate. Clashes between Christians and Muslims continue to pose a challenge to forging an attachment to an overarching Nigerian identity.

Ideology

Ideology has never been as central in Nigeria as in other countries. Politics tends to be personalized, with leaders' characteristics considered more important than their policy positions. Under military rule, the government was happy if the general population showed no interest in politics. This pattern is not unique to Nigeria. As discussed in more detail in Chapter 5, most authoritarian regimes place much less emphasis on ideology and citizen involvement than do totalitarian and democratic systems.

This idea of limited interest in ideology is a generalization. Within the Nigerian federal system, some regional governments are more aggressive in pushing a social blueprint. This is most true in the boundary areas between the largely non-Muslim south and the largely Muslim north. The internal division between those who wish to codify the rules and regulations of Nigeria into a version of Western law and those who wish to base their decisions upon Islamic law has divided the country along philosophical as well as religious lines and has contributed to the overall sense of distrust and uncertainty that plagues the country.

Russia

Throughout Russian history, collectivism, emphasis on security and order, and deference to strong authority figures benefited successive nondemocratic regimes. At the same time, individuals tended to desire the collective to take care of them and were suspicious of people who got ahead. The Soviet experience exposed them to culture-altering events, such as the devastation of and ultimate victory in World War II, and the early-post-Soviet period was even more traumatic. Ideologically, both the Marxist vision of the Soviet period and the ideological free-for-all of the 1990s have given way to Vladimir Putin's more pragmatic determination to do whatever is necessary

to create an internationally respected and economically prosperous Russia.

Political Culture

For centuries before Vladimir Lenin seized power in the name of a workers' revolution in 1917, Russians had demonstrated deference to authority, collectivist tendencies, and support for security and order at the expense of freedom. These beliefs were complemented by a disconnect from politics, particularly among the country's rural population. Tsarist, Soviet, and post-Soviet Russian leaders have taken advantage of these traits. Other aspects of Russian political culture, such as the ambivalent attachment to an overarching national identity and the tendency to connect system legitimacy to economic and military performance, have created challenges for authorities.

The Russian people have a long tradition of emphasizing the collective over the individual. Russians are often suspicious of people who get ahead, perceiving their success as the result of illegal, or at least unethical, efforts. In many cases, Russians would rather be personally less successful than see someone else be more successful than them. A Russian "God talks to a peasant" joke (of which there are many variants) captures this attitude well:

> One day, God calls out to a peasant working in the field. He says, "My son, I will give you anything you wish for, but your neighbor will get twice of whatever you get." The peasant thinks about it for a little while and then asks God to strike out one of his eyes, leaving his neighbor totally blind.

In the post-Soviet period, suspicion of successful individuals and the failure of economic reform to greatly improve ordinary Russians' lives fed negative views about change. The wealthy "new Russians," discussed in Chapter 2, were disdained. When former Russian President Putin attacked the economic and political power of the super-rich oligarchs in the early 2000s, the confrontations were largely applauded by Russians, even if some understood Putin's efforts to be largely about consolidating his political power.

Boris Yeltsin, left, reads a statement from atop a tank on August 19, 1991, urging the Russian people to resist a coup against Soviet leader Mikhail Gorbachev by hardliners.
© AP Photo/File

"Did You Know?"

The Russian word for friend, друг (pronounced "drūk"), has a deeper meaning than its English counterpart. It implies a companion who can be counted on to help even if doing so places him or her in danger. This difference in meaning captures the importance of a small, tight circle of family and friends in Russian life. Particularly in the past, the harsh Russian climate and even harsher authoritarian and totalitarian political systems meant that the loyalty of a friend could mean the difference between life and death.

At the same time, Russians have a commitment to their own individual well-being not always found in collectivistic cultures. During the Soviet period, residents of communal apartments, which had private rooms where families resided and shared areas such as bathrooms, would often take great care of their own areas while leaving the communal areas dirty and in disrepair.

Centuries of dictatorial rule by tsars and Soviets reinforced Russians' strong attachment to security and order at the expense of liberty and freedom. Major events added to the cultural aversion to disorder and insecurity. The territory of the present-day Russian Federation has been invaded numerous times over the centuries—by the Mongols, the Lithuanians and Poles, the French, the Germans, and the Germans again. Much of Putin's ongoing popularity, even after he moved from the position of president to that of prime minister, is based on the belief that he is a strong leader who turned the chaotic situation of the 1990s into order, security, and prosperity.

The combination of deference to authority figures and a desire for security and order has affected views about the legitimacy of the political system. Tsarist governments worked to develop the belief that the tsar was the link between God and ordinary people. Beginning with the tsars and continuing to the present, the population also linked its belief in the right of the system to rule to the system's performance. Defeats in wars, such as the Crimean War in the middle 1800s, the Russo-Japanese War of 1904–1905, and, most devastatingly, World War I, weakened the legitimacy of the system, and military success boosted it. Economic success under Stalin and Khrushchev, and more recently under Putin, also brought legitimacy, while economic hardship from Brezhnev through Gorbachev, and continuing under Yeltsin, challenged it.

Russians have been conflicted about the meaning of Russian national identity since well before the Soviet period. Some supported a vision of national identity based on Russian ethnic identity that excludes people who are not ethnically Russian, and others advocated a civic national identity inclusive of ethnic minorities. As a result, attachment to an overarching political community has not been as strong as the Russian government would like it to be.

The different views of Russian identity led then-President Boris Yeltsin to convene a special committee to propose ideas about what could unite the Russian population—in other words, to define Russian national identity. Rather than the unified vision that Yeltsin had hoped for, the report included a large number of different and conflicting characteristics. In a telling indication of disagreements about Russian national identity, the committee ultimately concluded that trying to find such unifying factors is the most important thing that Russians can do to be unified.

Sources of Political Culture: Socialization, Experiences, and Events

Of the nine TIC countries, events and government-led socialization have arguably had the greatest impact on political culture in Russia. The Soviets took advantage of and reinforced existing Russian political culture as much or more than they set out to remake it. But they did try to remake parts of it. Under the Soviets, most aspects of people's daily life—schools, workplaces, social organizations, media, and so forth—contributed to socialization. Only private institutions like the family were excepted. The Soviet leadership used its control of socializing institutions to try to develop support for the regime.

In the post-Soviet period, socialization has been more difficult to manipulate. This was especially true before the ascendancy of Vladimir Putin. During Putin's tenure as president, the state reasserted its authority over the flow of information. Media were consolidated and in some cases brought under state control. Schools, cultural events, and social organizations increasingly embraced Russian nationalism and the greatness of Putin, distributing brochures about Putin's life to schoolchildren and prominently displaying his image on posters and his name on major city streets.

Furthermore, from 1985 to 2005 alone, Russia experienced a number of events that helped mold Russian's political values:

- A new Communist political leader, quite different from the previous leaders.
- A period of significant political, economic, and social reform.
- A nearly complete collapse of the economy.
- A coup against the Communist leader by those opposed to reform.
- The collapse of the political system.
- The territorial disintegration of the country.
- The institution of a new political system with a noncommunist leader.
- A violent conflict between branches of the new government that led to the use of military force against government officials.
- A new constitution.
- Democratic elections.
- An internal conflict leading to military intervention against a region of the country.
- Increasing instances of terrorism.
- The resignation of the president.
- The consolidation of power in the hands of the new president.

It is not surprising that such experiences have reinforced certain elements of Russian political culture, including a desire for stability and order even at the expense of personal freedom.

Ideology

Ideology was important in both tsarist and Soviet times. The government used control over communications in both periods to try to transmit its blueprint for society to the general population. Under the tsars, the most unified ideology occurred during the reign of Nicholas I, who propagated a three-headed ideology of Orthodoxy, autocracy, and *narodnost* (national identity). These three components highlighted the basis of tsarist rule: the tsar as the head of the Orthodox Church (formalizing the concept of divine right to rule), the tsar as the unquestionable and absolute leader, and the czar as the father-figure and unifier of the Russian nation. Although the tsars also struggled with the question of who belonged to the Russian nation, their efforts tended to emphasize ethnic Russian characteristics, including Orthodox Christianity, at the expense of a large number of ethnic minorities.

Ideology was even more central during the Soviet period. Official Soviet newspapers as well as other publications, such as scholarly journals, were compelled to fit their presentations into the framework of Soviet ideology. Scholars who studied the Soviet Union identified a number of components of official Soviet ideology, including, among others, the monopoly of political power by the Communist Party, atheism, and the superiority of economic planning. Vladimir Shlapentokh, in *A Normal Totalitarian Society*, distills the elements of Soviet ideology to two: socialism and Russian nationalism.[38]

One of the Soviet period's many legacies to contemporary Russia is suspicion of official government ideology. The population endured years of socialization about the correctness of Marxist-Leninist ideology, then experienced the collapse of Soviet Communism and learned how bankrupt the official ideology was. Imagine realizing that much of what you had come to believe about your country, its economic system, and its political leaders had been a lie!

China

China's long history and Confucian traditions produced well-developed cultural traits that have been encouraged by and supportive of its various nondemocratic political systems. Socialization and defining events over the last several decades have continued to have an impact on Chinese political culture in important ways. While the country's extensive history and tradition dilute the impact of sudden shocks—even those as seemingly significant as the 1989 Tiananmen Square massacre—government-led socialization has been a cornerstone of Communist Party rule in China. At the same time, the Communist Party long ago abandoned a commitment to economic planning and state-controlled development, though it shares with leaders of Russia the use of nationalism as an alternative to the economic ideology of the past.

Political Culture

Chinese political culture continues to reflect the values of **Confucianism** as well as the often complementary values stressed by the Communist government. Confucius was an educator in China around 500 B.C., and Confucian traditions emphasize hierarchy and respect for authority in all major social institutions. These include the family, in which males and elders are to be given particular respect. Confucius emphasized a series of dominant-subordinate relationships: leader-subject, parent-child, male-female, and old-young. When the Communists seized power, they selectively emphasized a number of Confucian beliefs about authority while challenging others. Mao was particularly critical of the idea that women should be subordinate to men, although the Chinese Communists did not work actively to abolish that view.

While believing in the general goodness of individuals, Confucianism emphasizes the fate of the entire society over individual well-being. Individuals are expected to work hard, but the idea that they should look out for themselves is discouraged much more than it is in political cultures such as those of the UK and the United States. At the same time, education is valued; according to Confucian thought, people are able to improve their social standing by improving themselves through education. This tendency to value education led the Chinese to develop a merit-based governmental civil service much earlier than most other countries.

The Communist period reinforced the ideas of the collective over the individual, particularly during the rule of Mao Zedong. With the economic reforms that began under Deng Xiaoping in the late 1970s, however, the Communist government stressed a combination of the Confucian idea of hard work with a newly found toleration of individual gain. In Geert Hofstede's political culture analyses, China still has a very low individualism score of 15, compared to an average score of 23 of the other Asian countries Hofstede analyzed. However, the introduction of capitalist economic principles has begun to weaken China's emphasis on traditional collectivism somewhat.

Another legacy of Confucianism is the emphasis on order and security at the expense of individual freedom. Social harmony—through a respect for those in positions of authority and responsible actions by those with authority—is highly valued. While Confucius encouraged individuals to better themselves through education, the idea was for them to use their skills in a disciplined manner to improve social conditions. Some scholars discuss these values as crucial to the relative long-term stability

---

Confucianism A set of beliefs based on the writings of Confucius that emphasize respect for authority, hard work, and an obligation by those in power to rule responsibly and in the interests of society as a whole.

of Chinese politics (the early to mid-twentieth century being the most notable exception). The government expected individuals to be loyal to their political leaders and to the nation as a whole.

As China has developed economically in recent decades, the traditional emphasis on order at the expense of freedom has begun to break down. Chinese culture remains far from most Western cultures on the order-freedom continuum, but the Chinese have become more materialistic. They may have even begun to develop what political scientists Ronald Inglehart and Christian Welzel call "self-expression values"[39]—orientations championing freedom from control and the importance of human choice—a circumstance that must concern the country's Communist leadership.

Confucian traditions benefited Chinese political systems throughout history by helping to generate strong beliefs in system legitimacy. Yet, the leaders of the system were not free to act in any way they wished. Confucianism combines an emphasis on traditional authority with an element of performance-based system legitimacy. According to Confucius, the authority of government officials was to be respected, but the government had an obligation to use its authority honorably. Natural disasters in China came to be viewed as heaven's displeasure with corruption or other failures in government performance.

Within the political community component of Chinese political culture, the Chinese people are, for the most part, patriotic and proud of their national identity. As in Russia, however, China's size and the considerable ethnic minority populations in the periphery of the country create complexities and tensions. As a result, neither the development of unified loyalty to the Chinese state nor attachment to an overarching Chinese national identity has been easy to inculcate, and the government remains suspicious of identity-based organizations.

The Chinese government has encouraged nationalism; during the last two decades, it has pushed the ideals of nationalism significantly more than those of socialism. This has worked for much of the population, but Chinese leaders remain concerned about ethnic divisions in China's outlying regions.

Sources of Political Culture: Socialization, Experiences, and Events

Prior to the Communist period, socialization was generally left to such social institutions as the family. With Communist rule came much more aggressive government-led socialization, including government control of education and of the flow of information through the mass media. Consistent with Confucian and Communist ideals, Chinese schools emphasize effort over ability. The global explosion of social media (Internet blogs, Twitter, etc.) has made the control of information more difficult. In addition, the many decades of Communist Party

rule undermined the ethic of hard work—a legacy Russia also continues to face—in that guaranteed employment and flattened income levels gave workers few incentives to work intensely. This failure to work hard was openly discussed in government-run newspapers, and it is part of the reason for the government's open support of capitalist practices today.

China has one of the longest recorded histories in the world. It has experienced numerous challenges and significant events over that time, underlining the importance of order and security. With strong governments came order and prosperity, while instability and violence appeared during periods of weak government. The Chinese people associated limits on government with times of social chaos, and successive governments encouraged these beliefs.

China's long history somewhat limits an individual event's potential to influence political culture, and any effect may be slow to materialize. The consequences of an event even as shocking as the June 1989 Tiananmen Square massacre may thus be long-term rather than immediate. This tendency is compounded by the government's efforts to control the flow of political information and manipulate the portrayal of an event. At the same time, Chinese political culture is becoming increasingly heterogeneous as new values unleashed by marketization and China's exposure to values from countries such as the United States have begun to penetrate the traditional and the early Communist political culture.

Consistent with the idea that Chinese culture is somewhat resistant to sudden shocks, China scores high on another cultural component that Geert Hofstede examines: long term orientation. This is the extent to which society has a long-term perspective about problems, overcoming obstacles with time rather than forcibly attacking them.[40] China's score on this component (118) is around three times higher than the average of all countries he examines and nearly five times higher than that of the United Kingdom!

IN THEORY AND PRACTICE

China and Ronald Inglehart's Postmaterialism Theory

Many comparativists credit Ronald Inglehart with advancing the discussion of political culture through his development of **postmaterialism theory**. In works such as his 1989 book *Culture Shift in Advanced Industrial Society,* Inglehart

---

Postmaterialism Theory A theory associated with political scientist Ronald Inglehart that emphasizes causes and consequences of differences between those who value freedom and quality of life and those who value order and veconomic prosperity.

sets out to explain the emergence of postmaterialist values—beliefs that include the importance of freedom over order and of the protection of the natural environment—and differences in attachment to these beliefs within and between societies.[41] Inglehart proposes that underlying values are largely shaped by life experiences during a person's teens and early twenties. Age cohorts who experience conditions of economic hardship in these years will be more concerned about security and order for the rest of their lives. Those whose formative years take place during economic prosperity will be more likely to favor personal freedom and to focus on noneconomic quality of life concerns such as the environment.

Inglehart's arguments extend the concept of political culture in two ways. First, while examining the extent to which countries differ on postmaterialist values, he also highlights differences within the population of a country. He demonstrates that different age cohorts have values that are distinct from one another and that remain largely stable over time. This challenges the idea that differences in core beliefs between young and old exist because people become more conservative as they grow older.

Inglehart also places culture in a much broader context than do most works on political culture. He develops a theory of the emergence of postmaterialist values, as well as a theory about the implications of this phenomenon. The implications include a global advance in postmaterialist beliefs, as economic development means more and more generations experience material comfort in their formative years, and consequent changes in government policies that reflect this cultural shift. As a result, Inglehart integrates economic development, culture, and political change.

While Inglehart initially developed his postmaterialism theory around changes in values in economically developed countries of the West, the theory has interesting implications for China. Over the last three decades, China's economic growth has been impressive. For many young Chinese, economic hardship is not the concern it had been for their parents. If Inglehart is correct, these conditions will challenge the traditional Chinese emphasis on order and stability at the expense of freedom. The student protests that took place at times in the 1980s—culminating with the Tiananmen Square uprising in 1989—may have been the first outward signs of this culture shift. Thus, the Chinese government's encouragement of capitalist economic development is a double-edged sword. The government needs economic success to foster its performance legitimacy. But, if Inglehart is correct, such success will also foster an increased desire for freedom from government control.

Ideology

With the economic reforms of recent decades, ideology has declined in importance in China. As David Lampton, a political scientist specializing in Chinese politics, put it in 2001, the ideological emphasis of socialism's superiority to capitalism had already by then "been dead for 10 or 15 or more years in any significant way."[42]

To the extent that an official ideology exists today, it combines appeals to nationalism, arguments about the merits of capitalism, and a claim that the Communist Party provides the best opportunity for continued economic development. Well over 50 million residents of China are official Communist Party members, but people join the party not because they share the vision of the Communist Revolution or the views of past leaders like Mao, but because it is a gateway to social and economic advancement. Thus, Communist Party members today behave more like rational actors and less like true-believer revolutionaries committed to an ideological blueprint for remaking society.

Iran

Elements of the Iranian political culture are consistent with non-democracy, but Iran's culture is less traditional in orientation than are the cultures of many other countries in the Middle East (and also less traditional than many Americans believe it to be). The 1979 Islamic Revolution and subsequent government socialization efforts left a deep imprint on political culture. Iranians have witnessed a largely undemocratic approach to politics for much of their history, but the ideological positions of the Iranian governments have varied significantly over time. Even during the post-1979 period, different Iranian leaders have displayed different views of economics and of political reform. Attempts to deepen the population's commitment to the ideological vision of the Islamic leaders of the 1979 revolution have become more prevalent in recent years, although the backlash against the results of the 2009 presidential election call into question whether such efforts have been successful.

Political Culture

Traditional Iranian culture encourages respect for authority and promotes vertical social relations. Historically, the leaders of the monarchy were seen as a source of law and largely above the law—at least until the Constitutional Revolution of the early 1900s introduced a parliamentary system. Religious leaders enjoyed similar respect. On both respect for authority and vertical social relations, however, Iran is less extreme than many of its neighbors. For example, one of the components of Hofstede's political culture framework is called the "power distance index" (PDI). A high PDI score indicates a society that accepts inequality in social standing. Iran's PDI score of 58 captures its nature as respecting authority but only to an extent. Its score places it well below the Middle

Eastern average of 80, but it is nearly twice as high as that of the UK.[43]

In most Middle Eastern countries, the collectivism versus individualism aspect of political culture leans sharply toward collectivism. In Iran, the individualistic mindset is somewhat more in evidence and seems on the rise, particularly among the urban young. Hofstede's political culture study gives Iran a score of 41 on individualism. This is above the Middle Eastern average, but still well below countries the United States and UK. Hofstede's data on "uncertainty avoidance" point to Iran as having a political culture that values stability and order at the expense of freedom but not as much as other Middle Eastern countries. Its score of 59 is well below the Middle Eastern average of 68.[44] Inglehart's survival versus self-expression score for Iran also indicates its relatively moderate position; it is more focused on self-expression than China and much more so than Russia.[45] Writing with Daphna Oyserman, Inglehart argues that Iran "shows a surprisingly pro-democratic political culture," and is approaching the "transition zone," in which mass political culture becomes harmonious with democratic approaches.[46]

Of all the dimensions of political culture, it is most difficult to find reliable data about political system legitimacy. The harsh punishments handed out to dissidents must be taken into account when attempting to gauge the true feelings of officials and citizens who express support for the theocratic regime. When on camera and through the government-controlled print media, the Iranian people often express great satisfaction with their government. Such statements are consistent with their acceptance of the government's legitimacy. They are also consistent with recognition of the government's coercive power.

On the other hand, the prominent successes in the 1990s of candidates associated with political reform are hard to understand if the masses had a deep belief that the system was legitimate. The massive protests following the 2009 elections went beyond dissatisfaction with the results and signaled unhappiness with the political system itself.

Attachment to the national political community is relatively strong in Iran. In addition to the national pride that comes from Iran's long history (before the 1930s, Iran was known in the West as Persia), the pre-revolutionary and post-revolutionary Iranian governments encouraged a strong national identity. For the most part, their efforts have been successful. Because of the nature of the Islamic Revolution, however, the local and regional religious institutions are among the most powerful political units in Iran. They are of social as well as religious importance and play powerful roles in determining public policy and garnering local support. In addition, as in Russia and China, attachment to an overarching national identity is much weaker among ethnic minority groups living in outlying regions of the country than among the rest of the population.

Sources of Political Culture: Socialization, Experiences, and Events

Iran's political culture has been shaped by a long history of nondemocratic rule, including the two most important recent periods: the monarchy under the shah and the theocratic government in power since the 1979 Islamic Revolution. The political culture is also shaped by the country's economic experiences since 1979 and the current government's strong socialization efforts.

Since the Islamic Revolution, the socialization role of religious organizations has taken on added significance. Likewise, the educational system has been used to foster support for the revolution. Iranian textbooks highlight the shortcomings of the previous regime and portray the United States and the West in general in a negative light. Yet, as in most countries, the family remains arguably the most important socializing institution. For example, when boys see, from an early age, how their fathers treat their mothers, and when the treatment of women in society reinforces what they see at home, they learn to place a correspondingly low value on gender equality.

Revolutions that succeed in overthrowing the political system and establishing a different approach to societal organization are fairly rare. The 1979 revolution was a success on both counts, which is why it was such an important event. The shah's move toward secular modernization was halted, and Ayatollah Khomeini's vision of a theocratic political system with a tight control over society became the blueprint for interactions between politics and society. Thus, as important as other events in Iranian history are for its current political culture, the 1979 revolution predominates.

The most important repeated experience was daily life during the Iran-Iraq War. The war lasted eight years, from September 1980 to August 1988, and had a significant impact on the values of the Iranian people. While Iranian political culture remains less traditional than some others in the Mideast, the Iran-Iraq War increased the focus on security and stability.

IN THEORY AND PRACTICE

Iran and Benjamin Barber's "Jihad Versus McWorld" Framework

As discussed earlier in the chapter, understanding the interplay between globalization and culture is important to discussions of political culture today. Many scholars have proposed theories about the causes and consequences of culture in an increasingly interconnected world. These include sociologist George Ritzer's "McDonaldization" theory[47] and Samuel Huntington's idea of the "clash of civilizations."[48] Perhaps the best example of a theory about the intersection of culture and globalization is laid out in Benjamin Barber's book, *Jihad versus McWorld*. As Barber provocatively states, "The planet is falling precipitously apart and coming reluctantly together at the same time."[49] Barber uses the term *jihad* to capture the "dogmatic and violent particularism"[50] that is an extreme form of the blending of identity politics with the concept of self-determinism. *McWorld* is Barber's term for the forces of globalization that increasingly pull people around the world together.

In many ways, these two movements spin in opposite directions. Yet, one of Barber's key contributions is to demonstrate the extent to which tribalism and globalism complement one another. Jihad movements oppose Western culture but are willing to use the tools of that culture to further their agendas. Barber predicted such uses of technology nearly a decade before al Qaeda and the insurgents fighting American forces in Iraq began to use it, stating that the "information revolution's instrumentalities are also Jihad's favored weapons."[51]

Iran provides an interesting example of the concept of the tensions between jihad and McWorld. On the one hand, much of the Iranian leaders' rhetoric is anti-Western (anti-American in particular), expressing fears that Western culture could infect Iran's Muslim society. On the other hand, Tehran's streets look more Western than do the streets of many other Middle Eastern capitals. In particular, the young, like their counterparts in the latter years of the Soviet Union, respect the West. It is no accident that support for reformers is based in this young, urban constituency.

The Iranian government has done an impressive job of isolating Iran from the cultural effects of globalization. But as the attitudes of the young indicate, they may do better by borrowing a page from what some call "glocalization"— working to mold globalization, rather than trying to prevent it from penetrating into domestic society.[52] As Iran specialist Mahmood Sariolghalam has put it:

> In the end, Iranians cannot avoid settling for a system that will be founded on a combination of Iranian nationalism, Islamic faith, and globalization. This outcome might be a contradiction in terms, but any Eastern culture that desires to coexist in a contemporary global context that is dominated by the West will have to navigate these apparent contradictions and adapt itself to them.[53]

Ideology

Iranians are no strangers to government-sponsored ideology. Under the shahs, the main ideology involved justification of monarchial rule. In the decades leading up to the 1979 revolution, a new focus was added: modernization based on the model of Turkey and its

secular political system and close relations with the United States.

The 1979 Islamic Revolution provided a new official vision. It advocated a theocratic state based on strict interpretation of Islamic law. Thus, while ideology is nothing new to Iran, its central role in Iranian politics reached new heights in recent decades, a trend that became even more pronounced after the election of Iranian President Mahmoud Ahmadinejad in 2005 and his reelection in 2009.

Think and Discuss

Is the globalization of culture good or bad? Why?

TIC Wrap-Up

The TIC cases demonstrate the importance of ideology and political culture, as well as the role of socialization, events, and experiences in shaping political culture over time. In the three cases with the most consolidated democratic systems—the UK, Germany, and India—political culture has played a particularly important role in shaping and maintaining democracy. The combination of working class deference and noblesse oblige, for example, has contributed to the evolutionary nature of British political development. Sharper ideological disputes in German history contributed to Germany's more radical swings in governance. India's political culture reflects the country's diversity. To the extent that generalization is possible, Indian political culture displays a balance between contrasting ideals, blending respect for authority with tolerance of inconvenience and acceptance of national "unity in diversity." In the UK, important events include terrorist acts, initially those connected to the Irish Republican Army and more recently the 7/7 bombings of 2005. Germany's numerous defining events and important repeated experiences helped push it to develop its social market economic approach. In both the UK and Germany, broad agreement on economic and social welfare policy has limited the instances of significant economic ideological confrontation since World War II. In India, ideological debates have continued under the broadly accepted framework of market economic reforms since 1991.

Political cultures differ among and within the three newer established democracies—Mexico, Brazil, and

***

Jihad versus McWorld Benjamin Barber's term for the tension between the forces of particularism, which draw on ethnic and tribal identity and local attachments, and the forces of globalization.

Nigeria. Mexico's regard for revolutionary figures combined with respect of authority to help maintain the PRI as the prevailing political party for much of the twentieth century. In contrast, Brazil's diverse political culture and the different sets of experiences and defining events of different groups in the country has made it difficult for any single group, other than the military during the periods of its rule, to dominate the political system. In each of the three countries, corruption threatens the functioning of the democratic system. Nigeria's negative experience with democracy as well as daily struggles with corruption, for example, have reinforced the population's desire for stability and order at the expense of freedom. In Mexico, the ideological pragmatism of the PRI was replaced after 2000 by more visible ideological divides among the three main political parties. Such divides are even more apparent in Brazil, where they contribute to the country's multiparty political system, and in Nigeria, where they are reinforced by religious differences within the population.

The three nondemocratic TIC cases—Russia, China, and Iran—demonstrate that political culture and ideology are no less important to semi-authoritarian and authoritarian systems. The Russian tendency to be suspicious of people who get ahead economically caused problems in the late Soviet and early post-Soviet periods for those hoping to reform the economic system to give individuals greater responsibility. China's Confucian view of society emphasized working hard for the good of the collective. Both the Russian and Chinese governments have taken advantage of the tendency for their populations to respect authority and defer to leaders who portray images of strength. The governments of all three countries have worked to socialize their populations to hold values consistent with the broad approach of the leaders, but important events and repeated experiences have interfered with the effectiveness of these efforts. In Russia and China, ideology has taken a backseat to pragmatic approaches designed to foster economic success. In Iran, ideological divisions between the ruling government hardliners and those supporting significant reform played out in the streets following the 2009 presidential election.

Think and Discuss

What are the similarities and differences among the political cultures in the TIC cases? What themes emerge from the ways political culture was shaped in them? To what extent does ideology in each reflect the underlying political culture?

COUNTRY SUMMARY

TIC Country	Key Features of Political Culture	Key Institutions of Socialization	Defining Events and/or Important Repeated Experiences	Ideologies
United Kingdom	Working class deference; noblesse oblige; more individualistic than much of Europe; ITAP feature on Almond and Verba's civic culture theory	Family; media; educational system	Evolutionary political history; 7/7 terrorist bombings in 2005	Fewer economic ideological differences since World War II; Thatcher emphasis on conservatism; parties stressing moderate positions do well in last two decades
Germany	More collectivistic than individualistic; principles like subsidiarity guide government social welfare programs	Family; media; educational system	World War I; Great Depression; World War II; Communist period in East Germany; reunification	Social market economy approach to economics
India	More individualistic than other Asian cases; fragmented; notion of "unity in diversity"	Family; educational system	Events surrounding independence; the partition; assassinations	Market-led economic development approach widely accepted

TIC Country	Key Features of Political Culture	Key Institutions of Socialization	Defining Events and/or Important Repeated Experiences	Ideologies
Mexico	Tensions in beliefs on authority and social relations; less individualistic than United States	Educational system; Catholic Church; family	Mexican Revolution; presidential elections in 1997 and 2000	Increasingly visible ideological divides over free market economics and free trade approaches
Brazil	Heterogeneous; evasion of power; *jeito*; security over freedom	Family; religious institutions	Military dictatorship, 1964–85; economic crisis; corruption scandals	Diverse, ranging from Communist to conservative and religious
Nigeria	Heterogeneous; acceptance of vertical social relations; collectivism over individualism; security over freedom	Family; educational system	British colonial rule; Nigerian Civil War (1967–70); military rule; latest chapter of democracy	More emphasis on political figures than policies; religious rule versus Western-type rule
Russia	Collective over individual; security and order at the expense of liberty and freedom; deference to authority figures	Government; media; schools; social organizations	Political developments between 1985 and 2005	Tsarist period: orthodoxy, autocracy, narodnost; Soviet period: Communism, atheism, economic planning; post-Soviet period: suspicion of ideology
China	Confucianism-based respect for authority; society over individual; order and security at expense of freedom; ITAP feature on Ronald Inglehart's postmaterialism theory	Government (through media and schools); family	Exposure to values from other countries (e.g., United States); economic reforms and high growth rates	Appeals to nationalism; merits of capitalism; pragmatism over ideological commitments
Iran	Respect for authority; vertical social relations; high levels of individualism for a Middle Eastern country, but stability and order at expense of freedom; ITAP feature on Benjamin Barber's "Jihad versus McWorld" framework	Religious organizations; educational system; family	1979 Islamic Revolution; Iran-Iraq War	Since the 1979 revolution, emphasis on legitimacy of the Iranian theocracy based on Islamic law

Spotlight on . . . Country	Key Features of Political Culture	Key Institutions of Socialization	Defining Events and/or Important Repeated Experiences	Ideologies
France	Revolutionary principles still important; liberty valued over stability, but comparatively horizontal social relations and collectivist orientation	Government (through schools, museums, and military); family; social organizations, often led by political parties	French Revolution remains defining event; establishment of Fifth Republic renewed the commitment to the ideals of the revolution, while also focusing on stability and order	Fewer ideological divisions between major political parties than in the past; strong secularism that opposes public displays of religion
Iraq	Desire for stability and order; some attachment to traditional values of obedience to authority; ethno-religious collectivism; commitment to democracy is visible, but depth of attachment is unclear	Family; religious organizations; government information efforts and manipulation of the media	Political culture affected in recent decades by repeated experiences of dictatorship, war, and occupation	Official commitment to democracy; differing views about role of religion in politics; economic ideological positions less clear, even among major political parties
South Africa	Cultural diversity; suspicion of political authorities but respect for traditional social structures; corruption; relatively strong sense of legitimacy of democratic system	Family; media; educational system	Apartheid period; struggle for end of apartheid; negotiated transition to democratic system	The African National Congress (ANC) is officially a Leftist political party, but its policies are progressive to moderate; race-based ideological positions and Afrikaner nationalism weaken with the end of apartheid

Research in Context

Immigration is a source of political tension not only in the United States but also around the world. Debates on immigration tend to focus on the impact on the host country (e.g., the potential for residents to lose jobs to new immigrants, the costs to school districts of educating immigrant children, the value of cheaper immigrant labor to domestic businesses) and on the immigrants themselves (e.g., the potential for immigrants to better themselves economically, the ability for them to escape political persecution, the damage that exporting illegal immigrants can cause them and their children). Little of the debate centers on the extent to which exposure to a new situation can affect immigrants' political values and the potential impact on their home countries.

Migration from Mexico and Political Culture in Mexico

A 2010 article in *Comparative Political* Studies by Clarisa Pérez-Armendáriz and David Crow examined the extent to which migration from Mexico to the United States and Canada affects political beliefs and behaviors in Mexico. The authors hypothesize that political beliefs in the migrants' home country can be shaped by migrants bringing "new political values and practices when they return home," by migrants providing information about their experiences to family and friends in their home country, and by information transmitted through networks within "high-volume migration communities."[54] The idea behind this third form of influence is that information channeled through the social networks feeds on itself, reaching a critical mass that affects those working within the network and others in contact with it.

Based on an examination of survey data collected in Mexico in 2006, the authors conclude that migration from Mexico generates increases in political participation in Mexico, more tolerance of identity-based and political differences, and more critical analysis of the shortcomings of Mexican democracy. This happens not only to those who spend time in the United States or Canada and return to Mexico, but also—and sometimes more strongly—to "stay-behinds" in Mexico who have direct or indirect contact with migrants across the border.[55] The authors conclude that their research provides "substantial support for the proposition that migrants impel the diffusion of democratic attitudes and behaviors across international borders by way of the three diffusion paths we examine—migrant returns, cross-border communication, and community-wide migrant social networks."[56]

So What?

With so much of the debate on immigration in the United States centering on impacts on the United States, Pérez-Armendáriz and Crow's research adds an interesting piece to the puzzle. While many American foreign policy experts have long supported the idea of having students from nondemocratic countries study in the United States as a way of "infecting" them with pro-democratic ideals before sending them home, similar arguments have not been made about immigration from countries like Mexico. But, if migration from Mexico can help deepen a commitment to democracy within Mexico, the benefits for the United States could be substantial.

Could migration from Mexico to countries like the United States and Canada really alter something as sticky as political culture within Mexico? As Pérez-Armendáriz and Crow point out, 10 percent of all people born in Mexico currently reside in the United States, but a high portion of those who enter the country each year return to Mexico.[57] Their research also indicates how even those who remain in the United States or Canada may play a role in altering Mexican political culture. Such changes may not come quickly. If Alexis de Tocqueville could be struck by the unique features of American political culture during his travels in 1831, however, it would be foolish to dismiss the potential impact today on those living and working in the United States for extended periods of time.

CONCLUSION

An appreciation of a particular country's political culture can be a powerful tool in understanding how that country can remain politically stable, even rigid, for long periods of time. Yet, as sticky as political culture is, it can be altered by important events, such as the September 11, 2001, terrorist attacks, or modified by long-term or repeated experiences, such as the Great Depression. Such shifts bring a new cultural structure and new implications for political institutions and the individuals who govern within them.

It is possible to criticize explanations of political outcomes that rely on political culture alone. One would certainly want to consider other explanatory factors, such as the economic structural factors examined in the previous chapter. Another potential criticism is the ecological fallacy—that collective concepts cannot explain individual behavior—discussed in Chapter 1. An additional critique is that measuring political culture is problematic, above all when the collective concept of culture is specified through the aggregation of individual-level data. The flip side of the ecological fallacy, often termed the **individualistic fallacy**, is based on the idea that collectives are not necessarily the sum of their individual parts. Summing individuals' values misses the group dynamics that can accompany the infusion of culture into the context of politics. Others argue against a focus on political culture because, they contend, the concept oversimplifies complex societies by relying on stereotyping as much as on empirically valid characterizations; it cannot explain rapid political changes; and politics shapes culture rather than the other way around. All these concerns are legitimate.

> **Individualistic Fallacy** The assumption that collective concepts like culture can be adequately measured by aggregating individual level data.

Yet, the underlying values and systems of meaning in different countries around the world are important components of the comparative study of politics. Consider the example of understanding a nondemocratic political system governed by a long-time dictator that appeared to collapse very quickly. Suppose the following series of events led up to the political system's collapse:

- Changing economic conditions and other repeated events led values to change slowly, under the surface, for a period of time.
- These slow changes were not mirrored by changes in the political system.
- Eventually, the difference between the cultural setting and the political reality caused legitimacy to evaporate, allowing a political entrepreneur to challenge the system.
- This opposition leader rallied mass opposition to the current leader and the political system itself, protests spread rapidly, and the leader resigned.

Political culture is a crucial element in this chain of events. Even if political culture is not sufficient to bring about such a major political change, it can fuel changes sparked by another factor.

Comparativists who emphasize the importance of political culture argue that underlying values and systems of meaning—particularly those about politics—shape political institutions and political decisions. Experiences may affect political culture, but political culture also gives meaning to many experiences. As such, political culture is a lens for viewing the world of politics. Perceived cultural uniqueness is also a central component of group identity, which itself can have important political consequences and is the topic of the next chapter.

KEY TERMS

Civic culture theory, p. 75
Collectivistic political cultures, p. 66
Confucianism, p. 86
Conservative ideology, p. 71
Cultural heterogeneity, p. 65
Cultural homogeneity, p. 65
Culture, p. 65
Defining events, p. 68
Horizontal social relations, p. 66
Individualistic fallacy, p. 94

Individualistic political cultures, p. 66
Islamism, p. 72
Jeito, p. 81
Jihad versus McWorld, p. 90
Libertarian ideology, p. 71
Marxist ideology, p. 71
Moderate ideology, p. 72
Noblesse oblige, p. 73
Political culture, p. 65
Political ideology, p. 70

Postmaterialism theory, p. 87
Progressive ideology, p. 71
Reactionary ideology, p. 71
Repeated experiences, p. 68
Social democratic ideology, p. 71
Socialization, p. 69
Subsidiarity, p. 76
Vertical social relations, p. 66
Welfare state, p. 71
Working-class deference, p. 73

Identity Structure

Ethnic Russians in Estonia protest the Estonian government's decision in 2007 to move a Soviet-era WWII monument. © Reuters

CHAPTER OUTLINE

Identity
Complementary and Cross-Cutting Identity Divisions
Government Responses to Identity Diversity

TOPIC IN COUNTRIES

Features in this chapter:

Spotlight on . . . Iraq: Complementary Identity Divisions in Iraq

In Theory and Practice: Cleavage Structure Theory and Russia

In Theory and Practice: Primordialism, Constructivism, and Identity in China

In Theory and Practice: Feminist Theory and Iran

Research in Context: Identity Politics in Turkey

LEARNING OBJECTIVES

After reading this chapter, you should be able to

- Describe the various types of politically relevant collective identities.

- Explain how various forms of identity work as sources of political mobilization.

- Describe the strategies a government may take in response to ethnic diversity, and explain the conditions under which these responses are likely to be more or less accommodating.

- Compare and contrast the major identity divisions in the TIC countries.

- Summarize the main findings of this chapter's Research in Context section.

One evening in the summer of 1996, an American professor conducting research in Tallinn, Estonia, was returning to his apartment. As he walked across the building's courtyard, two Russian men yelled to him, asking if he had matches. The professor ignored them, and as he started up the stairs, the Russians grabbed him and threw him against the wall. Words were exchanged, and the professor realized that he was being mistaken for an Estonian. When he explained that he was an American, the two men apologized. "We cannot let an Estonian ignore us like that when we speak Russian," explained one of the men.

The American professor's experience highlights the extent to which belonging to a particular identity group—or being mistaken as belonging to it—can affect the way people interact with one another. Identity group membership, whether real or imagined, is also relevant to politics. Understanding fully major political outcomes requires considering the extent to which individuals and groups are bound together through their identity.

Sociologists and social psychologists have long understood that membership in identity groups largely determines how a person perceives himself or herself as an individual. Put simply, humans have a need to belong, to be part of a collective "us." This desire to belong is both natural for members of a population and reinforced by the actions of social and political elites. The development and reinforcement of a sense of "us" also creates and reinforces a sense of "them."

As Chapter 10 discusses, individuals take political stances and actions partly as a result of self-interested, rational calculations. Groups to which individuals belong, however, provide collective interests for them to consider, while also offering emotional counterweights to individual rational calculations. Because belonging is a powerful sentiment, political elites often target identity in their efforts to mobilize support for their candidacies for office and their policy positions. Identity can also fuel mass protests and violence without significant elite guidance, especially in response to particular events. In May 2011, for example, a Christian church in Egypt was burned down after rumors circulated that a Christian woman who was married to a Muslim man was being held there.[1]

Identity

Identity is the set of characteristics by which individuals or collectives understand themselves and are known to others. For individuals, these characteristics include personality traits and the groups to which they belong (family, clan, ethnic group, etc.).

> **Identity** The set of characteristics by which individuals or collectives of individuals are known to themselves and others.

They give the individual a sense of who he or she is and allow others to recognize the individual both as a unique person and as a member of particular groups. Many characteristics, such as hair color, are not politically salient. Others, including race, ethnic identity, religion, gender, and sexual orientation, can be important in shaping individual political behavior.

The structure of politically relevant group identities in a society can also play an important role in political outcomes. Much of this chapter focuses on concepts and theories related to collective identity rather than individual identity. The extent to which a population is divided into identity groups with emotionally powerful bonds and how much those groups complement other identity groups can be critical to political stability. The existence of deep identity divisions also drives governments to adopt strategies to address identity diversity. These strategies can include policies designed to protect minority group cultures, to enhance minorities' socioeconomic standing, or to make certain forms of group identity less politically salient.

The types of shared values and beliefs outlined in the previous chapter help bind together major identity categories. In other words, identity often incorporates culture. Because members of an identity group do not get to know, or even meet, most of the other members of the group, they must "imagine" themselves as part of it.[2] Accepting that they have a shared culture is a crucial part of the process of imagining. As this chapter shows, however, some types of identity groups can more easily generate perceived cultural bonds than other types.

In-Groups, Out-Groups, and Perceptions of Threat

Membership Boundary The divide between individuals who belong to a group and those who do not.

In-Group A group (e.g., an ethnic group) to which a particular individual belongs.

Out-Group A group to which a particular individual does not belong but which is the same type of group (e.g., another ethnic group) as the in-group.

The establishment of a group identity creates a **membership boundary**. A membership boundary is the divide between the individuals who belong to a particular identity group and those who do not. Within this boundary, the group's members share an identity bond and come to see themselves as "we." Social scientists typically refer to the group to which such members belong as an **in-group**. But by defining who belongs, membership boundaries also define who does not belong, thus creating what is called an **out-group**. The belief that the members of the out-group are different from members of the in-group can be a powerful tool for creating the boundaries of the group. Often, the out-group is believed to be culturally or intellectually inferior, although sometimes members of the in-group have an inferiority complex in relation to the out-group. If members of an in-group view themselves as less educated or less wealthy than members of the out-group, they may envy the out-group. They may also blame their circumstances on the out-group, believing their own lack of education or wealth to be the result of discrimination.

The sharpness of the membership boundary between an in-group and an out-group is both a cause and a result of relations between the two groups. Groups that have exchanged bloodshed in the past are more likely to clash in the future than if they had not experienced an initial violent conflict. This is partly because of memories of the previous conflict, which group leaders may invoke when discussing the "other." It is also because the conditions that led to the original conflict may still be in place.

To mobilize members, group leaders often emphasize the threat that an external force poses to the survival of the group. This threat from outside the group can come from a different group of the same identity type (e.g., a neighboring ethnic group), from the government of the group's state of residence, or from larger external forces such as globalization. As discussed in the previous chapter, a group may see globalization as posing a threat to its cultural survival by eroding its values over time. Rival identity groups or the government can pose a more direct and immediate threat—perhaps to the very lives of the group's members. Whether an outside threat is or is not objectively real is irrelevant. Alleged out-group threats exemplify the idea that perception is reality.

Think and Discuss
Why is identity so effective as a tool for political elites who are trying to mobilize members of the general public?

Forms of Collective Identity

Because the various categories of identity create divisions between groups in a society, they are typically referred to as **social cleavages**. This chapter discusses the social cleavages that most comparativists consider to be the most politically relevant. Some identity categories, such as language, are excluded. Although some comparativists consider language divisions to be a kind of identity division,[3] there is scant evidence that language is itself a defining collective identity for most people. Instead, language often serves as a marker for ethnic identity. In addition, other groupings, such as age cohorts and caste, are not discussed in this part of the chapter but rather are addressed in the Topic in Countries (TIC) sections. Caste, which exists as an identity category in a few countries in the world, is introduced in the section on India, as India is the only TIC case in which caste creates a primary identity divide.

> **Social Cleavages** The categories of identity that create us-them divisions in a society.

National Identity

National identity is one of the most important forms of identity. It is so central to understanding major domestic and international political outcomes that it was part of Chapter 1's coverage of key concepts in comparative politics. The membership boundaries of the nation and the shared cultural features that unite its members are often based on many of the other collective identity categories—ethnicity and religion, for example—discussed in the subsequent sections of this chapter. The key difference between the two ideal types of national identity, ethnic and civic, is the extent to which national identity is defined in ethic terms. Because national identity unites collective identity bonds, attachment to territory, and the belief in the right to political control over that territory, it is a particularly effective tool for mobilizing the general population.

Race, Ethnicity, Tribe, and Clan

A number of identity types extend the idea of kinship and "blood ties" to groups much larger than traditional familial groups. Four such group identities are highlighted here: race, ethnicity, tribe, and clan. The success of portraying members of these groups as related to one another by blood varies by geography and culture. Yet, the ability for racial, ethnic, tribal, and clan leaders to invoke biological connections among members can produce an emotional spark unmatched by any other group identities, with the possible exception of religion.

In some situations, perceived differences associated with racial group membership can influence how individuals view each other and can have political implications. In other settings, racial diversity within a group has no impact on personal interactions.
© Phil Date/Shutterstock.com

Race

The first major kinship category is **race**. Race is one of the most complicated and contested forms of identity. In the natural sciences, the term has a generally accepted meaning: races are subspecies (divisions of a species of animal), the members of which typically develop biological differences due to geographic isolation.

Applying the concept to humans, however, creates a number of difficulties. First, in an increasingly globalized world, it is difficult for large segments of the human population to remain geographically isolated. Second, even in earlier periods of history when intermarriage among different peoples was much less common, groups often intermingled, making objective identification of racial boundaries unworkable. Finally, unlike divisions within species of animals, separation of humans across geographic distances does not result in significant differences in skills or intellect. Thus, while the

> **Race** A large identity group whose members are perceived to be distinct on the basis of genetically transmitted physical differences.

concept of race has been socially established as an important identity category, it is much less objectively supported for humans than for subspecies of other animals.

Applied to humans, *race* is defined as a large human population perceived to be distinct from other such groups on the basis of genetically transmitted physical differences. The words *perceived to be* in the definition are very important. Because each racial group is so large and has so much diversity within it, race is arguably the least objective, most socially constructed form of identity. Anthropologists and sociologists, for example, point out that someone considered "white" in one setting may be considered "black" in another setting. The key is not whether the physical differences are real, but that people believe that they are real.

People believe in the existence of racial differences for two reasons. First, certain physical differences that people associate with race do exist, at least if one is focusing on extreme variations in such differences. For example, people closely associate skin color with race. Ordering photographs of people's faces, many of which would look similar, on a black-white continuum can be difficult, yet most individuals would recognize a significant difference between the pictures at each end of the continuum. Second, the historical construction of racial membership boundaries included powerful myths that the physical differences reflected important genetic differences. These myths generated stereotypes about intellectual potential, work ethic, and so on. Over time, differences in appearance became markers for racial boundaries, these boundaries were linked to racial stereotypes, and race became socially (and thus politically) relevant.

Ethnic Identity

Ethnic Identity The sense of belonging to an ethnic group; also known as ethnicity.

While race was arguably the most important group identity in the twentieth century, **ethnic identity**, also referred to as ethnicity, has almost certainly been the most important group identity of the last several decades. It has provided the emotional spark for the global reemergence of ethnic nationalism, has given politicians a ready-made tool for mobilizing supporters, and has been at the center of controversies over the right of minority groups to practice and protect their cultures. Donald Horowitz, one of the most important scholars of ethnic conflict, writes:

> In divided societies, ethnic conflict is at the center of politics. Ethnic divisions pose challenges to the cohesion of states and sometimes to peaceful relations among states. Ethnic conflict strains the bonds that sustain civility and is often at the root of violence that results in looting, death, homelessness, and the flight of large numbers of people. In divided societies, ethnic affiliations are powerful, permeative, passionate, and pervasive.[4]

Ethnic Group A large collective sharing a common history and culture whose members are believed to share a common descent.

What is ethnic identity, and what makes it so powerful? Ethnic identity is the sense of belonging to an **ethnic group**, which is a large collective sharing a common history and culture whose members are believed to be connected through common descent. Ethnic groups use numerous markers to differentiate between in-group and out-group members. These markers include, but are not limited to, language, family names, dialect, dress, and religion. Ethnic identity is typically ascribed rather than chosen. It is difficult, and sometimes impossible, to penetrate an ethnic group even if one learns and adopts the group's culture and practices.

Ethnicity is a strong form of identity because it connects three qualities: tightly shared cultural understandings, beliefs in kinship bonds, and perceptions that an "other" poses a threat to the group's survival. These three aspects combine with a fourth, the existence of ethnically heterogeneous states, to make ethnicity a central social cleavage and a source of significant conflict around the world.

First, culture is as central to ethnic identity as it is to any of the group identities discussed in this chapter. Ethnic groups contain a common set of cultural features that help bind members together. The features help in-group members recognize each other, although out-group members can also use them to identify the individuals as ethnically different. In this way, ethnic groups differ from racial groups, which tend to be much more culturally heterogeneous.

Second, ethnic identity bonds go beyond culture to include perceptions of shared kinship. Although members of racial groups also feel some degree of blood ties, racial groups are often too large for members to maintain a strong sense of shared kinship. Thus, most scholars see the ethnic group as the largest social group that still evokes family ties. As Donald Horowitz puts it, "the language of ethnicity is the language of kinship."[5] As a consequence, ethnic leaders can effectively portray the group as a large extended family that is united by a past of shared descent, a present of shared experiences and deep loyalty of members to one another, and a future (including descendants not yet born) of shared fate.

The image of ethnic boundaries as a perimeter dividing contrasting extended families leads to a third important distinction about ethnicity. Although any identity group may believe that its survival is threatened, ethnic identity's understandings of common descent and blood ties give this perceived threat added emotional salience. Ethnic groups can come to see a threat posed by the "other" as jeopardizing not only their common values and beliefs but also the survival of their ethnic extended family. In such instances, it is understandable when ethnic group members support extreme actions against the source of the threat.

The fourth aspect that contributes to making ethnicity a central social cleavage and a source of significant conflict is the existence of ethnically heterogeneous states. Few countries are anywhere close to being ethnically homogeneous. Most have at least one significant ethnic minority and often more than one sizable group. In some countries, including Nigeria, no ethnic group makes up a majority of the population. The existence of multiple ethnic groups within the territorial boundary of a state combines with the ethnicity's emotional potency to push it into the middle of politics. If, as discussed in Chapter 1, politics is indeed about "Who gets what?", ethnic identity is a common answer.

Tribal and Clan Identity

The smallest of the group identities associated with shared blood ties are tribes and clans. A **clan** is a kinship group made up of several families related to each other either by a common ancestor or through marriage. Clans often have a recognized leader who mediates conflicts within the clan and to whom clan members owe loyalty. The term *clan* is derived from the Scottish word *clann* (meaning family). Clan ties were historically important for the Scots, and they continue to remain important to people of Scottish descent around the world. For the most part, however, clan identity is much less important today among Europeans than it is in the Middle East, Central Asia, and Africa. In Africa, Somalia provides an example of clan ties overwhelming the effort to construct a strong national identity based on a shared ethnic Somali identity.[7]

A **tribe** is larger than a clan, although it is also a collective whose members believe that they can trace their heritage to a single ancestor. Compared with ethnic groups, tribes tend to be more geographically contiguous and compact, as well as more culturally homogeneous. They may have a single recognized leader, although their political organization tends to be less structured than that of a clan. In some countries, both tribal and clan affiliations are important, and tribes typically include anywhere from a few to many clans.

The term *tribe* has fallen out of favor with political scientists. It carries a stigma because it has often been used to refer to groups that are perceived to be economically and culturally backward. The term is also used for groups of such varying sizes, from hundreds to millions of people, that in many cases either *ethnic group* or *clan* would be a more appropriate designation.

Religion

Throughout recorded history, religion and politics have been tightly bound together. With the exception of such theocracies as Iran and the Holy See (Vatican City), today's religious leaders are generally less directly involved in governing than were religious

"Did You Know?" Seeming to understand the electoral ramifications of identity, Tony Sanchez, a candidate for governor of Texas, said in September 2001, "Issues are important, but they are not as important as the fact that this is an opportunity to vote for one of your own."[6]

Clan An identity group made up of a number of families who are believed to be related through birth or marriage to a common ancestor.

Tribe An identity group that is similar to a clan but larger; sometimes made up of a number of clans.

leaders of the past. Yet, religion remains an important part of individual identity and a significant social division. At the mass level, people who practice religion ardently tend to be more socially and politically conservative than those who do not.

Religion An organized system of beliefs and devotion regarding a spiritual force or forces.

Religion is an organized system of beliefs and devotion regarding a supernatural force (God) or forces (multiple gods). Most major religions are monotheistic, believing in a single deity. An individual can practice a faith, but, like culture, religion requires a collective of such individuals or, in the words of political scientist Thomas Reese, "a community of believers."[8] Religion also requires some form of institutionalization, a regularized set of practices flowing from the exercise of religious beliefs. Religion can have an emotionally powerful cultural pull because it is based not only on beliefs but also on faith. Often, when faced with events or settings that are inconsistent with certain beliefs, individuals change their beliefs. This is much harder in the case of faith, since by definition it is something that one believes without empirical support and even in the face of incongruent observation.

Religion provides answers for questions otherwise unanswerable. Faith is the belief that the answers are not just reasonable but are the Truth. This deep belief makes religion the most important collective bond within many people's individual identity. It also makes the us-them divide between religious groups potentially sharp. The members of the other religious group are not just different; they do not accept the Truth. In many religions, the in-group portrays itself as a "chosen people"; out-group members are thus not chosen. The ideas that the other group has not been chosen and lacks understanding of the Truth can combine to generate intolerance, discrimination, or violence against the other group's members.

The most politically important religions globally include Christianity, Islam, Judaism, Hinduism, and Buddhism. Although found throughout the world, most of them dominate particular regions—for example, Islam in the Middle East, Christianity in Latin America, and Hinduism in India—or are regionally concentrated, such as Buddhism in Asia. Religious divisions between a majority of the population and minority groups are increasingly commonplace.

Confucianism is not treated as a religion in this chapter due to its lack of formal structure and organized worship, although the previous chapter contained a discussion of Confucianism as a centerpiece of East Asian political culture. If deemed a religion, Confucianism would be one of the world's five largest religions.

Christianity

Historically and presently one of the world's most influential religions, Christianity has the largest number of adherents. Christians can be found in all regions of the world, making up an estimated 2.2 billion people or nearly one-third of the world's population. Christianity is less at the center of domestic politics in majority-Christian countries than it was in the past. Yet, it remains a political force globally due to its size and, in some of its branches at least, its defined hierarchical structure and moral code.

Like other large religions, Christianity has mainstream and fundamentalist believers, along with a number of members whose beliefs only weakly influence their behavior. Some believers support the intertwining of politics and Christian doctrine, while others favor a sharper separation of the religious and governmental spheres. Also, like other religions, Christianity is divided into a number of different groups, though it is possible to roughly place them into three broad categories: Roman Catholic, Protestant, and Eastern Orthodox. These three groups share important beliefs, summarized in statements such as the Nicene Creed and Apostles' Creed, but have divergent practices and some important contrasting positions on certain tenets of their faith. Of these major Christian groups, Protestantism has the greatest variety of beliefs and practices and, consequently, a large number of denominations.

Islam

Islam is the world's second largest religion, with around 1.7 billion adherents. Muslims make up about 25 percent of the world's population and the majority of the population in more than four dozen countries. As with other religions, only a portion of Muslims are extraordinarily devout. For devout believers, Islam provides a blueprint for life. Practicing Muslims observe a code, the Five Pillars, that summarizes the most central beliefs and practices, including prayer five times per day, fasting during Ramadan, and a pilgrimage to Mecca at least once during one's life. In some Muslim-majority countries, *Sharia* (Islamic law) has become a central foundation of government policy. Like Christians, however, not all devout Muslims favor Islam's incorporation into the political system.

Also like Christianity, Islam has significant internal divisions. The most notable is between Shiite and Sunni Muslims.[9] Shortly after the death of Muhammad, the founder of the religion, Shiites and Sunnis split over who should succeed him, with Sunnis supporting Abu Bakr, the elected first caliph, and Shiites supporting Muhammad's cousin, Ali. Around 85 to 90 percent of Muslims are Sunnis, but in some countries, such as Iran, the majority are Shiites.

While many Sunnis are devout, a much smaller portion support more radical variants of Sunni Islam such as Wahhabism and Deobandism. Centered in Saudi Arabia, Wahhabism is hostile to modernization and supports a return to traditional Islamic values and practices. Deobandi Islam, a form practiced by the Taliban of Afghanistan and a segment of Pakistan's population, has similar fundamentalist characteristics.

Think and Discuss

How are Islam's Five Pillars—the belief that "There is no true God except Allah, and Muhammad is the Messenger of Allah," prayer five times per day, fasting during Ramadan, charity to the poor, and a pilgrimage to Mecca at least one time during one's life—similar to and different from the core "pillars" of Christianity?

Judaism

Though Jews are much fewer in number than Christians and Muslims, Judaism has had a major impact on international politics. Some of the most internationally important conflicts of the past century involved the persecution of Jews in predominantly Christian countries and tensions between Jews and Muslims in the Middle East. Since Israel's founding, the failure of surrounding countries to accept the new state as legitimate has sparked a series of wars between Israel and its Arab neighbors. These conflicts were exacerbated by the failure of the international community to constitute a Palestinian state—as the UN General Assembly had originally supported—alongside Israel. Though the groundwork was in place for a Palestinian state at the end of the first decade of the twenty-first century, its creation is unlikely to resolve tensions between Jews and Muslims—and Christians—in the Middle East in the near future.

Christians, Muslims, and Jews share a common religious heritage. All three are monotheistic. More than any other religion, however, Judaism carries a strong sense of identity based on common descent that makes Jewish identity as much ethnic as religious. Religion is often a marker of ethnic boundaries, but for Jews it is the central criterion of their identity. With the emergence of Zionism, a movement that developed in Europe in the 1800s advocating a Jewish state in the region around Jerusalem, Jewish identity became a national identity as well. After the Holocaust, the Zionist cause was accepted by the leading countries of the time, and the state of Israel emerged in 1948.

The Western Wall ("Wailing Wall") in Jerusalem, one of Judaism's most sacred sites.
© J van der Wolf /Shutterstock.com

Hinduism

Hinduism is the third largest religion, currently constituting around 15 percent of the world's population. Scholars believe that it is more than three thousand years old. Hindus are primarily located in India and Nepal. Hinduism is less formally structured than either Christianity or Islam, and unlike many religions, it is not closely associated with a single individual (Jesus, Muhammad, etc.).

Mohandas Gandhi emphasized the peaceful, nonviolent components of Hindu thought in his mobilization of the Indian population to the cause of India's independence from British control. His emphasis on a combination of noncooperation and nonviolence became one of Gandhi's most important and lasting legacies. More recently, however, Hinduism has become the central identity component of nationalist movements in India that advocate violent struggle against other religious groups in South Asia, particularly Muslims in Pakistan. As a result, the Hindu-Muslim divide has fed the conflict between India and Pakistan over the disputed territory of Kashmir.

Buddhism

Like Hinduism, Buddhism originated in India. Unlike Hinduism, it spread far east of India: southeast to Sri Lanka and through Vietnam; east into much of China, the Korean peninsula, and as far as Japan; and northeast into Tibet and Mongolia. Around 400 million people practice Buddhism, including an increasing number of people in North America and Europe. Its political relevance comes from its emphasis on nonviolence and its encouragement of challenging authority, especially if that authority is perceived to have strayed from the path of wisdom, virtue, and discipline that Buddha emphasized.

As is the case with Confucianism, some balk at labeling Buddhism a religion because there is no focus on the worship of a creator. The religion is associated with a single individual, Siddhartha Gautama, who came to be known as the Buddha. Buddhists consider him to be a wise leader—the term *Buddha* means "enlightened one"—who came to his understandings through personal introspection rather than through intervention by God.

As a result, the centerpiece of Buddhist beliefs is not faith but self-reflective experience. Its principles (including ideas about suffering being the result of obsession with achieving one's personal desires) are less rigid and detailed than the dogma of other major religions. It is possible to practice Buddhism and still be a member of another religion; most people would consider it impossible to identify oneself simultaneously as Christian, Muslim, and/or Jewish. At the same time, the religion is more organized than Confucianism. There are formal structures (e.g., Buddhist monasteries), and adherents typically practice the religion at regular sessions that emphasize meditation and involve a group leader.

Sex/Gender

Many teachings in the world's major religions concern expectations of and relationships between men and women. The identity divide between men and women is also important in its own right. When comparativists discuss this identity division, they typically use the term *gender*. While *sex* is the appropriate term for biological differences between men and women (individuals as male or female), **gender** involves the perceived differences (masculine or feminine) that help shape the identity groups of male and female. In other words, gender differences entail supposed physical and psychological traits, expected roles, and socially acceptable behaviors. Some of the physical differences between men and women are readily apparent. More controversial, but gaining support among some biological scientists and psychologists, is the extent to which men and women process and react to information differently. Regardless of the extent to which such physical and psychological differences are real, their translation into social expectations about different types of behavior transforms them into gender differences. What a society considers masculine roles—and how rigid the boundaries are between masculine and feminine roles—can differ greatly from one country to another.

The term *gender* is also used to refer to differences in political behavior between men and women, as in the phrase "the gender gap." In the United States, women are generally less conservative than men.[10] This also appears to be the pattern in some Islamic countries, probably in part because conservative interpretations of Islam support subservient social roles for women. In many other countries, however, the gender gap takes the opposite form. In Eastern Europe and the former Soviet Union, women tend to be more conservative than men. In the postcommunist transition, women were

Gender A term that refers to social understandings of traits, roles, and behavioral differences between men and women and to differences between them in political attitudes and behavior.

hurt by social upheaval and economic reform much more than men, contributing to their suspicion of reform and preference for maintenance of the status quo.

Economic development and its accompanying social changes influence social and political attitudes among women, including their desire to participate in politics. Certain trends fed the feminist movements of the 1970s and 1980s, which generated additional opportunities for women and raised the consciousness of many women about gender relations. As more women entered the workforce, politics became more crucial to their daily lives. As educational opportunities for women improved, they gained skills necessary for effective political participation.

Gender has also become a more prominent social divide because of globalization, which has brought a greater awareness of the treatment of women around the world. The increased reach and effectiveness of international organizations such as the United Nations, for example, has placed the status of women on the international political agenda, complementing domestic pressures for women's rights. In most countries, women are much better off than they were a century ago. (The Nineteenth Amendment to the United States Constitution, which guaranteed women the right to vote, was ratified only in 1920.)

Class

Political scientists consider class divisions to be among the most important social cleavages. Class differences are a fact of life in nearly every country in the world. As discussed in Chapter 2, Karl Marx believed that understanding class divisions was essential to understanding politics. A key to Marx's predictions about the collapse of capitalism was awareness by members of the working class (the proletariat) of the extent to which the capitalist system exploited them and other members of the working class. This awareness, what Marx called "class consciousness," set the stage for the proletariat to overthrow capitalism and its allies in the political system.

Historically, class consciousness among the workers has played a role in uprisings, such as the Bolshevik Revolution in Russia in 1917. Even more, however, such uprisings involved elites leading the action in the name of the working class, or took the form of peasant uprisings not to overthrow the economic system but rather to seize land for their own use. Spontaneous uprisings among the lower classes with the goal of overthrowing the existing system have been few and far between. On the other hand, economic issues—working conditions, wages, number of hours worked per week, unemployment, and so on—have been a source of political mobilization. They spurred the widespread development of trade unions in the twentieth century, and they continue to play a role in shaping electoral results, especially in Europe.

Intrastate Regional Identity

In many countries, political attitudes and deeply held beliefs among members of the general population differ markedly depending on region, and much of the work in political science on mass attitudes in specific countries includes analyses of regional variation.[11] While differences in attitudes do not necessarily equate to differences in identity, people can develop strong attachment to the region in which they live.

For some people, this attachment develops into an important part of their identity. In the United States, for example, it is not unusual for individuals to incorporate their region of residence into their personal identity. Those who have lived in different states but in the same general region of the country for a significant portion of their lives may see themselves as southerners or midwesterners. Those who live their entire lives in a single U.S. state are more likely to adopt a state identity over a regional one (seeing themselves as a Wisconsinite or a Floridian).

Those who live in outlying regions of a country often see residents of the central region as the other, especially if the central region is home to the capital city of the country. Political science studies indicate that those living in border regions commonly believe that those in the center—and certainly those in the capital—are privileged. They see the capital as not only the seat of political power but also as the area that receives the most attention from government officials. In Canada, center-periphery relations take an interesting twist. Many residents of the province of Quebec see the province of Ontario as the privileged center. Residents of Ontario consider Quebec to be the most privileged region. For residents of Canada's western provinces (and, to a lesser extent, residents of the Maritime provinces), both Ontario and Quebec make up the privileged center. The fact that nearly every Canadian prime minister has come from Ontario or Quebec reinforces this perception.[12]

Although a regional identity is less likely to be a person's primary identity than is another identity group discussed in this section, identification with region of residence can reinforce other group identities. It is not unusual for an ethnic or religious group, for example, to be concentrated in a certain region of a country.

Transnational Regional Identity

The increasing interconnectedness among states in the international political system can also foster a form of transnational regional identity. The existence of this form of identity has been most obvious in Europe. The European Union (EU) is far ahead of any other regional organization in marshalling transnational integration among its member-states. It should not be surprising, therefore, that the EU considers the development of a strong attachment to European identity to be increasingly important.

How attached ordinary people are to such an identity, however, is another story. For the EU to succeed in its ultimate desire to create something akin to the United States in Europe, the populations of EU member-states will have to accept themselves, first and foremost, as European. In other words, European identity must become more than transnational. It must become an overarching national identity. "Europeanness" is a long way from superceding the existing national and subnational identities in Europe, but the extent to which people see themselves as European in a meaningful way does vary across the countries of Europe and among individuals in EU member-states.

Complementary and Cross-Cutting Identity Divisions

Each of the identity divisions discussed in the previous sections is noteworthy for its ability to shape political outcomes around the world. As effective as these particular group identities can be in mobilizing individuals politically, identities become even more powerful when they reinforce one another. Class divisions, for example, are less politically relevant today than in the past. When class boundaries coincide with other forms of identity (ethnic, regional, etc.), however, they can become highly salient. The other group boundaries are reinforced by the economic differences between "us" and "them." On the other hand, when an individual belongs to two or more types of identity groups that pull him or her in different directions, the ability to mobilize that individual politically using any of these identities is weakened.

Complementary Identity Divisions

Complementary Identity Divisions Identity divisions that coincide with one another for large numbers of individuals; also known as complementary or accumulative social cleavages.

Situations in which group identity boundaries coincide with one another are known as **complementary identity divisions** (sometimes called "complementary social cleavages" or "accumulative social cleavages"). Complementary divisions commonly involve ethnic minorities and majorities. Often, two ethnic groups speak different languages. They may also believe they are racially different from one another, may have different religions, and may live primarily in different regions of the country. The us-them boundaries of each form of identity—ethnic, racial, religious, and so on— correspond to and reinforce one another. The likelihood of conflict, including violent conflict, is great in cases of strong complementary identity divisions.

Spotlight on ... IRAQ

Complementary Identity Divisions in Iraq

Although the prospect that Iraq's political system would develop into a stable democracy looked more promising at the start of 2011 than it did at any point since the 2003 American-led invasion, many reasons remained for scholars of democratization to be uncertain about the future of Iraqi democracy. One reason in particular is relevant to this chapter: the presence of complementary identity divisions in Iraq. (Other reasons are discussed in more detail in Chapter 11.)

Even before the invasion of Iraq, significant tensions existed among the major identity groups: Kurds, Sunnis, and Shiites. As Figure 4.1 shows, these groups tend to be regionally concentrated. The Kurds mostly live in the northeastern quarter of the country. Other than in the area around Baghdad, where they live alongside Sunni Muslims, most of the Shiite Muslims live in the eastern and southeastern regions of Iraq. The Sunni population is concentrated in the north-central and western areas of the country.

Although other types of identity do not tend to reinforce these identity divisions further, Iraq is an example of the extent to which complementary lines between region and ethnic or religious identity can have significant political consequences. The deep social divisions posed a challenge to agreeing on a set of institutional arrangements for the new democratic system. Even after passage of the referendum on the Iraqi Constitution in October 2005, Sunni leaders continued to oppose many of its provisions. The complementary divide between region and ethno-religious groups has also been reflected in election returns, and they have consequently made forming a government after general elections difficult.

FIGURE 4.1   **Regional Concentrations of Iraq's Ethno-Religious Groups**

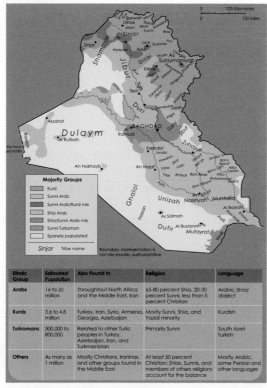

Ethnic Group	Estimated Population	Also Found In	Religion	Language
Arabs	16 to 20 million	Throughout North Africa and the Middle East, Iran	65-80 percent Shia, 20-30 percent Sunni, less than 5 percent Christian	Arabic (Iraqi dialect)
Kurds	3.6 to 4.8 million	Turkey, Iran, Syria, Armenia, Georgia, Azerbaijan	Mostly Sunni, Shia, and Yazidi minority	Kurdish
Turkomans	300,000 to 800,000	Related to other Turkic peoples in Turkey, Azerbaijan, Iran, and Turkmenistan	Primarily Sunni	South Azeri Turkish
Others	As many as 1 million	Mostly Christians, Iranians, and other groups found in the Middle East	At least 50 percent Christian: Shias, Sunnis, and members of others religions account for the balance	Mostly Arabic, some Persian and other languages

© University of Texas Libraries

Cross-Cutting Identity Divisions

At other times, group identity boundaries do not coincide with one another. Instead, the members who make up one major type of identity group are different from those who belong to another main type. Such situations are known as **cross-cutting identity divisions** (also referred to as cross-cutting social cleavages). For example, a significant portion of ethnic Ukrainians in the eastern part of Ukraine speak Russian better than they do Ukrainian. For these individuals, ethnicity and language do not complement each other. Because the major identity groups do not reinforce each other, a society with strong cross-cutting identity divisions tends to have fewer violent political conflicts than one with strong complementary identity divisions. Note that gender is almost always a cross-cutting division. It lines up with socioeconomic class, to an extent at least, in many countries around the world, but the other most politically potent forms of identity—ethnicity, race, religion, and region—are always cross-cut by the gender divide.

One can also think about how cross-cutting divisions affect a particular individual. Belonging to membership groups with different sets of members can pull an individual in different directions over major social issues and create conflicting loyalties. The competition between the collective identities weakens the ability of each of the identities to serve as a tool for getting that individual to believe or act in a particular way. For example, the religious beliefs of a group may include a strong commitment to nonviolence. At the same time, the members' ethnic group may be involved in a violent conflict with another ethnic group. In such instances, ethnic loyalty will often, but not always, win out over religious beliefs. Even so, it is unlikely that members will abandon their religion. Instead, the religious beliefs may weaken the ethnic loyalty, perhaps leading individuals only to tolerate, but not actively support, acts of violence against the other group.

Government Responses to Identity Diversity

Diversity of identity groups directly affects political outcomes like elections, but it can also lead governments to adopt policies to address the political and social challenges it poses. Governments have a significant range of options. This section focuses on racial and ethnic diversity and uses the example of a government controlled by the majority identity group and its policy alternatives in response to the presence of a sizable minority group or groups. As displayed in Figure 4.2, the variety of government options regarding an ethnically and/or racially diverse population can be laid out on a continuum from least to most accommodating to the minority groups.

Genocide

The most severe action taken against a group is to attempt to eliminate the members of the minority by killing them. When such an action is aimed at a large portion or an entire group of people, it is known as **genocide**. In the last century, genocide was used by the Turks' against Armenians during World War I, the German Nazis against Jews during World War II, the Hutus against the Tutsi in Rwanda in 1994, and the government of Sudan and government-supported militia against residents of the Sudanese region of Darfur.

FIGURE 4.2   **Possible Government Responses to Ethnic or Racial Diversity**

| Eliminate minority group identity | | Tolerate minority | | | | Cultivate minority group identity |

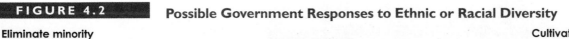

| Genocide | Ethnic cleansing | Assimilation | Integration | Accommodation | Ethno-federalism | Recognition of independence claims |

Least tolerant   **Most tolerant**

Ethnic Cleansing

One step up from genocide is **ethnic cleansing**. Ethnic cleansing campaigns can involve killing minority group members, but the government's central goal is to remove the minority from its territory rather than to eliminate the group entirely. Military or paramilitary units may be used to drive a minority across the border into another country. Ethnic cleansing is common in situations of ethnic conflict involving majority and minority groups. When the North Atlantic Treaty Organization (NATO), launched a major air campaign against the government of Yugoslavia in 1999, it argued that the military strikes were needed to stop an unfolding ethnic cleansing campaign against ethnic Albanians living in the Yugoslav region of Kosovo.

Ethnic Cleansing Efforts to remove an entire ethnic group from its territory.

Assimilation

The next step along the continuum is **assimilation**. A government policy of forced assimilation compels a minority group to abandon existing cultural characteristics and take on those of the majority group. Rather than attacking the individuals who compose the minority group in an effort to eliminate the group or force it from the state's territory, assimilation attacks the minority group's identity. Once the group's unique cultural features have been eliminated, disappearance of the group's identity is not far behind. As an example, in the early part of the twentieth century aboriginal children in Canada were forced to live in boarding schools. This intentional separation from their parents was designed to sever aboriginal cultural influences.

Assimilation A government response to identity diversity that forces a minority group to abandon its cultural characteristics and take on those of the majority group.

Integration

Less extreme than assimilation is a policy of **integration**. Integration does not seek to eliminate the minority group or its culture. Rather, the minority recognizes and accepts that the majority group will be culturally privileged in exchange for the majority's recognition of the minority's right to practice its culture. The majority's language may be the medium of instruction in schools or used in government meetings, and its religious symbols may be prominently displayed publicly. Such integration "bargains" were a centerpiece of postindependence Malaysian politics and, more recently, at the forefront of relations between the Estonian and Latvian governments and their Russian-speaking minorities.[13]

Integration An approach to managing identity diversity that allows minority groups to continue to practice their culture in exchange for accepting that the majority group's culture will be dominant.

Accommodation

The next approach is best labeled **accommodation**. Accommodation involves greater cultural freedom for members of the minority group, including a degree of cultural autonomy, as well as extensive rights or privileges for them, including the right of minority group children to attend schools in which instructors speak the minority group's language. Group privileges may include programs generally labeled "affirmative action" policies in the United States. These policies give certain preferences to members of minority groups—special treatment in hiring, quotas for certain government positions, and so on—and are often designed to address past discrimination against the minority.

Accommodation An approach to managing identity diversity that involves a degree of cultural autonomy and extensive rights or privileges for minority group members.

Ethno-federalism

The next approach along the spectrum is **ethno-federalism**. The idea behind an ethno-federal approach is to give a minority more than just cultural autonomy. The minority receives territorial autonomy with a high degree of control over a particular region. Like other forms of federalism, ethno-federal systems do not give complete power to the group to control the region in any way it sees fit, but specific powers are designated to the regional government that the central government of the country

Ethno-federalism A government response to identity diversity in which a minority receives territorial autonomy in exchange for not pursuing complete independence.

cannot take away. Ethno-federal arrangements exist in a number of countries around the world, including Belgium, Canada, and Russia.

Those who support such an approach argue that it is a way to prevent full-fledged ethnic nationalism leading to territorial secession. Ethno-federalism, however, has not had a great track record of placating minorities or of holding the state together. Chapter 1 put forward the two questions that nationalists have to answer in their pursuit of mass support for their cause: who belongs to the nation, and what territory should the nation control? By linking territory to ethnic identity and by drawing the homeland of an ethnic minority on the map, ethno-federal approaches answer both questions. It is possible that ethno-federalism will appease a disgruntled ethnic minority. It is also possible, however, that once the minority gets a taste of territorial control, it will desire to take the next step to complete independence. If so, ethno-federalism has done the nationalists' job for them by helping define the minority nation's membership and territorial boundaries.

Recognizing Independence Claims

If the minority pursues secession and the creation of an internationally recognized independent state, the majority must decide whether to accept the territorial partition of the state it presently controls. The most accommodating approach that the majority-controlled government can take is to recognize minority claims for territorial independence. Such acceptance is relatively rare, especially without a successful armed struggle by the minority or the intervention of the international community. Peaceful divorces sometimes occur, such as the relatively harmonious dismemberment of the Soviet Union in late 1991 and the dismantling of Czechoslovakia into the Czech Republic and Slovakia in 1993. More typical examples include the violent breakup of Yugoslavia, the on-and-off violence between Ethiopia and Eritrea, and the intervention of the international community to secure independence for East Timor.

Think and Discuss

What factors might lead a government to take more tolerant or less tolerant actions against ethnic, racial, or religious minorities? What strategies has the American government used in response to ethnic, racial, and religious diversity?

TOPIC IN COUNTRIES

Identity divisions, their complementary or cross-cutting nature, and government responses to them have had important effects on political outcomes across the Topic in Countries (TIC) cases. As one would expect, the particular patterns of identity divisions and the specific identity-related initiatives of governments have varied among the different cases and over time within the same case. As a result, when reading these sections, look for

- The major identity divisions in each TIC country.
- The extent to which identity divisions are complementary or cross-cutting in each of the TIC cases.
- Patterns of government responses to identity division across the cases, as well as patterns in how such responses have changed over time.
- Major theories associated with identity, discussed in this chapter's "In Theory and Practice" boxes.

The United Kingdom

Identity is a focal point of British politics. Separation from continental Europe, the territorial proximity of the main ethnic groups, and, at least among Protestants, religious commonalities have combined to aid the development of an overarching British national identity. Subnational identity divisions have an impact on political outcomes as well. Class had been the most salient division, but ethnicity and religion became more prominent in recent decades. Earlier in British history, the government engaged in forced assimilation efforts. Today, even in the aftermath of the 7/7 (July 7) terrorist acts of 2005, the government pursues integration and accommodation toward minority identity groups.

Identity Divisions

During much of the twentieth century, class cleavages were the dominant British social divisions. The divisions were typically between the middle class (executives, managers, and other white-collar workers) and the working class (skilled and unskilled manual laborers and the very poor). These class boundaries still roughly correspond to divisions in support for the two main political parties. The Conservative Party has generally had significantly greater support from the middle and lower-middle classes, while skilled and unskilled workers have supported the Labour Party, though class has become less politically salient over the last several decades.

Ethnicity and religion moved to the fore in British politics in the 1960s and 1970s. Ethnic identity divisions in the United Kingdom (UK) involve the main groups that British identity has comprised over the past couple of centuries—the English and the three Celtic groups (Scots, Irish, and Welsh)—and new immigrant populations. In the twentieth century, the main religious division in the UK was between Protestants and Roman Catholics, particularly in Northern Ireland. Over the last several decades, the issue of minority immigrant groups has become a focal point of British political discourse. The waves of immigrants from former British colonies have brought not only new ethnic identities to the UK but also religions such as Hinduism and Islam. Approximately 1.5 million Muslims and 500,000 Hindus live in the UK today.

Complementary cleavages are less prominent in the UK than in most of the other countries highlighted in this text, but they do exist and their reinforcing nature has consequences for British politics and social relations. Ethnicity and region complement each other somewhat, with English and Celtic ethnic groups concentrated in their respective regions of the country. This complementary cleavage between ethnicity and region has helped to fuel a nascent Scottish nationalism, along with a less successful nationalist movement in Wales, and it has contributed to the push to pursue the policy of "devolution," discussed in more detail in the next chapter.

Within Northern Ireland, religion and location of residence have complemented one another and have helped fuel tensions between the two sides. The Protestant population in Northern Ireland sees itself, first and foremost, as British, while Catholics maintain a stronger attachment to their Irish identity.

Like other European countries, complementary identity divisions also penetrate into politics via the issue of immigration. The newer immigrants have complementary boundaries involving ethnicity, religion, and class. As early as the 1970s, these immigrants were political targets, and anger toward them produced laws to slow immigration. The 7/7 train and bus bombings in 2005 deepened these identity divisions by bringing the presence of Muslims in the UK to the front of national consciousness.

Government Responses to Identity Diversity

In the past, the British government pursued assimilation, ethnic cleansing, and even quasi-genocidal actions against minorities. As time went on, assimilation, including the encouragement of English settlement in Scotland, gave way to integration and accommodation. Today, the British government encourages ethnic minority identity, although there is still a strong desire for ethnic and racial minorities to see themselves, first and foremost, as British.

This concern for loyalty and attachment to British identity took a more assimilationist turn following the 7/7 events. Much like in the United States after September 11, 2001, Muslims felt the need to prove their loyalty and attachment to British national identity. Some minority group leaders even proposed adopting an American-style system of hyphenated group names (Indian-British, Pakistani-British, etc.),[14] believing this would highlight the common British bond across the UK's various ethnic groups. Others feared it would weaken national British identity by drawing even more attention to subnational collective identities. Although the national government seemed open to the idea initially, the ensuing controversy stalled the proposal.

Germany

German national identity has long been defined in ethnic terms. Partly as a result, ethnic minorities have faced varying degrees of government-sponsored and society-led discrimination and even genocide, as in the case of Jews before and during World War II. Class remains somewhat important in affecting voting patterns, but the complementary nature of ethnicity and religion and their connection to issues like immigration create some of the greatest challenges for the German government today.

Identity Divisions

In the nineteenth century, romantic philosophers conceived of German identity in terms of blood or heritage as a way to compensate for the absence of natural borders and the delayed establishment of politically recognized external boundaries. The question "who is a German?" took a malignant form with the Nazi government's declaration of the *Volk* community whose membership was limited to so-called Aryans, those of German blood. Given the historical connection between ethnic and national identity, it is perhaps not surprising that ethnicity remains an important internal identity division in contemporary Germany, along with religion, class, and intrastate regional identity.

Part of the reason ethnicity remains a salient identity is the significant amount of immigration in the first decades of the Federal Republic. During the 1960s, Germany experienced a labor shortage, and the government responded by instituting a guest worker policy that attracted immigration from southern and Eastern Europe. Today 7.3 million persons, or 8.8 percent of the population, are immigrants and their descendants. At 1.8 million persons, Turks make up the largest minority group.[15]

Religious differences have been an important cleavage that has marked the country's development. Germany was the birthplace of the Protestant Reformation in the sixteenth century, and official state policy under Chancellor Otto von Bismarck in the nineteenth century sanctioned persecution of the Catholic Church. In the post–World War II period, Germany saw increased secularization. a trend evident across Europe. Today, the major religious divide in Germany is between the Christian majority and the Muslim minority.

Class has been a major cleavage in Germany since the Industrial Revolution in the nineteenth century. Class polarization was a major reason for the destruction of the Weimar democracy and the rise of Adolf Hitler. In the post–World War II period, the East German Communist regime officially oversaw a classless society, though differences in status and life chances remained, particularly between ordinary citizens and high-ranking members of the Communist Party (officially known as the Socialist Unity Party). In West Germany, widespread economic prosperity and generous welfare state policies did much to defuse class conflict. Still, the major parties of the Federal Republic continue to draw core supporters from specific classes (see Chapter 9).

Regional affiliations have long been a feature of German society. A strong sense of regional identity remains among residents of various *Länder*, especially Bavaria. In addition, the experience of living under distinct regimes for forty years left deep economic, political, and psychological imprints on western and eastern Germans, creating a wall in their minds that continues to divide Germans.

As in the UK, complementary cleavages pose less of a political threat in Germany than in some of the other TIC countries. Religious and regional identities are correlated, with Catholics concentrated in the Rhineland and the south and Protestants in the north and east, but these divisions have faded as a source of conflict. Regional and class divisions also coincide somewhat. Following unification, severe unemployment in the east created a new class divide between generally more prosperous western Germans and their poorer eastern brethren.

Today, ethnicity and religion are the major complementary cleavages. Most ethnic Germans are of Christian background, while most of the Turkish minority identifies as Muslim. Class and ethnicity also correlate among the Turkish minority. Turks are more likely to be in occupations of lower socioeconomic status and to be less educated than native Germans.

Government Responses to Identity Diversity

Government policies toward diverse identities have spanned the continuum from genocide to efforts at accommodation. During the twentieth century, Germany's citizenship law revolved around the view that German national identity was based on ethnicity. This made it difficult for immigrants and their offspring born on German soil to integrate into German society. The Nazi regime took this ethnic conception of German national identity to its extreme, defining the Volk in racial terms and engaging in the genocidal policies of the Holocaust.

After 1949, the Federal Republic sought to atone for Nazi atrocities by pursuing a generous policy toward immigrants seeking asylum from persecution in their home countries. The influx of asylum seekers in the 1990s sparked violent responses from native Germans, particularly in the east, where unemployment was rampant. Unemployed youth were attracted to extreme-right groups, which blamed immigrants for Germany's economic malaise. The violence prompted the government to tighten its asylum laws.[16] At the same time, citizenship policies remained highly restrictive, making it difficult for immigrants to integrate into German society.

A new citizenship law in place since 2000 extends citizenship to immigrant children born on German soil and provides for an easier naturalization process. Intended to help integrate the German-born offspring of earlier waves of Turkish guest workers, it has led to an increase in the number of naturalized citizens.[17] Overall, however, the effects of the new citizenship policy have been limited. Only a small portion of the immigrant population has naturalized, and Turks continue to face social exclusion on a number of fronts, as seen in high school dropout rates, low socioeconomic status, residential segregation, and low rates of intermarriage with ethnic Germans.[18] Addressing these issues requires labor market and education policies, not just changes to requirements for receiving citizenship.

India

Given India's diverse population, the degree of political and social stability it displays is a notable accomplishment. Several components of India's identity mosaic, including caste, religious, ethnic, and regional memberships, have been especially important in shaping the country's politics. The government continues to work to integrate and accommodate the less advantaged groups in society. At the same time, the government has answered demands for greater territorial autonomy inconsistently, with responses varying from repression to acceptance of new ethno-federal territorial divisions.

Identity Divisions

India's founders realized that its multidimensional diversity could not be ignored during the postindependence nation-building effort. Consequently, Indian democracy and national identity were built on the notion of unity in diversity. Though sometimes belatedly, tolerance has often trumped intolerance, and the Indian people have accepted diversity as a key feature of national character. At the same time, the periodic electoral success of the Bharatiya Janata Party (BJP), whose official ideology equates Indian identity with Hinduism, is evidence that not everyone accepts diversity as India's defining trait.

As noted in Chapter 3, each major identity group in India gives rise to elements of its own political culture and contributes in some fashion to the complexity of the composite Indian political culture. Indeed, the diversity refers principally to the numerous identities that sometimes challenge and other times reinforce national identity. The intensity, scope, and longevity of these identities vary from group to group.

The greatest identity challenges came immediately before and after independence. In the months leading up to independence, more than 450 princely states were integrated into the Indian union, but that process did not mean the immediate abandonment of the identities of those princes and states. Furthermore, the partition of India led to the movement of millions of Hindus from Pakistan to India, millions of Muslims from India to Pakistan, and the death of an estimated quarter of a million people. The partition also exacerbated the division within India between those who identified themselves as Hindu and Muslim. Both regional and religious identities have continued to influence political outcomes.

A train is set on fire during violence in November 2006 by *Dalits* ("untouchables"), who were protesting vandalism of a statue of Bhimrao Ramji Ambedkar, an Indian political leader who played a central role in drafting the constitution and was a member of the untouchable category of the caste system. © AP Photo

Many other significant identities exist as well. India has long been characterized by a **caste** system that, put simply, divides society into four groups, each of which has values and other attributes that distinguish it from the others. The caste system grew out of Hinduism, but manifestations of the hierarchy and cultural differences have affected Muslim and Christian communities in various parts of the country as well. The four main castes are the *Brahmin* (scholar-priests), *Kshatriya* (warriors), *Vaishya* (merchants), and *Sudra* (poor peasants and workers), while another group, *Dalits* (untouchables), is treated as beneath the lowest caste category. In addition, numerous *jati*, or groups, fall within these categories in different parts of India. Although the caste system has been officially outlawed, it continues to be socially and politically important.

India has been called "the most socially heterogeneous nation-state of modern times,"[19] and although its wide array of group identities guarantees that identity has an impact on political outcomes, the complexity also limits the extent to which identity boundaries coincide. Generally speaking, Indians have multiple identities at all times. Some reinforce each other; others often do not.

Religious, regional, caste, ethnic, and gender "entrepreneurs" in India have realized the importance of identity and have sought to politicize their particular identity categories. Any success they have had has often been at the local or regional level, where instances of complementary cleavages are more common. For the country as a whole,

---

Caste A hereditary identity category, primarily in Hindu society, that divides individuals based on social functions associated with each group.

the organization of broad identity movements has been hampered by the failure of identity boundaries to coincide. As comparativist Ernst Haas puts it:

> India has been saved by the fact that the divisions among its people, though numerous, are noninclusive; almost every individual belongs to more than one primary group and derives his or her identity from multiple sources. These multiple identities are not usually aggregated under a single master identity; they remain separate and separable. The result is an enormous network of cross-cutting social cleavages that inhibit the formation of super-ordinate claims to exclusive identities.[20]

Haas's use of the word *saved* highlights the importance of cross-cutting identity divisions to India's relative stability and successful experience with democracy.

Government Responses to Identity Diversity

The Indian government has responded in multiple ways to the politicization of various identities. Affirmative action has been a response to the exclusion of those who identify with, or who are identified as, a lower caste or tribe. Some seats in educational institutions and jobs with the government are reserved for Scheduled Castes (SC), Scheduled Tribes (ST), and Other Backward Classes (OBCs). Women have reserved seats in local government. Efforts have been made to reserve seats for Muslims, too. As the proportions of places being reserved for these groups have grown, some Brahmins have demanded reservations so that opportunities remain for them, and the courts have stepped in to place limits on the portion of seats and jobs that can be reserved for specific groups.

Various tools have been used to deal with the demands of regional groups. At times, the Indian government has imposed President's Rule, whereby the central government replaces the government of a federal unit. At other times, the central government and/or the government of the federal unit have provided financial and other forms of aid; have added new federal units; have created governments in separatist regions and given them limited powers; have given a variety of special privileges, such as steering government employment to indigenous people; have imprisoned regional leaders; have co-opted separatist leaders; and have used the army to suppress such movements.

Similarly, the central government has used a wide range of tools to deal with other non-national identities. From 2002 to 2007, the president of India was A. P. J. Abdul Kalam, a Muslim; in 2007, a woman, Pratibha Devisingh Patil, was selected to be president. The symbolism of these selections fostered greater national identity among Muslims and women.

Mexico

Varying estimates of Mexico's different ethnic groups complicate efforts to grasp ethnic identity's importance, while the importance of class and religion is more easily observed. Class, ethnicity, and region provide Mexico's most salient complementary identity divisions. This identity intersection has driven government initiatives regarding the indigenous population. Past efforts at assimilation have given way to more accommodating approaches since the establishment of democracy.

Identity Divisions

In large part because of its colonial experience, Mexican national identity contains a number of discordant components. It is anchored in mestizo identity, a collective identity that formed through the mixing of native and European peoples in the centuries since the Spanish conquest.[21] Advocates of a civic Mexican national identity have struggled with how to address native cultural rights, yet there is a deep pride in native Indian civilizations of the past. Like its Canadian counterpart, Mexican national identity is partially "defined by opposition to the United States,"[22] yet many Mexicans respect and even envy what they see as the affluent American lifestyle.

Between 60 and 80 percent of the Mexican population is estimated to be mestizo. As much as 30 percent of the population identifies itself as indigenous—often referred to as "Indian"—and little more than 10 percent of the population speaks indigenous languages and maintains other openly indigenous cultural markers. Most Mexicans argue that the ethno-racial divide is not nearly as sharp as in countries such as the United States. At the same time, many still associate European features with privilege, while those perceived to look indigenous (including dark-skinned mestizos) are subject to negative stereotyping and open discrimination.

Religion is more important to members of the general population in Mexico than in most of the TIC countries, and the vast majority of people are Catholic. The extent to which religion divides the population in identity terms is relative to how deeply Catholic individuals are. Mexicans' depth of attachment to religious identity affects their attitudes about the Catholic Church's role in society, and thus its role in politics.

Despite the social importance of ethnicity and religion, class is arguably the most important identity cleavage in terms of its political effects. A large portion of both the urban and rural Mexican population is poor. In the past, the one-party system prevented class divisions from driving political outcomes. In today's system, however, class lines increasingly coincide with political lines.

Regarding complementary identity divisions, region correlates with other collective identities in Mexico. The north and center of the country are much more urban and industrial than the south, which still relies heavily on agriculture. Northern economic development has fed a more individualistic capitalist spirit than is found in other parts of the country.

Region and class also complement indigenous identity. Class divisions and different levels of education between the indigenous minority and the rest of the population reinforce this identity boundary, although the presence of a large number of poor in the ethnic majority weakens the potential for class to strongly complement the ethnic cleavage. The Indian population has tended to be concentrated in the south-central and southeast of the country, with pockets in the northwest. An increasing portion of the indigenous population, however, now lives in Mexico City, joining others from the countryside who have moved there in hope of finding a better life. Due to the lingering stereotypes connected to skin color, finding such a life in Mexico City is especially difficult for dark-skinned Indians.

Government Responses to Identity Diversity

The indigenous population and its culture provide the main diversity question in Mexico. In the past, Mexico pursued assimilation, showing little concern for its Indian population. Areas in which the population did not assimilate were left to fend for themselves economically and educationally. Mexican government statistics that label a smaller portion of the population as indigenous than many scholars believe to be the case are a remnant of this approach.

Mexico's blossoming democracy seems to have bolstered the movement toward accommodation, and the erection of statues of Aztec leaders across Mexico in recent years is one sign of the government's efforts to rediscover the native past. The conflict in the region of Chiapas that began in 1994 elevated the plight of the Indians within the national consciousness and sparked a deeper attachment to indigenous identity. Following the uprising, various Indian groups formed the National Indigenous Congress (CNI). The organization became active politically, but it could not stop passage of an indigenous rights law that most indigenous groups felt set back their cause rather than improving it.

Brazil

In the absence of a strong, overarching national identity, the types of social identity discussed in this chapter have been of great significance to Brazilians. The deepest and most intractable social cleavages in Brazil are class and race. In part because of severe economic inequality (see Chapter 2), most of the Brazilian government's focus has been on addressing class differences, while lingering problems related to race have failed to generate an aggressive government response.

Identity Divisions

By the late 1800s, the Brazilian government began to see the development of an overarching national identity as an important goal.[23] By then, and even more as time went on, the demographic characteristics of the people living in Brazil, particularly the significant racial, ethnic, and regional differences within the population, made achieving this goal difficult. Instead of making it easier to develop an overarching civic national identity, the lack of shared cultural features among the population made the already-difficult task of agreeing on a set of unifying national cultural features more challenging. Consequently, although Brazil is closer to the definition of a civic nation than to an ethnic one, it continues to struggle to build a unifying civic national identity.

From its origins as a slaveholding colony, Brazilian society has been marked by profound divisions between the wealthy few and the masses of poor. As Brazil developed economically, a substantial middle class emerged, mostly in the cities. (Agriculture is still dominated by large landowners.) Nevertheless, Brazil remains one of the most unequal countries in the world, and inequality has grown over the last decade of neoliberal economic reform.

Ethnicity is another obvious cleavage. Brazil is a country of immigrants from many parts of the world, including some 25 million of Italian heritage, 10 million of German descent, and 10 million Lebanese. The Brazilian city of São Paulo has more ethnic Japanese than any city outside Japan.[24] Ethnic identity mostly finds peaceful expression in cultural communities, particularly towns or areas within a large city where immigrants of the same national origin live, and discrimination against specific groups of immigrants is rare.

Brazil is the largest Catholic country in the world, with nearly three-quarters of its population declaring themselves Catholic on the latest national census. Because of the dominance of Catholicism, religion was not historically a salient social cleavage. However, the rise of Protestant sects, mainly Pentecostals, has created a new identity cleavage. Almost 15 percent of Brazilians belong to one of Brazil's many Pentecostal churches, and their increasing numbers have made them a political force.

Race has also become more important politically over time. Brazil is a society of ex-slaves and ex-slaveholders. Today, "Brazil has more people of African descent than any country besides Nigeria."[25] Yet, people were not split by law or custom into two "races." Instead, individuals can be described by over a dozen racial terms identifying shades of skin color and facial features. The Brazilian census did not even include a question about racial identity until 1940. Today, Brazilians can identify themselves on the census as white (54 percent), brown/mixed race (39 percent), black (6.2 percent), or other (1 percent).

Most scholars now believe that Brazil's claim of "racial democracy" was a myth. Color is strongly correlated with economic and social status. Blacks have twice the unemployment rate of whites. Women and children also suffer disproportionately from poverty, unemployment, and lack of educational opportunities. The usual cause is abandonment by a husband or partner. If the woman is also black, the obstacles are even greater.

Government Responses to Identity Diversity

Because the Brazilian government did not recognize race as a salient social division until recently, past government policy could best be described as integration. No active efforts were made to force minority groups to conform to a national standard of behavior, language, or religious affiliation, as in assimilation. On the other hand, by not acknowledging racial divisions, the government failed to address very real racial discrimination and economic challenges faced by the descendants of slaves.

Brazil is only now beginning to recognize the problem. Strange though it might seem to Americans, the first affirmative action quotas in Brazil (saving places at university for students of color) were not adopted until 2003, amid huge controversy. The government of former President Lula da Silva moved more in the direction of accommodation, seeking to address programs specifically to black Brazilians. However, the dominant focus of his administration was poverty. Brazilian governments tend to classify their social policies in terms of class rather than race, even if the two categories substantially overlap. It is too early to tell whether President Dilma Rousseff's government will continue this pattern.

Nigeria

Ethnicity and religion have been the most politically important identity cleavages in Nigeria prior to and since gaining its independence from the UK. These divisions have proven to be a challenge to building an overarching Nigerian national identity. The government has shifted its identity diversity approach since independence, and contradictory approaches have sometimes overlapped.

Identity Divisions

Nigeria is one of the most ethnically heterogeneous countries in the world. Ethnic discrimination is common, including in hiring and the awarding of contracts. Nigeria has hundreds of different ethnic groups, though some of the smallest might be better described as tribes. Members of the three largest groups, the Ibo (or Igbo), Hausa-Fulani, and Yoruba, have especially strong attachments to their ethnic identity. Combined, they make up nearly two-thirds of the Nigerian population.

Like governments of many of the other multiethnic African states, the Nigerian government hoped to foster a sense of national identity to unify the population in the postcolonial period. This effort was hindered by economic difficulties (which tended to pit ethnic groups against one another), government corruption, and the decision by the postindependence government to create internal political units that reinforced the dividing lines in the population.

Over the last two decades, religion has increasingly become the topic of significant political debates in Nigeria. About half the population is Muslim, around 40 percent is Christian, and about 10 percent practices traditional indigenous religions or no religion. Hostilities between Muslims and Christians have revolved around the presence of foreign Christian missionaries and the adoption of Sharia in Muslim regions of the country. (Chapter 7 contains a more detailed discussion of the structure of Nigeria's legal system, including the implementation of Sharia in the north.) Local political elites have intentionally exacerbated religious tensions in an effort to mobilize supporters.

Comparativists interested in the topic of identity, particularly the way complementary social cleavages pose challenges to governments, have studied the Nigerian experience extensively and have analyzed the events leading up to the outbreak of the Nigerian civil war in 1967. Their research points to the consistency of the Nigerian events with cleavage structure theory's assertion that complementary social cleavages are politically destabilizing (see the "In Theory and Practice" box on Russia later in this chapter). The Nigerian experience shows how ethno-federalism can increase the political importance of ethnicity, encourage ethnic nationalism, and help spark violence. Because nationalism unites identity and territory, internal political boundary designs that also involve both identity and territory risk fanning nationalist sentiments.

Nigeria's struggles to develop a clear multiethnic national identity that cultivates mass attachment relates to the complementary nature of its identity divisions. Nigerians are citizens of Nigeria regardless of their ethnic background. The challenge is how to get ordinary Nigerians to accept this identity and place it at the top of their collective identity loyalty hierarchy. These difficulties stem from deep complementary cleavages, divisions that are more robust in Nigeria than in any of the other TIC countries.

Ethnicity and region are strongly complementary, a feature that has existed since long before independence. Members of the Hausa-Fulani are concentrated in the north; Ibo tend to live in the southeast; Yoruba generally live in the southwest. Religion reinforces these ethnic divides, since the Hausa-Fulani are generally Muslims, while large portions of the other two groups are Christians.

Government Responses to Identity Diversity

The Nigerian government undid the ethno-federal approach after the Nigerian civil war of the late 1960s and actively tried to develop attachment to an overarching Nigerian identity, moving in a less tolerant direction on the spectrum of policy options discussed earlier in the chapter. On the other hand, assimilation was impossible because no single ethnic group made up the vast majority of the population, and the government (civilian and military alike) feared minorities' perceptions that it did not respect their cultural practices. As President Olusegun Obasanjo pointed out in his farewell address in May 2007, the government stressed harmony and unity rather than uniformity.

Because of its prominence as a form of collective identity, religion has been at the center of Nigerian government action. At times, the government has tried to make religion less visible, including by means of a lightly enforced ban on published religious advertisements and control over religious television and radio programming. At other times, the government has supported religious expression, lifting its restrictions on religious programming and accepting the injection of religion into regional and local politics. Although the Nigerian constitution prohibits lower levels of government from establishing official religions in their regions, Muslim parts of the country are allowed to implement Sharia through local laws and a Sharia-based court system. Regional governments in Nigeria's north noticeably increased their use of Sharia following the reestablishment of democracy in 1999. The Sharia question highlights one of the difficulties that governments of diverse countries face: accommodating the culture of a minority may require tolerating practices that appear highly intolerant.

Russia

Like Brazil, Russia's ethnic diversity has led to dissonant views of Russian national identity and incongruent nation-building efforts. Nearly all the major identity cleavages discussed in this chapter are important in Russia. Partly due to Russia's ethno-federal arrangements, complementary identity divisions are most evident between ethnicity and region. The government's responses to identity diversity have changed over time, from efforts at assimilation in the past to a collection of policies with differing benefits to minority identity groups.

Identity Divisions

The topic of Russian national identity has been the focus of intellectuals and government officials in Russia for centuries.[26] Many Russian nationalists, including those in the pre-Soviet period, have emphasized an ethnic national identity. In this vision, ethnic Russians (*russkie*) form the nation's membership boundaries, whether they live in Russia or not. Alternatively, other nationalists and most Russian government officials have sought a more civic form of national identity encompassing Russia's minorities. In this variant, citizens of Russia (*rossiiskie*) constitute the nation.

Class divisions in Russia have become increasingly important since the collapse of the Communist system. During the Soviet period, class was not a central identity division, although Communist Party members—especially those at the top—lived like the upper classes of non-Communist countries. Today, there is a visible rich class, particularly in the largest cities.

Religion is also an important basis of collective identity, particularly since the collapse of the Soviet Union. In the pre-Soviet era, the Russian Orthodox Church was strongly connected to the tsarist state. Although the Orthodox Church and the Soviet government had, to put it mildly, an uneasy relationship, the post-Soviet Russian government has passed laws that privilege long-established religions such as Orthodox Christianity. The second largest religious group is Muslims, who make up as much as 15 percent of the population.[27] A number of high profile incidents across Russia, including the September 2004 attack by Islamic terrorists on the Beslan school in an autonomous republic of the Russian Federation, have led ordinary Russians and even the government itself to rashly link the country's Muslim minorities to terrorism.

As important as class and religion are, they remain less central to Russian politics than ethnicity. Ethnic cleavages had a significant effect on politics before the collapse of the Soviet Union, and their importance in contemporary Russia is one of the many enduring legacies of the Soviet period. Although officially a state based on Marxist principles, the Soviets emphasized ethnic identity by creating written languages for ethnic minorities that did not have them and including ethnic identity in people's internal "passports"—identity documents that the government gave Soviet citizens. Today, around 80 percent of Russia's population is ethnically Russian. The country's minorities tend to be concentrated in certain parts of the country, especially along Russia's long southern border.

Complementary identity divisions are limited somewhat by the frequency of interethnic marriage, particularly between ethnic Russians and members of non-Russian ethnic minorities. In addition, class divisions only recently solidified in a way that can complement ethnic identity. But coinciding divisions along ethnic, religious, and regional lines are still conspicuous, with race also playing a role in deepening the ethnic divide. Most ethnic Russians are Orthodox Christians, while many ethnic minorities belong to other faiths.

Russia's federal system—inherited from the Soviets—includes many regions named for ethnic minorities and considered the groups' homelands within Russia. These regions make up a majority of the Russian territory, though they contain less than 20 percent of its population. The effects of this territorialization of ethnicity are muted in many regions of Russia, however, by the presence of large numbers of ethnic Russians living in them.

By the first decade of the twenty-first century, Chechens, the group that the Russian region of Chechnya is named after, had become Russia's most discriminated-against group. The Chechens exemplify the way ethnic identity can be tied to perceptions of race. Chechens and other Muslim minorities from the southern part of Russia are generally darker skinned than ethnic Russians from regions like Moscow and St. Petersburg. Many Russians consider them to be "black," even though they look little like groups labeled black in other countries.

Other minorities, such as those from the far east of Russia, have strongly Asian features. In this case, however, race is as much cross-cutting as complementary to ethnicity. Intermarriage over the last two centuries has meant that many ethnic Russians, particularly outside of the northwest (European) part of the country, share Asian features with the ethnic minorities.

IN THEORY AND PRACTICE

Cleavage Structure Theory and Russia

Cleavage structure theory emphasizes identity complexity within a society, using the extent to which the population is divided into complementary instead of cross-cutting identity groups to explain political outcomes. The theory maintains that the role of identity as a political force is heightened when identity divisions complement one another. Majorities and minorities become "permanent." When identities cross-cut one another, identity is much less salient, and political elites have a harder time using group identities to mobilize people for political activities or in support of particular policies.

Arend Lijphart is one of a number of comparativists who have used cleavage structure theory to study democracy in societies with sharp social divisions.[28] According to Lijphart, cross-cutting divisions facilitate democracy. Since no permanent minorities exist, it is unlikely that any individual will always be on the losing side of votes using a majority rule mechanism. By contrast, identity traits of the candidates can drive electoral results far more than the candidates' policy positions in societies with sharp complementary identity cleavages. As Donald Horowitz so eloquently puts it, in such settings an election becomes a census.[29]

Cleavage structure theory can help explain tensions between ethnic groups and even drives by one or more groups to secede from the state in which they reside. The Russian Federation faced both kinds of situations after 1991. If cleavage structure theory is correct, relations with the ethnic Russian population and government should be more strained for groups with complementary divisions that make them highly distinct from ethnic Russians. One way to examine this possibility is to look at two groups, Chechens and Tatars, who share many features (e.g., both practice Islam) but differ in the extent to which their identity divisions complement one another and create a sharp us-them division between the group and ethnic Russians. Political scientist Elizabeth Fromberg made precisely this comparison when seeking to understand why the Russian government negotiated a treaty on autonomy with Tatarstan but took military action against Chechnya. The resulting violence within Chechnya and by Chechens in other parts of Russia became one of the central issues of post-Soviet Russian politics. Fromberg hints that the leaders involved and their calculations in deciding what actions to take (addressed in this book in Chapter 10) played important roles in the different outcomes, but argues that the central reason is the sharper, more complementary identity divisions between Chechens and Russians than between Tatars and Russians.[30]

The Chechens came under Russian control in the middle 1800s, after a fierce decades-long fight against the expansion of the Russian Empire into their territory. They tended not to intermarry with Russians over the next century and a half and resisted assimilation, thus maintaining a strong sense of themselves as ethnically different from Russians. Chechens made up 70 percent of the population of Chechnya in the 1990s. The Tatars and Russians have a longer relationship—from the 1500s to the present—that includes significant intermarriage. Tatars were open to assimilation, with many Tatars adopting the Russian language. Those who practiced religion tended to maintain their Islamic identity but were more secular than other Muslims.[31] Tatars and Russians were also more evenly split within Tatarstan in the first post-Soviet decade, representing 48 percent and 43 percent of the population, respectively).[32] In other words, regional divisions complemented the Chechen-Russian identity boundary to a greater extent than the boundary between Tatars and Russians. With Chechens also having a worse socioeconomic standing than the Tatars (making them even less similar to the Russians),[33] cleavage structure theory appears to provide a compelling story about relations between Russians and the Tatar and Chechen minorities within the Russian Federation.

Government Responses to Identity Diversity

Government officials deciding how to address Russia's ethnic and religious diversity face the problem of multiple ideas of what it means to be Russian. In the

---

Cleavage Structure Theory An approach that explains political outcomes, including violence and democratic stability, by the extent to which identities are cross-cutting or complementary.

past, an ethnic conception of national identity existed alongside an openness to ethnic assimilation. Some Jews chose to become Russians by converting to Orthodox Christianity; members of other minority groups learned to speak Russian, adopted Russian customs, and changed their last names to make them sound Russian. The tsarist government encouraged such behavior and even engaged in forced assimilation at times by, among other things, banning non-Russian languages from being spoken publicly in parts of the empire. The Soviets also encouraged non-Russians to learn Russian, while accommodating minority cultures to a large degree. Since the Soviet Union's breakup, the Russian government has pursued a mixed bag of diversity-related policies. The Russian ethno-federal system has been maintained, for example, but other policies favor ethnic Russians. Police often target ethnic minorities, especially those living in large cities outside their home republics, such as Chechens in Moscow.

China

The combination of ethnic diversity and the concentration of minority groups in China's periphery has made an overarching Chinese national identity difficult to establish. Like Russia, China is a country with new class divisions, a renewed emphasis on religion following the abandonment of Marxist ideology, and regionally concentrated ethnic minorities. The central complementary cleavage in China is between ethnicity and region. In response to its identity divisions, the Chinese government has engaged in a balancing act between integration and accommodation on the one hand and repression of ethnic minorities on the other.

Identity Divisions

China has the oldest recorded continuous history of any civilization, and the Chinese are proud of their long history. While the Chinese government has encouraged this kind of outward-looking national pride, the Communist government is concerned about nationalism by China's minorities, many of which see themselves as distinct nations deserving control of their own territory. Three regions, Taiwan, Tibet, and Xinjiang, have particularly been the focus of the Chinese government and the international community. Of the three, Taiwan is the biggest concern to international observers due to the potential for a large-scale military conflict between the Chinese government and the American-supplied Taiwanese government.

Class is a growing identity cleavage in many parts of the country. China's embrace of capitalism has brought significant wealth over the last several decades, but this wealth has been far from evenly distributed. A new, prosperous middle class has emerged alongside a small upper class. The majority of the population, however, remains poor by international standards. As in Russia, many of the poor resent the newly wealthy and perceive them as a symbol of widespread corruption.

China's emphasis on materialism, focus on economic development, and increasing interconnections with countries across the globe have produced a sense of loss in many Chinese. Like Russians, they face chaotic social problems in an ideological vacuum. In response, some have turned to religion, rediscovering traditional spiritual and cultural beliefs such as Confucianism with its blueprint for an orderly society. An estimated 100 million practice Buddhism, and some have turned to Christianity. The government has tried to control religion, not so much because of its ideological opposition to religion as because of fear of religious groups' ability to mobilize the population against state policies and officials. The government officially recognizes a number of groups, but it has had difficulty preventing groups it does not officially recognize from practicing their religions.

While class and religious divisions pose difficulties for the Chinese government, ethnicity arguably remains its greatest challenge. The government recognizes more than fifty different ethnic groups. The vast majority of the population is Han Chinese, a category that encompasses significant linguistic and cultural variation. Ethnic minorities do not make up a large percentage of China's overall population, but with that population approaching 1.5 billion, small percentages translate into large numbers. If these roughly 100 million members of China's ethnic minorities had their own country, for example, it would be one of the fifteen most populated countries in the world. China's minorities tend to be concentrated in border areas.

In the west of China, relatively small ethnic groups make up the majority of some regions' population. This is most obvious is the Xinjiang Uighur Autonomous Region, a huge area bordering India, Pakistan, Kyrgyzstan, Kazakhstan, Russia, and Mongolia. A large portion of its people is ethnic Uighur, a Turkic-speaking group that is primarily Muslim. Nearly all Uighurs in China live in Xinjiang. Like Chechnya in Russia, the combination of Islam and acts of violence has prompted the central government to label Uighur nationalists as Muslim terrorists.

Although class does not strongly reinforce ethno-regional divides, minorities believe that they are discriminated against economically. Economic development has altered their ways of life, partly due to increasing numbers of Han Chinese workers settling in the outlying regions, and the minorities feel they have gained little economically. Uighurs in Xinjiang, for example, perceive the increasing presence of Han Chinese in their region as disrupting their culture and argue that Han control the best jobs and ultimately send this wealth out of the region.[34] Such perceptions about economic neglect and the concentration of economic benefits in the hands of the Han Chinese fuel desires for greater autonomy and even independence.

Government Responses to Identity Diversity

Historically, the Chinese government has been suspicious of ethnic minority groups. The Chinese have often perceived such groups as not only different but also inferior. Assimilation was consequently less of a priority for the Chinese rulers than for the Russian tsars, since by definition it would have meant diluting the cultural supremacy of the Han Chinese. Yet, the Communists have not completely neglected their minorities. For example, the government has linked ethnic identity and territory by designating five regions and dozens of smaller areas as autonomous territories.[35] By emphasizing the unique cultures that make the minorities "others," the government reinforces the image of Han Chinese as a single, unified ethnic group.

At the same time, the government has shown concern over the potential for ethnic identity to turn into ethnic separatism, especially in oil-rich western provinces such as the Xinjiang region. The Communist government has restricted open expressions of Islamic faith in Xinjiang. It has prohibited traditional Muslim dress, the teaching of Islam to children, and even public prayer during Ramadan. Chinese police routinely harass Muslim clerics. These policies have made the practice of Islam less visible but have increased its standing as a centerpiece of Uighur identity.

IN THEORY AND PRACTICE

Primordialism, Constructivism, and Identity in China

The question of where identity comes from is the source of a major divide in the study of identity. The different positions can generally be grouped into two rival theoretical perspectives. The first approach, which social scientists label **primordialism**, holds that collective identity divisions are based on deep-rooted features (blood ties, physical appearance, etc.) that lead us-them identity boundaries to form naturally and that have divided people for thousands of years. While many scholars today criticize the primordial approach, it had supporters within the scholarly community.[36] Recently, the strongest support for the primordial view of identity has come from the media and government

officials. Reporters and pundits are fond of primordial explanations because their unnuanced nature about a given identity conflict allows them to keep the story simple: "These groups hate each other today as they always have." Government officials like primordialism because it releases them from having to address identity conflicts in their own country or other countries around the world: "If they just hate each other, what can we do?"

The counter to primordialism is **constructivism**. This approach argues that identity is a social construction. While there are several strands of constructivism, cultural anthropologist John Comaroff argues that all share the idea that social identities "are products of human agency."[37] In other words, how people define each other as us or them—including what identity markers are emphasized—is not natural. It is the product of conscious effort by elites to label individual members of society and make those labels socially and politically important, and it can be quite fluid.

Between the primordial and constructivist extremes is a theoretical position that Ronald G. Suny, a specialist on ethnic and national identity in the former Soviet Union, has called the "**radical middle position**."[38] It is a middle ground position because it accepts parts of both primordialism and constructivism. It acknowledges that identities are socially constructed, but it also recognizes that elites engaged in such "construction projects" have a limited range of options. This perspective is called radical because it deviates from the extreme constructivism that dominated disciplines such as sociology at the end of the twentieth century.

Although research from psychology supports the idea that humans have a natural tendency to divide themselves into groups and place importance on these groups, scholars seeking to understand identity have been hostile to a purely primordialist approach that emphasizes collective identities as natural and downplays the role of social construction of identity. China is the oldest civilization still in existence. As such, one might expect primordialism to explain Chinese identity divisions well. On the other hand, if primordialism fails to explain the political relevance of identity in the Chinese case, it would seriously call into question the general usefulness of the theory.

After taking power in China, the Communists sent researchers across the country to determine which groups should be officially recognized as ethnic minorities. Although

---

Primordialism A theoretical approach that maintains that identity divisions are based on deep-rooted features (blood ties, physical appearance, etc.) that have naturally divided people throughout history.

Constructivism A theoretical approach that maintains that identity divisions are not natural but rather are the product of elite efforts to define individuals as falling into different identity groups and to make such divisions politically relevant.

Radical Middle Position A theoretical approach that incorporates elements of constructivism and primordialism, accepting that social and political elites play a central role in creating and triggering identity while highlighting the way in which historical events and existing circumstances constrain such efforts.

more than four hundred groups applied for such recognition, only forty-one (later expanded to fifty-five) were granted it. Most of those that did not receive recognition were lumped into the Han Chinese category.[39] In addition, the government worked to highlight unifying features of the Han and supported the widespread use of Standard Mandarin (the Beijing dialect of the Mandarin language).

The process involved in the government's official sanctioning of some ethnic groups is more consistent with constructivism than with primordialism. On the other hand, the attempts to culturally and linguistically homogenize the Han Chinese have been far from successful, providing some support for primordialism. If anything, linguistic differences have deepened in recent years.[40] As with many other cases of the emergence and maintenance of identity, Chinese elites have played a significant role in the construction of ethnic identities but have been unable to create identities in any way they choose. The Chinese case supports neither a pure constructivist nor a pure primordialist theoretical approach but instead seems best explained by the radical middle position between primordialism and constructivism.

Iran

Iranian national identity is deeper and more coherent than most national identities in the Middle East. The divide between Iranians with a strong attachment to traditional Islamic teaching and practice and those who desire a more secular society drives Iran's religiously dominated political discourse. Ethnic and gender divides are also evident. Complementary identity divisions include region and ethnicity, though the intersection of age, education, and urban residency has important political implications. The Iranian government's response to ethnic and religious diversity has included significant discrimination, principally against minority religions.

Identity Divisions

The Iranian population is both aware and proud of its national culture.[41] This is due in part to the long history of the Persian people (the largest ethnic group in Iran). Like China, Iran is home to one of the world's oldest civilizations; the earliest Persians appeared in the area of modern-day Iran as long as four thousand years ago. Nonetheless, tensions in Iranian national identity abound. Prior to the Islamic Revolution, efforts to unify the population behind an overarching national identity incorporated a secular, modernizing focus similar to nation-building in Turkey. Since 1979, Shia Islam has moved to the front and center of nation-building efforts.

Government institutions and policy decisions reflect the dominant religion in the Islamic Republic of Iran. Human rights groups and the U.S. government have frequently reported poor treatment of religious minorities, including Sunni Muslims, Jews, and Christians. Jews and Christians make up well under 1 percent of the population, but Sunni Muslims may be as much as 10 percent.

Because Iran is 99 percent Muslim, casual observers often fail to appreciate its degree of ethnic diversity. Persians make up a slim majority of the population. Azeris form as much as one-fourth of it. They are the majority ethnic group of Azerbaijan, a country neighboring Iran to the north.[42] Fewer in number, making up around 8 percent of the population, ethnic Kurds are an ongoing source of concern for the Iranian government.

Tensions related to gender have also become conspicuous. The Iranian government has pursued more conservative policies regarding the status of women in recent years, and many women who support political and social reform in the country have openly protested. The intersection of religion and gender is likely to remain a central issue in Iranian politics in the years ahead.

Complementary identity divisions are less notable in Iran than in a case like Nigeria, but they are still important. The main complementary division in Iran involves ethnicity and region. Kurds are concentrated in two regions, with one group in the northwest along the border with Iraq and the other in the north near the border with Azerbaijan. Likewise, the large Azeri minority tends to be concentrated in Iran's north. The regional concentration of these minority groups has been a concern for the Iranian government, which fears that the groups' ethnic identities may develop into ethnic nationalism.

Although this chapter has not discussed age and type of locality as forms of identity, attachment to religion in Iran varies significantly by age and by residence in a large urban area or elsewhere. The strongest supporters of former Iranian President Khatami's efforts at social and political reforms were young urban women.

IN THEORY AND PRACTICE

Feminist Theory and Iran

A number of theoretical perspectives related to identity highlight specific group identities. The most prominent is

> **"Did You Know?"**
> Nearly every major capital city in the world has a Sunni mosque. Tehran does not. The lack of a Sunni mosque is a point of contention between Shiites and Sunnis in Iran. The U.S. State Department and various international organizations estimate that as many as one million Sunnis live in and around Tehran.

feminist theory, which focuses on the status of women in society and within the political process. It is based on the assumption that the structure of society, which in many cases involves male domination of economic, social, and political institutions, is perpetuated by the society's positive view of masculine traits. Feminist comparativists are also concerned with how comparative politics studies feminist issues. In *Theorizing Feminist Policy*, for example, political scientist Amy Mazur lays out a framework for studying government policies from a feminist perspective. She proposes several components to what she calls "feminist comparative policy" research, including a renewed focus on patriarchal state structures and the use of gender as an analysis category.[43]

Acceptance of feminist theory suffers somewhat from its prescriptive nature, in which empirical claims (e.g., pay disparities between men and women) and normative appeals (the need for greater equality) at times become closely intertwined. Rather than objectively testing the assumptions of the theory, empirical feminist research sometimes finds anecdotal examples that support the theory's contentions.[44] Feminism also suffers from what it highlights: the continued presence of males in many of the positions of power within the political science discipline. Although this is changing fairly rapidly, the pace in political science has been slower than in most other social sciences.

Iran reflects feminism's central contentions better than most other countries. A large portion of society and an even larger portion of government officials see women as second-class citizens. To many westerners, the idea that girls can be forced to marry as young as age nine—often to men three or four times their age—is shocking. The ongoing clash between traditional ultraconservative norms and desires for a more modern society is perhaps most evident in terms of the social and political status of women.

At least among the middle class, the Iranian gender gap in attitudes is much like it is in the United States, with women more likely than men to oppose conservative government officials. The conservative trend of the early 2000s troubled many Iranian women—especially better educated women in the capital city of Tehran. They had seen Ahmadinejad firsthand when he was mayor of the city prior to his victory in the presidential election, and they may have anticipated what would come next. Shortly after taking office, Ahmadinejad encouraged local officials and the national government to curtail women's rights. Proposed policies included segregated walkways and, in some cities at least, the creation of separate parks for men and women.

Even before Ahmadinejad's election, it had become clear that Iran's reestablishment of strongly conservative social views on gender roles was a dangerous tightrope act. On June 12, 2005, days before the presidential election, thousands of women engaged in a sit-in at the University of Tehran to protest the government's increasingly hardline positions on gender and specific provisions in the Iranian constitution that justified discrimination against women.

The government's attempt to turn back the clock on women's rights may strengthen gender as a form of identity. Whether this will radicalize a substantial number of women enough to risk their personal safety by pushing back against the Iranian government is difficult to predict. The example of Afghanistan under the Taliban is not encouraging. Either way, insights from feminist theory can help explain what underlies the conditions facing Iranian women. Mazur's proposed framework for studying government policies from a feminist perspective seems especially relevant. It is hard to imagine understanding Iranian domestic politics without focusing on issues like the patriarchal state structures and using gender—the social and governmental views of "masculine" and "feminine" traits—as a category of analysis.

Think and Discuss

In your opinion, which theory related to identity presented in this chapter's "In Theory and Practice" boxes is most convincing? Why?

Government Responses to Identity Diversity

Unlike the case in many countries in the world, Iran's constitution specifies an official religion, Shiite Islam. The government officially recognizes certain religious minorities; Jews, Christians, and Zoroastrians have a small number of reserved seats in the *Majles* (Iran's national assembly). Discrimination against these groups and others is common. The election of President Mahmoud Ahmadinejad and his subsequent anti-Israel statements did not bode well for Jews in Iran. Iran's religious police monitor Christian churches, though probably less to intimidate the Christian believers than to prevent Muslims from entering the churches and potentially converting to Christianity.

Ethnic minorities arguably face less government discrimination than do religious minorities, although the government carefully monitors groups that are large and concentrated enough to develop nationalist movements. The Azeris and Kurds are two such groups. Both have at least limited contacts with their ethnic cohorts in neighboring countries. The international community has increasingly taken note of the fate of the Kurds over the last two decades, and a violent crackdown against Kurdish activists in the west of Iran in 2005 drew international criticism.[45] Kurdish leaders were again targeted following the uprisings in Iran in 2009, and a number were executed following hastily conducted trials.

Feminist Theory An approach that focuses on the importance of gender, the actions of men and women in positions of power, and obstacles facing women in achieving economic, social, and political equality.

COUNTRY SUMMARY

TIC Country	Most Politically Important Identity Types	Complementary Identity Divisions	Government Responses to Identity Diversity
The United Kingdom	Formerly class; today ethnicity and religion	Ethnicity and region; ethnicity and religion; less central than in some TIC cases	Assimilation in the past; integration and accommodation today
Germany	Formerly class; today ethnicity and religion	Ethnicity and religion; less central than in some TIC cases	Genocide under the Nazis; integration and accommodation today
India	Religion and caste	Less central than in some TIC cases; when present, typically at the regional level more than nationally	Attempts to integrate previously discriminated against groups; mixed response to autonomy/independence claims
Mexico	Class, ethnicity, and religion	Ethnicity, region, and class	Assimilation in the past; integration and accommodation at present
Brazil	Class, race, and religion	Class and race	Programs designed to target the class divide; less focus on addressing racial discrimination
Nigeria	Ethnicity, religion, and region	Ethnicity, religion, and region	Initial ethno-federal approach abandoned; integration and accommodation today
Russia	Increasing class divisions, ethnicity, and religion	Ethnicity and region; ethnicity and religion for Muslim minorities; ITAP feature on cleavage structure theory	Forced assimilation efforts in the past; mixed set of policies today
China	Increasing class divisions, ethnicity, and religion	In some cases, ethnicity and region or even ethnicity, region, and religion	Suspicion of regionally concentrated minority groups due to fear of minority nationalism; ITAP feature on primordialism, constructivism, and the "radical middle position"
Iran	Religion (Shiite vs. Sunni), ethnicity, gender; ITAP feature on feminism	Ethnicity and region (Azeris and Kurds); intersection of age, education, and urban residence has political consequences	Repression of minority religions; targeting of Kurdish population and arrest of Kurdish leaders

Spotlight on . . . Country	Most Politically Important Identity Types	Complementary Identity Divisions	Government Responses to Identity Diversity
France	Focus on universalism limits appeals to subnational identity; but ethnicity and religion remain important identity divides	Religion and ethnicity (especially among Muslim residents); class and ethnicity (particularly for immigrant minority groups)	Emphasis on secularism drives government repression of public expression of religion
Iraq	Ethnicity, religion, and region	Ethnicity and region (especially for Kurds); religion and region (between Sunni Muslims and Shiite Muslims)	History of repression and even genocidal actions; efforts at accommodation today; three majority Kurdish governorates (provinces) make up the Kurdistan Region, led by the Kurdistan Regional Government
South Africa	Race, ethnicity, and gender	Race and class (though less today than under apartheid); ethnicity and language; ethnicity and region	Apartheid system legalized racial segregation and discrimination; postapartheid accommodation policies focusing on affirmative action; government recognition of eleven official languages

TIC Wrap-Up

In the United Kingdom and Germany, the salience of particular identities has shifted from a focus on class to a focus on ethnicity and religion. In India, the Hindu-Muslim divide has been central from before the partition that separated Pakistan from India to the present time. The case of India also adds the complex identity category of caste into the mix. Complementary identity divisions are less prevalent and play a less central role in shaping political outcomes in the UK, Germany, and India than in many other TIC cases. In both the UK and Germany, immigration has created new complementary boundaries between ethnic and religious groups. In India, the mix of disparate identities generates cross-cutting rather than complementary identity divisions for the most part, with instances of complementary divisions confined mostly to the regional level.

Across their histories, government responses to diversity in the UK, Germany, and India have differed sharply. For the most part, the approaches have evolved in a more accommodating direction. This is most evident in the case of Germany following the Nazi period. However, the treatment of minority immigrant groups—particularly Muslim minorities—remains an area of controversy in all three states. This issue in the UK and Germany represents a broader pattern across Europe, where the continent's Christian and largely secular majority struggles to come to terms with the religious practices and notable religious differences of Muslim residents. With independence, India took steps to address its caste system and created affirmative action programs for other traditionally underprivileged groups. At the same time, India has sometimes taken harsh measures against groups, particularly when the government perceives that the groups' desire for greater control over their own affairs threatens the country's territorial integrity and fragile national unity.

As in the European TIC cases, ethnicity has important effects on political outcomes in Mexico, Brazil, and Nigeria. Much more than in the UK and Germany, however, class remains a notable divide in Mexico and Brazil, with other collective identities like religion also playing consequential roles at times. In Nigeria, the religious divide is primarily between Muslims, who live mostly in the north of the country, and Christians. In both Mexico and Brazil, class divisions complement other identities, including regional, ethnic, racial, and gender. Members of indigenous groups in Mexico, for example, are dramatically poorer than members of the nonindigenous population. In Brazil, color and class have a strong correspondence. The main ethnic groups in Nigeria are regionally concentrated, with the religious divide between Muslims and Christians deepening the identity divisions further.

As in many countries, the approach to ethnic diversity in Mexico, Brazil, and Nigeria has varied over time. In Mexico and Brazil, there has been greater emphasis on more tolerant approaches. In Mexico, this has meant moving from an emphasis on assimilation to more acceptance of the accommodation of identity differences. In Brazil, the past nonrecognition of race as an identity category has given way to identity programs designed to make up for previous and ongoing discrimination. The pattern in Nigeria is more complicated. Nigeria initially pursued an ethno-federal approach, though it abandoned that arrangement after it became clear that reinforcing ethnic identity with internal territorial divisions was a recipe for the collapse of the newly independent state. At the same time, it has rejected any idea of assimilating the various ethnic groups into a single identity, leaning more toward accommodation under an India-style theme of unity in diversity.

Russia, China, and Iran all face a multitude of identity divisions. In China and Russia, class divisions and, to a lesser extent, religion, have emerged as identity factors over the last two decades. In Iran, the divide between different groups of Muslims (such as between the majority Shiite and the much smaller Sunni populations, as well as between the more fundamentalist believers and more secular ones) has become increasingly salient. Gender is also an important identity issue as women struggle to gain social and political equality in Iran. Complementary identity divisions exist in Russia and China, though not as sharply as in some countries. In Russia, there is some correspondence between ethnic identity and region and, in parts of the country, between ethnic identity and religion. In China, ethnicity, region, and religion correspond in some cases, most starkly in the case of the ethnic Uighurs, a Muslim minority concentrated in the Xinjiang region. In Iran, region and ethnicity correspond as well, causing the government to be concerned about the potential for ethnic Kurds and Azeris to develop nationalist aspirations.

Russia and China have struggled to develop a national identity that unites their many subnational identity groups. National identity in Russia is more nuanced and puzzling than in most other countries. As a result, policies aimed at addressing ethnic diversity have at times appeared to lack direction, with approaches varying from repression and assimilation to accommodation and ethno-federalism. Compared with Russia, China has viewed the idea of cultivating, or even accommodating, ethnic and religious diversity with considerable suspicion. Likewise, the Iranian government has often chosen to repress minority identities rather than accommodate them. These actions are more visible against religious minorities than ethnic ones, but even ethnic minorities have faced pressure to conform socially and support the regime politically.

Research in Context

Because of its potential impact on major social and political outcomes, identity is a central topic of social science research generally, and of comparative politics research in particular. Although past studies of identity politics tended to emphasize the power and repressive nature of the state and, correspondingly, the weak and repressed nature of identity groups, scholars have increasingly come to see identity groups as potentially potent political actors. Often employing case studies of particular countries, such research shows how identity groups challenge democracies and non-democracies alike with their ability to articulate demands and mobilize people in support of them.

Identity Politics in Turkey

Turkey is one of the most interesting present-day countries for scholars interested in identity. From its evolving relationship between Islam and the state, to ongoing tensions over ethnic minorities, to its thorny pursuit of EU membership, the country displays many of the major concepts involving identity presented in this chapter. A recent article by Gokhan Bacik, an international relations professor at Zirve University in Turkey, tackles the question of Turkish identity politics head on.[46]

Bacik's study highlights the extent to which understanding identity politics in a country like Turkey involves examining multiple factors. Not only does he focus on actions of, opportunities for, and constraints on the state, but he also focuses on the actions of various identity groups. Conceptualizing identity groups as interest-seeking, he pays particular attention to their interaction with the Turkish government. He argues that the interest-seeking groups form a "second axis" of identity politics that emerged in the late 1990s, around the same time Turkey began to take seriously its pursuit of EU membership.

One of the more interesting parts of Bacik's article discusses the relationship between Turkey and Armenia. This relationship remains tense for a number of reasons, but the predominant one is the ongoing debate about the Armenian genocide, the killing of an estimated 1 to 1.5 million Armenians living in Turkey during and immediately after World War I. Because the Turkish state has long denied the Armenian genocide (even Bacik refers to it as the "so-called Armenian Massacre"), the Turkish government's ability to reach out to its Armenian population, or to the government in neighboring Armenia, has been limited. However, Bacik recounts how the 2007 assassination of a leading Armenian intellectual, Hrant Dink, in Turkey altered the country's identity politics landscape. Turks joined protests of the assassination, and thousands of Turks attended the funeral, with some even carrying signs that read "We are all Armenians."[47]

So What?

Bacik's research highlights the complexity of the intersection between identity and politics. By providing a better understanding of identity politics in Turkey, the article provides a valuable source of information for policy makers in the United States and Europe who are interested in Turkey—a NATO ally and an applicant for EU membership. The discussion of the positive changes in Turkish-Armenian relations are a reminder that not all long-running disputes are fated to resist resolution.

By focusing the discussion on the relationship between the state and major identity groups, Bacik also provides a helpful model for scholars seeking to understand other countries. He demonstrates how the state and identity groups in Turkey interact, how these interactions affect future efforts at addressing identity-related issues, and the potentially important role of events like the assassination of Hrant Dink. In doing so, Bacik's study of Turkey reminds comparativists that a complete understanding of how identity affects political outcomes requires investigation of the ways identity constrains and offers opportunities to both the state and identity group leaders.

CONCLUSION

Identity matters in politics. This makes sense, considering identity's role in shaping how individuals view themselves and those around them. This chapter discussed collective identities that, along with national identity, have the greatest effect on politics: ethnicity, race, religion, region, gender, and class. These are just some of what individual identity involves. Age cohort, sexual orientation, occupation, level of education, and other traits combine with personal beliefs to form an individual's identity.

The TIC countries provide many lessons about identity and politics. Ethnicity is an important identity division in each of them. Russia and China highlight how religion can emerge more forcefully as part of people's identity in times of chaotic social transformation and ideological upheaval. Particular events can reenergize us-them boundaries, as in the UK after the 7/7 bombings and in Russia after the Beslan school tragedy. The cases also show that governments in different countries can take disparate actions in response to identity diversity, that different governments in the same country can develop alternative approaches over time, and that sometimes one country can have contrasting policies at the same time.

Perhaps most of all, the cases indicate that when identity divisions complement one another, identity politics is not only the norm but also a powerful feature of a country's domestic politics. Deep complementary divisions pose policy challenges for a government. A deep sense of shared identity provides opportunities to mobilize people to act on the basis of that identity, such as encouraging citizens to turn out and vote for a candidate who is "one of us."

Identity is not only a tool that elites use to secure political office. An important theme of this chapter is that identity is an underlying structural factor that constrains political leaders as much as it provides opportunities. In addition, while identities are socially constructed—largely through the action of intellectual and political leaders—the radical middle position between primordialism and constructivism asserts that such elites cannot craft and use identity in any way they see fit. Past incidents, current circumstances, and existing identity boundaries all affect how elites can create or mold collective identities and use them for political ends.

To conclude, three important reminders are in order. First, all societies are divided by collective identities. There is no perfectly homogeneous society in which everyone belongs to the same identity groups. Every sizable population has a "we" and a "they."

Second, individuals can be divided by the multiple components of their personal identities. An individual can be, simultaneously, American, of Irish ancestry, Christian, white, English-speaking, a resident of the Midwest, female, middle class, and any number of other categories, and that individual can prioritize these identities when defining herself. Just as cross-cutting cleavages may internally divide large groups, so too may individuals have numerous, often conflicting politically relevant elements to their identities.

Finally, identity plays an important role in politics, but, like other structural factors, it does not completely dictate how people will behave politically. It is only one piece of the puzzle of understanding political outcomes. The following chapters take a step toward completing this puzzle by moving away from economic and social structures and toward the foundation of the political process. This next step begins in Chapter 5 with a discussion of governmental institutions as structures. Like economic and social structures, the design of governmental institutions provides political leaders with a combination of constraints and opportunities.

KEY TERMS

Accommodation, p. 109
Assimilation, p. 109
Caste, p. 113
Clan, p. 101
Cleavage structure theory, p. 118
Complementary identity divisions, p. 106
Constructivism, p. 120
Cross-cutting identity divisions, p. 108

Ethnic cleansing, p. 109
Ethnic group, p. 100
Ethnic identity, p. 100
Ethno-federalism, p. 109
Feminist theory, p. 122
Gender, p. 104
Genocide, p. 108
Identity, p. 97
In-group, p. 98
Integration, p. 109

Membership boundary, p. 98
Out-group, p. 98
Primordialism, p. 120
Race, p. 99
Radical middle position, p. 120
Religion, p. 102
Social cleavages, p. 99
Tribe, p. 101

CHAPTER 5

Political Systems and Their Rules

Men eating at a restaurant in Moscow in 1972. RIA Novosti

CHAPTER OUTLINE

Political Institutions
The Constitution: A Regime's Rules for Making Rules
Levels of Government

TOPIC IN COUNTRIES

Features in this chapter:

Spotlight on . . . France: The French Combination of Majoritarian and Consensus Democratic Features

In Theory and Practice: Veto Points in the United Kingdom

In Theory and Practice: Political Change in Mexico and Easton's Systems Theory

In Theory and Practice: China and Skocpol's *States and Social Revolutions*

In Theory and Practice: Iran and Rational Choice New Institutionalism

Research in Context: Origins of Constitutionalism in Latin America

After reading this chapter, you should be able to

- Define key concepts such as political institution, democracy, authoritarianism, totalitarianism, and federal versus unitary systems.

- Explain the role of a constitution, and understand the concept of constitutionalism.

- Discuss the general type of political system and important constitutional issues in the TIC cases.

- Categorize each TIC case as having either a unitary or a federal system.

D uring the Soviet period, Russians sometimes told the following joke among friends:

A man walks into a dining hall, looks at the menu, and orders the beef dinner. The woman behind the counter replies, "We don't have any." The man looks at the menu again and orders the chicken. The woman behind the counter replies, "We don't have any." The man looks at the menu a third time and orders the borscht (beet soup). The woman behind the counter shakes her head and says, "We don't have any." The man slams down the menu and says, "Is this the menu or our constitution?"

This joke captures the frustration many Soviet citizens felt about the difference between what was written in their constitution and the practice of the Soviet government. It also raises an important point for the comparative study of politics: political institutions matter, but the way they work may differ significantly from the official "rules of the game." The comparative study of politics has long centered on the role of governmental institutions, a subject "central to political science since its inception."[1] Such institutions frame the actions of political leaders, constraining them and creating opportunities for them at the same time. The institutions emerge and change at different points in time, sometimes complementing one another and other times coming into conflict. Even the various components of a single political institution, such as a national legislature, may have different goals, different formal rules, and different norms.

This chapter highlights general concepts related to political systems, political institutions, and the rules that govern them. The discussion includes the major types of political regimes—democracy, totalitarianism, and authoritarianism—as well as the arrangements between different levels of government. It also involves a number of theories that attempt to explain how institutions are formed, how they change or persist over time, and what difference their design makes in determining political outcomes.

Political Institutions

Institutions direct much of our daily lives. Among their effects are shaping how we dress in a particular setting, creating rules for social networking interactions, providing moral guidance about relationships, and filtering and restructuring world events into "the news." Social scientists define the term **institution** in different ways. Most political scientists envision institutions as "purposive organizations" (created for a particular purpose) and the formal rules that structure them. Other social scientists, particularly sociologists, may conceptualize institutions as informal norms, social understandings, or longtime customs (e.g., the "institution of marriage"). Both views share the understanding that an institution involves rules that govern individual behavior. Thus, institutions are sets of rules that take the form of purposive organizations or informal norms and that shape individual behavior.

Institution A set of formal or informal rules, often taking the form of a purposive organization, that shapes individual behavior.

Political Institution A set of rules or a purposive organization created to establish or influence rules that apply across society.

Political systems are made up of political institutions. A **political institution** is a set of rules or a purposive organization created to establish or influence rules that apply across society. Political institutions are unique because their rules "reach outward," seeking to control the actions of people who do not necessarily participate in the institutions themselves.[2] Most social institutions, on the other hand, have rules designed to govern only the behavior of participants. In addition, as discussed in Chapter 1, one of the key features of the state is its sovereignty. This means that the rules produced by the state's political institutions take precedence over any conflicting rules from other social institutions. Political institutions include governing organizations, such as national or regional legislatures, as well as other organized groups like interest groups and political parties. In this chapter, unless otherwise stated, the term *political institution* refers to governing bodies.

Regime Types

From ancient philosophers on, scholars studying politics have focused on how political institutions come together to form a political system, or regime (see Chapter 1). The events of World War II and the early cold war period pushed comparativists to concentrate on nondemocratic political systems and to compare them to the democratic systems of the West. Scholars were particularly interested in a relatively new type of political regime: totalitarianism. This was one of three general regime types that political scientists identified at the time, along with democracy and authoritarianism. In more recent decades, the variants within each of these three types have drawn attention. Scholars began to categorize some real-world political systems as hybrids of the main types, leading to labels like "semiauthoritarianism" and "semidemocracy." The broad descriptions of the three main regime types in this section are ideal types. They provide a measuring stick with which to compare political systems, even though the pure form of the regime may not be realized in practice.

Democracy

Democracy A regime type that involves the selection of government officials through free and fair elections, a balance between the principle of majority rule and the protection of minority interests, and constitutional limitations on government actions.

There are many ways to think about **democracy**. A vague statement like "government of, by, and for the people" might be quickly dismissed as unhelpful. Yet, it points to an important difference between democracy and nondemocratic systems: citizens participate in the governing process in a democracy, and their participation can influence the kinds of policies the political system produces. This participation is generally a mixture of direct and indirect forms. In both newly minted and long-established democracies, citizens increasingly have a direct say in major political decisions through participation in referenda. Their participation in shaping government policies can also be indirect, as in the selection of representatives to serve in government on behalf of the general population.

Selection of Government Officials through Free and Fair Elections

The first defining characteristic of modern democracy is mass involvement in the selection of representatives through elections. Chapter 8 presents other ways in which elites and masses are linked, but elections remain the central vehicle for mass involvement and an essential force for holding government officials accountable for their actions. Elections are a necessary feature of democracy, but their presence is far from sufficient to label a system democratic. Totalitarian systems and even many authoritarian ones also hold regular elections.

What distinguishes electoral practices in democracies from those of nondemocratic systems is that the nondemocratic systems exclude large portions of the population from participating (e.g., South Africa during apartheid) or do not provide voters with a real choice between candidates. Political scientist Robert Dahl labels the portion of the adult population that is eligible to vote as a system's "inclusiveness"; he calls the extent to which they have a real choice between candidates as the system's level of "contestation."[3] Representative democracies are political systems that have high levels of both inclusiveness and contestation.

A related, and probably more common, way to think about elections in a democracy is the extent to which they are free and fair. In free elections

- Individuals have the ability to vote.
- Their votes are made in secret.
- Candidates have the ability to run for office.
- Candidates have the ability to campaign for office by providing information to voters.

Fair elections require

- Voters to have access to impartial coverage of the campaign in the media.
- Voters to have reasonable access to polling places.
- The vote of each eligible voter—and only of eligible voters—to be counted.
- The vote of each eligible voter to be counted equally.
- The losing candidate to acknowledge and accept the results (including, if necessary, a peaceful transfer of power from one set of ruling elites to another).
- The electoral process to be administered and monitored by an impartial body of electoral specialists.

All these things must occur without significant restrictions, governmental interference, or other attempts at intimidation. The elections must also be meaningful, selecting the officeholders for the political system's positions of real power.

Think and Discuss
Look at the list of criteria associated with free and fair elections. How do American elections measure up based on these criteria?

The Balance of Majority Rule and Minority Protection
A second feature of democracy is that it balances the principle of majority rule with the protection of minority interests. Dahl calls this provision "Madisonian democracy," named for James Madison's preoccupation with balancing majority and minority power in the design of the American political system.[4] For the most part, democratic representatives are chosen based on the idea that those who receive the most votes should win. Likewise, laws are generally produced by democratic governments when a majority of the elected officials support the provisions.

There are also often protections against what might be called mob rule or, for Madison, "majority tyranny." The intensity of the masses is taken into account in some electoral systems, and the activity of interest groups reflects their members' intensity (as well as their other resources, such as money). In addition, constitutional provisions may check the majority's ability to dictate policy. In the United States, majority tyranny is limited by the large number of requirements for a bill to become a law. These steps can lead what Dahl calls a "tentative majority" that can break apart in the face of an intense minority.

Limitations on Government Action
A third feature of democracy, and another way that majorities can be limited, is the constitutional prohibition of certain government actions. These so-called negative rights—freedoms that government cannot take away from the people—include freedoms of speech, religious practice, and assembly. A democracy requires that people be free to criticize governmental action. This is part of the free flow of information necessary for voters to hold government officials accountable. It also means that the communication media must be free to investigate and criticize without fear of reprisal. The degree of freedom the media enjoy is a strong indicator of the level of democracy in a particular political system.

Variants of Democracy

The institutional differences between one democracy and another can be significant. In a unitary democratic system, the central government has complete autonomy over all lower levels of government, and no powers are reserved for those lower levels; in a federal democratic state, lower levels of government retain designated powers that the central government cannot take away. These two options are discussed in more detail later in this chapter.

Democratic systems can be presidential, where the executive and legislative branches are separated both in their selection by voters and in the exercise of their powers. Democratic systems can also be parliamentary, where the legislative and executive branches are fused and the chief executive serves only with the consent of the legislature. These two approaches are a central topic of Chapter 6.

Democratic systems can have politically powerful judicial branches with the authority to overturn legislative initiatives as unconstitutional. Alternatively, their judiciaries can be restricted to resolving disputes about the violation of laws already on the books, with no authority to evaluate whether new laws comply with the constitution. Such judicial arrangements are a focus of Chapter 7.

Democracies may vary in how they bring interest groups into the political process. In a pluralist system, such as the United States, multiple interest groups compete for the attention of representatives through lobbying and campaign contributions. In a corporatist system, the government selects key organizations to represent major social groups, and their representatives sit at the table with government officials crafting policy affecting their groups (see Chapter 8).

Democracies can elect their legislative representatives through the use of first past the post (FPTP) district systems, in which the candidate with the most votes in the district wins a seat in the government; through proportional representation (PR) systems, in which political parties receive seats in a legislative body in proportion to how well they do in the elections; or through a hybrid of these approaches. Electoral arrangements and their consequences are major themes in Chapter 9.

The various institutional arrangements can be combined in different ways. Scholars have given labels to particular institutional combinations. One valuable distinction, described in greatest detail by political scientist Arend Lijphart, is between **majoritarian democracy** and **consensus democracy**. Lijphart distinguishes between these two forms of democracy by examining ten criteria. Table 5.1 summarizes these features.

"Did You Know?"
Australia and Belgium have compulsory voting. Citizens who fail to vote can be fined or jailed. Although critics might consider the practice undemocratic, it contributes to very high voter turnout rates (roughly 95 percent in Australia).

Majoritarian Democracy A democratic system combining strong executives, few checks on the power of the majority to pass laws and amend the constitution, and conflictual politics between two major political parties.

Consensus Democracy A democratic system that unites proportional representation elections, a multiparty system, and diffusion of power across branches and levels of government.

TABLE 5.1	Majoritarian and Consensus Democracy

Features of Ideal-Type Majoritarian Democracy	Features of Ideal-Type Consensus Democracy
• A first past the post (FPTP) plurality electoral system • A two-party system • A powerful executive • Control of the chief executive and cabinet by a single party rather than through a coalition of political parties • A pluralist approach to the incorporation of interest groups into the political process, in which groups compete against each other • A unitary and centralized government • A unicameral legislature • A flexible constitution that can be changed by a simple majority • No judicial review of legislation • A central bank under the control of the executive	• A proportional representation (PR) electoral mechanism • A multiparty system • Coalition governments • A balance of power between the legislature and the executive • A corporatist system of interest group representation • A federal and decentralized government • A division of power between two equally strong legislative houses • Rigid constitutions that are difficult to amend • Judicial review of legislation • An independent central bank

According to Lijphart, the consensus combination leads to more cooperation and compromise rather than to the politics of conflict found in the majoritarian approach. The British political system is close to the majoritarian ideal type, and Germany's democratic system approximates the consensus democracy ideal. The American political system, on the other hand, mixes features of the majoritarian and consensus approaches. Lijphart claims that most scholars believe that consensus democracy provides better representation and protection of minority views, but that majoritarian democracy leads to more effective government. Lijphart challenges this view, arguing that consensus democracy is better at representation and equally effective in maintaining order and managing the economy.[5]

Robert Dahl describes four sets of democracies based on electoral arrangements and the presidential or parliamentary approach. The **European model of democracy**—similar to Lijphart's consensus democracy—combines parliamentary and proportional representation arrangements. The **Westminster model of democracy**—similar to Lijphart's majoritarian system—joins a parliamentary approach with first past the post district voting. This kind of system is in place in the United Kingdom (UK) and many former British colonies, including Canada. The **American model of democracy** brings together presidentialism with FPTP district voting in legislative elections. Finally, the **Latin American model of democracy** is the combination of a presidential system with a PR electoral system for the legislature.[6]

Even Dahl's categories are imprecise; a number of exceptions are found in Europe and Latin America. Nevertheless, Dahl's and Lijphart's efforts to create middle-range categories (below the level of democracy in general but above the level of an individual country) are valuable. The additional categories allow more effective comparison of one democracy with another. They also serve as a helpful reminder that the American version of democracy is far from the only option. It is, in fact, unique among democracies, with features such as political party primaries, in which voters choose who runs under a party label in the general election instead of letting the parties decide, that seem downright odd to those unaccustomed to them.

European Model of Democracy A term used by Robert Dahl to discuss democratic systems that combine parliamentary and PR arrangements.

Westminster Model of Democracy Dahl's term for a democratic system that combines a parliamentary approach with a FPTP (plurality) electoral system.

American Model of Democracy Dahl's term for a democratic system that combines a presidential system with FPTP district voting in legislative elections.

Latin American Model of Democracy Dahl's term for a political system that combines presidentialism with a PR electoral system.

Spotlight on ... FRANCE

The French Combination of Majoritarian and Consensus Democratic Features

The cover of one of the most influential texts on the French state, *L'État en France de 1789 à nos jours* by Pierre Rosanvallon, is illustrated with a locomotive labeled ETAT ("state"). Moving forward through history, the locomotive suggests continuity and power within a regularized constitutional framework. Such a suggestion is somewhat ironic, given that France has had five republics, three kingdoms, and two empires as well as the Vichy state (the French government during the Nazi occupation) since the Revolution of 1789. In other ways, however, the metaphor is appropriate. Despite the many constitutional changes, the French state has evolved through an increasingly accepted view of the proper constitutional order for the country. This agreement appeared first in norms and practices, much like the British constitution. Later, the agreement became manifest through written documents and laws, such as the Constitution of the Fifth Republic adopted in 1958.

The Fifth Republic combines aspects of majoritarian and consensus democratic systems and integrates various procedures and arrangements from nearly all of the previous constitutions. Its constitution, which provides for strong executive and legislative functions, along with a bicameral parliament with senators selected by a special electoral college, appears to favor some degree of consensus. A number of agencies serve in advisory roles in the legislative process, quasi-judicial bodies review proposed laws and administrative actions, and there is a broad consensus on many of the basic principles of governance and policy.

On the other hand, the French presidency is powerful. The president can, for example, submit a proposal for a referendum, sending a law directly to the people for a vote and bypassing the government and the legislature. Consensus in practice also depends on the results of national elections. When the party of the French president controls a majority in the National Assembly and the Senate, the president can control legislation and administration by appointing a prime minister who administers the laws and directs legislation, acting as the representative of the nation to protect the constitution and arbitrate disputes, and serving as the leader of his or her party to implement a policy agenda.

Totalitarianism

Totalitarianism A regime type defined by an effort to remake society using an official ideology, a single mass political party, a secret police force employing terror against the population, a monopoly over means of communication, a monopoly over weapons in society, and a command economy.

The second major regime type is **totalitarianism**. Though far different from democracy, it also differs greatly from the ideal authoritarian system. This type of political system was a central preoccupation of scholars following World War II, since the two real-world examples that came closest to the totalitarian ideal were the Nazi German system under Hitler and the Communist system of the Soviet Union under Stalin.

Features of Totalitarianism

Two of the most important works on totalitarianism in political science are Hannah Arendt's *The Origins of Totalitarianism* and Carl Friedrich and Zbigniew Brzezinski's *Totalitarian Dictatorship and Autocracy*.[7] One of Arendt's major contributions to the discussion of totalitarianism is the idea that a totalitarian system seeks the "atomization" of society, except when performing party-sponsored functions. By atomization, Arendt meant the breaking down of society into its component parts (individuals) who become unable or unwilling to join together with other individuals to form autonomous groups. Controlling the way in which individuals relate to one another by atomizing society is a crucial step in the efforts of the totalitarian government to radically alter social and/or economic relations in the country.

This does not mean that people in a totalitarian system are apolitical. Like democracy, totalitarianism is a system that emphasizes mass mobilization. In other words, it seeks the active participation of the masses in support of its goals. While democracy allows significantly more autonomy for citizens about whether and how they will participate in politics, totalitarianism completely shapes the form of that participation.

Friedrich and Brzezinski are best known for outlining six basic features of a totalitarian system. The first feature is an official ideology. Totalitarian ideology includes a blueprint for restructuring society and justification for the monopoly of political power. It emphasizes the place of the state in world historical development; the struggle with other states or systems of government; the state's past, present, and future greatness; and the state's people (or at least much of its population) as a superior race.

The second characteristic is the existence of a single political party that has a monopoly on political power in the system. This party is part of the rulers' effort at total control of society. Previous political organizations, even volunteer organizations, are either destroyed or brought under the control of the party. In the systems closest to the totalitarian ideal, this party is headed by a single person.

The third feature is the reliance on terror to maintain order. Totalitarian systems seek to build legitimacy, but their willingness to terrorize the population—making people afraid even to talk with family members about problems with the political system—makes them unique. An essential part of totalitarian terror is the use of a secret police force. Because they seek to remake society, totalitarian governments are ruthless in dealing with political and cultural opponents. The secret police force is their main tool in this repression.

The fourth feature is complete control of communications. One could argue that it is impossible in practice to control all communications in society. But manipulating the flow of information (e.g., through control of the official media) is important for justifying the actions of the government, building support for the social blueprint, and enhancing the system's legitimacy.

The fifth feature is control over the means of force in society. This is, arguably, less important as a defining feature of totalitarianism than the previous four, since other types of regimes, including many democracies, attempt it as well. For Friedrich and Brzezinski, however, it is an important part of totalitarian systems' complete control over society.

The final trait of totalitarianism identified by Friedrich and Brzezinski is a command economy. In a command economy, decisions about what products to produce and how much to charge for products are controlled by government officials. This control over the economy allows the government to direct economic resources in a manner consistent with its efforts to remake society. It also aids in dominating all aspects of people's lives and means that the workplace can become a tool for socialization.

Variants of Totalitarianism: Fascism and Communism

Totalitarianism has two main varieties: fascism and Communism. **Fascism** is a form of totalitarianism that emphasizes racial, religious, or ethnic superiority and engages in militarism. The dominant state is justified as crucial to develop fully the capacity of the superior race or ethnic group, maintain a pure culture, and/or fight internal or external enemies who threaten the dominance of the superior group. **Communism** emphasizes collective ownership of the means of production in an effort to end the exploitation of the working class that is inherent in capitalism. In Communism, the dominant state is justified as crucial to the elimination of the capitalist class and the protection of the Communist system from external (anticommunist) threats.

Authoritarianism

The final major regime type is **authoritarianism**. The two real-world political systems most identified as approaching the authoritarian ideal are Spain under Francisco Franco (1939–75) and Chile under Augusto Pinochet Ugarte (1973–88). As an ideal type, authoritarianism shares some features with totalitarianism but has many distinct features as well.

Features of Authoritarianism

The first feature of authoritarianism is the presence of a dominant leader or small group of leaders. This leader may rule through a political party, or the leader may shun political parties altogether. In general, much less emphasis is on political parties in authoritarian systems than in either of the other two major regime types.

The lack of emphasis on political parties is a result of the next feature of authoritarian systems: limited political participation. Authoritarian leaders prefer a depoliticized population. The less people think about politics and the more they go about their normal lives without wanting to change the political system, the better for the authoritarian leader. Ideally, an authoritarian leader only has to mobilize the population in rare instances, such as to demonstrate support of a particular policy.

This does not imply that authoritarian systems seek to atomize the population like totalitarian systems do. A third feature of authoritarian systems is a degree of autonomy of society from state control. People cannot do whatever they want, but there is not a desire to control all possible activities. Voluntary associations and other groups may be allowed to form. If a group becomes a threat to the system or the leader—by working on political issues or otherwise accumulating significant power—it is either co-opted or eliminated. Likewise, not all communication is controlled by the authoritarian state. Censorship of the media exists, but it often takes the form of citizen self-censorship: reporters know they will be arrested if they write something unflattering about the leader. The government does not take direct control over all media content.

Fascism A variant of totalitarianism based on militarism and an emphasis on remaking society along racial, religious, or ethnic lines.

Communism A variant of totalitarianism in which the state owns the means of production and seeks to remake society in the name of the working class.

Authoritarianism A regime type defined by its rule by a single leader or small group of leaders, limited political participation, existent but limited autonomy of society from state control, lack of an overarching ideology, and limited control over the economy.

Nazi troops stand in formation while top Nazi officials make their entrance during a Nazi Party rally in 1935. © Heinrich Hoffmann/George Eastman House/Getty Images

Military Authoritarianism A type of authoritarian system, most common in Latin America and Africa, in which the government leaders are also military leaders.

Party Authoritarianism A type of authoritarian system that involves the control of an authoritarian system by a single political party.

Bureaucratic Authoritarianism A type of authoritarian system that occurs in countries where the economy is modernized enough to require authoritarian leaders to work closely with a large bureaucracy that has expertise on policy matters.

Semiauthoritarianism A political system in which elements of democracy are integrated into an otherwise authoritarian system.

Semidemocracy A political system that is similar to semiauthoritarianism but has more democratic features.

The fourth feature of authoritarianism is the general lack of an ideology. Authoritarian systems may focus their activities on a particular goal, but this goal is usually something like restoring order to a chaotic situation, eliminating government corruption, or improving the country's economic performance. This goal is not a blueprint for remaking society.

Finally, there is often limited control over the economy. Authoritarian political systems commonly exist side-by-side with free-market economies. The economy may be regulated, and people who might try to translate their economic power into political power are watched. But there is not complete control and state economic planning as in a totalitarian system.

Variants of Authoritarianism

Variants of authoritarianism include military, party, and bureaucratic. Political scientist Juan Linz has emphasized the first two of these variants; Guillermo O'Donnell has stressed the third.[8] **Military authoritarianism** is common in many parts of the world, including Latin America and Africa. Linz argues that militaries are often privileged in authoritarian systems, but in a military authoritarian system, the rulers themselves come from the military. **Party authoritarianism** exists when political life in an authoritarian system is organized and run through a single political party. Although the dominant party is more important than parties are in most authoritarian systems, this form of authoritarianism lacks some of the features that would allow one to label it totalitarian (e.g., command control of the economy). Mexico under the Institutional Revolutionary Party (PRI), which dominated politics in that country for much of the twentieth century, is an example of a party authoritarian system. **Bureaucratic authoritarianism**, according to O'Donnell, is found in societies with high levels of modernization. The modernization requires the political leaders, who may be members of the military, civilians, or both, to rely on experts ("technocrats") to assist them in creating and administering government policy.

Semiauthoritarianism/Semidemocracy

A final regime type is, in many ways, a hybrid of two others. Increasingly, scholars of political regimes and regime transitions are pointing to the prevalence of **semiauthoritarianism** or **semidemocracy**. The difference between the two hybrid types is largely a matter of degree. Both labels refer to systems in which the components of democracy are openly incorporated into an otherwise authoritarian system. For example, in a semidemocracy, elections exist but are limited, the judiciary is not fully independent, and the media are only partially free.

In the past, such systems were often seen as a stopping point on the way either to a full-fledged authoritarian system or a fully democratic one. Today, scholars recognize that semiauthoritarian systems are much more stable than they had appeared to be. Authoritarian leaders have learned how to allow degrees of both contestation and inclusiveness without directly putting their power at risk.

At the same time, the "color revolutions" of the first decade of the twenty-first century—the "Bulldozer Revolution" in Serbia (2000), the "Rose Revolution" in Georgia (2003–2004), the "Orange Revolution" in Ukraine (2004–2005), the "Tulip Revolution" in Kyrgyzstan (2005), and even the unsuccessful "Green Revolution" in Iran (2009)—demonstrate the danger for an authoritarian system when citizens believe they should have a real say in the selection of government officials. These uprisings included hundreds of thousands of protesters; toppled leaders in Serbia, Georgia, Ukraine, and Kyrgyzstan; and sent a message to the leaders of Iran. A leader of a semiauthoritarian system may still try to steal an election to maintain power, but the color revolutions highlight the risk in doing so. The general population may not always sit idly by and watch events unfold. These revolutions also make clear that the populations of countries with nondemocratic political systems may be aware of more democratic institutional arrangements in other countries.

The Constitution: A Regime's Rules for Making Rules

During the early decades of political science, scholars paid a great deal of attention to formal institutions. As a result, constitutions were a favorite topic. Political science has since gained a greater appreciation of the importance of informal institutions and the rules that political institutions create that cannot be found in the constitution. That said, constitutions remain an important topic, often serving as the starting point for comparativists seeking to understand the workings of a particular political system.

A **constitution** acts as the official "rules of the game" for a political system. If followed, the constitution prevents laws from being passed arbitrarily. It includes a list of positions of governmental authority, the specific powers of these positions, and rules for making new rules—the process for creating laws or passing constitutional amendments. By laying out the official powers of the various governmental institutions, a constitution also places restraints on government officials. In the U.S. Constitution, for example, certain powers are given only to the legislative branch.

Constitution A set of understandings about the functioning of a particular political system, which includes the description of official major government bodies and positions, the powers these positions have, and the process for making new laws.

Rule of Law

Many formal rules and limits on governmental power are ignored by leaders, particularly in authoritarian and totalitarian systems. Without doubt, a constitution is much more effective when it is followed. When its rules are adhered to, a constitution adds legitimacy to the system, conferring what Max Weber called legal authority (see Chapter 1). Citizens may not like a specific law, but they accept it as legitimate because they believe that the process through which laws were made is itself legitimate. Following the consistent process for passing laws is also an important part of the condition known as **rule of law**. Rule of law involves the government's belief (and practice) that it has to follow laws even as it is making new ones. The concept extends beyond lawmaking, also referring to society's lack of tolerance of corruption and its acceptance of the idea that agreements such as signed contracts are binding.

Rule of Law A condition in which laws are passed according to the constitution, government officials are not above the law, and society respects contracts as legally binding.

Constitutionalism

The term **constitutionalism** refers to the idea that constitutions are designed to limit the power of government, that government officials must follow the laws of the land, and that upholding these limitations and following these laws is a key source of legitimacy. The concept of constitutionalism also includes the idea that provisions in a constitution—the rules for making new rules—are above ordinary law. Ordinary laws must conform to constitutional provisions. These constitutional stipulations can be changed, but in most democracies this requires an elaborate process, well beyond just having a majority of the national legislature support the changes. Constitutionalism is at the heart of the American political system, as well as that of other democracies.

Constitutionalism The belief that constitutions should limit government power, that government officials must obey the country's laws, and that a government's legitimacy comes from obeying these limitations and laws.

To be effective, the limits must be clearly understood. As a result, most constitutions are written down in a single document, and most are long and detailed. Largely because it is one of the oldest written constitutions in existence, the U.S. Constitution is comparatively short and vague about many aspects of day-to-day governing. Over time, officials writing new constitutions have used their own and other countries' experiences to generate more (and more detailed) constitutional provisions. The vagueness of the U.S. Constitution is part of the story of its success. The ability to interpret its wording and evolve over time has enhanced its durability. On the other hand, this has also led to major disputes. As the large number of five-to-four Supreme Court decisions over the last two decades attests, interpreting the U.S. Constitution is not a simple matter.

Think and Discuss

Is the U.S. Constitution really as vague as the discussion above suggests? Provide specific examples from the U.S. Constitution to support your position.

Levels of Government

An important aspect of a political system laid out in most constitutions is the relationship between the central government and lower levels of government in the country. The question of levels of government involves three topics: unitary versus federal systems, local government, and devolution. Though people normally think of the central government when discussing features of a state, governments exist at many levels. In the United States, city councils and village boards exist alongside the governments of the fifty American states and the federal government. International governmental organizations such as the United Nations also produce policy decisions that they intend states in the international community to follow. The European Union (EU) has absorbed a portion of its member states' sovereignty. In considering levels of government, comparativists examine the various functions of central and lower-level governments and the relationship between the levels.

Unitary versus Federal Arrangements

Unitary System A political system in which the central government has authority over lower levels of government, and lower levels have no powers reserved for them.

Federal System A political system that provides lower levels of government with designated powers that the central government cannot take away.

Reserved Powers Powers designated to a particular level of government that another level of government cannot take away.

Shared Powers Powers held by both the central and the lower levels of government.

Confederation An affiliation of two or more states involving a relatively weak central governing authority set up to facilitate cooperation between them.

In any country, the relationship between the levels of government generally falls into one of two categories: **unitary system** or **federal system**. The difference between a unitary and a federal relationship centers on whether there are territorial units within a state that have specific powers that the central government cannot take away. If such units exist, the system is a federal one. In a federal system, lower-level government powers may be **reserved powers** for the lower levels alone. This is the approach of the American federal system. The federal and lower levels of government may also possess certain **shared powers.** This is more typical of the German federal system. Either way, certain powers exist that the central government cannot take away from the lower levels. In a unitary system, the central government has complete authority over lower levels of government; any powers held by the lower levels can be taken away by the central government.

In a federal system, sovereignty is shared between the central government and regional governments within the state. Is the EU a federation? For the moment, it is not a federal or a unitary state, since it comprises multiple internationally recognized states. Instead, it comes closer to the definition of a **confederation**—an affiliation of two or more independent states, in which the states' governments are much stronger than the central governing authority set up to facilitate cooperation between them. As time goes on, the EU may come to resemble a federal state. Its efforts toward the integration of European countries have involved not only expansion of the organization to include new member-states but also a deepening of the interconnectedness of existing member-states.

What are the advantages of a federal system over a unitary one? Giving powers to lower levels of government makes it easier to govern a very large country. It is no accident that the physically largest countries in the world tend to have federal arrangements, while few very small countries have adopted this approach. In addition, a federal system better accommodates regional differences in policy preferences and can help guard against the concentration of political power. Finally, as discussed in Chapter 4, when the territorial units within the boundaries of the state cut across deep social divisions rather than complement them, they can help overcome the social divisions.

Disadvantages include a lack of uniformity in policy across the country. This can be a problem for citizens who travel from one part of the country to another. In the United States, state governments control the creation of most electoral rules, even for federal elections. How one registers to vote in Wisconsin, for example, may be different from how one registers in Texas. In addition, although American interest groups are prevalent at the federal level, their power can be more exaggerated at lower levels of government. Finally, if territorial lines within the country correspond to deep social divisions, federalism reinforces those divisions. Comparativists debate whether this makes violent conflict and attempts to break apart the state more or less likely.

Local Government

All states, whether federal or unitary, include local government. Though central governments receive the bulk of the attention in comparative politics, much day-to-day governing takes place locally. Think about the extent to which local government decisions affected what you did today. Bus fares, placement of stop signs and crosswalks, and assignment of policing duties, among other things, were likely decided at the local level. One of two central tasks of local government is to provide local services such as schools, roads, water, and sewerage.

Local government's second task is to implement and enforce decisions of higher levels of government. These decisions can take the form of unfunded mandates, in which the local government did not make the policy but is expected to cover the costs of implementing it. A sizable commitment of funds from higher levels of government may assist local officials in these activities. Though enforcement of laws and administration of government programs is often more effective at the local level, the central government often has an easier time raising money for such supervision.

Local governments have powers to make such decisions because it is practical for them to do so. A central or provincial government can, or should, try to tackle only so many issues. Making political decisions at the local level can also give the decisions more legitimacy. Although residents rarely participate in local government meetings, at least in the United States, there is a sense that the local officials have the best interests of the community in mind.

Because of certain advantages to local governance, even unitary systems allow local governments to make a number of policy decisions and to enforce many others that the central government has made. Thus, a unitary system does not necessarily produce feeble local governments. What a local government in a unitary system lacks is sovereignty in that, unlike the central government, it does not have the ability to control its own affairs.

Devolving Powers from Central Governments to Lower Levels

Devolution involves the transfer of power from a central government to lower governments, usually at the regional (provincial) level. This process does not necessarily turn the system into a federal one, though that can be the ultimate result if the devolved powers become enshrined as rightfully belonging to the lower-level governments. The reason that devolution does not automatically lead to federation brings us back the topic of sovereignty. In devolution, the central government does not necessarily surrender its ultimate sovereignty to the lower level of government. If the powers are not reserved to the lower level, then they may be taken back at any time.

In practice, however, once power is given to a unit of government, taking it back is difficult. Even if a central government has maintained the right to take back devolved powers, it may decide that it is politically impossible to do so. As the Topic in Counties section below makes clear, this is a particular concern for leaders in the UK, where devolution has significantly increased the power of regions like Scotland.

> **Devolution** The process of transferring power from a central government to lower governments, which does not necessarily turn the system into a federal one.

TOPIC IN COUNTRIES

This chapter has described general concepts related to political systems, political institutions, and the rules that govern them. As we explore the Topic in Countries (TIC) cases, look for

- The extent to which the nine TIC cases are democratic, semiauthoritarian, or authoritarian.
- The changes in the regime types of the TIC cases over time.
- The differences in the approach, length, and importance of the constitutions of the TIC cases.
- The use of federal and unitary approaches across the TIC cases.

The United Kingdom

An irony of the British political system is that it is both a model of democracy for many countries and a system that some believe borders on dictatorship in practice. Its standing as a democratic model comes from its own early development of parliamentary democracy—the British parliament is known as the "mother of parliaments"—as well as its work with formerly British colonies to design their postindependence political systems. The portrayal of the UK as a quasi-dictatorship comes from its majoritarian qualities.

The Political System

The British political system is the real-world expression of the Westminster model of democracy. It is also so close to the pure form of Lijphart's majoritarian democracy that Lijphart uses the labels "majoritarian democracy" and "Westminster democracy" interchangeably in one of his best known books.[9] The UK remains one of the most majoritarian democratic systems in the world. It has even been dubbed an "elective dictatorship" because a majority party controlling the House of Commons, and thus, the position of the prime minister, has the ability to pass its legislation at will.

Why, then, is the British system considered democratic? First, majoritarian democracy is still democracy. Leaders are selected by the general population through free and fair elections, minority interests are somewhat protected, and the power of government is limited—both constitutionally and, particularly important for the British case, culturally. Members of the prime minister's party can check the power of the prime minister by pressuring the party leadership to rethink a proposal. This happened in 2004, for example, with a controversial bill to ban hunting with dogs. The presence of a formal and visible opposition and the ability of members of Parliament to openly question the prime

British Prime Minister David Cameron responds to criticism during Question Time on November 24, 2010. © REUTERS/ Parbul TV via Reuters TV

minister and cabinet officials during Question Time also keeps the prime minister's government in line by showcasing a viable alternative to its control.[10] In addition, as the 2010 British elections demonstrated, the prime minister's party may not always win a majority of the seats in the House of Commons. Consequently, the new government of Prime Minister David Cameron must function in less majoritarian ways than its predecessors.

IN THEORY AND PRACTICE

Veto Points in the United Kingdom

One of the most important theoretical perspectives about political institutions is the theory of **veto points**, identified most closely with political scientist George Tsebelis. Veto

Veto Points Individuals or collective political bodies whose failure to accept a policy change results in the rejection of the proposed change.

points are individuals or collective bodies (e.g., legislative chambers) that must agree to a policy change before it is adopted; their failure to accept a proposal amounts to a veto.[11] Tsebelis argues that systems with many veto points are likely to have much policy stability, since one of the veto players can likely prevent a major policy change with which it disagrees.[12]

Parliamentary systems generally have fewer veto points than do presidential systems (see Chapter 6), and unicameral (single-chamber) legislatures have fewer veto points than bicameral ones. But Tsebelis contends that the makeup of the executive and legislative branches is not the entire story. One must also understand the party system and ideological divisions between the main parties. If a president is from the same party as the party controlling the legislature, there could be fewer veto points than in a parliamentary system ruled by a coalition of small parties (what he calls "partisan veto players") with divergent ideological views.

During her time as British prime minister, Margaret Thatcher took steps to dramatically curtail the UK's "welfare state" provisions. Thatcher was able to decrease the government's role in the economy and government social welfare programs, which she thought fostered dependency on the government. The social welfare protections had served as the backbone of government economic policy throughout the post–World War II era. Though the "welfare state retrenchment" had begun under the Labour Party government preceding her, Thatcher's government turned their modest reforms into a full-scale policy shift.[13]

Because of the form of Britain's parliamentary system, there were few checks on Thatcher's ability to pursue these changes. The House of Commons was controlled by the Conservative Party, which Thatcher led. The House of Lords could get in the way and slow the reform process down, but the members of the House of Lords were also mostly Conservatives. Thus, the UK's small number of veto points—indeed, it often appears to have only one veto point—afforded the opportunity for significant policy change, and Thatcher took advantage. Although the veto points perspective cannot explain the timing of the major welfare reform under Margaret Thatcher or why she believed it was a good policy change, it does help explain how her desire for such reform became a reality.

The Constitution

The constitution is one of the most confusing features of the British political system. Like other aspects of British politics, it is the result of protracted evolution.[14] Unlike nearly every other democracy in the world, the UK's constitution was not the result of a constitutional convention, and it is not written down in a single document. Instead, it is a collection of government acts, legal opinions, and generally accepted norms and customs. Written components include old documents such as the Magna Carta and newer acts of Parliament designed to remake the political system.

How can a system function without a single document containing the political rules? The British constitution works partly because of British political culture's emphasis on the importance of tradition, respect for authority, and sense of obligation by elites to act responsibly. It is easy to think that written rules are superior to understood norms, but the latter can actually be more powerful—and certainly harder to get around. Thus, the combination of constitutional flexibility and cultural responsibility fosters political stability in the UK even though a partly unwritten constitution might produce chaos elsewhere.

When the Labour Party led by Tony Blair won the 1997 parliamentary elections, it marked the end of nearly two decades of Conservative Party control. Though perhaps not predominant in the minds of the voters, one of the central positions of the Labour Party platform was a substantial overhaul of the British constitution to make the system more effective and accountable. In short, its vision was of a less majoritarian and more consensus-based political system.

According to British political scientist Matthew Flinders, constitutional reform can be cosmetic, moderate, or fundamental.[15] Labour's rhetoric called for many fundamental changes, and some have called what Labour has done a "quiet revolution."[16] In truth, the reforms tended to be moderate or even cosmetic. Parliament did consider many constitutional reform bills, there were successes on devolution (discussed later in this section), and government was able to institute some reforms of the House of Lords (including a dramatic reduction in the number of hereditary peers). Other substantial reforms stalled, however, due to weariness about the amount of time being devoted to the subject compared with other issues more salient to the general public.[17] Even the efforts to more fundamentally alter the House of Lords hit roadblocks in the 2000s. Looking at Lijphart's criteria, Flinders claims that the combination of reforms that have occurred and those that have stalled has in many ways made the system more majoritarian.[18]

Levels of Government

Despite the existence of the UK's four main regions and the distinct identities of the societies within them, the British state has long been considered unitary. The issue of how much control the regions should have over daily political decisions has been a source of tension, however, and for more than a decade the British government has been actively involved in the process of devolution. Indeed, the only area in which Labour Party constitutional reforms can be clearly called fundamental is the shift in the division of powers between central and regional levels of government.

The early years of the process included a number of important parliamentary acts, such as the Referendums Act (1997), which allowed residents of Scotland and Wales to vote on the question of increased regional powers; the Scotland Act (1998), which established an elected Scottish Parliament; the Government of Wales Act (1998), which did the same thing for Wales; and the Northern Ireland Act (1998), which authorized a referendum and regional government based on the April 1998 Good Friday agreement.

As many observers expected, the process of enhancing self-governance in Northern Ireland faced a rocky road. Prior to 1972, Protestants in Northern Ireland controlled a powerful regional government. Its powers included overseeing policing in the region, which led to oppression of Catholics who supported the union of Northern Ireland and the country of Ireland to its south. Protests in the late 1960s and early 1970s, including the reestablishment of the Irish Republican Army (IRA) in 1971, brought erratic responses from the central government. At times, the British army worked to protect Catholics; often it worked with the regional government to repress them. The British government eliminated the Northern Ireland parliament in 1972, instituted a Protestant-Catholic regional executive in 1974, and then quickly abandoned those efforts after Protestant workers staged a series of crippling strikes. London's direct rule continued until the 1998 Good Friday agreement laid the groundwork for reestablishing some degree of local rule in Northern Ireland. Despite the deep divisions and the failure of earlier efforts to increase regional control, the implementation of devolution provisions in Northern Ireland gained momentum in the decade following the Good Friday agreement.

Though events in Northern Ireland garner more attention in the United States, devolution in Scotland has been more pronounced, and the regional government has a comparatively large amount of power. The 1998 Scotland Act authorized the formation of a Scottish Parliament. Under the terms of the act, the 129 members of the Scottish Parliament (MSPs) can pass laws covering a range of issues. The parliament even has limited authority to levy taxes.

Devolution for Wales and England is another story. The National Assembly of Wales is, in terms of official powers, weaker than both the Scottish and the Northern Irish assemblies. It has begun to act more independently over the last decade, although this has often taken the form of its Labour Party's acting more like the old Labour Party—that is, to the left of the New Labour Party that former Prime Minister Tony Blair cultivated. The attempt to bring devolution to England has faced the most serious hurdles. Perhaps because the English are used to controlling the national government or because the proposed multiple regional assemblies in the English region lacked real legislative authority, few in England have been passionate about having their own regional assemblies. A referendum in 2004 to create an elected regional assembly in the northeast of England was soundly defeated, drawing less than 50 percent of the vote.[19]

The UK's devolution policy has made it possible for regions to have greater control over their own affairs, but it has not yet transformed the system into a federal one. The issues on which the Scottish Parliament can pass legislation, for example, are known as "devolved matters"; they are not called reserved powers, as in a federal system. Instead, the 1998 Scotland Act used the term "reserved matters" to refer to issues left to the central government—that is, subjects about which the Scottish Parliament cannot pass legislation—which include foreign affairs, defense, national security, and employment. Though one can reasonably expect powers at the regional level to be maintained or even strengthened in the future, there is no assurance of this unless a constitutional shift accepts the principle of reserved powers for the regions of the UK. Thus, the British devolution process provides an important example of a unitary system with strengthened powers for lower levels of government that has not fully transformed into a federal system.

Germany

Germany has been home to a variety of regime types, from totalitarian to democratic. Its current constitution lays out the features of a consensus democracy. This includes its strong federal system, which takes the shared powers approach to federalism.

The Political System

Over the last century, Germans have experienced three regime types: semiauthoritarianism, both types of totalitarian regimes (the fascist variant under the Nazis and the Communist variant in East Germany following World War II), and democracy. A democratic regime took root in West Germany after 1949 and has was extended to the east following unification in 1990. Germany today exemplifies Lijphart's consensus democracy.

The Second Reich (1871–1918) was a semiauthoritarian system. It had the veneer of parliamentary institutions, but the emperor and his appointed chancellor had the real power.[20] The Weimar Republic that followed was an unstable democracy, fatally undermined by a polarized society unwilling to support it. It also suffered from a constitutional design that granted the president emergency decree powers at the expense of the prime minister and parliament and an electoral system that brought party fragmentation and unstable governments.[21]

The fascist variant of totalitarianism came during the rule of the National Socialist (Nazi) Party from 1933 to 1945. National Socialist ideology preached the superiority of an ethnically and racially defined nation; the regime glorified and pursued militarism; and the population was mobilized through the Nazi Party and its affiliated societal groups, and was subordinated through terrorism and propaganda. After the division of Germany in 1949, the Soviet Union constituted the German Democratic Republic (East Germany) as a Communist totalitarian regime. Under the Communists, the East German economy was centrally planned, and the population was controlled by secret police and the manipulation of the flow of information.

The democratic regime established in the Federal Republic (West Germany) in 1949 provides the basis for Germany's current democracy. This system deliberately dispersed state power as an antidote to the centralized state under the Nazi dictatorship.[22] The combination of coalition governments, federalism, and the representation of interests under corporatism has led comparativists to view Germany as the model of a consensual democratic political system. The system requires a high degree of negotiation and compromise among key actors involved in making and implementing policy. One reason for this is Germany's electoral system, which combines FPTP and PR elements (see Chapter 9). This electoral arrangement creates a multiparty system consisting of two large parties and several smaller parties, in which coalition governments are the rule.

Compromise is also necessary because German federalism affords substantial powers to the territorial units below the level of the federal government—the *Länder*. They are represented in the upper house (Bundesrat) of the parliament, share certain powers with the federal government, and play a significant role in administering federal legislation.

Another way the German system encourages cooperation is the federal government's reliance on interest groups to implement laws on its behalf. This obviates the need for a large federal bureaucracy. Instead, as discussed in Chapter 3, the government accords these groups substantial autonomy to manage their respective sector of the economy or domain of public policy and consults them regularly when formulating policy.[23]

The Constitution

The constitution of the Federal Republic, often referred to as the Basic Law, marked a conscious break with the lawlessness of Germany's Nazi past and established the German system as a democracy under the rule of law.[24] Thus, the constitution spells out a number of individual rights and freedoms, including a right to privacy and a right to choose one's occupation, as well as a right to political asylum. Likewise, it acknowledges the important

role of political parties to form the will of the people and the obligation of the state to "protect the natural sources of life," and it declares the Federal Republic a "democratic and social federal state."[25]

This latter clause represents a synthesis between two principles, one in which the state respects individual rights and equality, and another that recognizes the legitimacy of organized interests. The emphasis on legitimate organized interests allows the state to regulate the economy in a social direction but at the same time discourages detailed government intervention or state planning.[26] The balance between broad social welfare protection and limits on government action laid out in the German constitution is a hallmark of Germany's consensual approach to democratic governance.

Levels of Government

German federalism has been termed "cooperative federalism" or "interlocking politics," labels that emphasize interdependence and cooperation rather than exclusive powers for different levels of government.[27] Under this type of federalism, the national government enacts legislation but relies on the governments of the sixteen Länder to implement federal laws. The two levels of government also engage in joint tasks in a number of policy areas. State and local governments receive a specified share of federal tax revenues, while fiscal equalization procedures redistribute revenues from richer to poorer states. However, the Länder have primary jurisdiction in specific policy domains such as education, environment, media, cultural affairs, and law enforcement.[28]

The governments of Länder have also vetoed about 60 percent of federal legislation through their representation in the Bundesrat, far higher than the 10 percent figure that the constitution's framers envisioned.[29] Critics charge that the veto power of the Länder has encouraged legislative gridlock. In an effort to speed up the legislative process, the federal government and the Länder agreed to constitutional reform of federalism in 2006. That agreement constricted the reach of the Bundesrat's veto, but, in exchange, the federal government accorded the Länder enhanced control over policies concerning education, environment, and regulation of business opening hours.[30]

India

India gained independence from British control in 1947. Like many other British colonies, it began independence as a parliamentary democracy. Unlike many of those colonies, India has sustained its democracy throughout nearly the entire period of independence. Its constitution is long and detailed, and it has been heavily amended. Its federal system, while granting the central government significant power, contains a great deal of variation in the design of regional and local governments.

The Political System

India has been a relatively stable democracy since independence, with the exception of the June 1975 to March 1977 period of "the Emergency," when Indira Gandhi seized power. In the elections of 1977 after democracy was restored, voters punished Indira Gandhi's Congress Party, resulting in the first prime minister not from the Congress Party since independence. Today, regular elections are held, people can organize and protest, the press is largely free, and governments change. As a result, India's political system is regularly labeled "the world's largest democracy."

The system continues to change—sometimes in ways that undermine the democracy label, and sometimes in ways that reaffirm it. Formerly, the system was dominated by a single party and controlled by a relatively small group of politicians. Today, no party can obtain a majority, and representation extends to formerly marginalized groups. In the past, the Indian parliament was conducted with great decorum; today, it faces increasing disruption. The political system has also faced enormous challenges, including severe poverty in the midst of great wealth, riots and protests, assassinations and suicides, a backlog of court cases, and corruption. That India remains a democracy is a remarkable accomplishment.

The Constitution

After several years of debate, a constituent assembly adopted the Indian constitution in 1950. Its many provisions are spelled out in such great detail that it is widely believed to be the longest written constitution of any country in the world. The constitution's Preamble declares India to be a "Sovereign Socialist Secular Democratic Republic."[31] The word *socialist* describes the goal of the framers of the constitution, although many of India's policies have moved the country away from socialism. The other words, *sovereign*, *secular*, *democratic*, and *republic*, are appropriate descriptors of the political system today.

Two features of the Indian constitution are worthy of note. First, it provides for considerable centralization of power. The powers given to the central legislative bodies, for example, include the authority to amend the constitution and break up the federal units. Second, the detailed nature of the Indian constitution has meant that legislators have had to amend it frequently to accomplish their goals. By 2007, there were ninety-four amendments.

Levels of Government

The Indian political system is federal in form, with twenty-eight federal units below the level of the federal government, each with its own legislature. Yet, it differs from federal systems in the United States and elsewhere in that the central government in India possesses considerably greater power relative to the lower units of government.

As is typical of federal systems, India has three levels of government. At the center is a bicameral parliament (discussed in detail in the next chapter). Symbolizing the interdependence of the executive and legislative branches in a parliamentary democracy, the Indian constitution defines the president as a part of the parliament, and the president appoints a prime minister capable of controlling a majority of the seats in the lower house of parliament, the Lok Sabha.[32] Below the central government are the federal territorial units, each with its own legislative body and executive. There are also local governments. The constitution assigned the task of instituting village government to the federal territorial units, which meant that local government developed slowly and unevenly across the country. Constitutional changes in the 1990s, meant to clarify and standardize local governments in rural and urban areas, met with mixed success.[33]

Mexico

Long considered a party authoritarian system, Mexico is today considered a moderately successful democracy. Like the U.S. political system, Mexico's system has checks and balances. This was not a factor for much of the twentieth century because of the dominance of the Institutional Revolutionary Party (PRI), but the specifics of the constitution have become more important since 2000. Mexico also has a federal system, although the features of Mexican federalism include important differences from the U.S. version.

The Political System

Mexico's current political system is the result of political liberalization in the 1980s and 1990s, which turned an authoritarian system under the control of the PRI into a semiauthoritarian system and, ultimately, a fledgling democracy heralded by the 2000 presidential election and victory of a non-PRI candidate, Vicente Fox. Today, Mexico is considered an unconsolidated democracy. Government corruption remains a problem, above all in the judiciary and police.

Fitting its status as both a North American and a Latin American country, Mexico's regime falls in between Dahl's American and Latin American models of democracy. Dahl's American model employs an FPTP district electoral system, while the Latin American model uses PR, and Mexico's legislative electoral arrangements combine FPTP district and PR approaches. (Mexico's president is directly elected by FPTP rules, with the candidate getting the most votes gaining office even if he or she fails to win a majority of the vote.) The result of Mexico's electoral arrangements is three large political parties and several smaller ones, with the largest parties holding the vast majority of the seats in both houses of the Mexican national legislature.

IN THEORY AND PRACTICE

Political Change in Mexico and Easton's Systems Theory

In its early decades (from the late 1800s into the 1930s), political science paid great attention to institutions, particularly on formal institutions. The focus was typically a country's constitution, which was seen as the foundation of the political structure, as well as the institutional expression of political culture.[34] These efforts, which some now call **old institutionalism**, tended to be descriptive. When political science turned in the direction of behavioralism in the 1950s and 1960s, detailed descriptions of formal institutions were replaced by a focus on the broader process of translating political inputs into political outputs. Political scientists paid less attention to the political system's particular design than to the pressure and backing it received and the policies it produced.

The tendency to gloss over the characteristics of the institutions within the political system was most apparent in the work of David Easton, who treated institutional arrangements within the political system as a "black box." Rather than providing a detailed discussion of institutional arrangements or the actions of political leaders working within the system, Easton highlighted the demands and supports that enter a political system, which then translates them into policy outcomes. As portrayed in Figure 5.1, the process includes a feedback loop, as outputs (government policies) spark new demands and supports. Easton's approach came to be known as **systems theory**. In reality, it was much more of a model than a theory, highlighting what went into and came out of all political systems.

Although Easton's approach to modeling political institutions as a black box that turns inputs into outputs is simple, even simplistic, it does provide a framework for understanding important political outcomes. The approach stresses three forms of supports that flow into the system: supports for the government, for the regime, and for the political community, which refers to the extent of attachment to an overarching national identity.

In the last few decades of PRI rule in Mexico, all three sets of supports were strained. The population viewed the government as increasingly corrupt and ineffective and the system as stifling representation of their interests. The commitment to a unified Mexican national identity was also

---

Old Institutionalism A label for the traditional approach of political science to the study of political institutions, common from the late 1800s into the middle 1900s, which was highly descriptive.
Systems Theory The name given to the efforts by David Easton to model the political process as a set of inputs (demands and supports) that feed into the political system and outputs (policies) that flow from it.

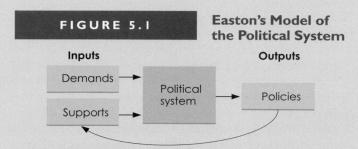

FIGURE 5.1   Easton's Model of the Political System

shaky. At the same time, demands on the system (Easton's other type of input) were increasing. The government tried to address increasing demands and shore up flagging support through policy initiatives and by allowing non-PRI candidates to win more and more local and regional elections. But these outputs were not enough to alter the configuration of inputs. Thus, even without knowing what was going on inside the black box of the political system, Easton's framework allows one to make some sense of the significant political reforms in Mexico. With supports decreasing, demands increasing, and outputs failing to feed back in a way that changed this pattern, the government was pressured to accept significant political liberalization.

The Constitution

Mexico's constitution is comparatively old. Officially known as the Political Constitution of the United Mexican States, it was originally written in 1917 and has been heavily amended since then. One of its lasting features is that it prohibits presidents or representatives in the national legislature from running for reelection. Like its American counterpart, the Mexican constitution provides for a number of checks and balances in a federal presidential system with a bicameral national legislature. In the past, when the PRI dominated the presidency and the legislature, these checks and balances were less relevant. Vicente Fox learned quickly that the Mexican presidency, which had appeared so powerful under the PRI, is not nearly as powerful when the president's party does not control the legislative branch. During his term in office, Fox was at the mercy of powers granted to the legislature in the Mexican constitution. Fox's successor, Felipe Calderón, faced similar problems during his term from 2006 to 2012.

Mexico's combination of presidentialism and a multiparty system is a recipe for gridlock. Although analysts of and participants in Mexican politics have discussed numerous dramatic political reforms,[35] the current gridlock-conducive system seems destined to remain in place. Reforming any system to increase the concentration of political power can be difficult. Those who believe that the reforms might threaten their political power will use their existing powers to block the reforms. In addition, changing the system to allow the president to force through reforms more easily sets the stage for a possible reemergence of authoritarianism centered on a strong president.

Levels of Government

Mexico is a federal system with thirty-one regional territories and one federal district, Mexico City. Like the United States, the regional territories are called states. (In an effort to avoid confusion over the use of the term *state*, this section refers to the regional territories by the equivalent Spanish word, *estado*.) A governor and legislature run the government of each estado, and localities within each have mayors and municipal councils. There are more than two thousand municipalities (*municipios*) in Mexico.

Estados have authority to pass laws and levy taxes, though they remain dependent on the federal government for much of their revenue. They also supply local governments with a large amount of revenue. In the past, this was one of many factors that contributed to corruption in Mexican politics. The Mexican constitution reserves certain powers to the federal government and prohibits the federal government and the estados from engaging in certain acts. According to Article 124 of the constitution, powers not discussed in the constitution fall to the estados.

There have been two noticeable differences between the American and Mexican federal systems since the adoption of the Mexican constitution in 1917. The more important of the two, the dominance of the PRI at all levels of government during the twentieth century, has changed dramatically over the last several decades. At the height of its power, the PRI controlled the federal government, the estado governments, and even most municipal governments in Mexico. This was significant in that it meant that the officially federal system behaved more like a unitary system. The first signs of cracks in PRI control appeared at the level of the municipios and then the estados. By the 1990s, it was not unusual for the PRI to lose elections at these levels, though the party did not surrender power at the federal level until 2000.

The second difference is that all the legislatures of the estados are unicameral (made up of only one house). Only one American state, Nebraska, has a unicameral legislature. The preponderance of unicameral legislatures in Mexico may sound trivial, but it played a role in helping concentrate the PRI's power. Though having to govern in a federal system makes total control of all levels more difficult, the PRI only needed to control the governorship and the single legislative house in each of the estados to dominate regional politics.

Brazil

Like many of its South American neighbors, Brazil experienced alternating periods of democracy and military authoritarian governments throughout much of the twentieth century. However, Brazil has maintained a stable democratic government since 1985, a period that included adoption of a new constitution in 1988. Like Mexico, Brazil is a federal system. Its distribution of power to lower levels of government has allowed entrenched elites to maintain significant control over regional and local politics.

The Political System

Brazil's current political system is the product of a protracted period of liberalization that began at the initiative of the military government more than ten years before the first nonmilitary president was elected in 1985. At first, the military's goal was to ease public dissatisfaction by permitting a little more freedom to speak and to organize. Within this limited space, popular movements and independent unions began to emerge.

The military allowed elections for the legislature, but banned most leftist politicians and organized the rest into two legal parties—an "opposition" party known as the MDB (Movement for Brazilian Democracy) and a pro-military party known as Arena (Alliance for National Renovation). Neither party opposed the military junta; they were known in Brazilian circles as the parties of "Yes" and "Yes, Sir!" Nevertheless, Brazilians saw the less-servile MDB as an opportunity to express their opposition to the military government.

As popular support for the MDB grew, the military searched for ways to maintain control. Hoping to divide the opposition vote, it legalized additional political parties in the late 1970s. The effort failed. Most of the political opposition joined together in a broad national movement calling for direct elections of the national executive in 1985. When the military candidate lost the election, a new constitutional convention was called.

The slow pace of Brazil's transition and the still powerful position of the military and its conservative allies during the constitutional convention meant that Brazil's new political system included important safeguards for elites. The Latin American model of strong presidentialism with a legislature elected by proportional representation was followed in Brazil—at least with respect to the lower house of the national legislature, the Chamber of Deputies. Like deputies in the lower house, the president serves a four-year term. Members of the upper house (the Senate) serve eight-year terms. The federal territorial units (estados) elect three senators each, using a plurality system in which seats go to the three candidates who receive the most votes. (As with Mexico, the discussion of Brazil uses the term *estado*, which is also the word for state in Portuguese.) The length of senatorial terms, the constitutional powers granted the Senate, and the fact that rural conservative estados outnumber industrial and centrist estados have given powerful regional elites the ability to block many reform measures, such as land reform, that would damage conservative interests. Although some serious problems remain in Brazilian democracy, such as corruption, Brazil ranked higher in 2010 on Freedom House's ratings of the extent of democracy than all the other TIC cases except the UK and Germany.[36]

The Constitution

The 1988 Brazilian constitution (its seventh since independence) was a compromise between groups with very different visions of Brazilian society and how it should be governed. The result, according to former president Fernando Henrique Cardoso, was "a completely unrealistic wish list. It guaranteed outlandish 'rights' that Brazil simply could not afford, creating laws and expectations that would haunt the country's politicians for years thereafter."[37]

Among other provisions, the constitution's 245 articles guarantee federal employees job security for life after only two years of service. Generous health care, pension plans, environmental protection, family leave, and free education are constitutionally defined as obligations of the state. Article 227 grants children constitutional rights to "life, health, nourishment, education, leisure, professional training, culture, dignity, respect, freedom . . . as well as [protection from] all forms of negligence, discrimination, exploitation, violence, cruelty, and oppression." Article 229 defines the duty of parents "to assist, raise and educate their underage children and . . . the duty of children of age to help and assist their parents in old age, need or sickness."[38] As laudable as these goals might be, constitutional scholars have worried that the sheer impossibility of enforcing such rights undermines Brazil's efforts to establish the rule of law. Some provisions of the constitution had to be ignored, and if these could be ignored with impunity, other, more enforceable rights might also be ignored.

The Brazilian constitution also enshrined privileges for the outgoing military government that guaranteed it a continuing say in how Brazil would be run. As a result, although the army is under the authority of the president, there is no civilian ministry of defense to oversee military budgets and behavior; active-duty officers serve in the cabinet; and the military runs the aviation and aeronautics industries, as well as others critical to national defense.

Levels of Government

Brazil is a federal system with authority granted to lower levels of government to a great extent. The country is divided into twenty-six regional territories below the federal government, along with a federal district that is home to Brazil's capital, Brasília.

The constitution confers upon estados all powers not expressly reserved for the federal government. The estados establish their own constitutions; can tax, spend, and regulate freely; have their own flags and anthems; and share with the federal government the power to legislate

on important issues such as social security, education, and the environment. They can create their own "metropolitan districts," a level of administration between the estado and the municipal governments to facilitate management of large cities and neighboring communities.

At the same time, municipal governments have substantial financial and legal autonomy from the higher levels of government. The period of Portuguese colonialism combined with the extraordinarily difficult topography of Brazil to leave a legacy of "relatively greater municipal autonomy . . . [that] still distinguishes the Brazilian local government system from its counterparts elsewhere in Latin America."[39] The 1988 constitution further bolstered the position of municipal governments. The local government share of total government spending rose from 11 percent in 1980 to 18 percent in 1990, higher than in any Latin American nation other than Colombia.[40] By comparison, Mexican municipalities control only 3 percent of total government spending.[41] In many ways, these provisions have been among the most democratic achievements of post-1988 Brazil. Municipalities have become laboratories for experiments in participatory democracy.

There have been some problems. For one, the Brazilian constitution is unclear about the division of responsibilities between the levels of government.[42] Thus, the governor of São Paulo (one of the most diverse and economically important of Brazil's estados) shares responsibility with the mayor of the city of São Paulo for the provision of public transportation, education, and health care, among other public services. This arrangement leads to much confusion and creates incentives for governments to try to avoid responsibility by shifting it to other levels.

In the highly economically unequal country of Brazil, this type of strong federalism has also tended to preserve the privileges of some of Brazil's most wealthy and powerful elites. Many estados cover considerable territory but are sparsely populated. Large landowners historically have dominated the more rural areas of the country's interior. By giving governors broad powers, the system allows these landowners to control what amounts to small kingdoms. They have huge influence over local politics and protect their property rights against "outside" (i.e., national) influences.

Strong federalism has thus limited the federal government's ability to tap into local resources in order to finance programs to help the poor or to redistribute wealth and land. Compromises—such as those protecting military autonomy—may have been necessary to secure the consent of the military and conservative interests during democratization. By permitting elites to veto reforms of vital interest to Brazil's poor majority, however, the choice to give broad powers to lower levels of government has lessened the Brazilian federal government's effectiveness and, ultimately, the regime's legitimacy.

Nigeria

The previous three chapters highlighted the social and economic traits that make Nigeria a prototypical developing country: an underdeveloped economy, dependence on natural resource exports, a political culture unattached to democratic practices, and an ethnically and religiously diverse population. Likewise, its political structures represent the characteristics of developing countries. Nigeria possesses a politically unstable postcolonial history, personalized politics, and a pattern of military intervention in the political system. Its constitution emphasizes unity of its diverse population, while its federal system is designed to try to cut across, rather than reinforce, its identity divisions.

The Political System

The combination of majoritarian and consensus features makes Nigeria's political system look a lot like that of the United States, with a president, a vice president, and a bicameral legislature (whose houses are called the House of Representatives and the Senate) within a federal system. In a country as socially complex and economically challenged as Nigeria, emulating the U.S. approach of multiple checks and balances has created as many problems as it has solved. From 1999 to 2007, Nigeria was considered an established (but unconsolidated) democracy. Following the 2007 elections, observers became more reluctant to label the country a democracy. Although the circumstances leading to President Goodluck Jonathan's ascension to the presidency in 2010 cast a shadow on the 2011 presidential elections (see Chapter 6), international election observers were largely positive about how the 2011 elections were ultimately conducted.

Politics in Nigeria is highly personalized. Who holds a particular position can be more important than the official powers of that position. Until that changes and until corruption is greatly diminished, democracy will have a difficult time consolidating itself as the only regime type Nigerian elites and masses consider legitimate.

Nigeria is also affected by the challenge of its recent past. Postcolonial Nigeria has alternated between periods of unstable democracy and of military authoritarianism. An understanding of the current Nigerian regime is thus impossible without understanding the influence of the military (addressed in more detail in Chapter 7). It is difficult to consolidate democracy in a country with a tradition of military intervention in politics. The executive and legislature cannot focus only on each other; they must always be looking over their shoulders.

The Constitution

Including constitutions written by the British during colonial rule, the Nigerian constitution, developed to coincide with the reestablishment of democracy in 1999,

was Nigeria's seventh in roughly five decades. It was not dramatically changed from the constitution governing the political system during the last serious attempt at democracy in the late 1970s and early 1980s, although the number of regions in Nigeria's federal system was increased to thirty-six.

The Nigerian constitution is long and detailed. It has 320 articles, most of them several paragraphs in length. It includes a section on the obligations of the government, many of which relate to fostering unity in the country. Provisions throughout the constitution address social divisions in the country with particular political arrangements. These include the requirement that a successful candidate for the presidency obtain 25 percent or more of the vote in two-thirds of the thirty-six regions. Perhaps somewhat ominously, the Miscellaneous Provisions section includes the circumstances under which the president can declare a state of emergency.

Levels of Government

It is no accident that the current Nigerian constitution contains a number of detailed passages regarding establishing national unity and overcoming social divisions. Since the civil war of the 1960s, this has been a goal of subsequent governments, democratic and authoritarian alike, when considering changes to the political system. Chapter 4 laid out some of the ways that interior political boundaries associated with Nigeria's federal system initially reinforced existing social divisions from 1960 to 1967. The Nigerian ethno-federal approach led directly to the civil war in Nigeria that broke out in 1967 and eventually claimed as many as 1 million lives. The government learned from the civil war and abandoned the ethno-federal approach in favor of having the territorial boundaries within the country provide a cross-cutting cleavage—that is, the federal territorial units cut across existing ethnic and religious divisions.

An examination of two periods following the civil war, 1979–84 and 1992–94, is helpful for understanding the relationship between Nigeria's federal structure and ethnic violence. These two periods were similar to the years 1960–67 in many ways. Each period includes the span of one of the country's democratic republics and the first full year of the military regime that replaced it. Other variables—level of development, demographic features of the population, and so on—were relatively constant across these years. Yet, unlike during the 1960–67 period, the result of the regime transitions in 1979–84 and 1992–94 was not widespread ethnic violence.

The 1979–84 period began with Olusegun Obasanjo as leader of the military government. Obasanjo had come to power after the previous military leader, Murtala Muhammad, was killed in an unsuccessful coup in 1976. Muhammad had promised to return the country to democracy, a promise that Obasanjo fulfilled. Elections were held in the middle of 1979. Nigeria's Second

Republic was a presidential system, replacing the parliamentary approach of the early independence period. Another major change was a reform to the federal system designed to address the problem of ethnic divisions. The federal approach persisted, but the number of states was increased to nineteen. This and other provisions in the electoral laws of the country reduced the incentives for ethnically based parties. Though some violence existed in the Second Republic, political tensions were due much less to ethnic divisions than to widespread corruption. The general public correctly saw elections in 1983 as fraudulent, and people welcomed the coup that ended the Second Republic that same year.

The period of 1992–94 included the awkwardly named Third Republic—the aborted attempt at reinstating democracy in 1992 and 1993. Voters democratically elected regional governments and local councils, but the military never surrendered rule over the federal government. The transition toward the Third Republic began in the mid-1980s when Ibrahim Babangida came to power through yet another coup. He declared his intention to return the country to democratic rule. The military government also again increased the number of regions in the federal system, this time to thirty.

Presidential elections were held in June 1993, but Babangida did not like the results and promptly declared the election invalid. The Third Republic ended before it got started. Babangida's handpicked successor was overthrown in a coup that brought General Sani Abacha to power. Abacha ruled with a firm hand until his death in 1998, which paved the way for Nigeria's Fourth Republic in 1999. The Third Republic and its aftermath brought some violence, including significant government repression. Once again, however, the regime had not collapsed because of ethnic violence, and the violence was dramatically less than had been the case in the 1960s. At least in terms of limiting ethnic violence, the changes in Nigeria's federal structure following the civil war appeared to have been a success.

Russia

In 1993, the new Russian constitution heralded a new democratic system, one with significant power concentrated in the executive branch. It also retained Russia's federal system. In contrast to the UK (a unitary system engaged in devolution), power became more concentrated in the Russian central government under Vladimir Putin.

The Political System
Soviet-era institutions persisted into the early post-Soviet period, leading to a major confrontation in 1993 that ultimately involved the use of military force against the Russian parliament. The new system that emerged from this conflict concentrated power in the president's hands.

Following a period of minimal abuse of these powers under Boris Yeltsin, his successor, Vladimir Putin, who became president of Russia at the end of 1999, used them to turn Russia in an authoritarian direction.

Under Boris Yeltsin, Russians had witnessed two economic collapses, the first at the beginning of the 1990s and the second later in the decade; an attempted coup against Yeltsin, leading to the use of the military against members of the Russian parliament; the inability of the Russian military to gain control of the region of Chechnya; and a presidential election in 1996 marred by numerous irregularities. Even so, Russia was ruled through democratic institutions for the longest period in its history.

It is hard to dispute that Russia has become less democratic since 2000. It increasingly resembles an authoritarian system, with government opponents failing to win seats in parliament, prosecuted for criminal activities, or both. With Putin's political allies in full control of the legislative branch following elections in 2003, the Russian political system had even fewer checks and balances in practice than it had on paper. By the end of Putin's term in 2008, Russia had earned the semiauthoritarian label.

The Constitution
In the fall of 1993, President Boris Yeltsin ordered the Russian parliament to disband and eventually ordered military units to attack the parliament building to remove members who refused to do so. In December 1993, Russian voters approved a new constitution and selected members of a new lower house of parliament, the Duma. The new constitution eliminated the position of vice president but included a dual executive system with a prime minister as well as a powerful president.

In late 2005, President Putin announced that he would not seek a third term when his term ended in 2008. At the same time, he indicated that he could not let Russia degenerate into political chaos. Thus, while he could have chosen to step down quietly, as Yeltsin did, he also could have extended his stay in office by amending the constitution to allow a third term, or he could have ignored the constitution, suspending presidential elections to prevent political chaos. Instead, he shifted to the position of prime minister after his handpicked successor, Dmitry Medvedev, became president.

In the past, Putin had appeared to show less concern for the rule of law than many in the West—if not many in Russia—would have liked him to show. Yet, his decision to maintain power by following the letter of the Russian constitution, albeit creatively, points to his unwillingness to completely ignore the system's overarching rules. It is fair to question the depth of Putin's commitment to the rule of law. At the same time, the Russian system is not based solely on the arbitrary rule of a single person. This is one of the reasons that the system is best labeled semiauthoritarian, rather than authoritarian.

Levels of Government

Russia's current federal system is one of the continuing legacies from the Soviet period. The Russian Soviet Federative Socialist Republic (RSFSR) of the Soviet Union was the USSR's only union republic officially labeled a federation. Other republics contained autonomous regions, but none to the extent of the RSFSR. When Russia emerged from the collapse of the USSR as an independent state, it inherited these regions, some of which had more official autonomy than others, and some of which were named for particular ethnic minorities.

Today, eighty-three regions in Russia have various standing: twenty-one are republics, forty-six are oblasts, one is an autonomous oblast, nine are krais, and four are autonomous okrugs. Moscow and St. Petersburg are treated as distinct regions deemed "cities of federal significance." Each of the twenty-one republics—nominally the homelands of non-Russian minorities such as the Tatars and Bashkirs—has the right to its own constitution. The republics have been the home of greatest anti-Russian sentiment, including those like Chechnya that pursued independence from Russia. Oblasts and krais are more like traditional provinces of a federal system. Autonomous okrugs are ethnic subdivisions of oblasts or krais that have claimed, and been granted, special status.

As president, Boris Yeltsin relied on the regions' support in his struggles with other parts of the federal government. This resulted in demands for greater regional autonomy both following the events of October 1993 and after Yeltsin won reelection in 1996. Regional leaders cut deals on taxes with the federal government, and some signed their own foreign trade agreements. The regional governments also routinely ignored Yeltsin's decrees, and numerous regions adopted laws contrary to both federal law and the Russian constitution. Yeltsin began to challenge the regions late in his presidency.

Vladimir Putin spent much of his presidency looking for ways to strengthen the rule of the federal government. In 2000, Putin established seven federal districts, adding a new layer to the federal system. Each federal district brought together a dozen or so regions, providing an additional link between the central government and the regions. In September 2004, Putin pushed through a provision to eliminate direct election of regional governors. Instead, Moscow would now appoint them. In addition, the Russian government has encouraged the ongoing contraction of the number of regions. Mergers of regions took place in 2005, 2007, and 2008, bringing the total down from eighty-nine to the present number of eighty-three.

Though some regional leaders have complained, they have been unable to stop these tactics. Thus, Russia stands in stark contrast to the UK's devolution policy, which increased regional power but maintained the UK's status as a unitary system. The Russian central government has taken back powers from the regions but has maintained a federal structure.

China

China is an authoritarian system, but official rules and government positions mean more than they used to. Consequently, the constitution has increased in importance, though the Chinese political system is nowhere near the point where the rule of law is a defining feature. In terms of levels of government, China shares the UK's pattern of increasing power for the regions while maintaining a unitary system.

The Political System

China's political institutions have long frustrated students of comparative politics. The dual hierarchy of state and party administrators can be confusing, particularly since nearly all top government officials are also high-ranking members of the Chinese Communist Party (CCP). At least as important, for the first several decades of CCP rule the lack of correspondence between official government position and actual power was unmatched among world powers. Mao Zedong was CCP chairman, but he ruled more through his personal legitimacy as leader of the revolution than through his institutional powers. When Deng Xiaoping emerged as the leader after Mao's death, he held neither the position of government premier nor of general secretary of the CCP—the leadership position that replaced the position of chairman after Mao's death. Perhaps indicating where much of the real power lies in China, the most important official position that Deng held was chairman of the CCP Central Military Commission and its government counterpart, the state Central Military Commission. When Deng was replaced by Jiang Zemin as the country's most visible leader, it also signaled the growing importance of official positions of power. This trend has continued to the present.

Shortly after Mao Zedong died in the fall of 1976, his wife and three others, collectively known as the "Gang of Four," were arrested. This event marked China's move away from the ideologically driven system Mao had cultivated. Within two years, Deng Xiaoping had solidified his hold over the Communist Party, allowing him to introduce significant economic reforms.

Prior to Deng's encouragement of such reforms, most scholars had labeled China a Communist totalitarian system. Since the 1980s, China has begun to look more and more like a party authoritarian system. The government is much less involved in the economy than it was in the past, and it intrudes less into people's lives, as long as they do not speak out against it. The government has even allowed capitalists (e.g., private sector business owners) to join the Communist Party for the last several years.

Today, China's party authoritarianism lacks the ideological focus it had when it more closely resembled a totalitarian system. Nationalism underpins the government's claims to legitimacy. The government's goals include continuation of rapid economic development in the decades since economic reforms, enhancement of China's reputation as a global economic and military power, and maintenance of its domestic political power. Unlike the Soviet Union, China has successfully reformed its economy without losing control of the political system. How long the party authoritarian system can withstand pressures for further political reform is a central question facing Chinese political leaders.

The Constitution

The Chinese constitution demonstrates that long, detailed constitutions do not necessarily translate into democratic political systems. The most recent version, ratified in 1982 and amended twice since, is one of the longer constitutions in the world. It contains 138 articles that follow a long preamble. Unlike most preambles, which provide a short overview of the principles underlying the arrangements of the political system, the preamble to the Chinese constitution provides the Communist Party's take on the history of Chinese civilization and foreign relations. With official government positions mattering more than they did prior to the death of Deng Xiaoping, the institutional powers laid out in the Chinese constitution have also become more important. The constitution sets up a dual executive system, with a president considered to be the head of state and a premier (prime minister) who oversees the day-to-day governing of the country.

Like other constitutions, the Chinese version is only as effective as the government's willingness to obey it. Rule of law is far from established in China, and the judicial system remains a hostage of the political dominance of the Communist Party. There are signs that the Communist government is open to improvements in this area, partly because foreign businesses have made clear that corruption and the general lack of respect for contracts threatens China's further economic development. The 2008 Olympics in Beijing also provided an incentive for the Chinese government to appear more democratic, though those who hoped the Olympics might spur major political changes have been disappointed.

Levels of Government

Like Russia, China has a large number of regions that take different forms. Of the thirty-one regions, four are municipalities, five are autonomous regions for ethnic minorities, and the remainder are provinces. Unlike Russia, however, China is a unitary state. A number of comparative politics and economics scholars have noted a conspicuous shift in the balance of power between the central government and China's regions. Again, unlike Russia, this shift has increased regional powers at the central government's expense, particularly in recent economic policy, and it has coincided with the ongoing implementation of market economic reforms and the declining adherence to official ideology. Some economists have labeled this trend Chinese "fiscal federalism" or "federalism, Chinese style."[43]

Is China devolving powers to the regions? Is it becoming a federal system? The answer to the first question is a tentative yes. China has increased the powers of regional and local governments dramatically. But these changes have focused on economics. No longer an archetypal unitary state, China remains centralized politically. It has not devolved political power to its regions like the UK has. The second question is easier to answer. China is not yet a federal state. An act called the Law-Making Law of the People's Republic of China, adopted in March 2000 following seven years of work, appeared to set the stage for federalism by laying out the central government's exclusive legislating powers.[44] Yet, the law left the central government in position to control activities at the regional level if necessary. While opening the door for legislating by local governments in areas not explicitly presented as central government matters, it provided that the central government can override such actions with contrary legislation.

Thus, China remains a unitary system. Changes like the Law on Law-Making signal a shift away from central control. But greater powers for lower levels of government alone do not signal a transition to a federal system. Only when such powers are constitutionally granted and protected could one discuss federalism in China.

IN THEORY AND PRACTICE

China and Skocpol's *States and Social Revolutions*

While most political scientists were turning away from a focus on state institutions in the 1960s and 1970s, scholars such as Theda Skocpol set the stage for the reemergence of a focus on state institutions in political science. Her 1979 book *States and Social Revolutions* was a landmark moment in comparative politics, a trumpet blast calling for comparative politics to "bring the state back in." Skocpol set out to move beyond comparativists who focused solely on socioeconomic structure. The state was not just a dependent variable driven by underlying economic structures. It was also an independent variable—or at least an important factor in its own right, if not fully independent from other structures—affecting political outcomes like revolutions.

China is one of the three main countries that Skocpol examines in detail in *States and Social Revolutions*. Skocpol takes a different approach to her study of revolutions, arguing that three very different states—France, Russia, and China—had similar experiences leading to major revolutions. Skocpol emphasizes the way that international pressures and domestic opposition combined with the institutional arrangement of the state to cause the state to respond ineffectively to the challenges it faced.

In China, the leaders of the Manchu Dynasty were increasingly forced to rely on local leaders for military support. This led local landlords to demand greater autonomy, creating a vicious circle of increasing local control. When the central government finally tried to reestablish control, local landlords rose up and overthrew it. This ushered in the nationalist period, which ended with the Communist seizure of power in 1949.

Skocpol's explanation of the collapse of the imperial system has relevance for Chinese politics today. More and more, Chinese local and regional leaders have pressured the central government to expand the authority of lower levels of government. Skocpol's study shows how relying on local officials can undercut the ability of the central government to maintain control. Even if Chinese leaders have not read Skocpol (many of them probably have), they know their own history. Thus, while one could expect further decentralization in China, it will likely go slowly. CCP leaders have ushered in a number of reforms over the last few decades, but they have no desire to oversee the collapse of their political system.

Iran

Iran's political system is comparatively unusual, but it reflects the influence of Islam in the practice of day-to-day politics. This includes a constitution, adopted in 1979 and revised in 1989, that clearly places Shia Islam at the center of Iranian politics. As in China, Iran's government had granted more power to the lower levels of government while maintaining its unitary and authoritarian nature and subsequently showing a willingness to reconcentrate power in the hands of the central government.

The Political System
The 1979 Islamic Revolution shaped the political structure to a great extent. For much of the period following the revolution, discussing Iran's political system meant discussing the role of its religious clerics. This system of infusing religious ideology and religious leaders into the political system is a crucial feature of Iranian politics.

As covered in Chapter 1, comparativists label such an approach a "theocracy." For a time in the late 1990s and early 2000s, Iran began to resemble a representative democracy. This led many scholars in the United States to openly discuss the beginning of genuine democratization in Iran. Events in 2004 and 2005 called this optimism into question. Although the Iranian legislature included a large number of reformers between 2000 and 2004,

the religious clerics who determine which candidates are allowed to run for national office blocked most reformers from the ballot in 2004. Combined with the end of moderate-reformist president Mohammed Khatami's term in 2005, this signaled a return to conservatism.

By the middle of 2006, at the same time tensions with the United States were escalating, Iran seemed as far from being an emerging democracy as it had at nearly any point since the 1979 revolution. At the end of that year, however, elections to the Assembly of Experts—the body that selects Iran's Supreme Leader and advises him on various issues—pointed to renewed dissatisfaction with the hard-liners controlling the government. Although many reformers were prevented from running in the March 14, 2008, elections to the national legislature, the Majles, the success of those who were on the ballot hinted at continued problems for conservatives like President Mahmoud Ahmadinejad. When Ahmadinejad won reelection in mid 2009, those supporting reform took to the streets. Though the protests ultimately failed to dislodge Ahmadinejad, they provided a further warning to conservative elements in Iran about the future direction of the country.

IN THEORY AND PRACTICE

Iran and Rational Choice New Institutionalism

Even before Theda Skocpol's call for a fresh look at state institutions, other scholars had begun to look to organizational theory to better understand institutions and their consequences. This ushered in what came to be called **new institutionalism**. This term applies to studies that examine institutions as structures marking a political system's historical changes, shaping individual choices, or reflecting society's underlying values and identities.

For new institutionalists, political institutions are not a black box; political institutions do not simply aggregate interests, but reshape them.[45] In short, "institutions matter."[46] Writing in 1996, Peter Hall and Rosemary Taylor provided a helpful overview of the various theories identified with the new institutionalism movement.[47] Hall and Taylor's article points to three sets of new institutionalism theories: rational choice, sociological, and historical. **Sociological new institutionalism** sees institutions as

---

New Institutionalism A theoretical perspective emphasizing the importance of political institutional arrangements and the extent to which the political system represents historical changes, shapes individual choices, and reflects underlying values and identities.

Sociological New Institutionalism A theoretical perspective that sees institutions as reflecting society's underlying culture rather than as the product of rational choices in the pursuit of increased efficiency.

flowing from the underlying culture of the society in which they develop. As such, sociological new institutionalism would be a logical choice for comparativists who focus on the effects of political culture's stability and changes over time. **Historical new institutionalism** acknowledges that political institutions are the product of social forces, rational calculations, and political institutional arrangements that existed in previous periods. It highlights the importance of past decisions that created the political structures in which current and future decisions are made. It is particularly helpful to those interested in the historical evolution of political systems.

Rational choice new institutionalism takes institutions to be the product of rational calculations. It thus shares many elements with rational choice theory, a theoretical perspective discussed in detail in Chapter 10. These include the belief that "individuals and their strategic calculations ought to be the central concern of social science"[48] and the assumption that individuals are calculating and self-interested, seeking to maximize the likelihood that they will achieve their preferred outcomes. The rational choice form of new institutionalism also holds that institutions constrain rational individuals by narrowing the field of possible choices or by altering calculations about the costs and benefits of a particular strategy. Individuals facing such constraints may seek to change the institution in response. As a result, institutions are designed and updated by individuals in an ongoing effort to maximize the benefits and minimize the costs of working within a given institutional framework.

Because Iranian leaders are often portrayed in the West as religious fanatics incapable of rational thought, can rational choice new institutionalism possibly help explain Iranian politics? Applying this approach to Iran would certainly make one think hard about the portrayal of Iranian leaders like President Mahmoud Ahmadinejad. The result might be an acknowledgment that political leaders, Western and Middle Eastern alike, tend to be both rational actors and true believers. As they design institutions, they do so both because they believe in certain ideals and because they seek to maximize their goals. As they make decisions within institutions, they continue to pursue these goals, but their beliefs shape what they perceive to be appropriate at the same time that the institutional rules constrain their options.

The design of Iran's theocracy is no exception. It reflects religious leaders' commitment to the governance of Iran through their interpretation of Islamic law, but it also

points to their efforts to prevent reformist pressures, such as those that emerged during the 1990s, the early 2000s, and again at the end of that decade, from weakening their hold on power. Specific institutional arrangements, such as the position of the Supreme Leader and the role of the Council of Guardians, were carefully crafted to maximize the goals of the Islamic leaders of the 1979 revolution. These institutions do not always produce the most efficient and effective policies for the country, but they are politically—or, perhaps more to the point, theocratically—efficient. They combine to make Iran a theocracy, but they also help maintain it as such.

The Constitution

In December 1979, following the ouster of the shah, the mullahs (religious clerics) who emerged as the country's new leaders put in place a new constitution. In 1989, a revised constitution removed the position of prime minister. Despite such changes, the Iranian constitution continues to reflect the 1979 Islamic Revolution and helps validate its designation as a theocracy.

Among the provisions of the constitution are the establishment of Shia Islam as the country's official religion and the creation of the Supreme Leader position. The Supreme Leader is part of the Iranian executive branch but is more powerful than the other chief executive, the Iranian president. He is the ultimate arbiter

Iran's Supreme Leader Ayatollah Ali Hoseini-Khamenei, center, with Iranian President Mahmoud Ahmadinejad, right. © REUTERS/Leader.ir/Handout

---

Historical New Institutionalism A theoretical approach that focuses on institutional change over time.

Rational Choice New Institutionalism A theoretical perspective that contends that institutions are the product of rational calculations on the part of individuals and limit the options of rational individuals seeking to make efficient and effective policy.

of political questions in Iran. He is allowed to use his interpretation of passages in the Koran and other Islamic documents to rule on any issue under consideration in the political system. The Supreme Leader works with other theocratic bodies in the political system, including the Expediency Council and the Guardian Council, institutions whose powers are outlined in more detail in the next chapter.

Levels of Government

Iran is a unitary system. The country is divided into thirty provinces, which are further divided into smaller units analogous to U.S. counties and municipalities. As in the past, provincial leaders—known today as governors-general—are quite powerful. They are appointed by the central government's interior minister. Befitting Iran's status as a theocracy, religious representatives of the central government also have significant power within the provinces.

Beginning in the late 1990s, the national government increased the authority of local governments. This policy included finally following through on local elections, which had been promised in the 1979 constitution. When elections took place in 1999, they brought reformers to power in a large number of cities. Several hundred women were elected at the local level, forming the majority of the councils in some localities.[49] Local governments increasingly served as sounding boards for disgruntled citizens who felt unable to express their concerns directly to the national government.

Some label the process of increasing local government responsibility and accountability in Iran as "controlled decentralization." As in China, the strengthening of local rule does not approach the extent of devolution efforts in the UK. In addition, the trends at the national level in 2004 and 2005, where the pro-reform leaders were dramatically weakened, did not bode well for increasing liberalization and responsibility at the local level in Iran. Certain scholars of Iranian politics have predicted that, in an effort to deflect criticism, the central government will blame local governments for economic or other performance problems.[50] This would assist those in the central government who support turning back the policies of the previous decade that expanded local powers.

TIC Wrap-Up

When examining the political systems, constitutions, and levels of government of the nine Topic in Countries (TIC) cases, one finds many similarities and differences. The current political systems in the UK, Germany, and India are all consolidated liberal democracies, and they place great power in the hands of the prime minister (called the chancellor in Germany). Yet, they differ in many significant ways, including the overall extent to which they approach Lijphart's majoritarian and consensus democracy ideal types, with the UK closely approximating the majoritarian system, the German system embodying the consensus variant, and India falling in between.

Their constitutional approaches vary greatly as well. The British constitution contains unwritten elements. The German constitution, based on the legal blueprint for the Federal Republic (West Germany) after World War II, balances individual rights and collective interests. The Indian constitution has been heavily amended since its adoption in 1950, but the amendments have not undone the significant power of the central government.

These three countries also provide examples of the range of possible federal and unitary arrangements. The UK has a unitary system, although devolution of central government authority to the regions has been notable. Germany and India are both federal systems. Befitting its consensus-style democracy, Germany's federal system is based more on shared powers than on reserved powers, and the federal government relies on the regional governments to enforce national policies and administer federal programs. By contrast, India is a federal system in which the central government yields significant power.

Mexico, Brazil, and Nigeria all have democratic political systems, though the long-term survival of democracy in these cases, particularly Nigeria, is far less certain than in the UK, Germany, and India. Mexico, Brazil, and Nigeria share American-style arrangements that place many powers in the president's hands but also spread power to other national political bodies and levels of government. All three have had significant periods of authoritarian rule in their recent histories, with the shadow of recent military rule hanging over both Nigeria and, to a lesser extent, Brazil. Other challenges to long-term democratic stability, such as corruption, plague all three countries as well.

Brazil and Nigeria have had numerous constitutions since gaining independence. Their current constitutions were adopted relatively recently, and both constitutions are much longer than the U.S. Constitution. By comparison, Mexico's constitution more closely resembles its northern neighbor's, but it is still less than a century old, has been heavily amended, and includes interesting provisions such as prohibiting national political leaders from seeking reelection.

Given the relatively large size of their territories and populations, it is not surprising that Mexico, Brazil, and Nigeria are all federal systems. In Mexico, the long dominance of the Institutional Revolutionary Party (PRI) meant that its federal system functioned more like a unitary system in practice, but this pattern disappeared with the end of the PRI's domination over the Mexican political system. Brazil's federal arrangements have meant significant power for regional leaders, which has helped perpetuate the country's significant economic inequality. Nigeria's federal system has been altered several times—mostly by adding new federal territorial units—after the initial ethno-federal approach fueled ethnic violence and helped undercut postindependence democracy.

Russia, China, and Iran all fall far from the democratic ideal. Russia had a brief experience with democracy in the 1990s but moved steadily toward authoritarianism under the former president and then prime minister, Vladimir Putin. China's political leaders continue to keep democracy at bay, although the formal positions of power in the government correlate much more with actual political power today than in decades past. The Iranian system has sent mixed signals to those hoping for greater political freedom, leaning toward limited political reforms, followed by a retrenchment of authoritarian politics and renewed hints of the possibility of liberalization. Even when reformers were most visible, however, the government looked little like a liberal democracy.

The constitutions of Russia, China, and Iran demonstrate how, even in non-democracies, leaders worry about the official rules of the game. At the same time, all three highlight how one must be careful not to assume that a constitution faithfully outlines the actual allocation of, and limits on, political power. Rule of law remains shaky in all three countries.

Russia, China, and Iran also demonstrate the difficulties that the federal versus unitary distinction can pose. Russia remains a federal system, though the central government continues to consolidate power at the expense of the regional governments. China has a unitary system, yet regional authorities continue to gain power at the expense of the central government. Iran is also a unitary state, but local authorities had been granted noteworthy levels of autonomy, only to have the national government signal a move back in the direction of centralized control.

COUNTRY SUMMARY

TIC Country	Regime Type	Constitution	Levels of Government
United Kingdom	Mature democracy; majoritarian; Westminster system; ITAP feature on veto points	Includes unwritten components as well as a number of different written components	Unitary system, but with significant devolution of powers (particularly to Scotland and Northern Ireland)
Germany	History of various non-democratic systems; mature democracy today; largely a consensus system; combines European and Westminster features in its electoral rules	Written constitution known as the Basic Law in West Germany prior to reunification; divides power and establishes significant individual rights	Federal system with significant powers shared with the regions (Länder); the Länder represented in the federal government by the Bundesrat (the upper house of parliament)
India	Consolidated democracy; relatively stable since independence with exception of the Emergency (1975–77)	Adopted in 1950; very long, very detailed, and heavily amended; provides for significant centralization of power within a federal system	Federal system, but with a strong central government; 28 federal territorial units; efforts to standardize and clarify local government powers had mixed success
Mexico	Liberalization of the party authoritarian system under the PRI led to establishment of democracy in the late 1990s; 2000 presidential election represents democracy's founding election; ITAP feature on Easton's systems theory	Written in 1917; heavily amended; functioned as the official rules of the game for the PRI's party authoritarian system and the current democratic system; checks and balances in the constitution more obvious since 2000	Federal system; 31 regional units (estados) and one federal district; more than 2,000 municipalities (municipios) in the country

TIC Country	Regime Type	Constitution	Levels of Government
Brazil	Established democracy; despite democracy's being in place since 1985, many do not consider it to be a consolidated democratic system because of corruption and legacy of military rule	Current constitution adopted in 1988 (7th constitution in Brazil's history); long list of social and economic guarantees has caused problems for the democratic governments that followed its adoption	Federal system, with significant powers granted to regional and local governments; 26 regional units (estados) and one federal territory, which contains the capital city of Brasília
Nigeria	Established democracy (since 1999); fears of backsliding towards semidemocracy, partly due to electoral irregularities and the circumstances that resulted in Goodluck Jonathan becoming president in 2010	Constitution put in place in 1999; long and detailed; designed to foster unity and discourage regionalism, including provision requiring the president to receive at least 25 percent of the vote in two-thirds of the 36 regions to win	Federal system; number of regions increased over time, in large part to combat complementary divisions between identity groups and regional boundaries; 36 federal territorial units at present
Russia	Attempt at democracy in the 1990s broke down after Vladimir Putin became president at the end of that decade; generally considered to be semiauthoritarian today	Adopted in 1993 following the violent clash between then president Yeltsin and parliament; enshrined strong executive powers, placed in the hands of both a president and a prime minister	Federal system; at the start of post-Soviet period, there were 89 regions; today there are 83 regions, with more consolidation possible; since 2000, the federal government has weakened the power of the regions
China	Formerly a Communist system; today considered to be a party authoritarian one under the control of the Chinese Communist Party	Most recent version ratified in 1982; very long preamble that details the major developments of Chinese history; importance is limited by government's unwillingness to abide by its provisions when it is inconvenient to do so	Unitary system divided into 31 regions; regional authorities are more powerful than in the past, but central government tries to limit corruption at the regional and local levels; ITAP feature on Skocpol's *States and Social Revolutions*
Iran	Aspects of democracy, but most consider it a theocracy that is more authoritarian than democratic; ITAP feature on rational choice new institutionalism	Constitution in 1979 established the system's theocratic nature; new constitution in 1989; constitution gives significant power to the Supreme Leader	Unitary system divided into 30 provinces; governments supportive of reform emerged at the local level in the 1990s
Spotlight on … Country			
France	Generally considered a mature democracy; current system is the Fifth Republic; established in 1958, it combines majoritarian and consensus features	Constitution adopted in 1958 to coincide with the launching of the Fifth Republic; emphasizes the fundamental principles of the French Revolution, including popular sovereignty and secularism	Unitary system divided into 26 regions (further divided into 100 departments); local government relatively weak

Spotlight on . . . Country	Regime Type	Constitution	Levels of Government
Iraq	Established but fragile democracy; some consider the January 2005 elections as the founding elections of the democracy; others see Iraq as still in the transition period to democratic establishment	Written in 2005 and in force in 2006; fundamental principles include Islam as the official religion and also that no law may contradict the principles of democracy; establishes Arabic and Kurdish as the official languages of Iraq	Federal system, divided into 18 governorates; regions (a level above the governorates) can be formed from multiple governorates; the Kurdish region encompasses three of the northern governorates and is the only one currently recognized
South Africa	Following a period of liberalization starting in the late 1980s, democracy established in 1994; system has both consensus and majoritarian democratic features	Constitution adopted in 1996; founding provisions include universal suffrage, opposition to racism and sexism, rule of law, and a common citizenship	Unitary, despite its large size and diverse population; divided into 9 provinces; Gauteng is smallest but most populated province and contains the cities of Pretoria and Johannesburg

Research in Context

Constitutionalism is one of the many important concepts presented in this chapter. Some comparativists consider it to be one of the most essential components of a democracy. Others may not go quite so far, but clearly it is a concept of great significance when considering how to begin to examine the role of political structures in shaping major political outcomes. As a result, it is also at the center of a significant amount of comparative politics research.

Origins of Constitutionalism in Latin America

One such work is an article by Andrea Pozas-Loyo and Julio Rios-Figueroa in the April 2010 edition of the journal *Comparative Politics*.[51] Pozas-Loyo and Rios-Figueroa ask the question, "When and why can we expect constitution-making processes to produce an institutional framework that formally serves constitutionalism?" They begin their study by distinguishing between "unilateral" constitution-making processes—when a single major political group controls the process of making and/ or amending the constitution—and "multilateral" ones, in which more than one such group exists. They examine eighteen Latin American countries over the period 1945 to 2005.

Examining these eighteen countries over sixty years, Pozas-Loyo and Rios-Figueroa focus on the extent of judicial autonomy. Also known as judicial independence, judicial autonomy is the ability of judges to make decisions free from pressure by the legislature or executive (see Chapter 7). They point out that the eighteen countries show significant variation in such autonomy. In some, the official rules have not established judicial autonomy in the first place. Thus, the stereotype of Latin American judiciaries having independence on paper but not in reality is incorrect. The authors contend that one can trace the differences in how independent the judiciary is to the setting in which the constitution was created or in which the major parts dealing with judicial powers were amended. Their study finds that multilateral constitution-making processes led to the establishment of judicial institutions that were autonomous from the other branches of government and had strong authority over constitutional matters.

So What?

For comparativists interested in the concept of constitutionalism, Pozas-Loyo and Rios-Figueroa's findings have obvious importance. Why should an ordinary American citizen or a policy maker in Washington, D.C., care about this research on constitution-making in Latin America? If constitutionalism is a fundamental requirement of a successful democracy, then policy makers who push for making the spread of democracy around the world a key U.S. foreign policy goal should take note of this study.

If the American government can shape the conditions under which a fledgling democracy's new constitution is developed, Pozas-Loyo and Rios-Figueroa's research points to the importance of one of those conditions being a multilateral constitution-making process. Simply put, those wanting to see constitutionalism take hold in a new democracy should help ensure that two or more distinct political groups are involved in drafting its constitution. It would seem to make sense that the best new constitution would be one drafted by a single group that has stated, and even shown, its deep commitment to democracy. Yet, Pozas-Loyo and Rios-Figueroa's research on Latin American constitutional development indicates that the involvement of multiple groups—even some groups the United States does not support—may produce constitutional arrangements effective in limiting arbitrary rule by government officials in the long term. For U.S. citizens, who are also taxpayers helping foot the bill to pay for U.S. foreign policy initiatives, this research project points to the things that those crafting such initiatives should be taking into account.

CONCLUSION

This chapter introduced concepts and theories related to the political structural approach to comparative politics. This approach pays close attention to the institutional arrangements in a political system. It allows comparativists to categorize the political system in broad terms (democracy, totalitarianism, or authoritarianism), consider subcategories within these broad categories (majoritarian versus consensus democracy), and formulate causal arguments that place institutional arrangements at the center of understandings of political outcomes.

Like examinations of socioeconomic structures, approaches that focus solely on political institutions and their rules can be criticized. Such criticisms include the idea that institutionalists too often focus on describing the rules of the game and too rarely consider the socioeconomic reasons that the institutions look the way they do. As political scientist Adam Przeworski provocatively asks, "If different institutions are possible only under different conditions, how can we tell whether what matters are institutions or the conditions?"[52] It is indeed important to consider the origins of institutions, and most new institutionalists, regardless of the variant of new institutionalism they utilize, build a discussion of the emergence or evolution of government institutions into their discussions of political effects.

In addition, even if criticisms of examining political institutions to understand political outcomes make sense, one must be careful not to overreact. The structure of the political system—the arrangement of political institutions and the rules that govern decision making within them—matters because it provides the most direct setting in which political decisions occur. It is the closest structural component to the process of political decision making. As Przeworski also declares, political institutions can "prevent people from doing what they would have otherwise done or induce them to do what they otherwise would not have done."[53] This chapter's overview of the constitutions and institutional arrangements and their effects on politics in the TIC cases supports Przeworski's contention. In Brazil, for example, the large number of veto points has allowed wealthy local elites to protect their holdings. Even if the vast majority of Brazilians desire dramatic land reform, it is unlikely to happen without changes to the country's political arrangements.

The TIC cases also demonstrate that political institutions are not the entire story. The UK's combination of a partially unwritten constitution and increasing powers to lower levels of government in a unitary system is distinct. It works, fairly well at least, in the British case. Similar institutional approaches in other cases—cases with differing socioeconomic structures and distinct leaders—would likely produce very different outcomes.

Students of comparative politics should not ignore the socioeconomic structural forces discussed in the previous three chapters. But the arrangement of political institutions is an important factor that shapes the kinds of major political outcomes in which comparativists are interested. The next two chapters move beyond the general discussion of political institutions to examine particular arrangements involving governing institutions and variations in them from one country to another.

KEY TERMS

American model of democracy, p. 133

Authoritarianism, p. 135

Bureaucratic authoritarianism, p. 136

Communism, p. 135

Confederation, p. 138

Consensus democracy, p. 132

Constitution, p. 137

Constitutionalism, p. 137

Democracy, p. 130

Devolution, p. 139

European model of democracy, p. 133

Fascism, p. 135

Federal system, p. 138

Historical new institutionalism, p. 153

Institution, p. 129

Latin American model of democracy, p. 133

Majoritarian democracy, p. 132

Military authoritarianism, p. 136

New institutionalism, p. 152

Old institutionalism, p. 145

Party authoritarianism, p.136

Political institution, p. 130

Rational choice new institutionalism, p. 153

Reserved powers, p. 138

Rule of law, p. 137

Semiauthoritarianism, p. 136

Semidemocracy, p. 136

Shared powers, p. 138

Sociological new institutionalism, p. 152

Systems theory, p. 145

Totalitarianism, p. 134

Unitary system, p. 138

Veto points, p. 140

Westminster model of democracy, p. 133

Legislatures and Executives

India's Prime Minister Manmohan Singh shakes hands with Brazil's President Dilma Rousseff during their meeting at the BRICS (Brazil, Russia, India, China and South Africa) summit in Sanya, China, April 14, 2011.
© REUTERS/Press Information Bureau of India/Handout

CHAPTER OUTLINE

Parliamentary, Presidential, and Semi-presidential Systems
Legislatures
The Executive

TOPIC IN COUNTRIES

Features in this chapter:

Spotlight on . . . South Africa: The South African Chief Executive: Part of a Parliamentary, Presidential, or Semi-presidential System?

In Theory and Practice: The United Kingdom and Party Government Theory

In Theory and Practice: Brazil and Theories about Presidential Systems

In Theory and Practice: Nigeria and Theories about Presidential Systems

In Theory and Practice: Iran and the Theory of "Going Public"

Research in Context: Questioning Ministers in Parliamentary Systems

After reading this chapter, you should be able to

- Identify the main tasks of a legislative branch.
- Identify the main tasks of a political executive.

- Discuss the key features, advantages, and disadvantages of a parliamentary system, a presidential system, and a semi-presidential system.
- Describe the executive and legislative arrangements in the TIC cases.

On October 31, 2010, Dilma Rousseff of the Worker's Party (known in Brazil by its Portuguese-language acronym, the PT) defeated José Serra, the former governor of São Paulo, and became Brazil's first female president. Rousseff had the support of the outgoing Brazilian president, Luiz Inácio "Lula" da Silva. Lula was highly popular in Brazil, with support of around 80 percent at the end of his second term, but Brazilian law prevented him from seeking a third term. Lula also brought Rousseff the support of much of the PT's political organization, particularly in the less wealthy areas of Brazil. Rousseff's victory was far from a given, however, and she won partly because of her personal abilities.

Rousseff was known as the "Iron Lady" as an administrator and had most recently served as Lula's chief of staff. The daughter of a Bulgarian immigrant, she was a prominent member of an opposition movement against the Brazilian military government that ruled Brazil from the mid-1960s to the mid-1980s. She had been arrested in 1970 and tortured for three weeks, enduring electric shock and other abuse.[1] With Brazil's ongoing challenges and upcoming opportunities, including hosting the World Cup in 2014 and the Olympics in 2016, many Brazilians hope that her toughness will serve her and the country well.

The previous chapter addressed some of the basic differences between political systems, including the fundamentals of federal and unitary systems and their advantages and disadvantages. This chapter addresses another central topic regarding a country's political structure: the government's legislative and executive functions. As societies and political systems became more complex throughout history, it was almost impossible to concentrate all decision-making power in the hands of a single leader. Even Joseph Stalin, who may have made more daily governing decisions than any other political leader in the twentieth century, had under him an array of decision-making and enforcing institutions.

Nearly all political systems, democratic and nondemocratic alike, contain legislative institutions—the part of the government officially in charge of legislating (making laws). General hostility toward a political system is often aimed at this institution. The early history of legislatures was one of increasing power over time as they battled monarchs for input into governing decisions. More recently, the trend has been in the other direction, with executives once again becoming the initiators of policies and with legislatures increasingly ceding power to them.[2] Yet, in many democracies, legislatures remain the heart and soul of lawmaking and maintain significant control over the policy-making process. As a result, scholars and citizens alike often consider the legislature the most democratic of the branches of government.

Governments also must execute (implement) the laws that are adopted. The two general approaches to the challenge of creating and implementing government policy are presidentialism and parliamentarism. Familiar to students in the United States, presidentialism separates the executive functions from the legislative functions, creating two distinct branches of government with a president, such as Brazil's Dilma Rousseff, who serves as head of the government and head of state. The second approach, parliamentarism, links the executive and legislature tightly together, fusing the governing responsibilities that presidential systems separate. There is also a growing tendency to create hybrid semi-presidential systems with features of both. Before discussing some of the specific duties of legislatures and executives, it is helpful to discuss these broad approaches to fusing or separating the legislative and executive branches.

Parliamentary, Presidential, and Semi-presidential Systems

Parliamentary and presidential alternatives to democratic rule differ primarily on whether the executive and the legislature are separated or fused. The next part of this chapter underscores the basic differences between these two categories of democratic government. It also highlights the semi-presidential approach. When reading the descriptions of these approaches, keep in mind that the differences matter more in democracies than in non-democracies. In the case of Russia, for example, having a semi-presidential rather than a parliamentary system has an effect on political outcomes in the country, but the effect would be much greater if Russia was a functioning democracy.

Parliamentary Systems

Parliamentary System A political system in which the chief executive is directly responsible to the legislature and elections can be held at irregular intervals.

Prime Minister The label normally given to the chief executive of the government in a parliamentary system.

A **parliamentary system** is a conventional approach to democracy, particularly in Europe and Asia. The head of the government and the political system's chief executive is usually called the **prime minister**, but the position may also be referred to as premier (as in the case of China) or chancellor (in Germany). In a parliamentary system, there is a strong connection between the chief executive and the legislature— a fusion of the branches of government that is absent in presidential systems. This fusion creates several key attributes, including the process for selecting the chief executive, the separation of the head of government and the head of state, and the lack of fixed terms for the chief executive and national legislature.

Selection of the Chief Executive and Formation of the Government

The way the chief executive is selected is a defining feature of parliamentary systems. Constituents do not directly elect the prime minister. Rather, the **head of state** usually holds the official power to select the prime minister. The head of state is the official representative of a country and is typically a monarch or a president. In practice, the power of the head of state to select the prime minister is rarely more than a formality. The head of state makes the selection based on the results of parliamentary elections.

Head of State The official representative of a country to other countries, who may or may not also be that country's head of government.

Head of Government The chief executive who assembles and directs the cabinet officials or other heads of government ministries, agencies, or departments.

MP The acronym for member of parliament.

Coalition A group of political parties that formally agree to work together to pass legislation.

The new prime minister is the **head of government**. He or she forms and directs "the government" (the cabinet and other important ministry heads), overseeing the actions of these officials and coordinating their efforts to formulate new policies. In parliamentary systems such as the United Kingdom and Germany, the chief executive is a sitting member of parliament, an **MP**, as are other government ministers. This arrangement is completely compatible with the parliamentary democracy approach, but strange to those familiar with the separation of power between branches and legal restrictions preventing simultaneous service in multiple branches of government in countries like the United States.

When one political party wins a majority of seats in the parliament, the leader of that party usually becomes prime minister. If no party has a majority of seats, two or more political parties typically form a **coalition**. A coalition is a group of parties that agree to work together to pass legislation and occupy cabinet positions. When a coalition is needed to obtain a majority of seats, a head of state with the power to name the prime minister will generally not do so without a coalition agreement in place. The prime minister is almost always the leader of the ruling coalition's biggest party, but when a coalition is made up of several parties of roughly similar size, the prime minister could come from one of the smaller ones.

The formation of coalitions can involve some of the most intense political bargaining imaginable. The prizes in this bargaining are policy positions and **portfolios**, positions in the government associated with particular ministries. An individual may even be included in the government without heading a ministry or other government department. Such a person is called a **minister without portfolio**. Since those putting together a coalition seek to control a majority of seats in the legislature, small parties can become kingmakers, putting a coalition "over the top." In the process, such parties may be rewarded with government portfolios and policy victories that far exceed what the number of their seats in parliament would otherwise warrant.

The most common coalition is called a **minimum necessary winning coalition**. The party forming the coalition seeks only as many other parties as is necessary to control a bare majority of the parliament's seats. If a parliament has 100 seats, the minimum necessary winning coalition is one that controls 51 seats. Such a coalition requires strong **party discipline**, with members of a party following the directions of party leaders about how to vote on bills. In the example of a 51-seat ruling coalition, the defection of only one coalition member would cause the defeat of a government-sponsored bill.

A **grand coalition** involves two or more of the largest parties and gives the coalition control over a large majority of seats. Grand coalitions are rare. In most cases, the multiparty system's largest parties do not get along. Often one is a left-of-center party and the other a right-of-center party that disagree with each other about issues as basic as government's role in society. Their leaders may also personally dislike each other, making it difficult for one to accept the other as prime minister. When a grand coalition is formed, these issue and personality disputes often make it less stable than a smaller coalition. As a result, grand coalitions mostly occur only when government unity is seen as necessary to address serious economic, social, and political problems.

On rare occasions, the head of state may also accept the formation of a **minority government**. In this case, the main party or coalition does not include enough MPs to control a majority of seats. Each vote requires the government to put together a coalition specific to that decision. In most cases, this is a recipe for instability and gridlock. It can work, however, if the prime minister is very popular or if a smaller party has chosen not to be a part of the coalition but has much in common with the coalition's main party. It can also be seen as a temporary measure to forestall the new elections that most members of parliament fear.

Separation of Head of Government and Head of State

In a parliamentary system, the head of state is normally separated from the head of government, and the head of state is the much weaker of the two. The head of state—a weak president or a monarch—has little role in governing. Instead, as ceremonial executive leader, the head of state provides continuity. Though government leadership may change, the head of state is a symbol of stability for the masses. The general population may also see the head of state as "above politics," giving people something in the political system to support when normal politics gets particularly distasteful, as it often does around election time.

Irregular Intervals between Elections and Votes of Confidence

MPs have a stipulated term in office, but this term is the maximum amount of time before new elections must be held. Prior to that deadline, the prime minister could be removed or could call early parliamentary elections. This again may strike many Americans, used to congressional elections every two years and presidential

Portfolio A position in the government associated with a particular ministry.

Minister without Portfolio An individual considered to be a member of the government without heading a ministry.

Minimum Necessary Winning Coalition A coalition involving only the parties required to gain control of a majority of the seats in the parliament.

Party Discipline The extent to which members of a legislature follow the direction of their party leaders.

Grand Coalition A coalition involving two or more large parties that gives the coalition control over a large majority of seats.

Minority Government A situation in which the prime minister comes from a party that does not control a majority of the seats in the parliament, and no official coalition agreement exists that creates such a majority.

"Did You Know?" In perhaps the ultimate example of a figurehead leader, the queen of England is Canada's head of state. Technically, this means that the queen of England enacts all the laws of Canada and that the prime minister of Canada is selected by the governor general (the official representative of the queen). In reality, there is little interaction between the monarch and the Canadian government, although Prime Minister Stephen Harper did get the governor general to suspend the Parliament of Canada in late 2008, only two months after Harper was reelected, to avoid a no-confidence vote. Some Canadian politicians want to break these formal ties, and there is support in Canada to do so once the current queen dies or steps down.

elections every four, as odd. Because the government is accountable to the legislature in a parliamentary system, it needs the support of a majority of the MPs to remain in power.

In some systems, the failure of even one government-supported bill to pass warrants new elections. In most systems, that is only a warning sign to the government about its lack of support. In such cases, the prime minister might call on the minister most responsible for crafting the policy to resign. The prime minister may also choose to resign, leading the head of state to dissolve the parliament and order new elections or the formation of a new government from the existing parliament. Thus, it is possible for a new prime minister to be selected without a change in the parliament's makeup. The ruling party may choose a new leader—such as occurred in 2007 when Gordon Brown replaced Tony Blair as British prime minister without new elections—or different parties in the parliament may assemble a new ruling coalition.

Vote of Confidence A vote called for by the sitting government in a parliamentary system; if this vote fails, the government is forced to resign, and new elections may be held.

Vote of No Confidence A vote sponsored by the opposition, which results in the formation of a new government or the holding of new parliamentary elections if it passes.

Vote of Censure Another name for a vote of no confidence.

In addition to signaling displeasure by defeating a bill, the parliament can force the prime minister's hand. One such measure is called a **vote of confidence**. The government itself picks a particular vote that it considers to be a confidence vote and states that it will resign and call for new elections if it loses the vote. Many systems allow a second option, called a **vote of no confidence** or **vote of censure**. Those opposed to the government sponsor this motion, and it usually forces the government to resign if it passes. Again, the head of state is likely to call for new elections in such a situation, although rules about whether this must occur differ from system to system.

Failed votes of confidence or successful votes of no confidence that lead to new elections are relatively rare. Members of a party in the ruling coalition fear new elections, given that their party may lose seats and, consequently, may not be involved in the next ruling coalition. When a failed vote of confidence triggers new elections, an MP could also lose his or her own seat and be out of a job altogether. MPs, therefore, are hesitant to support challenges to governments in which their party is a coalition member and are very reluctant to do so if their party controls a majority of parliament seats.

In most parliamentary systems, prime ministers can also call for early elections in an effort to improve their party's position in parliament. This is often done formally by the government resigning, leaving the head of state with little choice but to dissolve parliament. Why would a prime minister force early elections, especially if the prime minister's party already holds a majority of seats? New elections "reset the clock" on the parliament's term, guaranteeing the prime minister a longer tenure in office if his or her party maintains control of the legislature. If the prime minister's party has become more popular since the previous election, it makes sense to capitalize on that popularity. This was the thinking in September 2008, when Canadian Prime Minister Stephen Harper moved to hold early elections to bolster the position of the Conservative Party. A prime minister may also seek early elections if bad news is on the horizon but has not yet become public. This is a dangerous move, however, as the campaign could bring the bad news to light and hurt the ruling party.

Prime ministers in charge of coalition governments are much less likely to pursue this course than those who head parties with a majority of seats. Unless the prime minister is very confident that new elections will result in the prime minister's party winning a majority of seats, the danger of not being able to assemble a ruling coalition after the election outweighs the potential gains. Other parties in the coalition government may not do as well in the election, or—perhaps angered by the early elections—they might defect to another party to form a coalition after the election. If the prime minister's party did not become part of the subsequent ruling coalition, the party could end up with more seats but much less power.

Think and Discuss
Is the lack of fixed terms in parliamentary systems a good thing or a bad thing? Why?

The Opposition

Because they fuse the executive and legislative branches of government, parliamentary systems formalize the idea of an opposition to the government more than do presidential systems. Broadly, all the MPs not from a party in the governing coalition are the opposition. Some parliamentary systems take this a step further, allowing the main opposition party or parties to form a **shadow government**. A shadow government is a set of MPs who would replace the current government ministers if the opposition were to win the next election. Because there is no need to pass legislation—and thus no need to create a genuine coalition—the members of the shadow government often come from the largest opposition party only.

Shadow Government A group of MPs who would replace the current government if the opposition party or parties were to win the next election.

Advantages and Disadvantages of the Parliamentary System

Parliamentary systems take a quite different approach than presidential and semi-presidential systems. With their unique features come advantages and disadvantages.

Advantage 1: Efficiency in Passing Legislation

With a lack of checks and balances, things get done more easily in a parliamentary system. There is less chance of gridlock, unless significant divisions develop within a ruling coalition. The path to passing a law can still be lengthy, but it is more clear-cut than in a presidential system. If a prime minister wants a law passed and that prime minister's party controls a majority of the parliament, the law is most likely going to pass. Even strong disagreements between members of a ruling coalition usually result in the formation of a new government rather than an endless stalemate.

Advantage 2: Clearer Accountability for Voters

The fusion of executive and legislative branches in a parliamentary system means that voters can more easily reward or punish those in office. If voters dislike the ruling party's policies, they can cast their ballots for a different party. As a result, government should be more representative than it is in a presidential system because it is held more accountable.

In reality, voters in parliamentary systems do not always have it so easy. Often the government in a parliamentary system is the result of a coalition of several political parties. Voters seeking to punish the government could decide to vote for one of the opposition parties instead. But are policy failures really the fault of all the coalition partners, or just of one or two of the parties? Voters who want to reward the government face a similarly difficult decision. Should the prime minister's party be repaid with a vote, or should one of the smaller parties that helped hold the coalition together be rewarded for its actions?

Disadvantage 1: Instability

Particularly if coalitions are needed to produce a majority, parliamentary governments can be highly unstable. Even majority party situations require strong party discipline to prevent government collapse. As a result, the prime minister and other leading government officials may be in office only a year before losing power, making it difficult for them to pursue their legislative agenda. In these cases, as in Italy for decades after World War II, much of the decision-making power shifts to the more stable portion of the executive branch, the bureaucracy.

Disadvantage 2: Concentration of Power and Hasty Decisions

The concentration of power in parliamentary systems can lead to efficient policy making, but it can also lead to hasty decision making. In a unicameral parliament controlled by a majority party, there is no check on the prime minister. Members of the prime minister's party face strong pressures to go along with government decisions. Repeated readings of the bill, which are supposed to result in thoughtful consideration and amendments, end up being formalities. For every American who complains about how difficult it is for a bill to become a law, a resident of a country with a parliamentary system wishes it was not so easy!

Presidential Systems

Many countries in the Americas and Africa feature a **presidential system**. Given the image in many people's minds of an all-powerful president, it is ironic that democratic presidential systems first emerged as a way of diffusing political power to avoid tyrannical rule. Three basic features of presidential systems achieve this diffusion: selection of the chief executive by the general electorate, fixed terms for the chief executive and legislature, and separation of powers between the executive and the legislature that results in two independent branches of government.

Direct Election of the Chief Executive

A defining feature of presidential systems is how voters select the chief executive. As Figure 6.1 indicates, this vote is separate from the selection of members of the legislature, though the two votes may be cast at the same time as part of a general election. If the system includes a vice president—some systems have more than one vice president; others have none—the vice president may also be elected through a popular vote at the same time.

In practice, the selection of the president does not always rest solely with the general population. In the U.S. electoral process, the members of the Electoral College cast the ultimate vote for the president. These individuals become electors on the basis of popular votes for the president within each state. Thus, the distinguishing feature of presidential systems is not that the masses directly choose the president; rather, it is that the selection of the chief executive does not depend on the outcome of legislative elections.

Fixed Terms for the Executive and Legislature

Presidential systems are noteworthy for the fixed terms of office. Voters who select a president in a system with a four-year presidential term expect another presidential election in four years. In addition, legislatures cannot remove presidents, other than through impeachment, and executives generally cannot force early legislative elections. For good or bad, the president and the legislature are stuck with one another until their terms expire.

Separation of Powers and Checks and Balances

American students grow up learning about the virtues of checks and balances.[3] All presidential systems separate legislative and executive powers, and many include provisions for the override of presidential vetoes or require the legislature's consent when

Presidential System A political system in which the general population votes for the chief executive, there are fixed terms for the chief executive and the legislature, and a separation of powers exists between the executive and legislative branches.

"Did You Know?"
Since its inception, Israel's parliament, the Knesset, has had a large number of small political parties holding seats, complicating the selection of a prime minister. Reforms in 1996 gave voters the power to directly elect the prime minister, an experiment that lasted until 2001. Direct election of the prime minister did not make the system presidential. The Knesset could still vote the prime minister out of office.

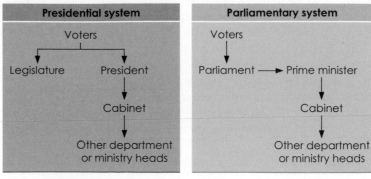

| FIGURE 6.1 | **Presidential versus Parliamentary Systems: Who Selects Whom** |

the president selects cabinet members. Presidents often still have at least as much independent power as the legislature, including the power to issue decrees that have the force of law.

Even in presidential systems without an elaborate system of checks and balances, one ultimate check is common: the power of the legislature to remove the president through **impeachment**. For at least three reasons, impeachment is generally neither simple nor common. First, voters select the president (and, as a consequence, the other top officials of the executive branch) for a term in office fixed by law. The legislature thus faces the burden of justifying not only the need to replace the chief executive earlier than scheduled but also the need for the legislature, not the voters, to make this decision.

Second, although the rules vary from country to country about which branch of government (legislative or judicial) triggers the impeachment process, impeachment is a major event. Unlike votes of confidence, which are customary ways of removing a government in a parliamentary system, nothing about impeachment is normal. Because the executive and legislative branches are separated in a presidential system, impeachment can be viewed as an attack on the executive. Mention of it can trigger talk of a constitutional crisis.

Finally, the impeachment process usually involves a lengthy investigation and legislative hearings prior to a vote to remove the official from office. Even after all this—and much to the relief of such leaders as former U.S. President Bill Clinton who have gone through it—the process may not result in a successful vote to remove the president from office. In such an instance, the impeachment process can damage relations between the legislature and the president beyond repair, and the general population may believe that members of the legislature engaged in a vindictive act that wasted time and money.

> **Impeachment** The process of removing a president in a presidential system, initiated by the legislature or judiciary.

Fusion of the Head of State and Head of Government

In a parliamentary system, the head of state is normally a different person than the head of government. This is largely moot in practice, since the role of head of state is often a figurehead position. In presidential systems, the president is usually both chief executive of the government and representative of the state to the outside world.

The Potential for Divided Government

Another distinguishing feature of presidential systems is the strong possibility of **divided government**. A government is divided when the president's political party is different from the party controlling the legislature. In such a scenario, the checks and balances can result in gridlock—the inability to pass legislation when each party blocks the actions of the other—or a "war of laws," in which acts of the legislature are countered by decrees from the president.

> **Divided Government** When the president's political party is different from the political party that controls the legislative branch.

Advantages and Disadvantages of the Presidential System

Because American students learn about their own presidential system from an early age, they often view it as having many advantages and few disadvantages. As they grow older, this view can change, particularly as the political system struggles to address pressing problems.

Advantage 1: A Check on the Majority Rule Aspect of Legislatures

Presidential systems include a role for the president in the legislative process. Seeing as legislatures make most decisions on the basis of majority rule, the president may be one of the only checks on a majority in a legislature that seeks to pass imprudent legislation. The president is, to use the term from the previous chapter, a veto point in the legislative process. This is most obvious in cases of divided government. Even when the president and members of a legislative majority are from the same party, however, presidents often take very seriously their role as a wall against the rapid charge of a particular piece of legislation. This also stabilizes a system over time, as presidential systems are less likely than parliamentary ones to hurriedly undo policies of the government officials who were previously in power.

Advantage 2: A National Mandate

A president is typically the only nationally elected government official. In parliamentary systems, voters only indirectly select the prime minister on the basis of legislative elections. Presidents can, therefore, claim national mandates in a way that is difficult for many prime ministers to match. This mandate comes in handy when the legislature is controlled by a party other than the president's, but also in times of national crisis.

Disadvantage 1: The Difficulty of Removing an Unpopular President

Thanks to the president's fixed term, a country with a sitting president who has become very unpopular has few options to remove him or her. The president may decide to resign, particularly if a constitutional crisis is looming. The legislature may also try to impeach the president, but as discussed earlier, this is a difficult and potentially destabilizing practice. Most often the country is stuck with the unpopular president until the next election.

Disadvantage 2: The Propensity for Gridlock

When the president's political party does not hold a majority of the legislature's seats, passing legislation can be very difficult. As Jimmy Carter discovered during his four years as U.S. president (1977–81), even having a legislature controlled by the president's own party is no guarantee that policies will pass quickly or resemble the original initiatives once they do. Those who dislike large government programs see this as a benefit. But when gridlock results in a government shutdown over budget disputes or the failure to respond in a timely fashion to a looming economic or military crisis, presidential systems can spiral out of control.

Disadvantage 3: Creeping Authoritarianism

Creeping Authoritarianism The gradual transition from a democracy into an authoritarian system; it is most typically seen in presidential or semi-presidential systems.

Many presidential systems increasingly concentrate power in the hands of the president over time, a process known as **creeping authoritarianism**. Even when no crisis triggers "authoritarianization," presidents tend to enjoy their power. They may become frustrated with the checks and balances built into the system and find ways to overcome them—including through amendments to the country's constitution. As presidential power increases, the legislature becomes little more than a rubber stamp, political opponents may face repression, elections may be rigged, and civil rights may be taken away from the general population.

Surprisingly, legislatures may go along with these steps, even supporting constitutional sanctioning of excessive presidential power. This is most likely when the president's political party has a majority of seats in the legislature, but it can also happen when a president becomes very popular. Students and policy makers in the West like to think that the general population dislikes political tyranny, but across time and in different settings, the masses have had a soft spot for charismatic and powerful chief executives. A president can project charisma in a way that a five-hundred-seat parliament cannot. In addition, because the president is both the head of state and the head of government, he or she is in many ways the symbol of the country. If challenges such an economic crisis arise in the country and the general population warms to the idea that concentrating power in the hands of a single leader is necessary to solve the problem, the president is the obvious choice.

Semi-presidential Systems

Semi-presidential System A political system that has both a directly elected president with significant powers and a prime minister who is responsible to the parliament (and, in some cases, to the president as well).

Sometimes, the political system combines the basic characteristics of both a parliamentary and a presidential system. Such a **semi-presidential system** has been used in several European countries, particularly by postcommunist states, but also in France,

Portugal, and Finland. The system has a prime minister who is responsible to the parliament—and often a member of it—as well as a directly elected president. The president may have the authority to remove the prime minister without the consent of the legislature. The president is separate from the legislative branch and is more than just a figurehead. In a semi-presidential system, the president is responsible for many, but not all, of the tasks of the chief executive in a presidential system. In some cases, all government ministers report to the prime minister. In others, some ministers report to the prime minister and others report to the president. Because both executive officials have important powers, comparativists also commonly call this a dual executive system.

A semi-presidential system requires more than the presence of both a president and a prime minister. Many parliamentary systems have figurehead presidents. Like parliamentary systems, semi-presidential systems generally separate the positions of head of state (the president) and head of government (the prime minister). As head of state in a semi-presidential system, the president is never just a figurehead. Both the president and prime minister have noteworthy powers.

In France, for example, the prime minister oversees the development of legislation by setting the agenda for almost all the meetings of the lower house of parliament, the National Assembly. While the French president can neither veto legislation nor fire the prime minister, the president is able to dissolve the National Assembly and force new elections, giving the office significant influence. It allows the president to pressure the prime minister and the National Assembly to work with him or her on key legislation, and it can lead the prime minister to resign if the two chief executives come in conflict with one another.

In democratic semi-presidential systems, the legislature can also have formidable powers. For example, although it not as strong as some legislatures, the French parliament is far from a powerless rubber stamp. Both the Senate and the National Assembly can institute inquiries into government actions. Even though the prime minister and other ministers cannot serve as members of either house, they must personally submit themselves to questioning by parliament.

Advantages and Disadvantages of the Semi-presidential System

The arguments for adopting a semi-presidential system include the idea that it brings together the best features of both presidential and parliamentary systems. The approach does have a number of advantages, but it also poses challenges to those governing the country and to voters trying to select political leaders who share their policy preferences.

Advantage 1: Providing Cover for the President
A semi-presidential system can shield the president from criticism. Unpopular policies can be blamed on the prime minister. Countries with semi-presidential systems, such as post-Soviet Russia and France after 1958, have often desperately needed stability; to the extent that a popular, stable president is a positive, the ability to deflect criticism onto a prime minister can be helpful.

Advantage 2: The Ability to Remove an Unpopular Prime Minister and Maintain Stability from the President's Fixed Term
In most semi-presidential systems, the parliament has the power to remove an unpopular prime minister. At the same time, the president in a semi-presidential system has a fixed term, which helps to stabilize the system. Theoretically, this offers the best of both worlds: responsiveness to the will of an unhappy electorate without the revolving door effect of some parliamentary systems.

Advantage 3: Additional Checks and Balances
Given their creativity in formulating a system with such diffuse power, it is surprising that the American founders did not think of the semi-presidential system. Though the

"Did You Know?"
Prior to the establishment of its current semi-presidential system in 1958, France was among the world's least stable parliamentary systems based on the duration in power of a particular government. During the Third and Fourth Republics (1870 to 1940 and 1946 to 1958), French governments lasted on average only around eight months. With the military poised to overthrow the government of the Fourth Republic in the late spring of 1958, Charles de Gaulle, a retired general who had led the Free French in World War II, became prime minister and tailored a new, idiosyncratic system of hybrids and compromises intended to secure a top-down transformation of society. Despite all the idiosyncrasies, more than 80 percent of French voters approved the Fifth Republic's semi-presidential structure in a national referendum. In January 1959, de Gaulle was sworn in as its first president.

president can dismiss the prime minister in most semi-presidential systems, this does not necessarily mean that the prime minister will blindly do the president's bidding. At a minimum, semi-presidential systems take the direct control of important segments of the bureaucracy away from the president, limiting the tendency of presidents to concentrate their power over time.

Disadvantage 1: Confusion about Accountability

Parliamentary systems give voters a relatively clear sense of who is responsible for policy successes and failures; presidential systems make this more difficult, particularly when there is divided government. Semi-presidential systems add another layer of complexity for voters.

Consider a situation in which a president and a prime minister belong to different political parties, the prime minister's party controls the parliament, the country's economy is performing poorly, and parliamentary elections are approaching. Voters might decide that the prime minister, as head of government, and the prime minister's party are responsible for the poor performance and might vote for another party. Then again, the president also has a role in economic decisions. To hold accountable the majority party justly, voters would have to first weigh the relative role in economic matters of the president, the prime minister, and the prime minister's party. The challenge is even greater in practice, since the countries in which semi-presidential systems are most common—for example, the postcommunist states—also tend to be those in which voters are least experienced with democratic elections.

Disadvantage 2: Confusion and Inefficiency in the Legislative Process

A basic distinction between parliamentary and presidential systems is the extent to which the executive is responsible to the legislature. In a presidential system, the executive is accountable to voters, while in a parliamentary system the legislature can dismiss the chief executive. In a semi-presidential system, the capacity for votes of confidence make the prime minister responsible to parliament, but the president may also have the power to dismiss the prime minister. The prime minister may find it difficult to formulate policy that pleases all those who need to be pleased. As a result, bickering between the president and the parliament can lead to incoherent policy and to the prime minister's becoming a sacrificial lamb. It is not surprising that semi-presidential systems often go through few presidents but many prime ministers.

Spotlight on . . . SOUTH AFRICA

The South African Chief Executive: Part of a Parliamentary, Presidential, or Semi-presidential System?

Hearing South Africa's chief executive called the president might lead one to believe that the country's democratic system is a presidential one. The chief executive is both the head of state and the head of government. The president must surrender his or her seat in the legislature upon being elected, consistent with the concept of separation of the executive and legislative branches in presidential systems. The South African constitution includes rules for the removal of the president for "a serious violation of the Constitution or the law, serious misconduct, or inability to perform the functions of office"—rules regarding impeachment that are common in presidential systems.[4] There is no second executive position as in a semi-presidential system (where the president is powerful) or a parliamentary system (where the head of state is typically a figurehead). There is, however, a deputy president (vice president) who replaces the president if the president resigns, dies, or is removed from office.

These features are common to presidential systems, but most scholars who study South Africa label it a parliamentary system. Why? The South African president is not directly elected by the people, as leaders of presidential systems usually are, but rather by the lower house—the four-hundred-member National Assembly—of South Africa's bicameral legislature. Yet, the chief executive's indirect election does not necessarily make the system a parliamentary one. The U.S. president is indirectly elected by the Electoral College, for example, but no one would label the United States a parliamentary system.

Instead, the case for labeling South Africa's system a parliamentary system lies in the context of how the president is chosen and the president's relationship to the legislature, including how he or she can be removed from office. Unlike the U.S. case, the selection of the South African president is driven by the results of the national legislative elections. The president is chosen from among the elected members of the National Assembly, just as prime ministers typically are in parliamentary systems. Likewise, the deputy president and government ministers come from the ranks of the National Assembly.[5]

If the method for selecting the president hints that the system is parliamentary, the ability of the National Assembly to remove the president with a simple majority vote of no confidence seals the deal. This provision, described later in the same chapter of the constitution that discusses the impeachment rules, indicates that the legislature can express no confidence in the cabinet excluding the president, in which case, the president must reconstitute the cabinet, or in the president and the cabinet. In that case, the vote of no confidence forces the president and the cabinet to resign. Thus, not only is the person who is chosen to be president dependent on the party makeup of the legislature, but the chief executive is ultimately responsible to the legislature, a hallmark of parliamentary systems. In 2008, the National Executive Committee of the African National Congress (ANC), the majority party in the National Assembly, requested the resignation of then-President Thabo Mbeki. An ANC member, Mbeki resigned to avoid being removed through a formal no-confidence vote.[6]

For these reasons, South Africa is best labeled a parliamentary system. The president's selection by the National Assembly and dependence on the ongoing approval of that body to remain in office contradict the core features of presidentialism. The lack of two chief executives belies the label of a semi-presidential system.

Still, South Africa reminds us that, regardless of the issue, a small number of categories—in this case, three—rarely captures all the countries of the world in a neat and tidy manner. South Africa has a political system with a chief executive who is called the president and who is both the head of state and the head of government, but who is chosen from the ranks of the national legislature. The individual must surrender his or her seat in the legislature if elected president, and yet is responsible to the legislature. The president can be impeached and removed through a two-thirds vote but can also be removed through a simple majority no-confidence vote. These features mean that students and scholars may struggle to agree on an appropriate label for South Africa. They also mean that South Africa is a useful case for considering various approaches to designing an executive, a legislature, and the relationship between them in political systems around the world.

Legislatures

Legislatures play an important role in governing the country in parliamentary, presidential, and semi-presidential systems. A **legislature** is a multimember body whose key responsibility is making new laws. The term comes from its members' legislating (lawmaking) role. In a democracy, legislators play a central role in policy creation. They are elected by the general public and are often called representatives. Most

Legislature A multimember government institution whose key responsibility is making new laws.

non-democracies also have legislatures, but the legislators often only appear to play an essential role in the development of national laws. Such legislatures give the government some legitimacy by appearing to be part of a constitutional power structure that represents the interests of the general public. In truth, legislatures in most non-democracies serve only to rubber stamp judgments of the executive.

Tasks of Legislatures

Legislatures' official responsibilities and their de facto power vary greatly from country to country. Even within democracies, their functions differ significantly, depending on whether the system is parliamentary or presidential. Still, all legislatures have certain tasks or responsibilities, including legislating; authorizing taxes; approving government spending; providing services to constituents or the general population; selecting, approving, and dismissing officials; and engaging in general oversight of the executive.

Legislating

The primary function of a legislature is to make laws. In presidential systems like the United States, this function is shared with the executive branch; the chief executive must approve of legislative initiatives before they become law. Presidents cannot force their policy preferences on the legislature, while the legislature cannot make laws without the support of the president except when enough members vote to override a presidential veto.

In a parliamentary system, a bill's passage requires only the legislature's approval. A bill may have to go through multiple readings, and many parliaments require bills to go through elaborate committee structures, but it is ultimately up to the legislature to determine the bill's fate. In addition, much of the work is done behind the scenes by the government ministries most connected to the policy issues of the bill, even before the bill is submitted. The vast majority of bills in parliamentary systems are submitted by the sitting government, and by the time the prime minister's government presents a bill to parliament, most of the potentially controversial issues have already been resolved.

Authorizing Government Taxing and Spending

The executive branch is in charge of administering government policy, but doing so costs money, and legislatures often have significant control over raising and spending government funds. Legislatures craft and approve tax policies, authorize the government to spend money on specific programs, and pass overall budgets. Thus, although making laws is the heart and soul of a legislature, its taxing and spending decisions are the guts. The best government program ever conceived has little chance of success if there is no money to fund it.

Legislatures in non-democracies have little real power in this area. They may officially authorize spending and can even participate in working out some of the details of revenue generation and distribution. But on important budget decisions, legislatures again do the leader's bidding.

Constituency Service/Ombuds Activities

Legislators also provide service by intervening on behalf of members of the general population. In countries with district-based electoral systems where legislators are elected to represent particular districts (see Chapter 9), this task is generally known as **constituency service**. In countries with proportional representation electoral systems, the actions are often called **ombuds activities**. The term is based on the Swedish word *ombudsman*, referring to an individual who provides assistance. Ombuds activities often involve members of the government advocating with government bureaucrats on behalf of an individual.

The amount of time a representative devotes to service activities varies from country to country and from legislator to legislator. Because voters in systems with

Constituency Service Legislators' activities on behalf of particular residents in their electoral districts.

Ombuds Activities Actions by legislators to address concerns of specific members of the general population in systems where the legislators do not represent particular districts.

electoral districts know who their representatives are, the representative are expected to make constituency service a central part of their jobs. Thus, service activities are more common in systems that choose representatives from electoral districts than in systems using proportional representation approaches. Within a given district system, representatives whose reelection prospects are less definite may also spend more time on constituency service. Successful constituency service activities build goodwill among residents of the district, and they can be effective stories on the campaign trail.

Selection, Approval, and Removal of Government Officials

Legislators often play important roles in selecting, approving, or removing other government officials, including key ministerial appointments in the chief executive's cabinet or judicial nominees. Some parliamentary systems also feature a weak president who is directly selected by parliament.

In parliamentary systems, the legislature removes executive branch officials through actions such as votes of no confidence, discussed earlier. In presidential systems, the legislature can remove the chief executive through impeachment, typically a much more involved process than a no-confidence vote. Similar moves may be made against other members of the executive branch or legislators accused of improper conduct in office, but the process is generally much less onerous than impeachment of a president.

Oversight of the Executive

Legislatures often oversee and investigate the activities of the executive branch. Government officials report to committees or to the legislature as a whole at regular intervals, and they may also be required to testify at special hearings. The special hearings often take place before regular legislative committees; the legislature may also authorize ad hoc commissions to direct investigations, such as the 9/11 Commission in the United States, which investigated the events leading up to the terrorist attacks on the United States in 2001. Regular reports and testimony are generally less newsworthy than extraordinary investigations. However, the questioning of government ministers in the British House of Commons during "Question Time," the time set aside during House of Commons deliberations for the prime minister and other ministers to respond to questions from MPs, is typically testy and can be an interesting political event to watch.

Other Aspects of Legislatures

Scholars who study the importance of legislatures and their design point to a number of other important factors. These include the number of members in the legislature, the length of the members' terms, whether the legislature is unicameral or bicameral, and the role of committees in the legislature's activities. The arrangements vary, and the particular combination of traits can have an impact on the legislature's effectiveness, the kinds of policies it produces, and its relations with the executive branch.

Number of Members

The sizes of national legislatures vary greatly around the world. Some legislatures have as few as a dozen members. Others, such as the Chinese legislature, have thousands. As a general rule, the larger the population in a country, the larger its legislature. This makes sense, because countries with more people often face more complex political choices. A larger number of members allows better representation of local interests in large and heavily populated countries, as well as a degree of specialization within the legislature. A legislative body with too few members in such a setting would overburden its members.

There is a point, however, at which a legislature becomes too big. It is hard to imagine genuine debate, a useful exchange of ideas, or efficient lawmaking in a legislative body with more than a thousand members. As a result, legislatures of that size, including in China, may not meet on a regular basis, relying instead on standing committees authorized to pass legislation on their behalf.

Length of Terms

The length of time that members serve varies from legislature to legislature and depends on the official length of a single term in office and legislators' prospects for reelection. In presidential systems, the term of office is fixed. U.S. House of Representatives members, for example, serve two-year terms. A more common term length around the world is four years. In parliamentary systems, terms can differ due to the provisions for the calling of early elections.

Even a short term length can lead to a long time in office if a member is continually reelected. "Career politicians," those who hold political office for much of their adult lives, are not unusual in the United States. As of 2011, the longest-serving member of the U.S. Senate was Daniel Inouye from Hawaii, who was originally elected in 1962 and was most recently reelected in 2010. John Dingell, representing Michigan's fifteenth congressional district, has served in Congress even longer. He was first elected in 1954 and also won reelection in 2010 at the age of eighty-four. Although there is more turnover in the U.S. Congress than many people think—the average House member serves about six terms, while the average senator serves only around two terms—American politicians remain in office longer than their counterparts in many other countries. This is largely due to the use of electoral districts rather than proportional representation voting (see Chapter 9), the existence of "safe seats" (congressional districts with boundaries drawn to ensure that the incumbent will win reelection), and the importance of money in the U.S. electoral process, which benefits incumbents.

Unicameral and Bicameral Legislatures

Unicameral The label for a legislature that has only one house (chamber).

Bicameral The label for a legislature that has two houses (chambers).

Most legislatures are made up of one or two houses (also known as "chambers"). A legislature consisting of just one house is known as **unicameral**. A system with two houses, such as the United States, has a **bicameral** legislature. Internationally, unicameral legislatures are not unusual. They make a great deal of sense in countries less concerned than the United States with separation of powers, those more eager for efficient lawmaking, or in unitary systems (discussed in Chapter 5) with no need to have members of the government represent different regions at the national level.

The two houses of a bicameral system are labeled the upper house and lower house. The relative power between the two houses varies. In some cases, the houses are almost equal in power. This is the case, for example, in the United States. More often, the lower house is the more powerful and the first to consider legislation. In these cases, the upper house may provide a check on the power of the lower house, but it rarely initiates government action. In extreme cases, the upper house is more like a rubber stamp. At best, it can delay legislation, but it cannot stop it.

Upper houses also vary in how members are selected. Even in democracies, the general population may not directly elect members of the upper house. In federal democratic systems, like that established in Germany, they may be appointed by the legislatures of the various regional governments. This was also the method for selecting members of the U.S. Senate before the Seventeenth Amendment, which established the direct election of senators, was ratified in 1913. In other cases, such as in Canada, the prime minister appoints upper house members in proportion to the population of the regions of the country. Thus, in many (but not all) democracies with bicameral legislatures, the upper house is less directly accountable to the general population than the lower house.

The previous chapter introduced the idea of veto points in a political system. Bicameral legislatures have one more veto point than do unicameral legislatures—and even more if committees are powerful. As a result, bicameral systems generally produce policy more slowly, sometimes falling victim to gridlock. The additional veto point can also check the ambitions of a majority party in the way a single-chamber legislature cannot. A majority party may represent the will of the majority at one moment but not necessarily the interests of the country in the long run. Bicameral systems are also more compatible with elements of federalism and can better represent local or regional interests at the national level.

The Power of Legislative Committees

A **committee** is a group of members in a legislative body that works on a particular set of topics. Most legislative bodies use committees to help craft bills prior to a final vote. They may also play important roles in the oversight process, with certain committees monitoring the activities of particular executive ministries, agencies, or departments. Committees allow legislators to develop and use expertise in certain issue areas, but powerful committees can also slow the process of formulating and implementing new policies.

Most committees are permanent groups that meet on a regular basis. Called **standing committees**, such groups often mirror the agencies, departments, or ministries of the executive. A committee that regularly addresses environmental issues would craft a bill on environmental protection. In addition, a legislature may create an **ad hoc committee** or commission to deal with a specific important problem that does not easily fit into the existing permanent committee structure.

The power of committees varies. The committees in the U.S. Congress are among the most powerful in the world. Some parliamentary systems, particularly in northern Europe, also grant a large amount of power to committees. Although the prime minister and the cabinet come up with the ideas behind most legislative acts, the committees in these countries hammer out many of the details and may even alter policy proposals dramatically during their deliberations.

The Executive

Though it is conceivable for a political system to lack a national legislature, no modern political system lacks an executive. Ordinarily, a single individual, known as the chief executive, heads the executive branch. These days, a chief executive is typically called president or prime minister. In the past, titles such as king, queen, tsar, and emperor were more common.

Domestic Political Tasks of Executives

The most important day-to-day activities of the executive take place in the domestic political arena. The executive administers government policy through a substantially sized segment of the government known as the bureaucracy. The executive also coordinates the development of new government policy.

Implementing Policies and Supervising the Bureaucracy

The executive implements and administers government policy. Effectively carrying out government policies is too big a job, even in a small country, for the chief executive and top ministers alone. As a result, the bureaucracy—a large body of unelected government officials working in government ministries and agencies—runs many of the day-to-day affairs of the state.

Ministers and agency heads directly oversee the various bureaucratic departments. The chief executive usually appoints and removes ministers, often with legislative approval; sometimes another executive such as the head of state performs this task. Chief executives in the British and German political systems are responsible for around one hundred such appointments. Along with the chief executive, the most important ministers form the **cabinet**. Cabinets can vary significantly in size, from half a dozen to two dozen or more members.

While the ministers and agency heads are often political appointees, the middle and lower levels of the bureaucracy are staffed by civil servants. Theoretically, civil servants objectively serve whomever controls the executive branch. Particular

Committee A group of members of a legislature that works on particular topics.

Standing Committee A committee that meets on a regular basis.

Ad Hoc Committee A committee that deals with special circumstances that do not fit neatly into the existing committee structure.

Cabinet The chief executive and most important government ministers.

bureaucrats may thus maintain their positions across a number of chief executives, providing a degree of stability and expertise within their policy area. (Chapter 7 deals with the structure and activities of bureaucracies in more detail.)

Coordinating Policy Development and Budgets

Even in a democratic system with a strong legislature separated from the executive branch, the executive plays a large role in budgeting and other policy making. Cabinet members work with their agencies to formulate recommendations. Using events such as press conferences or national addresses, presidents and prime ministers mobilize public support of their policy positions.

Though legislatures have ultimate control of the government purse strings in most democracies, the executive generally presents the budget for legislatures to consider. Voters are likely to hold the chief executive responsible for national economic performance. Thus, taxing and spending proposals garner much of executives' attention. Bill Clinton's 1992 internal campaign slogan—"It's the economy, stupid!"—typifies the president's preoccupation with economic matters in the United States.

In non-democracies and most parliamentary democracies, the executive is even more active in policy development. In a parliamentary democracy, the legislature may have a great deal of input on policies, or it may serve as almost a rubber stamp similar to its non-democratic counterparts. This is especially true when a single party controls a majority of seats in parliament. The chief executive oversees policy formulation and ensures passage of most policy provisions, playing the role of "chief legislator" as well.[7] Therefore, while no legislature fully controls the lawmaking process, in certain situations the executive may possess such power.

Foreign Policy Tasks of Executives

In addition to his or her important domestic political activities, the chief executive represents and leads the state in matters of foreign affairs, engaging in diplomatic efforts, treaty negotiations, and decisions about the use of military force. It is reasonable to concentrate power over negotiations and crisis management. Imagine a five-hundred-member legislature trying to negotiate with another five-hundred-member legislature to head off a looming international crisis! The executive also often takes the lead on more mundane, day-to-day foreign policy tasks, though again the legislature may maintain its oversight role.

As mentioned earlier, depending on the system, the official head of state may be a weak figurehead. In these cases, the head of state is the official representative of the state in international matters, but the head of the government actually coordinates foreign policy and takes part in international negotiations. In other systems, including presidential ones such as the United States, the chief executive wears both hats.

The decision to use military force is one of the most important decisions a chief executive can make, and in many countries, the chief executive also commands the military. This is the case in the United States, where the president is commander in chief of the armed forces. The U.S. Congress has the power to sanction military action abroad both by its constitutional power to declare war and its ability to regulate military expenditures through the War Powers Act. Even in the United States, however, there is a tendency to defer to the chief executive in decisions of war and peace. In countries without a tradition of civilian control of the military, including numerous nondemocratic systems and some unconsolidated democracies, the executive can have a difficult time keeping the military in check. In such cases, a leader must rely on close relations with top military officers, hoping that they remain loyal.

Think and Discuss

What is the most important power common to political executives? Why is it so important?

TOPIC IN COUNTRIES

As we explore the legislatures and executives of the Topic in Countries (TIC) cases, we will also examine their approaches to fusing or separating the legislative and executive branches. Look for

- The approach to democracy (or non-democracy) that each of the nine TIC countries takes—parliamentary, presidential, or semi-presidential.
- The power of the executive and executive-legislative relations in each of the TIC cases.
- How whether the president's political party also controls the legislature affects the practice of checks and balances in presidential systems.
- Major theories discussed in this chapter's "In Theory and Practice" features regarding presidential and parliamentary systems, voting in legislatures, and the power of the chief executive to take his or her message directly to the public.

The United Kingdom

The United Kingdom captures well many of the key ideas about a parliamentary system. In fact, it is often considered the model for other parliamentary systems around the world. As discussed in Chapter 5, countries that use parliamentary systems similar to the United Kingdom's are said to have Westminster parliamentary systems. This term comes from the Palace of Westminster, where the British parliament meets in session.

The emergence of **parliamentary supremacy**, also known as parliamentary sovereignty, was a key development in British history. Under parliamentary supremacy, no other domestic body of political power—neither the monarch in the past, nor the judicial system today—can block an act of Parliament. All that keeps Parliament in line domestically is a powerful cultural norm that individuals in positions of political power have a responsibility to act in the interest of the general public and the fear that voters will punish the government's party at the next election if it abuses its power.

The Legislature

Parliament is the center of British political power, and the House of Commons is the center of parliamentary power—so much so that the term *Parliament* is often used to refer to the House of Commons alone, rather than to the full bicameral legislature. Although Parliament was established in the middle of the thirteenth century, the House of Commons did not attain its fully

dominant position until 1911, when the Parliament Act stripped the House of Lords of veto power, replacing it with the power only to delay the passage of legislation.

In the House of Commons, 650 members of Parliament (MPs) sit on long benches facing the middle of the room. Because members of the government are also sitting MPs, these individuals have front-row seats near the prime minister during debates and are known as **frontbenchers**. MPs without seats in the government (or the shadow government) are **backbenchers**. The opposition party's MPs sit on benches across the room from the ruling party. As a result, the opposition party leader, an officially recognized position in the Westminster system, sits directly across from the prime minister. The opposition party members who make up the shadow cabinet sit across from their frontbencher counterparts in the ruling government.

The British take the concept of a parliamentary shadow government, introduced earlier in the chapter, seriously in other ways as well. Twenty days of each parliamentary session are designated "opposition days" when the opposition parties choose the subjects to be debated on the floor. Although these debates do not generally produce policy changes, they do allow the public to see those in the opposition party who would hold positions of power if that party were to win the next parliamentary election.

Because the prime minister usually enjoys a majority in parliament (the government following the 2010 elections being one of the exceptions), defeats on the floor of the legislature are uncommon. Amendments submitted without

---

Parliamentary Supremacy Also known as parliamentary sovereignty, a feature of the Westminster system in which no other part of government can block an act of Parliament.

Frontbenchers Members of the government who sit in the front row near the prime minister during parliamentary debates.

Backbenchers MPs who do not hold seats in the government (or the shadow government).

the support of the government rarely pass. Backbenchers occasionally break ranks with party leadership, but almost never if it could mean the defeat of the motion under consideration. As a result, the House of Commons has few legislative surprises. Successful motions of no confidence are particularly rare; the last one passed by one vote in March 1979. This led to the May 1979 elections that returned the Conservatives, under Margaret Thatcher, to power.

Members of Parliament also respect their constituency service obligations. Many of the activities concern the health care system, which is free to the general population but which can involve lengthy waits to receive care. Accordingly, many of the questions that MPs pose to cabinet ministers or the prime minister during Question Time relate to health care and often begin with short stories about constituents whose efforts to receive adequate and timely care were obstructed.

Parliament's upper house is the House of Lords. It has nearly 750 members, though this is hundreds fewer than in 1999. Traditionally, membership in the House of Lords was based on nobility. The British government also appointed members to serve alongside the nobility. These "life peers"—House of Lords members who serve for life but cannot pass on the positions to their children—received their positions as rewards for service to the country. Former Prime Minister Margaret Thatcher, for example, was named a life peer in 1992.

In 1999, the government reformed the House of Lords to abolish most hereditary lords. Only 92 of the more than 700 hereditary lords maintained their seats. During what was initially thought to be a transition period during which the House of Lords would be slowly turned into a more typical upper chamber of a bicameral legislature, the life peers, numbering more than 600, were retained. The other members of the House of Lords include bishops and archbishops of the Church of England. Prior to the establishment of the British Supreme Court in 2009 (see Chapter 7), the House of Lords also had a number of "law lords," judges who served as a court of final appeal for civil and criminal cases. When the reform process stalled, the government established a commission to make recommendations for the appointment of new life peers over time. During 2010, however, discussion about the need to push forward with more significant reform of the upper house heated up. The exact form that this new house will take remains unclear. It seems most likely that it will become a body of largely elected members serving lengthy terms.

IN THEORY AND PRACTICE

The United Kingdom and Party Government Theory

Political scientists have long tried to explain and predict patterns in legislative behavior, developing a number of theories, including George Tsebelis's theory of the importance of veto points discussed in the previous chapter, to help understand legislative outcomes. One such argument, known as **party government theory**, is associated with political scientists Gary Cox and Matthew McCubbins.[8] Their approach challenges the assumption that party unity is based largely on individual party members' preferences. Rather, Cox and McCubbins argue that legislative voting patterns are driven by the extent to which the majority party leadership controls which bills are voted on. Although Cox and McCubbins focus mostly on the U.S. Congress, where the majority party leadership controls the daily legislative agenda, the power to manage the legislative agenda is typically greater in parliamentary systems, especially where there is a single majority party rather than a ruling coalition.

Party government theory can be helpful in understanding legislative outcomes in the United Kingdom. In the House of Commons, practices like Question Time and opposition days provide a chance for debate on subjects that the government might prefer not to discuss openly. The opportunity for voters to glimpse what the opposition parties would do in power, however, does not translate into the consideration of opposition party bills for adoption. Instead, the government retains tight control over which bills get to become serious legislation. Thus, party government theory would predict stable voting patterns by MPs in a given session of Parliament, and indeed that is the case.

Westminster, home to British parliament. © Jupiter Images

Party Government Theory A theory that contends a legislature's rules about the majority party's control of the institution's actions drives the political outcomes emanating from it.

The Executive

The history of British political development centers on the relationship between the monarch and other competing sources of power. The monarchy has been an ever-present symbol of the English and British state. Only from 1649 to 1660, when the British civil war brought Oliver Cromwell to power, did it disappear. However, its presence has not coincided with the kind of absolute power enjoyed by monarchs in other countries. Since the signing of the Magna Carta in 1215, limitations on the monarch's power have been a centerpiece of British politics.

Today the monarch is little more than a ceremonial figurehead. The current monarch, Queen Elizabeth II, has a long list of official duties and powers, but none of them are genuine in practice. She can call for early parliamentary elections, but she does this only at the request of the prime minister. She must give her approval to all acts of Parliament, but a British monarch has not vetoed a piece of legislation since the early 1700s. She can meet on a regular basis with government officials and can even offer advice; the government has no obligation to listen. The queen also gives an annual speech before Parliament, much like the State of the Union address given by the U.S. President. There is one important difference between the two speeches: the queen delivers a speech written for her by the sitting prime minister and government, while the president gets to use his own speechwriters.

Why have a monarchy at all? That the monarchy has survived is testament to several features of British institutional development. British political changes tend to be evolutionary rather than revolutionary. Parts of the past system survive, even during periods of significant reform. The British place a high level of importance on symbolism in the conduct of politics. As chaotic and discourteous as debates in the House of Commons may appear to American students, the conduct of political business frequently becomes highly formal. The queen's annual address is one of the world's great political ceremonies, making the announcement of the entrance of the U.S. president onto the floor of the House of Representatives before the State of the Union address look trivial by comparison.

The prime minister is the chief executive of the political system. As is the case for all executives, the success of British prime ministers is driven by a combination of the prime minister's leadership style and institutional opportunities and constraints—the size (or existence) of a majority in Parliament, for example. The position is one of significant power, particularly when the prime minister's party controls a sizable majority of the seats in the House of Commons. Because of the fusion between the executive and the legislature in the Westminster system, the legislature scrutinizes the workings of the government much less than in most presidential systems. The prime minister can replace members of the cabinet and can even elevate a ministry to cabinet-level status without the consent of Parliament.

This does not mean the prime minister runs roughshod over the cabinet. Cabinet members meet regularly with the prime minister and play a central role in creating government policy. As a result, the British political system is sometimes referred to as "cabinet government" and the prime minister as "first among equals" in the cabinet. Debate in cabinet meetings can get heated, but once a collective decision is reached, members are expected to support it unconditionally. Cabinet members who speak out publicly against a policy introduced into the House of Commons are likely to find themselves out of the cabinet.

Germany

The parliamentary system of the Federal Republic disperses central government power and limits executive authority. This design was a deliberate response to the excesses of the Nazi regime's centralized dictatorship. Moreover, to avoid the defects of the interwar Weimar Republic, the current system situates primary authority for governing with the chancellor (prime minister), giving the president largely ceremonial duties.

Two features of the German political system—coalition governments and federalism—often require chancellors to compromise or face legislative deadlock and policy immobility. Coalition governments, made necessary when no party has a majority of the seats, require cooperation between political parties at the national level. As discussed in the previous chapter, German-style federalism requires cooperation between the different levels of government.

The Legislature

The German parliament is bicameral. The lower house, the Bundestag, is directly elected every four years. Party discipline is a feature of the Bundestag, which means that the governing coalition can normally expect the legislature to enact its program. On rare occasions, the chancellor has lost his or her majority in the Bundestag, and early elections have followed. Such episodes are rare not only because an early election poses risks to sitting Bundestag deputies, but also because Germany's "constructive vote of no confidence" makes such revolts harder to realize. Under this provision, the opposition must agree in advance on a successor to the chancellor for the vote of no confidence to count. The designers of the Federal Republic's political system included this safeguard to forestall the possibility of the unstable governments that had plagued the Weimar Republic.

The expression of federalism through the upper chamber, the Bundesrat, poses even greater challenges to the chancellor's rule than the need for coalitions. The Bundesrat's sixty-nine members are not directly elected by the people but are appointed by the *Land* governments and must vote according to their instructions. (*Länder* that are more populous have up to six Bundesrat delegates each; smaller ones have as few as three delegates.) Since Land elections occur in rolling fashion and on a different schedule from Bundestag elections, the chancellor faces the real possibility of opposition parties holding a majority of the Bundesrat's seats.

Also, the Bundesrat has formidable jurisdiction in the federal legislative process. Like the British House of Lords, the Bundesrat has delay powers, known as a **suspensive veto**, which the Bundestag can override. However, on matters directly affecting interests of the Länder, the Bundesrat wields an **absolute veto**; without its assent, the legislation dies. The German constitution's framers expected this to affect only 10 percent of federal legislation, but judicial decisions led it to encompass about 60 percent of federal laws.[9] A constitutional reform worked out by the federal and Land governments is expected to reduce this veto power.

The Executive

Germany's parliamentary system provides for a chancellor and a president, but real power rests with the chancellor. The president has formal power to appoint the chancellor, judges, and civil servants and to sign laws passed by parliament, though in all these capacities he or she is expected to respect the outcome of elections and the will of the chancellor and parliament. The office of the president, then, is largely ceremonial, and the occupant is expected to be "above politics." Unlike in the Weimar Republic, the president is not directly elected and cannot issue decrees, though he or she may declare an emergency that would allow the government to do so. The president is selected every five years by an assembly consisting of all deputies of the lower house of the parliament (Bundestag) and delegates from the Länder.[10]

Primary executive authority rests with the chancellor. The chancellor appoints the cabinet and is responsible for setting the policy direction of the government. Consequently, the Chancellor's Office is an important source of policy expertise. Consistent with parliamentary government, bills originate with the executive rather than with the legislature. The German chancellor faces constraints on his or her exercise of this authority, however, particularly compared with the British prime minister. Unlike the latter, who rules over a unitary system and usually enjoys a legislative majority in the House of Commons, the German chancellor faces coalition governments and federalism, both of which require negotiation and compromise to avoid deadlock.

Typical of parliamentary systems, the chancellor is normally the leader of the larger party that forms the government following Bundestag elections. Germany's mixed electoral system—with half the seats allocated on a single member district, simple plurality basis and the other half on a proportional representation basis—helps generate a multiparty system, which in turn makes coalition governments the norm. Most of the time, governments are of the minimum necessary winning coalition type, with either the Christian Democrats (CDU) or the Social Democrats (SPD) in coalition with a single smaller party.

The 2005 Bundestag elections made coalition-building much more complicated. The two major parties were nearly even in terms of seats. The erosion of electoral support for both the CDU and SPD, along with the entry of the small Left Party into parliament, made a minimum necessary winning coalition formed from either the CDU or the SPD with a second smaller party numerically impossible.[11] Following several weeks of uncertainty and negotiations among the political parties, a grand coalition between the CDU and SPD, only the second such coalition in the history of the Federal Republic, was created. The grand coalition, with the CDU's Angela Merkel serving as chancellor, remained in power from 2005 to 2009, when new elections allowed Merkel to form a more traditional German coalition without the help of the SPD.

India

Like Germany, India has a parliamentary and federal system of government with a bicameral national legislature. The largely ceremonial president takes a back seat to the prime minister, who governs with the consent of the lower house of parliament. While most parliamentary systems are often more efficient at passing legislation than presidential ones, legislative action in India is routinely held up by protests within parliament.

The Legislature

The Indian parliament is bicameral, with the lower house, the Lok Sabha (House of the People), being the paramount legislative body. Members serve for a maximum of five years, although a vote of no confidence may mean early elections. The upper house is the Rajya Sabha (Council of States). Its members serve six-year terms with one-third elected every other year. It meets continuously and is not disbanded if the government collapses and new Lok Sabha elections are held.

Suspensive Veto The power, often given to the upper house of a bicameral legislature, to delay enactment of legislation but not prevent it.

Absolute Veto The power of one component of the government, such as one of the legislative chambers in a bicameral legislature, to block a particular bill from being adopted.

Normally, there are three Lok Sabha sessions each year: the budget session (February-May), the monsoon session (July-September), and the winter session (November-December).[12] The speaker, elected by the members of the Lok Sabha, presides over the house. The speaker may not be from the dominant party in the coalition government. Considerable work on bills and other matters is undertaken through a committee system. The Lok Sabha has the sole power to pass monetary bills. If there is a conflict over other bills, a joint session of the Lok Sabha and the Rajya Sabha is held. Since the Lok Sabha has 545 seats and the Rajya Sabha only 240, the Lok Sabha's position is normally dominant.

One of the features of both bodies is that protests, common outside parliament, have moved into parliament and have taken up increasing amounts of time. In early 2010, for example, more than 30 percent of the hours of the Lok Sabha's budget session were lost to disruptions. The period ended with the passage of only six of the twenty-seven bills scheduled for the session.[13] Indians are increasingly frustrated by the inability of parliament to conduct business as it used to. The activities have even sparked debate among comparativists as to whether the disruptions are a "disease of democracy" or a "parliamentary ritual" that serves as a "crucial aspect of the performance of deliberation and representation in parliamentary debates."[14]

The Executive

The Indian prime minister is the head of government and normally, but not always, a member of the Lok Sabha. The chief executive overseeing domestic policy, the prime minister selects and heads the Council of Ministers and oversees the bureaucracy. Typical of parliamentary systems, the prime minister is also responsible for foreign policy.

As in most parliamentary systems, the Indian prime minister is usually the head of the party with the largest number of seats in the lower house of parliament. In 2004, however, Sonia Gandhi, the leader of the Congress Party, which was responsible for putting together the ruling coalition, decided not to become prime minister. Gandhi is Italian by birth, and some politicians perceived her background to have the potential for creating political problems. She deferred to Manmohan Singh (known to Indians as "Dr. Singh"). Singh, the first Sikh to become prime minister, was seen by members of various political parties as an honest and capable politician,[15] and following elections in 2009, he earned another term as prime minister.

India also has a president. The president exercises mostly formal, rather than real, powers on the advice of the prime minister and the cabinet. The extent of presidential power is contingent upon situational factors. The inability of one party to control the Lok Sabha during most of the last twenty years and the instability associated with coalition government have given the president greater discretion. When the Lok Sabha is evenly divided among potential coalitions or when the president dissolves parliament, the president has some discretion over the appointment of the prime minister.

The president signs laws, may address both houses, and is the commander in chief of the army. He or she appoints two members of the Lok Sabha to seats representing the Anglo-Indian community and twelve members of the Rajya Sabha. The president can also veto legislation, but a simple majority can override the veto. In extraordinary circumstances when parliament is not in session, the president may issue decrees on the advice of the prime minister, but they must be put before the parliament within six weeks of the start of its subsequent session.

On the advice of the prime minister, the president may also declare "president's rule" over a federal unit whose government is viewed as unable to function—a power that at times has been used for political ends—and is able to declare a state of emergency. (President Fakhruddin Ali Ahmed issued such a degree in 1975.) If not approved by parliament within two months, the state of emergency decree lapses. The expectation that the president would follow the advice of the prime minister was not part of the 1950 constitution, but the forty-second amendment to the constitution, which went into effect in 1976, specified that the president should act in accord with the direction of the Council of Ministers.

The president is elected for a term of five years by an electoral college that consists of all the legislators at the center and federal unit levels. The first woman to be elected president, Pratibha Patil, was chosen in 2007. The vice president serves for a similar period and is elected by a joint meeting of the Lok Sabha and Rajya Sabha. The vice president is the chairman of the Rajya Sabha and takes over the president's functions when he or she is unable to continue in the position.

In this image taken from India's Lok Sabha TV, opposition members, right, shout slogans, as Indian Prime Minister Manmohan Singh, standing at left, addresses the parliament.
© AP Photo/Lok Sabha TV

Mexico

As a presidential system, Mexico fuses the head of government and head of state into one position. Prior to the political liberalization of the 1980s and 1990s, the president ruled over Mexican politics with few checks on his power. The period of liberalization that culminated with Vicente Fox's victory in the 2000 presidential election changed the rules of the game. The system was still presidential, but the president could no longer easily overcome the political opposition.

Fox was the first Mexican president in seven decades not from the Institutional Revolutionary Party (PRI). He also became the first president during that period who was elected without his party controlling a majority of the seats in the national legislature. This feature, combined with Mexico's embrace of democracy, makes it impossible for the president to dictate to the legislature in the way that presidents could in the preceding era of PRI dominance. Fox and his National Action Party (PAN) successor, Felipe Calderón, have both struggled to govern in a presidential system whose previously hollow checks on presidential power have, over the last decade, proven highly effective.

The Legislature

Mexico's legislature, the Congress, is bicameral. The lower house is called the Chamber of Deputies. It has 500 members. The PRI, which had dominated the Chamber of Deputies for most of the twentieth century, lost its majority in 1997. Continuing the trend since the establishment of democracy, none of the political parties obtained a majority of the seats in the 2009 Chamber of Deputies elections. The PAN won only 147 seats (down from 151 in 2006), while the PRI took 241 seats, close to a majority and above its total of 224 seats in 2006. The PRI's success came mainly at the expense of the Party of the Democratic Revolution (PRD), which won only 72 seats after receiving 97 in 2006.

The upper house, the Senate, has 128 members: 4 each from Mexico's thirty-one states and 4 more from the Federal District of Mexico City. Senators serve six-year terms. Unlike in the United States, all the senators are elected at the same time, and the elections coincide with the presidential vote. The PRI dominated the Senate until 2000, when opposition parties won 68 seats. This success by non-PRI Senate candidates contrasts starkly with the period from the late 1920s to the late 1980s. During this period, only one non-PRI candidate won a Senate seat.

Like the president, members of Congress cannot be reelected for consecutive terms. However, they can sit out a term and then run again, and a good number do so. The rule preventing members of Congress from serving in consecutive terms means that they are much less experienced on average than representatives and senators in the United States. Some members of Congress in Mexico have been pushing to change the rule and allow members in both bodies to serve consecutive terms.

The two houses' powers are similar to those of their U.S. equivalents. The lower house has greater discretion over budgetary matters, while the upper house has a stronger say in foreign policy. Most bills must pass both houses, and it is possible to override a presidential veto. Compared with the United States, there is less oversight of the executive and fewer powers to challenge the executive's control of governmental appointments. This is partly due to the prohibition against consecutive terms, which causes members of both houses, sometimes early in their terms, to begin to look for positions they might hold when their terms end.

Congress has more powers to check the actions of the president than it has traditionally displayed. Until the 1990s, Mexican presidents dominated the activities of the legislative branch.[16] Presidents initiated well over 75 percent of all bills considered, and the PRI-controlled Congress never rejected a president-supported bill. This speaks to the institutional power of the president in Mexico, but even more to the PRI's domination of the political system. Because the PRI controlled both the presidency and a majority of seats in the legislature, the president operated much like a prime minister in a parliamentary system where one party controls the parliament. Since the late 1990s, however, the Congress has emerged as a much more significant part of the political system. With the PRI no longer in control of both the executive and legislative branches, legislators discovered their considerable constitutional powers. Tensions between the president and the Congress surfaced during the terms of Presidents Fox and Calderón, and the PRI's success in the 2009 legislative elections increased its willingness to confront the president. Unless the next president comes from a party that obtains a majority of the seats in Congress in 2012 (the PRI would be the most likely party), tensions between the legislative and executive branches are likely to continue.

The Executive

Despite the ability of the Congress to cause problems for the president, the Mexican presidency carries substantial powers. During the long period of PRI dominance, the system was often called a "six-year monarchy." (Mexican voters select a president for a single six-year term—referred to as the *sexenio*—and the president cannot be reelected.) In other words, PRI presidents had great power, but the president had to turn this power over to someone else after six years. During its period of control of the political system, the PRI thought little of this concentration of power. Since PRI candidates always won presidential elections (by fraudulent electoral practices, if necessary), a strong president was seen as an efficient way of managing the political system, a system that amounted to authoritarianism centered on a single party. By the time the PRI lost majority control of Congress in 1997, the system of dictatorial presidential rule had begun to evaporate. With Vicente Fox's election in 2000, it disappeared entirely.

Although the Mexican president must now share power with the other branches, the presidency has not become a feeble institution. Mexican presidents have more power to issue decrees—policy directives with the force of law that have a fixed expiration date—and to appoint government officials than their U.S. counterparts. The president tightly regulates foreign investment in the country, and the position even comes with the ability to influence the content of school textbooks. The secretaries of government departments that make up the cabinet handle many of the day-to-day administrative duties. Though the cabinet rarely meets as an entire group, the president works closely with individual cabinet members. Cabinet members have a fair amount of discretion, but they must tread lightly or risk alienating the president and being replaced.

Brazil

When the military surrendered power in 1985 after two decades of rule, many its opponents supported the creation of a parliamentary system. Instead, the 1988 Brazilian constitution maintained the presidential approach of the Second Republic (1946–1964). As noted in Chapter 5, the current Brazilian system is the result of a compromise between those who sought broader participation and decentralized democracy and those who wished to preserve political order and their own privileges. The result is a political system that frequently experiences deadlock between a powerful presidency and a fragmented legislature.

Brazil's political system resembles Mexico's in many ways, even sharing the names of the two houses of the national legislature: the Chamber of Deputies and the Senate. Yet, the Brazilian president has advantages and disadvantages compared to the Mexican counterpart. On paper, the president in Brazil has more power. Brazil has many more political parties in the legislature than Mexico, however, which can make it more difficult for the president to put together a coalition in the legislature to pass important laws quickly. On the other hand, the large number of opposition parties in the legislature makes it difficult for them to work together to oppose presidential initiatives. As Brazil demonstrated during the terms of President Lula da Silva, opponents have a particularly difficult time when the president is very popular.

The Legislature

Like the United States, Brazil has a bicameral legislature comprising the Federal Senate (the upper house) and the Chamber of Deputies (the lower house). Deputies serve four-year terms that coincide with the presidential term. Senators serve eight-year terms, with at least one-third of the Senate up for reelection every presidential election year; in alternate presidential election years, two-thirds stand for reelection.

The 1988 constitution also gives the legislature important powers to check the president. The approval of Congress is required to confirm treaties, declarations of war and peace, and declarations of a state of siege. Congress must authorize all presidential initiatives having to do with nuclear power, all radio or television concessions, and all grants of public land over a certain size. Senate approval is necessary to confirm Supreme Court justices, the attorney general, and presidents of the Central Bank. The Senate must also approve presidential proposals to increase the national debt. Presidential vetoes can be overridden with a majority of the legislature, as compared to the two-thirds majority required in the United States.

The constitution also grants the Brazilian Congress power to oversee the actions of the executive and the judiciary. Members of either house may summon an executive branch official to appear in Congress and answer questions. The Congress can impeach the president (and did, in the case of Fernando Collor de Mello in 1992). More frequently, the Congress appoints special parliamentary investigative commissions (CPIs). A CPI has full subpoena and investigative powers to ensure the disclosure of personal financial and telephone records, as well as the appearance of material witnesses before Congress. CPIs are used frequently for political purposes but also have produced significant accountability of executive branch officials, including the evidence used to impeach President Collor.

The Executive

The powers and selection of the Brazilian chief executive are similar to and different from those in other presidential systems. As in the United States, but in contrast to Mexico, the president serves a four-year term and may hold office for two terms. Also, unlike in Mexico, the president of Brazil is directly elected by an absolute majority of the vote. If no candidate receives a majority of the vote on the first ballot, which is the usual outcome, a second election between the first- and second-place finishers is held one month later. During that month, the top two candidates try to line up the support of the losing presidential candidates and their political factions in a process of coalition-building. Because the president is limited to two terms, the election may also be influenced by the wishes of a popular, term-limited incumbent. Such was the case in 2010 when Dilma Rousseff won the runoff election thanks in part to the active support of President Lula da Silva.

The Brazilian president controls the apparatus of the state, including the exclusive right to appoint and dismiss cabinet ministers, to fill and abolish federal government positions, and to declare a state of siege (although such a declaration must be approved by the legislature). The president presides over the National Defense Council, is supreme commander of the armed forces, and has broad legislative powers that go well beyond those of a U.S. president. He or she can directly introduce bills into the legislature, has the constitutional responsibility to introduce budget proposals, can veto bills either wholly or in part, and can issue provisional measures with the force of law (Article 62). Originally, the power to issue provisional measures was unchecked by restrictions on how long a provisional measure could last. However, legislators began to feel that presidents used this power indiscriminately to avoid taking important measures to Congress for legislative approval, and the article was amended in 2001 to give the Congress the right—though not the duty—to force the president to bring a specific measure to the legislature for debate.

IN THEORY AND PRACTICE

Brazil and Theories about Presidential Systems

The differences between presidential and parliamentary systems constitute a central theme of this chapter, and the consequences of adopting one or the other approach have been at the center of numerous debates over the last several decades. One of the most cited exchanges appears in a 1990 issue of the *Journal of Democracy*.[17] The debate captures two contrasting views about parliamentary and presidential systems in new democracies. This box addresses the first of these views, as articulated by Juan Linz. The second, Donald Horowitz's response to Linz, is the topic of the "In Theory and Practice" box on Nigeria on page 185.

Linz's argument, which can be labeled a **theory of parliamentary superiority**, is largely drawn from his observations of countries that, like Brazil, have strong presidents and divided legislatures. Such situations encourage political conflicts without providing the means to resolve them. Dramatic confrontations between presidents and legislatures have provided the context for military coups in Latin America. Even when conflicts do not result in breakdown, deadlock may cause presidents to legislate by decree. Linz also argues that presidential systems are too rigid and "zero-sum"—a gain by one side is always balanced by a loss by the other side—to produce healthy democracies. It is extremely difficult to get rid of an incompetent president who

has lost the confidence of the public, but in a parliamentary government, a no-confidence vote is generally all it takes to force new elections or the formation of a new government. Finally, the powers of the president represent an intoxicating prize that may tempt rivals to break the rules, cheat, lie, or commit fraud in their attempts to win the office.

These are legitimate concerns. In Brazil, acceptance of illegal campaign contributions played a part in President Fernando Collor de Mello's downfall in 1992. Moreover, no post-transition president has enjoyed anything close to a majority of his own party in the legislature. The result, as predicted, has often been presidential rule by decree. Alternatively, presidents have governed by bribing opposition congressional representatives to support their initiatives, an approach that encourages corruption and diminishes the legitimacy of democratic government. Less dramatically but more crucially, voters cannot expect their chosen president to be able to pass the policies he or she promises to enact. In a parliamentary system, either the parliament cooperates with the prime minister or the government falls. This powerful incentive for cooperation is missing in presidential systems.

Nevertheless, Brazilians have repeatedly chosen presidentialism over parliamentary government. Brazil tried parliamentary government twice, once during the monarchy, and again from 1961 to 1963. Neither experiment was a success. The first parliamentary government ended with the empire, the second with a referendum to restore presidentialism. Still, in 1993, a new proposal was floated to change the system to parliamentary government. Provoked by the collapse of Collor's government, some people argued that putting so much power in the hands of one person was dangerous. However, the ability of Congress to remove Collor through institutional means convinced most people that presidentialism could work, and parliamentarism was once again defeated in a public referendum. In each case, Brazilians chose stability over efficiency. As Chapter 9 spells out, Brazilian political parties are weak, and in such a context, parliamentarism may produce highly unstable governments. Presidentialism, Brazilians have argued, offers the stability of fixed terms with the ability to remove a criminal from office.

Nigeria

Postcolonial Nigeria has experienced alternating short periods of unstable democracy and long periods of only somewhat more stable military authoritarianism. For this reason, understanding the roles of the president and legislature is impossible without understanding the influence of the military. It is difficult to consolidate democracy in a country with a tradition of military intervention in politics (see Chapter 7). The executive and legislature cannot focus only on each other; they must always be looking over their shoulders.

Theory of Parliamentary Superiority Juan Linz's view that presidential systems encourage political conflicts without providing the means to resolve them.

Nigeria was a parliamentary system, with the British monarch as the official head of state, upon its independence from Britain in 1960. By 1966, when the military intervened for the first time, the country had cut its official ties with the United Kingdom. Drawing inspiration more from the United States than from its former colonial ruler, Nigeria turned to a presidential system when democracy was attempted for the second time in 1979 to 1983 and for the aborted Third Republic in 1993. It has maintained this approach for the current Fourth Republic that began in 1999. The first elected president of the Fourth Republic, Olusegun Obasanjo, was a former military leader. After serving two terms he stepped down, paving the way for his chosen successor, Umaru Yar'Adua, to be elected in a disputed vote in 2007. Yar'Adua's death in office led Goodluck Jonathan to assume the presidency in 2010. Jonathan won reelection in April 2011.

The Legislature

Nigeria's national legislature is bicameral. The upper house is the Senate whose 109 members serve four-year terms. Unlike in the United States, the entire Senate is elected at the same time; there is no staggering of members' terms. Three senators are elected from each of the thirty-six states and one from the Federal Capital Territory of Abuja. (The capital was moved from Lagos to Abuja in 1991.) The lower house, the House of Representatives, has 360 members elected to four-year terms at the same time as the Senate.

Elections to both houses last took place in April 2011. The elections were broadly praised by international observers as largely free and fair. The People's Democratic Party (PDP) again won majorities in both houses, though its majority in the Senate was noticeably smaller than the majority it had won in 2007. The PDP is the party of the current president as well as of the last two presidents. As a result, the potential for checks and balances in Nigeria's Fourth Republic has not been realized. Opposition politicians have criticized many actions of the PDP presidents. Unlike in Mexico, however, the opposition has been able to do little more than complain.

The Executive

The Nigerian presidency is a powerful position, particularly due to the dominance of the PDP in the two houses of the legislature. As in the United States, the Nigerian president is limited to two terms. The president can veto legislation, but the veto can be overridden. There are also important differences between the Nigerian and U.S. systems that reflect Nigeria's goal of reaching out to all segments of a diverse population. To avoid a run-off election, the president must win at least 25 percent in two-thirds of the country's thirty-six internal regions. The president oversees governmental affairs with the

help of a large cabinet of ministers, with members from all thirty-six regions. Finally, the vice president must come from a different region than the president. This provision became an issue for residents in the north of the country when Yar'Adua, a northerner, died in office and was replaced by Goodluck Jonathan, the sitting vice president, who is from the south. Yar'Adua's refusal to resign and hand over power to his vice president before his death only heightened the controversy surrounding this issue.

While observers had been concerned that the strong presidency and dominance of the PDP were leading to creeping authoritarianism, their views were more positive after the country's 2011 national elections. It is also important to place the current situation in context. Nigeria's latest attempt at democratic rule followed the reign of General Sani Abacha from November 1993 to his death in May 1998. The military leader who replaced Abacha, General Abdulsalam Abubakar, made good on a promise of genuine elections. General Olusegun Obasanjo, the former military ruler from the 1970s, came out of retirement to win the presidential election. He won reelection in April 2003 in what, by Nigerian standards, was a relatively free and fair electoral process. In June 2007, he stepped down following the election of Umaru Yar'Adua the preceding month. Outside observers and Yar'Adua's opponents criticized the 2007 presidential election as a step away from democracy. While some of the criticism of the 2007 election was justified, the election was also a milestone, representing the first time since independence that an elected Nigerian president peacefully handed over power to his successor. With international election observers largely praising the conduct of the 2011 national elections, it is possible that the move away from democracy, signaled by the 2007 elections, has been reversed.

IN THEORY AND PRACTICE

Nigeria and Theories about Presidential Systems

The "In Theory and Practice" box on Brazil introduced Juan Linz's arguments on the superiority of parliamentary systems. In response to Linz, Donald Horowitz argues that presidential systems can be more beneficial to new democracies than parliamentary ones. His **theory of presidential system design** criticizes Linz's characterization of presidential systems. Pointing out that Linz's emphasis on Latin American cases such as Brazil

---

Theory of Presidential System Design Donald Horowitz's argument that certain presidential system features can enhance political stability compared with parliamentary approaches.

ignores problems with parliamentary systems in Africa and Asia, Horowitz challenges Linz's association of presidentialism with winner-take-all electoral rules and the lack of coalitions in the legislature. He states that such features are the norm in certain parliamentary systems as well and points out particular approaches to selecting the president that can foster stability rather than limit it. Horowitz argues that choosing the president through a system that requires widespread support for the ultimate winner across different ethnic groups, for example, makes presidential elections a source of unity rather than division in ethnically divided societies.[18]

Nigeria is a particularly instructive case in which to examine the Linz-Horowitz debate. Following independence, Nigeria was a parliamentary democracy; from the Second Republic on, it employed the presidential model. Nigeria's presidential system was crafted in a way that addresses the flaws Linz highlights. For example, Nigeria established rules requiring successful presidential candidates to demonstrate considerable electoral support in more than one region of the country.

Horowitz's arguments help explain why Nigerians adopted the presidential system that they did, and Nigeria demonstrates how such rules can be applied in practice. At the same time, it is hard to call Nigeria a shining example of presidential system stability. The Second Republic collapsed after only a few years, and the Third Republic never got off the ground. While the Fourth Republic survived the transition of presidential power from Olusegun Obasanjo to Umaru Yar'Adua, the year preceding Yar'Adua's election was one of great turmoil, and many inside and outside of Nigeria questioned the fairness of the election. Thus, although Horowitz's theory clarifies certain choices made in Nigeria, the country's flawed experiences with both the parliamentary and presidential approaches demonstrate that neither Linz's nor Horowitz's theory fully explains democratic success and failure in countries like Nigeria.

Think and Discuss

The debates over the merits and limitations of presidential and parliamentary systems are presented in the context of developing countries with relatively new democracies. Some scholars have raised similar questions about countries like the United States. How different would American politics be if the United States had a parliamentary system instead of a presidential one?

Russia

After his election as president of the Russian republic of the Soviet Union (the RSFSR) in 1991, Boris Yeltsin had to work with a number of sources of power within the political structure. A new legislative body, the Congress of People's Deputies (CPD), was the Russian republic's

version of the body created by Mikhail Gorbachev at the Soviet level. A smaller bicameral legislative body, the RSFSR Supreme Soviet, met more often and had more power than the Russian CPD. There was also a government headed by a prime minister and responsible to the legislature. Add a constitutional court and a vice president—not to mention the Soviet government under the increasingly shaky control of Gorbachev—and it is clear that Yeltsin found himself in a complicated and challenging setting.

The Soviet Union collapsed at the end of 1991, and the RSFSR government became the government of post-Soviet Russia. Although Yeltsin was popular, the country faced a number of problems, including a horrible economy. The legislature gave Yeltsin strong powers to address the problems, including the ability to issue decrees related to the economy, but during 1992, relations between the parliament and the president began to break down. By 1993, hostilities were openly apparent. Yeltsin faced opposition from his own vice president and increasingly from the country's constitutional court. In early October 1993, the dispute boiled over; under Yeltsin's orders, troops surrounded the parliament building and took it by force.

In December 1993, a national vote ratified the new constitution and selected members of a new parliament. The new constitution established a semi-presidential system with a strong president and a comparatively weak prime minister. The vice presidency was eliminated. These changes led to significant stability in the position of the president, but because the president could easily dismiss the prime minister, there was a great deal of turnover of prime ministers. From early 1998 to late 1999 alone, Russia had five different prime ministers.

This trend continued under Vladimir Putin until he stepped down at the end of his second term as president—as he was constitutionally required to do—to serve as prime minister. While some thought Putin's choice signaled a major shift in the direction of a parliamentary system, Russia remained semi-presidential. Putin showed little interest in trying to dramatically weaken the presidency. With another presidential election looming in 2012, and Putin able to run for the position of president in that election after sitting out during his term as prime minister, Putin's reluctance to weaken the presidency made a great deal of sense.

The Legislature

Russia's parliament, the Federal Assembly, is a bicameral body. The lower house, the Duma, has been the more consistent of the two both in its powers and in the process of selecting its 450 members. In addition to its legislative duties, the Duma confirms the president's choice for prime minister, as well as other ministers, except for certain ministries related to security and the military.

The upper house, the Federation Council, has been more of a moving target since 1993. It has 166 members, two from each of Russia's eighty-three regions. From 1993 to 1995, members were elected by the general population. From 1995 to 2000, the chief executive and head of the legislature of each of the regions also served as the representatives to the Federation Council. This made it difficult for the body to meet on a regular basis. In 2000, Putin pushed through another change: the members are now permanent representatives selected by the regional governments. Thus, although the Federation Council shares the concept of representing regions within the country with the U.S. Senate, it has replaced the method of selecting members that the U.S. Senate now uses with the method the U.S. Senate originally used.

The Federation Council plays a much weaker role than the Duma in the formulation of policy. Its consent is not needed for bills other than those concerning defense and economic policy. Even on bills that it rejects, the Duma can override the veto by a two-thirds vote. This does not mean that the body has no teeth at all. It confirms border changes to the country or its regions, judicial appointments, and presidential decisions to declare a state of emergency. It can also authorize impeachment proceedings against the president.

The Executive

After the adoption of the 1993 constitution that enshrined Russia's current semi-presidential system, there was little attempt to balance the powers of the two chief executives. A prime minister who ran afoul of the president could begin looking for a new line of work. This is not to say that the official powers of the prime minister are insignificant. The prime minister oversees a large number of government ministries and formulates specific policy proposals. The president determines the government's overall approach, but the prime minister implements most policies. The prime minister also becomes acting president if the president resigns. Presidential elections must then be held within three months.

The powers of the Russian president include the ability to choose the prime minister. Unlike in a parliamentary system with a weak president, the power to select the head of the government is not just a formality. The president can also remove individual ministers at any time. The president makes cabinet appointments, including as high up as the deputy prime minister, without parliament's consent and can introduce bills in the assembly.[19] The president can veto bills passed by parliament, issue edicts (decrees) that have the force of law, and authorize a national referendum.

Additionally, the president directly controls the so-called power ministries: Defense, Interior, Foreign Affairs, the Foreign Intelligence Service, the Federal Agency for Government Communication and Information, the Federal Border Service, and the Federal Security Service (the current manifestation of the Russian secret police). The president also oversees the Security Council, the members of which are the president, the prime minister, representatives to the seven federal districts, the heads of the power ministries, a permanent secretary of the council, and other officials the president wants to include. Putin tended to stack its top positions with former intelligence and military officials, and he used it in his effort to strengthen the power of the central government versus the regions.[20]

There are some limitations on the president's power. Presidential decrees cannot contravene the constitution, and the legislature can overturn a decree by passing a contrary statute. A two-thirds vote by both houses of the assembly can override a presidential veto. The president needs the Duma to approve a nominated prime minister. If the Duma rejects three consecutive nominees, the president can dissolve the Duma and order new legislative elections. The president can be forced to remove a sitting prime minister if the Duma passes two votes of no confidence in the prime minister within three months. If this happens, however, the president can also again dissolve the Duma and call for new elections. Finally, as mentioned previously, the president is officially limited to two terms, a provision Putin abided by, surprising some observers and many Russian citizens as well.

Putin's move into the prime minister's chair also brought changes to the relative powers of the two chief executive positions. President Dmitry Medvedev had a harder time dominating the power ministries than did Yeltsin and, especially Putin. Following a military conflict in late 2008 between Russia and its southern neighbor Georgia, analysts interpreted the Russian government's decision to leave a large number of troops in Georgia as an example of Putin's increasing assertiveness in foreign policy.[21]

View of the Kremlin from the Moscow River.
© Jose Fuste Raga/Corbis

China

China is a semi-presidential system with both a president and a prime minister (known as the premier). There is also a dual hierarchy of state and party administrators, with nearly all top government officials also being high-ranking members of the Chinese Communist Party (CCP). For much of China's Communist period, official government positions corresponded little to actual political power. Mao Zedong was chairman of the CCP, but he ruled more through his personal legitimacy as leader of the revolution than through his institutional powers. When Deng Xiaoping eventually emerged as the leader after Mao's death, he held neither the position of premier of the government nor general secretary of the CCP, the party leadership position that replaced the position of chairman after Mao's death.

Following Mao's death, the official positions in the state institutions began to correspond more closely to actual political power. This process has accelerated in recent years. Deng's replacement as leader of the country, Jiang Zemin, took over Deng's positions as leader of the military while also holding the positions of president of the country and general secretary of the CCP. In a move that highlighted the growing importance of official government positions, China's current president, Hu Jintao, was vice president under Jiang.

With the increased importance of official governmental positions, students and scholars of Chinese politics must pay closer attention to which individual holds which political office. This does not mean, however, that one can look at those positions alone. Knowing the leaders' personalities and connections remains crucial to understanding Chinese politics.

The Legislature

China's national legislature is known as the National People's Congress (NPC). The Chinese constitution defines the NPC as "the highest organ of state power." Traditionally, the People's Congress served simply to sanction the executive's policies. This has begun to change as Communist leaders place more real power in the state institutions. In addition to its role in approving the government's economic plans, budgets, and other major policies, the NPC selects China's president and vice president, confirms the president's selection of a premier, and approves other major governmental appointments.

The NPC meets once a year. Provincial people's congresses and military personnel elect its nearly 3,000 members to five-year terms. Because the NPC is not in regular session throughout the year, and because its size would make it unwieldy for day-to-day legislating, much legislative work is ceded to the NPC's 175-member Standing Committee. The 1987 decision to give the Standing Committee the power to enact laws was designed to improve efficiency in legislating. In recent years, members have often been specialists either in law or in particular topics the Standing Committee is likely to address. Although the entire NPC must still adopt some laws, the Standing Committee now handles a large portion of legislation.

The Executive

Assessing the extent to which China's two chief executive positions, president and premier, balance each other can be difficult. China's President Hu Jintao is recognized as the country's leader. Yet, this is at least in part because he holds a number of other posts, including the position of General Secretary of the Chinese Communist Party (CCP). Since Jiang Zemin and now Hu Jintao have chosen to pair the position of CCP General Secretary with the state presidency, it is a sign that the presidency is far from a figurehead position. The president serves a five-year term, as does the vice president, who is currently Xi Jinping. Hu's second term as president ends in 2013, and by early 2011, there was speculation that Xi would be named his successor.

The premier is the chief executive of the Chinese government responsible for day-to-day governing. The current premier, Wen Jiabao, has held the position since March 2003, and like Hu Jintao, his term ends in 2013. The premier oversees the activities of the forty-five-member State Council, a cabinet-like structure that manages the large Chinese bureaucracy. The premier is assisted by four vice premiers. The premier and the State Council are charged with administering specific government policies, particularly domestic policies related to economic performance. The policies are influenced greatly by the CCP leadership's broad recommendations.

Consistent with the autonomous nature of the Chinese military (see Chapter 7), the state Central Military Commission is a group of state officials in charge of directing the armed forces. It mirrors a similarly named body in the CCP. While the CCP Central Military Commission sets general military policy, the state Central Military Commission oversees the military budget as well as appointments to top military positions. In the past, the president or party general secretary served as commander in chief, but now this position is given to the chairman of the state Central Military Commission. When Hu Jintao took over Jiang Zemin's other positions, he did not immediately become the chairman of the state and party Central Military Commissions. He instead held the vice chairman position. Jiang Zemin later surrendered his position as chairman of these bodies, marking Hu's control of most of the top positions in current Chinese politics.

Iran

For much of the period following the 1979 revolution, discussing Iran's legislature and president took a backseat to focusing on its religious clerics. Iran's theocratic features drove political developments more than the president's and legislature's institutional powers. Discussions of Iranian politics in the West focused on the position of the Supreme Leader, which for the decade following the revolution was Ayatollah Ruhollah Khomeini.

During the two terms of President Mohammed Khatami (1997-2005), many observers of Iranian politics saw Khatami's pro-reform rhetoric as marking a strong shift in Iranian politics. These observers put great stock—far too much stock—in the ability of the president to foster political reform. While focusing hope on the president of Iran is understandable, it is a flawed practice. Political power in the Iranian political system is dispersed in a more complex way than most casual observers understand. In many ways, it resembles a presidential system more than a parliamentary one, but the presidency is less powerful than other unelected institutions in the Iranian government. This includes the Supreme Leader, currently Ayatollah Ali Hoseini-Khamenei, who quietly is a more influential figure than President Mahmoud Ahmadinejad, even as Ahmadinejad garners headlines in the West.

The Legislature

Iran's legislature, the Majles, is unicameral. Prior to reforms that took effect in 2012, it had 290 members elected to four-year terms, with 285 of them chosen in electoral districts, and the remaining 5 seats reserved for members of the country's religious minorities. Starting with the Majles elected in 2012, the legislature will be increased to 310 seats. One of Iran's governmental bodies, the Guardian Council, must approve candidates running for seats in the Majles. As a result of this screening of candidates, the Majles is less moderate than it would be if all candidates were allowed to run. Conservatives have tended to control its ranks, except from 2000 to 2004, when a pro-reform Majles, working with President Khatami, pursued a number of social and political reforms.

In 2004, the Guardian Council used its powers to screen applicants to prevent another four years of reformist legislative initiatives. The Guardian Council blocked the candidacy of more than two thousand individuals it deemed unacceptable, including eighty who were serving in the Majles at the time. This represented half of all the candidates running. As a result, the population did not have the opportunity to make a genuine choice, and the legitimacy of the Majles was damaged. Turnout was low, thanks in part to calls by reformers to boycott the election. Conservatives swept back into control of a majority of the seats of the Majles.

The pattern was similar in 2008. Once again, the Guardian Council ruled out a large number of pro-reform candidates, leaving reformers to contest fewer than half of the seats. The result was a conservative majority that looked poised to continue to frustrate those in Iran and in the West hoping for liberalization of the country's theocratic regime. By the middle of 2011, it was still unclear how the Guardian Council would approach the issue of candidates for the Spring 2012 Majles elections. Given the harsh repression of pro-reform protesters following the presidential election in 2009, however, few observers expected the Guardian Council to welcome pro-reform Majles candidates in 2012.

The Executive

Following the 1979 Islamic Revolution, the leaders of Iran put in place a new constitution. The constitution created a system with a dual chief executive, but one very different from those discussed previously in this chapter. Instead of a president and a prime minister, the Iranian system included a president and a position known as the Supreme Leader. This individual is also considered to be a *faqih*, or "spiritual guide."

As the title indicates, the position of Supreme Leader carries tremendous power to shape legislative, executive, and even judicial outcomes in Iran. The first Supreme Leader was Ayatollah Ruhollah Khomeini. An ayatollah is a leading cleric—the word means "sign of God"—and Khomeini was recognized for his leadership in the effort to oust the shah, Iran's authoritarian leader prior to the 1979 revolution. Khomeini died in 1989 and was replaced by Ayatollah Ali Hoseini-Khamenei, the current Supreme Leader.

The Supreme Leader works closely with three bodies that straddle the line between executive and legislature. The first, mentioned in the previous section, is the Council of Guardians of the Constitution, or Guardian Council for short. The Guardian Council has twelve members, six of whom are specialists on Islamic law appointed by the Supreme Leader. The other six are selected by the national legislature, the Majles, from a group nominated by the High Council of Justice—Iran's version of a supreme court. The Guardian Council examines proposals from the Majles to determine whether they are consistent with the principles of Sharia (Islamic law). If the Guardian Council does not accept an act of the Majles, it is returned in order to be corrected. The Guardian Council also has veto power over candidates running for seats in the Majles.

The Expediency Council, whose members are appointed by the Supreme Leader, attends to clashes between the Guardian Council and the Majles. Disputes can arise when the Guardian Council returns a proposal and the Majles refuses to accept the Guardian Council's position. The Expediency Council was the brainchild of Ayatollah Khomeini, who was concerned when the Guardian Council blocked legislative measures that he supported. Declaring that commandments of the government may need to take precedence over Sharia in certain situations, Khomeini pushed for inclusion of the Expediency Council in the amended 1989 constitution. After reformers gained control of the Majles following the 2000 elections, the Expediency Council became a more central part of the Iranian political system, adding another check on the reformers by the more conservative elements of the executive. The Expediency Council is currently headed by former Iranian President Akbar Hashemi-Rafsanjani.

The eighty-six-member Assembly of Experts selects the Supreme Leader and advises him on various issues. It is, therefore, somewhat analogous to the Vatican's College of Cardinals, except that the Iranian people choose the Assembly of Experts in an election held every eight years. Candidates must be clerics, and the Guardian Council can block certain individuals from running. The most recent election took place in November 2006.

Although the Supreme Leader is the more powerful of the two chief executives, the constitution gives the president significant powers. Being directly elected also gives the president a degree of legitimacy that the clerics in many other institutions in the Iranian government struggle to achieve. The president oversees day-to-day government affairs and relies on a cabinet to formulate policy proposals, much like the other chief executives we have discussed. Certain cabinet officials are monitored by the religious leaders, including those working on defense and foreign policy and those overseeing cultural and social programs.

Iran's current president, Mahmoud Ahmadinejad, won a runoff against Rafsanjani in 2005 and against Mir-Hussein Mousavi in 2009. In many ways, Ahmadinejad is the converse of his predecessor, Mohammed Khatami. Khatami was a moderate reformer who won a convincing victory in 1997—getting almost 70 percent of the vote—against a conservative candidate supported by the religious establishment. He won reelection in an even more convincing fashion in 2001, with 78 percent of the vote. Khatami's victories were a warning to the clerics that many Iranians were ready for a more moderate approach to politics.

Ahmadinejad, on the other hand, is a conservative who defeated prominent and more moderate opponents. A large portion of pro-reform voters refused to participate in the 2005 election, aiding his victory. In 2009, his reelection sparked major protests (the so-called Green Revolution), which were a blow to Ahmadinejad's legitimacy at the start of his second term. At the same time, Ahmadinejad's electoral successes were a sign both to reformers, like Mousavi, and to more pro-business moderate-conservatives, such as Rafsanjani, that a sizable number of Iranians was ready to accept a more hard-line government. That government's repressive response to protests in 2011—part of the wave of protests against nondemocratic leaders across the Middle East—also signaled to the population that the government was willing to use force to hang onto power. If so, it may have to use it repeatedly. Events in countries like Egypt and Libya have shown that nondemocratic leaders should not assume that their hold on power is secure.

IN THEORY AND PRACTICE

Iran and the Theory of "Going Public"

Theories addressing a president's ability to set the legislative agenda draw on the concept of the "bully pulpit," the ability of a president to make direct appeals to the citizenry. One such theory, posed by Samuel Kernell, is the **theory of "going public,"**[22] which highlights the president's use of the mass media to promote particular policies.[23] Kernell's premise is based on the United States, but his argument can inform comparative politics studies as well. As electronic media around the world become more common, chief executives are turning more to radio, television, and the Internet to bolster support for their policies.

Does Kernell's theory apply to nondemocratic developing countries like Iran? Because of the existence of the Supreme Leader and bodies such as the Guardian Council, Iran's president is more constrained than most. The Iranian president not only has to worry about getting legislation on the agenda, but also has to worry that the Guardian Council may block an initiative even if it makes it out of the legislature.

Although the Iranian president does not have the institutional powers of other presidents, he does have the bully pulpit. Iran's former President Mohammed Khatami was well known for taking his message directly to the people. Though his vision of reform was ultimately unrealized, his reforms went further than many in the West expected. Were it not for his ability to go public and generate public enthusiasm for his ideas, it is unlikely that reforms would have been discussed so openly in Iran during Khatami's years in office.

Think and Discuss

Which of the countries examined in the TIC sections have the most interesting relations between the executive and legislative branches? Why?

TIC Wrap-Up

When thinking about executives and legislatures, the nine Topic in Countries cases can be placed into three groups based on their institutional arrangements. Although they look different in some ways, the political systems of the

Theory of "Going Public" A theoretical perspective that highlights the way that a president can promote specific policies by using the mass media to change public opinion.

United Kingdom, Germany, and India are all parliamentary. Each has a prime minister (in Germany known as the chancellor) with significant political power. Each also has a separate head of state (the queen in the United Kingdom, the president in Germany and India) with little real power over day-to-day politics.

Because the United Kingdom, Germany, and India are parliamentary systems, the legislatures at times appear to be rubber stamps for the will of the prime minister. Yet, the design and activities of the legislatures remain crucial to understanding important political outcomes in these countries. All three legislatures have the final say in crafting political policy, and even when the prime minister's party has controlled a majority of parliament's seats in the United Kingdom, the prime minister has not always been able to get his or her own way. In Germany and India, parliament creates challenges for the executive branch due to the German upper house's role in representing the country's regions and the tendency for spirited debate to slow down the policy process in India.

Of the nine TIC cases, four are presidential systems, in which the chief executive position, the president, is separate from the legislative branch. The Mexican, Brazilian, and Nigerian presidential systems resemble the American one in many ways. In all three, when the president's party controls a majority of seats in the legislature, the president can be powerful in setting the political agenda. In Brazil, the legislature has a difficult time working with the president and an equally difficult time controlling his or her activities. The Iranian system is more complicated. Because it lacks a prime minister, it is typically called a presidential system. However, its executive arrangements are complicated, and the power of the president is checked not only by the legislative branch but also by unelected executive positions designed to protect the system's theocratic character.

These four presidential systems highlight how a president can be constrained or aided as much by the partisan or ideological makeup of the legislature as by the official powers of the executive and legislative branches. In Mexico, what looked like a system with a powerful president increasingly resembled a recipe for gridlock. In Brazil, the highly divided legislature is often unable to organize effectively to thwart the president's agenda. In Nigeria, the presidential system that replaced Nigeria's initial parliamentary design gives the president great power, especially a president whose party controls a majority of the seats in the legislature. Even the authoritarian system of Iran, where the president is checked by unelected components of the executive, shows how a president and a legislature working in tandem can pressure for political change, and how a president with a hostile legislature can get little done.

Russia and China both employ semi-presidential political systems that combine features of the presidential and parliamentary approaches. Each has a president and a prime minister with substantial political powers. The president has been a more visible symbol of the regime than the prime minister, although with Vladimir Putin moving from the position of president to that of prime minister, this has changed somewhat in Russia.

The legislatures in the two semi-presidential TIC cases are relatively weak. In Russia in the 1990s, the bicameral legislature at times enjoyed causing problems for the president and prime minister, but in the last decade, the legislative branch of the Russian political system has increasingly acted as a rubber stamp of the chief executives' desires. Likewise, China's national legislature provides few checks on executive power and many rubber stamps of executive initiatives.

The Russian and Chinese semi-presidential systems concentrate significant power, both officially and in practice, in the hands of the executive. The presidency in the Russian system, a system designed by former President Boris Yeltsin and his supporters, has been the much more stable half of Russia's dual executive. In China, holding the presidency (especially if simultaneously serving as the general secretary of the CCP) has become associated with being the country's recognized leader.

COUNTRY SUMMARY

TIC Country	Parliamentary or Presidential	Head of Government	Head of State	Legislature	Legislative Houses
United Kingdom	Parliamentary	Prime Minister	King/Queen	Bicameral (with a weak upper house)	House of Commons (L); House of Lords (U)
Germany	Parliamentary	Chancellor	President	Bicameral	Bundestag (L); Bundesrat (U)

TIC Country	Parliamentary or Presidential	Head of Government	Head of State	Legislature	Legislative Houses
India	Parliamentary	Prime Minister	President	Bicameral	Lok Sabha (L); Rajya Sabha (U)
Mexico	Presidential	President	President	Bicameral	Chamber of Deputies (L); Senate (U)
Brazil	Presidential	President	President	Bicameral	Chamber of Deputies (L); Senate (U)
Nigeria	Presidential	President	President	Bicameral	House of Representatives (L); Senate (U)
Russia	Semi-presidential	Prime Minister (but president heads parts of government)	President	Bicameral	Duma (L); Federation Council (U)
China	Semi-presidential	Prime Minister	President	Unicameral	National People's Congress
Iran	Presidential (two chief executives; Supreme Leader holds significant power)	President (but Supreme Leader can affect day-to-day governing)	Supreme Leader	Unicameral	Majles (but Guardian Council and Expediency Council also oversee legislative decisions)

Spotlight on . . . Country

France	Semi-presidential	Prime Minister	President	Bicameral	National Assembly (L); Senate (U)
Iraq	Parliamentary	Prime Minister	President (a three-person Presidency Council was used in the initial period following the new Iraqi constitution)	Unicameral (but the Iraqi constitution calls for the future establishment of an upper house)	Council of Representatives (once established, the upper house will be called the Federation Council)
South Africa	Parliamentary	President	President	Bicameral	National Assembly (L); National Council of Provinces (U)

Research in Context

In discussing the United Kingdom, this chapter mentioned the practice of "Question Time"—members of parliament questioning the prime minister and other ministers. This practice is not limited to the House of Commons. While presidents are not often asked questions by members of national legislatures, MPs posing questions to ministers of the government is a basic feature of parliamentarism. Like many common political practices, however, the details of the practice differ from case to case.

Questioning Ministers in Parliamentary Systems

Although parliamentary questioning is a common and important feature of parliamentary systems, it had not been well-studied in a comparative manner. Two European political scientists, Federico Russo and Matti Wiberg, set out to change this by studying the practice of questioning government ministers in seventeen parliaments in Europe. Their results were published in a June 2010 article in the *Journal of Legislative Studies*.[24]

As discussed in the opening chapter of this book, some research projects, particularly when work on the topic has not previously been conducted, not only examine causal questions but also must first establish the existence of an interesting pattern in need of further examination. Russo and Wiberg's research allowed them to classify parliamentary procedures regarding the questioning of ministers, as well as to rank the effectiveness of the different approaches and examine the relationship between the pattern and the kinds of coalitions seen in the different parliaments. They identified differences such as oral versus written questions, the extent to which oral questions were spontaneous or presented in advance, and the length of time that ministers were given to respond to written questions.

Combining these different features, Russo and Wiberg constructed a scale of how much each parliament's questioning practices created the potential for information to be obtained from the government and the potential for promoting political confrontation. (Russo and Wiberg consider confrontation to be a positive feature that produces "lively debates" highlighting the differences between the government and the opposition.) Comparing these two dimensions, the authors identified three countries whose questioning practices had a high potential for generating information and confrontation: Sweden, Norway, and Finland. Other than this geographical pattern, the only apparent relationship they found was between the potential for information and the extent of coalition governments. Systems with frequent coalition governments were less likely to have questioning procedures that generated information than systems where one party typically won a majority of the seats.

So What?

The patterns of minister questioning practices in European parliaments might seem unrelated to the U.S. political system. Yet, the finding that coalition governments are less likely to exist in systems with questioning practices that generate useful information about the government has implications for long-standing critiques of the U.S. political system. Observers have criticized electoral arrangements like those in the United States for producing a small number of large parties. Such critics believe that the more parties there are in the legislature, the more voters can see the differences between the parties and align themselves with a party consistent with their own positions. In this view, debate and interaction between representatives from different parties provide voters with valuable information.

Russo and Wiberg's research provides reason to doubt that claim. At least when examining questioning of members of the executive—a form of oversight of the executive by the legislature—there is little reason to believe that a large number of political parties provides more information. Systems in which the large number of parties make coalition governments necessary had questioning procedures that were no more likely to lead to "lively debate" and were less likely to provide useful information about the government than systems in which one party controlled a majority of seats in the legislature.

CONCLUSION

Legislatures and executives are key components of a country's political structure. The division of powers between the legislature and the executive is among the political system's most important traits. Some comparativists contend that legislatures have lost the battle for political supremacy with executives. Legislatures in non-democracies regularly do the bidding of the executive without comment. In parliamentary systems, the fall of the government places members of the legislature in jeopardy; the members' party might lose its position as part of the ruling coalition; and the MPs might lose their seats if the collapse of the government results in new elections. Even in many presidential systems, there are incentives for legislatures to defer to the executive. As countries like Mexico demonstrate, however, one should not write the epitaph for legislatures so quickly. Powers on paper that had looked unimportant in the past can become important if the chief executive's party does not control a majority of legislative seats. In such cases, executives must work with the legislature or face crippling gridlock.

Executives and legislatures come into being and operate under rules that are followed, at least in most democracies. But they are also composed of individuals who have ideas, interests, and wills of their own. Just like a football game, the rules limit the actions of the participants, but they do not dictate the form of the plays. As a result, a fuller understanding of political outcomes requires not only an examination of how legislative and executive structures tend to operate but also familiarity with the individuals who serve in those institutions.

It also requires examining the broader structural context, including other political institutions, elected or otherwise. The next chapter covers the parts of government that, even in a democracy, are run by unelected officials. These institutions—the judiciary, the bureaucracy, and the military—are often as important to a country's daily governing as either its chief executive or national legislature.

KEY TERMS

Absolute veto, p. 180
Ad hoc committee, p. 175
Backbenchers, p. 177
Bicameral, p. 174
Cabinet, p. 175
Coalition, p. 162
Committee, p. 175
Constituency service, p. 172
Creeping authoritarianism, p. 168
Divided government, p. 167
Frontbenchers, p. 177
Grand coalition, p. 163
Head of government, p. 162
Head of state, p. 162

Impeachment, p. 167
Legislature, p. 171
Minimum necessary winning
  coalition, p. 163
Minister without portfolio, p. 163
Minority government, p. 163
MP, p. 162
Ombuds activities, p. 172
Parliamentary supremacy, p. 177
Parliamentary system, p. 162
Party discipline, p. 163
Party government theory, p. 178
Portfolio, p. 163
Presidential system, p. 166

Prime minister, p. 162
Semi-presidential system, p. 168
Shadow government, p. 165
Standing committee, p. 175
Suspensive veto, p. 180
Theory of "going public," p. 190
Theory of parliamentary superiority,
  p. 184
Theory of presidential system
  design, p. 185
Unicameral, p. 174
Vote of censure, p. 164
Vote of confidence, p. 164
Vote of no confidence, p. 164

Unelected Components of Government: Judiciaries, Bureaucracies, and Militaries

CHAPTER OUTLINE

The Judiciary
The Bureaucracy
The Military

TOPIC IN COUNTRIES

Features in this Chapter:

Workers stand in front of a collapsed pedestrian bridge outside the Jawaharlal Nehru Stadium in New Delhi, India, September 21, 2010. The collapse of the bridge was one of a number of problems surrounding the October 2010 Commonwealth Games, which India hosted. © REUTERS/Adnan Abidi

LEARNING OBJECTIVES

After reading this chapter, you should be able to

- Discuss the tasks of the judiciary, bureaucracy, and military.
- Describe how these unelected governmental components shape policy decisions.
- Discuss the advantages and disadvantages of judicial review.
- Discuss the benefits and drawbacks of a strong bureaucracy.
- Describe the roles that the judiciary, bureaucracy, and military play in the TIC cases.

In the fall of 2010, India hosted the Commonwealth Games, dubbed by India's media the "Shame Games." The governing body of the Commonwealth Games labeled the athletes' village "uninhabitable." Costs were dramatically higher than originally estimated, and a footbridge leading to the Games' main stadium collapsed.[1] Two months later, the first part of the film version of J. K. Rowling's *Harry Potter and the Deathly Hallows* was released.[2] At first glance, these two events appear to have little in common, but India's struggles and Rowling's novel cast a light on a broadly held perception of government bureaucracy: that it is inefficient and staffed with individuals lacking integrity and competence. Earlier in 2010, a survey of business executives ranked India's bureaucracy as the most inefficient in Asia, and critics of the Commonwealth Games fiasco argued that it was a "reflection of the incompetence of India's stifling government bureaucracy."[3] Rowling's attacks on bureaucrats were more subtle, appearing mostly in discussions of the fictional Ministry of Magic in a fictional story. Yet, in his study of the Harry Potter series' portrayal of bureaucrats, law professor Benjamin Barton contends that "Rowling's scathing portrait of government" was highly effective.[4] The unelected nature of bureaucracies undoubtedly contributes to their reputation as unaccountable and self-serving.

This chapter turns to the judiciary, the bureaucracy, and the military, three major political institutions whose officials are almost always unelected, in contrast to the legislature and the chief executive spotlighted in the previous chapter, whose members are typically elected. All three institutions are involved in the policy process. Their involvement ranges from carrying out policy to making numerous decisions on a daily basis that have the effect of law. How much the individuals who serve in these institutions actively create policy varies significantly from country to country. This chapter examines some of the factors that determine their level of involvement.

Like executives and legislatures, these three components of government are important in both democratic and nondemocratic systems. Although the judicial branch is typically controlled by the executive branch in nondemocratic systems, judges are still needed to rule in civil and criminal cases. Bureaucrats in nondemocratic systems need to worry about the extent to which their day-to-day decision making might alienate the chief executive, but non-democracies still rely on bureaucratic expertise. In all types of political systems, the military plays a crucial role in the defense of the country.

Because the judiciary, bureaucracy, and military are not directly accountable to voters, their roles and the oversight of their activities produce interesting tensions in democracies. On the one hand, giving significant power and autonomy to unelected government officials is undemocratic. On the other hand, an autonomous judiciary—free from the control of the other branches of government—is considered crucial to democratic governance. In addition, powerful bureaucrats and autonomous militaries threaten the consolidation of democratic rule. Yet, democracies rely on bureaucratic and military professionalism and expertise to implement, and even help develop, domestic and foreign policy. Micromanaging the work of the bureaucracy and military is likely to reduce the effectiveness and efficiency of both.

The Judiciary

The judiciary is commonly considered the third branch of government. It stabilizes the political system by solving disputes involving the country's laws. Courts often have to solve disagreements between citizens, but they can also settle conflicts between companies and governmental institutions, between different levels of government, and between institutions at the same level of government (e.g., disputes between the legislature and the president). Even in nondemocratic systems, courts sometimes play such roles, existing as an important arena of contestation among members of the ruling elite and between ordinary citizens and government officials of the non-democracy.[5]

Although comparative political works that addressed the role of the courts started to appear in the 1950s, only in the last two decades has the topic of judicial politics drawn significant attention from comparativists.[6] Today, comparativists interested in the courts seek to understand what influences a specific judicial decision (i.e., the rulings of members of a court as a dependent variable) and examine the role of the courts more generally in shaping political outcomes (i.e., the institution of the court as an independent variable).

Compared with the legislature or chief executive, the judiciary is supposed to be above politics. That is, its decisions are not supposed to be driven by political concerns. One of the most important concepts related to the judiciary, then, is **judicial independence**, the idea that the cases judges examine and their decisions are not the result of pressure from the legislature or the executive. Lifetime (or long single-term) judicial appointments enhance independence. When other officials can determine the cases that the court hears or can easily punish judges for their decisions, judicial independence is weak. Such punishments include removing judges from office in democracies and throwing them in jail (or worse) in non-democracies.

The extent to which other political actors accept judicial decisions is an important complement to judicial independence. Courts do not have their own police forces to enforce their decisions, and they cannot levy taxes to fund the policy shifts their rulings sometimes require. As a result, judicial independence does not mean much in practice without a commitment to enforce judicial decisions. In most of the world's democracies, other branches and lower levels of government accept and enforce judicial rulings. Political leaders recognize that failure to enforce judicial decisions with which they disagree would threaten the integrity of the entire political system.

An important distinction involving judicial rulings is the difference between **civil law** and **common law**. Of the two approaches, civil law is far more prevalent globally. Theoretically at least, in civil law systems judges narrowly interpret the law regarding the cases in question. Their ability to exercise individual judgment is limited. They rely on an existing legal code and supplementary laws passed since the code's adoption. In common law systems, judges' case rulings have the effect of law. These rulings are known as **case law**. Common law systems, such as in the United States, restrict a judge's flexibility through the principle of *stare decisis*—the idea that lower courts must adhere to higher court rulings and that previous court rulings on a topic provide a precedent that is largely binding on future decisions of courts at the same level of authority. Precedent is less important in a civil law system, as each judge is expected to apply the existing legal code to the particular case.

Judicial Independence The extent to which the judiciary is free from influence from the other branches of government.

Civil Law A legal system based on a strong adherence to existing statutes; judges have little discretion to interpret the law.

Common Law A legal system that allows judges more room to interpret the law, with their decisions setting precedents for lower courts and future court rulings.

Case Law The concept, found in common law systems, that judicial decisions have the force of law.

Stare Decisis The idea that a previous judicial decision creates a binding precedent.

Lawyers participate in an anti-government rally in Karachi, Pakistan, in April 2007, protesting the decreasing independence of the judiciary during the leadership of President Pervez Musharraf. Musharraf's removal of Supreme Court Chief Justice Iftikhar Mohammed Chaudhry the preceding month triggered a wave of demonstrations. Musharraf ultimately resigned as president of Pakistan in August of 2008.
© AP Photo/Shakil Adil

Judicial Review The power of the judiciary to rule on whether laws and government policies are consistent with the constitution or existing laws.

Constitutional Judicial Review The power to declare a law unconstitutional.

Statutory Judicial Review The power to judge whether government policies are consistent with existing government statutes.

Judicial Activism One or a series of rulings in which a court creates new policies rather than basing a ruling on a narrow interpretation of the legal question under review.

Tasks of the Judiciary

The main official task of the judiciary is to adjudicate, to settle disputes relating to existing laws. Courts are also responsible for sanctioning certain social activities, such as divorces, name changes, and inheritance distributions. In some countries, the judicial branch is much more powerful. It can overturn laws by declaring them unconstitutional or prescribe policy remedies to address problems brought before it.

Determining Violation of Law and Appropriate Punishment

The fundamental role of courts is to adjudicate laws by deciding the guilt or innocence of individuals charged with a crime. In some countries, judges are empowered to make these decisions entirely on their own, while in other countries, juries may be used to assess a defendant's guilt. Judges generally have the power to decide on appropriate punishments for those found guilty, though juries may also advise judges or even decide between punishment options, such as in capital punishment decisions in the United States.

Review of the Constitutionality of Existing Law and Policy

Judicial independence is especially important in the exercise of **judicial review**, the courts' authority to determine whether new laws or policies violate the constitution (**constitutional judicial review**) or contradict existing laws (**statutory judicial review**). A ruling that a particular law or policy is unconstitutional often leads the legislature to revise the law in light of the court ruling. This revised law will, legislators hope, achieve the policy goals of the original law and be acceptable to the court. In the case of a statutory review decision, the possibility that the legislature will solve a problem by passing a new law is even greater.

Interpretation of Vague Laws Passed by Other Branches of Government

All judicial decisions involve interpretation. No law is so clear or so obvious that everyone agrees about its intent and meaning, and some laws are less clear than others. Legislatures and chief executives faced with a controversial and deeply divisive issue often delegate authority over the matter to other parts of the government, including courts. One way to do this is to write vague laws that force the courts to fill in the blanks. This allows a legislator or chief executive to shift blame for an unpopular policy decision onto the judiciary.

In the United States, for example, the Americans with Disabilities Act (ADA) includes the provision that "All newly constructed places of public accommodation and commercial facilities must be accessible to individuals with disabilities to the extent that it is not structurally impractical." This does not specify which problems that individuals deal with on a daily basis are considered disabilities, nor what kinds of changes would be structurally practical or impractical. Not surprisingly, the ADA set the stage for numerous lawsuits about compliance with the law regarding new construction by public and private entities.

Creation of New Policies in Response to Pressing Social Problems

Another task of some judiciaries goes beyond filling in the blanks in vague laws. Sometimes in the context of a ruling on constitutionality, and sometimes as part of the resolution of some other kind of dispute, a court may choose to prescribe particular policy goals or even detailed policy provisions. In such cases, the court enters the realm of the legislator or bureaucrat. Those who dislike these actions deride them as "legislating from the bench." When judges dictate policy guidelines to other branches of government rather than basing their opinions on narrow interpretations of legal questions, their activities are often called **judicial activism**. An activist court is one that uses decisions before it to make sweeping policy changes.

In the United States, a classic example of judicial activism is the Supreme Court's 1954 *Brown v. Board of Education* decision. The court could have chosen to limit its ruling only to the school district in question; it instead ruled that racial segregation in U.S. schools was unconstitutional. Some associate activist courts with left-of-center policy prescriptions, but although it may sound like an oxymoron, conservative judicial activism is an increasingly recognized practice.[7]

Settlement of Civil Disputes and Disputes between Units of Government

In addition to ruling on criminal cases, judiciaries often resolve arguments—known as civil disputes—between individuals, between an individual and a company, or between companies. Civil disputes fall into a category known as **tort law**. A *tort* is a wrong or harm against an individual and can include instances of injury or nuisance. In many countries, individuals can sue companies or other individuals that they believe harmed them through negligence or other inappropriate behavior. Following the filing of a lawsuit by the harmed party, a court decides how to resolve the dispute.

> **Tort Law** Judicial action to address disputes involving torts (harms done to an individual), including injury and nuisance.

Courts also sometimes resolve disagreements between units of government. These may involve two levels of government in a federal system or two components of the government at the same level. In Pakistan, for example, the Supreme Court rules on disputes between the federal and provincial governments and between two or more provincial governments.

Legal Sanctioning of Particular Acts

The judicial system can also provide an official, legally binding decision to address other contentious matters—for example, child custody battles stemming from divorce—and to sanction specified actions that are not in dispute. Such actions include name changes, adoptions, divorces, and the distribution of property following an individual's death. For example, although private and government agencies may be involved in the process of matching children with new adoptive parents, a court decision may be required to finalize the adoption, giving it legal endorsement and authorization.

Think and Discuss

What is the most important task of the judiciary? What makes this task so important?

Organization of the Judicial Branch

In most political systems, the courts form a complex hierarchy. Courts at the same level of this hierarchy exist in different parts of the country, and courts at different levels can be located in the same city. A federal system is likely to have local, provincial ("state" in the United States), and federal courts, each with different responsibilities. In many countries, a single court sits at the top of this hierarchy. In the United States, the Supreme Court holds this position. It is both the final court of appeal and the ultimate authority on whether a particular state or federal law violates the U.S. Constitution. Other examples include Australia's High Court, Finland's Supreme Court, and Paraguay's Supreme Court of Justice.

In some countries, the two tasks of serving as the highest appellate court and as the constitutional arbiter are divided between two courts. The court that hears final appeals is sometimes known as the Supreme Court, while the other court is generally known as the Constitutional Court. Countries as different as Benin, Gabon, Lithuania, South Africa, South Korea, and Thailand have both a Supreme Court and Constitutional Court.

Advantages and Disadvantages of Strong Judiciaries

Establishing a strong judicial branch with important policy-making powers has advantages and disadvantages. This section presents two advantages and two disadvantages.

Advantage 1: A Check on Majority Tyranny

One important issue about democracy is how to balance majority rule and the protection of those in the minority. A politically independent court system can serve as a veto point (see Chapter 5) in a political system, checking the ability of the majority to easily impose its will. As legal scholar Jeremy Waldron relates, "Courts give reasons for their decisions, whereas legislatures do not, and this is a sign that courts, unlike legislatures, take seriously the issues of rights that they address."[8] While in the past many new democracies took minority protection less seriously than majority rule, a large number of democratizing countries in recent decades have implemented significant judicial review powers.

Advantage 2: A Key Component of the Rule of Law in Politics and Economics

Political systems in which the judiciary is subservient to the executive and legislative branches often struggle with developing and fostering the rule of law, in which laws are passed through a constitutional process, government officials are not above the law, and society respects agreements such as contracts as legally binding (see Chapter 5). In such cases, corruption may take the place of transparent, legally based government action.

The concept of rule of law extends to social and economic relations as well. For a country to develop economically, agreements such as contracts must be binding on those who enter into them. This is especially true if the government and the country's businesses hope to attract investment from outside individuals and companies. When the judiciary is beholden to the executive and when the executive itself is corrupt, rule of law is the last thing that drives legal decisions related to business practices.

Disadvantage 1: Power in the Hands of Unelected Officials

An important potential disadvantage of a powerful judicial branch is that government officials who have not been elected have significant discretion over government policy. If legislators and executives are constitutionally reckless in their policy making, giving strong powers to unelected judges might help alleviate the problem. But, in democracies at least, most elected officials have incentives to make good faith efforts to make policy consistent with the rules of the country's constitution. Blatantly violating the constitution would open the door for voters to hold them accountable at election time, so adhering to the constitution improves their prospects for being reelected, and it also protects the democratic system from which they derive their political power.

Disadvantage 2: The Potential to Advance a Political Agenda

A strong judiciary with constitutional and statutory review powers is built on the assumption that judges can objectively consider issues before them. This is not always the case. There is a danger that judges on a powerful court will let their personal political outlooks drive their judicial decisions. It is difficult to tell whether judges are overturning a law because they personally disagree with it or because they legitimately believe it violates the constitution. The observer's views tend to color interpretations of judicial rulings. People rarely level accusations of unfounded judicial activism at court decisions with which they agree.

The Bureaucracy

Judiciaries rule on violations and, sometimes, the constitutionality of laws, but it is up to the executive branch to oversee the laws' implementation. This job falls largely the part of the executive branch known as the **bureaucracy**. The bureaucracy comprises the various departments, agencies, or ministries of a government. Departments, agencies, and ministries are responsible for implementing policy in particular issue areas such as agriculture, labor, and the environment. Each of these issue-based components of bureaucracy is divided into layers based on responsibilities, tasks, and authority. Though technically part of the executive branch, the bureaucracy's power and autonomy from

Bureaucracy The large part of the executive branch dedicated to the implementation of government policy.

the legislative branch—and even from those at the top of the executive branch—has earned it the label of the "fourth branch of government."

Tasks of the Bureaucracy

As governments have taken on greater responsibilities in increasingly complex societies, bureaucracies have developed primarily to implement government policy. As governments have continued to grow in size and scope, the responsibilities of the bureaucracy have grown as well. Although a central task of the legislative branch is to oversee actions of the bureaucracy, the size of most bureaucracies today makes this difficult. In addition, as discussed in the previous chapter, many legislatures delegate responsibilities to the executive branch. As a result, in addition to executing laws developed by the legislature and top officials of the executive branch, bureaucracies play an increasingly important role in policy creation. As political scientist Stephen Brooks puts it, "The bureaucracy enters the policy process both early and late."[9]

Implementation of Laws and Policies

Officially, the central task of the bureaucracy is to execute laws and policies created by the legislature and chief executive. Laws and programs do not administer themselves, and it is hard to imagine how a government could do what it is expected to do—collect taxes, spend money, defend the country, and so on—without a large workforce to implement policies. At upper levels of the bureaucracy, implementation includes broad planning about how to administer policies. At the lower levels, it includes routine administrative duties, such as performing inspections of particular businesses or processing tax payments from individuals and corporations.

Interpretation of Existing but Vague Laws

Part of the way a legislature delegates to the executive branch is to pass vague laws. The lack of clarity in a particular law, intentional or unintentional, allows the bureaucrats to add specific details. Political scientists John Ferejohn and Charles Shipan argue that this happens more often than one might think. They claim that most statutes are "constraints" as opposed to "detailed directives" and that "relatively few governmental decisions are directly mandated by legislative acts."[10] The legislature and chief executive may want certain laws to be vague in the interest of efficiency, leaving the details up to those who know the most about the issue. Just as in the case of legislation that leaves the courts to fill in the blanks, those creating legislation requiring bureaucratic sorting out may also favor vague laws for political reasons. A vague law allows them to avoid taking a detailed stance on a controversial issue.

Agenda-Setting and Advising on Policy Specifics

Bureaucrats also play a significant role in policy creation. Sometimes, high-ranking members of the bureaucracy use their connections with legislators and the chief executive to stress certain broad approaches. Members of particular bureaucratic departments may emphasize the importance of their policy areas (e.g., transportation safety) within a broader policy concern (e.g., homeland security). They hope their efforts play a role in setting the policy agenda. Agenda setting is a primary step in the policy process. It provides the overarching framework for the policies generated by the political process.

As a developing policy is being drafted or an existing policy is being revised, bureaucrats provide detailed information to legislators or others in the executive branch. Legislatures and chief executives rely on officials in assorted bureaucratic departments for advice about issues within those departments' policy areas. As discussed in the previous chapter, legislative committees may call officials from the executive branch to testify. This is part of the legislature's oversight function, but it can also help the legislature formulate policy. In the United States, it is common for members of the bureaucracy to testify before congressional committees or subcommittees about particular bills.

Middle-level bureaucrats may give advice—broad or detailed, in person or through reports—to superiors in their department. The senior officials then craft policy recommendations that are submitted to the legislature for consideration. Officials directly below the level of minister, department secretary, or agency director can wield significant influence over policy by filtering suggestions from below before passing them on to the minister, secretary, or director. Likewise, the minister plays a similar role in filtering policy suggestions before passing them along to the chief executive or the legislature.

Policy Creation

Depending on the nature of the issue, bureaucracies sometimes have significant powers to create new policies from scratch. When specific rules governing an issue do not exist, the bureaucracy may be called on—or may decide on its own—to fill the void with new rules and regulations that have the force of law. The bureaucracy establishes the parameters of new government action, which become the prevailing and official policy unless preempted by a legislative or judicial response.[11] Such instances move bureaucrats well beyond their roles as implementers, agenda-setters, advisers, and interpreters. They become unelected legislators.

Think and Discuss

What is the bureaucracy's single most important task? What makes this task so important?

Organization of Bureaucracies

Bureaucracies are made up of various permanent bodies—ministries, departments, agencies, bureaus, and so on—that, taken together, constitute the majority of the executive branch. Officials at the top of each governmental section link the chief executive to the bureaucracy. The chief executive typically appoints these top officials. As a result, they generally serve in their positions only as long as that chief executive is in power. For personal reasons or because of poor performance, they may leave in the middle of the chief executive's term in office.

The U.S. federal bureaucracy has four types of government agencies: cabinet departments, regulatory agencies, government corporations, and independent executive agencies. The **cabinet departments** are most closely linked to the chief executive. With the exception of the Justice Department, headed by the attorney general, a **secretary** heads each of the fifteen departments of the president's cabinet. The most recent cabinet addition, Homeland Security, arose in 2002 in response to the September 11, 2001, terrorist attacks. In many other countries, cabinet departments are known as **ministries**, and they are headed by **ministers**. There are four times as many independent agencies as departments in the United States. These include the Environmental Protection Agency (EPA) and the Federal Reserve.

Middle- and lower-level bureaucrats are generally not political appointees. Instead, they are part of the national **civil service** and are known as **civil servants**. They are expected to serve in an objective manner regardless of who heads the executive branch. Unlike political appointees, civil servants ordinarily retain their positions through changes in the chief executive. Consistent with the idea of protecting civil servants from the politics of the governmental process, some countries have specific laws and regulations making it difficult for a civil servant to be fired. In the United States, for example, civil servants serve for a probationary period, after which they can appeal a dismissal to a government body such as the Merit Systems Protection Board.[12]

In most democracies, civil servants earn their positions through the **merit system**. A merit system allows individuals to enter and advance through the bureaucracy due to general competence (e.g., knowledge of the law), expertise in a particular policy field, and/or performance on the job. The opposite of a merit system is known as a **spoils system**. In a spoils system, even middle-level officials are political appointees who earn their positions through connections to government leaders or in return for favors done for such officials.

Cabinet Department A U.S. bureaucratic section closely tied to the president.

Secretary The head of a U.S. cabinet department, who is also a member of the cabinet.

Ministry The term used in many countries for a cabinet-level department.

Minister The head of a government ministry.

Civil Service The part of the bureaucracy made up of middle- and lower-level bureaucrats.

Civil Servant A middle- or lower-level bureaucrat hired for his or her expertise.

Merit System An approach in which members of the bureaucracy earn their initial positions and promotions on the basis of their qualifications and performance.

Spoils System An approach in which bureaucrats get their initial jobs and promotions on the basis of connections to top government officials or favors done for such officials.

In merit systems, bureaucrats develop their knowledge and expertise through educational training (often at the postbaccalaureate level), additional training once in the civil service, and experience from working for a particular agency over a period of time. Bureaucracies can differ significantly in their approach to training and qualifications. U.S. departments generally take a **specialist approach**, hiring individuals to fill specific roles. Such individuals are likely to remain in one department for their entire government careers. Other countries employ a **generalist approach**, in which individuals are hired for their general knowledge or legal expertise. Many European countries have a greater proportion of bureaucratic employees with law degrees than does the United States. In generalist systems, bureaucrats are likely to move from one department to another over their careers.

Advantages and Disadvantages of Large and Powerful Bureaucracies

Despite the way many Americans criticize bureaucracies, most Americans appreciate many of the government programs that the bureaucracy administers. Generally, they also have favorable impressions of the specific civil servants with whom they have interacted.

Advantage 1: Stability

One advantage of a large and powerful bureaucracy is that it creates a degree of stability. In the United States, civil servants may hold positions across several administrations. In parliamentary systems going through a period of unstable governments—that is, periods when the prime minister and cabinet are replaced every few months—mid- and lower-level civil servants keep the government running. In such cases, bureaucrats also take on greater policy-making responsibilities than they possess during more stable times.

Advantage 2: Expertise

Combined with a system of hiring based on merit, bureaucratic stability allows individuals to develop a high degree of expertise in their policy areas, particularly in systems where officials often spend their entire careers in the same department. Sociologist Max Weber's vision of bureaucracy was a hierarchy of government officials, selected for their competence and promoted for their performance, who make impartial and sensible decisions based on established rules. For Weber, the expansion of the size and scope of bureaucracies was a rational response to increasing social and economic complexity.

Advantage 3: Impartial and Fair Application of Rules

Weber also saw bureaucracies as a way to move beyond arbitrary rule creation and enforcement. In European monarchies prior to the spread of democracy, government officials routinely used their positions to grant favors to those they knew or those with particular economic or social clout. For Weber, the ability to apply general rules to specific cases and thus reduce the likelihood of favoritism was a defining feature of bureaucracy, leading to principled and reasonable government deeds.[13] Bureaucracies are more likely to be fair and impartial when they are closely overseen by other government personnel. Thus, oversight of the bureaucracy is not only about ensuring that bureaucrats do not overstep their policy-making bounds; it is also about helping establish that their decisions about individual situations are consistent and evenhanded.

Disadvantage 1: Inefficiency through Overexpansion and Wasteful Spending

While Max Weber saw bureaucratic expansion as a rational response to increasing social complexity, others believe that bureaucrats desire to expand the bureaucracy's size and scope in order to benefit themselves. Increases in staff and budget put more resources under department leaders' control, making these officials more important and furthering their prospects for career advancement. This internal incentive to expand can lead departments to manipulate information to justify expansion. In addition, although governments occasionally recognize and publicly praise efficient and effective agencies, departments that use resources efficiently run the risk of having

Specialist Approach An approach to filling positions in the bureaucracy in which individuals are hired to fill specific roles in particular government departments.

Generalist Approach An approach to filling positions in the bureaucracy in which individuals are hired for their general knowledge or expertise, including advanced legal training.

their budgets cut. If an agency has not used all its budgeted funds, why give it the same amount of money next year?

While it seems like bureaucracies do not always do things as efficiently as private firms might, observing and measuring such inefficiency can be difficult. Unlike a small, local business working on a single project, government agencies face multiple goals and tasks at the same time. Singling out their economically inefficient handling of a particular small project, therefore, ignores what might have been an honest and equitable approach to the project as well as their better handling of other projects.[14] Uncovering anecdotes about a particular agency's program using tax dollars inefficiently is easy. Finding an alternative that spends tax dollars efficiently but still achieves the program's goals is often more difficult.

Disadvantage 2: Power in the Hands of Unelected Officials

One might tolerate inefficiency if bureaucracies were responsive when creating and enforcing policies. As the discussion of India and the Harry Potter series in this chapter's opening highlights, however, robust bureaucracies often cause concern in democracies because of potential partiality and a lack of responsiveness. Bureaucrats are not responsible to voters. The term *bureaucracy*, in fact, comes from the French word *bureaucratie*, referring to rule by unelected government officials (more precisely, rule by offices).

How one can best address this concern is unclear. Placing too many restraints on bureaucrats' decisions in an effort to make them more accountable limits one of their key strengths: their expertise on the issue at hand. In addition, there is tension between the goal of responsiveness and the goal of impartiality. Applying rules without taking into account the context of the individual situation—what some decry as a "rules are rules" mentality—can make an agency more impartial but also more distant and less responsive.[15]

Disadvantage 3: Resistance to Reform and Creative Solutions

What one person sees as stability and fairness, another person could label rigidity and narrow-mindedness. Bureaucracies tend to be rigid organizations that resist reform, the introduction of untested innovations, and creative responses to current problems. Reform challenges those currently in positions of power, that is, the individuals with the authority to approve reform proposals and oversee their implementation. As a result, a government department generally embraces only those reforms that increase its scope and power, and it welcomes only those innovations that do not involve performing new tasks. Bureaucracies typically do not look for, and in fact may actively run away from, creative solutions that involve bending rules, enduring unsuccessful outcomes, or establishing new precedents. Those presenting inventive requests to such departments face the frustrating response: "If I did it for you, I would have to do it for everyone."[16]

In his well-known book on bureaucracy, James Q. Wilson suggests that the inflexibility of bureaucracies should not be surprising. Bureaucracies are "supposed to resist" innovation; they were created to replace "uncertain expectations and haphazard activities" with stability, routine, and equal treatment of similar cases.[17] As a result, they tend to rely on preestablished rules, known as standard operating procedures (SOPs). SOPs lay out ahead of time how an agency should handle a particular type of problem when it arises. They are based on logic and past experiences and thus seem more efficient and less risky than trying to come up with new solutions on the spot.

The Military

In some ways, the military is much like any other part of the bureaucracy. It is hierarchical, it follows standard operating procedures, and it helps craft and implement policies in its areas of interest and expertise. In other ways, the military is quite different from other bureaucratic agencies. It is, potentially at least, the most imposing component of the state. Its significant control over the means of force gives it the ability to overthrow the existing government, assuming that military leaders turn against the government and lower levels of the military follow the direction of those at the top. Generalizing about the military and its role in the policy process is harder than generalizing about other bureaucratic departments. Of the various unelected government components, the military varies the most in how active its members are in determining policy. This variation exists across countries, but it can also exist within the same country at different points in time.

Some countries have a strong tradition of **civilian control of the military**. This means that the military does not control government decision making even about matters affecting it, such as military spending. In the United States, military decisions are ultimately made by nonmilitary leaders, including the president as commander in chief and the secretary of defense, who by law must be a civilian. In most cases of civilian control, the military does enjoy a degree of autonomy. Political leaders typically yield to military officers in matters of day-to-day operations and specific decisions during military conflicts, though civilian commanders in chief are sometimes tempted to micromanage military operations.

> **Civilian Control of the Military** A situation in which the military is subordinate to nonmilitary government officials.

Tasks of the Military under Civilian Control

Militaries under civilian control have two essential tasks: defending the country and developing into a professional fighting force. Historically, militaries have also been charged with controlling the territory of an empire. This is less common today, although militaries may emphasize developing the capability to deal with regional or international crises abroad. Militaries may also be expected to maintain order internally, but systems with civilian control of the military typically prefer to leave this task to the country's police.

Defending the Country

The primary purpose of a military is to provide security by deterring attack by an external force. Most states try to maintain a certain level of military strength and preparedness compared with neighboring states or other potential rivals. Increased military spending by one state can trigger corresponding increases in spending by a rival, leading to an "arms race" between the two. Civilian leaders make such decisions, but as in other forms of bureaucracy, the military can influence these decisions by manipulating information about its needs and the rival's capabilities.

Developing into a Professional Fighting Force

Another task of militaries is to professionalize their ranks, becoming more focused, more specialized, and better able to address military matters such as national security. In a professionalized military, both the officer corps and the lower ranks are well trained, often through the use of academies requiring years of education. In this way, the military becomes a specialized civil service, with those holding positions in the various levels of the hierarchy earning their positions by merit.

Controlling the Empire

Governments have also used civilian-controlled militaries for expansion into new territory or control of existing colonies. Until the middle of the twentieth century, European states used their military strength to support colonial expansion far from Europe and to subjugate the colonies. Other states, such as tsarist Russia, built empires by seizing neighboring territory. These empires consisted of a core area and a conquered periphery, with the periphery typically more culturally diverse and less developed economically than the core. Such expansive use of the military requires more military spending than does defensive security. It can also lead to **militarism**, the preoccupation with a strong military force and an

> **Militarism** A state's preoccupation with having a strong military force and being prepared to use it aggressively.

emphasis on the likely need to use it aggressively. In such situations, military leaders are likely to become more central to policy making, eventually threatening the practice of civilian control.

Think and Discuss
What is the single most important task of the military? What makes this task so important?

Military Rule and Praetorianism

Coup d'État The act of overthrowing an existing government.

In some cases, military officers intervene to overthrow an existing government and become the rulers of the political system, an act known as a **coup d'état**. Casual observers of foreign affairs often associate military coups with selfish power grabs by military officers. While the typical military coup is led by a single officer or small group of officers, it is not always a selfish power grab; nor is it always unpopular among the general population. When a country is experiencing a faltering economy or political chaos, citizens may be happy to exchange political rights for resurrection of the economy or restoration of order, at least in the short term.

The military may seize power for a number of reasons, including a government's poor performance, a faltering economy, or corrupt political leaders and bureaucrats. Mass unrest may be widespread, with strikes, protests, and violence. When military leaders point to such problems as justification for their seizure of power, they imply that they will remain in power only until the problems are resolved. In other words, the masses, civilian politicians, and the military leaders themselves often see military government as a temporary fix. In other cases, the military takes over with no intention of ruling for only a brief period of time.

Junta A collective comprising the heads of the various segments of the armed forces that oversees policy decisions in some military governments.

Military rule can take many forms. Some military governments install a democratic-looking assembly, with the military leadership handpicking its members. Others center on a single popular leader who typically holds the position of president. Still others are run by a **junta**, a group made up of the heads of the assorted components of the armed forces. Even in this case, power may become concentrated in the hands of one military leader over time. Juntas were common in military governments in Latin America during the twentieth century.

In recent decades, military rule has become less common, and military coups against new democracies have been less successful. Norms about civilian control have penetrated into a number of militaries that had not previously held such values. Military leaders may have also learned that running a country and trying to solve economic and social problems can be difficult and can drain military resources. Finally, establishing civilian control of the military has been a popular response to military governments that have committed human rights abuses.[18]

Even when the military does not have complete control of a government, it may have a great deal of say over its own affairs, including sizable control of defense spending decisions. The military's role in decision making may be obscured, as military leaders work with (or put pressure on) the official rulers behind the scenes. In countries where civilian control is weak, militaries can become heavily involved in policy making beyond military spending and security without openly seizing control of the government.

Praetorianism A political system in which the military is an active participant in politics.

Comparativists use the term **praetorianism** to describe a political system in which the military is an active and regular participant in politics, either openly or covertly.[19] Political scientist Samuel Huntington asserted that praetorianism is likely when the military is cohesive and independent of civilian control while civilian political institutions are weak and ineffective. In praetorian systems, even when the military does not directly control the government, the threat of military intervention is constantly on the minds of civilian leaders.

Spotlight on . . . IRAQ

Reconstructing the Iraqi Military and Reestablishing Civilian Control

Following the overthrow of the Iraqi government by the U.S.-led coalition in spring 2003, the process of agreeing on a new political system and putting it in place began. Part of this process involved reconstruction of the Iraqi military, which had been decimated by the invasion and officially disbanded by coalition forces in May 2003. Because of the military's key role in maintaining security and also because of its potential to intervene in domestic politics, the process of rebuilding the Iraqi military was slow. The Iraqi military required new weapons and significant training before the United States handed over domestic security control to it. Another major topic of concern was establishing civilian control over the reconstituted military.

Iraqi soldiers take part in a training course at an Iraqi military base south of Baghdad, Iraq, August 30, 2010. © REUTERS/Saad Shalash

Iraq was a praetorian country for much of the twentieth century. Its military had a history of intervention in politics; there was at least one coup d'état in Iraq during every decade from the 1930s to the 1960s. Saddam Hussein, the head of the Baath Party (the ruling party of Iraq's one-party state from 1968 to 2003) for nearly twenty-four years, had installed a form of civilian control over the military, serving as Iraq's president and its commander in chief. He used Baath Party networks to supply soldiers and clan connections to foster loyalty.[20] In this case, civilian control meant an increasingly militaristic state and also that the military served Saddam's desires.

This structure had important consequences. While the Baath Party controlled the military, Saddam had significant military decision-making authority. The normal vertical chain of command found in most professionalized militaries was replaced by one in which Saddam directed orders to any part and any level of the military. Some observers believe that this feature contributed to problems for the Iraqi military during the Iran-Iraq War (a conflict discussed in the TIC section on Iran later in the chapter).[21] It also meant that the military became involved not only in international conflicts, such as the lengthy war with Iran, but also in settling domestic political scores. Saddam used the military to attack the Kurdish population a number of times, most forcefully in 1988, as well as the Shiite population in the south of the country following the first Gulf War as punishment for its U.S.-encouraged uprising against Saddam's government.

Today, no single party controls the Iraqi government. In 2010, the lack of a majority party in parliament following the March 2010 elections led to a months-long stalemate over creating a new government. As the deadlock dragged on through the summer of 2010, Iraq's top military officer, Babaker

Zebari, criticized the planned withdrawal of U.S. forces as premature.[22] Two months later, reports from the region and observers in the West began to hint at the possibility of military coup in Iraq.[23] In November 2010, a U.S. Department of Defense report stated that a "significant gap" remained between the "minimum essential capabilities" of the Iraqi military and its condition at the time of the report.[24]

Although a new Iraqi government was eventually supported by a unanimous vote in parliament in December 2010, Prime Minister Nouri al-Maliki warned about the government's less-than-ideal composition, stating, "Given the circumstances it has been created under, this government does not satisfy the people nor the needs of our country."[25] In addition, what might be interpreted as either a step toward strong civilian control or a reason for concern, al-Maliki was also named acting defense, interior, and national security minister.[26] As his own comment about the new government highlights, his challenges as prime minister are numerous. Among them is the need to establish the Iraqi armed forces as a professional and depoliticized military, immune both from the belief in a right or duty to intervene in politics and from its use by government leaders for their own political ends.

Advantages and Disadvantages of a Strong Political Role for the Military

For those used to civilian control, military involvement in politics may have obvious disadvantages. But a politically active military can be beneficial. A military government may play up these advantages to justify its seizure and maintenance of political power.

Advantage 1: Making Tough Policy Decisions

While all governments prefer to be popular, military governments generally do not give citizens the chance to vote them out of office. This allows the military to make unpopular decisions that may be necessary for a country's long-term stability and improved prosperity. Government leaders who have to worry about being reelected, on the other hand, are often reluctant to make tough policy choices. In such cases, problems can slowly get worse as the government implements small policy changes when more serious reforms are needed.

Advantage 2: Restoring Order and Battling Corruption

The military's ability to make tough policy choices enables it to tackle corruption and instability more forcefully than democratic governments often can. Although military leaders may use their power for personal gain, some military governments have waged successful fights against corruption. In South Korea, for example, the military government of General Park Chung Hee made significant strides against corruption during the 1960s, before becoming increasingly repressive in the 1970s, leading to the general's assassination in 1979.

Disadvantage 1: Unwillingness to Surrender Power

Military leaders often seize control of the political system with good intentions: ending social chaos, fostering economic growth, or attacking embedded corruption. After they have achieved their stated goals, they are often reluctant to abandon control of the political system. As discussed in Chapter 1, holding political power has many advantages. In addition, although one could argue that a military government's successful completion of its mission ends the need for military rule, military leaders may come to believe that military rule is a superior form of government or that they personally are superior leaders. This is particularly likely in countries with a history of poor performance by elected officials.

Disadvantage 2: A Permanent Presence in Politics

Even when military leaders surrender power and help establish a democratic system, their presence in politics does not magically evaporate. Establishing a commitment to civilian control of the military takes time. One of the firm rules of the comparative study of politics is that once a military has intervened in domestic politics, it is likely to intervene again. Military officers and ordinary soldiers may believe they have a right or even a duty not to surrender themselves to civilian control and to intervene in politics again if necessary. Civilian leaders may support continued military involvement in politics, allowing the military great autonomy to set defense policy and provide input on internal stability in the country. Thus, for comparativists who study military involvement in politics, it is not unusual to find a country where the military has repeatedly overthrown the government and maintained a significant role in politics between its periods of direct rule.

TOPIC IN COUNTRIES

The unelected components of government outlined so far in this chapter play important roles in the Topic in Countries (TIC) cases. In the following section, look for

- The extent to which the judiciaries in the TIC cases are independent from the other branches of government.
- Trends in the growth or contraction of the bureaucracies across the TIC cases.
- The role of the military, historically and more recently, in the domestic politics of the TIC cases.
- The importance of the issue of corruption within the unelected components of government in many of the TIC cases.

The United Kingdom

Befitting its status as a mature democracy, the elected components of the British government have kept close watch on their unelected counterparts. Largely because of the notion of parliamentary supremacy discussed in the previous chapter, the United Kingdom (UK) has no tradition of judicial review. The creation of the new British Supreme Court in 2009, however, has set the stage for an increased role for the judiciary in British politics. The British bureaucracy has also been transformed by efforts to make it more accountable and effective. During the 1980s and 1990s, the country became an exemplar of reform aimed at privatization and greater bureaucratic efficiency. No such reforms were needed in the case of the British military. Compared to other countries around the world with sizable armed forces, the UK is one of the closest to an ideal type case of civilian control of the military.

The Judiciary

The UK uses a common law approach, and its extensive and complex judicial branch tries civil and criminal cases. Like its fused executive and legislative branches, a portion of the judiciary has historically been fused with the legislature. In the past, the highest British appeals court was the Appellate Committee of the House of Lords. Twelve Lords of Appeal in Ordinary (more commonly called the Law Lords) decided on legal matters, with their decisions binding on all lower courts.

As part of the overhaul of the British political system under the government of Tony Blair, the Constitutional Reform Bill became law in March 2005. This law has altered the tradition of a fused legislature and judiciary by, among other things, creating a new UK Supreme Court, which convened for the first time in 2009. Consistent with the British political system's theme of evolutionary change, the first justices of the Supreme Court were former Law Lords, who then surrendered their seats in the House of Lords.

Another interesting feature of the judiciary is the relative absence of judicial review authority. An act of Parliament is, by definition, constitutional. This does not mean that the Law Lords never weighed in on parliamentary acts, and one would expect judicial intervention to continue to increase rather than decrease in the years ahead. One reason for this is the amplified role of European judicial bodies in the wake of continuing European integration. In addition to the European Court of Justice and the European Court of Human Rights that are "now regularly reviewing British legislation for compatibility with international obligations,"[27] the Law Lords increasingly use European standards to evaluate acts of the British Parliament. In December 2004, for example, the Lords' Appellate Committee declared that the Anti-terrorism, Crime and Security Act, passed by the British government in 2001, violated the European Convention on Human Rights, of which the UK is a signatory. Although the Law Lords' ruling did not invalidate the law, it placed great pressure on then-Prime Minister Tony Blair's government to address the concerns in the ruling and led the government to replace the law the following year.

As comparative law specialist Tom Ginsburg points out, the idea that commitments to the European Union mean that acts of Parliament are no longer completely sovereign has opened the door for a broader role for the judiciary. Ginsburg argues that if Parliament lacks complete supremacy, the traditional objection to judicial intervention by the British "is much less potent."[28] In the years ahead, it will be interesting to see whether the British Supreme Court will more forcefully attempt to establish a role for itself as a check on Parliament.

The Bureaucracy

At the height of the postwar settlement in Europe, during which the political Left accepted capitalist economics in exchange for acceptance of large welfare state programs by the political Right, the British bureaucracy reached its peak size. Nearly 750,000 people were employed in the British civil service. With Margaret Thatcher's reform efforts in the 1980s, the size of the bureaucracy declined dramatically to fewer than 500,000.

A centerpiece of Thatcher's reforms, and what allowed the reduction in bureaucracy, was the privatization of a large number of formerly government-run programs and businesses. Privatization efforts targeted a variety of government entities from utilities to public housing projects. Thatcher's commitment to reducing the size and scope of government shaped her term in office, and it lasted beyond her tenure. While shrinking the bureaucracy, Thatcher also listened to bureaucrats' desire for greater autonomy and performance rewards. Bureaucrats gained more autonomy but were also held more responsible for the results of their activities. These reforms maintained the British bureaucracy's strong culture of impartiality and subordination to the elected officials above them, but they also gave bureaucrats an increased ability to exercise discretion over government policy details.[29]

IN THEORY AND PRACTICE

Bureaucratic Autonomy Theory and the United Kingdom

Bureaucratic autonomy theory addresses the way bureaucracies develop autonomy over time. It holds that bureaucrats try to maximize their department's independence by emphasizing its objective, civil service components, developing formalized decision-making rules, and controlling information that might be used in oversight of its activities.[30] According to this approach, bureaucrats are most vulnerable to control by superiors when they are first hired or just after a new department's creation. They have not had time to develop expertise and a record of performance, and rules designed to limit their autonomy may still be effective. Once they become established and their expertise becomes recognized, officials are more difficult to control. As experienced bureaucrats, they become hard to replace.[31]

Even before Margaret Thatcher's reforms encouraged greater autonomy in exchange for improved performance, the British bureaucracy was already autonomous. This was due in part to the existence of the **permanent secretary** position in the British system. This position is the highest ranking official below the minister and is held by a senior member of that ministry's civil service. A permanent secretary generally retains the position even if the minister is replaced. The permanent secretary and subordinate deputy secretaries and undersecretaries form what is known as the British Higher Civil Service.[32]

According to bureaucratic autonomy theory, British bureaucrats should defend their independence in part by controlling information. Permanent secretaries often filter information from subordinates, but they have also employed the technique of burying the minister or prime minister with paper in an effort to prevent the minister from commenting on specific recommendations. Together, these techniques have given permanent secretaries the ability to influence the details of government policy, as well as the de facto ability to delay or even kill policy initiatives.[33]

The Military

Though by no means the largest, the British military is one of the world's most powerful armed forces. It is also a model of a professionalized military strongly accepting

Bureaucratic Autonomy Theory A theory that contends that bureaucrats emphasize their professional civil service expertise and control information in order to make oversight of their activities more difficult and maximize their independence from political control.

Permanent Secretary A senior member of the British civil service, just below the position of minister, who usually continues in this position if the minister is replaced.

of civilian control. The prime minister and Ministry of Defence determine military policy. Participation in the Iraq War became controversial among the general British population, but the idea that political leaders make such decisions is uncontroversial among the members of the military.

This is somewhat ironic given the country's history. The military first began to encourage professionalism in the early eighteenth century. Prior to that, British military forces had employed militias. While this was adequate for defense of the country, it was impractical for the running of an overseas empire. The British military became a professional force to be feared both for its discipline and, eventually, its technical expertise. A culture of professionalism also developed, reinforced by the combination of domestic political stability and a largely external focus (the two world wars, the cold war, the Iraq War, etc.).

The major exception to this generalization was the use of the military to maintain control of Northern Ireland. British troops were sent to Northern Ireland in 1969 in an effort to contain the growing violence, but their presence did little to weaken the resolve of Catholics opposed to British control. Serving in this capacity made maintaining military morale difficult.

Germany

Although Germany shares the UK's status as a mature democracy, its approach to integrating the unelected components of government into its democratic political system is different from that in the UK. Its judicial branch is far more powerful than that its British counterpart. Its bureaucracy today is also much less centralized than that of the UK, although the German bureaucracy historically played a significant role in the country's economic development. The central government broadly guides the actions of civil servants at the regional level, who make up the vast majority of the country's bureaucratic personnel. The German military—a fixture in politics prior to World War II—fully accepted civilian control only after that war, a practice that continued following reunification in 1990.

The Judiciary

The Federal Republic of Germany was founded on the principle of a *Rechtsstaat*, or a state based on the rule of law.[34] This principle stands in stark contrast to the lawlessness of the Nazi regime and its politicization of the legal system through the appointment of Nazi Party members throughout the judiciary. The post–World War II constitution delineates basic rights of individual citizens and societal groups and provides for an independent judiciary.

The Federal Constitutional Court, Germany's equivalent of the U.S. Supreme Court, exhibits substantial authority and independence from the executive. The court possesses judicial review over other branches of government and has the authority to act as the final arbiter of disputes between regional and federal levels of government. Justices can only be removed by the federal president on the recommendation of the court itself. In response to the country's tumultuous past, the court is charged with protecting the constitutional and political order against antidemocratic forces. The court used this authority to ban far-Left and far-Right parties that it deemed were a threat to democracy in the 1950s and 1960s.[35]

The organization of the judicial system reflects the influences of Germany's own brand of federalism. Eight of the sixteen justices to the Federal Constitutional Court are appointed by the upper house of parliament, the Bundesrat, the other eight by the lower house, the Bundestag. This arrangement gives voice to both the governments of the *Länder* and the political parties.[36] In contrast to the structure of the judiciary in the federal system of the United States, there are no separate federal and *Land* courts in the German federal system, with the exception of the Federal Constitutional Court. The remaining courts in Germany are established by the Länder. Germany also has an extensive system of specialized administrative courts that adjudicate labor and social welfare disputes.[37]

The Bureaucracy

The German bureaucracy played a significant role in the country's political and economic development. Germany became a nation-state and an industrial power in the late nineteenth century. Its Prussian administration sought to catch up with the more advanced industrial states of Britain and the United States.[38] Sociologist Max Weber's archetype of a modern bureaucracy, discussed earlier in the chapter, was modeled on the Prussian administration.

The bureaucracy in the Federal Republic is far more decentralized than its predecessors under the imperial and Nazi regimes. At the federal level, the administration is small, especially when compared with other European countries, accounting for only about 10 percent of all civil

Justices of the German Federal Constitutional Court stand in a courtroom in Karlsruhe, Germany, on August 9, 2005.
© AP Photo/Michael Probst

servants in Germany.[39] This compactness reflects the fact that the primary task of federal civil servants is to formulate policy by drafting government bills and administrative regulations. Consistent with the German conception of federalism based on "interlocking politics," implementation of federal law rests primarily with the Länder.[40] Despite its hierarchical structure, the top levels of the bureaucracy have little leverage over the actions of the lower levels.[41]

The Military

The military played a dominant role in German society and politics in the country's modern history. The Prussian military's values of order, hierarchy, and obedience permeated broader German society in the nineteenth century.[42] An aggressive foreign policy culminating in World War I reflected the German generals' influence in politics. Following Germany's defeat in World War II, the armed forces were discredited, and their numbers and mission were subsequently circumscribed. Under the Federal Republic, the armed forces came under firm civilian control, with the defense minister in command during peacetime and the chancellor serving as the commander in chief during periods of war.[43]

From the days of Prussia's efforts against Napoleon, all young men in Germany have faced compulsory military service. This practice ended in the summer of 2011, thanks to a new policy that Chancellor Angela Merkel's government approved in late 2010, which also aimed to reduce German forces from 250,000 to 185,000. This policy change is consistent with public opinion in Germany, which since World War II has opposed a large military. From German's rearmament during the 1950s to the decision to send troops to Afghanistan in 2003, any notable increase in German military activity has been controversial. The Green Party's acceptance of peacekeeping missions in the 1990s—breaking its long-standing commitment to pacifism—was a wrenching decision for its members. After participating in UN peacekeeping missions in the 1990s and 2000s and as members of the coalition forces in Afghanistan in the spring of 2011, Germany decided not to join the United States, UK, and France in establishing a no-fly zone in Libya to assist forces opposing the government of Muammar Qaddafi.

India

Most scholars who study India consider it a consolidated democracy. Compared to the UK and Germany, however, India's unelected components of government pose challenges to its democratic credentials. This is most true of the Indian bureaucracy, which has both sustained governance when political instability has arisen and, as the opening anecdote to this chapter highlighted,

contributed to popular frustration with government due to its inefficiency. The judiciary has been active in challenging the actions of legislatures and developing its power of judicial review. The military has largely stayed out of politics, except when used by the government to put down political uprisings.

The Judiciary

The judiciary has played a significant role in the governance of India. Using its powers of judicial review, it has been a check on Indian legislators. By encouraging a certain type of litigation, described later in this section, it has provided a tool for greater civic involvement in governance.

The Supreme Court, headed by a chief justice, is situated at the top of India's judicial hierarchy. High Courts, responsible for individual federal territorial units or groups of federal units, come next. Below that are three or four levels of civil and criminal courts in rural and metropolitan areas. Although the range of consultation on the appointment of justices has varied over time, the chief justice and other Supreme Court justices are appointed by the president on the advice of the prime minister and cabinet. The president appoints High Court judges after consultation with the chief justice of India, the chief justice of the High Court, and the governors of the federal territorial units that fall under the courts' jurisdiction. Governors appoint judges in their territories after consultation with the responsible High Court and the public services commissions.

The most significant source of tension between the courts and the legislature surrounds the authority to declare laws unconstitutional. Initially, the Supreme Court recognized the right of the Lok Sabha and Rajya Sabha to amend the constitution at will. In 1967, it decided in the *Golak Nath* case that the Fundamental Rights laid out in the constitution were supreme, and the legislature could not make laws that violated them. Responding to the court's action, the parliamentary bodies passed the Twenty-First Amendment in 1971, which gave the Lok Sabha and Rajya Sabha the power to amend any part of the constitution. In 1973, the amendment was challenged in the *Keshavananda Bharti* case, and the Supreme Court held that parliament could amend the constitution but could not alter the constitution's basic structure—a precedent that continues to guide the court's review of legislation.[44]

A second source of tension comes from the Supreme Court's encouragement of public interest litigation (PIL). Exact parameters for what constitutes PIL are not laid out in Indian law, allowing for significant judicial interpretation. Essentially, any litigation with the stated purpose of protecting the public interest could qualify. This includes cases designed to force government officials to enforce laws—PIL cases often target the executive and legislative branches—or to protect the citizenry from dangers such as pollution and terrorism. Rather than restricting such cases to claims by the specific victims of alleged violations of public interest protection, PIL cases can be filed by anyone.

The Indian judiciary also puts up with an immense backload of cases and an extreme shortage of staff. In the middle of 2009, Indian Prime Minister Manmohan Singh stated that clearing the case backlog was the judiciary's largest challenge, while the other pressing problem was the three thousand vacant judge posts across the country.[45] The following year, there were still tens of millions of cases pending in India's courts.

The Bureaucracy

During the colonial period, the Indian Civil Service (ICS) was referred to as the "steel frame" that held India together. Its successor, the Indian Administrative Service (IAS), continues the tradition of careful selection of leading civil servants. Although it has lost some of its prestige, the top echelon of administrators in India constitutes a very select group. There are estimated to be more than 19 million public sector employees, though only five to six thousand are found in the IAS.[46] Of those who apply for such positions, only about 0.01 percent are selected. Around half the positions are reserved for underrepresented groups, contributing to a shift in the social makeup away from a cadre dominated by urban, Westernized, upper-class men.[47]

About 70 percent of the IAS officers are assigned to serve the governments of the federal territorial units. To foster a sense of national identity, half of those in a given federal territorial unit are supposed to come from another of the territorial units. Because languages used in the various federal territorial units differ greatly and the IAS officers are unlikely to be able to use many of them effectively, adherence to this distribution rule has become difficult. This has led to the observation "that the services are increasingly becoming 'all-India' in name only."[48]

The "brain drain" to the private sector is another problem affecting these IAS officers and the bureaucrats serving under them. Civil servants are paid little, so entering the private sector is alluring and has resulted in the loss of highly qualified personnel. Indian politics specialist Bimal Jalan has referred to this trend as an "atrophy . . . of the Indian civil services," with the remaining officials displaying a combination of "non-accountability, corruption and ineptitude."[49]

The Military

The Indian armed forces contain around 1.3 million troops, a significant portion of whom are stationed in Kashmir, the disputed region that has been the primary source of tension between India and Pakistan in recent decades. Including the large numbers of reserve and paramilitary forces, India has the second largest military in the world, next to China. The Indian military possesses nuclear weapons and the ability to deliver them.

With these features, the military could wield significant political power, but the armed forces have remained essentially apolitical. Rather than directing the political system, they have, on numerous occasions, responded to the direction of elected political leaders. They regained control of Hyderabad in 1948 after its leader announced his intention to join Pakistan. They fought wars with Pakistan in 1947–48, 1965, 1971, and 1998. They fought China in 1962, went to Sri Lanka as a peacekeeping force in 1987, and blocked an attempted coup in the Maldives in 1988.

Mexico

Compared with the significant reforms of the electoral process and the fundamental changes in executive-legislative relations in Mexico over the past two decades, the roles of and problems with the Mexican judiciary, bureaucracy, and military have changed little. The judiciary is still coming into its own as an autonomous institution, and the Mexican bureaucracy has resisted efforts at significant reform. Because Mexico already had strong civilian control of the military during the period of dominance by the Institutional Revolutionary Party (PRI), relations between the military and the civilian government have remained largely unchanged during Mexico's ongoing democratization.

The Judiciary

Mexico has a civil law tradition and a history of judicial subservience to other branches of government. The writers of the Mexican constitution intended the judicial branch to serve as a check on the legislature and executive, but in practice, it was controlled by the executive in general and the president in particular. The Senate tended to rubber stamp the president's judicial selections during the era of PRI dominance. Showing the lack of judicial independence, the justices of the Mexican Supreme Court typically resigned after a presidential election, allowing the new president to handpick new judges, even though they were able to serve for life according to the constitution.

The judicial branch became more independent in the 1990s, largely as a result of judicial reforms under President Ernesto Zedillo in 1994. These changes were adopted in part because PRI leaders thought they might lose control of the federal government. In particular, they feared that the loss of the presidency would allow their opponents to use a weak judicial branch to support reprisals against them. Thus, the reforms that included judicial review powers became the PRI's "insurance policy."[50] Mexico does not yet have a fully independent judiciary. The practice of judicial review is relatively new, and a culture of judicial independence is still evolving. Mexico's judiciary has come a long way, however, from the body that automatically authorized executive decisions in the past.

The Mexican judicial system also reflects the country's federal arrangements. Each *estado* has its own judiciary, with powers to rule on the basis of laws passed in that estado. The structures of the estados' courts are not uniform, however, and the reform process affected judicial systems in different ways.[51] Corruption in law enforcement institutions, including the courts, remains a larger problem in some of the estados than in others.

The Bureaucracy

The bureaucracy played an important role in the PRI's dominance of Mexican politics. The president appointed a large number of bureaucrats, with top bureaucratic positions tending to go to the most loyal members of the PRI or those most owed political favors. The appointees in turn appointed a number of officials below them in their departments, again taking into account how the appointments benefited themselves and the PRI. Even those who served for long periods of time in the bureaucracy tended to bounce around within it, going where their political connections led them. Thus, the Mexican bureaucracy was more political machine than merit-based civil service, and the general problem of political corruption found a particular home within the Mexican bureaucracy.

As with the judiciary, changes began to take place during the liberalization of the 1980s and 1990s. President Carlos Salinas de Gortari stressed professionalism in key departments (energy, treasury, etc.) even before Presidents Zedillo and, even more so, Vicente Fox worked to shake up the system of PRI-connected officials. The nature of the bureaucracy was one of the many elements of the Mexican system that Fox sought to change when he became president in 2000. He led by example, appointing people to his cabinet who were not close friends and proposing a Transparency Commission to investigate allegations of corruption involving government officials. At the beginning of Fox's term, one of his economic advisers estimated that up to 10 percent of the 2.5 million government employees received paychecks but did no work for the government.[52]

As Fox's term came to an end in 2006, many considered his efforts to deal with the bureaucracy a failure. He had said that those in the government who lacked a professional, team-oriented attitude would be fired. Instead, the bureaucracy's culture remained largely unaltered, and its slow response time and corruption continued to harm economic development. When Felipe Calderón became president, it still took nearly two months to open a new

business in Mexico, compared to less than a week in Canada and the United States.[53] Some estimates placed the total value of bribes to Mexican government officials at more than $11 billion annually, more than 10 percent of Mexico's gross domestic product.

The Military

With the possible exception of postcolonial Africa, no region of the world has been associated with military intervention in politics more than Latin America. Until recently, military rule was common in Latin America, particularly from the 1940s to 1980s. In a few of the countries—including Guatemala, Haiti, Honduras, Paraguay, Peru, and especially Argentina—the military governed more than once during this period. Mexico challenged this pattern. It did not have a military government during the middle part of the twentieth century. Mexico's revolutionary history in the nineteenth and early twentieth centuries was followed by more institutionalized politics during much of the twentieth century.

This was reflected in the role of the military in politics. In periods of revolution and social upheaval, the military was a significant political actor. With the emergence of the PRI, the military took a backseat to the dominant political party and the position of the Mexican president. This trend has continued during the ongoing transition from authoritarianism toward a consolidated democracy.

IN THEORY AND PRACTICE

New Professionalism Theory and Mexico's Drug War

Some political scientists argue that the extent to which militaries intervene in politics is inversely related to their level of professionalism. The more a military resembles a professional force concerned with defense of national security, the less likely it is to get involved in political matters. Others have countered that professional militaries may actually be more committed to issues such as economic development and the expulsion of corruption from politics than are the governments they replace. As a result, professionalized militaries may be more likely to intervene in domestic politics to address domestic governmental failures.

Writing in the 1970s, comparativist Alfred Stepan attempted to resolve this tension. His approach, which came to be known as the **new professionalism theory**, highlights the importance of the military's perception of its

---

New Professionalism Theory The theoretical perspective, advanced by comparativist Alfred Stepan, which maintains that whether a professionalized military will intervene in politics depends on whether it sees its mission as primarily defending against external or internal threats.

mission. Stepan proposed that professionalism draws militaries away from politics only when the main threat to society and the political system comes from outside the country. When the military perceives a significant internal threat (economic crisis, violent protests, etc.), professionalism leads military officers to support intervention into politics to improve government performance or restore order.[54]

The greatest challenge to Mexico's military today is its use in the country's "war" against drug cartels. According to Stepan's new professionalism theory, the increasing use of the military to address drug-related instability may have long-term negative consequences. Using the military to maintain order within Mexico means its mission has become primarily internal, rather than defense against an external threat. While not guaranteeing military intervention into Mexican politics, this shift in focus increases the risk of civilian control of the military breaking down. If this were to happen, Mexico would again stand as an exception to the pattern of civil-military relations across Latin America. This time, however, it would be as an outlier from the growing acceptance of civilian rule in other parts of Central and South America.

Brazil

The complexity and diversity of Brazilian politics are reflected in its unelected components of government. Taken as a whole, the courts have a fair amount of autonomy, and the public has gained confidence in them, but they remain heavily overworked and underfunded. Brazil has been an established democracy for longer than Mexico, but like Mexico, its bureaucracy is resistant to greater transparency and responsiveness. The penetration of the military into the Brazilian political system has been a difficult pattern to break. Even today, a quarter century since the establishment of democracy, the country strains to assert civilian oversight.

The Judiciary

The Brazilian judicial system is complex. In addition to estado and municipal courts that deal with ordinary criminal and civil matters, Brazil has a federal court system, regional courts of appeals, the Supreme Federal Court with authority to rule on the constitutionality of federal or estado laws and actions, and the separate Superior Justice Tribunal that functions as the top court of appeals for nonconstitutional issues. Parallel court systems deal with issues involving labor law and electoral law, and there is also a separate system of military courts.

Of these courts, the most powerful is the Supreme Federal Court. The court is composed of eleven justices appointed by the president and approved by the Senate. It may declare an action or a law unconstitutional and is responsible for hearing cases involving top public officials

(such as the president or members of Congress) charged with criminal acts. The Supreme Federal Court has, therefore, significant ability to check the legislature or the executive, as well as the governments of the various estados.

The Supreme Federal Court is also relatively autonomous, in part because justices have life terms until they reach the mandatory retirement age of seventy. Although a new independent tribunal was created in 2004 to monitor the behavior of all judges (who used to monitor themselves), this tribunal has yet to demonstrate real clout. That its members serve for only two years and are limited to two terms suggests that it may lack the ability and expertise to be a serious investigative tool for the other branches.

Nevertheless, the Brazilian judiciary is overworked and underpaid. Brazil has roughly one judge for every 23,000 Brazilians, in contrast to one judge for every 9,000 people in the United States and one judge for every 3,500 people in Germany.[55] Brazil also inherited a civil law system from Portugal. Higher court decisions were not binding on lower courts until 2004; even now, the court must declare a "summary judgment" to make a specific decision binding. Thus, if many people are affected by the same government action, every one of them might have to file an individual case before the Supreme Federal Court in order to get relief. Needless to say, this increases the number of cases.

Ironically, increased public confidence in the judiciary has exacerbated its heavy workload and hurt its efficiency. As confidence in the courts has grown, litigation has increased. In 1989, 6,622 lawsuits were filed in the Supreme Federal Court.[56] In 2003, the court received 109,965 cases.[57] This proliferation of cases was a central reason for the 2004 constitutional reform that enabled the court to make its decisions binding on lower courts. At the same time, the lingering problems in the judiciary have limited the extent of increased public confidence in the legal system. Surveys of Brazilian business managers conducted by organizations such as the World Bank have found that a large portion lack confidence in the court system's ability to resolve their disputes in a timely fashion.[58]

The Bureaucracy

Many of the problems facing the judiciary are replicated in the Brazilian bureaucracy, which continues to face widespread perceptions that it is too cumbersome and deeply affected by corruption. Brazil's score on the

---

"Did You Know?"

The United States is exceptional in its widespread use of juries for a broad range of civil and criminal cases. In Brazil, for example, most cases brought to court are decided by a single judge. Normally, only cases involving crimes against people are expected to go to juries.

Corruption Perception Index, which measures perceptions of public corruption around the world, is 3.5 out of 10, where 10 represents a completely "clean" government; Brazil comes in 72nd in the world (out of 180 countries) in this corruption rating.[59]

The Brazilian bureaucracy can also be very inefficient. According to one study, starting a business in Brazil is even harder than in Mexico, taking an average of more than four months.[60] Surveys over the last decade or so indicate that a higher percentage of senior business managers in Brazil believe that interpretations of regulations are inconsistent and unpredictable than in any of the other TIC cases.[61]

The Military

One of the biggest challenges for Brazil's democracy has been reining in the military and forging civilian control. The 1988 constitution enshrined privileges for the outgoing military government, guaranteeing it a continuing say in how Brazil would be run. Although the Brazilian army is under the president's authority, no civilian ministry of defense oversees military budgets and behavior. Active-duty officers serve in the cabinet. The military runs the aviation and aeronautics industries, as well as other industries critical to national defense.

In addition, the military has retained formal control over the military police, the branch of police responsible for public order. Unlike most police forces, Brazilian police are divided into the military police, who arrest people and patrol the streets, and the civil police, who investigate crimes. Both forces are officially at the disposal of governors (not mayors or municipalities), but few observers view the military police as being fully responsible to civilians.

One of the most serious human rights issues in democratic Brazil has been a very high rate of killing by police. A large number of alleged criminals, as well as bystanders, die each year in shootings that critics call irresponsible and abusive, with little effective punishment of officers involved. In three of Brazil's estados, police were responsible for over 15 percent of all homicides from 1994 to 2001.[62] Police in the densely populated estados of Rio de Janeiro and São Paulo killed nearly ten thousand people between 1999 and 2004, in situations described officially as "resistance followed by death."[63] In some locations, the rate at which police officers kill citizens has risen since the transition to democracy. At the end of the decade of the 2000s, these abuses continued to undermine both the rule of law and popular trust in the Brazilian government.

Slowly, the civilian government has assumed more oversight of the military. Military budgets have been slashed to just 2.6 percent of GDP; top military commanders have been added to the list of people who may be tried for criminal offenses by the Supreme Federal Tribunal; and military officers, including the military police, may be charged in regular criminal courts (rather than military courts) if prosecutors judge their crimes to be unrelated to their military functions. Human rights watch groups have increased pressure on politicians to reclassify some acts of killings by the police as ordinary murders, and the overall rate of killings by the police has declined modestly since the mid-1990s. Nevertheless, the military remains a powerful actor within Brazilian society, incompletely subject to civilian oversight.

Nigeria

Nigeria's unelected components of government pose a greater challenge to the development of democracy than is the case in any of the five other democratic TIC cases—the UK, Germany, India, Mexico, and Brazil. The Nigerian judiciary is still recovering from corruption and neglect under the periods of military rule. The bureaucracy is among the most corrupt in world, with prevalent favoritism along ethnic, regional, and family lines. The Nigerian military, while not in power at the moment, is never far removed from political power. Former president Olusegun Obasanjo took steps following his election to weaken the autonomy of the military, but he and his successors have discovered that, to an even greater extent than in Brazil, the long history of military rule continues to lurk in the background of everyday politics.

The Judiciary

Consistent with its federal system, Nigeria's judiciary has both federal courts and regional courts. The Supreme Court is the country's highest court, responsible for handling appeals from the Federal Court of Appeals, which itself hears appeals from lower federal courts and regional courts, including the country's various Sharia (Islamic law) courts. The Supreme Court also handles disputes between regions and between a region and the federal government.

During the long period of military rule, the court system was both controlled and neglected.[64] The military preferred its own courts to those associated with the civilian political system. The neglect, including poor pay for judges, contributed to corruption in the judicial branch. To its credit, the federal government has taken steps to address the problem, including working with international organizations such as the United Nations to study the Nigerian system and make recommendations for judicial reform. In 2001, the UN and Nigeria launched the Strengthening Judicial Integrity and Capacity project as part of the UN Office on Drugs and Crime's Global Program against Corruption (GPAC).

Another major concern is the controversy over the actions of courts in many northern Nigerian regions.

Following laws in these regions, which themselves are based on Islamic law, the courts have ordered amputations, floggings, and even death by stoning. The stoning sentences were overturned by appeals courts, largely on procedural grounds, thus avoiding an appeal to the federal level. Whether the appeals court decisions reflect a waning desire to implement Sharia in the north is unclear. Many analysts believe that a federal court, perhaps even the Supreme Court, may ultimately have to decide whether extreme Sharia-based sentences are constitutional.

The Bureaucracy

Perhaps more than any other aspect of Nigerian politics, the bureaucracy reflects the underlying problems and challenges facing Nigeria. As two Nigerian scholars contended in 2004, corruption in the Nigerian bureaucracy mirrors corruption in Nigerian society, with the result that "corruption is a permanent integral feature of bureaucracy" in the country.[65]

Favoritism in the bureaucracy tends to correspond to family ties or ethnic and regional lines. The emphasis on local and family connections poses challenges to developing a merit-based bureaucracy. Disciplining ineffective or corrupt officials becomes a challenge when an elder from the individual's home area intervenes.[66] Favoritism along ethnic lines is both a feature of corruption and part of the government's efforts to foster ethnic diversity in its ranks. Because Nigeria's north is underrepresented among those training for government jobs compared to its portion of the population, individuals from the north tend to be privileged in filling many positions. This policy does not sit well with those in the south.

The Military

Over the last several decades, the Nigeria military has had a greater presence in politics than the military of any of the other TIC cases. Of the first forty years of Nigeria's independence, only around ten years were spent under civilian rule. This changed with the election of Olusegun Obasanjo (himself a former military leader) as president in 1999. Obasanjo's consecutive terms marked the longest period of civilian rule since independence despite some rocky times: members of parliament called for him to resign or face impeachment in 2002, for example. One of Obasanjo's first policies as president was to retire dozens of top generals who played major roles in the previous military government.

Still, in a country with a deep-rooted tradition of military rule, the rule of any civilian government is tenuous. Prior to Obasanjo's return, scholars debated whether the military leadership would actually allow the country to try democracy again, while also questioning whether civilian rule could last for any sizable amount of time even if they did.[67] Military leaders feared the loss of prestige and control over military policy that would accompany democratization, as well as the potential for democracy to reopen ethnic and religious tensions in the country. The military also benefited from controlling the government purse strings.

At the same time, the Nigerian military has valued its image as an institution of reform, willing to hand over power to a democratically elected civilian government once order was restored and corruption addressed.[68] For this reason, Nigerian officers committed to a professionalized military may resist a renewal of military involvement in politics. One lesson of past periods of military rule is that the military is more likely to be infected by the epidemic of corruption than to put an end to it. Leaders in the 1980s and 1990s such as Ibrahim Babangida and Sani Abacha were among the most corrupt political leaders in the world. Abacha oversaw glaring violations of human rights and possibly pilfered as much as $5 billion from the government during his five years in power.

Russia

During the first decade or so of the post-Soviet period, most employees of the unelected components of the Russian government were Soviet-era judges, bureaucrats, and soldiers. As a result, these components of the Russian government carried with them legacies of the Soviet period. For the Russian judiciary, this meant a desperate shortage of judges and lawyers, the lack of appropriate pay for judicial officials, and an ongoing reluctance to embrace the rule of law. For the bureaucracy, it meant corruption and a focus on connections rather than competence, a situation that appeared to worsen in the decade that followed as former Soviet officials were replaced by those who owed their loyalty to Vladimir Putin and his increasingly authoritarian approach to Russian politics. The military has struggled to overcome numerous problems, including its loss of status as one of the two most powerful militaries in the world and its use within Russia's borders to twice attempt to put down a separatist uprising in Chechnya. At the same time, the post-Soviet Russian government has largely continued the tradition of civilian control of the military established during the Soviet period.

The Judiciary

A common theme in Russia's development as a fledgling democracy following the Soviet collapse was the need to establish the rule of law. This not only meant that government officials should follow the country's constitution and laws, but it also meant that the legal system needed an overhaul. Russian judges—typically holdovers from the Soviet legal system—were underpaid, not used to real autonomy, and not used to making decisions aside from political considerations. As a result, rule of law and a more professional judiciary were slower to develop than other institutional practices of democracy.

The Constitutional Court became a respected body in the years following the new Russian constitution in December 1993. Like other aspects of Russian politics, however, the court felt its autonomy increasingly threatened by the reforms of the Putin era. Although it has maintained a degree of independence, the 2007 decision of the Duma (the lower house of the Russian legislature) to move the court from Moscow to St. Petersburg, over the opposition of the Constitutional Court justices, was symbolic of increasing pressure on the court by the executive and legislative branches. Even the backers of the law to authorize the move did not argue that it would help the performance of the court. Instead, they argued that the move to St. Petersburg "will upgrade the political status of Russia's second-largest city and Putin's hometown."[69]

Other judicial components have struggled even more. The replacement of old judges and the acceptance of a culture of professionalism among those who remained have been slow processes. Judges were notoriously corrupt in the 1990s, ruling in favor of the side that paid them the most. Russia lacked a sufficient number of qualified judges, but the shortage of prosecutors and defense attorneys was even worse. Some estimates placed the number of independent lawyers in Russia as low as twenty-five thousand. Contrary to the view of U.S. law by many Americans, justice in Russia would benefit from more lawyers, not fewer.

IN THEORY AND PRACTICE

Russia and the Theory of Inverse Judicial Power

A central political science question about the judiciary is why some courts are aggressive policy makers and others defer to the executive or legislature. The **inverse judicial power theory** argues that the courts' power is inversely related to the power and unity of the other branches. Courts are more likely to be activist when the other branches are weak and lack coherence. Political scientist John Ferejohn argues that judicial activism is most likely when the "legislature is too fragmented to react,"[70] and Cornell Clayton adds that in times of legislative weakness, the power to legislate can "relocate itself to other institutions, such as the courts."[71] Clayton calls this theoretical perspective a "separation of powers" approach, because it highlights constraints on the judiciary in terms of the other branches rather than in terms of the constitutional powers of the judiciary itself.[72]

This theory can help us understand the challenges currently facing the Russian judiciary. In 2002, halfway through President Putin's first term, a report on Russia by the International Commission of Jurists stated that "One of the principal problems confronting the judiciary is the undue influence of the executive on composition of the courts."[73] With the creeping authoritarianism that occurred during Putin's two terms as president, it is hard to imagine how the judiciary could have become more autonomous. Increased threats to judicial independence emerged alongside the increasing hold of Putin's United Russia party over both the executive and legislative branches in the Russian Federation.

Think and Discuss
Which of the theories discussed in this chapter seems most convincing, and why?

The Bureaucracy
For years following the breakup of the Soviet Union, the vast majority of Russian civil servants were leftovers from the Soviet system, and Communist leaders controlled appointments to the state bureaucracy. They did this in part through the *nomenklatura* system: selecting individuals from a preexisting list of names (the nomenklatura). The official nomenklatura contained as many as 1.5 million names of such individuals (sometimes called the *nomenklaturshchiki*) at the end of the Soviet period, and around 1 million bureaucrats in the Russian government were inherited from its ranks.[74] This list represented the fusion of the merit and spoils systems. Although it was disbanded at the end of the Soviet period, its legacy remains.

The nature of the Russian bureaucracy as a holdover of Soviet nomenklaturshchiki has began to change, as many of these bureaucrats have retired. Both Boris Yeltsin and Vladimir Putin had promised to trim and improve the ranks of the bureaucracy in the early post-Soviet period. Their actions, especially Putin's, fell short of the rhetoric. The number of bureaucrats swelled rather than contracted during Putin's tenure in office, as he used positions in the bureaucracy to reward those who displayed political loyalty.

Although the 1990s saw some movement toward a more merit-based and honest bureaucracy, the move away from democracy under Vladimir Putin reopened the door to corruption and a spoils system. A 2006 World Bank report highlighted Russia as one of the few postcommunist countries in which corruption, including payments to government officials, worsened from 2002 to 2005.[75] In April 2005, Mikhail Khodorkovsky, a billionaire arrested and tried by the Russian government on charges of embezzlement and tax evasion, lashed out against what he called the

---

Inverse Judicial Power Theory A theory that explains judicial activism as a function of the relative power of the courts compared to other branches of government.

Nomenklatura System The method of controlling bureaucratic appointments during the Soviet period by selecting individuals from a preexisting list of names (the nomenklatura).

"criminal bureaucracy" in Russia.[76] Few ordinary Russians had sympathy for Khodorkovsky, although many shared his view of the bureaucracy. Khodorkovsky's case drew new international attention in 2010 when the Russian government pursued an additional set of charges against Khodorkovsky designed to keep him in prison longer. The court's ruling in December 2010, which found Khodorkovsky guilty of the new charges, was a blow to those who had held out hope that external pressure on Russia would lead to a not guilty verdict.

The Military

The Russian government inherited from its Soviet counterpart a weakened military with a long history of submitting to civilian control. Its mission was clearly externally focused. Not only had the cold war provided a strong external enemy, the United States, but Soviet ideology stressed internal harmony. The twin ideas of subordination to civilian rule and the lack of a need for the military to solve internal problems were transmitted into the culture of the military through Communist Party penetration and oversight.[77]

Late in the Soviet period, military force was used several times in attempts to solve internal problems. On April 9, 1989, troops were sent in to disperse protestors in Tbilisi, the capital of the Soviet republic of Georgia. In January 1990, Interior Ministry units, KGB (secret police) forces, and regular military troops were used in the republic of Azerbaijan. In January 1991, similar steps were taken in Lithuania—by then openly hostile to Soviet rule—leading to the deaths of seventeen individuals who defended republic government buildings. Some officers openly criticized the government's use of the regular army against Soviet citizens in such cases.

In August 1991, the military was mobilized to maintain order during the attempted coup against Soviet leader Mikhail Gorbachev. Unlike the previous events, in which the military was following the orders of civilian leaders, this time the defense minister, Marshall Dmitry Yazov, was a key participant in the planning and execution of the coup. Other military leaders opposed the coup and worked to prevent certain orders from being carried out. The division in the military was one of the central causes of the collapse of the coup and ultimately of the Soviet Union.

The central events in the intersection of military and political matters in post-Soviet Russia concerned the republic of Chechnya, a region of Russia that sought independence. The Russian military intervened twice in Chechnya, first from 1994 to 1996 and then beginning in 1999. Though the second intervention was much more successful than the first, Chechnya has remained a problem for Russia. The permanent stationing of troops during the 2000s led to a number of casualties even after the military had largely gained control of the region. Only at the end of the decade did Russia finally remove combat troops from the region, placing the issue of domestic security in the hands of Chechnya's police force under the control of the pro-Moscow regional government.

China

All three unelected components of government in China have come under pressure to reform while remaining loyal to the Chinese Communist Party (CCP). Some of the reform efforts in recent decades have targeted the judiciary and have been hampered on a number of fronts, not the least of which is the extent to which serious reform of the courts threatens the CCP's hold on political power. As a result, the judicial system remains under heavy CCP control. While the Chinese government has pursued market reforms of the economy to improve economic performance, reform of the Chinese bureaucracy, which remains large and less than efficient, is representative of the dissonance between the booming private sector and still-potent public sector in China. Following the death of Mao Zedong, the military became increasingly independent from the government. This seems less true in recent years, as a greater emphasis on developing the military into a more professionalized fighting force has opened the door to greater civilian control.

The Judiciary

In some ways, the Chinese judiciary functions like those of other authoritarian countries, trying individuals accused of crimes but saying little about laws passed by the government. Following Mao's death, the excesses of the Great Proletarian Cultural Revolution (Mao's final effort at dramatic reform from 1966 to 1976 in which tens of thousands were executed) led some to reconsider China's legal system. Change was slow, but the 1999 Chinese Supreme Court announcement of a five-year plan to reform the judicial system seemed to point to an acceptance of the need for significant change. Some in the government understand the importance of a properly functioning legal system for economic performance and efforts to deal with increasing social tensions, while others are concerned about the political consequences of weakening the CCP's control of the judiciary.[78] At the end of the five-year reform plan, the Supreme Court claimed that most of its components had been adopted, but most analysts believe that China is a long way from the "fair, open, highly effective, honest, and well-functioning" judicial system the court had promised.[79] For the government, the dangers of taking the concept of rule of law seriously outweigh the benefits.

Thus, a central question remains: the extent to which the Chinese judiciary will be allowed to function relatively independently from the CCP and state leadership. The National People's Congress can remove Supreme Court officials, and local people's congresses can remove local judges. In addition, as in Russia, judges are few in number, poorly paid, and often corrupt. The court system is overwhelmed by an explosion in civil cases. Millions of civil cases are filed annually, and in 2009 alone, the national court system saw more than thirty thousand cases filed regarding copyrights, trademarks, patents, and other intellectual property disputes.[80]

The Bureaucracy

Both because China's legislative branch has little real power and because the Chinese system has required such a large bureaucracy, bureaucrats in China have more day-to-day power than do their counterparts in many other countries. At the same time, they have been at the mercy of Communist leadership decisions about major reforms. From Mao Zedong's Great Leap Forward to Deng Xiaoping's overhaul of the economic system, Chinese officials have not always been able to count on the stability that most bureaucrats prefer.

Deng's successors, Jiang Zemin and Hu Jintao, have emphasized stability and technical expertise to an even greater extent than Deng had. Unlike Mao and Deng, both Jiang and Hu were **technocrats**, government officials who rose through the ranks of the bureaucracy as experts in their field rather than because of their ideological fervor. During the middle decades of the Communist period, technocrats were in conflict with **reds**, those known for their fervent commitment to Communist ideology, about the proper path of Chinese economic development. As China's economic reforms continued, the technocrats largely won out over the reds. Even with its significant economic reforms, China has maintained one feature borrowed from Soviet Communism: the nomenklatura system. Some estimates put the number of names on the Chinese government nomenklatura list as high as 10 million. This is many more than in the USSR at the time of its collapse, though similar in terms of percentage of the population.

The Military

Partly because the Communists came to power after a lengthy civil war, the People's Liberation Army (PLA) has played a central role in Chinese politics since 1949. CCP leaders such as Mao Zedong and Deng Xiaoping believed that the military should be under CCP control, but the party and the military were highly intertwined. Top CCP officials also held top positions in the Party Central Military Commission and its counterpart commission in the state. Some consider this part of a successful effort by the CCP to co-opt and subordinate the military, but the record on civilian control of the military has been mixed at best. Prior to the end of the 1980s, the Chinese military gained

Technocrats Bureaucrats who emphasize technical expertise and often have significant scientific knowledge.

Reds Bureaucrats in Communist countries who are more committed to Communist ideology than to technical expertise.

China's Peoples' Liberation Army (PLA) soldiers parade outside a military barracks in Hong Kong to celebrate the anniversary of the establishment of the PLA.
© Mike Clarke/AFP/Getty Images

greater autonomy, in terms of controlling both military policy and its own finances, than its Soviet counterpart.

The crackdown against protestors in Tiananmen Square in 1989 also had a great effect on the military and its relationship with the government. Some in the government questioned the military's loyalty in the aftermath of Tiananmen Square, and surveillance of the army by the Communist leadership increased after 1989. Among the reforms that the government pressed the military to accept was to reduce its commercial holdings. Historically, the Chinese military had maintained a number of economic enterprises, designed in part to help fund military spending. In addition to concerns that such holdings in the increasingly capitalist Chinese economy would breed corruption in the military, allowing the military too much financial independence was viewed as a threat to CCP control of the PLA. The efforts to limit the military's commercial holdings were largely completed by the start of the 2000s.

In other ways, the government appeared to become more dependent on the military and less able to control it following Tiananmen Square.[81] In 1990, the military budget was increased by more than 15 percent, and by the start of the following decade, the Chinese government began to make clear its commitment to a professionalized military capable of protecting China's interests at home and, if necessary, helping pursue those interests abroad. This commitment has included, in the words of U.S. Admiral Robert Willard in early 2010, an "aggressive program of modernization . . . supported by a military budget that has grown annually by double digits over the last decade."[82] It remains to be seen whether this effort at professionalization through modernization opens the door to greater civilian control of the 3-million-strong PLA, or whether it represents a government desperate to keep the military happy.

Iran

The extent to which Iran's unelected components of government function autonomously and professionally is constrained by the country's theocratic system and its prevalent corruption. Iran's judiciary plays a key role in enforcing the system's Islamic law–based ideology. Blurring the lines between the public and private sector, various organizations work closely with the Iranian bureaucracy in particular economic endeavors. This leads to personal gain for the business class, the bureaucrats, and many of Iran's top religious officials. Iran's military has been more of a puzzle. At times it is weak and divided, and at other times, it is difficult to control and potentially politically threatening to the civilian religious leadership, particularly the component of the military known as the Revolutionary Guards.

The Judiciary

The Iranian judiciary is an important part of the theocratic regime. It provides the government with some legitimacy, yet its rulings tend to support the government's more conservative elements. The courts have been used to ban moderate publications and arrest those who publish pro reform messages on Iranian Web sites. The courts do not have judicial review authority; that power is reserved for the Guardian Council and, to an extent, the Expediency Council and Supreme Leader. The judiciary is not independent from the Supreme Leader, who has constitutional authority (Article 57) to oversee the judicial branch. The Supreme Leader makes his views on many issues well known, sometimes via "briefings" to members of the judiciary, and the selection of judges for top judicial positions is tightly controlled.[83] Thus, while the Iranian constitution talks about judicial independence, its preamble also states clearly that the judiciary is to enforce "ideological conformity" and prevent "deviations within the Islamic nation."

Prevention of deviation can take extreme forms. Iran has one of the highest execution rates in the world, and it has been known to execute minors.[84] Judicial decisions have been particularly harsh against women. In one well-documented case, Atefeh Sahaleh Rajabi, a sixteen-year-old from the city of Neka, was hanged in public in August 2004. She was denied access to a lawyer during her trial and was reported to be suffering from mental illness. The judge, Hadji Rezai, used apparently forged documents to claim that she was twenty-two. The judge actually put the noose around the girl's neck, saying he sentenced her to death in part for her "sharp tongue" in court. Unlike many of the Sharia-based death sentences in Nigeria that have been overturned by religious courts, the Iranian Supreme Court upheld the sentence. The young man accused of having sex with her received one hundred lashes and was set free.[85]

The Bureaucracy

Iran's history of a large and important bureaucracy dates back centuries. The current Iranian government strives to control the bureaucracy and use it for political purposes. Just as with the judiciary, part of the way that top government officials in Iran control the bureaucracy is through the selection of individuals committed to the ideology of the rulers. Emphasizing ideological loyalty, however, can have its costs. Bureaucrats are also expected to be experts in their fields, and finding a combination of ideological commitment and expertise can be difficult. Similar to the "red versus technocrat" debate in China, the Iranian bureaucracy has the potential for a "mullah versus technocrat" debate, particularly at the middle and lower levels. (A mullah is an Islamic religious teacher, but the word is also used for the more conservative Muslim clerics who hold important positions in the government.)

For now, two things appear to be keeping the Iranian bureaucracy from fracturing into such a conflict. First, an interesting alliance has developed between the business class in Iran—known as the *bazaari* class—and the religious establishment. The nexus for this relationship are the *bonyads*, which are, officially, charitable organizations. These groups blur the line between state and society, as they are technically autonomous but work closely with the bureaucracy and other government officials and control huge portions of the economy. Some estimates suggest the bonyads control up to 40 percent of the country's economy. In the middle 2000s, the worth of one bonyad alone, the Mostazafan va Janbazan foundation, was calculated to be upwards of $12 billion.[86] The bonyads bring together wealthy businessmen, who see the value in working with the mullahs, and religious officials, who benefit from the wealth of bonyads. Second, both the mullahs and technocrats benefit from bureaucratic corruption. The corruption involving the bazaari class and the religious establishment in economic and social matters provides the potential for bureaucratic positions to generate significant personal gain.

The Military

Since the Islamic Revolution in 1979, the Iranian government has worked hard to maintain control of the military. Many officers who had been loyal to the shah were executed, other purges took place during the 1980s, and the war with Iraq helped to weaken and demoralize the military further.[87] In short, Iran was experiencing the opposite of the situation that Samuel Huntington described as leading to praetorianism. Rather than a strong military and a weak civilian government, Iran had a weak and fractured military alongside strong civilian political institutions. This pattern has become even more pronounced after the solidification of conservative control over the elected positions of the national legislature and the presidency in 2004 and 2005.

While it has taken advantage of the internal divisions within the Iranian military, the theocratic government of Iran has also worked to indoctrinate the military. Part of this effort has involved establishing and increasing the importance of the **Islamic Revolution Guard Corps** (IRGC, or "Revolutionary Guards"). The IRGC began as an informal militia recruited from groups who were among the strongest supporters of the 1979 revolution. Its numbers swelled in the decades following the revolution, and it eventually became treated as a regular professional military. The government established a separate IRGC academy, gave the IRGC tasks commonly reserved for regular forces such as border patrol, and allowed it to enforce dress codes and other practices related to Sharia.[88] Some worry that the IRGC has become too powerful, making it increasingly difficult for the government to control its ranks.

Despite efforts at socialization within the military, the officers and ordinary soldiers have not always supported the Iranian regime. Though no military coup has taken place since the Islamic Revolution, statements by retired military officers in support of free and fair elections and executions of members of the Revolutionary Guards following charges of espionage led some scholars to weigh the possibility of the military's more direct involvement in Iranian politics.[89] Even without a coup, military dissatisfaction could fuel mass uprisings. If a future "Green Revolution" event materializes and orders are given for police or Revolutionary Guard units to disperse protesters through violent means, one might imagine elements of the military turning against other units of force to defend the protesting masses. While an intriguing possibility, the successful use of force in early 2011 against antigovernment protesters signaled that such an event remains unlikely in the near term.

TIC Wrap-Up

An examination of the political impact of the unelected components of government points to similarities and differences across the nine Topic in Countries cases. Historically, the British judiciary has been fused to the legislative branch, although potentially important changes have begun to be implemented. In Germany,

Islamic Revolution Guard Corps Military units in Iran that were originally formed as an informal militia but became increasingly important in the maintenance of internal order in the country; known by the acronym IRGC or as the "Revolutionary Guards."

on the other hand, the country's courts, including the Federal Constitutional Court, are separated from the legislative and executive branches and have considerable power. The bureaucracies in the UK and Germany have been both large and powerful. Despite forces supporting a reduction of their political clout, particularly in the UK, they remain important to political outcomes in both countries. The histories of the British and German militaries provide quite different examples of the military's role in politics. The UK remains an archetype of civilian control of the military, developing a professional military force in large part because of its large overseas empire until a half-century ago. Germany's military is subservient to its civilian leaders today, but a tradition of militarism, from the Prussians through the Nazis, required an aggressive effort at civilian control that significantly limited Germany's military activities until relatively recently.

The judiciaries of Mexico, Brazil, Nigeria, and India have many differences but share in struggling to be autonomous, appropriately staffed and funded, and free from corruption. The bureaucracies of these four countries exhibit a certain level of competence and professionalism but fall short of the level citizens would prefer. Like the judiciaries, corruption and inefficiency remain a problem in all four countries' bureaucracies. The experience with the militaries of these four countries has greater variation. Both Mexico and India have seen minimal military involvement in politics. Until relatively recently, the military has been a visible feature of politics in Brazil and, especially, Nigeria.

In Russia, China, and Iran, the judicial branch has little autonomy from the legislative branch and even less from the executive branch. The three countries' bureaucracies reflect past political practices and contemporary political dictates. In all three, the upper levels of government keep close watch over the bureaucracy. Unlike oversight in democratic countries like the UK and Germany, efforts to craft an efficient and impartial bureaucracy in semiauthoritarian and authoritarian countries like Russia, China, and Iran take a back seat to political connections and demonstrations of loyalty to the political leaders. The militaries of Russia, China, and Iran have all been used by their governments to help maintain control of their countries, yet the extent to which the governments fully control their militaries differ. Russia has used its military to put down the uprising in Chechnya, while maintaining civilian control. In China, the tradition of fusing the top leadership of the military and the Communist Party has been maintained, but the military seems to be moving in the direction of greater professionalism. The leaders of Iran's theocratic system have tried to contain the military and use it to serve their purposes. They have been only partially successful.

COUNTRY SUMMARY

TIC Country	Judiciary	Bureaucracy	Military
United Kingdom	Common law approach; parliamentary supremacy concept limits judicial power; new UK Supreme Court in place since 2009	Decrease in size but increase in autonomy under Thatcher; importance of permanent secretary position; ITAP feature on bureaucratic autonomy theory	One of the world's most powerful militaries; strong civilian control; military is professionalized and has an external focus, except for its use in Northern Ireland
Germany	Federal Constitutional Court with judicial review authority; organized according to German brand of federalism	More decentralized today than in past; comparatively small in size at the federal level	Dominant role historically; much smaller role since World War II; compulsory military service ended in 2011
India	Historically served as a check on legislators; tensions between the Supreme Court and legislative branch over the power to amend the constitution	Indian Administrative Service (IAS) serves as the select group at the top of a huge public sector; growing problem of brain drain to private sector	Second largest military in the world (after China); possesses nuclear weapons; typically follows political leaders rather than intervening in politics
Mexico	Civil law tradition; subservience to other branches of government; more independent since 1990s, but not fully independent	Developed more as a political machine than a merit-based civil service; largely unsuccessful at professionalizing the bureaucracy; corruption remains a problem	Significant in revolutionary periods; civilian control during PRI period; ITAP feature on new professionalism theory and use of military to fight growing drug-related violence
Brazil	Civil law system; Federal Supreme Court on top of federal court system; estado and municipal courts; judges overworked and underpaid	Perceived as corrupt, inefficient, and cumbersome; bureaucratic hurdles get in the way of business development	Remains a powerful actor; moves toward civilian rule, but military remains incompletely subject to government oversight
Nigeria	Supreme Court on top of a federal and regional court system; significant corruption is a legacy of periods of military rule	Largely corrupt; favoritism related to family, ethnic, and regional lines; spoils system more than merit-based bureaucracy	History of a strong presence in politics; civilian control tenuous, but some officers see military rule period as corrupting the military
Russia	Under pressure from executive and legislative branches; culture of corruption and unprofessional practices; ITAP feature on inverse judicial power theory	Nomenklatura legacies; corruption and spoils system under Putin's leadership	History of civilian control over military; military active in resolving internal problems, including Chechen conflict
China	Rule of law remains weak; dependent on the CCP and the state; large numbers of civil cases	Remains controlled by the CCP; nomenklatura system; "red versus technocrat" debate	Since 1949, CCP and military intertwined; makes civilian control over military challenging

TIC Country	Judiciary	Bureaucracy	Military
Iran	Supports the theocratic regime; judicial review authority resides in Guardian Council; little to no judicial independence	"Mullah versus technocrat" debate; alliance between business class and religious establishment	Fractured military; use of military as a socializing institution; growing importance and autonomy of the Revolutionary Guards
Spotlight on . . . Country			
France	Heavy reliance on civil law; limited nature of judicial power	Expanded over time; officially merit-based yet highly elitist in the past; slightly less elitist today	Relationship with government historically complex; political involvement sporadic, but hints of lingering militarism
Iraq	No clear legal tradition or precedents; lacked independence under Saddam; falls short of international standards for rule of law, fairness, and due process; lack of public confidence	Some turnover in membership but still largely made up of veteran technocrats; bureaucracy seen as corrupt, opaque, and fragile	Collapse of the military after 2003 invasion; need to establish professional and depoliticized military
South Africa	Combination of customary and common law; rule of law suffered during apartheid; level of judicial independence questionable	Inexperienced; poor efficiency and competence in meeting government goals; legacy of corruption, particularly among regional bureaucratic officials	Instrumental in sustaining the apartheid system; was the most advanced and professional military in Africa at the end of the apartheid period; potential to challenge political authority but reluctant to date

Research in Context

Previous chapters, as well as this chapter, have highlighted the concept of rule of law. In addition to its general importance for understanding American-style democracy, it has been at the center of a large body of research on the democratization efforts of postcommunist states. Across Eastern Europe and the former Soviet Union, countries inherited judiciaries that had little experience with autonomy from the executive branch and even less with government officials who accepted that the laws of the land applied to political leaders as well as the general public. In this context, scholars have emphasized the importance of rule of law and theorized about the best way to achieve it.

Like many works in political science, much of this research has emphasized the importance of formal institutional arrangements, such as the creation of new bodies designed to protect judges from pressure—what some have called "political interference"[90]—from other branches of government. These formal institutions, the argument goes, help deepen a judicial culture consistent with the rule of law. In addition to research works from scholars, organizations ranging from the European Union to Freedom House to the American Bar Association's Central European and Eurasian Law Institute have emphasized the importance of formal institutional arrangements designed to cultivate the rule of law.[91]

The Origins of Postcommunist Judicial Culture

Can new formal institutions reshape the culture of the judiciary in postcommunist states? Some scholars, including Daniel J. Beers, were skeptical. In his winter 2010 article "A Tale of Two Transitions" in the journal *Demokratizatsiya*, Beers questions whether formal institutional arrangements are the main story behind the development of a rule of law–conducive judicial culture.[92] In this article, Beers examines survey and interview responses from four hundred judges in Romania and the Czech Republic. He chose these two countries for his research because they took very different paths. Romania engaged in a major overhaul of its judicial system, focusing on new formal institutions based on the advice of outside observers. The Czech Republic engaged in more modest reforms, which Beers labels as "far less sophisticated" than Romania,[93] directed by domestic officials with significant input from members of the judiciary.

Despite the external advice to and greater effort at reform in Romania, Beers found that the Czech judges had attitudes and underlying values more in line with the rule of law. He linked these differences to disparities between the levels of trust in the institutions designed to protect the interests of the judges of the two countries. Despite a grander approach to developing such institutions in Romania, judges in Romania felt less sure about the effectiveness of the formal institutional changes than did their counterparts in the Czech Republic. As Beers puts it, "formal rules and guarantees of independence are only effective when judges believe in the credibility of such rules."[94]

So What?

Why should American policy makers—or ordinary citizens—care about Beers's research on judges in two Eastern European countries? As mentioned in the introduction to this section, scholars, nongovernmental organizations, and international governmental organizations had been pushing formal institutional design as a key to getting the rule of law to take hold in the postcommunist region. They made specific proposals for complex institutional arrangements, and they spent money to help other countries implement the proposed changes.

The results of Beers's self-described "theory-building inquiry" provide guidance to those who advise governments of new democracies about the proper form of their institutional arrangements. His research points out the importance of allowing domestic government officials to play a central role in the reform of their systems. Trusting in the formal rules is important for efficient and effective outcomes from any political institution, and Beers's research highlights the link between keeping institutional reforms home-grown and simple and developing trust in the new institutions by the officials who have to work within them. Political practitioners interested in fostering democracy abroad and students of comparative politics should pay careful attention to this lesson.

CONCLUSION

This chapter provided an overview of the three main types of unelected government institutions. All three have the potential to play important roles in policy creation: judges "legislate from the bench," bureaucrats frame agendas in their policy areas or craft specific policy provisions, and the military pressures government officials or even forces them from power. The involvement in politics of all three also has advantages and disadvantages. Unelected officials can make tough decisions, protect minority interests, and utilize their expertise, but they can also impose their personal views and resist efforts to limit their influence.

Think and Discuss

Do the advantages of powerful unelected officials outweigh the disadvantages?

The discussion of these unelected components in the TIC cases makes clear that different countries can have very different experiences with unelected governmental institutions. The TIC cases also highlight the relationships between these institutions and the legislature and chief executive and how these relationships change over time. In Germany today, for example, the power, autonomy, and accountability of Germany's unelected branches are firmly embedded in its wider democratic institutions. Its independent and powerful judiciary, less centralized bureaucracy, and civilian-controlled military represent a substantial change in the nature of these institutions compared with the imperial and Nazi dictatorships.

Finally, the cases show how the judiciary, bureaucracy, and military play important roles in democratic rule but also pose challenges to it. Because voters cannot hold unelected officials accountable for their actions, such officials are even more vulnerable to the temptations of corruption than elected officials, though temptations can be limited through efforts such as increasing the number of judges and paying them reasonable salaries. Other changes are broader and even more difficult to bring about, such as fostering a strong attachment to the principle of rule of law. Interestingly, the question of independence versus control differs across the three types of institutions. Corruption appears less likely for a judiciary when it is independent from executive branch control. In the case of the bureaucracy and the military, on the other hand, greater executive and legislative oversight appears to be an important part of the solution. Thus, in a country such as Brazil where all three unelected components of the state enjoy significant formal powers and autonomy from the elected branches, these powers are not always exercised efficiently or appropriately, resulting in problems for the consolidation of democracy.

KEY TERMS

Bureaucracy, p. 200
Bureaucratic autonomy theory, p. 210
Cabinet department, p. 202
Case law, p. 197
Civilian control of the military, p. 205
Civil law, p. 197
Civil servant, p. 202
Civil service, p. 202
Common law, p. 197
Constitutional judicial review, p. 198

Coup d'état, p. 206
Generalist approach, p. 203
Inverse judicial power theory, p. 218
Islamic Revolution Guard Corps, p. 222
Judicial activism, p. 198
Judicial independence, p. 197
Judicial review, p. 198
Junta, p. 206
Merit system, p. 202
Militarism, p. 205
Minister, p. 202

Ministry, p. 202
New professionalism theory, p. 214
Nomenklatura system, p. 218
Permanent secretary, p. 210
Praetorianism, p. 206
Reds, p. 220
Secretary, p. 202
Specialist approach, p. 203
Spoils system, p. 202
Stare decisis, p. 197
Statutory judicial review, p. 198
Technocrats, p. 220
Tort law, p. 199

CHAPTER

8

Political Participation and Approaches to Linking Elites and Masses

CHAPTER OUTLINE

The Elites and the Masses
Connecting Elites to Masses
Social Movements, Interest Groups, and Civil Society

TOPIC IN COUNTRIES

Features in this chapter:

Spotlight on . . . South Africa: Civil Society before and after Apartheid

In Theory and Practice: Disturbance Theory and Mexico

In Theory and Practice: The Military-Industrial Complex in China

In Theory and Practice: The Collective Action Problem and Iran

Research in Context: Measuring Interest Group Participation in European Union Politics

Protesters opposed to the government of Muammar Qaddafi chant slogans during a protest in Benghazi, Libya, February 25, 2011. © REUTERS/Suhaib Sale

LEARNING OBJECTIVES

After reading this chapter, you should be able to

- Discuss the difference between elites and masses and describe different ways that the idea of an elite is conceptualized in comparative politics.
- Describe different forms of political participation and give examples from the TIC cases.
- Discuss the differences between programmatic and clientelist linkage and between an interest group and a social movement.
- Characterize alternative arrangements for incorporating interest groups into the policy-making process.
- Analyze various approaches to linking elites and masses in the TIC cases.

In March 2011, the mass protests against authoritarian governments that developed across the Middle East and North Africa reached Libya. People took to the streets in protest against Libyan leader Muammar Qaddafi, who had led the country for more than four decades. The opposition to Qaddafi was strongest in the northeast of the country, particularly in and around the port city of Benghazi. In early March, in the city of Ras Lanuf west of Benghazi, volunteer fighters tried to stall the advance of pro-Qaddafi elements of the Libyan military. Brandishing guns they had looted from a military base, the volunteers, mostly young men, took part in the most extreme form of unconventional political participation: taking up arms against the sitting government.

As opposition to Qaddafi became a leading news story, and as Qaddafi's supporters took violent actions against the antigovernment rebels, the United Nations voted to impose a no-fly zone. Military action to enforce the no-fly zone, taken by mostly Western government military forces and led by NATO, slowed down Qaddafi's advances and gave the rebels hope. Because NATO countries opposed placing their own troops on the ground in Libya, however, the success of the anti-Qaddafi uprising ultimately came down to the efforts of the Libyans who opposed Qaddafi's rule. In mid August, anti-Qaddafi forces attacked the capital and drove Qaddafi into hiding. Their successful attack took so long to happen because the rebels were initially not as well armed or organized as Qaddafi's supporters. As former Libyan soldier who was training the volunteers fighting in Ras Lanuf had explained five months earlier, "They need a leader. We don't have enough leaders."[1]

A basic attribute of government is that a relatively small number of individuals are selected—or select themselves—to make policy decisions for the rest of the population. In most countries, political structures link this small group of leaders to members of the general public. The extent to which the populace takes advantage of these structures, or challenges the existing structures by creating new channels of participation, varies from country to country and among individuals within the same country. Seeking to understand these patterns is a core undertaking of comparative politics. The fourth section of the book, which starts with this chapter, shifts the focus to individuals and their role in the political process. It considers the differences between political elites and masses, various ways in which the general public can participate in politics, and institutional approaches such as interest groups that link elites and masses.

Comparative politics often focuses on elections and political parties as the hallmarks of democratic mass participation and elite-mass linkage. Elections and parties are important, and the next chapter examines them in detail. But between the frenzied episodes of democratic electoral politics are long periods of everyday politics worthy of study. Elites and masses are also linked in many ways in nondemocratic systems. In such systems, mass participation is typically limited. As events in countries like Libya demonstrate, however, unconventional forms of mass participation can emerge quickly, sometimes around an opposition leader and at other times without much leadership at all.

The Elites and the Masses

Much of the study of politics involves examining the relationships between political, economic, and social leaders—elites—and members of the general public—the masses. The way people with the most political power rule over, are linked to, or are constrained by ordinary citizens in a particular country plays a crucial role in shaping that country's major political outcomes. Thus, whether we define politics as "the set of activities that organizes individuals, systematically resolves disputes, and maintains order in society" or as the process of determining "who gets what," politics is about elites and masses.

The Political Elite

A **political elite** is a group of individuals who are far more involved in day-to-day political decisions than is the rest of the population. Those who hold official government positions, those who can influence such leaders because of their social or financial standing, and those who can shape public opinion related to government policy are all part of the political elite. Not everyone in this group is equally powerful, but all can affect political outcomes far more than ordinary citizens. The percentage of the population that falls into the political elite varies from country to country. In many countries, including the United States, it is far less than 1 percent.

Political Elite Individuals who are far more involved in, and have a far greater impact on, daily politics than the rest of the population.

As with many political science concepts, defining the term *political elite* is easier than identifying the people who fall into it in practice, especially in cases of individuals who do not hold official governmental positions. How might one determine whether people without official positions are part of the political elite? One possibility is to look at decision-making processes and see which people appear to be wielding influence. This is what Robert Dahl did in *Who Governs?*, his landmark study of local decision making in New Haven, Connecticut.[2]

Debate over whether there is a single elite or several competing elites further complicates the issue. Sociologist C. Wright Mills, influenced greatly by Max Weber, argued that the elite is relatively unified. Mills stressed the idea of a **power elite**: a single elite made up of political, economic, and military leaders. He contended these three groups act in unison to rule the political system.[3] Mills did not argue that the members of this elite participate in a great conspiracy, but rather their similar social backgrounds give them similar goals and values. On the other hand, in *Who Governs?* Dahl argued that groups of elites compete against each other for policy victories, and no single group always benefits from governmental decisions.

Power Elite An elite made up of political, military, and economic leaders working in unison to control the government and produce policies that serve its interests.

Another question to consider is how similar the elite is to the masses in terms of socioeconomic status and political orientation. If the members of the elite differ greatly from the masses socially, some observers worry the elite cannot adequately represent the masses. It is hard to represent people to whom one cannot relate. Others feel that this is not an issue if elites have incentives, such as reelection, to diligently represent the mass public.

A third question concerns whether membership in the elite is open or closed. If it is open, new people have access to mechanisms to help them work their way into the elite on their own. The previous chapter, for example, discussed the use of merit systems in selecting bureaucratic officials. These systems allow people without family connections

© Harley Schwadron

Nepotism Favoring relatives in granting positions or distributing resources.

Masses Members of the population who are not involved in day-to-day governing.

Political Participation The process of engaging in activities that are intended to influence the selection of officials and the policies that they create.

Conventional Participation Political participation that does not advocate or promote political or social instability, that existing political institutions can effectively channel, and of which the political elite approves.

Unconventional Participation The set of political activities not approved by the political elite, including strikes, boycotts, and terrorism.

or other personal advantages to earn their way into government positions. If the elite is closed, the elite itself chooses its new members, opting for those who fit with its values and goals. In this case, family members of the current elite often become the elite of the future. Such favoritism shown to relatives in the granting of official positions is known as **nepotism**. Nepotism is common in developing countries, particularly those in which clan or tribal identity is politically salient.

Think and Discuss

Is it good or bad for a democratic political system to have a strong political elite?

The Masses and Their Political Participation

In contrast to the political elite, the **masses** are not involved in day-to-day governing. They do not hold official positions, and they generally know less about and have less interest in politics than the elite. Unless large numbers of them act together, such as by voting or participating in a social movement, they also lack social, economic, or political resources to play a major role in policy making. Members of the masses are political participants. **Political participation** refers to the set of activities intended to influence the selection of officials and their policies. If politics is about who gets what, individuals participate in politics in the hope of getting what they want.

Mass political participation is found in all variants of democracy, where, at a minimum, the general population takes part in selecting key government officials. Totalitarian systems also emphasize mass political mobilization, but in a much more controlled manner. Only ideal type authoritarian systems do not feature mass involvement as a cornerstone of politics. In practice, however, even authoritarian leaders seek to make the public feel as though it is participating in the selection of officials and playing a role in the creation of government policy. In short, all systems either want masses to participate or want them to think they can participate.

Conventional versus Unconventional Participation

Political participation can be conventional or unconventional. **Conventional participation** is the set of activities that political elites accept and that existing political institutions are able to channel effectively. Because it involves working with existing mechanisms for linking the general public to the political system, conventional participation does not advocate or promote social instability. The activities that a government leader of one political system would consider conventional participation might not be the same activities that a leader of another system would deem conventional. Leaders of nondemocratic political systems, for example, are likely to be suspicious of any kind of political participation other than the activities the state has created and tightly controls. Within democracies, most political scientists agree on the kinds of activities that they consider conventional participation. Such activities include voting and belonging to political parties or other social groups.

Unconventional participation is participation in activities of which political elites do not approve, often because such participation is politically destabilizing. Such behavior includes strikes, boycotts, violence, and terrorism. Categorizing less extreme forms of protest, such as signing petitions, as unconventional can be difficult. Some scholars include such less extreme forms in their list of unconventional participatory activities,[4] while others do not. It can, therefore, help to think of unconventional and conventional participation as end points of a range of political activities (see Figure 8.1). France provides an example of how unconventional participation need not undermine the political system. On multiple occasions in recent years, French

| FIGURE 8.1 | Examples of Unconventional and Conventional Political Participation |

Terrorism	Engaging in violent protests	Participating in a strike	Signing petitions	Writing a letter or editorial	Contributing money to a candidate	Joining a political party	Voting

Unconventional   Conventional

farmers have used tractors and other farm equipment to block the streets of Paris and have dumped milk rather than bring it to market. They took these actions to protest proposed reductions in government farm subsidies and low European milk prices.

People who engage in unconventional activities often feel alienated by the political system and believe that political participation through normal channels is pointless. Protest allows them to bypass these channels, providing what political scientist Russell Dalton calls a "direct-action technique of confronting political elites, instead of participating within a framework defined by elites."[5] Alienation does not justify the most extreme types of unconventional participation, but it is important to understand how alienation and a lack of legitimacy lead some to see unconventional participation as a reasonable response to their social and political situation.

Nonparticipation

A number of individuals choose not to participate in the political system at all. Even in democracies, a portion of the population does not participate on a regular basis. These individuals often feel alienated from politics, have little understanding of political events, and have no interest in trying to understand them better. Gabriel Almond and Sidney Verba labeled these people "parochials" in their book *The Civic Culture* (discussed in Chapter 3). In many countries, nonparticipants are overwhelmingly young, poor, less educated, and members of ethnic minorities.

People who do not participate share a sense of frustration with people who turn to unconventional participation, but key differences exist between the two groups. Those who engage in unconventional participation have more knowledge of and interest in politics, and they often find themselves mobilized by leaders of a particular political movement. This chapter's "In Theory and Practice" boxes discuss other notions about people's political participation.

Comparing Mass Participation in Different Countries

The portion of people who participate more than others and people's overall participation levels (e.g., turnout rates in elections) vary from state to state. States can also differ in how effectively they channel mass participation in ways that do not threaten political stability. In states with strong and effective political institutions, increases in mass participation help the system by providing information about the general population's desires. Such participation improves the political system's legitimacy.

On the other hand, undisciplined mass participation can be destabilizing. In the late 1960s, Samuel Huntington published an important work on economic development and its political effects, *Political Order in Changing Societies*, which framed political stability as a function of the political system's ability to channel mass participation.[6] Huntington stressed the way that economic and social development can lead the general population to demand a greater say in their government. He argued that the inability to adequately address demands for increasing participation is destabilizing and can cause the political system to collapse.

Connecting Elites to Masses

Masses are tied more closely to elites in democracies than in authoritarian and totalitarian systems. Yet, elites and masses in all systems are somewhat interdependent. The masses depend on the elite to govern and to distribute resources. In a democracy, the population must consent in order for members of the elite with official positions to maintain political power.

Programmatic or Clientelist Linkage?

Broadly speaking, the two main approaches to linking elites and masses are programmatic and clientelist.[7] Programmatic linkage is often associated with political parties and elections, while clientelism is generally seen as unrelated to political groupings such as parties. In fact, both forms of elite-mass linkage sometimes involve parties and sometimes do not. The key difference is whether elites are linked to masses through stated policy positions or through personal connections.

Programmatic Representation

Programmatic Representation Linking the general population to the political elite through institutions such as political parties that stress particular political programs.

One approach to linking elites and masses common in democracies involves politicians representing a large portion of the population through the stands they take on government policies. This method of elite-mass linkage is often referred to as **programmatic representation**. To decide who they want to represent them, the people assess the programs spelled out in political party platforms and the performance of individual political leaders. In other words, individuals seeking public office represent segments of the general population through "programmatic appeals and policy achievements."[8] In such systems, numerous people represent individual members of the general public and/or serve as an outlet for their frustrations with the political system. Americans, for example, can express opinions to and seek help from the president, members of Congress, state legislators, local government leaders, and bureaucrats at the various levels of government.

Clientelism

Clientelism Linking elites and masses through patron-client relationships.

Masses are not always linked to elites as part of a large group. They can also be connected as individuals in a one-on-one, patron-client relationship. In systems based on patron-client relationships, known as **clientelism**, patrons look out for the clients' interests. The client receives certain benefits, which are either material goods held privately by the patron or public goods (government money) under the control of the patron in his or her capacity as a governmental official.[9] In exchange, the client owes the patron support at election time or in other ways.

In clientelism, everyone except those at the very top of the elite has a patron. In other words, there are patron-client relationships between members of the elite. In the context of elite-mass linkage, however, it is appropriate to think of the client as an ordinary citizen and the patron as a member of the political elite.

Clientelism is most pervasive when an individual is unable to receive the services a patron provides from a different political official or from a broader governmental or social institution. Consequently, the extent to which a political system operates through clientelist arrangements depends on the structure of the political system, on social relations more broadly, and on features of the country's population. Those in rural areas or with little education, for example, are more likely to become clients than educated city dwellers. As comparativist Herbert Kitschelt puts it, "Vote-rich but resource-poor constituencies receive selective material incentives before and after elections in exchange for surrendering their vote."[10] They lack the skills or opportunities to receive benefits outside the clientelist framework. But, as Kitschelt points out, there can also be wealthy clients. In such cases, "resource-rich but vote-poor constituencies provide politicians with money in exchange for material favors."[11]

The previous chapter discussed the extent to which corruption among unelected officials is a problem in a variety of countries. Clientelism can foster such corruption, which is one of the reasons political scientists tend to view clientelism as something that contaminates political life.[12] Although political officials are not alone in being able to provide things people want, their public position gives them significant advantages in this regard.

Clientelist systems need not, by definition, involve high levels of corruption. Patrons with a commitment to public service may use their positions for their clients' benefit rather than for their own. In practice, however, clientelism and corruption seem to go hand in hand. Governments implement programs targeting particular groups or locales and make rules governing social and economic behavior. In doing so, they spend money and employ a large number of bureaucrats to oversee policy implementation. Having control over how these resources are distributed can give senior political officials significant influence.

Clientelism is most common in nondemocratic systems. It is important to note, however, that some democracies have elements of clientelism as well. These are often remnants of more extensive clientelist arrangements during a previous nondemocratic period. Japan, Italy, and Mexico, for example, have maintained a degree of clientelism in otherwise democratic systems. In other democratic countries, clientelism exists more at the local level than at the national level. The presence of machine politics in major American cities is less common today than in the past, but in small American towns, knowing people in positions of power remains an important part of political outcomes.

Elite-Mass Linkage, Information, and Representation

Whether a linkage is more programmatic or more clientelist, the public can use it to send messages about policy preferences to elites. In patron-client systems, the information flow from the bottom to the top of the patron-client hierarchy can be good. People know how to get in touch with their patron. In programmatic systems, the political elite gets information from the public either from opinion polls or from the **attentive public**, the people who follow political events, belong to politically germane organizations, and engage in high-effort participation such as sending letters, calling their political leaders, or participating in public protests. The attentive public is generally different from the rest of the mass public in its life experiences and political attitudes. Thus, even though a clientelist system provides weaker incentives for the elite to respond to the masses than a programmatic system, clientelism can, arguably, provide a better gauge of public opinion and the desires of the masses.

> **Attentive Public** The part of the general population that is not part of the political elite but is more involved in politics than the rest of the masses.

Social Movements, Interest Groups, and Civil Society

The attentive public also plays a key role in social movements, interest groups, and civil society. While ordinary citizens play a role in these activities and organizations, the elite and the attentive public ultimately drive social movements, interest groups, and civil society organizations. These three concepts are at the center of studies of political participation and elite-mass linkage.

Social Movements

When a sizable portion of the population participates in activities related to a general socioeconomic or political issue, the activities are known as a **social movement**. Members of social movements share general concerns related to politics, economics, and society. They work to promote or resist broad socioeconomic or political changes through informal networks that organize activities such as public protests.

Traditionally, social movements formed around economic issues, such as workers' movements seeking better working conditions, higher wages, and a shorter workweek. After World War II, these traditional issues began to take a backseat to other quality-of-life issues such as women's rights and environmentalism. The activities addressing these topics came to be known as **new social movements**. They have tended to be even less coordinated than the traditional economic-based movements of the past, and organizations working on the issues have been generally shorter lived. New social movements became a central focus of comparativists in Western Europe in the late twentieth century, but their research drew heavily upon the work of American comparative politics scholars such as Ronald Inglehart and his ideas about a postmaterialist culture shift (see Chapter 3).

> **Social Movement** An informal network sharing a common viewpoint; working to promote or resist certain political, economic, or social changes; and engaging in activities such as mass protests.
>
> **New Social Movements** Large movements that emerged following World War II to address noneconomic issues, such as women's rights and the environment.

The membership of social movements is less clear than that of specific organizations. Individuals and groups combine to pursue their shared goals in a social movement, and this membership is often fragile and constantly varying. In his classic 1978 work on social movements, *From Mobilization to Revolution*, Charles Tilly characterized social participants as falling into four categories. "Zealots" are so devoted to the movement that they will participate despite the costs. "Run-of-the-mill" participants are sympathetic to the cause, but they participate on and off and only when they expect to get more from the activities than their participation costs them. "Misers" support the general goals of the movement but are willing to participate only if they expect a significantly greater return than the costs of participating. Finally, "opportunists" have no real attachment to the cause but participate in the movement's activities for purely personal gain.[13] More recently, Friedhelm Neidhart and Dieter Rucht have distinguished among different types of members and supporters of a social movement in a slightly different manner. In declining order of participation and sense of attachment to the movement, they label these individuals core activists, participants, contributors, and sympathizers; and they claim that the latter two groups are not real members but rather are part of the movement's "supportive environment."[14]

Interest Groups

Interest Group An organization whose members share concerns about an issue and work to shape government policies, but do not seek governmental office.

An **interest group** is similar to a social movement, but it is both more organized and more focused than a social movement. Interest groups are specific organizations with fairly well-defined memberships. The members share concerns about a particular issue and work toward the adoption of policies consistent with their position. Interest groups seek to shape policies without pursuing governmental office. Thus, while one could speak of the environmental movement as a social movement, a group such as the Sierra Club is an interest group; the broad set of activities in support of human rights is a social movement, whereas Amnesty International is an interest group.

Interest groups provide the ruling elite with information about the wishes of major segments of the population. They serve as messengers between political leaders and the population at large, providing political leaders with some sense about how the general public feels about certain issues and how intense people's feelings are. Yet, it is wrong to assume that interest groups represent the opinions and desires of the population as a whole. Just as members of the attentive public tend to be the people who contact politicians directly, so do they tend to be the ones to participate in interest group activities or provide financial support for the activities.

The characteristics and approach of interest groups vary significantly across countries and within them. In general, the effectiveness of an interest group depends on its organization, the size of its membership, and the number of other resources, especially money, that it has at its disposal. Almost by definition, large, well-organized, and wealthy interest groups are important players in politics.

Types of Interest Groups

A vast number of different interest groups operate around the world. Political scientists tend to focus on three main types: economic groups, advocacy groups, and local issue groups. An **economic group** forms for financial or occupational reasons and represents particular sectors of the economy. Economic groups include major labor unions, business groups such as the chamber of commerce, and interest groups representing farmers. The importance of unions varies from country to country, although in economically developed countries their membership and influence have generally declined over the last several decades. In almost every country, farmers continue to have more political clout than their percentage of the population would indicate. They produce an important good, which is a form of resource for the group, and they can punish the government by withholding their products if they do not like what the government is doing.

Economic Group An interest group that forms around shared economic interests and represents particular sectors of the economy, including labor unions and business groups.

An **advocacy group** centers on a particular issue or cause that its members believe is an important political or social issue for the country as a whole. Examples in the United States include the National Rifle Association (NRA) and environmental groups such as Greenpeace and the Sea Shepherd Conservation Society (SSCS).[15] Because members often see little financial benefit from achieving their goals, advocacy groups are often less well organized than economic groups. The NRA is an exception. It is one of the best organized and most powerful American interest groups.

A **local issue group** forms because of concerns with "backyard" issues, such as the proposed location of a new landfill in a town. The topics that such groups focus on are known as **NIMBY** (not in my backyard) issues. Such groups generally do not expand to become players on the national political scene. They also tend to be fairly short-lived, dissipating once the issue has been addressed. This does not mean that they are ineffective. Local issue groups are often successful because members are passionate about the topic and close to the action, and local governments cannot afford to ignore even a relatively small number of vocal residents.

The Organization of Interest Groups: Pluralism, Corporatism, and State Control

In addition to different types of interest groups, the way that interest groups are organized in relation to the state varies among countries. In some, interest groups are largely autonomous from state institutions; they interact with the state through efforts to convince political officials to adopt particular policies. In other cases, major interest groups are brought more directly into the political process. They are given seats at the table as partners alongside government officials. In still other states, state institutions control interest groups, which function as extensions of the state, providing another way that the masses are linked to the state.

The first arrangement, and the one most familiar to Americans, is **pluralism**. In a pluralist system, interest groups are autonomous. They lobby the government to take their side on policy but are not officially involved in the decision-making process. Instead, they compete with one another for the attention of government officials.

Because interest groups in pluralist systems generally form on their own without state assistance and without the state's sanctioning them as the official interest groups for particular issues, pluralist systems have a large number of interest groups, spreading out interest groups' political power.[16] Even within a single issue area such as environmentalism, there may be a number of competing groups. The political system is designed to receive information from this large and diverse set of interest groups, though in practice not all groups have equal influence.

Within democratic political systems, the main alternative to pluralism is **corporatism**. Although its name might lead one to believe it involves the domination of corporations, its defining feature is how certain interest groups are more closely connected to the state than occurs in pluralism. In a corporatist system, the state recognizes one or two groups in important sectors (business, labor, farming, etc.) as official interest groups. This is known as a **peak organization**. Such interest groups are often umbrella organizations that themselves are made up of a number of smaller groups, and they may represent significant portions of the general population.

In corporatism, interest groups do not simply lobby the government. They actually participate in writing and debating the merits of proposed policies. Peak organizations affected by the policy partake in crafting it. Significant debate may take place, but the emphasis is on finding a cooperative solution to the policy problem that the main interest groups can all support. When a bill finally comes up for a vote on the floor of the national legislature, the main organizations in the major social sectors have already had their say and, theoretically, support the bill.

Political scientists typically discuss two main variants of corporatism related to interest groups' power compared to the state and to the process of bringing the groups into the decision-making process. In **state corporatism**, the state brings certain interest groups into the process; the groups are "junior partners" in the policy-making process, and their range of activities may be limited. The other variant is **societal corporatism**, in which the major interest groups emerge fairly autonomously, tend

Advocacy Group An interest group that forms around a particular issue or cause its members believe in and that seeks to influence government policy at the national level.

Local Issue Group An interest group that forms to address a specific short-term issue in a community.

NIMBY An acronym for "not in my backyard" used to highlight the positions of many local issue groups.

Pluralism An approach to organizing interests in which groups form autonomously, lobby government officials, and compete with other groups engaged in similar activities.

Corporatism An approach to organizing interest groups in which the state officially recognizes certain large interest groups as the representatives of large segments of society and brings the leaders of those groups to the table as policy is being created.

Peak Organization A large interest group given official status in a corporatist system.

State Corporatism A variant of corporatism in which the state recognizes the main interest groups; the groups have little autonomy, and they are "junior partners" during policy making.

Societal Corporatism A variant of corporatism in which the main interest groups form independently of state action, force the state to accept them in the policy-making process, and have greater autonomy from state control.

to drive the policy-making process, and are thus the "senior partners" in that process. The state is brought in to arbitrate disputes among the major groups and to legitimate their decisions, rather than the other way around. In other words, in societal corporatism the dominant interest groups force themselves into the policy-making process, while in state corporatism the state sets the rules of the game. It invites interest groups into discussions about government policy, and even creates interest groups if they do not already exist or cannot be easily co-opted by government leaders.[17]

Societal corporatism is considered more democratic than state corporatism, which is often associated with authoritarian governance. Societal corporatism has been more common in northern European democracies, while state corporatism has flourished at times in authoritarian systems in Latin America and Asia. Because societal corporatism is seen as the less traditional approach, emerging only in the middle of the twentieth century, some use the label **neo-corporatism** to refer to this variant.

Neo-corporatism A label used to refer to societal corporatism.

A cornerstone of both types of corporatism is the state's endorsement of certain "official" groups. As comparativist Philippe Schmitter puts it, peak organizations are "recognized or licensed (if not created) by the state and granted a deliberate representational monopoly."[18] In such systems, other groups are left out of the policy-making process. Not surprisingly, members of the groups that are left out may turn to more unconventional forms of participation. They may also transform themselves in a way that allows them to access other conventional channels of participation.

Traditionally, for example, the major official groups in European corporatist systems represented business, labor unions, farmers, and sometimes established religion. New social movement groups, such as environmentalists, were excluded from debates over policy, even policies about which they cared deeply. Their displeasure produced two results. First, some groups transformed themselves into political parties as a way of forcing themselves into the political process. This is an important part of the story behind the emergence of Green Parties in Europe. Second, their protests about the nature of the corporatist system led to reforms, making the system more open to these new social forces.

State Control System An interest group system in which the state creates and controls the main interest groups; groups have no autonomy from the state.

The final form of interest group–state relations is the **state control system**. This approach is most common in totalitarian or strong authoritarian systems. The state control approach goes beyond state corporatism. Official interest groups are present, but they are creations of the state and under its complete control. They have no autonomy, and they exist to serve the interests of the state.[19] The state uses the groups to enforce its decisions and provide some legitimacy. This does not mean that the relationship is completely a one-way street. Government officials may also look to the groups for information as they make policy decisions. Thus, while the interest groups are largely an arm of the state, they also allow the state to link itself to the masses and gather information about mass attitudes and policy preferences.

It is possible to put the four arrangements just discussed on a spectrum based on the groups' degree of autonomy from the state. Figure 8.2 presents such a spectrum. Pluralism is associated with complete autonomy from the government, while the state control system features no autonomy at all.

Advantages and Disadvantages of Pluralism

Pluralism and corporatism are distinct and in many ways contrary alternatives to interest group organization. As a result, the advantages of one tend to correspond to the disadvantages of the other, and vice versa. This section, therefore, only focuses on the advantages and disadvantages of pluralism.

FIGURE 8.2   **Interest Group Systems and Autonomy from State Control**

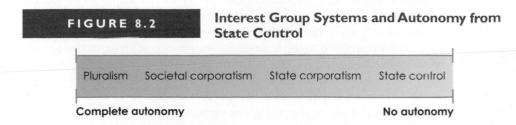

| Pluralism | Societal corporatism | State corporatism | State control |

Complete autonomy   **No autonomy**

Advantage 1: A Marketplace of Ideas. One of the strongest claims in favor of pluralism is based on the idea that, in the end, competition between rival interest groups produces better policy. Unlike corporatist policy making, where the state creates a virtual monopoly for certain interest groups, pluralism forces groups to make the strongest possible arguments in favor of their positions. Even groups with roughly similar ideas compete against one another for the adoption of their version of the policy. In theory at least, the result of such competition is that the policy that emerges is based on the best, most reasoned argument about the issue.

Advantage 2: Even Minor Groups Can Be Heard. Corporatism relies on peak organizations to represent society. Pluralism allows any group to try to influence the policy process. In pluralism, small groups are not excluded just because they do not represent privileged sectors of society, such as labor and business. This does not guarantee that small groups will have the levels of access and influence that large groups do. The characteristics of a group, such as membership size and financial resources, can affect the extent to which its pleas are heard. However, pluralism does give even small groups the opportunity to try to be heard by those in positions of political power.

Disadvantage 1: Inefficiency through Competition between Similar Groups. The flip side of pluralism as a marketplace of ideas is the view that it encourages inefficient competition among similar interest groups. Each of two environmental groups with slightly different views of a proposed bill, for example, may work against the other group to maximize the chance that its specific position is adopted. A united front would lead to a more efficient use of resources.

One could respond that nothing prevents such groups from working together, and cooperation sometimes occurs, particularly when there is much at stake. But because the groups are autonomous from the state, they rely on members' support, and a group that works too closely with or, worse, appears to be dependent on a group with similar policy concerns can see its members defect to the other group. Pluralism thus encourages groups to work for policy successes independently of those with related policy preferences.

Disadvantage 2: Money Talks. The competitive lobbying that is the centerpiece of pluralism involves providing information to officials. The information that an interest group provides does not necessarily present a complete or balanced picture. Rather, a group is likely to present information that supports its position. This would not be a problem if all sides in a debate had equal resources with which to get their messages out and had equal access to government officials. Particularly in the United States, equality of both resources and access is far from the norm. Those with more, especially with more money, can better get their messages across through direct lobbying efforts and through indirect lobbying—using information campaigns to encourage the masses to put pressure on their political officials, leading the officials to support the position of the interest group. Groups with more money can also contribute more to political candidates. While it is difficult to prove that campaign contributions in the United States have a direct effect on policy positions, solid evidence shows that campaign contributions do improve a group's access to political officials once they take office.

Civil Society

Related to the idea of interest groups and autonomy from the state is the concept of **civil society**. Political scientists use the term *civil society* in a number of ways. Most commonly, it refers to the array of voluntary social organizations not controlled by the state. The voluntary autonomous organizations themselves are called **civil society organizations (CSOs)**. Examples in the United States include service organizations (the Rotary Club), local fraternal societies (the Lions Club), groups catering to personal hobbies and interests (chess clubs), and groups with more political relevance (such as national interest groups like the NRA and American Association of Retired Persons [AARP]).

Civil Society A term used to refer to the array of groups that are both autonomous from the state and that people join voluntarily.

Civil Society Organizations (CSOs) The voluntary autonomous organizations that make up civil society.

In an ideal-type totalitarian system, there is no civil society. In an authoritarian system, the nonpolitical segments of civil society may be abundant, but groups that look politically threatening are either co-opted into or crushed by the state. In democratic systems where interest groups are organized through pluralism, the politically salient portion of civil society is generally strong. In democratic corporatist systems, the politically relevant component of civil society is usually weaker, since the state privileges certain groups over others.

A problem with the concept of civil society is the question of how autonomous from the state a group should be to be considered part of civil society. We might exclude peak organizations in state corporatist systems from civil society, but what about nongovernmental organizations at the local level that receive significant funding from the state? As is often the case, some arguments about civil society among comparativists boil down to different conceptualizations and different approaches to measuring the concept.

Think and Discuss
In what ways can civil society organizations be a force for instability and intolerance?

Spotlight on ... SOUTH AFRICA

Civil Society before and after Apartheid

Nondemocratic political systems often constrain, or outright prohibit, the development of civil society organizations (CSOs). As a result, periods of liberalization under an authoritarian political system and the first years of a newly established democracy often generate an explosion in the visible indicators of civil society. South Africa poses an interesting test of this pattern of civil society development, since the apartheid system allowed relative freedom for white citizens while restricting political participation by blacks. Even with this atypical feature, idea that changing "political opportunities"[20] affects civil society development holds in South Africa. In the early 1980s, when South African President P. W. Botha engaged in political liberalization, black civil society in South Africa rapidly caught up with the white population's counterpart.

The separate civil societies were fundamentally different, however, in their outlook. While white civil society largely supported the apartheid government, the emerging black CSOs formed a cohesive "anti-apartheid civil society."[21] Put another way, CSOs among the minority white population supported the regime, while CSOs among the majority black population were strongly opposed to the existing political system. This racial dividing line within civil society changed after the new postapartheid government came to power in 1994. From that point forward, black civil society and white civil society (along with a small number of integrated groups) contained both antigovernment and pro-government elements. In October 2010, an unprecedented gathering of representatives from South African CSOs praised the South African constitution but sharply criticized the government's implementation of constitutional protections for the country's less fortunate.

One of the important lessons from the South African case involves the influence of external actors in civil society development. Although the emergence of numerous and effective CSOs is easier when the government allows them rather than does all it can to prevent them, civil society also expands as the result of the availability of financial and other resources. In South Africa, as in many lesser-developed or middle-income countries, these resources include support from foreign governments and international nongovernmental organizations. Donor countries and organizations make aid available due to their assumption that a vibrant civil society contributes to democratic and economic development.[22]

Aid from foreign governments was more common in the late-apartheid period, when Western governments financed many antiapartheid groups. After 1994, much of this aid was redirected to the new South African government, although a portion of foreign aid to the government was tied to its willingness to work with CSOs.[23] Some foreign government aid is still given directly to CSOs, such as grants from the French government's Civil Society Development Fund. Much of the direct support to CSOs, however, comes from international nongovernmental organizations based outside South Africa, such as the Open Society Foundation and the Charles Stewart Mott Foundation. Without such support from these sources, civil society in the late-apartheid and postapartheid periods may still have blossomed. There is little doubt, however, that their blossoming would have been a much slower process.

The final lesson is that pro-democracy CSOs can become victims of their own success. Once their main goal of establishing a new democracy has been achieved, some struggle to redefine themselves. Others cannot adjust to losing the external financial support they had relied on during the struggle against the previous nondemocratic government. Still others succumb to a form of brain drain, as their leaders take positions in the new government.[24] Some CSOs fall victim to all these problems and either disappear or struggle to remain relevant. In the case of South Africa, some of the more important organizations in the late-apartheid period have been ineffective since 1994, while others continue to have a significant impact on government policy.[25]

TOPIC IN COUNTRIES

Given how fundamentally different the organization of the political systems of many of the Topic in Countries (TIC) cases are, it should not be surprising that the cases also vary greatly in how and how much the masses participate, how the elites and masses are linked, and how politically relevant their social movements, interest groups, and civil society organizations are. In the following sections on the TIC cases, pay particular attention to

- The different levels in political participation and the variation in the use of unconventional participation among the TIC cases.
- The extent to which elites and masses in the TIC cases are linked through programmatic representation or clientelism.
- The presence of social movements and the importance and organization of interest groups across the TIC cases.
- Differences in the size and political relevance of civil society in the TIC cases.

The United Kingdom

The actions of the British mass public, as well as the United Kingdom's (UK's) political elite, are shaped by the cultural principles of noblesse oblige and working-class deference (discussed in Chapter 3). The British public tends to accept the system's legitimacy. Part of the reason is the extent to which British political leaders take their responsibility for the population's welfare seriously. The country's politics has evolved from being based largely on clientelism in the pre-democracy period to linking elites and masses through political parties and debates over ideas. While less dramatic and drawn out than its change from a clientelist to programmatic system, British interest group participation has changed over time as well, from a more corporatist approach to one with noticeable features of pluralism.

Political Participation

In general, voting rates in the UK are higher than in some other mature democracies but lower than in many other European countries. Turnout has varied, driven partly by differences in mass perceptions of the competitiveness of the elections and the level of dissatisfaction with the ruling party. There has also been a general downward trend since the early 1990s. After World War II, turnout rates were above 70 percent of registered voters for parliamentary elections and often near or above 80 percent. In 2001, turnout dropped below 60 percent, and it rebounded only slightly to 61.4 percent in 2005. The trend continued in 2010, with turnout topping 65.5 percent in the May 2010 parliamentary elections.[26] As in other mature democracies, including the United States, conventional participation rates are much lower for younger citizens than for older ones.

With the exception of the violence in Northern Ireland, student-led violent protests against government spending cuts, and riots in London and other large cities in 2011, the UK has had few instances of unconventional political participation over the past few decades. However, fitting with working-class deference, a large percentage of the population chooses not to participate in British politics. Russell Dalton's examination of mass participation in the UK, the United States, West Germany, and France found that, other than voting, the British public participates at comparatively low levels.[27]

Programmatic versus Clientelistic Linkage

In the days of feudal lords, clientelism dominated the lives of ordinary people. What people received came from their lords, and unquestioned loyalty was expected in return. Even as the British political system became more democratic, clientelism remained an essential way in which British masses and elites were linked.

Today, programmatic linkage has largely replaced clientelism. Political parties and specific political leaders stake out ideological positions and seek the support of the electorate based on their performance in office and stated policy goals. Activities such as the prime minister's Question Time help citizens get a sense of political leaders' ideologies and positions on specific policies. In addition, the strength of British political parties, including their ability to dictate which of their candidates runs in a particular electoral district, makes it difficult for prominent politicians to engage in clientelism at the expense of the interests of the party.

Interest Groups, Social Movements, and Civil Society

The fairly low levels of overall participation in the UK do not indicate a lack of social movements or interest group membership. In the past, Britain was much more corporatist than it is today, with several peak organizations. Among Margaret Thatcher's reforms was an effort to reduce the direct impact of groups by reducing the number of government boards where interest groups were directly involved in crafting policy. This especially weakened the power of unions. As with many of Thatcher's other reforms, her attack on corporatism survived the years of Labour Party control of the British government under Tony Blair.

The result of corporatism's decline is a greater emphasis on lobbying and a greater role for small groups. Unlike the United States, little lobbying occurs around the final vote on a bill. Instead, interest groups focus on the initial draft of a proposed policy and the period of time between readings of the bill in the House of Commons. Groups can have a strong impact on details but typically cannot stop a bill from passing. The strength of British interest groups is aided by the district voting system. Groups stress how their members in the MP's district support or oppose a policy.

Along with the new social movements common to other Western European countries in the 1960s to 1980s, immigration has sparked social movements in the UK on both sides of the issue. Prior to the 1980s, anti-immigrant groups had drawn some of their support from the Left (due to concerns about working-class and union employment). When Margaret Thatcher made immigration a central part of the Conservative Party platform, anti-immigrant groups became increasingly associated with forces of the political Right. Of course, many other people from the Right see escalating immigration as a benefit to British businesses. As in other Western European countries, the process of European integration has fostered growing concerns that the UK is increasingly unable to guarantee jobs for long-time residents, to protect its culture, or to ensure its national security.

The UK has a substantial civil society.[28] Among the various types of social movements, the most prominent have been peace, environmental, women's, and immigration-related movements. The peace movement, a force during the Vietnam War and an antinuclear weapons forum during the cold war, reemerged during the Iraq War. Even after Prime Minister Tony Blair, who had been one of the strongest allies of the United States on the issue both before and after the invasion of Iraq, stepped down in favor of Gordon Brown, the anti–Iraq War movement worked to mobilize citizens in London against maintaining a significant presence in Iraq.

Germany

Germans vote in large numbers but also participate in other conventional—and occasionally unconventional—ways. Like the UK, Germany's approach to linking elites and masses has changed from being centered on personal connections to being based on programmatic representation. Societal corporatism has been the principal structure of relations between interest groups and the state in the Federal Republic.

Political Participation

Voter turnout in the Federal Republic averaged about 87 percent from the 1950s through the 1980s and nearly 80 percent in the 1990s.[29] Compared with voting, participation in other types of political activity has been lower. West Germans withdrew from organized activities in the years immediately after 1945, a natural reaction to coerced participation under the Nazi regime, but their participation in voluntary group activities rebounded in due course. In the 2000s, nearly 60 percent of Germans in the western part of the country participated in some type of organized group activity in a given year, which is on par with or even better than other Western democracies. A similar citizens' withdrawal from organized groups appears to have occurred in the east since reunification, but without the subsequent increase in participation that occurred in West Germany. As a result, participation in all types of groups remains lower among easterners than westerners.[30]

Although most political activity in the post–World War II period has been conventional, periods of unconventional politics occurred in both East and West Germany. The German Democratic Republic (East Germany) outlawed independent political groups and harassed, jailed, or expelled dissidents to prevent broader opposition movements from emerging, but unconventional political activity occasionally flared up. In 1953, for example, workers in major East German cities struck against the regime and its harsh policies. Soviet tanks quickly crushed the revolt. As in other Western European countries and the United States, portions of the mass population in

West Germany became radicalized in the late 1960s and the 1970s. The resulting demonstrations were often peaceful, though some generated violent clashes with police. Postwar West Germany also experienced more extreme behavior. Extremist movements on the Left and Right have very small memberships, but their presence and message have caused unease among mainstream parties, political elites, and ordinary citizens.

Programmatic versus Clientelistic Linkage

Clientelistic relationships dominated feudal society in Germany during medieval times. Programmatic parties with clearly articulated, class-based, ideological programs emerged in German politics from the latter half of the nineteenth century until World War II, and they continue to provide a major link between political elites and masses today. Following World War II, however, the two major parties of the Federal Republic—the Christian Democrats and the Social Democrats—muted the class content of their programs, and their messages became more similar in order to attract as many voters as possible. In short, they became catch-all parties to appeal across class, religious, and regional lines in order to win elections.[31]

In the German Democratic Republic, the Communist Party initially employed Marxist ideology as the basis of its programmatic appeal to the masses. Like other Communist Parties, however, the regime relied on privilege and clientelism in its later decades to create an elite whose loyalty derived from the perks of party membership, such as travel to the West and access to scarce consumer goods.[32]

Interest Groups, Social Movements, and Civil Society

Peak associations representing major economic interests such as labor, business, and the professions negotiate policies with the state. This sometimes occurs in formal roundtable forums but often is more informal. German societal corporatism extends beyond the realm of policy formulation to encompass policy implementation as well. These peak associations, as well as those representing the main religious denominations in the area of social welfare, implement policies and administer their particular domain of industrial relations or the welfare state on behalf of the government. In doing so, they enjoy substantial autonomy from state interference as long as they fulfill their public obligations to implement the law.[33]

Western Germans after World War II and eastern Germans after 1990 loathed group participation in the years immediately following the end of totalitarian rule. Previous dictatorial regimes had suppressed voluntary associations, and civil society was weak. State control was a hallmark of Germany's experiences with both the fascist and Communist variants of totalitarianism.

Civil society reemerged in the Federal Republic over time, aided by the societal corporatist system of interest group representation. From the 1960s to the present, social movements representing university students, anti-nuclear forces, pacifism, feminism, and environmentalism organized to bring about political change. The Green Party emerged from these social movements in the late 1970s.[34]

India

As might be expected in a democratic country with a diverse population of over a billion people, portions of the masses in India are very actively engaged in a variety of political and social venues. The masses use an assortment of methods to achieve an array of goals both through direct action and by influencing political leaders. Both the unconventional and violent and the conventional and nonviolent approaches to mass political participation can be found in India today. Programmatic approaches to elite-mass linkage have been conspicuous in politics since independence. Unlike some of the other democratic TIC cases, however, such efforts have not always been based on nationwide appeals. Particularly in recent years, regional programmatic appeals have grown in number and effectiveness. As in the UK, the organization of Indian interest groups has evolved away from variants of corporatism and toward pluralism.

Political Participation

The general population of India participates though conventional channels, though at lower rates than the European countries discussed in this section. Turnout for parliamentary elections has averaged slightly under 60 percent, but has been quite stable. From 1952 through 2004, it was never lower than 55 percent and never higher than 65 percent. Both the low numbers and their relative stability are due in large part to the longtime dominance of the Indian National Congress (INC) Party in these elections.

Examples of unconventional participation in India are numerous. Many political organizations engage in confrontational politics to publicize their interests. Of all countries across the globe, India has the most disruptions of normal life caused by efforts to get political leaders to act—or not to act. The words used in the English press for many of the disruptions are borrowed from Hindi and other indigenous languages. There are *bandhs* (in which all businesses and other normal activities are blocked), *gheraos* (in which leaders are surrounded and kept where they are for long periods of time), fasts, *yatras* (processions that may move through a large part of the countryside advocating some sort of action), *hartals* (in which a general strike occurs), rail and road *rokos* (in which trains and cars are not allowed to move), and many other forms.[35] Each involves a demand for action on an issue of interest to the participants.

Phoolan Devi, a candidate for parliament, speaks at a political rally in Mirzapur, India. Devi became a hero in India among low-caste Hindu women after serving eleven years in prison for the murder of a group of upper-caste men who had raped her. © AP Photo/Saurabh Das

Other unconventional acts have been less peaceful. Along with various secessionist movements, groups that forcibly take land from landlords have operated outside the formal political system for decades. In the late 1960s, the Naxalite movement (a violent Communist movement linked to Maoist thought) was born in West Bengal. Despite massive efforts of the government to stamp it out, Naxalites, or similar groups, have spread to almost half of India's federal units. The fact that such militant movements continue to operate reflects both the absence of the real political representation of many very poor rural inhabitants and the continuing role of violence as a form of unconventional participation in India.

Programmatic versus Clientelistic Linkage

At the start of independence, the dominant INC appealed for support by offering a social democratic program, that is, involving both the development of a hegemonic public sector and the allowance of some private enterprise. The Communist Party of India sought followers by advocating the advancement of workers and peasants. Still other parties championed alternative national and local issues. Over the years, domestic and international problems and pressures reduced the appeal of the INC program and led to a substantial rise in the number of parties with a variety of alternative policy objectives. In response, by the early 1990s, the INC formally began advocating a liberalized economy. By the late 1990s, its primary challenger was the Bharatiya Janata Party (BJP), whose appeal was its call for building a society based upon Hinduism. Regional parties pushing programs designed to benefit regional interests continued to multiply.

Clientelism may not be as significant in India as it is in other parts of the world, but deference to power is a widespread feature of the country's various cultures. In addition to making programmatic appeals, politicians promise social group leaders special benefits in exchange for the votes of the group's members. As a lure, they also reserve jobs and seats in educational institutions for supporters. A so-called creamy layer of privileged individuals in the Scheduled Caste/Scheduled Tribe category has developed, indicative of the small group of beneficiaries linked by clientelism.

Interest Groups, Social Movements, and Civil Society

In the early period following independence, the INC developed its own student associations, peasant groups, and trade unions (characterized as "state-dominated pluralism"). Over time, interest group representation in India transitioned to a form of "authoritarian corporatism" during the Emergency (1975–77) and to a form of "competitive pluralism" in subsequent years.[36] Today, numerous interest groups, such as unions, have affiliations with political parties in most sectors of the economy. For example, student groups have been active in all parts of the country on many different issues. These groups have produced future leaders of many of India's political parties, and they compete with each other for prominence. There are groups advocating the interests of traditionally discriminated-against minorities, women's advocacy groups, civil liberties groups, environmental groups, Hindu-nationalist-oriented groups, and many others, including thousands of NGOs, many funded from abroad, representing a wide range of interests.

Social movements have developed in India over the years seeking to block dam building, to stop deforestation, and to stop privatization of public companies, among other causes. Separatist movements demanding either secession from India or a separate federal unit have developed with varying intensity for decades. Ever since federal unit boundaries were established with the implementation of the States Reorganization Commission's report in 1956, demands for changes, sometimes peaceful and sometimes violent, have occurred. From the 1960s to 2000, additional federal territorial units were added to the Indian federal system in an effort to quell uprisings.

Mexico

The move away from authoritarianism in the late twentieth and early twenty-first centuries has affected mass participation in Mexico. Conventional participation has declined following the energy of the liberalization period leading up to the establishment of democracy at the end of the 1990s. The Institutional Revolutionary Party (PRI) controlled the federal government for much of the twentieth century, in part through its extensive use of clientelist arrangements, and Mexico is retreating, albeit slowly, from that clientelism. Like other aspects of Mexican politics, the nature of social movements and the structure of interest group representation are changing, with a slow move away from corporatism organized through the PRI.

Political Participation

Participation in legislative elections has varied greatly. The highest turnout in the legislative elections was during the period of liberalization before Mexico had established its democracy. As is the case in the United States, Mexican turnout for legislative elections tends to be higher in years that there are presidential elections. In the presidential election years of 1994, 2000, and 2006, turnout was 78 percent, 63 percent, and 58.9 percent respectively. In non-presidential-election years, turnout was lower: a bit under 58 percent in 1997, only 41.7 percent in 2003, and 47.8 percent in 2009.

Unconventional activities like the Chiapas uprising (see the In Theory and Practice feature on pages 244–245.) have also become more visible in recent decades. Controversy following elections can also drive protests, as it did when the runner-up challenged the official vote count in the 2006 presidential election. Compared with other Latin American countries, however, the Mexican population is less likely to engage in unconventional political activities. Survey data has pointed to the percentage of Mexican respondents indicating that they had attended a political demonstration being lower, in some cases much lower, than respondents in Argentina, Brazil, Chile, Colombia, Peru, Uruguay, and Venezuela.[37]

Programmatic versus Clientelistic Linkage

On top of the many other obstacles facing opposition parties during the period of PRI dominance, the political system's roots in clientelism put opponents of the PRI at a particular disadvantage. Non-PRI candidates had to fight for electoral support with neither the institutional organization nor the access to state resources required to turn clientelism into a national political strategy.

Clientelism was especially crucial in linking PRI elites to the poor and rural population. Programmatic appeals meant less to these groups than direct and immediate economic benefits. The benefits were distributed through the *cacique* (a Spanish term for the local party boss), who expected political support for himself and for the PRI in regional or national political activities, such as presidential elections, in return.

Mexico's democratization has increased the importance of programmatic linkage. As political scientist Jonathan Fox puts it, the Mexican transition provided an opportunity to examine the transition from "clients to citizens," in which "poor people gain access to whatever material resources the state has to offer without having to forfeit their right to articulate their interests autonomously."[38] While the PRI's grip on the federal government has declined dramatically, it continues to use local clientelist methods in large parts of the country. In other areas, the PRI has lost its control of local politics through clientelism only to see another major party, typically the National Action Party (PAN) or the Party of the Democratic Revolution (PRD), adopt its former tactics. The result, claim researchers such as comparativist Tina Hilgers, is that "the unwritten rules of clientelism" continue on as "a solidly established—albeit informal—institution" in Mexican politics.[39]

Interest Groups, Social Movements, and Civil Society

Comparativists long considered Mexico a corporatist country, but one that differed both from an ideal state corporatist system and an ideal societal corporatist one. While connected to the state, Mexican interest groups were more tightly connected to the PRI itself, which set up and largely controlled them. As a result, some called Mexico a case of **party corporatism**,[40] like many Communist countries in Europe and Asia in the twentieth century.

As with many of Mexico's other political reforms, the changes in interest group connections with the government have been controversial among those who benefited from the old arrangements. Official unions strongly resisted policies that threatened the PRI and their connections to it because their claim to influence in the state depended both on incorporation in the PRI and on PRI control of the state.[41] Likewise, many of the old guard members of the PRI resisted weakening connections with labor unions that they had so effectively mobilized in the past to support the party's dominance.

Genuine social movements in Mexico were difficult during the era of PRI dominance, but they did exist. University students pushed for a more democratic political system in the late 1960s, a social movement that the government, not yet ready for liberalization, decided to crush. The result was the death of around three hundred protesters. Peasant uprisings, involving seizures of land loosely coordinated by leftist organizations in Mexico, took place in the early to mid-1970s.[42] The rebellion in the state of Chiapas in the mid-1990s was the definition of a social movement based on unconventional participation. In recent years, the increase in drug-related violence has sparked a new social movement mobilized around opposition to the drug cartels.

The leader of the Zapatista National Liberation Army (EZLN), Subcomandante Insurgente Marcos gives the victory sign to supporters as he marches from the U.S. Embassy to the main Zocalo plaza in Mexico City, on May 1, 2006. Marcos joined calls to boycott U.S. goods in what was dubbed "A Day without Gringos," an action timed to coincide with a call for immigrants to boycott work, school, and shopping in the United States. © AP Photo/Moises Castillo

IN THEORY AND PRACTICE

Disturbance Theory and Mexico

Political scientists have spent a great deal of time theorizing about who participates in interest groups and social movements and how such groups form and mobilize members. One of the first scholars to address this question was David Truman in a 1951 book called *The Governmental Process*.[43] Truman argued that interest groups form as a response to social and economic change, particularly when such development creates a "disturbance" in society. As a result, his ideas came to be known as **disturbance theory**.

Though it does not completely explain the uprising in Chiapas in the mid-1990s, disturbance theory does provide some insight. The implementation of the North American Free Trade Agreement (NAFTA) clearly fueled the Chiapas explosion. On January 1, 1994, coinciding with NAFTA's implementation, the Zapatista Army of National Liberation (EZLN) seized four towns. NAFTA embodied what EZLN

Party Corporatism The variant of corporatism in Mexico during the PRI's dominance of the Mexican political system.

Disturbance Theory A term for the theory developed by David Truman that interest groups form from economic and social changes that create disturbances in society and lead those who share concerns about the problems to form groups to solve them.

leaders saw as Mexico's failure to address problems facing the country's peasants that were exacerbated by globalization. Thus, while not the original source of the disturbance around which EZLN mobilized, NAFTA's implementation was a trigger for the violent uprising.

Brazil

Brazilians continue to participate in the conventional channels of their democracy, but unconventional participation is not uncommon. One of the key reasons for the high level of unconventional behavior is Brazil's failure to develop a strong political party system. With the noteworthy exception of the Brazilian Workers' Party (PT), Brazilian political parties lack clear programmatic profiles or institutionalized linkages to interest groups, unions, and social movements. Brazil's system of labor representation developed through state corporatism, while other autonomous groups compose one of the most vigorous civil societies in Latin America.

Political Participation

Brazilians participate in conventional activities such as voting at relatively high levels. Dilma Rousseff's victory in the runoff round of the 2010 presidential election saw turnout of 78.5 percent of registered voters. Such conventional participation, however, does not mean that all Brazilians are happy with their political system and its responsiveness. Partly as a result of the ineffective linkage between masses and elites in Brazil, popular participation frequently involves unconventional action, including, at one extreme, "self-help" activities seeking to avoid state contact and, at the other, mass protests directed at the state. Brazilians are nearly twice as likely as Mexicans to say they would attend a demonstration or occupy a building; they are first or second in Latin America in their willingness to engage in most types of unconventional political action.[44]

Unconventional participation has been prevalent in the arena of organized labor. Consistent with his rhetoric, Brazil's former president, Luiz Inácio "Lula" da Silva, got his start as a militant union organizer. An example the effectiveness of unconventional participation involves the Unified Workers' Central (CUT), which became nationally known for its defiant rejection of military rule. Its confrontational approaches forced wage concessions and salary increases from employers. The CUT's success in winning material improvements for its workers led to the use of more militant methods by other unions, even those that did not share its radical ideological perspectives.

Programmatic versus Clientelistic Linkage

Most of the linkages between Brazilian elites and masses are highly personalistic and clientelistic between individual politicians and their local client groups. In some cases, these relationships last for many years. In others, groups bargain with different politicians every electoral cycle to see who will offer the most for their votes.

The combination of prevalent clientelism and largely nonexistent efforts at programmatic linkage has had important political consequences. Specifically, it makes creating and enacting clear policy agendas very difficult for Brazil's legislature. Instead, most politicians spend their time in office trying to grab enough "pork" (i.e., state resources) to keep their clients happy up to and during the next electoral cycle. In order to enact any significant new policies, government leaders, including the president, have to play along with the game of pork-funded clientelism.[45]

Although clientelism is strong in Brazil, its long-term stability is not guaranteed. In contrast to France and Mexico, where clientelism is stronger at the local level than at the national level, some Brazilian local governments have adopted initiatives that challenge clientelist practices. One such initiative, "participatory budgeting" (PB), is a system that allows citizens to take part in meetings where they select from various general policy directions, vote on specific policy initiatives, and elect "PB delegates" who represent them in additional meetings with other such delegates, representatives of local organizations, and government officials.[46]

Along with Brazil's blossoming civil society, participatory decision-making institutions such as PB represent an emerging challenge to the dominance of Brazilian clientelism over the development of government policy and the distribution of state resources.[47] Research on the attitudes of the PB delegates indicates that they believe support from other PB delegates and from representatives of civil society organizations is more important than support from government officials.[48]

Interest Groups, Social Movements, and Civil Society

Unlike in the Mexican case, corporatism in Brazil did not tie unions and other class-based organizations to the state through a political party. Instead, Brazil developed a state corporatist approach in which the system of peak unions resulted from top-down state direction. Although formal state support systems discouraging pluralistic competition are not in place for other types of organizations, many have adopted the format of peak organizations in order to be heard more clearly at the national level. The systems that developed in the estados mirrored that at the national level.

Some of the traditional labor unions, such as the General Workers' Central (CGT), continue to operate much as the corporatist system intended, as more or less passive supporters of the state. Others, such as CUT, have developed along much more confrontational lines. The unions that today belong to the CUT were once traditional co-opted labor unions such as the CGT, but internal rebellions led by the powerful metalworkers' unions in the São Paulo region of Brazil began to challenge the military regime in the late 1970s. While a model for the use of unconventional tactics in Brazil, the CUT is far from an anti-system organization: it originally founded the Workers' Party (PT) and continues to dominate its leadership.

Most of Brazil's social movements developed more autonomously from the state than labor unions and in some cases have been quite confrontational. Particularly since the 1970s, nongovernmental organizations within the country have worked to raise awareness of many pressing national problems and to mobilize the population to support actions to address them. These include movements on the environment, homelessness, and AIDS, as well as the *Movimento dos Trabalhadores Sem Terra* (MST) or "Landless Movement." Considered the largest social movement in Latin America, the MST has pressured the government to address the significant inequality in land ownership in Brazil, particularly in some of the larger and more rural estados. Its activities that have gained the most attention are those designed to bypass the political process entirely, such as the forceful seizure of land and the establishment of agricultural cooperatives beginning in the mid-1980s.

Along with Mexico and Chile, Brazil has one of the most vibrant civil societies in Latin America. According to the World Values Survey, Brazil would be classified as having a strong civil society, weaker than that of the United States or the UK, but stronger than that of Italy, France, Japan, or Spain.[49] Yet, the individual civil society organizations, though numerous, have not been effectively linked to political elites.

Nigeria

The optimism some have displayed about Nigeria's democracy has been based on several factors: visible conventional participation, a decrease in ethnic violence (compared to some periods of Nigerian history), and a tentative resolution to the oil-related violence in the Niger Delta region. Concerns regarding elite-mass linkage however, remain. As discussed in Chapter 4, elite-led violence between Christians and Muslims continues. The Niger Delta cease-fire is fragile. Clientelism contributes to the corruption that plagues Nigerian politics. Interest groups are growing in importance but, like the country's civil society organizations, are still developing.

Political Participation

Nigeria's democratic leaders have sought to direct mass participation into conventional outlets like voting. To an extent, they have been successful. Although turnout for the 1999 presidential elections was only slightly over 52 percent, it increased to 69 percent in 2003 before falling to an estimated 57.5 percent in 2007.[50] Ethnic conflict is also less severe than in the early postindependence period. On the other hand, increasing instances of electoral fraud since 1999 threaten to create significant disillusionment among the general population and depress future rates of conventional political participation.

In addition, violent unconventional political participation remains a problem. In the Niger Delta region of Nigeria, for example, groups have engaged in unconventional activities while also seeking international support over the issues of oil drilling, resulting negative environmental effects, and limited redistribution of the oil wealth to local residents. Some protests have been relatively nonviolent, such as occupations of ChevronTexaco facilities by unarmed female villagers in 2002 and 2003. More recently, other groups in the Niger Delta engaged in more violent protests, threatening "all-out war" with the Nigerian government and attacking international oil company personnel and facilities.[51] These actions have periodically forced other oil companies, such as Shell, to halt operations. While Nigeria reached a cease-fire agreement with the main Niger Delta group in 2010, subsequent disagreements cast doubt on the ability of the government to contain such unconventional forms of participation in the long run.

Programmatic versus Clientelistic Linkage

Clientelism provided a structural support for authoritarian military leaders such as Ibrahim Babangida, but such leaders also worked to deepen clientelist ties. Oil revenues greased the clientelist system, providing significant resources for patrons to give to their clients, after skimming a significant portion off the top for themselves. Like other aspects of Nigerian politics, tribal and family connections play an important role in clientelist practices, and clientelism remains especially prevalent in smaller towns and in the countryside.

Even during periods of democratic rule, parties have been organized more along clientelist lines than as programmatic mechanisms for linking elites and masses.[52] As in other countries where clientelism is widespread, the political parties act mostly as umbrellas for the collection of local and regional political machines. Despite promises by former president Olusegun Obasanjo and his successors of significant reform and efforts to attack corruption, Nigerian politics remains more about who you know than about what politicians stand for.

Interest Groups, Social Movements, and Civil Society

Like other groups in Nigerian society, interest groups tend to be organized through tribal-based clientelism, though some broader groups exist that are designed to represent segments of the population in regions of the country or even the country as a whole. Some of the strongest are economic organizations, both more traditional groups representing business and labor and those connecting members of particular professions. At times, unions have been strong and independent; at other times, repressed. The Nigerian Labor Congress, the country's largest union organization, has organized successful unconventional activities, including general strikes, to pressure the government.

During periods of military rule, the government repressed social movements, specific interest groups, and the leaders of both if they posed a threat to its rule. Some social movements and groups were allowed to function, often by finding sympathetic officials in the military government who desired a transition back to democracy. Since the reestablishment of democracy in 1999, social movements have become even more visible, including ethnic minority movements, women's movements, and youth movements. The youth movements are divided between those favoring peaceful collaborations and "ethnic militias."[53]

Thus, while interest groups and social movements are still underdeveloped, the presence of civil society in Nigeria is a reality. However, Nigeria demonstrates that one should not assume that all civil society organizations or social movement activities are "civil." Some of the more organized associations are designed to unite people along ethnic and religious lines, playing a role in reinforcing the already deep social divisions in the country, while others have increasingly turned to violence in their unconventional political activities.

Russia

In the early post-Soviet period, scholars studying mass political participation in Russia believed that the country had the potential to develop a pattern of participation "familiar in the established democracies but alien under the old Soviet system."[54] While such optimism appeared warranted in the early 1990s, by the end of that decade patterns of participation had begun to change. Personalities and connections dominated ideas, and clientelism, a long-standing Russian tradition, was solidified under Vladimir Putin. Interest groups exist but struggle to shape government policy due to the state's significant presence in, and self-interest regarding, the economy.

Political Participation

By the end of Putin's second term as president, the frenzy of the initial political transition from 1990 through 1993 had been replaced by a system in which the government, while popular, was increasingly seen as a distant elite. The belief that ordinary citizens could affect political outcomes was declining, and nonparticipation was becoming a way of life for many. Putin and his political allies had to work hard to convince people to turn out to vote for his successor, Dmitry Medvedev, in 2008.

As a result, turnout for presidential elections, which was near 69 percent in 1996 and 2000, dropped to 64.4 percent in 2004. Although it officially increased to 69.7 percent in 2008, many observers questioned this figure. There were numerous reports of voting irregularities across the country and of managers pressuring their workers to turn out. In the region of Ingushetia, for example, the official turnout rate for the previous December's parliamentary elections was 98 percent, and the president of the region, former KGB agent and Putin ally Murat Zyazikov, predicted a similarly "massive" turnout for the 2008 presidential vote.[55] While Ingushetia's official turnout was reported as over 92 percent, independent observers estimated that the region's actual turnout was as low as 3.5 percent.[56]

Some Russians have turned to unconventional participation methods. Even in the early post-Soviet period, survey results indicated that Russians were comparatively open to unconventional participation.[57] Actual participation in one or more of what comparativists Ronald Inglehart and Gabriela Catterberg call "elite-challenging actions," however, was lower in the post-Soviet period than before and during the collapse of the Soviet system.[58] While most Russians eschew unconventional tactics, terrorist attacks by supporters of independence for the region of Chechnya included the Moscow theater hostage crisis in 2002 in which more than one hundred people died and the school hostage crisis in the city of Beslan in 2004 that ended in the death of more than three hundred children and adults.

Programmatic versus Clientelistic Linkage

The collapse of the Soviet system discredited the idea that politics should center on a single ideology. With few exceptions, political parties were fragile and often issued vague policy platforms. It was particularly difficult for voters to develop firm attachments to parties in favor of market economic reforms. Instead, Russian politics was highly personalized. Parties formed around popular individuals, and personality triumphed over policy substance.

During the Soviet period, clientelism was less about connecting the elite to the masses than about connecting the different layers of the elite to each other. Within the Communist Party, the key to moving up was to know someone at a higher level. With the Soviet collapse in 1991, personal political ties remained central in Russian politics. Organized crime, with its own brand of clientelism, became a fundamental part of Russian life in the early post-Soviet period and bled into the halls of government. President Putin cracked down on corruption but rarely targeted his own political associates. Instead, he used the existence of corrupt clientelist practices as an excuse to target political opponents, while quietly supporting such practices by his political allies.

In addition to traditional clientelism, pre-Soviet, Soviet, and post-Soviet Russian society has been organized through a system based on *blat* (the Russian word for "connections"). Although the blat system did not extend to ordinary people to the same extent that it functioned at the elite level, ordinary citizens were not excluded from it. Even those without membership in the Communist Party knew people with the ability to provide access to a particular good or service—or at least knew someone who knew someone with such an ability. The person who received a benefit through his or her connections (in Russian, *po blatu*) was not necessarily expected to return the favor immediately or through monetary payment. Rather, blat was a system of interactions in which favors were eventually repaid in one form or another over time.

Interest Groups, Social Movements, and Civil Society

Independent interest groups emerged during the early post-Soviet period, but Russia never developed a highly pluralist arrangement. The business community developed close ties with the government, and the line between the government and private companies, as well as organized criminal groups, was at times difficult to discern. Private businesses first benefited from the privatization of state property and then watched as the government began to increase its presence in the economy as an owner of large businesses. Although state corporatism may be the best descriptor of the present Russian interest group system, the renewal of a state control system is not difficult to imagine.

In the late Soviet period, social movements became widespread. Mikhail Gorbachev's policies allowed a genuine civil society to emerge. People followed and talked about political events, and they participated in a large number of conventional and unconventional political activities. Environmentalists, for example, protested past and present Soviet policies, and their collaboration with nationalist movements in a number of union republics played a role in the USSR's ultimate collapse.

Following that collapse, Russian social movements faced a number of challenges. Many in the general Russian population were politically burnt out, the economy was a mess throughout the 1990s, and the creeping authoritarianism of the Putin period made autonomous activity and unconventional participation potentially more costly than it had been under Boris Yeltsin. As a result, local and national political elites increasingly manipulated social movements for their own ends.[59]

Blat The Russian word for "connections," used to describe the prevalence of clientelism and interpersonal relationships in which favors are exchanged between elites, between elites and masses, and between members of the general population.

China

Because China's Communist Party (CCP) still attempts to control the political system tightly, conventional participation has less of an impact in China than in many of the other TIC cases. In China, a form of programmatic linkage existed in the past when the CCP worked to convince the general population that its vision was correct. Linkage in today's China is more pragmatic than programmatic. As with other one-party systems, the CCP has been highly suspicious of autonomous organizations, especially of interest groups concerned about government policy.

Political Participation

The Chinese population has often seen participating in officially sanctioned activities as more of a duty, or simply in people's personal self-interest, than as a right. However, it would be a mistake to assume that the Chinese avoid conventional participation. First, as discussed in more detail in the next chapter, China allows relatively open elections at the village level. Whether this will spread to higher levels of government remains to be seen, but the village elections have given at least some Chinese a taste of participating in elections where the outcome is not predetermined. Second, citizens often take steps to report lower-level government officials whom they believe are unresponsive, ineffective, or corrupt. These actions include letter writing or in-person appeals to higher-level authorities, as well as efforts to use local media outlets—and increasingly the Internet—to put pressure on the individual official in question.

Unconventional participation has also had a notable impact on Chinese politics. The best-known incidents have been on a large scale, such as the June 1989 Tiananmen Square uprising. The government's harsh response to the demonstration effectively limited similar actions for years afterward. Instead of massive protests in the largest cities, subsequent protests were often small and concerned with local issues.

During the 2000s, unconventional participation mostly took the form of protests in rural areas of China, often against corrupt local officials, specific economic conditions in the region, or government-approved land seizures for development. Government estimates put the number of what Chinese officials call "mass group incidents" in the tens of thousands annually at the beginning of the twenty-first century.[60] From 2003 to early 2008 alone, around fifty thousand protests over land seizures and poor compensation were reported. In 2009, the Chinese government adopted a law designed to better handle grievances by farmers involved in land disputes. The law went into effect in 2010, and early that year the Chinese government also promised increased government spending in rural areas. Yet, throughout 2010 and into 2011, rural protests continued.

Programmatic versus Clientelistic Linkage

In one-party systems, the party typically uses an official ideology to link itself to the masses. In China, the importance of ideology has been on the decline since the death of Mao Zedong. Once the CCP allowed capitalists (business owners) to be members, it was hard to see how the party based itself on Communist ideology. Some programmatic elements remain, but rather than Communist ideology, the CCP emphasizes economic development and nationalism.

Clientelism and personal connections have a lot to do with how people interact with government officials and how government officials interact with each other. Clientelist arrangements have always been part of politics under the rule of the CCP, especially at the local level.[61] Even with the introduction of post-Mao economic reforms, clientelist connections never went away. In fact, as corruption has become an increasingly serious problem in Chinese politics, clientelism has become even more evident. In a setting where the government directly controls much less of the country's wealth than it used to, government officials are still able to use their positions of authority to improve their personal social and economic standing.

As in the blat system in Russia, ordinary Chinese have often relied on their personal connections to get things they need. Known as the *guanxi* (pronounced gwan-shee) system, the use of personal networks in China has subtle differences from its Russian counterpart. Many Russians view engaging in blat transactions as pleasurable, while Chinese view the performance of services through guanxi as a social responsibility. At the same time, the loss of blat is more serious than the loss of guanxi, often being perceived as a matter of life and death.[62]

Guanxi also shares many features with blat. Both imply repeated exchanges between individuals who are familiar with each other, and both combine trust and cooperation with power and domination.[63] Also like the Russian system of blat, guanxi has declined slightly in its use and importance with the development of a market economy. Connections remain important, but in both countries, corruption can often involve large sums of money and increasingly includes payments to strangers.

Interest Groups, Social Movements, and Civil Society

The CCP-led government has co-opted, created, and directly or indirectly controlled nongovernmental organizations. Yet, far from involving the absolute state control common to one-party systems, the interest group system appears more corporatist. Interest groups in China are used and closely watched by the state, but they are no longer completely controlled by it. This approach has

worked to limit the size and organizational capacity of individual protests, if not their overall numbers. By continuing to curtail civil society groups that might organize larger protests, the Chinese government has prevented pockets of discontent from turning into effective social movements.

As economic and social interests gain more power and become more autonomous from the state, interest groups may seek to co-opt government officials rather than the other way around. China specialist Bruce Dickson points out that some scholars see China losing control of interest groups to the extent that societal corporatism will come to replace state corporatist arrangements.[64] China is not there yet; government officials still keep close watch on politically relevant interest groups. It will be interesting to watch how interest groups relate to the state in the future.

IN THEORY AND PRACTICE

The Military-Industrial Complex in China

For political scientists who study interest groups, an important set of arguments concerns the concept of subgovernments. These arguments, which one could collectively call **subgovernment theory**, emphasize how interest groups concerned about a particular issue create a "subgovernment" by working closely with interested legislators and bureaucrats who have the authority to make decisions regarding that issue. Theories about subgovernments often discuss them as an **iron triangle**. The term *triangle* captures the way in which a subgovernment's components are connected, while *iron* refers to how a subgovernment prevents other entities from penetrating the triangle.

As Figure 8.3 shows, an iron triangle is made up of a government agency working on a certain issue, those responsible for producing legislation on the issue and overseeing the agency (e.g., Congress in the United States), and interest groups that work on the issue. Because these groups control large amounts of information, policies and government spending may reflect their shared interests. As discussed in the previous chapter, the agency's tasks may include both regulating the interest groups and making significant policy decisions. Government agencies in the United States help perpetuate iron triangles by including pet projects of key members of Congress in their budget requests.[65]

Subgovernment Theory A theoretical perspective that emphasizes the extent to which interest groups concerned about a particular issue create a subgovernment by working closely with interested legislators and bureaucrats.

Iron Triangle A set of three groups with similar interests on a particular topic: government agencies, those responsible for overseeing the agencies, and interest groups pushing for particular policies related to the work of the agency.

Guanxi The Chinese term for the system of personal connections that shares some features with the blat system in Russia.

FIGURE 8.3   **An Iron Triangle**

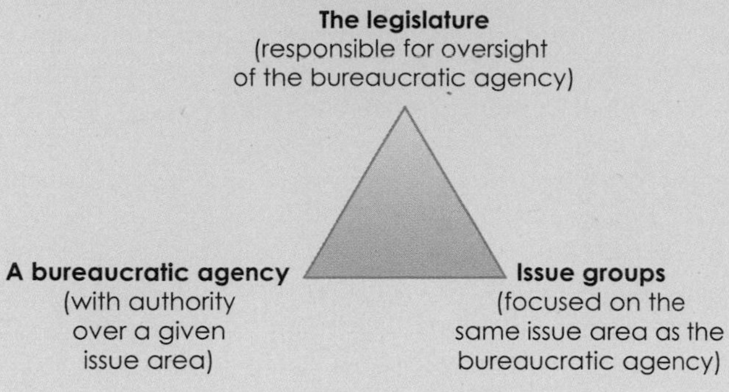

The legislature
(responsible for oversight
of the bureaucratic agency)

A bureaucratic agency
(with authority
over a given
issue area)

Issue groups
(focused on the
same issue area as the
bureaucratic agency)

A well-known example of an iron triangle is the **military-industrial complex (MIC)**, a term made famous by U.S. President Dwight Eisenhower in his farewell address. In the U.S., the MIC involves Congress, defense contractors, and the military and related executive branch entities such as the Department of Defense. These three components have the potential to control information about military capabilities and needs and have a shared interest in maximizing defense spending. The military wants spending increases to improve effectiveness and better protect soldiers. Members of Congress view defense spending increases as a chance to get money for their districts. Contractors like that more defense spending increases profits.

The CCP both closely monitors the activities of the Chinese military and allows it a certain degree of autonomy. Can subgovernment theory help explain this? Is there an MIC in China? Observers of China often use the MIC label, but until the late 1990s, it was difficult to fit China into an iron triangle framework because the military controlled all three corners of the triangle.

Following the launch of economic reforms, the government began to discuss the need to privatize weapons production. In 1998, Chinese leader Jiang Zemin announced an end to the practice of military control of weapons production. As a result, civilian enterprises, both state-owned and privately controlled, have largely taken over arms production under careful government regulation.[66] This has made the MIC in China more typical in that the military has become a consumer of weapons, with production shifting to weapons manufacturing industries, and with the process overseen and financed by the government.

Think and Discuss

To what extent does the logic behind the concept of an MIC make sense? What might prevent the three groups from working together to increase defense spending?

Military-Industrial Complex (MIC) A hypothesized form of iron triangle in the U.S. in which the military and Department of Defense, Congress, and defense contractors control and manipulate information to justify increased defense spending.

Iran

Supporters of the Iranian Islamic Revolution saw the shah as too secular, too isolated, and too authoritarian. Accordingly, the 1979 revolution was about reinvigorating the practice of Islam in the country and increasing representation of the general population within the halls of government. When revolutions have multiple and discordant goals, it is not unusual for one goal to be sacrificed for another. In Iran, the goal of making Iranian society less secular and more Islamic quickly took precedence over the goal of making Iranian politics more democratic. Clientelism in Iran predated the Islamic Revolution. It survived the disruptions that the revolution unleashed, and it has become a particularly noticeable feature of Iranian politics since Ayatollah Khomeini's death in 1989. In a system like Iran's, it would be unusual to find a large civil society with a wide array of social movements and interest groups functioning independently of the state. Some interest groups, however, are granted significant autonomy, and a small number of social movements function despite the government's opposition.

Political Participation

Despite Iran's limited (at best) democratic features, people do participate. The 2005 presidential election garnered almost 60 percent turnout, and the election in 2009 saw a huge turnout, estimated at more than 85 percent. The power of unelected bodies like the Guardian Council and their ability to limit the extent of contestation in national elections, however, mean that many Iranian citizens have turned to unconventional participation or, more often, have chosen to withdraw from politics.

Mass protests occasionally materialize in Iran, such as the sizable pro-democracy demonstrations that took place in 1999, 2002, and 2003 and important protests in support of women's rights in 2005 and 2006. The best-known recent example of large-scale unconventional participation came in the aftermath of the June 2009 presidential election. After the incumbent, Mahmoud Ahmadinejad, was declared the winner with around 62 percent of the vote, supporters of his main challenger, Mir Hossein Mousavi, took to the streets. The resulting Green Revolution (named for the color used by Mousavi's campaign) failed to force Ahmadinejad's resignation. These unconventional actions sent a strong signal to the government that the support for reform evident during the presidency of Mohammed Khatami (1997–2005) had not disappeared, particularly among younger Iranians. Because the protesters were disproportionately young and often spread news to each other using new media sources, the 2009 uprisings also came to be called the "Twitter Revolution."

Despite the ongoing, and arguably growing, frustrations of many Iranian citizens, the nature of the political system makes large-scale unconventional actions infrequent. Not only does unconventional political behavior carry potentially significant costs, but also the system is designed to make most Iranians believe that unconventional participation is unlikely to achieve its goals. Consequently, the Iranian masses are most likely to engage in conventional participation or to choose not to participate at all. Like the unconventional forms of participation, nonparticipation has been common among younger urban residents of Iran.

Programmatic versus Clientelistic Linkage

According to sociologist Kazem Alamdari, Ayatollah Khomeini's death in 1989 marked the end of populism and the blossoming of clientelism.[67] Clientelism has formed around rival government power bases, such as former president Akbar Hashemi Rafsanjani, and it corresponds to a "combination of the patrimonial and the saintly, in which both traditional and religious relations between superior and subordinates have been revived."[68] Heavy regulation of the economy and a powerful bureaucracy have reinforced clientelism, hurting Iran's chances to use its oil wealth to benefit the general population.

At the same time, programmatic appeals have a certain importance. Those vocally supportive of an overhaul of Iran's theocracy are unlikely to be allowed to run for political office and may be jailed. However, Iranian voters have become sophisticated at picking up on subtle differences in what candidates in Majles, the Iranian legislature, or presidential elections say about social relations, gender, the economy, and global interconnections.

Interest Groups, Social Movements, and Civil Society

The structure of interactions between the state and interest groups in Iran is difficult to categorize. A narrow range of groups that the state believes aids its cause function in a quasi-pluralistic manner. Those that perform regime-supportive functions are allowed to keep a good deal of the wealth they generate and/or receive significant financial support from the government. Other groups are more closely tied to the state in a form of state corporatism. Some are wholly the creation of and tightly controlled by the state, while still other potential groups are repressed and prevented from engaging in political activities.

Like narrower interest groups, some broad social movements exist outside government control, particularly the movement for increased rights for women. At the same

time, as discussed in the "In Theory and Practice" box in this section, it is dangerous to engage in unconventional participation in Iran. In addition, Iran's political institutions are designed to insulate the government from popular pressure. While the president and Majles may feel some need to respond to popular demands, the existence of institutions such as the Supreme Leader and the Guardian Council reflect the idea that the clerics in the Iranian government know better than ordinary citizens what is in the best interests of the country.

IN THEORY AND PRACTICE

The Collective Action Problem and Iran

Many political scientists who work on political behavior related to interest groups and social movements focus on how rational individuals would behave based on the circumstances in which they find themselves. Chapter 10 discusses the role of rationality in political outcomes in greater detail. Here, it is necessary to consider the difficulty of getting rational individuals to engage in collective activities, such as participating in interest groups. While scholars like David Truman believe that interest groups form naturally (see the "In Theory and Practice" box on Mexico on pages 244–245), others have questioned whether sacrificing time and money to work on a particular cause is rational for any individual. This was the topic of a classic work on interest groups and one of the most influential social science works in the second half of the twentieth century: Mancur Olson's 1965 *The Logic of Collective Action*.[69]

Olson sought to understand why individuals join a group if membership imposes costs—membership dues, time commitments, and so on—but the benefits generated by the group are broadly available to nonmembers. With costs targeted to individual members but benefits spread out to everyone, individuals have strong incentives not to join the organization. The problem posed by these incentives to "free ride" is known as the **collective action problem** (also sometimes called the "free rider problem"). Olson's work helped make the collective action problem a central social science concept. The implications of targeting or spreading out costs and benefits of collective actions help clarify the tactics of membership in groups, such as one of the most important interest groups in the United States, the AARP.

Collective Action Problem The difficulty of getting a rational person to participate in a collective activity if the costs of participating are targeted to those who participate but benefits generated are available to the general public; also sometimes called the free-rider problem.

In comparative politics, Olson's ideas help us understand the difficulties of organizing political activity in many countries. Iranian interest groups are fewer in number and function less openly than their counterparts in more democratic systems. Those that do prosper often generate sizable revenues from their activities, and group members are allowed to keep a large amount of this wealth for themselves. In such circumstances, the collective action problem is less severe than it is for most interest groups. Rather than collective benefits, the groups' activities produce concentrated benefits, which more than outweigh the costs of participating in the activities.

For groups that challenge the Iranian system, however, the collective action problem is more severe than normal. These groups seek benefits spread across the general population, but the costs of participating in social movement and interest group activities are concentrated on the participants. In Iran, such costs are not just money and time. Individuals who challenge the state and its conservative social order risk arrest or even death. Unless President Ahmadinejad is successful in challenging the wealth-concentrating nature of the current Iranian system, one would expect interest groups that play the game of clientelism and corruption to continue to thrive and those that seek social and economic reform to continue to struggle.

TIC Wrap-Up

Across the nine Topic in Countries cases, levels and forms of political participation, patterns of clientelist and programmatic linkage, and the presence and organization of social movements and interest groups display similarities and differences.

Political participation in the UK, Germany, and India is often conventional, yet all three have seen instances of unconventional participation over the last several decades. These incidents of unconventional participation rarely threaten the overall stability of the political systems of the consolidated democracies. At the same time, the growth of violence related to the situation of immigrants has concerned leaders in the two European cases, while in India the government has been unable to put an end to the many instances of unconventional participation by radical Communist groups.

Personal connections and clientelist relationships were central to the political systems of the UK and Germany long ago, but programmatic appeals became more important over time. The pattern of programmatic appeals replacing clientelism also emerged in India. The Indian case highlights the importance of not necessarily associating corruption, which is still a problem in India, with an extensive system of clientelist interactions between citizens and political elites.

The UK, Germany, and India show how social movements can play a visible role in politics and also the extent to which approaches to interest group organization can vary within democracies. In both the UK and Germany, environmentalism, the peace movement, women's groups, and broad mobilization on both sides of the immigration issue have been part of the landscape of domestic politics. In India, the desire for greater regional autonomy has been a major issue driving social movement development, along with the environment and concerns over the treatment of *Dalits* ("untouchables") in the caste system. Relations between the state and interest groups are based on societal corporatism in Germany. In the UK and India, the trend has been away from corporatism and toward pluralism.

Living in relatively young democracies, the populations of Mexico, Brazil, and Nigeria are to an extent still getting used to the ability to participate in conventional ways that can have meaningful results. The voting rates in Brazil, the eldest of the three democracies, have been both the highest and the most consistent over the past two decades. The three countries have shared prevalent instances of violent unconventional participation in recent years, often from groups that believe that they have been abandoned by the political system.

Mexico, Brazil, and Nigeria also share a long history of clientelist approaches to elite-mass linkage and a continuation of these practices even during the current period of democracy. Democracy has brought some increased importance to programmatic appeals, but elites and masses continue to be linked through clientelism more than through programmatic alternatives.

With democratization, interest groups and social movements in Mexico, Brazil, and Nigeria have gained renewed importance. Along with Mexico's slow retreat from clientelism, the old corporatist system dominated by the Institutional Revolutionary Party has become notably weaker over the last decade. Brazil's corporatist system, on the other hand, has largely survived democratization, partly because it was tied to the state rather than to a single political party as in Mexico. Not all interest groups have agreed to play by Brazil's corporatist rules, choosing confrontation over cooperation. With the return of democracy to Nigeria, as imperfect as it may be, interest groups, which had existed to an extent even during military rule, have become increasingly important. In all three countries, democracy has helped foster an increasingly conspicuous—though, in Nigeria's case, still developing—civil society.

The governments of the Russian Federation, China, and Iran closely monitor mass participation and seek to direct it in ways supportive of the regime. Although these three systems are far from models of free and fair elections, citizens find other ways to participate. These include conventional participatory activities, such as presenting grievances to government officials, and unconventional activities, from nonviolent protests to violent clashes with the police or military.

Clientelism and the general importance of personal connections is a dominant theme in Russian, Chinese, and Iranian politics. In Russia, programmatic approaches failed to take hold in the early post-Soviet period. In China, elites and masses are increasingly distant politically and are primarily linked through clientelism. Both Russia and China also have their own versions of patronage-based linkage systems, blat and guanxi, respectively, which link masses and elites as well as link members of the general population with each other. In Iran, clientelism drives many political outcomes, though subtle programmatic appeals related to political and social reform can affect electoral results.

Despite facing co-optation and outright repression, interest groups and social movements continue to exist in Russia, China, and Iran. Their autonomy from the state and their impact on political outcomes in these countries is more limited than in most of the other TIC cases. In Russia, social movements and autonomous interest groups, which exploded onto the scene during the late Soviet and early post-Soviet periods, have increasingly become targets of the government under Vladimir Putin. In China, interest groups are brought into politics through a corporatist approach. In Iran, some groups that are seen as supportive of the regime have some control over their own affairs, although the development of new interest groups and social movements remains a challenge. Those likely to be perceived as potentially threatening to the theocratic system find it hard to recruit members.

COUNTRY SUMMARY

TIC Country	Political Participation	Programmatic versus Clientelist Linkage	Interest Groups, Social Movements, and Civil Society
United Kingdom	Lower levels of conventional participation than in other European countries; unconventional participation exists but is relatively rare	Clientelism existed in the past, largely connected to the feudal system; programmatic linkage dominates today	Less corporatist than in the past; greater emphasis on lobbying, especially early in a bill's development; many social movements, including ones surrounding immigration today; vibrant civil society
Germany	High levels of voting, lower levels of other conventional participation; incidents of unconventional participation throughout German history, but less common today	Past clientelism connected to feudalism but also existed in East Germany under Communist rule; programmatic linkage today, but largest parties' platforms became more similar over time	Societal corporatist system of interest group organization; social movements formed around environmentalism and peace; civil society was limited after World War II in West Germany and after Communist rule in East Germany, but increased over time
India	Conventional participation at rates lower than in Europe; unconventional participation activities are common	Emergence of the INC and the BJP led to programmatic appeals; clientelism less common than in other developing countries, but does exist	INC controlled interest groups until the 1970s; more traditional pluralism today; social movements develop but do not always last, often forming around environmental or regional autonomy issues

TIC Country	Political Participation	Programmatic versus Clientelist Linkage	Interest Groups, Social Movements, and Civil Society
Mexico	Voter turnout high during liberalization period; lower once democracy was established; Mexicans less likely to engage in unconventional participation than others in Latin America; Chiapas uprising is an exception	PRI used clientelism to help maintain its dominance over Mexican politics; clientelism remains today, but competitive party politics has increased the importance of programmatic appeals	System of party corporatism under the PRI; liberalization weakened this system; social movements under the PRI uncommon, but 1960s student protests; social movement opposing drug-related violence emerging today; visible civil society; ITAP feature on disturbance theory
Brazil	High turnout rates in elections; organized labor-led unconventional participation	Clientelism is the primary form of elite-mass linkage; local governments working to undermine clientelism through participatory budgeting	State corporatist approach to interest group organization; numerous social movements around social problems; the Landless Movement (MST) has coordinated land seizures; vibrant civil society
Nigeria	Moderate turnout rates in elections; unconventional participation is common, especially in the Niger Delta region	Military governments used and deepened clientelism; clientelism has remained important during democracy, with local party officials relying on it	Interest groups often tied to a region or identity groups; national presence for key labor organizations; social movements and civil society have reemerged under democracy, but some groups have turned to violence and other forms of unconventional participation
Russia	Moderate to high turnout, but some local officials add to the official numbers to look good; less unconventional participation than in the 1990s, but terrorist acts related to Chechnya continued into the 2000s	Collapse of USSR discredited ideology; post-Soviet politics has been highly personalized; clientelism did exist in the Soviet Union, reinforced by the long-standing emphasis on blat (connections)	Interest groups have limited independence; system today is somewhere between state corporatism and state control; an explosion of social movements and civil society in the late Soviet and early post-Soviet periods died down over the following decade
China	CCP encourages and controls conventional participation; unconventional acts include many localized protests; no major, regime-threatening events since Tiananmen Square in 1989	Clientelism is primary form of linkage; most common at the local level, but exists at all levels; similar to blat system in Russia, Chinese rely on guanxi (personal networks) for many things they need	Interest groups no longer completely controlled by the state; social movements limited by the government's suspicion of any regime-threatening aspects of civil society; ITAP feature on the military-industrial complex

TIC Country	Political Participation	Programmatic versus Clientelist Linkage	Interest Groups, Social Movements, and Civil Society
Iran	Moderate to high voter turnout rates (2009 turnout was very high); some unconventional protests, including the Green Revolution protests following the 2009 presidential election	Clientelism increasingly common since Ayatollah Khomeini's death in 1989; subtle programmatic differences signal to voters which candidates may be supportive of political reform	Quasi-pluralist approach for regime-supportive interest groups; social movements are limited due to government repression; occasional mass activities on the issue of the treatment of women; ITAP feature on the collective action problem

Spotlight on . . . Country

TIC Country	Political Participation	Programmatic versus Clientelist Linkage	Interest Groups, Social Movements, and Civil Society
France	Moderate to high turnout levels, especially for presidential elections; unconventional participation is common, especially by labor unions, farmers, and students	Complicated mix of programmatic and clientelist political organizing; patronage practices common at the local level	"Concertation" approach, where interest groups are brought into negotiations but results less binding than in corporatism; social movements and civil society are weak by European standards, but new social movements have developed
Iraq	Moderate to low turnout in national and regional elections; Sunni population demanding more representation after initially withdrawing from Iraq's developing democratic arrangements; women increasingly participating in politics	Under Saddam, Baath Party ruled through clientelism and repression; clientelism continues today, with identity-based connections prominent; personalized politics continues, but with some programmatic differences between political parties	Interest groups developing slowly; Islamist movements appeared during the U.S. occupation, but less influential today; women's movements have struggled to find broad support; with foreign assistance, civil society groups have begun to emerge, but many are hesitant to criticize government officials
South Africa	Voter turnout comparatively high; struggle against apartheid included unconventional forms of participation; since 1994, unconventional actions have decreased but not disappeared	Clientelism prevalent, particularly at the regional and local levels; dominance of the African National Congress (ANC) weakens the potential for a programmatic alternative	Corporatist approach, with unions and business groups connected to the National Economic Development and Labour Council (NEDLAC); some social movements opposing neoliberal economics exist; civil society groups formed the Movement for Good to encourage volunteerism

Research in Context

As highlighted in the opening chapter of this book, the scientific research process involves identifying interesting research questions, defining key concepts, gathering data, making sense of the data with categories to group the information in meaningful ways, and hypothesizing about and investigating the relationships between variables to explain the resulting patterns. Each part of this process is important. It makes little sense, for example, to try to understand the causes of a particular pattern before one knows whether such a pattern exists. In addition, looking at how the observations or values for a particular variable fall into different categories can point to new research questions one might not have considered. The research project summarized in this section identifies patterns and raises questions for study.

Measuring Interest Group Participation in European Union Politics

In 2010, four scholars who study the European Union (EU)—Arndt Wonka, Frank Baumgartner, Christine Mahoney, and Joost Berkhout—published a research article in the journal *European Union Politics*.[70] The article, "Measuring the Size and Scope of the EU Interest Group Population," summarizes findings from a new data set the researchers created of organizations that lobby EU political institutions. Thus, their project was a data-gathering and categorizing exercise. It tested no hypotheses, and the article says little about existing comparative politics theories related to lobbying and interest groups. Yet, the project's data have the potential to play an important role in inspiring a variety of new research projects on how interest groups affect political outcomes in the EU.

The researchers tackled this data-gathering and organizing exercise because existing measures of groups lobbying the decision-making institutions of the EU were flawed. Simply put, there was no valid data set that combined the different existing lists of lobbying groups registered by the EU. The researchers combined information from three such lists, eliminated duplicate entries, and checked the validity of the remaining 3,700 entries.

In a very important step for spurring future research, they also categorized the groups they identified by the type of interest each group represents and each group's country of origin. Their article presents some of these findings, including the finding that corporations are the second most common type of lobbying group (behind "professional associations and interest groups"). Groups representing regions (including municipalities) within the EU constitute the third most common type. For those interested in how the EU interacts with subnational political units of EU member states, this finding indicates that studying how such subnational units lobby the EU could be an important area of research.

Perhaps the most interesting findings come from their breakdown of the country of origin of each lobbying group. Not surprisingly, the three most common countries of origin are the three largest EU member states: the UK, Germany, and France. But, perhaps not so expected, the United States was tied for the fourth most common country of origin for groups lobbying the EU. The United States had more EU-registered lobbying organizations than seventeen of the twenty-seven EU member states combined.[71]

So What?

Some comparative politics research projects have less potential for impact on the American public than others. At first glance, this project would appear to be one of the lesser-impact ones. Yet, it is possible, particularly given the finding in the data set about the large number of American-based organizations, that the data could spark new research projects on how U.S. interests are injected into EU policy debates. With the strong political, economic, and security connections between the United States and Europe, such research projects might play a role, however large or small, in shaping future European-American relations. Thus, there is a potential indirect impact on the United States by fostering research about American public policy. At this stage, it is unclear how effectively the data set will stimulate new research projects, but more information for comparativists to use is always better than less.

It is also important to consider the study's potential importance for other populations. The value of the research to EU citizens, for example, could be significant. The authors claim that one potential use of the data set would be to help determine how democratic the inner workings of the EU are, and how EU officials might reform the organization to better represent the views of member states' populations.

CONCLUSION

This chapter explored the concepts of elites and masses, alternative forms of mass participation, and ways that political elites are linked to the general population in different countries. The forms of participation and linkage range from the public and malicious (such as terrorism), to the quiet and difficult to observe (such as backroom interest group lobbying).

In the 1950s, C. Wright Mills portrayed the United States as having a society with an "increasingly unified . . . elite of power," a middle level comprised of a "drifting set of stalemated, balancing forces," and a bottom that is "politically fragmented" and "increasingly powerless."[72] One could argue that this portrayal fits developing countries such as Nigeria and Iran better than the United States. Even in those countries, however, at least some of these "powerless" members of the "bottom" of society seek to influence the political system by means of both conventional and unconventional participation, through the support of interest groups, and by working with international organizations to further their cause.

By examining forms of participation and elite-mass linkage, this chapter also marked the beginning of a progression in the book toward the idea that that one should take into account individuals and their decisions as causal factors affecting political outcomes. This focus continues across the next two chapters, on parties and elections (Chapter 9) and on leadership and individual decision making (Chapter 10).

KEY TERMS

Advocacy group, p. 235
Attentive public, p. 233
Blat, p. 248
Civil society, p. 237
Civil society organizations (CSOs), p. 237
Clientelism, p. 232
Collective action problem, p. 251
Conventional participation, p. 230
Corporatism, p. 235
Disturbance theory, p. 244
Economic group, p. 234
Guanxi, p. 249

Interest group, p. 234
Iron triangle, p. 249
Local issue group, p. 235
Masses, p. 230
Military-industrial complex (MIC), p. 250
Neo-corporatism, p. 236
Nepotism, p. 230
New social movements, p. 233
NIMBY, p. 235
Party corporatism, p. 244
Peak organization, p. 235
Pluralism, p. 235

Political elite, p. 229
Political participation, p. 230
Power elite, p. 229
Programmatic representation, p. 232
Social movement, p. 233
Societal corporatism, p. 235
State control system, p. 236
State corporatism, p. 235
Subgovernment theory, p. 249
Unconventional participation, p. 230

Women in Tehran, Iran, fill in their ballots for the Majles (national legislature) election, March 14, 2008.
AP Photo/Vahid Salemi

CHAPTER OUTLINE

Political Parties and Party Systems
Elections and Electoral Systems

TOPIC IN COUNTRIES

Features in this chapter:

Spotlight on . . . France: Elections in a Semipresidential System

In Theory and Practice: Duverger's Law and British Elections

In Theory and Practice: Realignment Theory and Germany

In Theory and Practice: Party Organization Theory and Mexico

Research in Context: Islamic Parties and Islamic Politics in Indonesia

After reading this chapter, you should be able to

- Describe how political parties differ from interest groups.
- Differentiate among the types of party systems.
- Characterize the alternative electoral arrangements used in democratic elections, and explain the relationship between electoral systems and party systems.
- Describe the party systems and key electoral outcomes in the Topic in Countries cases.

In February 2008, Ali Eshraghi was informed that he would not be allowed to run for a seat in the Majles, Iran's national legislature. He had registered to run, but his candidacy was rejected by an Interior Ministry committee. The committee's ruling was the first step of a three-stage process of vetting potential Majles candidates. In some ways, Eshraghi's fate was not unique. He was one of more than two thousand candidates rejected by the committee. What made his story exceptional were his family ties. Eshraghi was the grandson of Ayatollah Ruhollah Khomeini, who was Iran's Supreme Leader from the 1979 Islamic Revolution until his death in 1989.

Eshraghi publicly questioned the decision and criticized investigations during the vetting process, during which neighbors were interviewed about his personal life, "including if he shaved, smoked and what kind of car he drove."[1] The outrage over his situation forced a reversal, and Eshraghi was allowed on the ballot. He ended up withdrawing from the race before the election, however, after stories about his personal life began circulating on Iranian Web sites. Although the committee's decision had been overturned, the initial rejection of Eshraghi's candidacy shows the degree to which the leaders of Iran's theocracy fear anyone who may support political and social reform. It also shows how, even in a political system like Iran's, elections matter.

The previous chapter introduced the concept of elite-mass linkage by focusing on topics such as conventional and unconventional participation, clientelism, and interest groups. This chapter looks at the process of selecting candidates for political office and the grouping of those candidates within political parties in much more detail. It turns to the important structures that link masses and elites that were not focused on in the previous chapter: political parties, party systems, elections, and various alternative electoral arrangements, including those in Iran that prevented Ali Eshraghi from running for a seat in the Majles.

Political Parties and Party Systems

Political parties are the most politically relevant groups in most political systems. A **political party** is an organization that seeks political office, typically through participation in elections. Those competing for and holding office openly share the label of their political party. The pursuit of political office is a key difference between parties and interest groups.

> **Political Party** An organization that articulates its stance on a large number of policy positions and runs candidates for political office.

In addition, while an interest group tends to focus on a single issue, a political party must make its positions known on a large number of issues. In political science, the phrase that captures this is the need for parties to "articulate and aggregate interests." In his famous work on political parties, the French scholar Maurice Duverger pointed out that such articulation not only helps link parties to their followers but also binds together the smaller units of a national party (branches, local organizations, etc.). As Duverger puts it, a party "is not a community but a collection of communities."[2] The specific interests and communities that parties aggregate are typically related to one another as part of an overarching ideological perspective. As discussed in Chapter 3, ideological divisions within a society are often reflected in the varying broad perspectives of that society's major political parties.

The Value of Political Parties

Political parties receive a great deal of criticism, and they have generally declined in strength around the world over the last several decades.[3] However, they also have important functions. For example, political parties are a central link between the elites and masses, especially in democratic systems. Many parties present an overall vision about the relationship between government and society, as well as propose specific policy changes that they plan to implement once in office. This combination of broad ideological views and policy-specific positions means that political parties are crucial facilitators of the programmatic linkage approach discussed in the previous chapter.

Parties also simplify the decision-making process for voters by bringing together politicians who share similar views. A party label carries a rough summary of that party's candidates' ideological leanings. Because parties make their general views known, voters need not learn the specific policy positions of every candidate. In Germany, for example, a voter for whom environmentalism is the most important issue may vote for a Green Party candidate, even without knowing much about that candidate.

Without party labels, it would also be harder to hold political leaders accountable. If voters know that a certain party is in charge, and those voters do not like how things are going in the country, they can punish the party in power by voting for another party. In presidential systems, voters can punish a sitting president fairly easily by voting for someone else. Determining the culpability of individual legislators requires a more nuanced understanding of voting records and political power struggles than most voters possess.

Although the existence of parties that stress ideology-based policy preferences makes programmatic connections between elites and masses easier, not all political parties or party systems are based on the idea of programmatic linkage. Many early parties were highly clientelist.[4] Today, members of some political parties still spend more time and effort promising favors to clients in exchange for support in an upcoming election than they do trying to earn their votes through discussions of ideas and policies. Other political parties continue to center themselves around the personality and popularity of their party leaders more than they emphasize their policy positions.

Party Identification

Party Identification An individual's attachment to a particular political party.

Because of the importance of political parties, comparativists also study **party identification**, individuals' attachment to specific political parties. Voters with strong party identification typically support candidates from that party in election after election. Weak party identification has positive and negative effects on a political system. The less people identify with parties, the more fluid the system is, and the larger the swings in the makeup of the government from election to election. Weak party identification also tends to make politics more personalized with the candidate's image becoming more important than the policies the candidate's party stands for. However, weak party identification can also indicate voters who are more moderate, who are paying attention to policies rather than blindly following a party label, and who thus hold parties and candidates more accountable from election to election.

Party Systems

The collection of the main parties in a country makes up that country's **party system**. When looking at party systems, scholars focus on the number of major parties and how polarized they are (how far apart they are on major issues). Comparativists normally put a particular country's party system into one of five categories: one-party, one-party dominant, two-party, two-and-a-half party, and multiparty.

There are many reasons that one country's party system differs from another. For comparativists who study political parties and elections, the two most important factors that influence of the type of party system are the form of the country's electoral system and the extent to which there are sharp identity or ideological divisions within the population. Different electoral arrangements—such as those discussed later in this chapter—provide voters with different incentives, including how much sense it makes to support a smaller political party. Deep social or ideological divisions within a population give a political party a way to differentiate itself from other political parties. Given the potential political power of identity (see Chapter 4) and the political importance of ideology, it makes sense that a country's political parties often reflect such divisions.

The nature of a country's party system also has important consequences. These include its effect on major political outcomes like political stability. Usually, political systems with more parties and with parties that are more polarized are less stable than systems with fewer parties that are more similar to one another on key issues. On the other hand, the more options for a voter to find a match between his or her own political views and those of a political party, the more attached to the political system that voter may become.

The discussion of party systems assumes that parties are important in all countries. However, in some countries, particularly authoritarian systems or very small countries, political parties play a small role or no role at all in elections and in the organization of policy making in the national legislature. The "no-party" system approach is far from the norm around the world, but it has been present in Iran.

One-Party Systems

In totalitarian and some authoritarian systems, a single party coordinates government activities and mobilizes mass support. Such cases are examples of a **one-party system** or single-party system. One party systems have no competitiveness; if elections are held, only candidates from the one party are on the ballot. Voters are not free to remove their support from the ruling party and give it to another.

Comparativist Giovanni Sartori emphasizes that, beyond sharing the core feature of a single party, one-party systems vary greatly in practice: they are "more or less oppressive, more or less pervasive, more or less intolerant."[5] He distinguishes among three types: totalitarian, where the party is ideological, coercive, and destructive of autonomous groups; pragmatic, where the party has much less ideological focus, coercive capacity, and desire to destroy autonomous groups; and authoritarian, which falls between the other two. One could lump his pragmatic and authoritarian categories together, but his point is valuable. The ruling party does not function the same way in all one-party systems, and political leaders do not have the same kinds of goals. Even the same one-party system can evolve from one type to another over time. For example, for several decades after the Communist Revolution China was close to Sartori's totalitarian variant; it is now much more like his authoritarian category of one-party systems.

One-Party Dominant Systems

It is also possible for one party to dominate for long periods of time without completely controlling all aspects of politics. Other political parties are not banned, and a combination of smaller parties may even receive a sizable percentage of the vote, but only the main party is expected to win elections and control the government. Comparativists label this as a **one-party dominant system**. Sartori called such a party "hegemonic"; other parties in the system are "secondary" or "second class."[6] One-party dominant systems can conceal sharp differences within the main party. Factions

Party System A label based on the number of prominent political parties in a country.

One-Party System A party system in which one political party controls the government and voters have no option to choose an opposition party; also known as a single-party system.

One-Party Dominant System A party system in which one large party directs the political system, but small parties exist and may compete in elections.

within that party take the place of the open competition of different parties. The conflicts within the dominant party, however, are generally behind closed doors, which helps foster political stability. The masses are less likely to be drawn into political conflicts than in a system with more equally powerful parties.

One-party dominant systems can exist in both democratic and nondemocratic regimes. In a democratic system, this party system can emerge following a country's independence and/or establishment of democracy, when the key individuals associated with bringing the country its independence or its democracy form a political party. This was the case in India following independence, when the Congress Party (INC) dominated. It was also the case in Japan for much of the period since World War II; the Liberal Democratic Party (LDP) dominated electoral politics until losing control of the government to the Democratic Party of Japan in 2009. When the massive earthquake and tsunami hit Japan in the spring of 2011, many argued that the response of the government reflected its relative inexperience. As relatively minor players in Japanese politics during the latter period of LDP rule, leaders of the Democratic Party of Japan had no firsthand experience in crisis decision making.

In a nondemocratic political system, a one-party dominant system can develop when an otherwise one-party system allows small, nonthreatening parties to exist. In other cases, the government of a nondemocratic system may tolerate smaller parties in the hope of boosting its legitimacy among the general population. This was the case in Poland under Communist Party rule. Sometimes this strategy works. The dominance of the Institutional Revolutionary Party (PRI) in Mexico for much of the twentieth century was partly due to its popularity, even though other, smaller parties existed and garnered some support. Showing the authoritarian nature of the Mexican system, the PRI also engaged in undemocratic manipulation of the political system and elections.

In the case of nondemocratic political systems, one could argue that whether the party system is one-party or one-party dominant makes little difference. Either the main party will control the political system (as in a party authoritarian system), or parties will be relatively unimportant to how the system is run. Examples such as Mexico, however, point out that what appears to be a minor difference can later become important. Because alternative political parties existed and were allowed to compete in national, regional, and local elections, voters who had become disillusioned with PRI rule had ready-made outlets for the expression of their frustration.

Two-Party Systems

Two-Party System A party system in which two main parties compete for majority control of the government; small parties may exist but play no role in national electoral outcomes.

In a **two-party system**, two large parties compete with one another for control of the government. One or the other will gain a majority of the seats in the legislature, making coalition governments unnecessary. Other very small parties may exist, but their success does not translate into a notable number of seats in the national legislature, nor does their degree of electoral success influence which of the two main parties ultimately controls that legislature.

The United States is the classic example of a two-party system. Small "third" parties, such as the Green Party and the Libertarian Party, compete for political office. Only on rare occasions does such a party take a seat even in state government, not to mention at the national level. At times, a strong independent candidate will swing the result of a presidential election (as Ross Perot and Ralph Nader arguably did in the United States in 1992 and 2000, respectively). As the next section discusses in more detail, the electoral system for congressional elections encourages the perpetuation of a party system where the two main parties receive nearly all the votes in U.S. legislative elections.

Two-and-a-Half Party Systems

Two-and-a-Half Party System A party system in which two large parties exist alongside a third party that receives a smaller but notable share of the national vote.

The **two-and-a-half party system** concept was introduced to political science by Jean Blondel in a 1968 article about party systems in Western democracies.[7] As awkward as it is, the term *two-and-a-half party system* stuck, largely because it captured an important feature of these systems: Though a third party exists and has influence, its vote totals and number of seats in the national legislature are significantly lower than those of the two main parties. Blondel differentiated between two-party and two-and-a-half party systems based on the percentage of the national vote that the two main parties receive and the size of the third party compared with the first two over time. Blondel considered the United States a two-party system because the Republicans and Democrats combined earned around 99 percent of the national vote from 1945 to 1966.[8] Blondel also considered the United Kingdom (UK) a two-party system based on voting patterns from the mid-1940s to mid-1960s.[9] Once Blondel's differentiation between two-party and two-and-a-half party systems took hold, however, comparativists increasingly labeled countries like the UK and Canada two-and-a-half party systems.

In two-and-a-half party systems, one of the two largest parties usually gains a majority of the seats in the national legislature. Thus, even though it receives a sizable percentage of the national vote, the third party in a two-and-a-half party system usually does not gain a large enough number of seats to force the creation of a coalition government. Its electoral fortunes still matter from election to election, however, because the votes that one of the large parties loses to the third party determine which of the two large parties controls the government. In addition, when other small parties begin to secure seats, the presence of this third party can prevent a majority government. If this were to happen for a number of subsequent elections, it would mark the transformation of the party system from a two-and-a-half party system to a multiparty one.

Multiparty Systems

The final type of party system is the **multiparty system**. This term is used when a political system has more key parties than does the two-and-a-half party system. Although two of the parties may be larger than the others, these parties are far from dominant. None of the largest parties generally gains a majority of the seats in the national legislature; coalitions are the norm. Generally every decade or so, each of the two largest parties has the opportunity to serve as the main party in a ruling coalition government.

In his famous work on parties and party systems, Duverger reminded his readers that multiparty systems should not be confused with systems in which little party identification exists among the general public.[10] Party identification in multiparty systems can be relatively stable over time, particularly when the main parties reflect deep social divisions. Because the number of relevant parties is greater in a multiparty system, however, even small changes in their electoral fortunes can transform the makeup of the legislature. Consider, for example, a party that earned forty of one hundred seats and formed a coalition with a smaller party that had twelve seats of its own. In the next election, if the large party lost only three seats, it would be unable to form the same coalition to control a majority of the legislative seats, even if the smaller party ended up with the same number of seats.

Figure 9.1 summarizes the differences among party systems on two dimensions: the importance of small parties and the dominance by the largest party in the political system. As one moves from a one-party system to a multiparty type, small parties become increasingly important. In contrast, a single party's ability to dominate the political system wanes.

> **Multiparty System** A party system with several important political parties, none of which generally gains a majority of the seats in the national legislature.

FIGURE 9.1   Political Party Systems

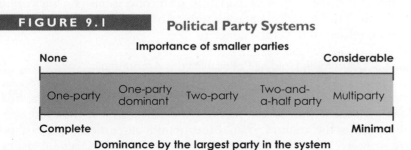

Advantages and Disadvantages of a Large Number of Political Parties

Consider the advantages of a system with many key parties compared with the American-style two-party system. Where the multiparty approach is strong, the two-party system is weak. Likewise, the disadvantages of a multiparty system correspond to the advantages of a two-party system.

Advantage 1: Better Representation of the Masses

The greater the number of political parties, the better the options for voters. Assuming that the parties make their policy views known, the existence of more parties translates into a greater opportunity for voters to find a party that matches their particular combination of views. If a voter is economically liberal but socially conservative, for example, a multiparty system is more likely than a two-party system to have a party with corresponding positions.

Advantage 2: Better Representation of Minority Interests

Along with providing better options, multiparty systems better reflect societal divisions. Smaller groups need not join with larger ones to have a chance to gain seats in a legislature. Thus, increasing the number of major parties increases the likelihood that minority groups will be represented in the national government.

Disadvantage 1: Political Instability Due to Fragile Coalitions

The more parties with seats in the national legislature, the less likely that one party will hold a majority of the seats. In other words, multiparty systems create the need for coalitions to gain the necessary minimum number of seats to pass legislation. In such situations, coalitions become increasingly unstable. Having only a few defections among legislators in a ruling coalition can be enough to kill a policy proposal. Disputes among ruling parties can be fierce, as each party sees itself as key to sustaining the coalition. The result is instability and, in parliamentary systems, the strong possibility of early elections.

Disadvantage 2: Undue Influence of Small and Extreme Parties

Two-party systems tend to force the main parties to the political spectrum's center. If one party's positions become too extreme, the other party will win control by gaining the support of voters on its side of the spectrum and those in the center. Alienating moderate voters, the other party will have the support only of more extreme voters on its side of the spectrum. Next time, this party will likely learn from its mistake and move toward the center as well.

In a multiparty system, there is less need to win the support of moderate voters in order to be influential. As a result, multiparty systems do not encourage parties to moderate their policy positions, and they provide little incentive for people from different groups to find common political ground. In multiparty systems, small and extreme parties often hold seats in the national legislature and have the potential to become key players in the coalition process discussed under disadvantage 1. A larger party might need a small, extreme party to put together a coalition government. In the bargaining that ensues, the small party can gain concessions on issues of importance to it. In the case of parliamentary systems, the small party may also ask for a cabinet position related to its central concerns.

Disadvantage 3: Difficulty in Holding Political Parties Accountable

A final disadvantage is the challenge a large number of parties poses for voters seeking to reward or punish leaders for performance in office. Following from the first two disadvantages, coalitions with several parties can be the norm. If voters are unhappy with the direction of the country, should they punish all parties in the coalition or just the largest party? What if the leader of a small party in the coalition claims that the small party disagreed with the rest of the coalition on a controversial policy, but supported it in order to get a concession on another policy? While a large number of parties give voters more options at election time, they may also make choosing the best party on the basis of government performance a difficult proposition.

Elections and Electoral Systems

One of the main differences between a political party and other types of political organizations is that party members seek political office. The most common way to do this, even in many non-democracies, is through elections. An **election** is a form of conventional mass participation in which individuals express preferences for candidates or political parties seeking political office. It is the primary way that members of a national legislature are selected around the world. In many countries, the chief executive of the government is also directly elected.

While some people grumble about the conduct of political campaigns in the United States, elections are a particularly important form of democratic participation. Democratic elections give ordinary citizens a direct say in determining the leaders of their government. As Adam Przeworski so succinctly puts it, "democracy is a system in which parties lose elections."[11] In other words, unlike elections in nondemocratic systems, where results are predetermined, in democratic systems an election can remove a ruling party or sitting president from power.

Types of Electoral Systems

Elections are considered the backbone of democracy, but there is little agreement about the best set of rules for translating votes into legislative seats. Electoral arrangements can generally be divided into two categories: proportional representation (PR) and first past the post (FPTP). As discussed in Chapter 5, these electoral system types can be combined with the distinction between presidential and parliamentary political systems to create different categories of democracy. These categories include American-style democracy (combining FPTP voting with a presidential system), Westminster democracy (FPTP and parliamentary), Latin American democracy (PR and presidential), and European democracy (PR and parliamentary).

In PR systems, the percentage of votes each party receives nationally determines its percentage of seats in the legislature. FPTP systems pick representatives individually, with the candidate who wins the most votes in a certain region of the country securing the seat, regardless of how that candidate's party performed elsewhere. Many variants of these two main types exist, and a number of countries incorporate hybrid systems that bring PR and FPTP together. Germany, for example, combines PR and FPTP voting. Each voter has two votes, with one vote counting toward each type of electoral arrangement.

Proportional Representation (PR)

In a pure **proportional representation (PR)** system, the percentage of the vote a party gets becomes the percentage of the seats that the party secures in the legislature. For example, if the legislature has one hundred seats and Party X gets 25 percent of the national vote, it would receive twenty-five of the one hundred seats for its members. Prior to the election in PR systems, a party typically produces a list of candidates who would hold the seats it wins. In the case of Party X, the first twenty-five individuals on the list would become members of the legislature; number twenty-six on the list would not. The leader of the party (the potential prime minister if the system is a parliamentary one) would be listed first.

Although most PR systems allow political parties to construct their own ordered lists of candidates, some countries allow voters to have a greater say in this part of the decision. In an **open list proportional representation (open list PR)** system, for example, voters choose the party they prefer and also, within that party, the specific candidate they prefer. One of the TIC cases, Brazil, uses a form of open list PR in which voters cast only one vote for either a party or a candidate.

Election A form of conventional mass participation in which the population selects among various individual candidates or political parties seeking political office.

A regular (closed list) PR ballot, used in 1994 in the first democratic elections of postapartheid South Africa.
Per-Anders Pettersson/Getty Images

Proportional Representation (PR) An electoral system in which voters cast their votes for political parties and the percentage of the vote that each party receives translates into the percentage of seats that the party receives in the legislature.

Open List Proportional Representation (Open List PR) An electoral system in which voters cast a vote for a particular party but also play a role in the decision of which candidates receive the seats earned by that party.

The pure form of PR encourages a large number of small parties. In the one hundred person legislature, a politician who believes that he or she could form a party and get even 1 percent of the vote would secure a seat in the legislature. Consequently, a pure PR system could lead to dozens of similarly sized parties, unstable coalition governments, and chaotic legislating. In practice, such extreme problems do not occur, partly because most PR-based electoral systems do not rely on a pure PR approach. Instead, the rules of how votes translate into seats are amended to discourage a large number of small political parties.

One of the central ways that PR systems deviate from their pure form is by setting a **threshold**. A threshold is the minimum percentage of the vote that a party must receive in order to secure even one seat in the legislature. Israel has had one of the lowest thresholds of any country (1 percent into the 1990s; 2 percent today), but the most common threshold around the world is 5 percent. A 5 percent threshold means that a party that receives even 4.99 percent of the vote earns no seats. With a 5 percent threshold, it makes little sense for a politician to form a party that is likely to get only 1 percent of the vote. The threshold rule thus encourages small parties to combine forces with other small parties to guarantee that the threshold is cleared. This reduces the overall number of parties to a more manageable number, improving stability and the ability to generate policy effectively.

Large parties also benefit from the threshold when smaller parties fail to clear it. The votes for the parties that do not clear the threshold become void. As a result, the percentage of the seats for the parties that do cross the threshold is greater than their percentage of the vote. A party that receives 40 percent of the vote in the election, for example, could end up with a majority of the seats if several small parties do not reach the 5 percent barrier.

An Iraqi electoral worker counts ballots from the parliamentary elections on May 3, 2010 in Baghdad, Iraq. Iraq switched to an open list PR system just prior to this election.
Muhannad Fala'ah/Getty Images

First Past the Post (FPTP)

The other basic form of electoral system is the **first past the post (FPTP)** system. In FPTP, voters typically do not vote for political parties. Rather, they cast votes for individual political candidates who are running for seats linked to relatively small electoral districts. The candidate who receives the plurality of the vote—the most votes—in that district earns the seat from the district. This form of election is familiar to most Americans; it is what the United States uses to select members of the House of Representatives, and it is the model for most state and local government elections as well.

Pure FPTP systems use a plurality rule rather than a majority rule. The individual selected from the electoral district is the one who receives the most votes, even if that person does not receive a majority (over 50 percent) of the votes. As a result, FPTP systems are sometimes called "plurality systems." Just as the pure PR system can produce a large number of small parties, a pure FPTP system can result in a large number of candidates, with the winner earning the seat with a small percentage of the vote. For example, even if only five candidates were running for office in a pure FPTP system, it is possible for a candidate to win with just over 20 percent of the vote. This is a concern, since an extreme candidate with a loyal base of followers could secure a seat even though the vast majority of the voters would not want that candidate in office.

To help avoid this possibility, some countries amend the plurality rule through use of a **runoff**. In a runoff, the two candidates who receive the most votes in the first round of voting compete again. The candidate who gets a majority of the vote in this second round is elected. As a result, a runoff system is also known as a **majority** or **majoritarian system**, because a majority of the voters, in either the first or second round, must support a candidate before he or she can hold political office. In majoritarian systems, extreme candidates rarely win elections because voters have a chance to vote against those candidates in the second round. The runoff approach is not only used in legislative elections. Runoffs are common in presidential elections around the world as well.

Threshold A rule in PR systems that forces parties to receive a certain percentage of the vote before they receive seats in the legislature.

First Past the Post (FPTP) An electoral system in which voters select a particular candidate for each office, and the candidate receiving a plurality of the vote wins.

Runoff An election in which the two candidates who receive the most votes in the first round compete in a second round.

Majority (Majoritarian) System Another name for a runoff system, since a candidate needs a majority of the vote in the second round to win.

Another variation in the FPTP approach involves voters selecting a candidate from each party in a **primary election** to compete as that party's candidate in the general election. Primaries are common in the United States, but they are relatively rare in other parts of the world. To those unused to the system, the American reliance on primaries seems strange in that they allow voters, not a political party, to decide which candidate runs under the political party's label in the general election.

Single-Member Districts versus Multi-Member Districts

An important consideration in understanding how PR and FPTP systems work in practice is whether representatives are chosen from single-member districts, multi-member districts, or from the country as a whole. FPTP systems often, but not always, involve the selection of only one person from each electoral district. When voters in each electoral district choose only one representative, the system is also often referred to as a **single-member district (SMD)** system or even just a "district system." Using SMD and FPTP interchangeably, however, can be misleading. FPTP rules can be used in multi-member districts as well as single-member ones.

Although PR rules do not make sense in an SMD system (there is no proportionality if only one seat is available to win), SMD elections can involve more than just adding up single votes to see who received the most. In a **preference system**, for example, voters are allowed to rank candidates seeking office in an electoral district. In single-member districts, this approach is typically called the **alternative vote (AV)** approach. In elections using AV, the first step involves counting the first-place votes from all ballots. If no candidate receives a majority of the votes, the candidate who finished last is removed, and the second-place vote totals are added to the first place votes. If there is still no candidate with a majority, the process is repeated with the third-place votes and so on until a majority of votes has been secured. Such a system benefits candidates who are everyone's second choice but few people's first choice.

An alternative to the use of single-member districts is the **multi-member district (MMD)** approach. In MMD systems, several candidates are selected from a single electoral district. These districts are larger than they would be in an SMD system but smaller than the country as a whole (though some consider PR voting for the entire country to be a form of MMD). In MMD systems, the districts sometimes all select the same number of candidates; for example, five candidates earn office from each district. In other cases, the number of seats filled by the districts vary across the country.

Just as it is incorrect to use FPTP and SMD interchangeably, one should be careful not to use MMD and PR interchangeably. Different approaches are available for choosing the representatives from districts in an MMD system. Particularly in districts with a large number of seats, a PR approach could be used; a party might secure more than one seat from the same district depending on its performance in that district. A FPTP approach could be used with the three highest vote recipients in a three-seat district being elected. The FPTP approach could be combined with a threshold requirement. In this case, voters may get to vote for as many candidates as there are seats from the district, but to win one of the seats, a candidate must secure above a certain percentage of the vote. Although the MMD approach generally provides different groups in a particular area of the country, including minority groups, a better chance to be represented by the candidate of their choice, a threshold requirement forces candidates to have broad support in the district to be elected.

The idea behind the preference system can also be combined with MMD systems to determine which group of candidates earns seats from the MMD. The combination of a preference arrangement and multi-member districts is known as a **single transferable vote (STV) system**. Rather than a majority of the votes (as in the case of preference systems used in SMD systems), candidates in a STV system have to earn a certain predetermined portion of the total votes cast to be elected. While some scholars label STV systems as a form of PR, the resulting distribution of seats is generally far less proportional than in a traditional PR system based on a national party vote.[12] Ireland uses STV in its national legislative elections.

Primary Election An election for a particular political office in which candidates from the same political party compete against each other for the right to represent the party in a general election.

Single-Member District (SMD) An electoral district in which voters choose only one representative, often using the plurality rule to determine the winner.

Preference System An electoral system that allows voters to rank candidates in a district race and uses the rankings to determine who fills the seat from that district.

Alternative Vote (AV) A preference system approach used in single-member districts.

Multi-Member District (MMD) A system in which more than one candidate is selected from a particular electoral district.

Single Transferable Vote (STV) System An electoral system that combines preference voting with multi-member districts.

Finally, some MMD arrangements are designed to allow the party finishing second in an electoral district to receive at least one seat from that district, even if candidates from the party finishing first receive more than one seat. This is known as a **second past the post (SPTP)** rule, or the principle of the first minority. It is designed to address the situation where a party finishes second in many FPTP races and gets no seats from them. This rule is used in Mexican Senate elections.

Hybrid Systems

Some electoral systems combine FPTP and PR approaches by dividing the total seats of the legislature into two groups. Which representatives hold the seats in the first group is determined by the outcome of FPTP district voting. The remaining seats are distributed based on the results of a separate PR vote. This approach is often called a **hybrid electoral system**, because voters cast two separate votes, one in a FPTP race and the other for a political party in a PR contest. In the PR vote, voters do not have to support the party of the candidate they chose in the FPTP district vote. This hybrid system benefits voters who like a particular party in general but feel a strong attachment to a candidate of another party. Russia used a hybrid system in the early post-Soviet period, and the hybrid approach remains in use in Germany in elections for the Bundestag.

Advantages and Disadvantages of PR Electoral Systems

Governments in many countries have reformed their electoral systems with the goal of making FPTP systems look more like PR systems. This is due to the belief that PR systems offer substantial advantages. This section focuses on the advantages and disadvantages of PR systems, which, because PR and FPTP take such opposite approaches, correspond respectively to the disadvantages and advantages of FPTP systems.

Advantage 1: Minority Interests Are Represented

Even with a threshold in place, PR systems allow small parties to win seats. This gives the small parties a platform to voice their concerns. As a result, PR systems often better capture support for newly emerging issue areas such as environmentalism that become a central focus for one or more small parties. The PR approach can also make small parties important political players. Since PR systems allow more parties to hold seats in the legislature, it is rare for a party to secure a majority of the seats. As a result, coalition governments are common, and small parties can receive important cabinet positions and policy victories in exchange for helping the coalition control a majority of the seats in the legislature.

Advantage 2: Women Are More Likely to Be Elected to Office

FPTP systems tend to generate fewer female representatives in national legislatures. One could argue that a number of other causal factors may be at play here, including the possibility that countries that are more culturally patriarchal also happen to have FPTP electoral systems. However, the evidence that PR plays a role in female participation is hard to dispute. In every country in which women hold at least 25 percent of legislative seats, PR is used in the selection of the legislature.[13] In addition, in countries such as Russia and Germany that have used hybrid electoral arrangements, more women have held PR-linked seats than FPTP-districts seats. One reason for this difference is that it is easier for gender quotas to be applied in PR. When a party can decide which individuals hold the seats that the party wins, it is easier to reach a particular target for officeholder diversity. Although some countries with electoral gender quotas use FPTP voting, FPTP electoral systems make it more difficult to translate an increase in the number of female candidates into an increase in the number of women holding political office.

Second Past the Post (SPTP) An electoral system, also known as the principle of the first minority, that reserves seats in a particular body for the party that finishes second in a district election.

Hybrid Electoral System An electoral system that combines PR and FPTP methods by dividing the legislature into separate groups of PR and district seats and having voters select both a party and a candidate.

Advantage 3: Emphasis on Ideas over Personalities

PR systems lead voters to select among political parties rather than individual candidates, making the policy positions of the parties arguably more important than in FPTP systems. It becomes impossible for a candidate to run as an independent in a PR system. Of course, party leaders are often well-known individuals, and it is certainly possible for voters in PR systems to select a party based on how they view the party leader. PR does not, therefore, eliminate the importance of individuals and their personalities. Compared with FPTP systems, however, PR systems do make personalities less central than ideas and policy positions.

Disadvantage 1: Too Many Small Parties with Disproportionate Importance

Thresholds make it more difficult for small parties to win seats, but even in systems with a 5 percent threshold, it is not unusual for one or more parties that received less than 10 percent of the vote to hold seats. Such parties can become kingmakers of coalition governments and, therefore, wield much more influence than their electoral support justifies. While FPTP systems can shut small parties out of the legislature, PR systems can give them a disproportionate amount of power.

Disadvantage 2: PR Facilitates Extremist Parties

While PR electoral systems give small parties in the center of the political spectrum a chance to be heard in the halls of the legislature, they provide similar opportunities to small extremist parties. Depending on how high the threshold is set, a far-Left or far-Right party with the support of only a few percent of the population could earn seats in the legislature. One could argue that this should not be a major concern for those considering the relative merits of the PR approach, since such parties are usually not brought into coalition governments. At the same time, giving extremist parties any seats can allow their members to disrupt legislative proceedings or find other ways to broadcast their policy positions from the stage of the national legislature. A counterargument is that bringing extremist groups into the official governmental institutions tends to make them less extreme. As discussed in the previous chapter, when groups and their supporters are shut out of conventional forms of political participation like elections, they are more likely to consider unconventional, violent forms of participation.

Think and Discuss

Does a PR system's advantages, such as doing a better job of representing the interests of minority groups, outweigh its disadvantages, such as potentially giving small parties the ability to hijack the process of creating and maintaining a ruling coalition? Why?

Spotlight on ... FRANCE

Elections in a Semipresidential System

Like Russia, France has a semipresidential political system with a dual executive that includes significant powers for both the president and the prime minister. Voters select a president and also vote separately for the lower house of the national legislature, the National Assembly. The members of the National Assembly are elected to five-year terms but, like members of other parliaments, can also face early elections if parliament is dissolved—a power held by the French president. Members of the upper house, the Senate, are selected by an electoral college to six-year terms, and the Senate cannot be dissolved early.

The French electoral process for the president is majoritarian with two rounds of balloting if necessary. The two top candidates advance to a second round if no candidate receives a majority of the first-round vote. The National

Assembly uses a modified FPTP format, again using a majoritarian approach. Parties field candidates in single-member districts, and candidates who win the most votes cast, provided the number corresponds to at least 25 percent of the number of registered voters, are elected outright in the first round. When no candidate in a district meets these criteria, legislative candidates with vote totals of at least 12.5 percent of registered voters advance to the second round. This complicated system is an innovation of the Fifth Republic, designed to allow for both programmatic and charismatic party appeals. Typically, intense negotiations emerge when three candidates qualify for the second round.

The system can sometimes produce surprises in the first round. In the first round of presidential elections in 2002, for example, voters scattered their ballots among sixteen candidates. With massive abstentions, no one, not even sitting President Jacques Chirac, received more than 20 percent of the vote in the first round. Combined, candidates from parties of the far Right garnered more than 20 percent, while those to the left of the French Socialist Party earned more than 23 percent, including nearly 10 percent for two Trotskyite parties. As a result, Socialist candidate Lionel Jospin was knocked out, and in the second round, Chirac faced the extremist founder of the National Front, Jean-Marie Le Pen.[14] Spurred on by massive demonstrations of high school students against Le Pen, voters gave Chirac his second term over the man infamous for denying that the Holocaust happened and for physically assaulting a female opponent.[15]

TOPIC IN COUNTRIES

France is not alone in providing interesting examples of parties and elections. The Topic in Countries (TIC) cases cover the range of party systems and demonstrate the various approaches to electoral systems. In this chapter's TIC section, look for

- The major political parties in each TIC case.
- The type of party system in each TIC case.
- The electoral arrangements used at the national level.
- The results of recent elections.

The United Kingdom

The British political system has long had two major political parties vying with each other to control the government. The system has also long been considered a two-and-a-half party system rather than a two-party system because of the electoral success of one or more smaller parties. In 2010, the UK moved even more sharply away from a two-party system (and perhaps even from a two-and-a-half party system), as neither of the two main political parties secured a majority of the seats in the House of Commons. In 2011, voters participated in a national referendum to determine whether elections to the House of Commons would continue to employ a SMD-FPTP system or whether the UK should instead adopt an AV system.

Political Parties

When Maurice Duverger wrote his study of parties and party systems (see the In Theory and Practice box on Duverger at the end of this section), scholars had not yet differentiated between two and two and a half party systems. As a result, he labeled the British system as a two-party system, but one with unique features compared to the U.S. system.[16] In recent years, the UK's party system has become even more different from the classic American-style two-party variant. For example, the British system now has a solid third party that regularly secures a sizable percentage of the national vote but, because of the FPTP electoral system, has often held relatively few seats in Parliament. Thus, most comparativists now describe the UK as a two-and-a-half party system, the only such system among the nine TIC cases.

The two largest political parties in the United Kingdom are the Labour Party and the Conservative Party. The Labour Party, often calling itself New Labour since the mid-1990s, is the party of the two previous prime ministers, Gordon Brown and Tony Blair. It held a majority of the seats in the House of Commons directly after World War II, for much of the 1960s and 1970s, and from 1997 to 2010. The Conservative Party, also referred to as the "Tories," controlled the government for much of the 1950s and in the 1980s and early 1990s. During that time, many voters saw Labour as far to the left of center. Blair succeeded in his efforts to move Labour toward the center, capturing many working-class voters who had supported Margaret Thatcher and the Conservatives in the 1980s.

The third major party in the UK today is the Liberal Democratic Party. It formed when the Liberal Party and the Social Democratic Party (SDP) combined in 1988. The Liberal Party had existed since the 1800s. Its "liberal" label came from its support of economic liberalism, meaning free trade and government nonintervention in the economy. In other words, it was a right-of-center party. The SDP, on the other hand, was a left-of-center party established in 1981. As one might expect given the backgrounds of the two parties that created it, the Liberal Democratic Party's policy positions have not always been easily cast as left or right of center. It appeared to have moved to the left of the Labour Party on a large number of issues including the environment, but it agreed to work with the Conservatives after the 2010 parliamentary elections.

Elections

As in other parliamentary systems, the prime minister is the leader of the party that secures a majority of the seats in Parliament or, more recently, the main party of a coalition controlling a majority of the seats. Unlike in many parliamentary systems, however, voters select individual candidates in districts through FPTP arrangements rather than by casting votes for a political party. Interestingly, the UK almost adopted a single transferable vote (STV) system after World War I. This system is used in Northern Ireland in local elections and to select representatives to the European Parliament.

On May 5, 2011, British voters participated in a national referendum on replacing the FPTP system with an AV system. The campaign was vigorous, with both supporters and opponents of the proposed changes working hard to convince voters to support their position and to get those voters

British Prime Minister David Cameron delivers a speech in London against the proposed change to the UK's electoral system, April 18, 2011. Oli Scarff - WPA Pool/Getty Images

to the polls. Although in the weeks leading up to the vote some thought that the referendum might pass, nearly 68 percent of voters opposed the change to an AV system. In some ways, the results were unsurprising, since leaders of the two major parties opposed the reform.

The country's two largest parties opposed the change to an AV system because both have historically benefited from the existing FPTP approach. The FPTP system has tended to create an artificial majority for the largest party and has caused problems for smaller parties such as the Liberal Democrats. Even in 2010, when no party won a majority of seats in the House of Commons, the Liberal Democrats received around 23 percent of the vote across the country as a whole but won only 8.8 percent of the seats. On the other hand, in the "landslide" victory that brought Tony Blair and the Labour Party to power in 1997, Labour won only 43.2 percent of all votes cast but earned 418 seats, a sizable majority.

FPTP rules have helped to prevent minority governments or coalition arrangements and to maintain the UK's two-and-a-half party system. Yet, in the days leading up to the May 5, 2005, elections for the British House of Commons, it was unclear which of the two main parties would win, and some believed that a coalition government would be necessary. Instead, FPTP once again translated a popular vote minority into a legislative majority. Maintaining its majority party status, Labour controlled fewer seats than it had since 1997.

In 2005, Labour won only 35.2 percent of the vote nationally, a full 8 percent less than in 1997. The Liberal Democratic Party won 22 percent of the vote and, more important, nearly 10 percent of the seats in the House of Commons. These successes led party leader Charles Kennedy to hail the 2005 elections as signaling the Liberal Democrats as a "real alternative" to Labour and the Conservatives in the future.[17] Given the sharp regional divisions in the UK, with the two main parties combined earning only around 75 percent of the national vote and the Liberal Democrats' vote totals within 10 percent of the second largest party, it was possible to imagine a shake-up in British electoral politics in 2010, even one that would require a coalition government to control Parliament.

That is precisely what happened in the May 2010 general election. The Conservatives won the most seats in the House of Commons, and their leader, David Cameron, became British prime minister. By securing only 306 of the 650 seats in the House of Commons, however, the Conservatives failed to gain the majority necessary to pass legislation without the help of other political parties. The Labour Party held nearly 260 seats, while the country's third largest party, the Liberal Democrats, won 57 seats. After nearly a week of bargaining and intrigue, the Liberal Democrats and the Conservatives announced a coalition agreement. One of the major components of the agreement was a compromise involving the national referendum on replacing the British FPTP system with a preference system to allow voters to rank candidates rather than simply select one.

IN THEORY AND PRACTICE

Duverger's Law and British Elections

Maurice Duverger believed that electoral systems have two basic consequences, which he labeled psychological and mechanical. Psychological consequences relate to how voters and candidates behave in light of electoral rules; mechanical consequences concern how the votes in an election translate into seats in the legislature.[18] One of Duverger's claims, that FPTP systems encourage two-party systems, has so much logical and empirical support behind it that it is known as **Duverger's law**.[19] Even Duverger argued that the idea that a FPTP system encourages a stable two-party system "approaches ... a true sociological law."[20]

Why would FPTP arrangements encourage a two-party system? For a multiparty system to remain in place over time, smaller parties must be able to translate votes from the general public into some seats in the national legislature. With FPTP rules, small national parties tend to get votes across a large number of electoral districts but win the elections in few or even none of those districts. As a result, voters become increasingly reluctant to "waste their votes" on third parties, deciding instead between the two main parties.

Electoral results in the UK cast doubt on Duverger's law. If Duverger's proposition were indeed a law, the FPTP electoral arrangements used by the British should have produced a two-party system and a majority party in control of the House of Commons. Instead, the British system has long been a two-and-a-half party system, and the election results in 2010 failed to produce a majority government.

What explains the ability of smaller parties to garner notable vote totals? Part of the answer lies in powerful regional divisions, sometimes fueled by ethnic nationalism. The importance of regionalism in the UK points to the need to amend Duverger's law to consider the role of identity divisions that break down along regional lines. If supporters of smaller parties are concentrated in particular parts of the country, candidates from the small parties can actually win a majority of the votes (and thus seats) in a number of electoral districts. In a close election, the ability of the Scottish National Party (SNP), for example, to do well in Scotland disrupts Duverger's calculus about FPTP arrangements, as do the local parties that often win seats from districts in Northern Ireland. Even more important, the Liberal Democratic Party tends to do well in certain regions in the northern and southwestern parts of the country.

If future British elections continue to give neither of the two main British parties majority control of the House of Commons, the country would fall into the multiparty system category. This trend has already been seen in India, where strong regional parties emerged over time. Even with FPTP rules in place, India developed a multiparty system. Were the UK to do so as well, Duverger's law would clearly need to be amended: FPTP systems encourage two-party systems except in countries with strong regional divisions.

Think and Discuss

Does the existence of regionally strong third parties in the UK have implications for the United States? Could American third parties be successful if they adopted a regional strategy rather than trying to run as national parties?

Germany

Over the last eight decades, the German population has experienced the extremes of party politics, including one-party systems like the Nazis and, following World War II, the Communist Party in East Germany, as well as the multiparty system of the Federal Republic. Befitting its consensus democracy label (see Chapter 5), Germany's largest political parties need the support of smaller parties to form governing coalitions. More recently, coalitions have included both a grand coalition and, more often, a minimum necessary winning coalition of either the Right or the Left.

Duverger's Law The label given to Maurice Duverger's argument that FPTP electoral systems generate two-party systems.

Political Parties

German parties transmit their policy stances to voters through their platforms, which they issue in advance of elections. The two major parties are the Christian Democratic Union (CDU) on the center-right and the Social Democratic Party (SPD) on the center-left. The CDU affiliates with its sister party in Bavaria, the Christian Social Union (CSU), which is the more socially conservative of the two. The differences between the CDU and SPD have been less distinct than one might expect from programmatic parties.

Like the Democratic and Republican Parties in the United States, the CDU and SPD are known as **catch-all parties**. Political scientist Otto Kirchheimer has described a catch-all party as one that softens its ideology and moderates its policy stances to appeal to more than one group in the electorate. The aim is to draw in a broad swath of voters, especially moderate voters.[21] The CDU's support, for example, cuts across class and religious lines. It controlled the chancellorship from 1949 to 1969, 1982 to 1998, 2005 to 2009 as part of Germany's most recent CDU-SPD grand coalition, and since then as head of a more traditional coalition government.

The SPD was initially rooted in the working class and committed to socialism. Its stance alienated many voters, and in 1959, it accepted capitalism and the welfare state in order to broaden its electoral appeal. The strategic shift led to the SPD's participation, with the CDU, in the Federal Republic's first grand coalition from 1966 to 1969. Subsequently, the SPD became the lead party in a ruling coalition with the Free Democratic Party (FDP). Under the leadership of Willy Brandt and later Helmut Schmidt, the SDP-FDP coalition controlled the Bundestag, the lower house of Parliament, until 1982, when the FDP joined a coalition government with the CDU headed by Helmut Kohl. Although the SPD was out of the government for the next sixteen years, its catch-all nature allowed it to maintain strong support among trade unionists while also appealing to the middle classes, setting the stage for its return to power in 1998.

A number of smaller parties fill out Germany's multiparty system. The FDP attracts professionals and the self-employed with its message of limited government and the free market. It has been the kingmaker in coalition governments for much of the post–World War II period. The Green Party first entered the Bundestag in 1983 on a program of environmentalism, feminism, democracy, and peace. It counts the younger university-educated strata (particularly teachers) among its supporters. Though it

had been in coalition governments in the *Länder* (the federal territorial units within Germany), the Green Party was not a coalition partner at the national level until 1998, when Chancellor Gerhard Schröder of the SPD formed a coalition government with the Greens that lasted until 2005.

Following German unification in 1990, the former Communist Party of East Germany transformed itself into the Party of Democratic Socialism (PDS) and won some Bundestag seats from the reunited country's new eastern Länder. Since 2006, the PDS has been superseded by the Left Party, which consists of dissident left-wing Social Democrats who bolted from the SPD and joined forces with the PDS to contest the 2005 election. The two groups formally merged as a single party in 2006.

Elections

Germany employs a hybrid electoral system, combining FPTP and PR for Bundestag elections. A voter gets two votes, one of which is a vote for the representative of the electoral district and the other a vote for a political party. Many voters make tactical choices and accordingly split their votes between two different parties in the hope of securing a desired coalition government. Half of the 598 Bundestag seats are distributed based on single-member districts and a simple plurality (FPTP) of the votes for individual candidates. The other 299 seats are filled by party lists on the basis of the party vote. Threshold rules prevent small splinter parties from winning representation. Thus, a party must win at least 5 percent of the party vote nationally or three single-member districts in order to win any seats.

The number of seats that a party wins in the FPTP district vote is deducted from its percentage of seats won by PR, although this is calculated based on the party's performance in each of the Länder rather than nationally. The overall effect of the electoral system is to allocate seats, roughly, as if it were a PR-only system. As a result, the German electoral system is often called "personalized PR." This provision helps smaller parties, which typically fail to win in the FPTP district races but finish above the 5 percent threshold in the PR vote.

One of the more interesting rules of this system concerns this distribution of seats in the Bundestag when a party secures more seats through the FPTP district vote than it would have earned if the electoral system were PR-only. The party is not required to forfeit these "overhang" seats. Instead, they are added to the total number of seats in the Bundestag. As a result, following the 2005 elections the Bundestag had 614 total seats, and after 2009 it had 622 seats.

Germany's complex hybrid electoral system produces a multiparty system and coalition governments.[22] The head of the largest party in the coalition becomes the German chancellor.[23] Most of the time, a coalition is forged by one of the larger parties and one of the smaller parties. However, as mentioned earlier, there were two instances of grand coalitions between the two largest parties, the CDU and SPD, in 1966 to 1969 and 2005 to 2009.

IN THEORY AND PRACTICE

Realignment Theory and Germany

Realignment theory concerns how certain elections shake up political systems, altering ("realigning") long-term levels of support for major political parties.[24] The theory emerged when a number of scholars, including V. O. Key and E. E. Schattschneider, noticed that a regular pattern of continuity in American elections was followed by occasional significant change. Elections in which the outcome radically alters the political landscape of a country for decades are known as **critical elections**. Looking at U.S. political history, critical elections appear to take place roughly once every three decades. In other countries, such a pattern is less identifiable. Still, most democratic systems have seen one or more elections that represented a realignment of the electorate.

Some scholars believe that the 2005 election pointed to a realignment of the German party system, albeit one that is more complex and possibly more protracted than the "ideal" shift at the heart of realignment theory. The party system fragmented in 2005. That election produced a "hung parliament" with no clear-cut winner. Both the SPD and CDU lost support to the smaller parties. Neither of the two larger parties could muster a majority coalition government with just one of the smaller parties alone; in fact, several coalition possibilities involved three parties. After weeks of tough negotiations, the CDU and SPD settled for a grand coalition.

The two main parties' predicament was driven by the appearance of a new party. Some left-wing SPD members, disappointed with Schröder's market-oriented policies, quit the party and formed an electoral alliance with the PDS in the east. Together, they won more than 8 percent of the vote in the 2005 election and fifty-four seats in the Bundestag. The groups formalized their electoral alliance in a merger as the Left Party in 2006. Unlike the PDS, the Left Party enjoys electoral support in both west and east, as *Land* elections in 2008 demonstrated.

Hence, this new party has placed the SPD in a difficult bind. By participating in the grand coalition, the SPD alienated its traditional left-wing and labor union supporters,

---

Realignment Theory A theoretical perspective that contends that the fortunes of major political parties remain stable for long periods, followed by a dramatic change.

Critical Elections Elections that mark the beginning of a realignment.

who began to vote for the Left Party in Land elections. In response, the SPD's leader, Kurt Beck, took an increasingly radical stance on labor market and welfare state policies and even contemplated forming a coalition government with the Left Party in the Land of Hessen. This shift strained its relations with the CDU coalition partner and made governing more difficult. Even worse, opinion polls indicated that centrist voters were beginning to desert the SPD to the benefit of the CDU. With Bundestag elections looming in 2009, the SPD changed tack by dumping Beck in September 2008 and installing a more centrist leadership team.[25] It did not work; the SPD lost the 2009 elections and saw the CDU form a coalition government without it. Given this fragmentation of the party system and the new players that it brought, German politics appears to be headed into a more uncertain period in the near future.

India

From a one-party dominant system at the time of independence, India eventually transformed into a multiparty system. This occurred both because of the emergence of a strong second major party and because of the growth of regional parties. Elections are a major undertaking in a country like India, but they have largely succeeded in linking elites and masses in the world's largest democracy.

Political Parties

India has six national parties, identified as such by the Indian Election Commission because they have achieved a set minimum level of support across federal units. The most prominent national parties are the Indian National Congress (INC, also known as the Congress Party or, simply, Congress); the Bharatiya Janata Party (BJP); and the two Communist Parties—the Communist Party of India (Marxist) (CPI[M]) and the Communist Party of India (CPI).[26] Other types of parties are categorized by the commission as "state parties," those that get a set minimum number of votes in a federal unit, and "officially recognized parties," those that don't meet the minimum number. Many independent candidates run for office as well.

The INC, founded in 1885, was the dominant party in the country until the end of the Emergency in 1977 (see Chapter 5), when it lost the national election for the first time. Since then, it has remained a key, but not consistently a dominant, player in the struggle for national power and for regional power in many parts of the country. Its character has changed over time in at least two respects: from a party in which regional leaders held extensive power to one in which power was centralized in the party leader, and from advocating social democratic policies to fostering a liberalized economy. Like the CDU and SPD in Germany, the INC in India has been labeled a catch-all party, with a range of policies designed to draw votes from the diverse communities that constitute the Indian population. Today, the INC's main national rival is the BJP. The BJP espouses a religious/cultural ideology known as *Hindutva* that equates Hinduism with Indian nationalism. When the BJP came to power in 1998 as the leader of the coalition called the National Democratic Alliance, it behaved much like the INC had. Many attributed this to the constraints on it imposed by secular parties in its coalition.

There are also two major Communist Parties, the CPI and the CPI(M). The CPI(M) broke away from the CPI in 1964. The CPI(M) is the more significant party and has controlled the federal unit of West Bengal for decades, has alternated in power in the state of Kerala since 1957, and has governed in Tripura. The secular nature of the Communist Parties leads them to support Congress and oppose the BJP.

Regional parties have grown substantially in number, power, and importance. They control the legislative assemblies of many states. By their nature, none of them is likely to become a dominant national party. However, their support has become essential to the INC and the BJP in the construction of ruling coalitions at the center.

Elections

Elections to the Lok Sabha are mammoth undertakings. They require the delineation of 543 constituencies, the issuance of hundreds of millions of photo ID cards to registered voters, and the establishment of approximately eight hundred thousand polling stations. About 5 million polling personnel and security forces are involved in running a general election. In recent Lok Sabha elections, the turnout has been about 60 percent, meaning around 400 million voters went to the polls.[27]

Elections occur at least every five years for the Lok Sabha and the legislative assemblies. A candidate for the Lok Sabha runs in one of 543 single-member districts. (The Lok Sabha has 545 members but two are appointed as representatives of the Anglo-Indian community.) No fewer than two weeks for campaigning is allowed, but the campaigns are very short compared with countries like the United States. Voting in national elections is held over at least three days because of the difficulty of supervising such a huge event. Election to the Rajya Sabha is by a complex system of voting by elected officials.

Because of the inability of national parties to win majorities in the Lok Sabha, electoral alliances are often developed with regional parties prior to an election. In such cases, the national party and the regional party divvy up districts so that they do not run candidates who compete against each other. The bargaining is often difficult, and defections sometimes occur when the likely candidate of a party is not allowed to run in a district because his or her party has allotted the district to its alliance partner.

One relatively unique feature of elections in India is that the proportion of poorer people who vote seems to have increased over time relative to that of the wealthy. Some observers see this trend as indicative of a deepening of democracy. At a minimum, it shows that the poor are not as alienated as they are in many countries, including many democracies, and believe that their participation can make a difference.

The 2004 general election surprised the ruling National Democratic Alliance led by the BJP. The BJP called the election early because it thought circumstances

Residents stand in line to cast their vote in Shilla Koraibari, located in the Indian state of Assam. © AP Photo/Amit Bhargava

were favorable for a victory. Yet, the INC received over 103 million votes of the nearly 390 million votes cast and won 150 districts, while the BJP got only 86 million votes across the country and won 130 districts. The INC did even better in the subsequent election in 2009. It won more than 200 seats alone, and its United Progressive Alliance coalition controlled 280 of the Lok Sabha's 545 seats. Even with the INC's recent successes, these figures highlight the strength of regional parties, the seat-sharing electoral alliances, the necessity of coalition government, and the scale of the democratic electoral event in India.

Mexico

For much of the twentieth century, Mexico was a one-party dominant system under the control of the Institutional Revolutionary Party (PRI). The Mexican party system has changed greatly from its one-party dominant roots, although with elections looming in 2012, the PRI reemerged as a force in Mexican national politics.

Political Parties

Writing in the mid-1970s, Giovanni Sartori viewed Mexico as a one-party dominant system with the PRI serving as a "clear-cut case of [a] hegemonic party that permits second class parties as long as, and to the extent that, they remain as they are."[28] Clearly, the smaller parties in Mexico did not accept this bargain, and, increasingly in the decades after Sartori wrote, neither did the leaders of the PRI. Today, whether Mexico is heading toward a two-and-a-half party system or a stable multiparty system remains an open question. Mexico's electoral arrangements make a multiparty system more likely than in other presidential systems; the three largest parties all have significant representation in the national legislature, and most scholars consider Mexico a multiparty system.

The PRI controlled Mexican politics by appealing to a large number of groups. Its oxymoronic name shows its attempt to appeal to a broad constituency, as does the name selected for its 2006 electoral alliance with the Green Party: the Alliance for Mexico. At the peak of its success, the party reached out to multiple sectors in society: labor, peasant, military, and "popular" (middle class). Its link to these major segments of society, and its clientelist dealings with individuals at the local level, helped it mobilize significant support at election time. If that was not enough, the PRI-led government manipulated election returns to guarantee continued PRI control.

As discussed in Chapter 5, the PRI's surrender of control of the political system was a slow process overseen by party leaders such as President Carlos Salinas in the late 1980s and early 1990s and Ernesto Zedillo for the rest of that decade. Its descent included the assassinations of a presidential candidate and other party officials, the loss of control of a number of state and local governments, the loss of the presidency in 2000, and an especially poor showing in the 2006 elections that at the time dropped it to third place in Mexican federal politics.

Parties that control a country during a long period of authoritarian rule have certain advantages. The PRI's name recognition, organizational head start, and clientelist connections at the local level are significant assets in open electoral competition. It remains a force in local politics. At the same time, compared with its two main rivals, the PRI is a more national party and does not need to rely on strength in particular regions for its electoral success. Legislative elections in 2009 pointed to the PRI's growing relevance. Thus, the PRI is not only unlikely to disappear from the political scene, it may have the best chance of any of the three largest parties in Mexico of gaining control of the presidency and the legislature at the same time.

During the 2000s, the National Action Party (PAN) became the leading party in Mexico at the federal level. Its candidates won the presidential contests in 2000 and 2006, and it controlled the largest portion of seats in both houses of the legislature until 2009. Viewed as both pro-business and pro-Catholic, the party has strong support in the industrial north. It began its ascent as a national political force by winning races for governor in certain states in the north and west. While the party held fewer than eighteen mayoral offices in the mid-1980s, a decade later it controlled around 250. It was Vicente Fox's victory in the 2000 presidential election that signaled both the broad appeal of the PAN and its potential to replace the PRI as the leading party in the country.[29]

The other major party in Mexico is the Party of the Democratic Revolution (PRD). The PRD-led Alliance for the Welfare of All nearly won the presidency in 2006 and made significant gains in the national legislative elections. It offers a left-of-center alternative to the PAN's right-of-center policy positions and has a strong base of support in the south and east of the country.

IN THEORY AND PRACTICE

Party Organization Theory and Mexico

In 1984, Joseph Schlesinger proposed a way to understand how parties are organized and, more broadly, how they behave in democratic political systems.[31] Schlesinger's **party organization theory** considers three key features of political parties: that they are market-based, that their

---

Party Organization Theory A theory that highlights the similarities and differences between political parties and businesses, interest groups, and government agencies.

policies provide collective benefits, and that their work is performed in large part by unpaid volunteers.

Schlesinger contended that, like businesses, parties are market-based organizations that trade certain goods for a desired resource.[32] While businesses engage in economic exchange, elections involve political exchange. Voters help parties gain office, and parties try to adopt policies those voters favor. Schlesinger points out, however, that the policies are collective benefits, generating a collective action problem (see Chapter 8). Finding people to take on the costs of party work is difficult if they receive the policy benefit even if they do not do the work. Parties are partially able to overcome this problem because the most important people in the party do directly and personally benefit from its success: they become the officeholders. As a result, they accept the organizational costs and act as the party's "entrepreneurs."[33] These entrepreneurs play a central role in party organization. Others gain less directly, and lower-level party members, especially unpaid volunteers, are typically less dedicated to working for the party over the long term.

Thus, parties are like businesses in their market-based exchanges, like interest groups and government agencies in that they produce collective goods, and like interest groups in their reliance on workers who are compensated indirectly. Schlesinger argues that this unique combination of features makes political parties function through "organized trial and error."[34]

At first glance, the creation of the PRD in Mexico appears to be a good example of Schlesinger's emphasis on entrepreneurs. A number of left-leaning former PRI officials founded the party, including Cuauhtémoc Cárdenas Solórzano, the son of a former PRI leader and president of the country. Trying to follow in his father's footsteps, he sought the PRI's nomination for president in 1988. When he did not receive it, he formed an electoral alliance of leftist parties to compete against the PRI candidate, Carlos Salinas. Many contend that Cárdenas actually won the election—claims supported by survey data and a mysterious shutdown of the computerized vote counting system on election night—but Salinas was named the official winner.

The experience led Cárdenas to form the PRD and to compete again in the 1994 and 2000 elections. He finished third in 2000, partly because some PRD members defected to support the candidacy of Vicente Fox. The PRD also worked to distance itself from the idea that it was only a vehicle for Cárdenas's pursuit of the presidency, an effort that appeared to be paying off by 2006. While the party has moved beyond Cárdenas, it is clear that without his personal interest in becoming president and his resulting efforts to take on the PRI, the PRD would not exist today.

At the same time, there is more to the story of Cárdenas's entrepreneurial efforts than pure personal ambition. Cárdenas and his allies were neither seeking political power entirely for its own sake nor acting on belief in a perceived birthright for Cárdenas to be president. Cárdenas never

expected to come as close to winning the presidency in 1988 as he did. In addition, by challenging Salinas, Cárdenas lost the chance of serving in a comfortable public servant position. He received constant death threats, some of his closest friends were murdered, and he spent much of his inheritance on an exhausting political campaign.

Thus, the example of Cárdenas and PRD shows the importance of political party entrepreneurs, but it also challenges the view that such entrepreneurs accept the costs of party formation only because they expect the personal benefits to more than outweigh the costs. Cárdenas deemed fundamental policy differences with Salinas, especially over the proper extent of market reforms in the economy, important enough to venture into entrepreneurial, party-forming activity that, at times, appeared to be as fruitless as it was costly.

Elections

The presidential election in Mexico is an FPTP national vote. While the Mexican political system resembles the American system in a number of ways, it has no electoral college and no estado-by-estado winner-take-all approach. The national election and the emerging multiparty system mean that, as happened in 2006, a candidate could be elected president with less than 40 percent of the national vote.

Elections for the bicameral Congress are more complex and include a hybrid approach combining FPTP and PR for the 500-member Chamber of Deputies, 300 of whom are elected through FPTP arrangements and 200

Supporters of presidential candidate Andrés Manuel López Obrador, from the Party of the Democratic Revolution (PRD), take part in a protest against the inauguration of Mexican President Felipe Calderón on December 1, 2006, in Mexico City. In the center, one supporter holds up a sign reading "Andrés Manuel López Obrador: The Real President of Mexico." © Yuri Cortez/AFP/Getty Images

through PR. Senate elections also combine FPTP and PR arrangements: the 128 senators are selected based on a tally of votes within the thirty-one estados and the Federal District, as well as the country as a whole. Parties nominate two-person slates in each state, and voters select their preferred pair. The pair that receives the most votes wins two Senate seats from the estado (and the Federal District). An additional Senate seat from each estado (and the Federal District) comes from a second past the post arrangement. It is given to the party that finishes second in the voting in that estado. Finally, 32 more senators are chosen based on the total votes across all the states. Divided on the basis of PR, these remaining senators are not linked to a particular state but are considered senators-at-large.

As presidential elections in many countries do, the 2006 vote for the Mexican president highlighted the country's regional divisions. The winner, Felipe Calderón of the PAN, defeated Andrés Manuel López Obrador, who represented an alliance that included the PRD. López Obrador, riding the wave of electoral success by left-of-center politicians in Latin America in the past decade, barely lost the election. The official vote count gave Calderón 35.9 percent to López Obrador's 35.3 percent. Despite López Obrador's claims of massive irregularities—claims challenged by European Union election monitors[30]—and protests by López Obrador's supporters when he was not declared the winner, Calderón succeeded Vicente Fox at the end of 2006. Calderón's support came largely from the north of Mexico, while López Obrador's support was concentrated in the south.

The country's last two legislative elections in 2006 and 2009 highlighted the unstable nature of the party system. In the 2006 Chamber of Deputies election, PAN candidates won the most districts (137). Receiving around 33.5 percent of the vote, the party also picked up nearly 70 more seats based on the results of the PR voting. The PRD-led Alliance for the Welfare of All won almost 100 of the district races. Receiving around 29 percent of the vote, it secured another 60 seats based on PR. Showing what appeared at the time to be its weakening popularity and organizational strength, the PRI-led Alliance for Mexico won only 64 seats from the FPTP district races. However, it picked up almost 60 additional seats from the PR vote after gaining over 28 percent of the vote nationally.

In the Senate in 2006, the PAN ended up with 52 seats (32 from FPTP, 9 from SPTP, and 11 from PR). The PRD's Alliance for the Welfare of All won 36 seats (22, 4, and 10), while the PRI's Alliance for Mexico won 39 seats (10, 19, 10). Mexico's second past the post rule benefited the PRI greatly, with nearly half of its alliance's Senate seats earned through SPTP in 2006. The New Alliance Party gained the remaining Senate seat on the basis of the PR arrangement.

The PRI made a stunning comeback in the July 5, 2009, federal elections for the Chamber of Deputies, falling just short of majority status by capturing 241 of the 500 seats. Its 135-seat increase came largely at the expense of the PAN, which lost 59 seats, and the PRD, which won 54 fewer seats than in 2006. It is not clear whether this was a one-time event or if the fortunes of the PRI have turned around for the long term. Consequently, the legislative and presidential elections scheduled for 2012 have the potential to once again reshape the Mexican political scene.

Brazil

The diversity seen in other aspects of Brazilian society is reflected in its political parties, party system, and electoral arrangements. Brazil uses a variety of electoral systems, depending on which type of office the election is designed to fill. The large number and fragile nature of Brazilian parties is conspicuous given the country's more than two-decades-old democratic system. The instability of the party system contributes to Brazil's struggles to consolidate its democracy.

Political Parties

Since 1990, the year of the first national elections following the transition to democracy, no political party has succeeded in winning more than 20 percent of the vote or 22 percent of the seats in the Chamber of Deputies. On average nineteen parties have been represented in the Chamber since 1988; there have never been fewer than eighteen parties represented. The ideological spectrum is correspondingly wide, ranging from far right monarchist parties to far left Communist and Trotskyite parties.

Moreover, the parties that participate in the system are themselves unstable; they disappear, split, merge, and form new parties with some frequency. Politicians frequently change their party affiliations before, during, and after elections. In this sense, the Brazilian party system after transition has looked much like the Russian party system during the 1990s, with voters straining to identify party programs and individual politicians more politically relevant than most parties.

Nevertheless, four major parties have stood out over time. Two of them have been among the top vote getters since the first 1990 legislative election: the Brazilian Democratic Movement Party (PMDB) and the Liberal Front Party (PFL). The PMDB is a successor of the Movement for Brazilian Democracy (MDB), which competed in rigged elections during the military dictatorship. As its name suggests, the MDB attempted to resist the military government from within the system, and it retains a centrist political stance. The PFL is a successor of the other, more pro-military party permitted under the military dictatorship, the Alliance for National

Renovation (ARENA). It remains a right-of-center political party, though it changed its name to *Democratas* (Democrats) in 2007.

The other two major parties have placed among the top four vote getters in each of the last three legislative elections, and both have won the presidency at least twice. The Workers' Party (PT), which currently holds the presidency, is the older and more leftist, founded by labor union organizers and social movement leaders in 1980. Of all Brazil's parties, the PT is the most ideologically coherent, most strongly connected to civil society organizations, most disciplined, and most committed to social change. Its politicians are much less likely to switch parties midstream, as a history of party activism is considered important for winning party candidacies. The Brazilian Social Democratic Party (PSDB) occupies a middle ground between the PT and the PMDB. Originally part of the PMDB, its founders split from that party in order to create a party with a more coherent, center-left ideological platform. The PSDB's most important leader, well-known sociologist Fernando Henrique Cardoso, was president of Brazil from 1994 to 2002.

Elections

At the national level, Brazil uses three different electoral systems. The president is chosen through a majority (runoff) system. If no presidential candidate receives a majority of the vote in the first round, a runoff between the top two candidates is held one month later. Senators in Brazil are elected through FPTP. Members of the Chamber of Deputies, the lower house of Congress, are selected through the open list variant of PR. In Brazil's open list approach, voters may cast a simple party vote, approving any candidate from that party, or they may choose a specific candidate. Most choose a candidate. The percentage of seats a party receives is determined by the sum of the votes received by all of the party's candidates, and the ranking of the candidates is determined by the number of votes they individually receive. The candidates who take office are the most popular within their party; the party calculation only determines how many of them will be seated.

Proportional representation results in a larger number of parties in the legislature; therefore, it is nearly impossible for the president to win a legislative majority of his or her own party. Under these conditions, some presidents have resorted to issuing provisional decrees. Another technique is the liberal use of bribes and favoritism in handing out government offices to individual legislators who agree to cooperate with presidential initiatives. These perverse results of the electoral system hamper the consolidation of Brazilian democracy.

The most recent Brazilian elections brought a new president, Dilma Rousseff, a PT candidate and former president Lula's chosen successor, to power. She won in a runoff election and took office on January 1, 2011. As was the case with Lula before her, Rousseff does not control the majority of the seats in Congress. In the 2010 elections, the PT won 88 seats in the Chamber of Deputies, more than any other party, but this amounted to only 17 percent of that house's seats.

Nigeria

Of all the consequences of military intervention in Nigerian politics, one of the most important has been its effect on political parties. At least since the civil war, which ended in January 1970, military leaders have been deeply suspicious of political parties. Rather than seeing them as a crucial vehicle for linking elites and masses, parties have been perceived to be undisciplined, divisive, and instruments of corruption.[35] With the establishment of democracy, a large number of political parties sought office. By 2007, the party system had appeared to have solidified itself as a one-party dominant system under the control of the People's Democratic Party (PDP). Elections in the spring of 2011, however, showed cracks in the PDP's dominance. Although it maintained its status as the majority party in the legislature and held on to the presidency, its victory was narrower than many had expected and sparked postelection protests by supporters of the opposition.

Political Parties

In 1991, when a transition to democracy was supposedly underway, the government banned numerous existing political parties, creating instead two official parties. This attempt at a forced two-party system demonstrated both a lack of appreciation for more subtle ways to influence the development of party systems and the view that large catch-all parties were superior to smaller parties representing narrower interests. In its next attempt at fostering a stable democratic transition, the military government initially recognized nine political parties. In line with its efforts to prevent ethnically concentrated parties, the government required parties to open membership to all individuals, regardless of ethnicity or religion, carry names free of ethnic or regional affiliation, and have "functional branches" in at least twenty-four of Nigeria's federal units.[36] Ultimately, the government ruled that only three political parties met the criteria for official registration. Two of them, the PDP and the All People's Party (APP), were created to a large extent from scratch. The third party, the Alliance for Democracy (AD), had its roots in an earlier political party associated with the Yoruba ethnic group. The PDP was the most important party in the first decade following the reestablishment of democracy in 1999. The APP reemerged in 2003 as the All Nigerian People's Party (ANPP).

During the first several years of the Fourth Republic, the number of political parties exploded. While the PDP, ANPP, and AD remained the three most prominent parties, around thirty Nigerian groups met the definition of political parties by 2003. This prompted the president of the country, Olusegun Obasanjo, to call for steps to reduce the number of parties. If he had feared a Brazil-style fragmentation that would prevent effective cooperation between the executive and legislative branches, these fears turned out to be unfounded. Despite more than fifty active parties by 2008, the PDP has had no problem establishing itself as the country's majority party. After the 2007 presidential and legislative elections, it was in firm control of both the executive and legislative branches of the Nigerian government, though its showing in the 2011 elections indicated a decrease in support.

In 2009, an important new political party, the Congress for Progressive Change (CPC), was created. The party formed around General Muhammadu Buhari, who was a leader of Nigeria's military government for nearly two years in the middle 1980s. Buhari had initially aligned himself with the ANPP and was the ANPP's candidate in the 2007 presidential elections, but he supported the creation of a new party after ANPP leadership decided to work closely with former president Yar'Adua following the 2007 elections. The CPC's base of support is in the north of the country. Buhari, its candidate in the 2011 presidential elections, finished second behind Nigeria's current president, Goodluck Jonathan.

Elections

Nigeria's electoral rules are straightforward, particularly in the case of the National Assembly. Candidates for the lower house, the House of Representatives, run in single-member districts and are selected on the basis of FPTP. For the Senate, each of the thirty-six federal territorial units is divided into three districts and selects three senators using FPTP rules in each district, without a threshold requirement. The Federal Capital Territory, home to the country's capital city of Abuja, selects only one senator.

The People's Democratic Party (PDP) did well in the 1999 elections that marked the reestablishment of democracy, winning a majority of governorships, a significant number of seats in the National Assembly, and the presidency under Olusegun Obasanjo. Obasanjo received over 62 percent of the vote in 1999 and nearly 62 percent in 2003. In 2003, the PDP received over 54 percent of the popular vote in the House of Representatives elections and gained control of more than 200 of its 360 seats. It also took a similar portion of the national vote in the Senate elections and won 76 of the 109 seats. The 2003 elections demonstrated that ethnic and regional divisions had not been purged from

Nigerian electoral politics. Obasanjo's main challenger in 2003, Muhammadu Buhari, was not only a former military ruler of Nigeria but also an ethnic Fulani and a Muslim. Not surprisingly, his support was heavily concentrated in the north.

The PDP increased its control of the legislative branch as a result of the elections in 2007. Although Nigeria's electoral commission had not posted the official results almost a year later, others estimated that the PDP won over 70 percent of the seats in both the House of Representatives and the Senate.[37] The many concerns about the 2007 elections expressed by the opposition parties and outside observers caused some to argue that, like Russia, Nigeria was on a path leading away from democracy.[38] The 2007 vote also highlighted the deepening regional concentration of party support, at least for the smaller parties. Following the elections, for example, representatives from the Action Congress (AC), the successor to the AD, held every House seat from the region of Lagos as well as all three of its Senate seats.

The May 29, 2007, presidential vote that brought President Umaru Yar'Adua to power offered an example of what consolidated democracies take for granted: a sitting democratically elected president peacefully turning over the reins of power to a newly elected president. After Yar' Adua died in office on May 5, 2010, Vice President Goodluck Jonathan officially took over as Nigeria's president. Jonathan had been serving as acting president because of Yar'Adua's health problems.

In April 2011, Nigeria held both legislative and presidential elections. Following significant instability, both elections were delayed by one week. Official returns in the legislative elections were slow to be reported, and voting for some legislative seats was delayed until the week following the presidential vote. The PDP retained its majorities in both houses. The results, however, indicated a decrease in support for the ruling party compared to 2007. In the presidential vote one week later, Goodluck Jonathan's victory was sizable: he received around 59 percent of the vote. His closest challenger, who again was Muhammadu Buhari, received just under 32 percent. Even more important, Jonathan won more than 25 percent of the vote in thirty-one of Nigeria's thirty-six federal territorial units. (Presidents must win at least 25 percent of the vote in two-thirds of the regions.) Examining the extent to which the 2011 elections were free and fair, Western observers considered both the legislative and presidential contests an improvement over 2007. On a more pessimistic note, the deep regional divide in the voting and the violence that followed the 2011 elections brought fears that the country might be slipping toward civil war, though by the middle of 2011 observers were less concerned than they had been in the spring.

Russia

During its first post-Soviet decade (1991–2000), the Russian party system was difficult to grasp. Some parties did relatively well in one election before virtually disappearing in the next. Only two parties consistently cleared the 5 percent threshold in parliamentary elections, and party identification was extremely fragile. This began to change with President Putin's emergence on the political scene at the end of 1999. By the time Putin had won reelection in 2004, Russia appeared headed for a one-party dominant system controlled by the United Russia Party. Dmitry Medvedev's election as president in 2008, and Putin's subsequent appointment as prime minister, confirmed the appropriateness of the one-party dominant label.

Political Parties

Russian political parties during the post-Soviet period can be placed into four groups. The first is actually a single party, the Communist Party of Russia, which has remained a visible player in Russian politics since the Soviet collapse in 1991. Prior to the period of creeping authoritarianism under Putin, it was the most popular party in the country and won the largest percentage of the party vote in the 1995 and 1999 parliamentary elections. Its supporters are largely older and rural voters, those most hurt by the economic changes in the country since the Soviet period.

The second group consists of nationalist parties emphasizing a strong state and a strong international reputation. The classic example is Vladimir Zhirinovsky's Liberal Democratic Party (LDP), created with the blessing of the Yeltsin government partly as an alternative to the Communist Party for those displeased with economic reform. The nationalists also included the Fatherland–All Russia (OVR) Party, affiliated with the popular mayor of Moscow, Yuri Luzhkov, in the late 1990s. Luzhkov later defected to Putin's United Russia Party, and the nationalist parties have been less important since Putin's consolidation of power after the 2000 presidential election.

The third group is made up of pro-Western, pro-reform parties. In the early 1990s, the main reform parties were Russia's Choice (headed by a former prime minister, Yegor Gaidar) and Yabloko (led by the economist Grigory Yavlinsky). Many observers of Russian politics expected these parties to do well in elections after the Soviet collapse, but their performance fell short of expectations. Yabloko maintained its presence as a small but important party until the early 2000s, but the successor party to Russia's Choice, Russia's Democratic Choice, failed to clear the 5 percent threshold in the 1995 parliamentary elections. At the end of the 1990s, it reemerged as the Union of Right Forces,

which cleared the threshold in the 1999 elections but not in 2003.

The final group is made up of pro-government parties. In the early 1990s, these overlapped somewhat with the reform parties. President Boris Yeltsin refused to form—or even really endorse—any party in 1993, though most believed he hoped that Russia's Choice would win the elections. In the middle of the 1990s, the main pro-government party was Our Home Is Russia, a party supportive of political reform but mostly concerned with improving the prospects of the Yeltsin administration and the prime minister at that time, Viktor Chenomyrdin.

By the end of the 1990s, the pro-government "party" was a hastily thrown together group known as the Unity Bloc. Putin, who had recently been appointed prime minister by President Yeltsin, openly, but unofficially, supported the bloc. This new party was formed to challenge the other major parties in the 1999 parliamentary elections and pave the way for Putin's presidential victory in 2000. By 2003, this pro-government party had taken the name United Russia. The party did well in the 2003 parliamentary elections and has helped facilitate Putin's control over Russian politics ever since.

By the middle of 2007, United Russia was poised to become the central party of Russia's emerging one-party dominant system. In December 2007, United Russia dominated elections to the Duma, Russia's lower house of parliament, and in March 2008, United Russia-supported Dmitry Medvedev won the presidential election and became Putin's successor.

Elections

The Russian Federation has had many important elections since its emergence from the collapse of the USSR. In addition to a national referendum in April 1993 and ratification of the new constitution in December of that year, parliamentary elections were held in 1993, 1995, 1999, 2003, and 2007 (with the next election scheduled for 2011). Presidential elections were held in 1996, 2000, 2004, and 2008 (and are scheduled for 2012). Several central themes emerged across the course of these elections. Pro-market and pro-Western political parties performed terribly in the parliamentary elections of the 1990s. On the other hand, the Unity/United Russia Party, associated with Vladimir Putin, performed well after 2000. Although elections in the early post-Soviet period had elements of bring free and fair, elections since 2000 have been increasingly criticized for their undemocratic character.

In Russia's first parliamentary elections, held in December 1993 to coincide with the vote on the new constitution, voters selecting members of the Duma had two votes: one for a candidate in a district and one for a party. Half of the Duma's 450 seats came from the district vote using FPTP rules, and the other 225 were based on the party vote using PR. Pro-reform parties did worse than expected. They saw each other as their main rivals and attacked each other rather than working together. Russia's Choice ended up with around the same number of seats as Zhirinovsky's LDP. The LDP won the PR vote handily, securing around 24 percent compared with 15 percent for Russia's Choice and 13 percent for the Communists. Independents won a large number of district races, reflecting the personal nature of Russian politics.

In 1995, voters again selected members of the Duma through the hybrid arrangement, this time for four-year terms. More parties ran in 1995 (forty-three, compared with only thirteen parties or blocs of parties in 1993), but only seven earned seats in the Duma. Of the roughly 2,800 candidates who ran in the 225 district races, more than 1,000 ran as independents. The Communist Party did best in the elections, and its portion of the party vote increased to 24 percent in 1995. Yet, it earned only around 150 of the Duma's 450 seats, far short of a majority. The percentage of the vote for the LDP dropped significantly, as the Communists replaced the LDP as the party of people seeking to protest Yeltsin's policies.

In the final elections before Yeltsin stepped down as president, the Communists continued their strong showing. They again won around 24 percent of the party vote. The surprise was the upstart Unity Bloc, informally affiliated with then-Prime Minister Putin, which won 23 percent of the PR vote. OVR also did well, earning 13 percent of the vote in part due to extremely favorable coverage from Moscow-based television stations.

In 2003, United Russia won the election, earning 37.6 percent of the vote. This gave it 120 seats from the PR vote alone. In combination with another 102 seats from district races and sympathetic independent candidates, the party controlled over 300 seats in the Duma. This marked the first time since the collapse of the USSR that a single party could count on the support of a majority of the members of the Duma. The Communists and the LDP earned about 12.5 percent and 11.5 percent of the party vote, respectively. Yabloko failed to clear the 5 percent threshold for the first time, along with the Union of Right Forces. The pro-reform parties of the 1990s had largely disappeared from Russian politics.

The process of party system consolidation continued in 2007, the first parliamentary election under the new PR-only electoral system. Four parties received enough votes to qualify for seats in the 450-seat Duma. Of the four, United Russia dominated the elections, receiving over 64 percent of the vote and 315 seats. Two of the other parties that cleared the threshold, the LDP and A Just Russia, received 40 and 38 seats, respectively, but both were widely viewed as pro-Putin. As in 2003, the only serious opposition party was the Communist Party of Russia, which received less than 12 percent of the vote and 57 seats. Shortly after the elections, United Russia and other pro-Putin parties pledged their support to Putin's handpicked successor, Dmitry Medvedev, to replace Putin as president in 2008.

The outcome of the presidential contests reflected the trend toward a one-party dominant system as well. In 1996, President Yeltsin won reelection in a runoff against the head of the Communist Party, Gennadi Zyuganov. In 2000, acting-President Putin, who had become president when Yeltsin unexpectedly resigned on New Year's Eve of 1999, sought election for his first full term. Putin won 53 percent of the vote in the first round, making a runoff vote unnecessary. Communist Party leader Zyuganov received 30 percent of the vote, showing the still solid core of Communist supporters in the country. In 2004, Putin was reelected, capturing 69 percent of the vote in the first round. Despite claims of electoral irregularities, the real story was how the Putin campaign controlled information prior to the vote. The Russian electronic media became Putin campaign outlets, and most of the candidates campaigned as if part of a predetermined process. In March 2008, Dmitry Medvedev ran as Putin's chosen successor and won handily. Putin actively supported Medvedev's candidacy, and Medvedev indicated that Putin would be the country's prime minister. With presidential elections on the horizon in 2012, many analysts were predicting that Putin would run once again for president. In late 2010 and early 2011, however, there was some indication that Medvedev preferred to seek reelection himself and have Putin remain prime minister.

China

Every other TIC country discussion in this chapter contains a discussion of multiple political parties. In China, the Chinese Communist Party (CCP) is the only party allowed to function openly. China is, consequently, a classic example of a one-party system. Elections at the local level offer a glimpse of democracy, but elections at the national level are indirect and tightly controlled by the CCP.

The Political Party

Though far from the ideal type of a totalitarian system, the Chinese Communists have learned from the fate of the USSR, have understood the dangers of allowing political opposition, and have maintained a monopoly of political power for themselves. The leadership of the CCP was officially in the hands of the chairman until the position was abolished in 1982. Mao was party chairman from 1949 until his death in 1976. He was also general secretary of the CCP during this time. In the Soviet Union, the general secretary position became synonymous with the leader of the country. Because official position was still less important than personal prestige in China during Deng Xiaoping's tenure, he was not general secretary but was still recognized as China's real leader.

Most major policy decisions are made in the top collective body in the party, the Politburo. The Politburo has between twenty and thirty members and sets both party and national government policy. While open debate is not something the CCP encourages, the discussions behind closed doors in the Politburo can be lively. The Politburo also has a smaller standing committee that makes decisions when the entire body is not meeting. Below the Politburo is the Central Committee, which is the part of the party that officially selects the Politburo members. More often than not it rubber stamps decisions of the Politburo and the leader of the country—including decisions about who should be added or taken off the Politburo—more than it pushes the Politburo on policy or genuinely shapes its membership. Today, the Central Committee has more than three hundred members. Below the Central Committee, but technically the highest organ of the CCP, is the party congress. The party congress meets every few years and officially picks the Central Committee (though in reality it is picked for the congress), and it ratifies major policy changes the CCP is proposing.

Elections

Though China is a one-party state, not all elections are meaningless. The government has resisted pressures to liberalize politically at the national level, but it does give some voters a say at the local level. The practice of allowing more-genuine elections in small towns began in 1980 when village elders in two rural counties sought greater control over practices they saw as hostile to traditional Communist farming practices. The result was "villagers' committees" (also called village committees), bodies that did not control state resources but did set certain policies within their communities.[39] Within two years, villagers' committees were in the constitution, though open elections to determine who held positions on them took longer.

Far from all of China's 930,000 villages participated in open villagers' committee elections during the 1990s. Many village leaders resisted implementing the reform entirely, and many of the villages that have instituted competitive elections have met only the bare minimum official government requirement of one more overall candidate than open position to fill.[40] Still, the long-term importance of these elections should not be dismissed.[41] Just as the large urban special economic zones had been a way of experimenting with capitalism before its more general acceptance, the selection

of village officials through competitive elections is an experiment in self-government. While the CCP tightly controls the nomination of officials for the indirect election of leaders at higher levels of government, candidates for village elections are not always those preferred by local CCP officials.

Iran

Following the Islamic Revolution in 1979, Iran looked to be heading toward a one-party or one-party dominant system. Instead, parties were replaced by loose electoral alliances. Even though it is largely considered an authoritarian system, elections in Iran matter. Though the range of candidates is narrowed prior to the vote, the results, as well as protests over certain results, can point to underlying trends in Iranian society.

Political Parties

Following the 1979 Islamic Revolution, two of the most important Iranian political parties were the People's Mojahedin Organization of Iran (PMOI) and the Islamic Republican Party (IRP). PMOI, which advocated a blend of socialist ideas and Islamic character, became a key member of the National Council of Resistance of Iran (NCR), an umbrella organization formed in 1981 to oppose the retreat from democracy following the revolution. NCR was forced to leave Iran—the organization is based in Paris at the present time—while PMOI was based in Iraq from 1986 until the American invasion in 2003. It has tried to maintain an active presence in Iraq since then, but its membership has dwindled, and the Iraqi government launched a crackdown on the PMOI in 2009.

Though Ayatollah Khomeini never belonged to the IRP, he supported it during and after the revolution. IRP leaders played a major role in drafting the post-revolution constitution. They also intimidated the other, smaller political parties through threats and, at times, violence. By the end of 1980, only the PMOI remained a serious challenger to the IRP. The two parties turned on each other, with violent clashes, bombings of party offices, and assassinations of leading party officials. In the end, the IRP emerged on top, and remaining PMOI leaders fled the country.

Iran was poised to become a one-party dominant or even one-party system in the early 1980s. In 1986, however, the IRP became divided, apparently over both economic policy and how uncompromising the government should be with the West. In response, the party's leaders—including the then-Iranian president and current Supreme Leader of the country, Ali Khamenei, and the man who would be president following Khamenei, Akbar-Hashemi Rafsanjani—asked Ayatollah Khomeini to support the disbanding of the IRP. He agreed, and

Iran's political system was transformed, with political parties playing a much less central role.

The Iranian constitution permits political parties and other organizations. However, it states that the parties cannot violate principles of "freedom, sovereignty, and national unity" or question the Islamic foundations of the state.[42] The government has used this statement to justify banning established political parties that threaten its vision of a theocratic Iranian state. Perhaps partly as a result, less structured electoral alliances have been the norm prior to elections. A conservative alliance, Islamic Iran Developers' Council (Etelaf-e Abadgaran-e Iran-e Eslami), for example, did well in the 2004 elections to the national legislature, the Majles, but it did not always act in unison following them.

Candidates who openly advocate democratization or a secular government are banned by the Guardian Council. Those that the Guardian Council allows to run generally fall into three groups. Hard-liners, such as current Iranian president Mahmoud Ahmadinejad, support an extreme theocratic state and question the vast wealth of the business sector in the country. Pragmatic conservatives, including former president Rafsanjani, support the regime as it is currently constituted, including its relationship with the business class. Moderates, such as former president Khatami and the runner-up in the 2009 presidential election, Mir Hossein Mousavi, favor an increase in political and social freedoms within the broad framework of an Islamic state.

Elections

Iran is an authoritarian system, and the level of electoral contestation for the Majles and the presidency is significantly curtailed by the Guardian Council. Even so, elections matter in Iran. A more moderate legislature, particularly if combined with a moderate president, can put pressure on the more conservative unelected components of the government. Success of pro-reform candidates also tell the government, the broader population, and observers outside Iran that many citizens continue to support a less hard-line approach to politics and social policies.

After candidates register to stand for election to the Majles, there is a two-month period of review, during which their "legitimacy" is determined by the Guardian Council, following initial screening by two other unelected bodies. Those who are approved run in electoral districts and vie for 285 of the 290 Majles seats, while the remaining 5 seats are set aside for religious minorities. Many of these districts have only one Majles seat, but the district of Tehran has thirty, which shows the size of Tehran compared to other cities in the country. No other electoral district in Iran has more than 6 seats.

In the first round of voting, a candidate must clear a certain threshold (currently 25 percent) to win a seat. If more candidates clear this threshold than the number of seats from the district, the top vote getters receive the seats. If not enough candidates clear the threshold to fill a district's seats, a second (runoff) round of voting takes place to fill the remaining seats. Twice as many candidates as open seats compete in the second round, with the candidates getting the most votes in the first round being the ones who face off in the second round.

Moderates did well in elections during Khatami's two terms as president, gaining control not only of the presidency but also of the Majles from 2000 to 2004. The pragmatic conservatives and hard-liners, on the other hand, have done particularly well since 2004. The Guardian Council's decisions to bar many reformist candidates from seeking legislative or presidential office have played a role in the hard-liners' successes. The actions of the Guardian Council were controversial both inside and outside the country, and reformers organized a boycott that drove down turnout in 2004. The Guardian Council repeated its efforts to keep reformers off the ballot in the 2008 Majles elections, helping conservatives maintain control despite growing disenchantment with President Ahmadinejad.

In the 2005 presidential race, Ahmadinejad was a surprising finalist, finishing in the top two in the first round of voting despite receiving less than 20 percent of the vote. In the runoff, Ahmadinejad won handily, gaining nearly 62 percent of the vote against his opponent, Akbar Hashemi-Rafsanjani. Rafsanjani had been president of the country from the late 1980s to the mid-1990s. Ahmadinejad portrayed him as a supporter of the corrupt, wealth-concentrating status quo and himself as a supporter of policies designed to help ordinary Iranians.[43] Western observers have tended to focus on Ahmadinejad's anti-U.S. and anti-Israel statements and his more hard-line interpretation of social and cultural practices in the country. In the end, however, the 2005 election was as much about economics as about Islam or Israel.

In 2009, Ahmadinejad's approach, and the results of the presidential vote, shared features with the 2005 election. In June 2009, Ahmadinejad defeated Mousavi and two other candidates. The outcome of the election, in which Ahmadinejad reportedly received nearly 63 percent of the vote, sparked the protests in large cities across the country, particularly in Tehran, known as the Green Revolution (see Chapter 8). Although his victory and the collapse of the Green Revolution secured another term in office for Ahmadinejad, the protests suggest a base of support for a future pro-reform candidate.

COUNTRY SUMMARY

TIC Country	Main Parties	Party System	Electoral System*
United Kingdom	Conservatives Labour Liberal Democrats	Two-and-a-half party; possibly emerging multiparty	FPTP for House of Commons; ITAP feature on Duverger's law
Germany	Christian Democratic Union/ Christian Social Union (CDU/CSU); Social Democrats (SPD); Free Democrats (FDP); The Left Alliance '90/ The Greens	Multiparty	Mixed (PR and FPTP) for Bundestag; Länder governments select Bundesrat; ITAP feature on realignment theory
India	Indian National Congress (INC, "Congress"); Bharatiya Janata Party (BJP)	Multiparty	FPTP for the Lok Sabha; regional governments select Rajya Sabha
Mexico	National Action Party (PAN); Party of the Democratic Revolution (PRD); Institutional Revolutionary Party (PRI); ITAP feature on party organization theory	Multiparty; formerly one-party dominant (under PRI)	Mixed (PR and FPTP) for Chamber of Deputies; FPTP/SPTP-MMD for Senate FPTP for president
Brazil	Worker's Party (PT); Brazilian Democratic Movement Party (PMDB); Liberal Front Party (PFL); Brazilian Social Democratic Party (PSDB)	Multiparty	Open list PR for Chamber of Deputies; FPTP-MMD for Senate; FPTP-majoritarian (two-round) for president
Nigeria	People's Democratic Party (PDP); All Nigeria People's Party (ANNP); Congress for Progressive Change (CPC); Action Congress (AC)	Emerging one-party dominant	FPTP for House of Representatives; FPTP-MMD for Senate; FPTP (with threshold rules) for president
Russia	United Russia; Communist Party of the Russian Federation; Liberal Democratic Party (LDP)	One-party dominant	PR for Duma; Regional governments select Federation Council; FPTP-majoritarian (two-round) for president
China	Chinese Communist Party (CCP)	One party	Indirect for president and premier; FPTP-modified majoritarian (two-round, 33%) for local elections

TIC Country	Main Parties	Party System	Electoral System*
Iran	No meaningful parties compared to the other TIC cases; a large number of officially recognized political organizations that support particular candidates; electoral alliances form prior to elections for the Majles	"No party" system, but multiple electoral alliances	FPTP-modified majoritarian (two-round, 25%)-MMD for Majles; FPTP-majoritarian (two-round) for president

Spotlight on . . . Country

France	Union for a Popular Movement (UMP); Socialist Party; Democratic Movement; National Front	Multiparty	FPTP-majoritarian (two-round) for president; FPTP-modified majoritarian (two-round, 25%) for National Assembly; indirect elections for Senate, with senators selected by a 150,000-member electoral college made up of local and regional officials
Iraq	Many small parties, but major alliances include State of Law Coalition; Iraqi National Movement (INM); National Iraqi Alliance (INA); Kurdistan Alliance	Multiparty system, with many small parties; electoral alliances are common	Open list PR-MMD (18 districts with different numbers of representatives from each) for Council of Representatives; at least 25% of members of parliament must be women
South Africa	African National Congress (ANC); Democratic Alliance (DA); Congress of the People (COPE)	One-party dominant	For National Assembly, half the seats come from open list PR-MMD races in 9 districts; remaining seats come from a PR based on results of national vote Indirect elections for Council of Provinces, with the provincial assemblies of each of the 9 provinces selecting 10 members; indirect for president (selected by National Assembly)

*Unless specified, FPTP means plurality voting and single-member districts.

TIC Wrap-Up

In addition to sharing a history of undemocratic political systems, Iran, China, Russia, and Nigeria currently have either one main political party or no main parties. In Iran, a system that had been heading in the direction of a one-party dominant system became instead a no party system. China is a classic one-party system, while Russia and Nigeria each currently has one dominant party plus other parties that receive a noticeable portion of the vote.

The remaining five TIC cases are all two-and-a-half or multiparty systems. Only in the UK is one of the major parties likely to control a majority of seats in the national legislature on a regular basis, and even so the 2010 elections failed to produce a majority party in Parliament. A multiparty system was historically not the case in India and Mexico. Both countries had one-party dominant systems, under the Indian National Congress and the Institutional Revolutionary Party, respectively, which became multiparty systems as other parties increased their share of the vote.

Electoral systems employing proportional representation are common around the world, particularly in many European countries. Yet, among the nine TIC cases, only Brazil and Russia use a PR approach in selecting representatives to their legislatures' lower houses. Brazil's PR approach is different from those in many countries, as voters can select a party but also have the option to rank candidates on that party's list. Russia's system is more pure PR, but Russia came to this approach relatively recently. In the first portion of the post-Soviet period, Russia used a hybrid system, combining PR and FPTP district votes to select members of the lower house of parliament, the Duma.

Four of the TIC cases, the UK, India, Nigeria, and Iran, use FPTP arrangements in their legislative elections. The UK and India are parliamentary systems, in which the results of these legislative elections determine the selection of the chief executive. Like other presidential systems, Nigeria holds separate elections for a president and for legislative representatives. In its Majles elections, Iran combines the SMD and MMD approaches, with many districts having only one legislative seat and others having as many as thirty. The most important rule in Iran's elections is the requirement that candidates be approved by the unelected Guardian Council in order to appear on the ballot.

Germany and Mexico provide examples of how PR and FPTP approaches can be combined in unique ways. The rules for election to the lower house in Germany, the Bundestag, are complicated. The system gives some seats to candidates on the basis of FPTP-SMD rules and others through PR rules. Because the two larger parties fail to secure a majority of the seats in the Bundestag, coalition governments are the norm. In Mexico, both the Chamber of Deputies and the Senate are elected through a combination of FPTP and PR.

At the national level, China has the least democratic elections of any of the TIC cases. The most interesting developments in Chinese elections have taken place at the local level. Far from all of China's villages have participated in the democratic experiment. Yet, such elections could, perhaps, plant a seed that grows into greater support for democracy at the national level.

Research in Context

While some comparative politics research tests existing theories by examining a number of cases, other studies focus on clarifying concepts or proposing a different way to measure concepts. Sometimes, the journal articles that result from such research can make the reader think more carefully about both a concept and how it might be measured.

Islam has become a major topic in political science in general and comparative politics in particular. How one goes about examining the political relevance of Islam in a country is not easy to determine. Particularly in a nondemocratic system, it may be difficult to determine Islam's political impact. A policy outcome might be the result of the government responding to the perceived desires of its Muslim population, or the government may simply have been using elements of Islam to justify policies that it believes help it remain in power. In more democratic systems, the power of "political Islam" is often assessed by electoral support for Islamic parties and their resulting presence in a national legislature or ruling coalition. Thus, the "political" part of "political Islam" is associated with elections.

Islamic Parties and Islamic Politics in Indonesia

In 2010, Sunny Tanuwidjaja, a political science graduate student at the time, published an article on Islamic politics and Islamic political parties in Indonesia.[44] Tanuwidjaja's article assessed the widely held claim that Islam was becoming less politically important in Indonesia. In addition to survey data pointing to increasing secularization, the main evidence for this belief was the declining electoral success of Islamic political parties in the country. In 1955, such parties captured 44 percent of the vote, but this percentage decreased to just over 36 percent in 1999—arguably the first democratic elections since 1955—and then rose to slightly to 41 percent in 2004, before dropping below 30 percent in 2009.

In his article, Tanuwidjaja argues that even though Islamic parties did not do as well at the polls in 2009 as they had earlier, one must be careful about concluding that Islam was in decline as a political force. Looking at policy outcomes in the country at both the national and local levels, and the policy positions of major parties in national elections, tells a very different story from that told by the election outcomes. Not only were a number of laws that the Islamic parties had been pushing adopted in the country, but other major parties, especially two of the main nationalist parties, Golkar and the Demokrat Party (PD), were also openly courting Muslim voters leading up to the 2009 elections. As Tanuwidjaja puts it, "The two parties—which identify more closely with nationalist and secular ideologies—are shifting their party positions by becoming more accommodative towards religious agendas."[45] With nationalist parties articulating such positions, the decline in support for Islamic parties need not signal that voters were tuning out Islamic political messages. Rather, more conservative Islam-focused voters now had other outlets that accepted many of the voters' policy preferences but offered other reasons to support them, such as expertise in government, favorable economic policies, and a likelihood of winning the election, that the Islamic parties could not match.

So What?

In the United States, the rhetoric surrounding Islam often contains broad-brush claims. Some supporters of the political Right have called Islam a violent religion and have claimed that nearly all Muslims support terrorism against the United States. The political Left has been quick to dismiss claims that predominantly Muslim countries pose a significant threat to the United States. Tanuwidjaja's research tackles the important issue of Islam's influence on the domestic politics of countries outside the United States, examining it in the world's most populous Muslim country.

Tanuwidjaja's article reminds those interested in Islam in other countries that they need to look deeper than they sometimes do. Islamic political parties are not necessarily growing in strength, and helping establish democracy in formerly nondemocratic Muslim countries does not guarantee that Islamic parties will control the government. Neither do their declining electoral fortunes in a country like Indonesia signal that their influence is decreasing. Declining vote totals for Islamic parties can, and in the case of Indonesia appear to, reflect other parties adopting Islamic parties' policy positions. This strategy has worked in Indonesia because many Muslim voters neither blindly follow Islamic parties nor ignore their religion as they examine the aggregated and articulated interests of those seeking electoral office.

CONCLUSION

Comparativists who are interested in mass participation and elite-mass linkage commonly examine political parties and elections in democratic political systems. In democracies, parties and elections are part of a complex relationship. Parties and their candidates compete for office in elections. Electoral rules partially determine which (and how many) parties and candidates are successful. In addition, changes in patterns of a country's electoral outcomes, as well as changes in its party system, can represent other fundamental changes in its political structure. No part of Mexico's transition to democracy has been more visible than the move from a one-party dominant system controlled by the PRI to a system based on genuine multiparty competition.

Social divisions in many democracies affect the nature of parties and party systems, but the practice of voting can deepen social divisions. In new democracies in particular, electoral politics and identity politics frequently become intertwined. In Nigeria, the PDP's control of the national government masks strong regional showings by other parties, which increasingly turn to identity-based appeals to head off the PDP's growing dominance.

Nondemocratic systems also generally incorporate both political parties and elections. China shows how a dominant political party can be the vehicle for authoritarian political control, although other nondemocratic leaders appear increasingly compelled to hold national elections. As countries such as Iran and, increasingly, Russia demonstrate, however, political leaders often work both openly and behind the scenes to prevent these elections from being genuine contests that threaten the ruling government's control of the state.

Think and Discuss

The previous chapter discussed non-electoral mechanisms for linking elites and masses. This chapter focuses on political parties and elections. Which of these sets of mechanisms are more important for understanding mass participation and how masses are linked to elites? Why?

The next chapter focuses more closely on individuals and their decisions. Up to this point, we have seen various accounts of the way that individual leaders matter to a political system, how elites and masses interact, and some of the factors that influence individuals' decisions to participate or not participate in collective political activities. At the same time, the starting point for these discussions has been structures: economic, cultural, identity, and political. Chapter 10 moves squarely to the choice side of the structure versus choice framework, focusing on individuals and their political decision making.

KEY TERMS

Alternative vote (AV), p. 267
Catch-all parties, p. 273
Critical elections, p. 274
Duverger's law, p. 272
Election, p. 265
First past the post (FPTP), p. 266
Hybrid electoral system, p. 268
Majority (majoritarian) system, p. 266
Multi-member district (MMD), p. 267
Multiparty system, p. 263

One-party dominant system, p. 261
One-party system, p. 261
Open list proportional representation (open list PR), p. 265
Party identification, p. 260
Party organization theory, p. 276
Party system, p. 261
Political party, p. 259
Preference system, p. 267
Primary election, p. 267

Proportional representation (PR), p. 265
Realignment theory, p. 274
Runoff, p. 266
Second past the post (SPTP), p. 268
Single-member district (SMD), p. 267
Single transferable vote (STV) system, p. 267
Threshold, p. 266
Two-and-a-half party system, p. 262
Two-party system, p. 262

Leadership and the Importance of Individuals in the Political Process

Adolf Hitler, left, shakes hands with King Boris III of Bulgaria, 1941.
© DIZ Muenchen GmbH, Sueddeutsche Zeitung Photo/Alamy

CHAPTER OUTLINE

Leadership and the Importance of Individuals in the Political Process

Decision Making: Rational and Otherwise

TOPIC IN COUNTRIES

Features in this chapter:

Spotlight on . . . South Africa: The Leadership of Nelson Mandela

In Theory and Practice: India and Incrementalism

In Theory and Practice: Rational Choice Theory and the Mexican Government's Support of NAFTA

In Theory and Practice: Deng Xiaoping, Tiananmen Square, and Elite Learning

Research in Context: The Leadership Styles of David Cameron and Margaret Thatcher

LEARNING OBJECTIVES

After reading this chapter, you should be able to

- Describe the basic features of the choice approach.

- Discuss the differences among leadership traits, skills, and style.

- Discuss the strengths and weaknesses of focusing on leadership as a way of understanding political outcomes.

- Explain rational choice theory and propose criticisms of it.

- Provide examples from the chapter about the importance of specific individuals in shaping political outcomes.

During World War II, Bulgaria was under the leadership of King Boris III. Hoping to be able to regain territories in Macedonia, Greece, and Serbia that Bulgaria had lost in earlier wars, the king agreed to an alliance with Nazi Germany. As part of dealing with Nazi Germany, the Bulgarian government secretly agreed to send at least twenty thousand Jews to Poland, where they were to be placed in concentration camps. The majority were to come from the regions Bulgaria had seized from neighboring countries but between six thousand and eight thousand were to come from Bulgaria itself.

As the deportation process was about to begin in Bulgaria, the vice president of the Bulgarian National Assembly, Dimitar Peshev, went public about the secret plan.[1] Forty-two others in the legislature signed a letter to the king and Prime Minister Bogdan Filov asking that the deportations be stopped. Peshev's actions led leaders of the Orthodox Church in Sofia to speak out, and mass demonstrations broke out in opposition to the plan. While some in the Bulgarian government began discussing a new plan to deport all of the nearly fifty thousand Jews in Bulgaria,[2] the king instead ordered Bulgaria's Jews to be put into internal exile within Bulgaria, many in labor camps, rather than turning them over to the Nazis. Although more than ten thousand Jews from Bulgarian-controlled neighboring regions had already been deported, the king's refusal to follow through with the plan to deport the Jews inside Bulgaria as well—a decision sparked by Peshev's courageous choice to speak out against the deportation plan—saved the lives of thousands.

To this point, much of this textbook has focused on the economic, social, and political settings within which political outcomes occur. As important as these socioeconomic and political structures can be, political outcomes are, most directly, the result of political choices made by individuals—many by political leaders such as Dimitar Peshev and King Boris III, others by ordinary citizens. Political scientist Eric Selbin highlights the importance of both elite and mass choices in revolutions:

> Leaders play a unique role in social revolutions, organizing the population, and perhaps most importantly, articulating the vision—the ideas and ideals—around which they rally. The population, in turn, responds to these entreaties or not; if they do, it is they who determine how far and how fast the process unfolds and often shape the efforts of the leaders to their reality.[3]

This chapter addresses the importance of individuals in politics. Most history text-book accounts of specific political events (revolutions, wars, dramatic policy reforms, etc.) emphasize individuals and their decisions, but structural explanations typically receive more attention in comparative politics.[4] In this book, the concentration on individuals and their decisions is referred to as the **choice approach**. In other books, it is known as focusing on "agency," referring to the idea of individuals as agents of political change.[5] Other terms comparativists use to refer to the choice approach include *elite-focused explanation*, *micro-approach*, *intentionalism*, *voluntarism*, and *decision-making analysis*.

Individual-based explanations of political outcomes spotlight two distinct ideas. The first centers on the concept of leadership and holds that the traits of individual polit-ical figures have a big impact on political outcomes. History is often taught through an examination of the actions of great leaders. Of course, bad leaders are no less important, and not all political decisions are good ones. Leaders' misperceptions can play important roles in political outcomes. Given the emphasis of studies of leadership on the style and background of political leaders, the first part of this chapter's Topic in Countries (TIC) sections highlights the characteristics of the countries' current leaders.

Arguing that individual leaders' traits are crucial to political outcomes is problematic. How can one develop and test theories about unique leaders at different points in time and in varying settings around the world? The choice approach anchors itself to indi-viduals, but it does not stop there. The ultimate goal of most scholars employing choice theories is to understand political action in a general sense. The discussion of a particular leader, for example, is placed in the context of broader understandings of leadership.

This is also true of those who focus on the second half of the choice approach's dual nature: individual decision making. Theories about decision making seek to explain how individuals, in general, approach the process of making political deci-sions. Such theories are based on generalizable ideas (e.g., that humans act ration-ally to maximize the likelihood of realizing their personal interests). Explanations of specific political events—such as a country's democratization—might highlight indi-vidual action, but theorizing about democratization requires moving into the more generalizable realm of decision making. In addition to presenting a number of theo-ries about decision making, this chapter's TIC sections examine how individuals have shaped important political events in each country by analyzing a decision in light of how rational it appears to have been.

Choice Approach A broad approach to understanding political outcomes that emphasizes concepts such as leadership and individual decision making.

Leadership and the Importance of Individuals in the Political Process

The traits of the individuals who make political decisions have an impact on the form those decisions take. One of the key ways that political decision makers in positions of power differ from one another is in their ability as leaders. Thus, a great deal of work across social science disciplines has been conducted on the topic of leadership.

Leadership is the ability to influence members of a particular group to achieve a set of defined goals, ideally without making them feel that they are being forced. Successful leaders hold positions of authority but also have the ability to convince or inspire those they lead to take certain actions. This ability might come from a leader's captivating style—psychologist Howard Gardner states that leaders must be good "storytellers"[6]—or it may result from an effective argument about the necessity of the task at hand. Note that the perceived value of charisma in leadership potential echoes Max Weber's discussion of charismatic authority, introduced in Chapter 1.

Leadership The ability to influence a group to achieve goals through the combination of a position of authority, effective argumentation, and charisma.

Leadership Traits

Political scientists utilize a number of concepts and perspectives on leadership, includ-ing many that were originally developed in disciplines like psychology and business administration. Across these different perspectives, one can identify three important themes: successful leaders have certain common character traits, successful leaders develop certain skills that contribute to their effectiveness, and successful leaders tend to have particular leadership styles that help them to reach their goals.

Those who emphasize **leadership traits** view the ability to lead as driven by particular inborn traits such as general intelligence rather than by learned skills. Trait theory proposes that an individual possessing these traits can more effectively achieve key policy goals. Although this view of leadership has been around since the early 1900s, it has failed to gain wide acceptance. In addition to recognizing that leadership may involve more than innate features, scholars have not been able to agree on the exact list of essential traits or how to identify and measure them.

> **Leadership Traits** Innate personal qualities that make for a successful leader.

Leadership Skills

Rather than search for natural and fixed characteristics, other social scientists turned their attention to **leadership skills**, focusing on attributes of leaders that can be learned and developed. These include technical knowledge about the subject in question, the ability to work well with people, and the capacity to grasp a problem conceptually and express a vision about addressing it. These individual attributes create competencies that drive leadership outcomes.[7]

> **Leadership Skills** Qualities that can be developed, such as technical expertise and the ability to work with others.

Leadership Style

The concept of **leadership style**, which is connected to arguments from psychology about the importance of personality, considers how leaders approach relationships with colleagues and subordinates. One can consider, for example, the extent to which a leader is relationship-oriented or task-oriented. Leaders who combine both orientations are more likely to be successful at achieving their policy goals than those who possess one or neither. This view of leadership is a common approach to examining leaders in studies of business management, educational administration, and health care.

> **Leadership Style** The approach a leader takes when interacting with those working for him or her, including task-oriented behaviors and relationship-oriented behaviors.

Spotlight on ... SOUTH AFRICA

The Leadership of Nelson Mandela

South Africa's Nelson Mandela was one of the most important world leaders of the last century. He helped bring an end to the apartheid system in South Africa, governed South Africa as its first postapartheid president, and represented to the world the concept of racial equality and the struggle against political repression.[8] Born Rolihlahla Mandela (he received the name Nelson later as a boarding school student), the future South African president became politically active during the 1940s in the African National Congress, where others noted his discipline and work ethic.[9]

As an emerging leader in the struggle against apartheid, Mandela's adherence to a vision of equality is one of the main leadership traits that shaped him. As many other great leaders have also done, he developed the self-perception of being a person who could save his people from their current hardships. At his trial before being imprisoned during apartheid, Mandela defended his use of sabotage as a response to the white government's repression of black South Africans:

> Some of the things so far told to the court are true and some are untrue. I do not, however, deny that I planned sabotage. I did not plan it in a spirit of recklessness, nor because I have any love of violence. I planned it as a result of a calm and sober assessment of the political situation that had arisen after many years of tyranny, exploitation, and oppression of my people by the whites.[10]

His resulting imprisonment made him a global symbol of struggle against apartheid, the system of legalized racial segregation in South Africa that was finally dismantled in the early 1990s.

In the postapartheid period, Mandela became the first president of a democratic South Africa. His track record as president is more open to debate than is his role in ending apartheid. Some argue that he was a more passive president than his rise to power would have predicted, which ultimately weakened the office of the South African president for his successors.[11] Most scholars, however, see his legacies as largely positive. He was a forceful advocate for democratization in Africa, and he is part of the reason that the continent is far more democratic than it had been in the past.[12] He relinquished power voluntarily, something far from the norm across Africa. He also contributed to a favorable image of South Africa in the rest of the world, aiding its postapartheid transition and, among other achievements, helping it secure the 2010 World Cup.

Decision Making: Rational and Otherwise

In addition to emphasizing concepts such as leadership and the characteristics of successful leaders, political science research based on the choice approach often concentrates on features of the decision-making process. Within this body of research, decision making is generally viewed as a largely rational process. However, aided by insights from disciplines such as psychology, a growing number of political scientists have become skeptical of the idea that individuals routinely employ rational calculations to make political decisions.

Rationality

Rationality A condition in which people base decisions on reason and logic, leading them to act in ways that they believe will maximize their personal interests.

Rationality is arguably the most important, and most controversial, concept related to political decision making. Rationality is a condition in which people base their decisions on reason, taking logical steps in an effort to maximize their interests. Comparativists who emphasize rational decision making generally contend that rational decision makers are self-interested and that their interests are concrete and material, such as gaining more economic wealth, although some contend that people's interests may be less objective things such as power or even emotional well-being. Whatever the specific interests, individuals operating in a fully rational manner determine and rank their goals, assess their options' costs and benefits, and choose the option that they believe maximizes the likelihood of achieving their most important goals with the fewest costs.

The idea of rational political decisions makes a fair amount of sense when thinking about political elites, although it is less clear that the masses engage in rational calculations as they formulate their political choices. In political science studies that focus on rational decision making, rationality is typically assumed rather than empirically tested. Most actual tests of the idea of rational decision making do not inspire confidence that individuals, particularly the mass public, in fact make rational political decisions.

Scholars who emphasize individual rationality are often interested in understanding collective political outcomes. Such collective decisions include voting and joining political organizations. The approach of examining collective outcomes via individual rational decisions came to political science by way of economics, which is one of the reasons that interests are often defined in economic terms.[13] Voters, for example, are assumed to make their assessments about candidates on the basis of their own economic well-being, a process usually referred to as **pocketbook calculations**. These

Pocketbook Calculations Voters' assessments made on the basis of their personal economic well-being.

are either **retrospective calculations**—"Am I better off than I was four years ago?"— or **prospective calculations**—"Will I be better off in the future?" Other voters may take into account the well-being of society as a whole, which is known as making **sociotropic calculations**. Sociotropic calculations can also be prospective or retrospective.

Bounded Rationality

A number of social scientists have challenged whether fully rational decisions are possible. In the late 1940s, for example, political scientist Herbert Simon proposed the concept of **bounded rationality** as a challenge to the dominance of "comprehensively rational" models in economics.[14] Simon's notion of checks on full rationality, which earned him the Nobel Prize in economics, emphasizes the extent to which individuals are constrained in their decision making, particularly by cognitive limitations.

The bounded rationality concept does not hold that people are stupid. Rather, it asserts that greater demands are placed on, and more information is available to, decision makers than they can possibly digest in a fully rational manner. Short-term memory, computation skills, and attention are finite. These limits are more important the more difficult the decision-making task. Simon is particularly known for the idea of **satisficing**, a decision-making model that states that humans select the first option they find that satisfies their aspirations rather than conducting an exhaustive search for the best choice, which is what an "ideal" rational decision maker would do.

Non-rationality

Some political scientists contend that even bounded rational decisions are few and far between. Influenced by psychology more than economics, they focus their study of political decision making on situations and settings in which individuals might act less than rationally. Such views highlight psychological tendencies that interfere with people's ability to process information and make a choice based on logic and reason.

Cognitive Dissonance

Cognitive dissonance is a psychological concept with important political implications. People do not like to hold obviously contradictory positions or engage in obviously inconsistent behaviors. The dissonance between incongruous positions or behaviors—like playing a white and black key that are next to each other on a piano at the same time—is hard for many people to tolerate, particularly over time. So far, this sounds like rational thinking, but it may not be. Evidence from psychological experiments shows that people's initial position on an issue influences their interpretation of additional evidence about that issue and can even lead them to reject this new information outright.

Groupthink

Another concept highlighted by those who question the idea of fully rational individual decision making involves the dynamics of making a decision in a group. Because politics involves interactions among individuals, how individuals behave in groups is an important question. **Groupthink**, for example, occurs when individuals succumb to pressure from the group of which they are a part. Their positions on an issue, and even how they come to view the issue, can be shaped greatly by the arguments of others in the group. They fear standing out and instead go along with the crowd. Like more extreme forms of mob mentality, groupthink typically has little in common with fully rational thought.

Retrospective Calculations Choosing candidates or parties to support on the basis of recent performance by the government.

Prospective Calculations Choosing candidates or parties to support on the basis of which politician or political party is expected to perform best in the future.

Sociotropic Calculations Assessments by voters that take into account the well-being of society as a whole.

Bounded Rationality The idea that humans are cognitively limited in important ways that restrict their ability to process information in a comprehensively rational manner.

Satisficing Choosing the first acceptable solution rather than searching for a best solution.

Cognitive Dissonance The idea that people do not like to hold obviously contradictory positions, which can lead them to reject additional evidence about a topic if it runs counter to their initial beliefs.

Groupthink Quietly going along with the apparent decision of the group even if one disagrees with it, due to a desire to "fit in."

Transference, Mood, and Emotion

While both cognitive dissonance and groupthink imply some element of conscious thought, scholars working in psychology and related fields are increasingly recognizing the extent to which decision making is influenced by important but unconscious processes. For example, concepts such as **transference** highlight the unconscious role of past experiences in present behavior. The process of transference is like a lens that filters initial experiences through past contacts or relationships with similar settings or individuals. As a 2007 *Science News* article put it, "A variety of evidence now suggests that the brain continually maps current experiences, such as interactions with new people, onto prior ones—namely, the thoughts, feelings, motivations, and relationship styles associated with important people from the past."[15] As a result, transference can significantly affect an individual's first impressions and behaviors both inside and outside of the political arena.

Beyond specific concepts such as transference, broader processes, such as **emotion** and **mood**, operate at a subconscious level but still affect people's ability to make rational choices. Although people often use the terms interchangeably, psychologists generally distinguish between mood and emotion. Emotions are intense, short-lived responses to specific events or objects. Moods are less intense but deeper and longer lasting feelings that may not be tied to particular events.

These deep or short-lived feelings, which psychologists often call "affective states," include joy, surprise, fear, anger, and shame. Empirical research supports the view that they interfere with rational thought in some cases and enhance it in others. Studies have shown, for example, that those in mildly positive moods not only make more positive judgments about things they confront but are also better at processing information than those in mildly negative moods. Fear can lead to interpreting events as more threatening. Frustration, the result of unfulfilled anticipation, is associated with support for aggressive responses.

Transference A concept that highlights the extent to which contact or experiences are filtered through past contacts or relationships with similar individuals or settings.

Emotion An intense short-term response to a specific event.

Mood Less intense than emotions but deeper and longer lasting feelings, which may not be tied to particular events.

TOPIC IN COUNTRIES

If leadership and decision making are as important as many comparativists believe them to be, a deep understanding of a particular country's politics requires getting a handle on its leaders' backgrounds and approaches to leadership and their most important decisions. Choosing who and what to highlight when providing a quick overview of a country's leaders and important decisions is difficult. Many countries have long histories of influential and well-known leaders, as well as ineffective and often forgotten ones, who provide equally interesting and valuable lessons about leadership. Each of the following Topic in Countries sections focuses on the country's current leader or leaders, as well as one example of an important past decision and how rational the decision appears to have been. (The feature on pages 310–312 also highlights important recent leaders in several of the TIC cases.) Leadership can change. Not only can early elections bring in new leaders of parliamentary systems, but this chapter was written prior to 2012 presidential elections in Mexico and Russia and an anticipated leadership change in China. As you read the following country discussions, be sure to look for

- The current leader or leaders of each of the TIC cases as of late 2011.
- An important previous leader from each country.
- A major decision from each of the TIC cases and how rational it was.
- Additional theories associated with leadership capabilities.

The United Kingdom

The political history of the United Kingdom includes many important political leaders, from monarchs of the past to previous prime ministers like Winston Churchill. Individuals have had a tremendous influence on the evolution of the British political system. In recent decades, leaders have included controversial and persuasive prime ministers such as Margaret Thatcher and Tony Blair, as well as more workmanlike prime ministers such as John Major and Gordon Brown.

Leadership: David Cameron

This section includes an overview of the background and leadership characteristics of current British Prime Minister David Cameron. Cameron and his connections to former Prime Minister Margaret Thatcher are also the topic of this chapter's Research in Context feature. The leader of the Conservative Party, Cameron became prime minister following the May 2010 parliamentary elections in which the Conservatives received the most seats in the House of Commons but fell short of securing a majority. He and Nick Clegg, the leader of the Liberal Democrats, reached an agreement to work together in Parliament. Their agreement allowed Cameron to take the prime ministership away from Gordon Brown of the Labour Party, who had been prime minister from 2007 to 2010 following Tony Blair's resignation.

While Brown was known as smart and detail-oriented but also as a less-than-inspiring leader (the *New York Times* stated that Brown possessed a "tortured, self-lacerating intensity"[16]), Cameron's qualities and leadership style remind many people of Tony Blair. Young (he was forty-three when he became prime minister), energetic, and well-spoken, Cameron also managed to present his party as a more moderate alternative to the ruling Labour Party during the campaign. He is viewed as "more pragmatic than ideological," a trait some attribute to his upbringing in rural England, which led him to value traditional family structures but remain open to alternatives to address a pressing problem.[17] He has family connections to the aristocracy, is distantly connected to the royal family, and was educated in elite schools, and others point to this lineage and background as generating a self-confidence that can get in the way of understanding policy complexities.[18] Unlike Blair, however, Cameron's party does not control a majority of the House of Commons, which means that his leadership abilities will be tested even more than Blair's were. He must not only lead the country but must also keep the Liberal Democrats content in their partnership with the Conservatives.

A Rational Decision? Margaret Thatcher and the Falkland Islands War

The daughter of a shopkeeper, Margaret Thatcher was elected to Parliament in her mid-thirties and became a part of the cabinet as education minister in her mid-forties. When she led the Conservatives to victory and became prime minister in 1979, she did so on a platform of controlling labor union influence and limiting the growth of government spending. While most known for these domestic policy changes and the related contraction of the size of the national government, Margaret Thatcher also carved a place for herself in British history with her strong foreign policy leadership. When Argentina seized the Falkland Islands in 1982, Thatcher had a number of options. Her own Foreign Office (the British equivalent of the U.S. State Department), British defense advisers, and even the U.S. government counseled her against trying to retake the islands. Without someone like Thatcher as prime minister, the United Kingdom would likely not have fought to regain the Falklands.[19]

How can one understand Thatcher's decision to use violence to regain control of the Falklands? While not denying that mood and emotion played a role, the Falklands decision may be an example of rational decision making. Thatcher weighed the costs of the war to the benefits of reclaiming the islands, maintaining the British reputation as a military power, and bolstering her domestic standing if the conflict ended successfully. Although she expected criticism from the rest of Europe, she knew she could count on support from British Commonwealth countries and on the United States at worst to remain quiet; indeed, the United States did more than that, providing useful intelligence to the British military.

Thus, once Thatcher came to believe that diplomatic efforts had little chance of success, she turned to what she took to be the best, albeit unpopular, decision: to pursue

Margaret Thatcher, known as the UK's "Iron Lady" during her time as prime minister, shown here addressing the Conservative Party conference in the city of Blackpool in 1985.
© BRIAN HARRIS/Alamy

a military response. Against the mountain of advice to continue to negotiate—and against public opinion, which was against military action—Thatcher mobilized the military. The ultimate British victory confirmed her international reputation as Britain's "Iron Lady." It also elevated her status domestically, helping lock up a sizable Conservative Party electoral victory in 1984.

Germany

German political history is full of important leaders, including Otto von Bismarck, who formed the modern German state, and Adolf Hitler, who turned its repressive apparatus against the rest of Europe and part of Germany's own population. Today, Germany's political system disperses executive power through coalition governments, federalism, and a policy-making process that grants key interest groups a strong voice in negotiating and implementing policy. Still, some chancellors have proven to be strong leaders. Their personalities and skills have transformed the political system's structural constraints into opportunities. Other opportunities to excel as leaders have come in the form of major challenges, such as those leading up to and following German reunification in 1990.

Leadership: Angela Merkel

The consensus democratic system of the post–World War II German Federal Republic has forced leaders to work with others. As a result, contemporary German leaders have been known more for their hard work and ability to bridge divides than for their charisma. Germany's current chancellor, Angela Merkel, is no exception. Hardworking and with a formidable intellect, she rose quickly

German Chancellor Angela Merkel gestures during a press conference in Berlin, Germany. © Andreas Rentz/Getty Images

through the ranks of the CDU to become party chair in 2000.[20] She is Germany's first female chancellor and the first chancellor of the Federal Republic from the east. Merkel is not a typical CDU politician in other respects. She is Protestant, divorced, without children, and a scientist with an advanced degree in physics.

Merkel honed her problem-solving skills in her earlier career as a physicist. She developed a reputation as a good listener who allows all sides to air their views before pursuing a consensus decision.[21] At the same time, she was seen as forward looking, understanding the benefit of many small steps in the same direction. In 2007, Henry Kissinger described Merkel's leadership style as "the art of accomplishing great goals through the accumulation of nuance."[22]

Merkel heads a coalition between the Christian Democratic Union/Christian Social Union (CDU/CSU) and the Free Democrats. Merkel's ruling coalition, formed after the September 2009 elections, succeeded the grand coalition between the CDU/CSU and the Social Democrats (SPD). That grand coalition formed in 2005 and lasted longer than many observers thought it would at the time, a tribute to Merkel's leadership efforts. Many believed that the chancellor would have great difficulty enforcing discipline on the two rival parties turned governing partners. At least for the first few years of the coalition, this was not the case. With a Bundestag election looming in 2009, the grand coalition became more fractious. Merkel's domestic leadership skills were put to the test and passed. Her party's success in the 2009 elections allowed her to form a more traditional ruling coalition.[23]

In addition to her domestic political successes, Merkel also showed herself to be a strong leader in foreign policy. European leaders viewed favorably her tenure as president of the European Union's Council of Ministers. She was able to repair relations between Germany and the United States, which had been badly strained by the Iraq War. As time went on, and as the European Union's financial troubles worsened at the start of the 2010s, however, some began to question whether her leadership traits had become a negative. By the middle of 2010, her physics background was portrayed as contributing to her tendency to be a "disinterested observer during political debates, preferring delay over action when conditions are uncertain."[24]

A Rational Decision? The German Currency Union

Helmut Kohl is most famous for his role in German unification and for being the German chancellor with the longest tenure in office. His achievements were strongest in the area of foreign policy, but his record in domestic policy, especially economic management, was less stellar. Kohl was not a charismatic leader, but he was an astute politician. In this context, one of his most important economic decisions, the German currency union, may be viewed as more rational than it first appeared.

Following the fall of the Berlin Wall in November 1989, the process of German unification proceeded at a dizzying pace. On October 3, 1990, German Unity Day, the German Democratic Republic (East Germany) ceased to exist, and its five *Länder* were incorporated into the Federal Republic, which had previously been West Germany and was now the name of the reunified country of Germany. One of the major decisions surrounding unification concerned the question of merging the two very different economies of east and west. Not only had East Germany been a centrally planned economy, but the living standards of its citizens had also been far below those of the citizens of West Germany.

With the disintegration of the Berlin Wall and the open border between East and West Germany, the specter of mass migration to the western part of the country haunted Chancellor Kohl and other West German politicians. Emigration was running at nearly fifty thousand easterners a month in the first two months of 1990.[25] The process of unifying the West German deutschmark with the East German ostmark thus became of paramount importance in staunching the flow of easterners.

In the weeks after the opening of the Berlin Wall, the ostmark rapidly devalued to 20:1, down from 2.5:1 in 1980 and 10:1 at the end of 1988.[26] A formal currency union between the two Germanys at a 20:1 rate would have left easterners with vastly reduced purchasing power, wiped out their savings, and given them a strong incentive to flee to the more prosperous western regions. In May 1999, to encourage easterners to stay put, the Kohl government implemented the currency union that valued the East German and West German marks at a rate of one-to-one (up to a set amount of savings).

The economic wisdom of this decision was suspect. West German economists and members of the Bundesbank, the country's central bank, opposed such a move, arguing that East German goods would be overvalued and that mass unemployment would follow. The currency union would also provide pressure for wage equalization between western and eastern workers, as easterners would now have to pay for goods at western prices. But politicians argued that attaining parity of eastern and western living standards was necessary to prevent political unrest and ensure a smooth process of unification. In the end, the central bank yielded to the Kohl government, while insisting on preserving its ability to set economic policy for united Germany free from subsequent political interference.

The dire economic predictions following currency union were largely borne out. The union helped eastern pensioners and those with savings, but at the cost of unemployment and economic decline in the east. After unification, labor unions demanded wage parity between east and west, and the competitiveness of eastern industry, which was far below that of the west, consequently suffered. As government subsidies and welfare state spending rose to absorb the costs of unification, the Bundesbank compensated for the ballooning federal deficit by raising interest rates. This induced a severe recession and accelerated the collapse of the economy in the eastern part of the country.[27]

The currency union decision demonstrates one of the difficulties in assessing a political decision's rationality. This decision was clearly questionable, perhaps even irrational, on economic grounds. But politicians have to worry about more than economic rationality. Although it generated significant economic problems that had been predicted well in advance, the choice to pursue a currency union across the newly unified Germany was, arguably, the most politically rational decision available to the German government.

India

All India's top leaders since independence in 1947 have achieved office through elections. For the first thirty years, the principal leaders came solely out of the Indian National Congress (INC). Although the INC has remained a key provider of leaders in the years since, other parties have successfully challenged the monopoly. Over the last couple of decades, the top leadership has come either from the INC or from the Bharatiya Janata Party (BJP), yet they rule through coalitions.

Since 2004 and the reemergence of the INC as India's leading political party, the country has had a form of dual leadership. Unlike the dual executive arrangements of countries such as Russia, however, only one of these leaders is the prime minister, the official chief executive. The other is the head of the INC. India thus demonstrates how an understanding of political leadership sometimes requires looking beyond government positions to focus on leaders of important political organizations.

Leadership: Manmohan Singh

When the INC won more Lok Sabha seats than any other party in the 2004 general elections, the party leader, Sonia Gandhi, decided against becoming prime minister and endorsed Dr. Manmohan Singh for that position. A Sikh born in 1932 in a part of the Punjab that is now in Pakistan, Singh earned a B.A. and an M.A. in economics from Panjab University in Chandigarh, another undergraduate degree from Cambridge University, and a Ph.D. from Oxford. He moved quickly through the professorial ranks at Panjab University, and he published widely on economic issues.

Manmohan Singh's career included a variety of positions in academia, the United Nations, and the International Monetary Fund (IMF), and with the Indian government as a governor of the Reserve Bank of India, among others. When the INC's Narasimha Rao became prime minister in 1991, he selected Singh as his finance minister. Responding to serious balance-of-payment problems, Singh instituted economic reforms that initiated a significant shift to a liberalized economy. Unlike most of his predecessors, he was elected to the Rajya Sabha, rather than the Lok Sabha, in 1991 and reelected since 1995 from the federal unit of Assam.

Singh first became prime minister on May 22, 2004. He was not at all viewed as charismatic, but rather as honest, intelligent, and, befitting his background, more a technocrat than a politician. In a country in which corruption is a prevalent part of political life, he developed a reputation as incorruptible. These traits, and the public's largely positive view of the performance of Singh's INC-led coalition, helped the INC to win the spring 2009 parliamentary elections and form a new coalition government. Singh became the first prime minister of India since Jawaharlal Nehru (prime minister from 1947 until 1964) to serve a full five-year term and then be reelected.[28]

Leadership: Sonia Gandhi

The leader of the INC parliamentary party and of the ruling United Progressive Alliance, Sonia Gandhi was born Sonia Antonia Maino in a village near Vincenza, Italy, in 1946. In 1964, she studied English at the Bell Educational Trust language school in Cambridge, where she met Rajiv Gandhi, who was at Cambridge University's Trinity College. He was Hindu, and she was Roman Catholic. They were married in India in 1968.

Rajiv Gandhi did not want to enter politics but was drawn in after his mother, Indira Gandhi, was assassinated by her Sikh bodyguards in 1984. Following her husband's assassination by a Sri Lankan Tamil in 1991, Sonia Gandhi also initially refused to enter politics. Six years later. after persistent pressure, she joined the INC, and she became its president the following year. In 1999, she was elected to the thirteenth Lok Sabha and chosen leader of the opposition. Three senior INC leaders, who subsequently resigned from the party, challenged her selection because of her foreign birth. (In fact, she was the third person of foreign birth to lead the Congress Party.) When the INC gained a plurality of seats in the Lok Sabha in 2004 and she refused to become prime minister, she was widely praised for the selfless act. Her decision shielded her from strong BJP opposition to a foreign-born person assuming the prime ministership. In 2007, *Forbes* magazine ranked Sonia Gandhi as the sixth most powerful woman in the world. She retained her position as INC party leader following the INC victory in 2009, and the following year *Forbes* named her the ninth most powerful person in the world, one spot ahead of Bill Gates and nine spots ahead of Prime Minister Manmohan Singh.

A Rational Decision? The Indo-U.S. Nuclear Agreement

In 1974, India exploded a nuclear weapon. In view of that event, the United States imposed sanctions on India, as a result of which India was unable to acquire nuclear technology and uranium from abroad and thus could not expand its nuclear power generation plants to provide electricity essential to its rapidly developing economy. In July 2005, Indian Prime Minister Manmohan Singh and U.S. President George W. Bush met and issued a joint statement about building a global partnership. Subsequent negotiations led to the Indo-U.S. Nuclear Agreement, made public in August 2007. The Bush administration initially sought to finalize the deal and get it to the U.S. Congress for ratification by the end of 2007. But Singh faced major obstacles within India, which delayed progress and forced extensions of the deadline.

Singh devoted more energy and political capital to getting the Indo-U.S. Nuclear Agreement adopted than to getting any other policy adopted during his first term as prime minister. He viewed the agreement as a way to better the lives of Indians and to improve India's position in the world, much as had the economic liberalization reforms he initiated in 1991 when he was finance minister. In October 2007, he appeared to have been defeated and announced that his government would "freeze" further consideration of the agreement.

The explanation had to do with political calculations. To prevent collapse, Singh's United Progressive Alliance (UPA) government needed the support of a group of parties on the left that was not a formal part of the alliance, primarily the two Communist Parties, the CPI(M) and CPI. Both opposed the closer ties with the United States that the nuclear agreement seemed to imply.[29] The UPA was unable to get the Left to give up its opposition, and the government feared that losing its domestic political allies would force new elections, a situation widely thought to benefit the fortunes of the Bharatiya Janata Party (BJP). Prime Minister Singh justified the retreat by saying that his government was not a "single-issue government."

The success of the Left in blocking the agreement was temporary. Believing the Indo-U.S. Nuclear Agreement was no longer a possibility and wanting to give Singh a face-saving exit, the Left allowed the UPA to go to the International Atomic Energy Agency (IAEA) to work out a safeguard agreement to facilitate access to nuclear fuel. By the end of June 2008, when the UPA-Left coordination committee again met, it became clear that Singh was determined to move forward and "unfreeze" the nuclear agreement with the United States.[30] On July 9, 2008, the Indian government submitted the proposed deal to the IAEA, initiating a process that culminated with U.S. Senate approval of the Indo-U.S. Nuclear Agreement on

October 1, 2008. When the Left publicly withdrew its support from the UPA government in response, Singh scheduled a confidence vote for July 22, 2008. After intense lobbying for support, Singh won on a vote of 275 to 256, although charges of vote-buying tarnished the UPA's success.

Manmohan Singh's "nuclear freeze" shows the extent to which political leaders will weigh the short-term political consequences of a major policy initiative. When Singh believed that the nuclear agreement threatened the survival of his government, he backed off. When it subsequently appeared that he could survive moving forward, he raised the issue again, forged ahead, and ultimately won the battle.

IN THEORY AND PRACTICE

India and Incrementalism

The theoretical approach that emphasizes **incrementalism** highlights how decision makers use a particular shortcut in setting government policy. The theory is most closely associated with Charles Lindblom, who argued that rational politicians do not start from scratch when formulating policy.[31] "New" policy is rarely new, but rather involves small, incremental changes to existing policy. Although the theory of incrementalism is related to the choice approach, it leaves little room for individual initiative. It assumes that most leaders will operate in a similar manner, regardless of who they are.

Take the example of local government budgeting. A city council must pass a budget, usually annually. This budget is broken down into various sections, and committees may formulate recommendations for the whole council about spending amounts for each of the sections. In making these recommendations, policy makers rarely ask whether an existing program is actually needed, and they rarely spend a great deal of time assessing the best possible budget amount for that program given their goals and the program's costs and benefits. Instead, they take the previous year's budget amount for that program and change the figure by some percentage downward or, more often, upward. In keeping with the idea of incremental policy adjustments, this change is usually fairly small, at least in percentage terms.

In crisis situations, significant policy changes sometimes occur quickly, but incrementalism accurately explains most policy making when no crisis or new problem has emerged. It clarifies, for example, why government programs are rarely eliminated entirely. It also helps us understand the growth in government spending over time. Though changes from year to year are usually made in small increments, the small increments add up. Over a long period of time, incremental

alterations can result in dramatic changes in the scope of a government program.

Although incrementalism guides economic policy development in some parts of the world, India's basic economic policies have developed in fits and starts. For the first fifteen years after independence, public sector development was emphasized. Some liberalization took place in the mid-1960s, followed by a return to emphasis on the public sector and to nationalization of industries in the late 1960s and early 1970s. In the remainder of the 1970s and the 1980s, limited and sporadic liberalization occurred. When the National Front government took power in 1989, it was divided on which way to take the economy, and major economic problems began to develop.

In 1991, India experienced its worst economic crisis since independence. Its many problems included a serious balance of payments deficit. This was also the year that a new INC government came to power. To get the financial resources the government needed, India was forced to turn to the IMF, which demanded serious liberalization of the economy, as it usually did with other developing countries in similar situations. The government responded positively to the demand, and 1991 is widely viewed as the start of real economic liberalization.

India's liberalization process has been less incremental than it has been a series of steps, both large and small. In the late 1990s, two governments were brought down shortly after being elected. Political forces on the right have fought fully opening the economy to "outsiders," while those on the left have fought privatization. Nevertheless, by the end of the term in office of the BJP-led National Democratic Alliance (NDA) government in 2004, the economy was growing at a rapid rate. To the surprise of many observers, the NDA lost the election. The victory of the INC-dominated United Progressive Alliance was attributed, in part, to the fact that poorer segments of the population had not benefited much from the economic growth occurring in the liberalizing economy—a situation that favored a greater economic role for the state.

Thus, India provides two important caveats to the use of incrementalism to explain domestic policy choices around the world. First, incrementalism is less likely to explain policy making immediately following a major policy shift, such as the IMF-inspired Indian emphasis on economic liberalization, than in periods of normal politics. Second, when rival political parties alternate control of the government, incrementalism is likely to take a backseat to ideological and electoral considerations. This certainly appears to be the case in India, where the democratic struggle for political power has contributed significantly to the fits and starts of liberalization.

Mexico

The struggle for independence from Spain and the subsequent Mexican revolution involved some of the most colorful individuals in history. It is ironic, therefore,

---

Incrementalism A theory of decision making that assumes that, other than during a crisis, government officials will make small changes to existing policy rather than start from scratch.

that more recent Mexican history involves a long period of stable governance under relatively bland leaders (an exception being Vicente Fox, president from 2000 to 2006). However, lacking flair does not mean that a leader is weak or unimportant. As during the last few decades in Germany, some of the most important individuals whose decisions have played a crucial role in shaping Mexico in recent years were leaders not known for their charisma.

During the period of dominance by the Institutional Revolutionary Party (PRI), Mexican presidents had the luxury of a deferential legislative branch. Since the establishment of democracy, presidents have had to work with legislatures in which their party did not control a majority of the seats. The challenge posed by divided government has been compounded by the emergence of new problems, such as increasing drug-related violence in the late 2000s.

Leadership: Felipe Calderón

When he became Mexico's president at the end of 2006, Felipe Calderón faced a mountain of challenges. These included a sizable portion of the population that was suspicious about the legitimacy of his election, a contentious legislature with the majority of seats held by parties other than Calderón's National Action Party (PAN), and an anti-immigration mood in the United States characterized by U.S. House of Representatives authorization of a seven-hundred-mile-long fence along a portion of the border. These early tribulations provided a strong test of Calderón's leadership abilities.

Calderón is the son of a devout Catholic, Luis Calderón Vega, who helped found the PAN before leaving it in 1980 because he believed the party had abandoned its Catholic roots in favor of big business.[32] Consequently, some feared that Felipe Calderón might turn away from the PAN's pro-business positions. For the most part, however, his Harvard education in law and business and his former position as head of the national development bank won over Mexican professionals at the same time that his campaign successfully struck blue-collar themes, including proposals to improve education, expand public health programs, and get tougher on crime.[33]

Calderón's tough-on-crime rhetoric was put to the test in the middle of his term as drug-cartel-related violence exploded across Mexico. The situation was so bad by the middle of 2009 that Calderón had to address claims that Mexico was a "failing state." In 2010, Mexico witnessed an estimated fifteen thousand deaths related to organized crime. At the start of 2011, contrary to the Calderón government's claims that the situation had improved, over five hundred people were killed in gangland-style killings in the first half of January.[34] With signs that the drug-related violence could continue into 2012, Calderón's mixed record could cost the PAN the 2012 presidential election at the end of his term.

A Rational Decision? Ernesto Zedillo and Liberalization

Ernesto Zedillo was the last president of the seven-decade reign of the PRI over the office. When he replaced Carlos Salinas de Gortari as president in 1994, he faced a number of serious adversities: Mexico's currency, the peso, was threatening to collapse, and the uprising in Chiapas struck at Salinas's vision of closer ties to the United States on the basis of economic liberalism. Arguably, his most serious challenge was to fulfill his promise to limit the power of the presidency and liberalize Mexico's authoritarian political system. Zedillo could have backtracked on the significant transformation of the regime. Instead, he set out to alter Mexican politics in three ways: by creating a greater balance of power between the presidency and the other two branches, by reforming the electoral system, and by devolving power to the *estado* governments. For these actions to work, he also had to reform the PRI and accustom it to not controlling Mexican political life.[35]

Zedillo surprised some observers by following through on his 1996 pledge that the following year's estado and national legislative elections would be free and fair, and the 1997 elections demonstrated that he was serious. For the first time in decades, PRI candidates for the lower house of the national legislature did not win a majority of the votes. The powerful position of mayor of Mexico City also went to a non-PRI candidate.

No single decision-making perspective can explain Zedillo's decision to push forward with political liberalization, partly because the choice involved a series of decisions. The process of liberalization had been underway for many years, so Zedillo inherited a Mexican system engaged in incremental choices by the ruling elite (see the In Theory and Practice feature on India for a discussion of incrementalism) that had built to the point that the country reached a crossroads: turn liberalization into democratization or turn back and reestablish authoritarian rule.

Zedillo's final decisions, particularly to allow the PRI to lose the presidential election, may be understood as examples of rational calculations in response to increasing domestic and international pressure. The United States was insisting that PRI leadership honor the results of the 2000 presidential election. Failure to do so risked significant strain between the countries, jeopardizing a relationship that Salinas and Zedillo had done much to cultivate. In addition, when the PRI openly stole the 1988 presidential election, it sparked national protests and did significant damage to the legitimacy of its rule.

Stealing another election, when it was clear to most observers that Fox would win if the election were fair, might have unleashed violent social protest and threatened to eliminate the PRI as a viable party in whatever system emerged from the chaos. Instead, when Vicente Fox won the 2000 presidential election, Zedillo publicly congratulated him. That he did so before Fox's PRI opponent conceded angered some in the PRI, but it also paved the way for a smooth transition of power from one set of ruling elites to another, solidified Zedillo's reputation as a reformer, and may have helped the PRI to remain a significant political force in newly democratic Mexico.

IN THEORY AND PRACTICE

Rational Choice Theory and the Mexican Government's Support of NAFTA

Much of this chapter's discussion of decision making has centered on whether individual political decisions tend to be rational. One of the most important theoretical perspectives in political science is based on the view that political decisions are, almost without exception, rational. The primary assumption of **rational choice theory** is that humans seek to maximize the likelihood of attaining their interests by weighing the costs and benefits of particular actions. The approach typically understands collective political outcomes as flowing from a set of individual decisions. The interest that an individual seeks to maximize need not be self-interest, though that is a common starting point for models of rational behavior. Note that rationality is more than just conscious thought. Being conscious of one's actions is not enough for those actions to be rationally based.

How effective is rational choice theory at explaining major political decisions? Mexico's decision to join the United States and Canada in the North American Free Trade Agreement (NAFTA) provides valuable insight into the strengths and limitations of rational choice theory. In 1990, Mexican president Carlos Salinas de Gortari supported a proposed free trade agreement with the United States, after having opposed it only two years earlier. After witnessing the success of an agreement between the United States and Canada, Salinas chose to aggressively pursue the idea of extending that agreement both in scope and to include Mexico.[36] NAFTA was born.

Rational choice explanations commonly assume that politicians seek to maximize the likelihood of reelection by taking policy positions that are popular, particularly with their political base. NAFTA had little public support when negotiations began. Unlike Margaret Thatcher's initially unpopular reforms, which were at least beneficial to her electoral base, NAFTA would hit farmers—a core component of the PRI's base—harder than any other economic

sector. One might conclude, therefore, that Salinas acted irrationally. As discussed in Chapter 5, however, political rules constrain or create opportunities for political leaders. One of Mexico's key institutional provisions, the single-term president, is particularly crucial. Because Mexican presidents serve only one term, Salinas had no electoral concerns to take into account.

Rather, it was in Salinas's self-interest to maximize his personal authority during his term in office. Salinas had come to power under allegations of vote fraud; he faced a troubled economy and led an increasingly unpopular PRI. He had little to lose by shaking up Mexican economic approaches and much to gain if new investment in the country sparked an economic turnaround. Salinas pursued a number of economic reforms—dubbed "Salinastroika" after the *perestroika* reforms under Mikhail Gorbachev in the Soviet Union. These reforms included the privatization of most state-owned companies in Mexico. Salinas also likely believed that NAFTA would make the United States even more willing to offer economic assistance to Mexico. In short, Salinas's personal fate was tied to maximizing Mexico's economic performance. If he believed that a trade agreement like NAFTA would improve Mexico's economic performance, his decision to support NAFTA was rational.

Scholars who view rational choice theory as too simplistic might ask at this point why Salinas believed that NAFTA maximized the likelihood of strong Mexican economic performance. Here one must consider Salinas's background and experiences. Born in Mexico City, Salinas had little direct knowledge of rural life. In addition, he attended graduate school in the United States, studying economics and politics at Harvard University. Finally, the world that Salinas saw around him was very different in 1990 than it had been only two years earlier. The collapse of Communism in Eastern Europe led many political figures to consider American-style economic neoliberalism as their only option.

Thus, rational choice theory provides some help in understanding Salinas's decision to encourage NAFTA, but this examination also raises questions about applying rational choice perspectives to particular settings. Traditional assumptions of political self-interest involving reelection do not apply in this case, requiring an adjustment of the assumption about Salinas's interests to fit the situation. This reconsideration of Salinas's interests makes it necessary to take into account various structural and leadership-related issues: institutional arrangements in Mexico, Salinas's education in the United States, and even the transformation of international politics with the collapse of Communism. The Mexican case highlights how examining decisions through the lens of rational choice theory can bring to light arguments that might otherwise be missed. At the same time, Salinas's decision to participate in NAFTA shows the importance of thinking carefully about the factors that shape perceptions of interests, costs, and benefits.

Rational Choice Theory A wide-ranging theoretical perspective based on the assumption that individuals make rational decisions to maximize their interests that is used to explain both individual political behavior and collective actions.

Think and Discuss
What factors not examined in the In Theory and Practice feature might explain Carlos Salinas's decision to support NAFTA?

Brazil

The weakness of most Brazilian political parties puts a premium on individual leadership. In Brazil's case, relying on leadership skills has produced both excellent leaders and spectacularly bad ones. It is too early to tell into which of these two categories Brazil's newest leader, and first ever female president, is most likely to fall. Her background and character provide hope, however, both to Brazilians and to those who see Brazil's fate as connected to the success or failure of its Latin American neighbors.

Brazil's presidents face a combination of challenges similar to their counterparts in Mexico: pressing national problems and the need to work with divided legislatures to try to fix them. The most recent Brazilian leaders also challenge the common view of presidents as coming from positions of social privilege; they forced their way into the political elite through a combination of hard work, leadership traits and skills, and the willingness to stand up to the military regime in the 1970s and 1980s, when many others chose to support the military government with their silence.

Leadership: Dilma Rousseff
On January 1, 2011, Dilma Rousseff was sworn in as president of Brazil. A close associate of the previous president, Luiz Inácio "Lula" da Silva, Rousseff won in a runoff vote. Given Brazil's demographic, economic, cultural, and political challenges, governing is no easy task. It takes a leader with both a strong personality and a good grasp of political tactics. Although her abilities as a backroom politician are unknown, Rousseff's toughness is not questioned.

As disclosed in Chapter 6, Rousseff was arrested in 1970 during the period of military rule in Brazil. An opponent of the military government, she was tortured for three weeks, including being subjected to electric shock. She is also a cancer survivor. The combination of her personality and Brazil's status as a growing economic power has caught the attention of observers from across the globe. In 2010, on the eve of her inauguration, *Forbes* magazine had already named her the sixteenth most powerful person in the world.

Rousseff's closeness to former president "Lula" da Silva has also been seen as an asset, and it certainly played a role in her election. Lula remained popular at the start of Rousseff's term, and many expected her to continue his economic policies. Within days of taking office, however, Rousseff signaled that she intended to pursue her own course at times. Her selection for the head of the Brazilian central bank hinted at important policy changes, and observers saw her as moving away from Lula's focus on stimulating government-run businesses and toward making Brazil more internationally competitive. The new direction was hailed by the IMF, another change from the Lula period.

A Rational Decision? Fernando Henrique Cardoso and the *Plano Real*
When Fernando Collor de Mello resigned in late 1992, he was replaced by his vice president, Itamar Franco, in the midst of an ongoing economic crisis. Since the transition to democracy, inflation had skyrocketed to over 1,000 percent per year. In 1993, inflation more than doubled to nearly 2,500 percent.[37] Despite efforts to restrain the rampant inflation—Brazil went through seven different currencies in eight years—nothing seemed to help. As Fernando Henrique Cardoso would later note, "By the time Itamar took office, many economists believed that Brazil's inflation problem could not be solved . . . it *was* tempting to just give up. However, Itamar did not have that luxury. . . . All of us had nightmares about people running around with suitcases full of worthless cash. This would cause unimaginable riots and social unrest."[38] In desperation, after going through three finance ministers in seven months, Franco turned to Cardoso, his minister of foreign relations. Cardoso tried to refuse. His less-than-delighted reaction when the press printed reports of his appointment as finance minister was, "Oh my God, I'm ruined. . . . What am I supposed to do now?"

Cardoso was not a professional politician, nor did he have training in economics. Determined to avoid what he called "the family business"—that is, politics—Cardoso got a Ph.D. in sociology and became a professor.[39] He would later establish a worldwide reputation as a neo-Marxist and a founder of dependency theory (see Chapter 2), which argues that poverty and underdevelopment in lesser developed countries is the result of exploitation by the advanced industrial democracies.

Cardoso approached his problem more like a professor than a politician, thinking that he "needed a clear diagnosis of the problem, a plan to end it, and then the political support to carry such a plan through." He found a team of economic advisers with the training he lacked.

"Did You Know?"

"Lula," the nickname of former Brazilian president Luiz Inácio da Silva, means "squid" in Portuguese. While Lula seems to have used the nickname from childhood—probably it was a diminutive of his first name, Luiz—his fans and critics later used it to refer to his uncanny ability to wriggle out of tight spots, including military prisons.

Remembering it later, Cardoso describes the intense effort that ultimately produced the new approach: "Untold gallons of coffee went into the making of the *Plano Real* [Real Plan]. We spent countless nights poring over economics textbooks, scribbling equations on chalkboards, and arguing until four in the morning. . . . For months we met secretly in people's homes and back offices. . . . Finally, by December 1993, we took a collective deep breath and announced a course of action."[40]

The plan would create a new currency (the *Real*), initiate a round of steep budget cuts, and reduce the practice of tying raises to inflation. "Naturally," says Cardoso, "almost everybody hated it." Cardoso spent the next few months campaigning for the plan on talk shows, at business conventions, in city council meetings, and, most importantly, among congressmen. Ultimately, the Real Plan passed, in his view, because "none of these congressmen had any better ideas of their own. [And] it dawned on them that they would lose their jobs unless they met society's demands to end inflation."[41]

Not only did the Real Plan work, dropping inflation below 20 percent in two years, but the process itself was eminently rational. Cardoso brought together a team of experts, determined logically that he had to take the politically unpopular but necessary step of drastically cutting the budget, and then sold it to reluctant congressmen on the basis of their own self-interest. The fact that seven previous plans had failed worked in Cardoso's favor: with each failure, more people became convinced that the hard choice was the only viable way to resolve a serious problem.

Cardoso's success led him to pursue the presidency of Brazil. He won election and held the office from 1995 to 2003. Despite his history as a leftist intellectual and critic of market capitalism, the Real Plan meant that Cardoso's presidency was best known for economic stabilization and economic reforms designed to embrace markets and reduce regulation. In other words, as president he downplayed the negative consequences of capitalism that he had emphasized as an academic. Cardoso saw this apparent about-face as a natural, rational extension of his previous arguments that Latin American countries could develop by working within the capitalist system.

Nigeria

Until recently, leadership in Nigeria has involved the military in one way or another. Much of the period since independence has been under military rule, and even the democratic interludes have produced elections of former military leaders. This includes Olusegun Obasanjo, a dictator turned democratizer, who reemerged twenty years after stepping aside for an elected government to win the presidency by way of a relatively free and fair election and become the first president of Nigeria's Fourth Republic.

President Goodluck Jonathan watches Nigerian troops parade during his inauguration ceremony in Nigeria's capital of Abuja, May 29, 2011. © AP Photo/Sunday Alamba

The three leaders since the establishment of the Fourth Republic have had different backgrounds, but they have faced some similar challenges, such as the need to tackle corruption. Unlike several of the other TIC cases, Nigeria's presidents have had the support of the legislative branch due to the growing dominance of the People's Democratic Party (PDP).

Leadership: Goodluck Jonathan

Goodluck Jonathan became Nigerian president upon the death of President Umaru Yar'Adua, himself the first civilian leader to succeed another civilian leader since independence. Elected in the spring of 2007, Yar'Adua became ill during his first term, and most of his powers passed to his vice president, Goodluck Jonathan, even before he died on May 5, 2010. There was discussion that Jonathan might not run in 2011, but he decided to pursue the PDP's nomination. In early 2011, delegates at the PDP party convention selected Jonathan to be the party's presidential candidate, and he won the April 2011 presidential election.

Yar'Adua had been from the north of the country, and Jonathan is from the south. Because Nigeria has an understanding that the presidency rotates between a northerner and a southerner, his ascendancy to the presidency bothered many in the north. Violence broke out, highlighting the complementary identity divides in Nigeria involving ethnic identity, religion, and region. While

Nigeria faces significant economic challenges and the glaring problem of corruption, defusing the explosive identity divide is Jonathan's greatest challenge. His modest, unassuming nature and results-oriented approach may be helpful in resolving the tensions.

A Rational Decision? The Nigerian Civil War

The Nigerian civil war of the 1960s had important structural causes, most notably the country's ethno-federal political structure. The British had established the system, and the postindependence Nigerian leadership chose to continue it. These decisions by political leaders indirectly produced the civil war.

A series of other decisions at various levels of the Nigerian government were even more important. The leadership of the southeastern province of the country, the region in which most of the Ibo ethnic group lived, could have sought greater autonomy short of independence. It instead chose to pursue independence. The leadership of the federal government had numerous alternatives in response to the demands, but it chose to confront them violently.[42]

It is tempting to argue that the Ibo nationalists' decision to pursue independence was rational. Nationalist elites are often portrayed as conniving and self-serving, and the Ibo ethno-nationalist leaders likely weighed the costs and benefits of pursuing independence. At the same time, when decisions leading to or in response to ethnonational violence are made, emotions often drive decisions as much as rational calculations. Frustration at the inability of an ethnic group to control its own affairs can trigger aggressive responses.

As violence becomes a real possibility and as the crisis makes pressure mount, information shortcuts such as stereotypes and historical analogies sometimes replace cautious, reasoned decision making. Often this results in misunderstandings about the other side's intentions, incorrect assessments of threat, and a rush to violence to defend the nation. The Nigerian civil war was no exception.

Russia

Many events in Russian history highlight the role of individuals in political outcomes. Going back to the tsarist period, decisions by various leaders to get involved in wars (e.g., the Crimean War), to respond to defeat in such wars (the emancipation of the serfs), and to stay in unpopular wars (Tsar Nicholas II and, later, Prime Minister Alexander Kerensky in World War I) radically altered the social, economic, and political landscape of the country. The early decisions of Communist leaders like Lenin and Stalin to accept an ethno-federal system in forming the Soviet Union continue to have implications today. The decision by government hard-liners to attempt to oust Soviet leader Mikhail Gorbachev in 1991, detailed later

Russia's Vladimir Putin, who served briefly as prime minister, two terms as president, and as prime minister a second time. Many observers believe he will seek the presidency again in 2012. REUTERS/Alexsey Druginyn/RIA Novosti/Pool

in this section, set the stage for the collapse of the Soviet Union. Russia's first two post-Soviet presidents, Boris Yeltsin and Vladimir Putin, played monumental roles in shaping Russia's post-Soviet economic, social, and political trajectory.

Leadership: Vladimir Putin

Since the collapse of Communism and the Soviet Union itself, two main domestic politics issues have been economic reform and political liberalization. Key decisions by Presidents Boris Yeltsin, Vladimir Putin, and Dmitry Medvedev moved Russia away from its Soviet-era economics but failed to move the country toward consolidation of democracy. Instead, under Putin, the Russian Federation turned sharply away from democracy during almost a decade of "creeping authoritarianism." Putin's move into the position of prime minister did little to change the country's political direction.

Following Boris Yeltsin as president of Russia at the end of 1999, Vladimir Putin placed his stamp on both the office and the entire Russian political system. Putin completed his second term as president in 2008. Through a deal with his handpicked successor, Dmitry Medvedev, Putin slid seamlessly from the office of president into the prime ministership. This change simultaneously transformed the Russian political system, shifting at least some power away from the presidency, and guaranteed that Putin would remain one of the system's central figures.

Born in Leningrad (now St. Petersburg), Putin studied civil law at Leningrad State University. He made his way into politics after a long period of service in KGB, the Soviet secret police. He spent five years in East Germany, where he was exposed to Western economic and political ideas. In 1991, he joined the administration of the St. Petersburg mayor—his former law professor—Anatoly Sobchak.

From there, Putin rose quickly through the Russian political system. Having received a federal government appointment in 1997, Putin got a major promotion when Yeltsin made him head of the Federal Security Service (the successor organization to the KGB). Yeltsin promoted Putin two more times. In August 1999, Yeltsin named him one of a string of new prime ministers. A few months later, when Yeltsin suddenly and unexpectedly resigned on New Year's Eve, Putin found himself the acting president of the country. Yeltsin apparently liked what he had seen in Putin. By elevating him to acting president, Yeltsin all but ensured that Putin would be elected in the presidential elections held in March 2000.

Putin is the kind of president Russians had been craving during the Yeltsin years. He is perceived as strong and energetic (he is skilled in judo and the sport of sambo, which combines judo and wrestling), decisive, and confident. As president, Putin has placed importance on gaining control of the breakaway region of Chechnya while restoring a sense of respect for Russia around the world. His tendency to favor those who share his St. Petersburg ties has concerned some in Russia, while his efforts to reestablish Russian greatness and authoritarian political practices have troubled many outside observers. By the early stages of Putin's second term, it was clear that he was focused on consolidating power in the central government and into his own hands. The Yeltsin-led experiment in democracy was facing a full-fledged assault from Putin, which culminated not with his seeking an unconstitutional third consecutive term, but rather with his resourceful move to shift power to the other half of Russia's dual executive system.

By 2010, speculation was rampant about whether Putin would run for president in 2012. Although the Russian constitution prohibits three consecutive terms, Putin made himself eligible once again to serve as Russia's president by taking a term off and serving as prime minister. At the start of 2011, most observers of Russian politics believed that this was the most likely scenario. However, statements in late 2010 from some of President Medvedev's advisers hinted that Medvedev might be interested in a second term. It seemed highly unlikely that Putin and Medvedev would run against each other.

After Putin surprised those who thought he would do whatever necessary to remain president in 2008, however, it is possible, if unlikely, that Medvedev will once again find himself on the ballot in 2012.

Leadership: Dmitry Medvedev

In late 2007, a number of political parties loyal to then-President Vladimir Putin, including United Russia, and Putin himself announced their intention to support Dmitry Medvedev in the March 2008 presidential elections. The move ended speculation that Putin would seek a third term as president. However, when Medvedev announced the following day that he would support Putin to be prime minister, what some had envisioned as a possible way for Putin to maintain control of Russian politics became reality. In the context of what many considered to be a "hyper-presidential" political system in the 1990s and during Putin's two terms, it seems strange to discuss Russian president Medvedev as secondary to Prime Minister Putin. Yet, few inside or outside Russia believe that Medvedev has been Russia's supreme political leader during his tenure as president.

Medvedev was part of Putin's St. Petersburg inner circle, served as his former chief of staff, and managed his successful 2000 presidential campaign. He is also used to serving in a position of power but letting Putin pull the strings: when Medvedev was chairman of Russia's massive energy company, Gazprom, many believed that Putin was calling the shots.[43] At the same time, given his support of free market economics and his vocal criticism of Russian governmental corruption, he helped smooth over strained relations with the United States.[44]

As president, Medvedev has rarely challenged Putin's authority. Occasionally publicly criticizing Putin for his handling of the economy or his slow reaction to crises like forest fires in the summer of 2010, Medvedev largely fell into step with Putin. This was perhaps most evident at the end of 2010 when a Russian court found former billionaire and Putin political opponent Mikhail Khodorkovsky guilty of additional charges largely designed to keep him in prison at the end of his initial term. Given the transparent nature of the trumped-up charges, human rights groups had hoped that Medvedev might intervene on Khodorkovsky's behalf.

A Rational Decision? The Coup against Mikhail Gorbachev

As events spiraled out of Mikhail Gorbachev's control in 1990 and 1991, he began to backtrack on some of his liberalization efforts. He appointed hard-liners opposed to reform of the Soviet system to key positions in the government. By mid-1991, however, Gorbachev tried once again to get ahead of the wave of reform and proposed a new treaty to hold the Soviet Union together.

The agreement to grant significant powers to the republics was the last straw for the hard-liners, who placed Gorbachev under house arrest while he was vacationing in Crimea in the USSR's Ukrainian union republic. Initially announcing that Gorbachev had asked to be removed from power, the coup leaders quickly made clear that they were acting to restore order to the country.

The coup leaders were, arguably, acting in a classic rational choice manner. By August 1991, Gorbachev had clearly abandoned the conservatives and thrown his support behind a revamped, and much less Soviet, Soviet Union. Seeking to protect both the Soviet Union and their personal political power, the coup leaders weighed the costs and benefits of doing nothing against the option of seeking to restore order by removing Gorbachev. Despite the costs of a coup, they believed it offered them the best chance of maximizing their goal of hanging onto political power.

In the end, the coup leaders made a number of mistakes and showed poor leadership skills. The mistakes included allowing Boris Yeltsin, a chief opposition figure, to rally the masses in Moscow against the coup. Giving rousing speeches, at times standing on tanks that had been ordered into the streets by the coup leaders, Yeltsin won over much of the population of Moscow and, more important, much of the military supposedly acting on behalf of the coup leaders.

The coup fell apart in a matter of days, and the fate of the Soviet Union was sealed. Gorbachev tried to maintain control of the country and save some sort of Soviet state, but his efforts to win the support of those in the middle failed to recognize the absence of a political middle. Yeltsin replaced Gorbachev as the de facto leader of the country, part of a process that would culminate with the dissolution of the Soviet Union at the end of 1991.

China

The importance of individual leaders is as evident in China as in any of the other countries examined in this textbook. Mao Zedong remade China, and his successor, Deng Xiaoping, remade it again. As discussed in previous chapters, one of Chinese Communism's stranger elements in the past was how an individual could be recognized as a leader without holding the official positions associated with leadership. This has changed, but the importance of leadership and the role of individuals in Chinese politics has not.

Since Deng Xiaoping, China's leaders have come from the post-revolution generation. Today, the torch is on the verge of being passed to yet another generation. These leaders are less attached to ideology than those of the past. They have instead chosen to run with Deng's emphasis on pragmatism and performance.

Leadership: Hu Jintao

Even more than Jiang Zemin's replacement of Deng Xiaoping in the early 1990s, the emergence of Hu Jintao marked the transition to a new generation of leaders. Born in 1942, Hu studied hydroelectric engineering and joined the Communist Party as a student in 1964 but did not receive a significant party position until the early 1980s. He gained attention later in the 1980s as party leader in Tibet, where he imposed martial law.

Hu became vice president of China in 1998. When Jiang Zemin stepped down as party general secretary in 2002 and president in 2003, Hu Jintao replaced him. Over the next two years, Hu solidified his control of the political system by succeeding Jiang as head of the party and state military commissions.

Hu's leadership style is that of a "soft-spoken technocrat."[45] Although pro-reform Chinese initially hoped that he was open to political liberalization, his first years as leader of China indicate that he is firmly opposed to significant political reforms. In addition, his past actions to stifle Tibetan independence are consistent with his more recently expressed position on independence for Taiwan. In early 2005, he told a party gathering that the people of Taiwan were "our flesh-and-blood brothers" and that the Chinese will "never compromise in opposing the 'Taiwan independence' secessionist activities."[46]

Hu's term, along with that of Prime Minister Wen Jiabao, ends in 2013. Unlike in Russia, there is no intrigue about Hu's running again. In early 2011, there was an emerging sense that Hu's replacement would be Xi Jinping. Xi became the country's vice president in March 2008 and was named vice chairman of the Central Military Commission of the Communist Party in October 2010. Both positions were held by Hu before he became president. This does not guarantee that Xi will replace Hu in 2013. If he does, however, it will add further evidence that China has institutionalized its approach to leadership succession.

A Rational Decision? Mao, the Great Leap Forward, and the Cultural Revolution

Mao Zedong will be remembered in China and around the world as one of the great leaders of the twentieth century, but two of his most important policy decisions ended in failure. In 1958, Mao launched the Great Leap Forward, designed to speed up China's economic development and reach Marx's vision of a Communist utopia before the Soviet Union. Chinese peasants, who were still the majority of the population, were organized into massive communes. Each community was expected to be as self-sufficient as possible, which led to the practice of installing backyard blast furnaces on communes so that each collective could produce its own steel. Within a year, Mao backed down and resigned as president, but he kept the all-important position of party chairman.

Less than a decade later, Mao encouraged the young to rise up against the country's political and social establishment in the Great Proletarian Cultural Revolution. The youth of China responded, setting up Red Guard units that terrorized the country. University professors and high school teachers were particularly targeted. Many were killed or committed suicide; many more were sent to the countryside to work as peasants. Once more, Mao eventually came to realize that he had made a mistake, although the policy remained officially in place until his death. Mao used the army to regain control of the situation, but not before a great deal of damage had been done.

It is hard to say that either of these major decisions was made in a fully rational manner; Mao clearly failed to think through all possible consequences. Instead, it is likely Mao was making decisions based on his view of Marxist ideology and his desire to apply Marxism in a more pure manner than did the Soviet government. Already by the time of the Great Leap Forward, and certainly during the Cultural Revolution, cracks had developed in China's relationship with the Soviet Union. Personal rivalry between the leaders of the countries at times shaped policy decisions, leading to rushed decisions, clouded judgment, and decisions based more on emotion than rational calculation.

IN THEORY AND PRACTICE

Deng Xiaoping, Tiananmen Square, and Elite Learning

One important theory related to the concept of rational decision making is that of **elite learning**. Elite learning theory holds that elites make adjustments based on previous political experiences. Simply put, elites learn. They remember past decisions that led to success and the context of those decisions, and they remember those that failed. They adjust their behavior to maximize the likelihood of success at present and in the future. In countries with unsuccessful democratization experiences, for example, mistakes made the first time can be corrected in subsequent democratization opportunities. This theory can be applied to decision makers' use of historical analogies or recent experiences in other countries.

Elite Learning A theory that political leaders learn from previous successes and failures and adjust their behavior accordingly to maximize the likelihood of future successes.

In 1989, as Communism was faltering across Eastern Europe, students in Beijing began protesting economic conditions. As their numbers grew and time went on, demands for political reform moved front and center. The Chinese government, under the leadership of Deng Xiaoping, initially tolerated the protests, which were centered in Beijing's Tiananmen Square. Once the protests began to draw as many as a million people in Beijing and spread to other major Chinese cities, Deng decided to listen to those in the government calling for a crackdown against the protesters. On June 4, 1989, the Chinese military regained control of Tiananmen Square and surrounding areas of the city, killing hundreds (perhaps thousands) of protesters and injuring thousands more in the process.

Another leader might have handled the Tiananmen Square incident differently, but it is a solid example of elite learning. Although the Berlin Wall would not fall until November 1989, already by early that summer, the Communist leaders of China had seen Communist parties lose power in several Central and Eastern European countries and Soviet troops complete their withdrawal from Afghanistan. Although one cannot attribute the exact timing of the crackdown to the Chinese leaders' knowledge of events unfolding in Eastern Europe, the Tiananmen Square crackdown came on the same day as Eastern Europe's first free election—in Poland—in four decades. What is clear is that the decision to suppress the protesters was not made in a domestic vacuum. The Chinese elites had learned: protests were rapidly bringing down Communist governments in Europe, and without a significant show of force, the Chinese Communist Party was in real danger of suffering the same fate.

Iran

The overthrow of the shah in 1979 marked a dramatic shift in Iran's domestic politics and international relations. The United States had played a role in the shah's coming to power in 1954, and the friendly relationship between the United States and Iran ended with his departure from the country. While moderates in Iran had hoped the shah's removal would bring democracy to the country, the emergence of Ayatollah Ruhollah Khomeini as the symbol of opposition to the shah set the stage for the rejection of democracy and the development of Iran's current theocracy.

Leadership: Ayatollah Ali Hoseini-Khamenei
The leaders of Iran's theocratic political system have displayed a mix of ideological zeal and pragmatism. They have also ranged from hard-liners to moderate reformers. Iran's system is further complicated by the visible presence of two leaders—the Supreme Leader and the

president—as well as a number of other powerful individuals. Focusing on the Iranian president, as Western media reports often do, paints a misleading picture of political leadership and decision making in Iran.

Born in 1939, Ali Hoseini-Khamenei became a religious leader and an ally of Ayatollah Ruhollah Khomeini. Imprisoned by the shah, he played an important role in the 1979 Islamic Revolution. Khamenei became commander of the Revolutionary Guard in 1979 and was elected president of Iran in 1981. The Council of Experts selected Khamenei to become *Rahbar-e Moazam* (Supreme Leader) following Khomeini's death in 1989. He holds tremendous power in the Iranian theocratic political system. He opposed efforts by Mohammed Khatami, Iran's moderate president in the late 1990s and early 2000s, to liberalize the country.

Leadership: Mahmoud Ahmadinejad

Iran's other chief executive is its elected president. The election in 2005 to replace Khatami brought Mahmoud Ahmadinejad to power as Iran's new president. Ahmadinejad won a runoff election against a less conservative candidate, Akbar Hashemi-Rafsanjani, who had served as president of Iran from 1989 to 1997, and won reelection in 2009 against an even stronger pro-reform candidate. His reelection sparked protests in the streets (see Chapters 8 and 9), but unlike the so-called color revolutions in other countries that toppled sitting leaders, Iran's Green Revolution failed to dislodge Ahmadinejad.

Ahmadinejad studied civil engineering in college, but after the 1979 revolution, he became more active in politics, joining the Islamic Revolutionary Guards and participating in covert operations against Iraq during the Iran-Iraq War. He served in local and regional political positions before being appointed mayor of Tehran in 2003. From his efforts as Tehran's mayor to roll back reforms in the city to his policies and statements as president, he is seen as a religious conservative. As a result, Ahmadinejad's 2005 victory marked the reestablishment of conservative clerics' control of the elected positions of government and the end, for the moment, of serious prospects for significant political reform.

Ahmadinejad has run largely populist campaigns, emphasizing the need to fight corruption and support the interests of the poorer segments of society. The approach has worked, and Ahmadinejad received nearly 62 percent of the vote in 2005. Reformers claimed vote rigging and intimidation, criticized the role of the Guardian Council in banning a huge number of potential candidates from running, and raised the possibility that Ahmadinejad's vote totals in the first round of voting were inflated to get him into the runoff.

The criticism in 2005 paled in comparison to the protests that followed his 2009 reelection where Ahmadinejad won with 64 percent of the vote in the runoff round. Even if the vote totals had not been manipulated enough to make a difference in the outcome, the demonstrations against his reelection were the largest protests since the 1979 Islamic Revolution. They signaled that, at least among segments of the population such as young urbanites, Ahmadinejad's brand of populism had worn out its welcome.

A Rational Decision? The Choice to Bar Reformist Candidates in the 2004 Majles Elections

Tensions between Mohammed Khatami, a political moderate and Iran's president from 1997 to 2005, and conservative clerics came to a head in 2004. Since the elections in early 2000, Khatami had had a pro-reform majority in the national legislature, the Majles. In the lead-up to the 2004 Majles elections, the legislature sought to pass laws strengthening presidential power. The Guardian Council sprang into action, disqualifying a large portion of the candidates, including reformers currently in the legislature. Ayatollah Khamenei ordered the Guardian Council to reconsider its decision, but many politicians remained off the ballot.

President Khatami also faced a decision in response to the actions of the Guardian Council. Having promised not to endorse the holding of a fraudulent election, he backtracked in the hope of clinging to the little power he had left. Instead, the elections sealed the fate of the reform movement, at least in the near term. Even the pro-reform candidates who were allowed to run did poorly, though this was partly because of the election's low turnout.

The actions of the Guardian Council can be effectively explained from a rational choice perspective. By 2003, conservatives were able to shape national political outcomes only through unelected government positions, such as the Supreme Leader and the Guardian Council. It is not hard to imagine discussions among the top conservatives about their goals, their options, and especially the costs of blocking pro-reform candidates versus allowing them to run. Given the successes of the reform movement—gaining the presidency under Khatami for two terms, gaining control of the national legislature in 2000, and making major inroads in many city governments—the costs of allowing reform to continue were too great.

In the short run, at least, the decision by Iran's hardliners worked. For all intents and purposes, the first post-Islamic Revolution reform era ended in 2004. Hopes for any serious steps toward democratization in the near term were dashed, and the theocratic nature of Iran's regime was solidified. In 2005, Mahmoud Ahmadinejad's election as president further deepened religious conservatives' political control of Iran.

SELECTED IMPORTANT FORMER LEADERS OF THE TOPIC IN COUNTRIES CASES

Tony Blair

Tony Blair rose to become one of the more influential prime ministers in British history through a combination of a vision to reform the British political system, his charisma and eloquence, and the sizable majority that his Labour Party held in the House of Commons. Becoming head of the Labour Party at the age of forty, Blair led the party to landslide electoral victories in the 1997, 2001, and 2005 House of Commons elections. With large majorities, he was able to enact many policies with ease and even begin to tackle problems many thought impossible to resolve, such as the makeup and role of the House of Lords.

Though less controlling in cabinet meetings than previous prime ministers, such as Margaret Thatcher, Blair developed a reputation for micromanaging—a change from the way the prime minister before him, John Major, let his ministers run their ministries with significant autonomy. Blair became less popular during his second term, partly due to opposition among the British public to the United Kingdom's participation in the Iraq War. He faced his biggest electoral challenge in the 2005 elections but again delivered, becoming the only Labour Party leader in history to win three straight elections.

© Matt Cardy/Getty Images

Vicente Fox

REUTERS/Tomas Bravo

Vicente Fox was president of Mexico during 2000–2006. His victory in 2000 was a surprise to many. This was not because Fox was unpopular (he was quite popular), but rather because he defeated a candidate from the formerly dominant political party, the PRI.

Born in 1942, Fox was raised on a ranch in the state of Guanajuato. Educated at Universidad Iberoamericana, the private Jesuit university in Mexico City, Fox also attended Harvard Business School. He became the president of Coca-Cola's Mexican division in 1979. After being elected to the national legislature in 1988, he ran for governor of Guanajuato in 1991 as a member of the PAN. Though some thought Fox won the election, the PRI candidate opposing him was declared the winner. Fox tried again in 1995, this time successfully securing the governorship. As early as 1997, he began discussing a run for president.

Fox's brash style and frank discussions of the problems of the political system won him the support of many in the general population. As president, however, this style led him to clash with members of other political parties who controlled a majority of the seats in the Congress. He responded by attempting to reach out to his opponents, even putting a number of members of the other main political parties in his cabinet. Many of his successful activities were a continuation of trends begun under the previous presidents, Zedillo and Salinas, but his political opponents in the legislature frustrated Fox's other attempts to reform Mexican politics.

Luiz Inácio "Lula" da Silva

© CityFiles/WireImage

Former Brazilian president "Lula" da Silva did not have the traditional background for a Brazilian president. One of eight children, he was born to a poor peasant family. His father left the family when Lula was a baby, and his mother later moved the family to the large industrial city of São Paulo in search of work. Lula did not learn to read until he was ten years old and attended formal school only through the fourth grade. By the age of twelve, he was working as a shoeshine boy on the streets. By nineteen, he was working in an auto parts factory, where he lost a finger on his left hand in an industrial accident. This accident—and the indifference with which factory owners treated his injury—turned him toward union organization, as did the influence of his older brother, a Communist Party member. His charismatic leadership and willingness to take risks propelled him to the head of the local steelworkers' union in 1978, when he was just thirty-three years old.

Over the next several years, Lula and the steel workers' union led a wave of protests against the authoritarian military regime and its repression of independent unions. They were joined in this effort by many civil society associations, neighborhood associations, and progressive Catholic activists. Pressure from Lula's radical leftist supporters helped convince the military to turn over power to what they hoped would be a much more moderate political party system in 1985. But Lula refused to cooperate. Declining to join the centrist antimilitary coalition, he led the way in founding both the Workers' Party (PT) and the main independent union federation, the CUT. He ran for president for the first time in 1989 and came within an inch of winning the election, demonstrating

the potential popular appeal of a candidate who not only spoke for common people, but also was one of them. It was largely the hope of electing Lula that kept his diverse coalition together. Without his personal leadership, it is unlikely that the PT would have been created or held together as a party for over twenty years.

Lula was finally elected president in October 2002—his fourth try at the office—and was subsequently reelected in 2006. His tenure as president was much less radical or revolutionary than many of his supporters hoped. He largely kept to the terms of IMF deals signed by his predecessors, although when they expired, he declined to sign another deal with the IMF. He distributed some land, but not as much as the Landless Workers' Movement wanted. He attempted to reorient public spending toward the poor, but without totally alienating the business class. In short, he was a pragmatist, understanding that Brazil needed foreign investment and trade even as he tried to change the terms in favor of Brazil. As a result, the Brazilian economy remained stable, but less change occurred in the structures of economic and political power than he originally advocated. One could argue that his greatest accomplishment was to demonstrate, both to Brazilians and to his critics in countries like the United States, that a leftist president need not bring economic or social collapse.

Boris Yeltsin

Boris Yeltsin was Russia's first postcommunist president. His rise to power during the Soviet period was long and rocky. Following years working in construction in the

© Andre Durand/AFP/Getty Images

city of Sverdlovsk, he was appointed Communist Party secretary of Sverdlovsk in the mid-1970s. This led to a position on the party's Central Committee in the early 1980s, his appointment as Moscow party boss in 1985, and a position in the powerful Politburo the following year. Once on the Politburo, Yeltsin made a name for himself when he publicly criticized perks and privileges for Communist Party officials.

This action and other disagreements with Gorbachev led to Yeltsin's removal from the body in early 1988 but won the hearts of many ordinary Soviet citizens. Yeltsin translated this popularity into electoral victories for a seat in the newly created Congress of People's Deputies in 1989, for a seat in and chairmanship of the Russian union republic's parliament in 1990, and for the position of president of the Russian republic in mid-1991. The collapse of the hard-liner-led coup against Gorbachev in August 1991 solidified Yeltsin's rise to prominence. He emerged as the most powerful figure in the Soviet Union and played a central role in negotiating its dismantling.

When the Soviet Union was relegated to history at the end of 1991, Yeltsin's position as president of the Russian republic of the USSR was transformed into the presidency of an independent country, the Russian Federation. Governing a country with a failing economy and regional secessionist movements, Yeltsin faced a number of hardships, including a struggle with the parliament in 1992 and 1993.

Yeltsin's leadership style combined toughness and occasionally fiery rhetoric with an ability to broker political compromises at key moments. As a result, he was the consummate survivor. He won reelection in the middle of 1996 despite very low popularity numbers early in the year. Yeltsin rejected discussions about seeking a third term and resigned from the presidency on his own terms on New Year's Eve of 1999. His record as a leader is mixed, but he remains one of the most dynamic and important figures of the late twentieth century.

Think and Discuss

To what extent do the backgrounds and leadership styles of the current and past political leaders highlighted in the TIC sections explain their successes and failures?

© Bettmann/CORBIS

Ayatollah Ruhollah Khomeini

Born in 1900, Ruhollah Khomeini studied religion throughout his life, becoming an ayatollah in the 1950s. An ardent opponent of the shah, he criticized the shah's connections to the West. He was arrested in 1963 and exiled from Iran in the mid-1960s. He first went to Turkey, lived in Iraq until forced out by Saddam Hussein in 1978, and finally settled in Paris. One of the shah's decisions, to strike out against Khomeini while he was in exile, played a role in Khomeini's political emergence. A prominent Tehran daily newspaper ran a fabricated letter attacking Khomeini. Instead of discrediting him, the letter's publication turned religious members of society more sharply against the shah's regime and vaulted Khomeini into the status of head of the political opposition.[47]

Khomeini was Supreme Leader after the 1979 Islamic Revolution until his death in June 1989. He oversaw Iran through the American Embassy hostage crisis and the Iran-Iraq War. He also issued a famous *fatwa* in February 1989 calling for the killing of Salman Rushdie, author of *The Satanic Verses*, which Khomeini deemed blasphemous.

COUNTRY SUMMARY

TIC Country	Current Leader or Leaders	Example of Decision Making and Its Rationality
United Kingdom	David Cameron (Prime Minister)	Margaret Thatcher and the Falklands Islands War
Germany	Angela Merkel (Chancellor)	Helmut Kohl and the German Currency Union
India	Manmohan Singh (Prime Minister); Sonia Gandhi (Leader of the INC)	Manmohan Singh and the Indo-U.S. Nuclear Agreement; ITAP feature on incrementalism
Mexico	Felipe Calderón (President, term expires in 2012)	Ernesto Zedillo and liberalization; ITAP feature on rational choice theory and NAFTA
Brazil	Dilma Rousseff (President)	Henrique Cardoso and the *Plano Real*
Nigeria	Goodluck Jonathan (President)	The Nigerian Civil War
Russia	Vladimir Putin (Prime Minister, expected to run for president in 2012); Dmitry Medvedev (President, term expires in 2012)	The Coup against Mikhail Gorbachev
China	Hu Jintao (President, term expires in 2012)	Mao Zedong, the Great Leap Forward, and the Cultural Revolution; ITAP feature on Deng Xiaoping, Tiananmen Square, and elite learning
Iran	Ayatollah Ali Hoseini-Khamenei (Supreme Leader); Mahmoud Ahmadinejad (President)	The choice to bar reformist candidates in the 2004 Majles election

Spotlight on . . . Country

France	Nicolas Sarkozy (President, next election in 2012)	Sarkozy and the decision to ban burqas in public
Iraq	Nouri al-Maliki (Prime Minister); Jalal Talabani (President)	Nouri al-Maliki and the decision on whether to maintain a U.S. troop presence in Iraq
South Africa	Jacob Zuma (President)	The 2011 Immigration Amendment Bill

TIC Wrap-Up

An examination of the present leaders of the nine TIC cases highlights how varied the backgrounds and leadership skills, traits, and styles of major political leaders can be. While British Prime Minister David Cameron achieved electoral success through charisma and persuasiveness, German Chancellor Angela Merkel and Indian Prime Minister Manmohan Singh demonstrate that successful leadership can also be based on technical competence and a reputation for being above politics, especially when, in the case of India, politics as usual involves corruption.

In Mexico, Brazil, and Nigeria, one leader's term is ending, another's has just started, and the third has won reelection amid controversy. Felipe Calderón's term as Mexican president highlights the extent to which emerging events, such as the drug-related violence that has spiraled out of control in Mexico, can pose nearly insurmountable obstacles to a leader. Brazilian president Dilma Rousseff faces challenges of her own, including leading Brazil from the shadow of a popular predecessor. In Nigeria, the violent protests following Goodluck Jonathan's victory in 2011 have created a challenge almost as great as Calderón faces in Mexico.

The cases of Russia, China, and Iran demonstrate how leaders of nondemocratic systems face opportunities and constraints similar to those in democracies. Vladimir Putin's tell-it-like-it-is approach has won the admiration of many in the country, but he has also been blessed by economic success driven by high oil prices for much of the previous decade. As in the case of Hu Jintao in China, economic performance–based legitimacy provides a leader like Putin with a valuable base of support, but it depends on continued economic success. In Iran, President Mahmoud Ahmadinejad faces limits on his ability to pursue his own policy path, as institutional arrangements in Iran give Supreme Leader Ali Hoseini-Khamenei significant power to shape major political outcomes in the country.

The overview of leadership in the TIC cases also highlights examples of important political decisions and how rational they appeared to be. These examples include decisions by former British Prime Minister Margaret Thatcher, former German Chancellor Helmut Kohl, and Indian Prime Minister Manmohan Singh. These leaders took controversial positions in the hope that it would pay off for their respective countries in the long term.

The decisions examined in the cases of Mexico, Brazil, and Nigeria are all important yet very different. In Mexico, former president Ernesto Zedillo decided to make and follow through with promises to liberalize the political system, setting the stage for the establishment of democracy. In Brazil, Fernando Henrique Cardoso faced the daunting task of devising a plan to curb Brazil's runaway inflation. In Nigeria, a series of decisions paved the way for the Nigerian civil war. Each of these cases shows how elites can make decisions in part, at least, as the result of rational calculations. Each also shows the extent to which the setting in which the decisions occur—external pressure, previous policy failures, and growing frustrations alongside increasing tensions—can make rational decision making more or less likely.

The examples of decision making in the Soviet Union just prior to its collapse, China, and Iran highlight how key figures in nondemocratic systems sometimes make choices designed to bolster their own position or to save the nondemocratic system. In the case of the Soviet Union, hard-liners in the Soviet government chose to attempt an overthrow of Soviet leader Mikhail Gorbachev, whom they saw as having become too supportive of political liberalization. In China, Mao Zedong made two choices designed to shake up the Communist system and mold it even more in his image, which ended up having negative consequences for him and his legacy. The China section also includes a discussion of Deng Xiaoping's decision to use violence against the Tiananmen Square protesters as an example of elite learning. The example from Iran—the Guardian Council's decision to reject a large number of moderate candidates from the ballot for the 2004 Majles elections—is more recent. Unlike the coup against Gorbachev and Mao's great reforms, it appears to have succeeded in its goals.

Research in Context

Although political scientists and other social scientists increasingly understand the importance of leadership style, less is known about how a leader develops his or her style. Case studies of particular leaders could point to broader lessons that one could examine in other cases. A recent research article on British Prime Minister David Cameron's rhetoric and leadership style provides such potential lessons.

The Leadership Styles of David Cameron and Margaret Thatcher

In 2010, Stephen Evans published an article in the *British Journal of Politics and International Relations* about the relationship between the leadership styles of David Cameron and Margaret Thatcher.[48] The article claims that observers who highlight the differences between David Cameron and Margaret Thatcher are missing interesting similarities in their view of the individual and the state, their rhetoric about government intrusiveness, and even their leadership styles. Cameron has tried to move the Conservative Party toward the political center. This is something that Thatcher largely rejected as a strategy but that Tony Blair pursued as leader of the Labour Party. At the same time, Cameron's approach to presenting his message to the British public has mirrored that of Margaret Thatcher. Evans argues that such parallels could be expected, partly because Cameron's formative years as a college student took place during Thatcher's second and third terms.

One of Cameron's approaches as leader of the Conservative Party particularly draws on the Thatcher model: using the view of state, society, and the individual as a way to distinguish between the UK's two main political parties. In his speech before the party conference in 2008, Cameron claimed that

> For Labour there is only the state and the individual, nothing in between. No family to rely on, no friend to depend on, no community to call on. No neighbourhood to grow in, no faith to share in, no charities to work in. No-one but the minister, nowhere but Whitehall, no such thing as society—just them, and their laws, and their rules, and their arrogance.[49]

So What?

How is Evans's study relevant beyond British leadership? It provides potentially generalizable lessons from the British case. For example, the concept of elite learning was highlighted earlier in the chapter, but Evans shows how leaders not only learn from past leaders' decisions but also emulate those leaders' approaches to framing issues and mobilizing supporters. By discussing in depth Thatcher's impact on Cameron during his college years, Evans also provides a generational argument about leadership emulation. One might not expect those who come right after a great leader to copy his or her way of framing issues or leadership style. Instead, only decades after that leader—when those who were in college when the leader was in power reach leadership positions themselves—might one expect a new crop of leaders who resemble the great leader of the past.

As a result, Evans's work can provide insight into American leaders and their sources of leadership style. Governing at nearly the same time as Margaret Thatcher, Ronald Reagan remains a hero to many conservative Republicans in the United States. Evans's conclusions about the relationship between Thatcher's and Cameron's leadership styles would imply that one could expect to see budding Republican leaders, now likely in their forties, mirroring the leadership style of Ronald Reagan in the years ahead.

CONCLUSION

The choice approach, with its emphasis on individuals and their decisions, stands in stark contrast to structural approaches in the field of comparative politics. As Jack Goldstone writes about the study of revolutions, "In the 1970s and 1980s, scholars studying revolutions focused their attention on long-term characteristics of states and societies that heighten their risk of revolution. . . . in focusing on these 'macro' or large-scale structural causes, scholars seemed to lose an appreciation for the critical role of ideas, and the decisions of key individuals, as elements that make revolutions happen."[50]

Over the next two decades, the pendulum swung away from structural approaches and toward an emphasis on choice. Though some scholars believe that rational choice theory solves the levels of analysis problem (allowing one to explain both collective events and those at the individual level), one must be careful not to underestimate the extent to which structures provide constraints on political decision makers. Although these constraints do not shape every individual political decision in the same way, they should not be ignored when looking at a given individual political decision.

Think and Discuss
The idea that leadership matters is a strong challenge to structural arguments discussed in previous chapters. At this point, which seem more important, structural arguments or choice arguments? Why?

Information problems also should be taken seriously. Scholars have addressed information problems in amendments to rational choice such as satisficing or incrementalism, both of which are discussed in this chapter. The idea that humans are creatures of emotion poses perhaps the greatest challenge to rational choice. Rational choice scholars cannot easily co-opt human emotions into their models. Taking emotion into account does not mean assuming that all political decisions are irrational. It does mean that one must consider the conditions under which political decisions are likely to be more or less rational.

While it is important to consider the role of individual leaders and how rational they are, a full understanding of broad patterns of political behavior and of particular political outcomes benefits from finding ways to integrate structural and choice-based explanations, a recognition that appears to be gaining momentum among comparative politics scholars.[51] Integrating choice and structure requires understanding both. Previous sections of the book introduced the political consequences of various economic, cultural, identity, and political structures. This section of the book and this chapter in particular have emphasized individuals and their choices. It is now time to bring structures and choices together more systematically. The next chapter integrates structure and choice arguments in the examination of the important comparative politics topic of democratization.

KEY TERMS

Bounded rationality, p. 295
Choice approach, p. 292
Cognitive dissonance, p. 295
Elite learning, p. 309
Emotion, p. 296
Groupthink, p. 295
Incrementalism, p. 301

Leadership, p. 292
Leadership skills, p. 293
Leadership style, p. 293
Leadership traits, p. 293
Mood, p. 296
Pocketbook calculations, p. 294
Prospective calculations, p. 295

Rational choice theory, p. 303
Rationality, p. 294
Retrospective calculations, p. 295
Satisficing, p. 295
Sociotropic calculations, p. 295
Transference, p. 296

CHAPTER

11

Regime Transitions

An Egyptian army officer is held on the shoulders of protesters in Tahrir Square in Cairo, Egypt, on January 30, 2011. Protesters called for an end to the three-decade rule of President Hosni Mubarak.
© Lewis Whyld/PA Wire URN:10110217 (Press Association via AP Images)

CHAPTER OUTLINE

Regime Transitions
Understanding Regime Transitions

TOPIC IN COUNTRIES

Features in this chapter:

Spotlight on . . . Iraq: The Prospects for Consolidation of the Imposed Iraqi Democracy

Research in Context: Studying Democratic Breakdown

LEARNING OBJECTIVES

After reading this chapter, you should be able to

- Define key concepts such as *regime transition*, *democratic breakdown*, and *democratization*.

- Discuss why democratization can be destabilizing for a country.

- Describe the characteristics of a consolidated democracy.

- Summarize the major explanations of democratization that focus on structures and choices.

- Outline the historical and recent experiences with regime transition in the Topic in Countries cases.

In early 2011, mass protests against authoritarian leaders broke out in the Middle East, starting in Tunisia and spreading to Egypt several days later. The Tunisian protesters forced the president to resign and flee the country. Protests in Egypt also resulted in the resignation of the country's long-time president, Hosni Mubarak. As discussed at the beginning of Chapter 8, popular unrest eventually spread to Libya, leading NATO to provide military support to rebels opposing the rule of Muammar Qaddafi. The protests reminded some observers of the Cedar Revolution that swept through Lebanon in 2005. Sparked by the assassination of the former Lebanese prime minister on February 14 of that year, the Cedar Revolution protesters forced Syria to withdraw its troops from Lebanon. It also reminded observers of the less successful Green Revolution in Iran in 2009, in which tens of thousands of Iranians protested what they believed to be a fraudulent election. Those protests came on the heels of the "color revolutions" in the postcommunist states, such as the Orange Revolution in Ukraine. The use of the word *revolution* appears to have been premature in several of these popular uprisings, including those in the Middle East. Yet, the street protests did open the door to possible regime transitions in countries that few thought to be viable candidates for such change only months earlier.

Protests like these have captured the attention of pundits and scholars alike. Comparativists interested in social movements have been especially intrigued by the increasing role of new media. The Internet has spread information about uprisings in several countries, while cell phones, Facebook, and Twitter have helped coordinate the protests. The spark for the protests in Tunisia may have been the release of American government documents on WikiLeaks, another prominent new media outlet, that documented Tunisian government corruption, and analysts were quick to ask whether the protests that brought down the leader of Tunisia marked the first "WikiLeaks Revolution."[1] After Mubarak resigned, reporters and analysts covering Egypt pointed to the importance of technology and social networking sites in the Egyptian uprising as well.

Regime transition is one of the central topics of comparative politics, arguably serving as the dependent variable in as many comparative politics studies as any other political outcome. Some instructors design introductory comparative politics courses entirely around regime transition because it serves as an effective anchor for the discussion of central comparative politics concepts, theories, and debates. It is, therefore, appropriate that this first chapter of the final section of the book is about how analyzing structures and choices can help us understand such cases as the successful efforts to remove the leaders of Tunisia and Egypt and the possible establishment of more democratic systems in both countries.

Understanding the causes and consequences of different political regimes is crucial to understanding politics. Because political systems matter, it is a good idea to know what factors influence their creation, consolidation, and collapse. The topic of regime transition also highlights the connections between comparative politics and international relations, as well as between political science and other social science disciplines.

Comparativists today have a superb opportunity to discover generalizable patterns regarding democratization; numerous examples have occurred over the last several decades. These recent regime transitions provide fertile ground for comparison. Comparative politics research regarding regime transitions focuses more on transitions to democracy than on the collapse of democracy. Likewise, this chapter centers more on democratization than on democratic breakdown.

A number of normative and empirical arguments hold that democracy is a superior form of government. They contend that people having a say in running their own lives is inherently good; that consolidated democratic systems are more politically and socially stable than their counterparts; and that, because democracies tend not to go to war against other democracies, increasing the number of democracies promotes peace.[2] As a result, in the last several decades, both the architects of American foreign policy and the leaders of international organizations such as the European Union (EU) have emphasized fostering regime change in certain countries in order to achieve various national and international political goals.

Democratization can have pitfalls. While mature democracies are politically stable, periods of transition to democracy can be chaotic, leading elites and masses alike to look back fondly at times of relative order and stability under a nondemocratic system.[3] Elections in new democracies may also produce awkward results. In 2006, for example, Hamas, a group the U.S. government labeled a terrorist organization, won elections in the Palestinian territories. In prior decades, democratic elections in a variety of settings increased ethnic tensions and brought ethnic nationalists to power.[4] Although a world in which every political system was democratic might be much more peaceful than the world today, recent history suggests that one should expect a number of civil wars and international conflicts on the way to that point.

Regime Transitions

Regime Transition The process of changing from one type of political system to another.

A **regime transition** occurs when one type of political system changes into another. Figure 11.1 displays a continuum of regime types, ranging from authoritarian to democratic. A regime transition involves movement in either direction from one category to another on this continuum. (Totalitarian systems are excluded from Figure 11.1, although, as some of this chapter's Topic in Countries discussions point out, transitions can begin from or end in totalitarianism as well. See Chapter 5 for definitions and a more detailed discussion of totalitarianism, authoritarianism, and democracy.)

Regime transitions vary in pace and extent. Some happen relatively quickly, such as the collapse of Eastern European Communist regimes in the late 1980s. In other cases, the process is more protracted. Mexico moved from authoritarianism to democracy over several decades. Some transitions are also more sweeping than others. Mexico's spanned the entire spectrum in Figure 11.1, but Russia's

FIGURE 11.1   The Continuum from Authoritarian to Democratic Systems

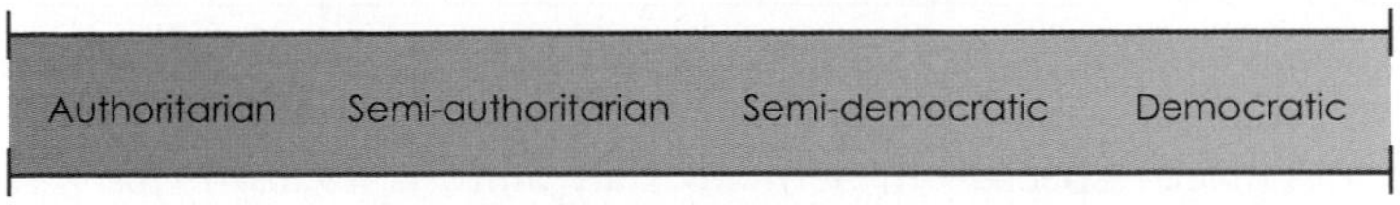

| Authoritarian | Semi-authoritarian | Semi-democratic | Democratic |

recent retreat from democracy has been less wide ranging. Although Russia is increasingly less democratic, many observers do not yet consider it a full-fledged authoritarian system.

Liberalization

Liberalization occurs when a nondemocratic system becomes politically more open and less repressive. The government expands individual rights and freedoms, often through official changes to the country's constitution or the enforcement of previously ignored constitutional provisions. Nondemocratic leaders may pursue liberalization for a number of reasons. They may seek to boost their legitimacy and believe that they can maintain control of the reform process. Some, such as China's Communist leadership, are able to maintain control while loosening some restraints on people's daily lives. Others, as in the case of Soviet leader Mikhail Gorbachev, are unable to contain the politically destabilizing forces that can surface during periods of liberalization.

There are degrees of liberalization. A country undergoing significant liberalization would move from left to right in Figure 11.1, but liberalization does not necessarily alter the category in which a comparativist would place the regime. Reforms that liberalize a nondemocratic system might move the country from one regime type (authoritarianism) to another (semi-authoritarianism), but they might also make an authoritarian system less authoritarian without clearly moving it out of the authoritarian category.

Liberalization The process of making a nondemocratic political system more open and less repressive.

Democratization

Democratization is a regime transition that establishes a stable democratic system. In Figure 11.1, it is a move from left to right across the continuum that reaches the democratic category and, if successful, remains there. Not all democratization processes are successful. **Incomplete democratization** occurs when a democracy exists for a short time and then collapses or slowly regresses. Examples of incomplete democratization are plentiful, particularly among less economically developed countries or countries with histories of repeated military involvement in domestic politics.

Like regime transitions in general, the pace of democratization varies. A nondemocracy may collapse in a matter of days, or it may evolve into a more democratic system over a long time, with liberalization ultimately leading to the establishment of a system recognized as democratic. The successful consolidation of a democracy is nearly always a protracted process, typically occurring in decades rather than years.

Democratization A regime transition that establishes a democracy and, if successful, a consolidated democracy.

Incomplete Democratization A transition in which a democracy is established but does not last for an extended period of time.

Waves of Democratization
Just as democratizations can vary from one case to the next, the global spread of democracy also varies over time. A noticeable surge in global democracy over a particular period is known as a **democratization wave**. Although political scientist Samuel Huntington was not the first to discuss the idea of global democratic surges and retrenchments, the concept of waves of democratization is most closely associated with his 1991 book *The Third Wave*.[5]

During a democratization wave, the number of new democracies exceeds the number of democratic breakdowns. Eventually, the balance may shift, bringing a contraction in the number of democracies. This reduction in democratic systems is

Democratization Wave A period in which the number of democracies around the world increases noticeably.

TABLE 11.1	Waves and Reverse Waves of Democratization	
Wave/Reverse Wave	**Examples**	**Period**
First Wave	American and French democracy; expansion of the franchise in Western democracies	1820s–1920s
First Reverse Wave	Rise of fascism in Europe, especially in Germany, Italy, and Spain, and also in Eastern Europe	1920s–1940s
Second Wave	Post–World War II occupation and decolonization in Africa and Asia	1940s–1960s
Second Reverse Wave	Resurgence of bureaucratic and military authoritarianism in Latin America, Africa, and Asia	1960s–1970s
Third Wave	Southern European, Latin American, and postcommunist democratizations	1970s–1990s
Possible Third Reverse Wave	Creeping authoritarianism in Peru under Fujimori and in some postcommunist states (e.g., Russia and Belarus); military coups in Africa (e.g., Niger and Gambia)	1990s–2000
Possible Fourth Wave	Mexico's 2000 presidential election; color revolutions (Serbia, Georgia, Ukraine, Kyrgyzstan); U.S.-led efforts at regime change in Afghanistan and Iraq; uprisings in the Middle East and North Africa in 2011	2000–present

Source: Modified from Samuel Huntington, *The Third Wave: Democratization in the Late Twentieth Century* (Norman: University of Oklahoma Press, 1991).

Reverse Wave A period with a sizable reduction in the number of democracies globally.

known as a **reverse wave**. Huntington points out that even when reverse waves have occurred, they have left behind more democracies than had existed prior to the original wave.[6] While several new democracies have developed in the last three decades, Huntington's historical framework implies that not all of the third wave democracies will survive; some will likely be swept away in a subsequent reverse wave. As Table 11.1 indicates, some observers believe that a reverse wave already occurred in the 1990s, followed by a new fourth wave of democratization.

Stages of Democratization

Democratization in a particular country occurs in stages. Some comparativists argue that the stages can overlap, while others see them as more distinct. Assorted democratization studies use different labels for the stages and disagree about the number. For the most part, however, there is agreement that democratization entails a nondemocratic regime breaking down, a democracy being instituted, and the democracy becoming stable and secure. As presented in Figure 11.2, comparativists often label these three stages as the breakdown of non-democracy, the establishment of democracy, and the consolidation of democracy. Although successful democratization involves movement through all three stages, it is not always easy to identity when a country has left one stage and moved into another.

Arriving at one stage of democratization also does not guarantee that a country will reach the next stage. Regime transitions are times of great uncertainty. When a nondemocratic system collapses, a new leader might reestablish the system or form a different nondemocratic system. Even when the population perceives the

FIGURE 11.2	The Stages of Democratization

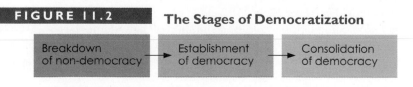

old nondemocratic government as very corrupt, government change without regime change is a distinct possibility. Likewise, the founding of a democracy does not guarantee its consolidation. Just as established non-democracies can break down, so too can established democracies.

The Breakdown of the Nondemocratic System. The first stage of democratization is the **breakdown of non-democracy**. This involves the slow liberalization or rapid collapse of a nondemocratic system. Comparativist Dankwart Rustow has called the breakdown of the non-democracy the "preparatory" stage of democratization.[7] This label captures the idea that the disintegration of the non-democracy makes the emergence of democracy possible.

Nondemocratic systems can break down in a variety of ways. Comparativist Terry Lynn Karl distinguishes between "transitions from above," in which the ruling elite liberalizes and effectively controls the political reform process, and "transitions from below," in which opposition leaders successfully organize unconventional mass participation in resistance to the non-democracy.[8] Comparativist Scott Mainwaring adds a middle category, in which the old rulers do not fully control the process but are able to participate in negotiations and protect themselves from retribution following the establishment of the new democracy.[9] In many ways, this is the story of the democratization of postapartheid South Africa.

Establishment of the Democratic System. During the second stage, the **establishment of democracy**, political elites establish the institutional framework for the new democratic system. The country typically adopts a new constitution, often in a national referendum. Because of the importance of the choices and decisions elites make during this stage of democratization, Rustow labels it the "decision stage."[10]

By emphasizing decisions, Rustow highlights the choice side of the structure versus choice framework. Consequently, his label fails to convey the extent to which the existing socioeconomic and political structures affect the decisions about the new institutional arrangements. It also fails to capture the way that the new democratic institutions become a central part of the country's political structure, constraining government officials in the new democracy and providing them with opportunities. The composition of the new institutions matter a great deal. A presidential system with FPTP electoral arrangements might work in one country but be disastrous in another. As a result, those designing a new constitution ideally not only look at examples of other democratic systems but also take into account their country's unique challenges and needs.

Consolidation of Democracy. The third stage of democratization is the **consolidation of democracy**. Democratic consolidation is one of the more thought-provoking concepts in comparative politics. Comparativists disagree on its causes and even how to determine whether it exists. In defining consolidation, scholars such as Juan Linz stress the lack of viable alternatives to the democratic system.[11] The government leaders and their political opponents expect democracy to endure and accept it as the "only game in town."[12] Accordingly, a consolidated democracy is very unlikely to break down and be replaced by a nondemocratic system. A breakdown would require a fundamental change in the political setting, such as the development of massive corruption or a severe economic crisis, to eliminate democracy's status as the only game in town and make the transition to a nondemocratic system a viable alternative.

As is the case with many political science concepts, the definition and measurement of democratic consolidation generates debate. Comparativists have identified several indicators of measurement:

- **Holding repeated free and fair elections.** When free and fair elections become routine, it is a strong sign that democracy has become the only game in town.
- **Peaceful transfer of power through elections.** Some comparativists believe that elections alone are not enough. A number of scholars suggest looking for a successful and peaceful transfer of power from one set of rulers to another. If democracy is, as political scientist Adam Przeworski claims, "a system in which parties

Breakdown of Non-democracy The first stage of the democratization process, in which the existing nondemocratic system erodes or collapses.

Establishment of Democracy The second stage of democratization, in which a new democratic system is developed and put into place.

Consolidation of Democracy A condition in which elites and masses alike see no viable alternative to an existing democratic system.

lose elections,"[13] not only opposition parties can lose elections. If an election results in a president or ruling party losing control of the government and if the rulers peacefully hand over power to those who defeated them, democracy would appear to be entrenched. But even this is not enough for some scholars, who need to see repeated transfers of power before labeling a democracy as consolidated. Political scientist Samuel Huntington, for example, prefers a "two-turnover" criterion, with those who peacefully replace the sitting government later turning over power to another set of leaders.[14]

- **Surviving a test.** A consolidated democracy can endure various threats or tests. Such tests include attempted coups (e.g., Spain in 1981); very close elections (e.g., Mexico in 2006); or severe economic hardships (e.g., a number Latin American countries in the 1980s, when democracy expanded despite a regional economic crisis).[15]

- **Adherence to the rule of law.** Following the constitution and accepting that no one is above the law—principles at the heart of the concept of rule of law—are also features of a consolidated democracy. It is not always easy to determine when the rule of law has taken hold in a country, but the more one sees what Lawrence Whitehead calls "durable compliance with rules and procedures,"[16] the more likely that democracy is consolidated.

- **Legitimacy.** Chapter 1 discussed legitimacy, the population's acceptance of the political system as having the right to produce binding rules for the society. It makes sense that the development of legitimacy would signal a democratic system's consolidation. It is unclear, though, how much legitimacy is necessary—that is, what portion of the population needs to accept the system as legitimate for democracy to be called consolidated.

- **Survival for a lengthy period of time.** Surviving for a period of time is not the same as stability, nor does it guarantee that democracy has become the only game in town. Still, the longer a democracy survives, the more likely that it will continue to survive.

The idea that even a consolidated democracy may break down at some point in the future has led some scholars to emphasize an additional stage of democratization: maturation. According to this view, a mature democracy has lasted so long and survived so many tests that it is unthinkable that it could collapse, even during economic or political crises.[17] The vast majority of democratization scholars, however, discuss only three stages of democratization and consider that mature democracies are simply more consolidated than others.

Think and Discuss

Which of the indicators of democratic consolidation would most convincingly indicate that a democracy is consolidated? Why?

Democratic Breakdown

It is not unusual for an established democracy to break down and be replaced by some form of nondemocratic political system. **Democratic breakdown** can happen over time, as in the cases of creeping authoritarianism discussed earlier in the book, or it can happen abruptly. Sometimes a democracy may exist for a lengthy period, appear to be consolidated, and still collapse. Instances of incomplete democratization in which the democracy is never consolidated are more common, however.

The seminal study of democratic breakdowns is a 1978 book edited by Juan Linz and Alfred Stepan that covers cases from Europe to Latin America, including Germany and Brazil.[18] In his introduction to the book, Linz proposes that, like democratization, democratic breakdown occurs in stages. He labels the first the **crisis stage**, in which a democratic government fails to address one or more pressing social problems. When a crisis is severe enough that it undercuts not just support for the government but for the legitimacy of the system itself, the typical result is the **breakdown stage**.

Democratic Breakdown When a democracy collapses or slowly transforms into a nondemocratic system.

Crisis Stage The first stage of democratic breakdown, when a crisis emerges that threatens an existing democracy.

Breakdown Stage The second stage in the process of democratic breakdown, when the democratic system falls apart.

According to Linz, this stage is reached when the sitting government, faced with mounting instability and diminishing legitimacy, chooses to strengthen dramatically the executive, to surrender power to the military, or to attempt to co-opt opposition forces that are uncommitted to democracy. These actions often fail to save democracy, transforming it into one nondemocratic system or another. The nondemocratic period that follows democratic breakdown may be a brief interlude, or it may last decades or longer.

Alternatively, the crisis stage may lead the democratic government to transform without a regime transition. Democracy survives, although it generally looks different from its previous incarnation. Linz calls this the process of **reequilibration**. It requires leadership untainted by the preceding crisis that can win over important political, economic, and social groups; the willingness of former leaders to turn over power to the new rulers and accept new policy directions; and a high level of passivity among the general population.[19] Such conditions do not frequently intersect. Consequently, reequilibration is far from guaranteed, and severe crises commonly result instead in a period of nondemocratic government.

> **Reequilibration** An overhaul of a democratic system in response to a major crisis.

Think and Discuss

Could democracy possibly break down in the United Kingdom? In the United States? How?

Understanding Regime Transitions

Over the past five decades, most comparative politics research on regime transition has focused either on specific structural conditions or on elite choices. Works studying democratization, for example, initially tended to emphasize economic structure as part of comparativists' "search for the necessary conditions and prerequisites for the emergence of a stable democracy."[20] Later, identity and culture took center stage among those emphasizing structure, while other researchers increasingly focused on the role of elites. Both structural and choice factors help explain regime transitions. Unfortunately, no necessary or sufficient causal factors appear to determine the outcome of democratization in all cases. Consequently, causal theories of democratization are, as a rule, probabilistic (see Chapter 1). They emphasize factors that make democratic establishment and consolidation more likely.

Structure versus Choice and Internal versus External

The overall set of causal factors related to regime transition can be divided two ways: structure versus choice, and factors within a country versus those outside that country. At times throughout the text, discussions of the structure versus choice framework have emphasized this second dividing line. For example, the overview of economic and cultural structures underscored the role of globalization in domestic economic development and political culture. Even the previous chapter's coverage of elite decision making pointed to the way elites in a country can learn from the decisions of leaders in neighboring countries, or how an important global leader's decisions can directly affect that country's political outcomes.

Taking into consideration the difference between internal and external factors aids in the application of the structure versus choice framework. The result is four sets of factors—internal structure, external structure, internal choice, and external choice—as presented in Figure 11.3.

Internal Structural Explanations

This book's discussion of internal structure is divided into economic, cultural, identity, and political structure. Likewise, when considering how internal structural factors

FIGURE 11.3 **Categorizing Structural and Choice Variables**

Structure versus choice / Internal versus external	Internal	External
Structure	Internal structure	External structure
Choice	Internal choice	External choice

might influence democratization, it is useful to distinguish among these four types of structural factors.

Economic Structure

Modernization theory (see Chapter 2) and its emphasis on capitalist economic development influenced initial democratization studies. In 1959, political scientist Seymour Martin Lipset published a seminal article on what he believed to be the social and economic requisites for democracy.[21] Lipset's claim that economic development is associated with democracy remains a central topic in the democratization literature. Even rough indicators of such development—for example, per capita GDP—reveal a strong relationship between development and democratization. Especially if one excludes states prosperous due to oil wealth, most stable democracies are much wealthier than most non-democracies. Excluding the oil states improves the relationship largely because oil states generally lack another key economic structural factor, a sizable middle class, which many democratization scholars believe makes successful democratization more likely.

Scholars discuss the development-democracy relationship in terms of both direct and indirect effects. Direct effects include economic power being spread out across the general population, which makes it more difficult for the government to engage in repression. Economic structure's indirect effects on democratization include conditions generated by economic development like urbanization and education. Economic development also provides a sense of security that makes it possible for people to value voting rights. When people are struggling to find food for themselves and their families, whether they had a say in the selection of their country's political leaders is often far from their top priority.

Political Culture

Chapter 3 presented five key components of political culture. Three of them—beliefs about authority, values regarding security versus liberty, and national identity—are particularly relevant to democratization. Existing beliefs about authority, such as deference to social elites and a strongly vertical social hierarchy, can make democracy difficult to establish. At the same time, Gabriel Almond and Sidney Verba argue in *The Civic Culture* that a certain degree of deference to authority (as in British political culture) increases stability in an established democracy because the masses are not regularly challenging the system's outputs and legitimacy.[22] Cultures valuing security over liberty pose a challenge to democracy. As a system of "institutionalized uncertainty" that emphasizes personal liberty, democracy is not necessarily conducive to social order, especially in its early years. If people prefer order over freedom, new democracies are vulnerable both to creeping authoritarianism and to a rapid breakdown such as by a military coup d'état. Cultures emphasizing national identity and attachment to the central government as the primary political unit enhance prospects for democracy. Without national unity, democratic practices can deepen divisions rather than overcome them. In his seminal piece on democratic transitions in 1970, Dankwart Rustow went so far as to call national unity a precondition of any democratic transition.[23]

Identity Structure

Explanations of identity structure and democratic transition often center on the form of identity diversity, or what Chapter 4 called cleavage structure theory. According to this perspective, when social divisions cut across one another, democracy is plausible. In contrast, democracy is tenuous when deep social divisions complement one another, such as when two ethnic groups speak different languages, have different religions, are concentrated in different parts of the country, and differ in terms of collective wealth. Democratic practices like elections foster candidates and parties that emphasize and reinforce these social divisions. Programmatic differences between parties give way to identity politics.

Other comparativists interested in identity structure and democracy explore whether certain collective identities are incompatible with democracy. Much of this work turns the spotlight on religion, most recently scrutinizing the relationship of Islam to democracy. When considering the role religion plays in a particular country's democratization prospects, one should ask three questions. First, because any strain of fundamentalism is arguably hostile to democracy, how prevalent is fundamentalism? Fundamentalists take religious texts literally, see religion as essential to society's proper functioning, and are commonly intolerant of opposing viewpoints. Listening to others' views and seeking compromise and cooperation are inconsistent with belief in an absolute "Truth" that should guide all political, economic, and social relations.

Second, have events possibly made past arguments about a particular religion less relevant at the present? Prior to the third wave of democratization, many believed that Catholicism was less compatible with democracy than Protestantism. Yet, most of the democratizations of the first half of the third wave took place in Catholic countries.

Third, to what extent does a country's main religion correlate with its overall culture? A dominant religion shapes a society's culture, but existing political cultural values about authority, security, and national identity may be distinct from that religion. Disputes over whether Islam is conducive to democracy bring to light the factor of attitudes toward women. When women are seen as second-class citizens, individuals may use elements of Islam to perpetuate those views, even if Islam itself did not create them.

Political Structure

Political structures affect democratization in several ways. The form of a nondemocratic regime can influence the nature and speed of that regime's dissolution. In addition, when a non-democracy breaks down, its institutional structures can leave lasting legacies with which the new democracy must contend. All the independent states that emerged from the collapse of the Soviet Union, for example, began independence with the constitutions and institutional composition they had used when they were Soviet republics.

Democratization specialists also pay a great deal of attention to the design of new democratic institutions and the implications that different arrangements have for stability and consolidation. Such design options include some of the major features discussed in Chapters 5 through 9: federal versus unitary systems, presidential versus parliamentary systems, judiciaries with constitutional review powers versus those without, pluralist versus corporatist interest group arrangements, and first past the post (FPTP) versus proportional representation (PR) electoral systems.

Some comparativists see federalism, including ethno-federal approaches, as beneficial for democracy. Nancy Bermeo argues that federal systems provide greater long-term stability for a new democracy given that they spread power across more layers of government, creating more arenas for political bargaining and giving regional political elites a greater stake in the survival of the democracy.[24] Others worry that federalism can deepen divisions and potentially lead to the breakdown of the state. Donald Horowitz, for example, takes a more cautious view. Horowitz advocates federal systems in deeply divided societies when the federation's internal territorial boundaries cut across identity group boundaries, but he opposes ethno-federal systems, which he sees as reinforcing already deep identity group divisions.[25]

Arguments over the relative merits of presidential and parliamentary systems have been among the most lively in comparative politics. Chapter 6 contrasted Juan Linz's theory of parliamentary superiority with Donald Horowitz's theory of presidential system design. Linz proposes that presidential systems are unstable and inhibit democratic consolidation by creating dual legitimacy problems and making it too difficult to remove a corrupt or incompetent leader. Horowitz counters that parliamentary systems have been unstable as well, arguing that the careful design of a presidential system's rules can address the weaknesses Linz identifies.[26]

Comparativists have done less work on the role of judicial review powers and on the implications of corporatist versus pluralist arrangements for successful consolidation. The concept of civil society, however, has garnered significant attention. In addition to definitional problems with the term (see Chapter 8), causal claims have been plagued by questions of tautology, causal direction, and contrary evidence. Some scholars, such as Robert Putnam, see civil society activities as crucial to the development of "social capital," which involves values such as tolerance and interpersonal trust that make democracies more stable in the long run.[27] Others point to the value of civil society as a counterweight to the state, making creeping authoritarianism or other forms of democratic breakdown less likely.[28] In contrast, Sheri Berman's case study of Weimar Germany (the democratic system between World War I and the Nazi seizure of power) demonstrates not only that civil society did not save the Weimar democracy, but also that it actively subverted it.[29] Extremists on both ends of the political spectrum used civil society groups to spread their messages and mobilize their supporters. Comparativists also disagree about the benefits of different electoral arrangements. However, there is general agreement that rules that create a vast number of small parties can make the early years of democratic transition less stable.

External Structural Explanations

Just as international relations scholars sometimes downplay the importance of domestic causes of foreign policy and international affairs, comparativists are often reluctant to regard external influences as playing a key role in domestic policy and other national political outcomes. Research on democratization, however, is one arena in which scholars have taken international influences seriously. These external factors include structural conditions, such as the nature of the international "polar system," direct imposition of democracy via military conquest, global economic processes, pressure from international organizations, and examples provided by neighboring states or states with similar demographic features.

The Importance of the International Polar System

For many international relations scholars, one of the starting points when examining the international political system is to look at its poles. A **pole** is a dominant state in the international system. The number and type of poles at a point in time forms the **polar system**. Those emphasizing the importance of polar arrangements (in the political science field of international relations, they are usually called "neorealists" or "structural realists") accept political scientist Kenneth Waltz's claim that the form of the polar system shapes the actions of states in the international system.[30] These scholars distinguish between four types of polar systems: unipolar, bipolar, tripolar, and multipolar.

Pole A dominant state in the international system.

Polar System The arrangement of poles—unipolar, bipolar, tripolar, or multipolar—at a point in time.

The existence of a unipolar or bipolar system would have the greatest impact on global democratization. A bipolar world has two poles, each of which dominates a large bloc of countries. While nonaligned countries may exist, they are typically much fewer in number than are countries that fall into one bloc or the other. If one of the two poles is hostile to democracy, other countries in its bloc are unlikely to be democratic. This was true of the Communist countries during the cold war, most of which were allies of and strongly influenced by the Soviet Union. However, the cold war also shows that a democratic pole in a bipolar system may tolerate non-democracies in its bloc to try to prevent them from falling under the sphere of influence of the other pole. During the cold war, the United States supported a sizable number of authoritarian governments, largely in the name of fighting the spread of Communism into those countries.

In the unipolar case, a single pole dominates globally, imposing its will on all other countries. If that unipolar country is a democracy, it might encourage democratic systems in other countries as well, though the main feature of the unipolar system is that the dominant pole will not tolerate challenges to its rule. Thus, the democratic pole in a unipolar world may look on quiet non-democracies more favorably than on vocal democracies. If the dominant pole is a non-democracy, it is hard to imagine that it would tolerate the global spread of democracy. The accompanying free speech and political organization in democratizing countries would almost certainly facilitate challenges to its global rule. A truly unipolar world has never existed. Some observers believe that the current international system is as close to being unipolar today as ever before, though most international relations scholars consider today's polar system to be an unusual hybrid of a unipolar and a multipolar arrangement. A large number of powerful states exist, but the United States is more powerful than the others.

Imposition through Conquest

A second external structural factor has been important both historically and recently. Regime change is not always a homegrown process driven by the structural conditions and elites of the country undergoing the transition. Numerous democratizations have been the result of military conquest and the conquering power's desire to establish a democratic system, including the often-discussed cases of West Germany and Japan after World War II; several colonial states, particularly British colonies, that were given democratic systems before independence; and a number of countries in which the United States fostered regime change through military action. In the last few decades, this latter group has included Grenada during Ronald Reagan's administration, Panama in George H. W. Bush's administration, Haiti during Bill Clinton's administration, and Iraq in George W. Bush's administration.

Many imposed democracies fail, partly because the domestic structural conditions identified in the previous section are lacking. British colonies have fared better than those of other European states partly because the British tended to spend more time working closely with the successor government during the transition period to independence. Yet, even the democratic record of former British colonies is far from stellar.

Spotlight on ... IRAQ

The Prospects for Consolidation of the Imposed Iraqi Democracy

In 2003, the United States led a coalition of countries in an invasion of Iraq. Unlike the earlier Gulf War, which had included a broader U.S.-led coalition that successfully drove Iraq out of Kuwait, the 2003 invasion was a preemptive effort involving a smaller number of countries. Based on the argument that

Iraq had failed to live up to United Nations mandates related to weapons of mass destruction (WMD), President George W. Bush claimed that Iraq posed a significant threat to regional and even global security. The invasion that followed succeeded in driving Iraqi President Saddam Hussein from power but failed to produce the WMD "smoking gun" the Bush Administration hoped to find.[31] As a result, the U.S. government increasingly emphasized another argument, one that had been mentioned prior to the invasion but was less central to the justification for going to war than the WMD issue: that bringing democracy to Iraq could plant a pro-democratic seed in the largely nondemocratic region of the Middle East.

The challenges in getting this seed to take root were substantial. The American-led efforts to craft and establish democracy in Iraq faced a problem similar to other imposed democracies. Because the democracy was not generated domestically, many in Iraq saw it as a foreign import. Imported democracies struggle to gain domestic legitimacy, particularly when they fail to solve pressing domestic problems. Beyond the emergence of a civil war involving major identity groups and organized attacks on American and other foreign soldiers in the country, domestic problems were numerous in Iraq.[32]

Stability in imposed democracies often requires a lengthy presence by the occupying country. In the case of Iraq, the United States had a significant military and security presence into 2011, eight years after the initial invasion. Even then, as it finalized plans to withdraw troops by the end of 2011, there were fears about the likely instability that would follow a final U.S. withdrawal. These fears were well founded; sectarian violence increased in the late summer of 2010, when the United States removed its combat troops. If Iraq's democratically elected government showed competence and stability, some of these fears might have receded. Instead, following the March 2010 elections, Iraqi leaders spent most of the rest of 2010 trying to create a stable ruling coalition.

None of this means that Iraq's experiment with democracy is destined to fail. New democracies are typically shaky in their early years, but many of them succeed in becoming consolidated democracies. When they are perceived to be someone else's imposed or imported system, however, they are especially fragile. If the system fails to produce solutions to pressing problems, the population, elites and masses alike, may begin to consider alternative forms of government.

Global Economic Structure

By the 1970s, some scholars began to respond to modernization theory with criticisms that came to be labeled dependency theory (see Chapter 2). Dependency theorists emphasized aspects of the global capitalist economic structure that discouraged democratic development. These arguments provided a solid explanation of the second reverse wave during which democracy retreated, particularly in Latin America and Africa.

Just as modernization theory does not explain the lack of democracy in some relatively developed states, dependency theory explains little about developing states that successfully democratize. With the onset of global democratization's third wave, those looking for external structural explanations began to turn away from dependency theory and toward arguments about the increasing importance of international organizations and "demonstration effects."

International Organizations and Their Membership Rules

One of the most noticeable markers of increasing globalization and regionalization has been the explosion in the number and authority of international organizations. International relations scholars distinguish between international intergovernmental organizations (IGOs), made up of internationally recognized states, and international nongovernmental organizations (NGOs), whose members are individuals and/or groups. Many international NGOs advocate democratization, reduced corruption, and the spread of respect for human rights. As political scientist Hans Peter Schmitz contends, such NGOs "diffuse democratic principles, support domestic allies, and exert pressure on authoritarian regimes."[33]

Of the two types of organizations, NGOs have been less effective at pressuring countries to liberalize and democratize than IGOs. The reason is relatively straightforward: IGOs can offer rewards and punishments not available to NGOs. One of the major rewards is membership in the organization itself. The use of standards for membership in an IGO is known as conditionality; in other words, receiving and maintaining membership is conditional on a country's meeting the standards of the organization. The best example of the use of membership as a reward for democratization is the EU. Becoming an EU member is a long and difficult process involving both negotiation and demonstration of changes required by the organization. For the EU, such standards include Western democratic practices.

Demonstration Effects

A final external structural effect involves states' providing models of democratization for other similar states. Democratization scholars typically refer to this process as demonstration effects or contagion. Many nondemocratic governments successfully resist pressures to liberalize and democratize, often by stressing to their populations the chaotic nature of such transformations and proposing the idea that the country is not yet ready for democracy. This becomes much less effective when neighboring or otherwise similar countries democratize. As a result, it is most difficult to be the first country in a region or one that is part of a group of similar states to democratize. Once the threshold is crossed by that first country, pressure increases on the others to follow this lead. In such cases, nondemocratic system collapse can "snowball,"[34] with each successive collapse taking less time than the previous one, as happened in Eastern Europe in 1989. The protests across the Middle East and North Africa in 2011 spread even more rapidly, although it remains unclear whether this example of demonstration effects will generate the number of successful democracies that the Eastern European uprisings did two decades earlier. Demonstration effects need not involve only countries that are neighbors. Spain's and Portugal's democratization in the 1970s was important for subsequent democratization in Latin America because it challenged the idea that democracy is difficult to establish in predominantly Catholic countries.

Internal Choice Explanations

Traditionally, structural explanations were more common in democratization research than were theoretical perspectives emphasizing individual and collective choices. The difficulty in generalizing choice-based explanations is one reason. But as tests of structural theories failed to generate a single widely accepted theory of democratization, the choice approach became more prevalent. Studies of specific cases of democratization seemed to confirm that the actions of individual decision makers were central to the breakdown of the nondemocratic system, the form of the democratic system that replaced it, and the prospects for democratic consolidation. As political scientist Michael McFaul put it:

> Inert, invisible structures do not make democracies or dictatorships. People do. Structural factors such as economic development, cultural influences, and historical institutional arrangements influence the formation of actors' preferences and power, but ultimately these forces have causal significance only if translated into human action.[35]

Intergovernmental Organizations (IGOs) Political organizations whose members are internationally recognized states.

Nongovernmental Organizations (NGOs) Political organizations whose members are individuals and/or groups.

Conditionality The creation and enforcement of standards for IGO membership.

Demonstration Effects The process in which a regime transition in one country sparks a parallel regime transition in a neighboring or otherwise similar country; also known as contagion.

Romanians stand on an armored carrier near Timisoara, Romania, on December 23, 1989. As demonstrations spread, Romanian troops sided with protestors against President Nicolae Ceaucescu. Ceaucescu and his wife were captured and executed on December 25, 1989.
© AP Photo/Dusan Vranic

The study of individuals generally focuses on four types of political elites that play important roles in different stages of democratization: the ruling elite in the nondemocratic system prior to its breakdown, the opposition leaders in the non-democracy prior to its collapse, the rulers of the new democratic system, and the leaders of institutions like the military that must side with the new democracy in times of crisis for it to become consolidated.

Leadership and Elite Choices in the Nondemocratic System Breakdown Stage

Structural factors and changes in them can create favorable conditions for the breakdown of a non-democracy, but the decisions of particular individuals turn this potential into reality. A leader may decide to liberalize; the head of the opposition may choose to organize mass protests. When the nondemocratic elites are dominated by people who support liberalization, a gradual opening of the political system can set the table for democratization. Such elites are typically called **reformers**, though comparativists also refer to them as moderates in the ruling elite or "soft-liners."

Reformers Members of the nondemocratic political elite committed to liberalization and possibly to democratization; also known as "soft-liners."

Hard-Liners Those who oppose reform and prefer to maintain or strengthen the current nondemocratic system; also known as "standpatters."

If, on the other hand, the non-democracy is controlled by individuals committed to the maintenance of the non-democracy at all costs—whom comparativists typically call **hard-liners** or "standpatters"—liberalization will not occur. Thus, many democratization scholars point to the importance of a split in the ruling elite between moderates and hard-liners, particularly when moderates gain the upper hand. When hard-liners continue to dominate a nondemocratic system, democratization is unlikely.

Rulers are not the only important individuals in a non-democracy. When opposition forces contest the rule of a nondemocratic government, the opposition leaders make decisions and take actions to enhance prospects for removing the nondemocratic leaders from power. Here again, comparativists distinguish between types of opposition elites. **Moderates** are those in the opposition who favor working with the ruling elite to facilitate a gradual transition to democracy, while **radicals** are unwilling to work with nondemocratic rulers. Radicals may instead support placing the rulers on trial once they are no longer in power, and they may even prefer another form of non-democracy. Prospects for a smooth and peaceful transition to democracy are enhanced when reformers dominate the government and moderates dominate the opposition.

Moderates Members of the opposition in a nondemocratic system who support cooperating with the government to encourage liberalization and democratization.

Radicals Opponents who are unwilling to work with the nondemocratic rulers.

Leadership and Elite Choices in the Establishment and Consolidation Stages

A relatively small number of individuals can play a large role in establishing a new democracy, including crafting its initial institutional arrangements. Their influence can be long-lasting. (Think about how often Americans focus on the intentions of the U.S. democratic system's founders.) Likewise, the leadership and choices of the initial leaders can be important for a new democracy's consolidation. In his work on postcommunist transitions, political scientist Shale Horowitz points out that the people who lead new democracies can be more important than the democracies' institutional design. Horowitz argues that strong presidential powers can improve a new democracy's prospects for consolidation if the powers are held by a leader committed to the democracy. If, on the other hand, the leader is ambivalent about or hostile to democracy, a strong president can promote creeping (or rapid) authoritarianism.[36]

Because the choices that elites make during the establishment and consolidation of democracy are so important, a number of works on democratization focus on decision-making topics such as bargaining and elite learning. New democracies are often the result of bargaining between reformers in the old government and moderates in the opposition, which produces a **pact** by the differing sides. In democratization, a pact is an official agreement about the rules for the new democratic system and the policy approaches it is expected to take. Pacts typically address specific issues, including economic and social policies. The pact-making process often excludes the most radical and most conservative political groups. The negotiations that created Venezuela's 1958 Pact of Punto Fijo, in which the political parties agreed to support the development of a democratic regime, for example, excluded the Communists. Pacts are helpful to democratization because they reduce the uncertainty surrounding elections and their aftermath.

Pact A negotiated agreement during democratization that often establishes the institutional arrangements of the new democracy as well as specific policy approaches to be adhered to by the democratic government.

Think and Discuss

Pacts are, in many ways, undemocratic. They involve a small group of individuals deciding both the institutional arrangements of a new democracy and key economic and social policies. Is it good to build a new democracy in such an undemocratic fashion? Why?

When comparativists study bargaining and pact-making during democratization, they often employ many of the decision-making theories discussed in the previous chapter. During negotiations, individuals on each side pursue institutional arrangements that they believe work to their benefit. Thus, rational calculations are likely during bargaining over the new system, though these calculations need not take the form of full-blown rational choice. Bounded rationality options like satisficing are common, especially if the various sides feel pressure to reach decisions in short order. Comparativists also often make use of the elite learning perspective to understand pact-making. In his study of Venezuelan democratization, for example, Daniel Levine contends that opposition leaders learned from their mistakes and were more willing to compromise than they had been in an earlier unsuccessful attempt at democratization. During the bargaining process, elites also learned to work together and to trust each other.[37]

The possibility of irrational decision making should also not be overlooked. Egos and emotions can interject themselves into bargaining during the process of democratization. Negotiators looking at those on the other side of the table see not only future rivals but also past opponents. Even more moderate opposition leaders may have spent time in jail, while reformers in the current government may have felt threatened by past opposition undertakings, such as the organization of unconventional mass political participation.

External Choice Explanations

The final set of causal factors associated with democratization is external choice. The leadership and decisions of elites outside a country can support or deter its democratization. Like their domestic counterparts, external elites who want a country to democratize face choices about whether and how to intervene in the democratization process. The choices can include whether to support sanctions against the nondemocratic government, to provide military support to pro-democracy forces, to engage in more direct intervention through military invasion, or to provide significant economic support once a new democracy is established. The 2011 uprisings in the Middle East required U.S. leaders to make such choices. President Barack Obama decided to provide military support to antigovernment forces in Libya. Facing a similar situation in Syria, he chose not to intervene. Elites making such decisions ordinarily weigh the costs and benefits of their actions carefully, taking the national interest of their own country into account more than that of the democratizing country. As with other choices, however, these leaders are subject to limitations on their ability to reach such decisions in a rational manner, including ego, emotion, and wishful thinking.

One debate about external choice concerns the collapse of Communist states in 1989 as a wave of liberalization and democratization spread across Eastern Europe. Determining who was most responsible for the downfall of the Communist systems remains relevant for a number of reasons, including its implications for the enduring U.S. foreign policy goal of fostering democracies in heretofore undemocratic regions of the world. Those who emphasize the role of external leaders usually point to one of three individuals as most central to European Communism's demise: Soviet leader Mikhail Gorbachev, U.S. President Ronald Reagan, and Pope John Paul II.[38]

Triggering Events

The factors discussed to this point can provide solid explanations of why a nondemocratic government might break down or a new democratic system might be established. They are less effective at predicting when a transition will occur. Even focusing

Triggering Events Incidents, such as the death of an authoritarian leader or a severe economic crisis, that initiate political transitions.

on leaders and their decisions provides, at best, a rough sense of the timing of a regime transition.

As a result, a complete understanding of regime transitions requires a sense not only of underlying causes but also of **triggering events**, the actions that provide the spark that ignites the fuel provided by the underlying causes. Triggering events are occurrences that directly affect the timing of a movement from one stage of the democratization process to another. Without the underlying causal factors, triggering events cannot generate a regime transition. At the same time, democratizations without major triggering events are few and far between.

Of the large number of possible triggering events, three stand out in the study of regime transitions. The first is the death of the leader of the nondemocratic system. An authoritarian system based on the rule of a single charismatic leader often becomes associated with that leader to such an extent that it may not survive the leader's death. A second common type of triggering event is a severe economic crisis, particularly one that emerges suddenly. An economic crisis can be the result of domestic forces alone, including poor government decision making, or it could result from the effects of other countries' economic problems. Protests and government responses to them can also trigger regime transitions. Once a sizable protest develops, nondemocratic governments face difficult choices. If they violently repress the protests, what may already be shaky legitimacy can evaporate. If they allow the protests to continue, they can spread to other parts of the country and give protesters time to better organize and coordinate their activities. Sometimes, orders to crack down on a protest are not followed, or one component of the state security apparatus (e.g., the army) defends the protesters from attacks by another (e.g., the police). Though such events need not result in a democratic political system, they often signal the end of the existing nondemocratic government.

Protests themselves may be triggered by internal or external events. The opener of this chapter, for example, discusses how material released by WikiLeaks may have sparked protests in Tunisia in 2011. Those protests helped trigger others across the Middle East, including the uprising that toppled Egyptian President Hosni Mubarak.

Structural and Choice Explanations of Democratic Breakdown

The various structural and choice-based factors related to democracy's establishment and consolidation can also play a role in its breakdown. According to Juan Linz, unresolved internal structural problems "are rarely the immediate cause of the breakdown" unless they cause the situation to deteriorate quickly.[39] When that happens, all bets are off. An opposition unsupportive of democracy may be able to mobilize large numbers of people, and the military may be unwilling to stand by and watch the social order crumble. More often, internal structural factors slowly eat away at democratic legitimacy, making an eventual crisis more likely.

Social and economic structural features can challenge democratic consolidation in several ways. Economic development followed by a severe economic downturn can frustrate citizens. In a new democracy, they may associate the economic failures with the democratic system. A political culture inconsistent with democracy may not prevent a democracy from being established, but it certainly can play a role in its termination. Lacking mass values supportive of democracy, elites favoring its abandonment may expect the population to be passive, or even supportive of actions to overthrow the democratic system. In such a case, democratic leaders may see little reason to protect the democratic system. In terms of identity divisions, democracy can be fragile when ethnic, religious, or linguistic identity divisions run deep. Consistent with cleavage structure theory (see Chapter 4), when complementary social divisions exist, a regionally concentrated minority may favor its region's secession from the state rather than working through that state's existing democratic system.

Domestic political structures also matter. Comparativists point to the relative merits of presidential versus parliamentary systems for democratic stability (e.g., the Linz-Horowitz debate discussed in Chapter 6). Democratization scholars also emphasize the importance of the military's acceptance or rejection of civilian rule and of the extent to which the judiciary is free from corruption and dominance by the executive branch. Finally, scholars argue that electoral rules make democracies less likely to break down when they foster party cooperation and prevent party systems that are both polarized and contain a large number of parties.[40]

Just as individuals and their decisions are important to the breakdown of a non-democracy, they are also central to the survival or demise of a democracy. Following Francisco Franco's death in 1975, for example, King Juan Carlos became head of the Spanish government. He oversaw a transition to democracy, eventually surrendering rule and appointing Adolfo Suárez as prime minister. In 1981, a group of military leaders staged a coup against the democratic government and sought to reinstall Juan Carlos as head of the government. The king chose to oppose the coup, publicly ordered the rest of the military not to support the coup leaders, and was crucial in saving the fledgling Spanish democracy.

Combining Structural and Choice Arguments

Getting a handle on democratization requires openness to combining structural and choice-based arguments. There are numerous possible combinations, such as the way economic development shapes political culture, which then affects elites' calculations about possible political reform. One case of democratization provides an especially useful example. An earlier section of the chapter highlighted Daniel Levine's contention that pact-making in Venezuela's second effort at democratization is a classic example of elite learning. Terry Lynn Karl's study of the same case emphasizes how changing structural conditions aided that pact-making.[41] While accepting the importance of elite bargaining and compromise, Karl argues that a significant increase in oil revenue prior to the democratic transition was the key to its success. The discovery of oil increased government revenues. Rather than having to fight over how to divide up the same "pie," the interested parties had a bigger pie. This structural change made pact-making easier, though it still took the actions of elites to secure the Venezuelan democracy.

TOPIC IN COUNTRIES

The Topic in Countries cases have a range of experiences with democracy. Some, such as the United Kingdom (UK), Germany, and India, are considered consolidated democracies. Others—specifically, Brazil and Mexico—are on the verge of the consolidated label but are held back by lingering problems. Countries like Russia and Nigeria have had periods of democracy, but comparativists increasingly view them as far from consolidated (Nigeria) or semi-democratic at best (Russia). Meanwhile, China and Iran have little to no experience with full-fledged democracy. As a result, the TIC cases provide an interesting set of countries in which to examine the impact of various internal and external structures and choices on regime type and regime transition. In the following cases, look for

- Differences in the TIC cases' experiences with democracy.
- The role of social and economic structures in fostering or weakening democracy.
- The impact of key individuals and their decisions.

The United Kingdom

The drawn-out nature of British democratization stands in stark contrast to events in many of the other TIC countries. The British political system evolved over centuries, moving away from a strong monarchy and toward expanded political rights and voting privileges for an increasing portion of the population. As political scientist Vernon Bagdanor maintains, even the British constitution is the result "not of deliberate design but of a long process of evolution."[42]

While a casual glance at the evolution of the British political system portrays a slow and deliberate march forward, a closer look reveals fits and starts. Scholars point to the Magna Carta (1215) and the Glorious Revolution of 1688 (as a result of which William of Orange oversaw a monarchy further restrained by Parliament) as important events in limiting the power of the British monarchy. Nevertheless, Britain remained dominated by the Crown, the aristocracy, and the Anglican Church at the end of the eighteenth century. Serious movement toward democracy began only in the 1800s. These reforms included important acts of Parliament in 1832, 1867, 1884, 1918, and 1928 that collectively expanded the franchise from less than 10 percent of the population to universal adult suffrage. As political scientists John Freeman and Duncan Snidal put it, while Finland moved to universal suffrage essentially in one step, reaching that point took the British "five separate reforms and a century."[43]

The development of the British political system coincided with other slow and evolutionary processes, including economic development, an increasingly pro-democratic political culture, and the emergence of an overarching British national identity. The Industrial Revolution brought capitalist development to the British Isles earlier than anywhere else in the world. The result was a large middle and working class and a comparatively prosperous population. In addition, economic development had important spillover effects on urbanization and education. In the arena of political culture, British society was slow to embrace mass participation. Working-class deference meant that ordinary citizens did little beyond voting, and the makeup of the electorate was still limited for much of the nineteenth century and into the twentieth century. During that same period, however, the UK did develop a significant civil society. With a general acceptance of an overarching national identity, and complementary cleavages less prominent than in the other TIC countries, the UK's identity structure became conducive to democracy. Finally, though one might question how well the UK's Westminster political system would work in other countries, it has been effective, stable, and a source of pride for the British.

Leadership and decisions also mattered. Ruling elites worked with opposition forces during the nineteenth and early twentieth centuries to exchange an expansion of political rights for commitment to the system and social stability. While the UK cannot point to a single pact like Venezuela's Pact of Punto Fijo, its history demonstrates how bargaining, cooperation, and concessions can facilitate a peaceful transition toward consolidated democracy, even if such cooperation emerges haphazardly rather than as part of a conscious plan for long-term democratization.[44] As in other European countries, rulers extended political rights when socioeconomic changes and legitimacy crises pushed them to reach out to those who had previously been excluded.

It is hard to believe that the UK's evolutionary democratization can serve as a model today. The general populations of most nondemocratic countries are unlikely to tolerate a century-long process of regime transition. Yet, it is equally unlikely that British democracy could be threatened, even by significant economic or social crises. The system is well ingrained, with the public used to participating in elections and the military accepting of civilian rule. This stability and legitimacy notwithstanding, the Labour Party felt the need to revamp key aspects of the system through constitutional reform in the late 1990s and early 2000s. Such efforts demonstrate that even leaders of a long-consolidated democracy may look for ways to improve the system's policy performance and representation of public opinion.

Germany

Germany has undergone a number of regime transitions since its establishment as a nation-state in 1871. The short-lived democracy of the Weimar Republic after World War I was superseded by the Nazi regime, one of the most brutal dictatorships in human history. Following World War II, a divided Germany experienced democracy and Communist totalitarianism. Democracy proved to be the stronger regime, taking firm root in the Federal Republic in the years after 1949 and extending to the east in 1990. Since then, it has withstood economic and political challenges. Both structural and choice explanations can help make sense of Germany's turbulent path of multiple regime changes.

Explaining the failure of the Weimar Republic (1919–33) has occupied many scholars of comparative politics. In seeking to understand democratic breakdown, political scientists have asked how a modern country—a leading industrial power with a middle class and one of the most progressive political systems of the time—could have slid so quickly and thoroughly into brutal dictatorship, and how it could have done so by legal means and with substantial popular support.

The character of Germany's class structure played an important role in Weimar's collapse. Under the "marriage of iron and rye," the industrial bourgeoisie in the west and the Prussian landed aristocracy in the east modernized Germany following its establishment as a nation-state in 1871. Rapid industrialization created a large working class and a substantial middle class, but the state outlawed the working class–based Socialist Party and the middle class "exchang[ed] the right to rule for the right to make money" and let the antidemocratic industrial and agrarian elites run the country.[45] Conservative elites survived into the Weimar period and supported the Nazi Party's rise. At the same time, many on the political left rejected democracy and supported the Communist Party, which had attempted to overthrow the nascent Weimar Republic's democratic system in 1919 and subsequently refused to cooperate with the more moderate Social Democratic Party. Class polarization grew more noticeable at the ballot box. In the regime's last years, antisystem parties of the Left and the Right—particularly the Nazi and Communist Parties—received the majority of votes, leaving democratic parties occupying a shrinking middle space.

In addition, although the Weimar political system was democratic, a democracy-supportive political culture was not broadly shared. Authoritarian values were deepened by Germany's defeat in World War I and the humiliating and punitive terms of the Versailles Treaty. Germans then had to endure two periods of severe economic hardship in less than a decade: the hyperinflation of 1923 that wiped out the savings of the middle classes, followed by the Great Depression of 1929 that ushered in mass unemployment and destroyed numerous businesses and farms. These events soured many Germans on democracy. In short, German society and politics during Weimar were highly polarized, and antidemocratic forces on the right and left became stronger as economic misery deepened during the Depression.

The Weimar Republic's political structures also contained flaws that paved the way for antidemocratic elements to take power. The constitution's provision for a dual executive granted the president too much power and the parliament too little. The electoral system fostered fragmentation among numerous splinter parties that made for unstable governing partners.[46]

Finally, triggering events combined with the deeper structural features of German society to tip the regime into dictatorship. These events included the intentionally set fire at the Reichstag (the Weimar system's parliament building) in 1933.[47] Adolf Hitler, then-chancellor of Germany, used the fire as an excuse to request sweeping emergency powers, which President Paul von Hindenburg authorized. The Third Reich was born.

Germany's second attempt at democracy arose from occupation by Britain, France, and the United States after Germany's defeat in World War II. The occupying nations invited Germany's democratic elites to draw up the Constitution of the Federal Republic. Rather than simply an external imposition, the construction of democracy was the result of conscious choices by German political elites to overcome the social divisions and mistakes that had destroyed the Weimar Republic. Konrad Adenauer, Germany's first postwar chancellor (and one of the longest serving), built the Christian Democratic Union (CDU) into a quintessential catchall party that successfully bridged regional, religious, and class divisions. Adenauer also worked with union leaders and employers to forge a "Social Partnership" system involving corporatist negotiations among them and legally sanctioned employee participation in the management of firms.[48] Moreover, the CDU's creation of the social market economy (see Chapter 2), which guaranteed private property alongside a generous welfare state, reconciled German conservatives and Social Democrats to democracy and capitalism.[49]

The German elites fashioned the political system in ways that structured conflict within democratic channels and encouraged bargaining and compromise. The proportional representation of the German electoral system produces coalition governments that require governing parties to negotiate solutions. Federalism requires the chancellor to bargain with the *Länder* to ensure passage of the government's legislative program. In addition, the

The fire at the Reichstag in Berlin that aided the Nazi Party's ascent to power in Germany. © Fox Photos/Getty Images

5 percent electoral threshold rule (discussed in Chapter 9) has prevented extreme splinter parties from gaining parliamentary representation. These political institutional designs have made governments in the Federal Republic more durable than those of the Weimar Republic.

Important structural elements have also strengthened democracy in the post–World War II era. West Germany's economic miracle of the 1950s and 1960s helped legitimize democracy. A democratic political culture took root, particularly after the passing of the Nazi-era generation. Finally, the partition of Germany after 1945 eliminated the conservative landed aristocracy's deleterious influence on politics. The landed elite found themselves in East Germany, where the Communist regime wasted no time in confiscating their land and stripping them of political power.

Today, Germany is a consolidated democracy, and its political system has been able to contain difficult challenges. Far-right parties have won seats in some *Land* parliaments in areas with high unemployment, but they have not cleared the threshold to win representation at the national level. The privatization of East German state enterprises, the settlement of thorny questions of property claims in the east, and the opening up of secret police (*Stasi*) files on citizens have all advanced under the rule of law. The fact that current Chancellor Angela Merkel is from the east provides further evidence of democracy's consolidation.

India

India is a regional military power and a potential economic powerhouse. With its booming population, it is on pace to overtake China as the world's most populous country over the next couple of decades. It is also a democracy, its most surprising feature. Other than a very brief period of authoritarian rule in the mid-1970s, India has been governed by a democratic system since its independence from the British. Given the theoretical importance of economic development for successful democracy, India's consolidated democracy has posed an interesting puzzle for comparativists.

The British ruled colonial India with a combination of coercion and compromise. While it is tempting to give the British credit for the compromise, the enormous size of the territory, sheer size of the population, and complexity of the society gave the British little choice. To rely on coercion alone would have required a continuous, massive, and costly display of force. The British do deserve credit for their support of certain democratic procedures during colonial rule. They allowed localities and some regions degrees of self-rule as early as the late 1800s, and the process accelerated in the first half of the twentieth century.

The acceleration of self-rule coincided with the emergence of the Congress Party (also referred to as the Indian National Congress, or INC) as a national political force. As highlighted in Chapter 9, the INC became a mass political party, reaching into all corners of India. While many attribute its success to Mohandas Gandhi, he was president of the party for only one year during 1924 and 1925; Jawaharlal Nehru was its president six times starting in 1929. Yet, Gandhi's impact on the party was substantial. His personal views and rational calculations about what was best for the INC and its goal of independence led the party to stress nonviolent resistance. This made it even more difficult for the British to justify coercive control.

Inspired by Gandhi and reinforced by Nehru, the party's openness to a diverse collection of leaders and supporters from across India's territory and social divides also fostered political cooperation and tolerance for identity and policy differences. The diversity of the party played a role in creating an overarching and largely civic Indian national identity, which helped India to achieve independence and institute a functioning postindependence democracy.[50] Independence came in 1947, the same year that a partition of India removed a significant portion of Muslim-majority territory, the western portion of which is now Pakistan and the eastern portion of which is now Bangladesh. Jawaharlal Nehru became India's first prime minister in 1947 (and held that position until his death in 1964). Continuing the Gandhi-inspired vision of broad and diverse membership, the party remained popular, indeed dominant, in Indian politics for the next several decades.

The first of the greatest challenges to India's democracy came in the mid-1970s. In 1975, widespread protests and strikes demanding Prime Minister Indira Gandhi's resignation followed an Allahabad High Court finding that she had misused government machinery in her election campaign in 1971. Although the court acquitted her of more serious charges, it ruled that as a result of her conviction the election was null and void, she had to vacate the seat, and she was banned from running for office for six years. In response, Prime Minister Gandhi asked President Fakhruddin Ali Ahmed to declare a state of emergency and suspend the democratic system. The official justification was that a threat to national security had arisen. Following nearly two years of authoritarian rule, Indira Gandhi held elections in 1977 that she thought the INC would win. Instead, the Janata Party won. Indira Gandhi surrendered power to her political opponents, and Indian democracy was reestablished.

More recently, a form of nationalism posed a second challenge to India's democracy. The Bharatiya Janata Party (BJP), in a coalition with a number of smaller parties, gained control of the government in 1998 and again in 1999 through appeals to Hindu nationalism, criticism of policies designed to protect and give preference to minority groups, and promises of a tough stance against Pakistan. The BJP's approach concerned Indian supporters of secularism, as well as outside observers, because it challenged India's past commitment to civic nationalism and an inclusive, overarching national identity. However, again showing the extent to which India's democracy is consolidated, when the BJP lost the 2004 elections, it peacefully turned over control to a coalition headed by the INC.

The presence of a ruling elite committed to democratic norms is an important factor in the establishment and initial stability of India's democracy, and many casual observers of the country and its history emphasize it. Focusing on the role of individual Indian leaders alone, however, is overly simplistic. Structural conditions in India are more complicated than they first appear, and choices and structures interacted in important ways in the years before and after independence. India's middle class, for example, is smaller in percentage of the population than the middle classes of many other consolidated democracies. But in a country of more than a billion people, a small percentage can equal a large absolute number. The effect of an emergent middle class may be as much about absolute numbers as about percentages.[51]

In addition, India is a deeply divided society, but cross-cutting divisions are as prevalent as complementary ones. Hindus are the vast majority (80 percent). But Hindus are linguistically and economically diverse, and the religion has many manifestations across the country. The caste system in India—officially outlawed, though still important—adds another dimension to social divisions, again cutting across linguistic lines and dividing Hindus from one another. Even ethnic divisions in the country are more localized than national, helping contain conflicts when they flare up.[52]

Finally, the partition is a valuable example of the intersection of choices and structures. According to political scientist Ashutosh Varshney, the choice to partition India and create Pakistan allowed India's British-style majoritarian system to work.[53] Although supporters may not have intended this outcome, the partition weakened the Hindu-Muslim divide enough to allow the cross-cutting divisions to have an effect. Without it, divisions between Hindus and Muslims might have been too deep for the democratic system to survive.

Mexico

Over its history, Mexico has had limited experience with democracy. In the nearly 690 years since the founding of the Aztec capital of Tenochtitlán, the three periods of democratic rule total fewer than three decades. Mexico's recent transition is a case of economic development and related changes altering the socioeconomic structure, setting the stage for government leaders to choose liberalization and the eventual establishment of democracy. In addition, a large part of the story of Mexico's democratization involves the role of external factors—both demonstration effects from democratizations across Latin America and pressure from the United States.

Mexico's liberalization and ultimate democratization mirrored underlying economic and social developments. At the time of the 1910 revolution, the Mexican population was largely rural and illiterate. By the 1980s, the population was more urban and educated, capable of and desiring a greater say in the country's political affairs. Mexico's citizens were less accepting of the dominance of the Institutional Revolutionary Party (PRI) than they had been in the past, particularly when the economy failed to keep up with their rising expectations in the 1980s. When the PRI's supremacy finally came to an end in 2000, Mexico had a more industrial, globalized economy and a more visible civil society than ever before.

Government and opposition officials' decisions and leadership were also crucial. Individuals such as Presidents Carlos Salinas and Ernesto Zedillo chose the liberalization path. Zedillo's presidency marked the final victory of the technocrat wing of the PRI—leaders of the party committed to economic reform and increased connections with the United States and willing to engage in political liberalization to achieve those goals. His presidency also brought some semblance of stability to Mexico after the chaotic 1994 campaign that saw the PRI's original candidate, Luis Donaldo Colosio, assassinated.

As Mexico liberalized in the 1980s and 1990s, elections became more important. The public joined opposition elites in believing that elections should be free and fair. Controversy and protests over the 1988 presidential elections were important triggering events. They pushed the government to back up its commitment to liberalization by establishing an independent body to oversee elections and by allowing non-PRI candidates to win a larger number of local, regional, and national races. This set the stage for 2000, the year of the Mexican democracy's "founding elections," in which liberalization gave way to established democracy.

Mexico was a latecomer to Latin American democratization, and it took a different path. Rather than the rapid democratization, democratic collapse, and renewed democratization efforts of other Latin American countries, Mexico's transition was more cautious and deliberate. Mexico reveals how committed reformers in the government, who are willing to allow the potential of underlying economic development to transform into the reality of democratic change, can play decisive roles in a successful, and relatively nonviolent, transition. Additionally, the Mexican case highlights the importance of the existing nondemocratic political structure. Unlike other Latin American countries with military authoritarian systems, Mexico under the PRI was a party authoritarian system. As such, it already had elections and other basic institutional practices that democracy requires. This does not take away from the importance of individual decisions, but liberalizing a system is easier when it is a matter of refining institutional features rather than tearing them apart and rebuilding them from scratch.

Mexico also demonstrates the importance of removing as much corruption from the electoral process as possible. A series of reforms from 1986 to 1996 resulted in nearly three hundred legal stipulations governing elections. The reforms included the creation of Mexico's Federal Election Institute (IFE), an independent body that oversees elections from the training of poll workers to the counting of votes, and the creation of rules allowing political parties to engage in careful surveillance of the casting and counting of votes.[54]

Mexico's elections have improved so much that in 2001 the head of the IFE was invited to write an article for the *Journal of Democracy* on the lessons Mexico could provide the United States regarding the disputed 2000 American presidential election![55] Though its democracy is not yet consolidated, Mexico's democratization process has been impressive. Its electoral process is, by most standards, free and fair. Accordingly, the country was able to weather the very close 2006 presidential elections and the protests that followed; passing this test makes the consolidation of Mexico's democracy appear increasingly likely.

Brazil

Brazil's democratic transition was largely managed from above by authoritarian elites, a form of democratization that comparativist Terry Lynn Karl calls "imposition."[56] Only at the very end did the military government find itself giving up more power than it had intended. Nevertheless, Brazilian democracy has since survived impeachment of a president, years of economic crisis and high inflation, and high levels of poverty and inequality. Just over ten years after the ratification of its newly designed democratic constitution in 1988, it also passed what Samuel Huntington considers a telling test for a democracy: two alternations of the ruling elites in power. Only the relatively high levels of corruption and the unstable party system keep some scholars from labeling Brazil a consolidated democracy.

The seeds of Brazil's 1985 democratic transition were present from the moment of the military coup in 1964. Faced with a somewhat erratic president, some military officers thought the army's interests would be better served by staying out of politics and protecting the military's institutional autonomy, while others felt that national security required removing him. The hardliners won this battle, but when no civilian replacement for President João Goulart who was acceptable to all sides could be found, the military took over directly. To appease the soft-liners in the military, Brazil's military junta never entirely scrapped the façade of democratic elections, though it strictly regulated who could participate in them and which offices were subject to election.

By 1974, six consecutive years of record growth, averaging 8.5 percent per year, had strengthened the position of reformers in the military. The military was popular because the country was doing so well. There would be little risk in opening up the political system in preparation for an eventual transition back to civilian control. In 1974, President Ernesto Geisel began a process of *distensão* (liberalization). By the late 1970s, however, the position of the military had deteriorated. The oil shocks and world recession of the 1970s had slowed Brazilian economic growth. Workers whose incomes had risen during the golden years of 1968 to 1974 now watched their wages erode under growing inflation.

Brazilian civil society began to mobilize. In 1977, the Movement against the High Cost of Living coordinated efforts by neighborhood associations and church-related grassroots organizations to petition the federal government to freeze the prices of basic foodstuffs and transportation. Simultaneously, metalworkers, led by future president Luiz Inácio "Lula" da Silva, pushed for a 34 percent wage increase after the military government admitted misrepresenting the inflation rates on which salary adjustments were based. In 1978, the metalworkers went on strike and won a 24.5 percent raise, sparking a wave of strikes in other sectors during 1978 and 1979. The Catholic Church openly supported the strikes. Increasingly, moderates in the official parties, intellectuals, and business sided with this broad multiclass coalition and demanded political liberalization.

Moderates in the military responded to the growing pressure by implementing further liberalization, known in Brazil as the *abertura*, which they hoped they could control. At the end of 1979, the military abolished the two official parties and permitted the registration of multiple parties in order to divide the opposition. Most of the opposition refused to take the bait, and the opposition parties together received a majority of the seats in the Chamber of Deputies in the 1982 legislative and municipal elections. Hard-line military factions fought further liberalization, launching fierce attacks on perceived "Leftist enemies."

At this juncture, the Latin American debt crisis hit, creating a severe recession across the entire region. In lieu of economic progress, further democratization was virtually the only thing the military could offer. Members of the congress, who selected the president, refused for the first time to endorse the military's nominee. Instead, they chose a respected moderate named Tancredo Neves. Although Neves died before he could be inaugurated, his successor, Jose Sarney, called for a constitutional assembly, which wrote the 1988 constitution that completed the transition to an established democracy.

Although the Brazilian economy grew during the military regime, economic growth did not trickle down to the poor. Inequality increased beyond its historically high levels. Political culture was not dramatically different in the late 1970s than it had been in the 1960s. The United States had supported the military coup of 1964; although the Carter administration (1977–81) criticized human rights abuses by the Brazilian military government, criticism largely ended with the election of Ronald Reagan. Pressure to democratize did result from the fall of the military regime in Brazil's neighbor and trading partner Argentina in 1983, but other military governments, like that of General Pinochet in Chile, remained strong. So why did Brazil democratize in 1985, and, more important, why has it remained democratic?

The factor that triggered the Brazilian transition, more than any other, was the increasing failure of the military government to provide economic stability and growth, and the resulting explosion of opposition from civil society. When hard-liners in the military attempted to roll back liberalization in the early 1980s, one of the reasons they failed was the 1982 debt crisis, which caused many former supporters of the regime, such as business, to change sides and back those who wanted a democratic transition.

Several factors explain the maintenance of Brazilian democracy. First, civilians of many different ideological persuasions had learned from the twenty-one years of military government that they did not like military rule. Although Brazil's military was less repressive than some, it still tortured, imprisoned, and murdered hundreds of Brazilian citizens. Second, the 1988 constitution provided a place within the system for most of the significant societal elites, including influential conservatives who were overrepresented in the Brazilian federal structure codified in the new democratic system. Along with other arguably undemocratic features of Brazilian democracy—some of which have been discussed in previous chapters of this book—the federal arrangements helped appease conservatives. Finally, the world began to be a much less friendly place for military governments, especially after the cold war ended. At the same time that officials from countries such as the United States were pushing for neoliberal economic reforms in the 1990s, they were also encouraging those reforms to take place within a democratic political structure. Such encouragement played a less direct role in Brazil's democratization than in Mexico's. Yet, like Mexico, Brazil serves as a reminder that while external factors can undermine democracy on occasion, they can also sometimes be a key part of the story of its establishment and path to consolidation.

Nigeria

Long considered by many analysts a country with great potential, Nigeria has disappointed its advocates both politically and economically. Endowed with abundant natural resource wealth, oil in particular, the country has failed to use its resources effectively to develop a vibrant economy with a sizable middle class. Its political system, which began independence as a democracy, has spent more years under military rule than under representative government and has seen more successful and unsuccessful military coups than free and fair presidential elections. Thus, Nigeria is a fascinating case for comparativists interested in democratization. In its fourth democratization attempt and its third established democracy in less than half a century,[57] the country provides an abundance of evidence about causal factors related to democratization and democratic breakdown.

Even a quick look at Nigeria's socioeconomic structures helps explain the country's unstable and unsuccessful experiments with democracy. It remains relatively poor, economically unequal, and largely rural, with barely a majority of the population literate and middle-class people few and far between. High population growth rates and a fate closely tied to the world price of oil has made crafting economic policies a challenge, a situation worsened by the country's lingering and significant corruption. Its deep identity divisions pose hurdles to democratic consolidation and help foster a deeply divided political culture in which the different cultural groups often seem to have in common only an acquiescence to corruption.

To make matters worse, elites in the government and military have placed maintenance of the democratic system below other priorities, including social stability, economic performance, and, unfortunately, personal gain. Nigeria's past experiences with democracy provide ample room for elite learning, and some lessons from past failures have generated transformations (e.g., the evolution of the Nigerian federal system) in the institutional arrangements of subsequent democratic systems. The potential for elite learning has been more than canceled out by a history of military involvement in politics and the failure to successfully promote a culture of civilian rule and military noninterference in political disputes. Given this history, military overthrow of the democratic system during a severe crisis—perhaps with significant support from the Nigerian population—would not be surprising.

Still, the country has had three periods of democratic rule. Nigeria's colonizer, the UK, wanted as many of its colonies as possible to begin independence as functioning democracies. The British worked with the Nigerians to conduct elections prior to independence, and they played a significant role in the design of the initial Nigerian democracy with its ethno-federal and Westminster parliamentary features. Even though many Nigerian elites have not demonstrated a commitment to democracy, others have. President Olusegun Obasanjo oversaw a transition to democracy in 1979 and won presidential elections in 1999 and 2003. These elections contained irregularities, but they were relatively free and fair, and Obasanjo's victories were large enough that the irregularities did not ultimately affect the outcome. Obasanjo rejected the use of unconstitutional means to remain in office beyond a second term and worked to save the Fourth Republic when the looming 2007 elections led to renewed political and social instability.

The Nigerian case shows the importance of tackling corruption following the establishment of a democracy. As in many other African states, political office in Nigeria is seen as the gateway to both direct and personal economic wealth. The direct wealth comes from skimming government funds before their distribution. The indirect wealth is a consequence of the ability to target state resources to loyal clients, which deepens an officeholder's political power and opens the doors to bribes and kickbacks. Neither is helpful to democratic stability.

Another Nigerian lesson is the importance of addressing social divisions in the design of a democratic system. With the structural and choice chips stacked against successful democracy, one could argue that it is a miracle that the Second and Fourth Republics survived as long as they did. Their relative success is partially due to the design of the Nigerian federal system, which scuttled the initial ethno-federal approach in favor of the use of internal political boundaries to cross-cut the country's deep social divisions. That these efforts have not been fully successful was demonstrated by the tensions over the 2007 presidential election and, more recently, the anger when Vice President Goodluck Jonathan, a southerner, finished the term of Umaru Yar'Adua, a

northerner, and then ran for reelection in 2011. Identity divisions remain strong, but at least the elections have not reinforced these divisions to the extent that they did in the past.

Russia

The collapse of the Soviet Union resulted in fifteen new countries. Their experience with democracy has varied greatly, from the development of consolidated democracies in the Baltic region to the failure of most of the central Asian states to consider democracy seriously. The largest of the fifteen successor states, Russia, has itself run the gamut of democratic experiences. Boris Yeltsin's use of the military to put down opponents in the parliament in October 1993 was undemocratic, but it created the stability necessary for the establishment of democracy. The new democracy functioned, if not perfectly, in the 1990s. Significant turnover among prime ministers, disputes between Yeltsin and the new parliament, and questionable campaign practices during national elections pointed to areas of weakness. Since 2000, Russia has backtracked from a deepening of its democracy, placing order above freedom and pursuing that order through a strong central government controlled by a formidable executive.

For comparativists interested in democratization, Russia provides two puzzles: why the country established a democratic system, and why the system appears to have fallen apart. One must consider both structural and choice factors in answering these questions. Although some elements of socioeconomic and political structure and certain decisions by political leaders made democracy possible, other socioeconomic and political conditions and decisions by subsequent leaders prevented its consolidation.

One can make a case that structural changes caused the liberalization and democratization in the late Soviet and early post-Soviet periods. Over the previous fifty years, the economy had developed dramatically—cultivating urbanization and increases in education—only to suffer a period of stagnation in which people's expectations for a better life were unmet. Soviet political structures also made liberalization difficult to control. The Soviet Union's ethno-federal arrangement created opportunities for provincial leaders to engage in political reforms beyond those sanctioned at the center.[58]

These structural conditions may have made reform more likely, but Soviet leader Mikhail Gorbachev still had to decide to pursue liberalization. Gorbachev's inability to foresee the destabilizing consequences of his political (*demokratizatsiya*), economic (*perestroika*), mass communication (*glasnost*), and international relations ("new thinking") reforms ultimately undid the Soviet authoritarian system and similar systems across Eastern Europe. Gorbachev expected greater legitimacy for the system and for himself. Instead, the reforms allowed people to see that many others in the country were as unhappy as they were. Soviet authoritarianism's collapse brought an establishment of democracy, rather than another form of non-democracy, largely because of the commitment of such Russian leaders as Boris Yeltsin.

During Yeltsin's tenure as president, there were hints that democracy might be in trouble. Yeltsin allowed media censorship and attacks against political opponents, though in lower levels than appeared after 2000. The system Yeltsin designed, which had few genuine checks on the president, made further concentration of power in the hands of the executive a distinct possibility.[59] He never built a strong political party committed to democracy during the 1990s, instead believing that he, as president, should be above party politics. Parties like the Communists and Liberal Democrats initially filled this void, followed by, even more effectively, Putin's United Russia Party.

Socioeconomic structural factors in Russia also hinted at incomplete democratization. Economic development under the Soviets did not produce a middle class, and the economic ups and downs of the 1990s generally did not either. Many Russians associated the periods of economic decline in the first half of the 1990s and in 1998 with Russia's new democracy. In addition, Russian political culture, historically hostile to democracy, did not change overnight once democracy was established. As Russians watched Putin consolidate power rather than democracy, most liked what they saw.[60] Early in Putin's second term, fewer than 30 percent of Russians felt that democracy was preferable to a strong leader.[61] Even those who supported democracy in the early 1990s, such as younger residents of big cities, began to sour on it in the subsequent decade.

The late Soviet and early post-Soviet periods were times of great division among political leaders, but Russia provides a counterexample to the idea that such situations automatically lead to bargaining and pact-making. Yeltsin's successful attack against his opponents in October 1993 made bargaining unnecessary. Yeltsin does not deserve all the blame for the lack of compromise. His opponents in the 1993 conflict did little to pursue a new system based on negotiation. Because they decisively won in 1993, Yeltsin and his advisers were able to impose their vision during the final design of the new Russian constitution without serious challenge. The Russian political system that emerged was a political structure that made creeping authoritarianism possible. Yeltsin's successor,

Vladimir Putin, used the resulting dual executive system with its substantial presidential powers to place Russia on the path to authoritarianism.

China

Unlike the other TIC cases discussed so far, China has had no significant experience with democracy. Thus, one could argue that it makes little sense to discuss Chinese democratization, especially because the timing of a particular instance of democratization is so difficult to predict in advance. Many comparativists agree, focusing instead on the factors that have, to date, allowed China to maintain its authoritarian system.

China specialist Bruce Gilley, however, contends that comparativists have a professional obligation to use their knowledge of general theories and particular cases to explain why democratization in China is or is not likely.[62] Given the extent to which global changes and transformation of socioeconomic structures in China are consistent with comparative politics explanations of democratization, he adds, the "burden of proof" is on comparativists who believe that China will not democratize.[63]

In addition, recent transitions in Asian countries and other parts of the world provide evidence about the kinds of factors that might influence Chinese democratization. For comparativists, Taiwan's democratization provides particularly strong substantiation. Both governments have aggressively fostered economic development, though the resulting middle class makes up a larger portion of the population in Taiwan than in

An estimated 100,000 students, workers, and other Chinese citizens protest at Tiananmen Square in Beijing on May 4, 1989. After another month of demonstrations, the Chinese government sent in military troops to end the protests on June 4, 1989. AP Photo/Sadayuki Mikami

China. The political cultures of the two countries are similar, with both heavily influenced by Confucianism and their authoritarian pasts. Both face ethnic tensions. In Taiwan, ethnic divisions have largely been between the native population of the island and those who came from the mainland, while in China's case, the divisions are mainly between the Han majority and minority groups on the periphery of the country. Sharp ethnic divisions can make democracy difficult to consolidate, but as the late Soviet period demonstrated, regionally concentrated minorities can also push for liberalization and play a role in the breakdown of the nondemocratic system.

China has so far avoided the demonstration effects from nine major Asian states—Bangladesh, Indonesia, Mongolia, Nepal, Pakistan, the Philippines, South Korea, Taiwan, and Thailand—that established democracies from the mid-1980s to the late 1990s.[64] Korean political scientist Junhan Lee points out that, other than in Pakistan, the establishment of democracy followed mass protests typically led by university students. Once again, China defied this regional trend. Its most conspicuous protests in Tiananmen Square in 1989 ended not in liberalization and democracy, but in a successful military crackdown.

Another interesting comparative case is Mexico. From the 1960s to the 1990s, Mexico lagged behind regional democratization trends. Unlike other authoritarian systems around it, Mexico's nondemocratic system concentrated political power in the hands of a single political party, using that party to penetrate into society and mobilize the population in support of the government. It also repressed a significant student protest by force and experimented with more legitimate elections at the local level before considering the liberalization of national politics.

While a comparison of Chinese conditions to those that sparked transitions in Taiwan and Mexico uncovers a number of parallels, there are also important dissimilarities. These help explain China's lack of democratization to date and provide lessons for comparativists about the potential for political reform in China and other non-democracies. For example, China appears to lack a significant split in the ruling elite. If anything, by 2007 the CCP leadership was more unified about the blending of economic openness and political authoritarianism than it had been at any point since Deng Xiaoping launched his economic reforms at the end of the 1970s.

Although technocrats like Hu Jintao have gained China's top leadership positions, their impact has been different from their counterparts' emergence in Mexico. Unlike technocrats in Mexico, who accepted political liberalization, the Chinese leaders have leaned on economic growth to provide performance legitimacy in their quest to maintain authoritarian rule. China has managed to avoid the economic downturn that sparked liberalization in Mexico. Consequently, no large gap between economic performance and aggregate popular expectations has occurred, although increasing inequality, including the novelty of noticeable urban poverty, poses a threat to the regime's ability to use economic growth to buy popular support. Perhaps to hedge its bets on economic growth, China's leaders have also appealed to nationalism. But just as history shows that high levels of economic growth cannot be sustained forever, nationalism does not always have a long shelf life.

China also demonstrates how some authoritarian leaders recognize the dangers that economic development poses to their rule and have taken steps to contain its effects. The CCP government has worked to prevent support for democracy from taking deep hold. The crackdown against protesters in Tiananmen Square demonstrated the will of CCP leadership to maintain control through force if necessary, but the CCP has also used more subtle methods. Agreements with software companies Google and Microsoft limited the opportunities of the Chinese population to access English-language news sites or use words such as *freedom* and *democracy* on Internet blogs.[65] During the uprisings in Egypt in 2011, the Chinese government blocked Internet searches about the Egyptian protests. Whether such actions will be enough to maintain China's authoritarian system or at least limit the transformation of its system to one that is semi-democratic are among the key questions about the next decade of Chinese politics.

Iran

The success of moderate reformers such as former president Mohammed Khatami, limited as it was, encouraged many who desire sustained liberalization in Iran. Such views were tempered when hard-liners successfully grabbed the reins of Iranian political power. While moderates can point to past electoral successes and while socioeconomic structural changes over the past three decades have made democratization more likely, it does not appear to be on the immediate horizon. The design of Iran's current nondemocratic political system has allowed leaders opposed to political reform to block liberalization efforts.

Khatami's tenure as president proved that reformers existed and could mobilize significant political support in Iran. What many scholars identify as the first step in democratization, the split in the ruling elite between hard-liners and reformers, was in full view in the late

1990s and early 2000s. Since 2004, the hard-liners have retaken control of the political stage.

It is not hard to imagine a Khatami-like figure emerging in the future. Had he won the election, the runner-up in the 2009 presidential election, Mir Hossein Mousavi, would have likely followed in Khatami's footsteps, or even gone farther down the reform path. Events over the last decade indicate that hard-liners will use their sizable institutional powers to try to prevent such an occurrence. Following the uprisings in Egypt, the Iranian government tried to block an announced rally in support of political reform. Despite threats against the protesters, thousands turned out anyway. Hard-liners in Iran's national legislature, the Majles, called for the arrest and execution of those associated with the protests, including Mousavi and Khatami.

The hard-liners have reason to fear the reformers. Iran's demographic changes since 1979, discussed in earlier chapters, are consistent with liberalization and democratization. The Iranian population is young, increasingly urban, and much better educated than in the past. Within two decades of the Islamic Revolution, the population changed from a rural majority to well over 60 percent urban. With population growth hitting its peak in 1986, large numbers of these urban Iranians are now in their twenties, the age at which unemployment and other economic problems can become intolerable.[66] Adding to their frustration, only around 10 percent of high schoolers are admitted to Iranian universities, even though literacy and education have improved in past decades.[67] These younger Iranians are generally more politically liberal and supportive of reform than older generations. Not surprisingly, they were the bulk of the protesters during the 2009 Green Revolution and had the technological know-how for effective use of new media.

Iran provides a telling example of how a split between reformers and hard-liners does not always result in significant reform. While former president Khatami and others favoring liberalization have had significant public support in the recent past, Iran's institutional arrangements allow hard-liners to trump most pro-reform efforts. The banning of reformist candidates and the resulting conservative transformation of elective Iranian political offices strengthened the hard-liners' control over Iranian politics, at least in the short run.

TIC Wrap-Up

The nine TIC countries have a wide range of experiences with democratization. As a result, they provide comparativists with a variety of lessons about the role of structures and choices in regime transitions. Two of the TIC cases, the UK and Germany, are considered long-consolidated ("mature") democracies. The UK's democracy emerged through slow, evolutionary change. Germany's consolidated democracy still deals with legacies of past totalitarian rule, but its legitimacy has proven ample and resilient. The case of India, also generally considered a consolidated democracy, is particularly compelling. Although its level of economic development defies the past model of successful democracies, its numerically large middle class and cross-cutting identity divisions and the role of pro-democracy leaders during and after the struggle for independence have helped its democracy to consolidate.

Mexico, Brazil, and Nigeria have all existed as democracies since 2000. While Mexico passed an important consolidation test in 2006, when the controversial outcome of a presidential election did not lead the democracy to break down, it remains too early to consider Mexico's democracy consolidated. Of the three, Brazil comes closest to meeting the criteria of a consolidated democracy. Because Brazil seeks to consolidate its democracy amid corruption and with a military that historically has been deeply involved in politics, however, scholars are reluctant to declare Brazilian democracy consolidated. At the other extreme is Nigeria, which has at times appeared to be drifting away from the established democracy category. Launched in 1999 after repeated and unsuccessful previous attempts, Nigeria's most recent democratic undertaking has faced structural conditions inconsistent with a strong likelihood of consolidating its democracy. Significant questions about the legitimacy of the 2007 national elections, for example, made many ask whether the appropriate question was not how Nigeria would consolidate its democracy, but rather if it was still a democracy at all. The much more favorable evaluations of the 2011 elections, however, renewed observers' confidence that democracy was still functioning.

Russia, China, and Iran are the three TIC cases furthest away from being considered established democracies. Even before the end of Vladimir Putin's first presidential term, Russia had begun to turn away from its democratic experiment. Events between then and the end of Dmitry Medvedev's term as president signaled a further drift toward authoritarianism. Neither China nor Iran has any significant experience with democracy, but both countries intrigue comparativists with their potential to move in a more democratic direction in the years ahead.

COUNTRY SUMMARY

TIC Country	Democratization Experiences	Important Causal Factors
United Kingdom	Long, evolutionary process of democratization; reforms in the 1800s expanded the franchise; House of Commons became the center of British government, with the monarch turning into a figurehead head of state; consolidated democracy today	Long process of economic development, but a high level of economic development today; values of noblesse oblige and working-class deference help create stability and allow changes to be gradual; leadership and elite bargaining, including the post–World War II settlement on welfare protections
Germany	A variety of political systems over the last century; democratic experiences include the Weimar democratic system between World War I and World War II, democracy in West Germany after World War II, and the democratic reunified Germany after 1990; consolidated democracy today	Economic development through the "marriage of iron and rye" stifled democracy in the late 1800s; economic collapse doomed the Weimar system; economic boom and elite-driven changes in political culture facilitated West Germany's democracy
India	Democratic system in place at the time of independence survived; brief period of authoritarian rule in the 1970s, followed by reestablishment of democracy; considered a consolidated democracy today	Low levels of economic development in per capita terms, but a sizable middle class today; identity divisions are sharp but localized, with identity lines crosscutting each other at the national level; strong elite commitment to democracy most of the time since independence
Mexico	Liberalization in the late 1900s led the party authoritarian system (under the PRI) to transform into a democratic system; the 2000 elections, when a non-PRI candidate won the presidency, marked the start of the democracy; democracy today is established but not yet consolidated	Economic development under the PRI created an emerging middle class; pressure from the United States after 1994 played a role in the transition; commitment to liberalization by PRI leaders allowed the transition to be cautious but deliberate; corruption remains a problem but has been less of a factor in elections than many predicted
Brazil	Following two decades of military rule, a new democratic system was established in 1985; system has remained democratic, but many observers continue to label it an established but unconsolidated democracy	Economic turmoil in the late 1970s eroded confidence in the military government; economic development under military rule failed to lessen severe inequality; workers and the Catholic Church led the push for ending military rule; strong powers given to the regions under the new democracy limit the potential for reform but give economically powerful elites a reason to support the democracy
Nigeria	Since independence, alternating periods of democracy and military rule; democracy reestablished in 1999 (the Fourth Republic); considered a fragile democracy today, but fewer concerns about creeping authoritarianism than a few years ago	Minimal economic development, complementary identity divisions, and severe corruption threaten the established democracy and make consolidation unlikely in the near term; with prevalent corruption, political elite's commitment to rule of law is crucial
Russia	Minimal experience with democracy prior to the 1990s; creeping authoritarianism under Vladimir Putin erodes the fragile democratic system established by Boris Yeltsin	Economic hardship during the 1990s coincides with the new post-Soviet democracy; economic successes during Vladimir Putin's first two terms coincides with erosion of democracy; the democratic system designed by Boris Yeltsin places significant powers in the hands of the president, making creeping authoritarianism easier

TIC Country	Democratization Experiences	Important Causal Factors
China	No significant experience with democracy; political liberalization does not accompany the economic liberalization of the last three decades	Growing middle class so far unwilling to push for democratic reforms; elite commitment to maintain authoritarian rule; Tiananmen Square crackdown limits unconventional mass participation, particularly in the capital; potential for democracy due to economic development and accompanying modernization, as well as sporadic uprisings in outlying regions
Iran	Following the overthrow of the shah in the 1979 Islamic Revolution, the theocratic system included limited democratic practices—such as an elected president and legislators—but restricted electoral contestation and had powerful unelected leadership positions	Economic development creates a visible urban middle class; possibility of a pro-reform leader emerging in the future exists, but current institutional arrangements and the failure of the 2009 Green Revolution make a liberalizing leader unlikely in the near term

Spotlight on . . . Country

France	History of alternating between democratic republics and nondemocratic systems; today's Fifth Republic regarded as a consolidated democracy	High levels of economic development and equality; some identity divides, particularly between immigrants and the rest of the population; values from the French Revolution still underlie the political system
Iraq	Moving toward an established democracy after years of U.S.-led occupation and internal instability	Economic problems and sharp identity divisions remain; very high portion of government revenue from oil sector; growing acceptance of the political institutional arrangements despite difficulties creating a government following the 2010 elections
South Africa	Democratization following the end of apartheid; some concerns about the possibility of a one-party dominant system with creeping authoritarianism; today, system is generally considered an established but not yet consolidated democracy	Class and identity divisions; lingering corruption concerns but a strong commitment to rule of law at the elite level; the establishment of a highly democratic constitution; leadership committed to democracy in late apartheid and early postapartheid periods

Research in Context

While the majority of the comparative politics research on regime transition over the last several decades has examined democratization, more recently there has been renewed interest in the topic of democratic breakdown. The success of democratization is part of the reason. As more democracies have appeared, more potential cases of democratic breakdown exist. The weakening of democracy in high-profile countries around the world, including the TIC cases of Russia and Nigeria, has also helped move the topic of democratic breakdown to the front burner.

Studying Democratic Breakdown

One recent study of democratic breakdown comes from Ko Maeda, a comparativist at the University of North Texas. In the October 2010 issue of the *Journal of Politics*,

Ko published an article titled "Two Modes of Democratic Breakdown: A Competing Risks Analysis of Democratic Durability."[68] As the title indicates, one goal of the study was to stress that democracies break down in one of two general ways. Ko labels the first "exogenous termination," which occurs when the government is overthrown by forces outside it, such as a military coup. The source of the breakdown need not come from outside the country, just from outside the sitting government. The other mode of breakdown is "endogenous termination," in which the leader of the democratic government initiates the breakdown. Ko argues that exogenous breakdowns have received more attention from scholars, yet breakdowns led by the government itself, such as the creeping authoritarianism in Russia, account for "40% of democratic terminations between 1950 and 2004."[69]

After establishing this pattern within the population of democratic breakdowns, Ko sets out to explain the variation in modes of democratic breakdown. He analyzes and tests two hypotheses by looking at 104 countries that had periods of democratic rule between 1950 and 2004. The first hypothesis focuses on exogenous breakdowns and contends that they are less likely in countries with high levels of economic development. The second hypothesis, in line with Juan Linz's theory of parliamentary superiority discussed in Chapter 6, proposes that endogenous breakdowns are more likely in countries with presidential democracies.

Ko's analysis provides support for both hypotheses. Although poor economic conditions do not increase the likelihood of creeping authoritarianism, they do make a military coup or other externally led replacement of the government more likely. In addition, the establishment of a presidential system increases the chance that the government itself will move away from democracy, but it does not increase the likelihood of an external overthrow of the democratic government.

So What?

Promoting democracy abroad remains a goal of U.S. foreign policy. Because successful democratization is a multistage process, encouraging it requires not only creating the conditions for the establishment of a new democratic system, but also helping ensure that the democracy lasts. Ko's research provides U.S. government officials with two important policy-relevant lessons. The first is that encouraging democracy in countries with low levels of economic development is less likely to produce consolidated democracies than doing so in countries with higher levels of development. This does not mean that the United States needs to write off lesser developed countries as lost causes, but it does suggest that substantial economic assistance to these countries is warranted to improve the odds that democracy will take hold.

The second lesson from Ko's work is that presidential systems increase the prospects for creeping authoritarianism. American advisers consulting with those who are designing a country's new democratic system should stress the importance of thinking carefully about whether a presidential system should be adopted and, if it is, how it should be designed. The goal should be to minimize the tendencies for gridlock in presidential democracies that, as Ko puts it, "tempt presidents into seeking unconstitutional measures to achieve their goals."[70] Ko himself does not investigate which institutional arrangements would best minimize this kind of temptation. Instead, he indicates that future research on the question of variation in democratic longevity should look within presidential systems to determine whether particular electoral arrangements or a specific set of legislative powers held by the president could weaken the tendency for endogenous termination.

CONCLUSION

No other comparative politics topic highlights the importance of structure and choice as clearly as regime transition. The three stages of democratization—the breakdown of a nondemocratic system, the establishment of a new democracy, and the consolidation of that democracy—result from the complex interplay of underlying structural factors and the decisions of political agents, both domestically and internationally. Economic development and the emergence of a middle class, for example, can both challenge the power monopoly of a nondemocratic government and lead to changes in the general population (e.g., education) that make citizens more accepting of democratic principles.

Certain cultural features can make democracy more or less likely. These include not only values directly tied to democracy, such as a comparative desire for freedom over a strong leader, but also related beliefs such as tolerance for differing opinions, interpersonal trust, and the desirability of social equality over a strongly hierarchal society. For example, an increasing body of comparative politics research points to a strong relationship between beliefs about women's equality and the establishment and consolidation of democracy.

There is also general agreement that deep identity divisions in a country pose challenges to democratic consolidation. The already unstable period of regime transition can be even more chaotic in such cases, particularly when the new democratic institutions have not been designed to encourage groups to reach across identity group boundaries. Finding ways to overcome deep social divisions gives democracy a better chance to survive.

Less consensus exists about whether particular identities make democracy less likely. For example, some contend that Islam is not conducive to democracy, but one should not blindly accept such claims. Even if one believes that elements of Islam contrast with democratic ideals, one can say similar things about elements of Christianity. Many observers questioned Catholicism's compatibility with democracy prior to the "third wave" democratizations in majority-Catholic countries. In addition, Islam is not the only source of identity for Muslims. Individuals can have strong religious identities but still identify themselves in other ways, such as through their national, ethnic, racial, linguistic, regional, or class identities.

Political institutional arrangements also affect democratization. The experiences of Nigeria demonstrate the importance of institutional design. Debates continue about the effects of unitary versus federal systems, presidential systems versus parliamentary ones, and FPTP versus PR electoral arrangements on democratic consolidation. Few debate, however, that the fit between a country's political structure and its socioeconomic structure matters.

The decisions and leadership of certain individuals have a significant impact on democratization. Some comparativists argue that choice factors, being closer to the process of democratization, are more directly related to democratization than structural ones. After focusing on structure from the 1950s to the 1970s, comparative studies of regime change have looked more to the role of leaders and their choices. Individuals and their decisions can drive a country toward democracy, but they can also prevent democratization. As democracy specialist Larry Diamond argues, "The principal obstacle to the expansion of democracy in the world is not the people of the remaining authoritarian states. The problem is the ruling elites who have hijacked the structures of state power and barricaded themselves inside."[71]

Structural and choice-based factors, both internal and external, also intersect. Domestic socioeconomic structures and international conditions shape leaders' abilities to consolidate new democracies, and affect whether nondemocratic ruling elites choose to liberalize or remain "barricaded" in their nondemocratic systems. Structures alone do not fully determine this process. Comparativist Sheri Berman puts it nicely: "Structural developments may be necessary to create an environment favorable to democratization and eventual consolidation, but unless powerful and determined local actors step up to lead the way, even weakened authoritarian regimes may find themselves with an extended lease on life."[72] In turn, the individuals' choices can alter the socioeconomic and political structures and their effects on regime transition. Thus, a full understanding of democratization and democratic breakdown, even in a single country, requires an examination of internal and external structures, choices, and their interaction.

KEY TERMS

Breakdown of non-democracy,
p. 323
Breakdown stage, p. 324
Conditionality, p. 331
Consolidation of democracy,
p. 323
Crisis stage, p. 324
Democratic breakdown, p. 324
Democratization, p. 321
Democratization wave, p. 321
Demonstration effects, p. 331

Establishment of democracy,
p. 323
Hard-liners, p. 332
Incomplete democratization,
p. 321
Intergovernmental
organizations (IGOs), p. 331
Liberalization, p. 321
Moderates, p. 332
Nongovernmental
organizations (NGOs), p. 331

Pact, p. 332
Polar system, p. 328
Pole, p. 328
Radicals, p. 332
Reequilibration, p. 325
Reformers, p. 332
Regime transition, p. 320
Reverse wave, p. 322
Triggering events, p. 334

CHAPTER 12

Comparative Public Policy

CHAPTER OUTLINE

Public Policy
Understanding Policy Outcomes

TOPIC IN COUNTRIES

Features in this chapter:

Spotlight on . . . Iraq: External Influences on Iraq's Judicial Training Program

Research in Context: Reform of the Budget Process in Italy

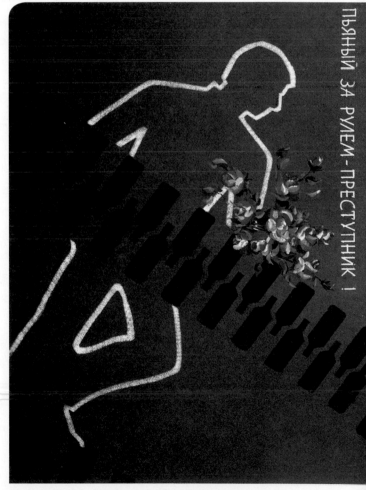

ПЬЯНЫЙ ЗА РУЛЁМ-ПРЕСТУПНИК !

Early in his leadership of the Soviet Union, Mikhail Gorbachev implemented a multi-facted anti-alcohol policy program that included informational posters like the one above. This poster states, in Russian, "A drunk behind the wheel is a criminal!" © Topham/The Image Works

LEARNING OBJECTIVES

After reading this chapter, you should be able to

- Explain the differences between domestic, foreign, and intermestic policy.
- Discuss the differences among first, second, and third order policy changes, and explain why third order changes are relatively rare.
- Explain how socioeconomic structures, political structures, and leadership can affect policy outcomes, and discuss the extent to which policy is made through a process of rational decision making.
- Discuss the major policy debates and key factors affecting policy outcomes in the Topic in Countries cases.

In 1985, Mikhail Gorbachev became general secretary of the Communist Party of the Soviet Union and thus the Soviet leader. Gorbachev initiated a number of significant policy reforms, many of which did not bring the results he had intended. His initial reforms sought to jump-start the economy. Among them was an attempt to reduce Soviet citizens' unparalleled consumption of alcohol. Economic development in the Soviet Union had stalled during the early 1980s, and the use of alcohol was an important reason for the country's economic troubles. Spending on alcohol was estimated to be as much as 20 percent of disposable household income, and drunkenness contributed to up to 90 percent of absences from work.[1]

The anti-alcohol policy, launched in May 1985, increased the drinking age, banned the sale of alcoholic beverages at many locations in the country; prohibited the sale of hard liquor on weekends; and instituted steep price increases on beer, wine, and liquor when and where it could be sold. On the face of it, the policy appeared to work. By October 1985, *Time* magazine was reporting that hard liquor sales had fallen by 15 percent, and wine and champagne sales had decreased by 25 percent.[2]

Like many policy initiatives, the anti-alcohol program had unintended consequences. Stores began running short of sugar and inexpensive cologne. The former disappeared as individuals began making their own alcohol, while the shortage of the latter came about as some alcoholics substituted cologne and other similar solutions for the suddenly more expensive liquor. The Soviet government also began running a significant budget deficit brought about by a sharp decline in government revenue from alcohol sales in state-run liquor stores. In 1988, the Soviet government ended the campaign.

If politics is the struggle for "who gets what," understanding it requires knowledge about how and why governments seek to address social and economic problems. Rarely do such efforts take the form of a single revolutionary change. Instead, they are the result of a large number of small decisions over time. These decisions concern how to address things that government leaders, and often the general public, perceive to be problems in need of solutions, such as alcoholism in the Soviet Union in the 1980s.

Policies are important political outcomes, and their study has become a core component of comparative politics over the last several decades. As a result, **comparative public policy** is a key subfield of comparative politics. Comparative public policy seeks to understand the causes and consequences of policy decisions, including why some governments act to solve certain problems that other governments refuse to address. As one public policy textbook puts it, comparative public policy is the "study of how, why, and to what effect different governments pursue particular courses of action or inaction."[3] Because many of the most important government policies relate in one way or another to the economy, significant overlap exists between the study of public policy and the study of political economy.

Given its focus on policy creation and implementation, comparative public policy looks closely at the inner workings of government institutions. This focus is often given its own label, **public administration**. While public policy scholars seek to understand policies, including the factors that affect variation in policy approaches, the study of public administration centers on the nuts and bolts of the government institutions that produce such policy.

The first of public policy scholars' two main tasks is to understand why particular policies are adopted. As Figure 12.1 indicates, this task centers on causal links between the structural and choice factors that comparativists believe influence policy and patterns in the resulting policies. Similar to other comparative politics topics, the study of policy adoption sometimes takes the form of a detailed analysis of a single case. One might, for example, examine the reform of budgeting in Italy, the topic of this chapter's Research in Context feature. While this type of study is helpful to those interested in that case, it can also generate ideas that scholars may use to examine other cases.

Case studies of policy are common, but they are far from comparativists' only option. Other comparativists look at multiple cases but restrict their analysis to a single policy area, such as education policy or spending on transportation. Those seeking to develop a more generalizable explanation of policy adoption may choose to compare a number of policies in one or more countries, using the comparative method. Still others may choose to engage in the study of a large number of cases, using statistical techniques to test theories about what factors influence variation in policy adoption. These studies often analyze a large number of policies in a variety of countries over a long period of time. Some of the most persuasive comparative politics research on public policy combines one or more of these approaches, uniting qualitative and quantitative analyses.

In addition to studying factors that influence policy adoption, comparative public policy scholars focus on consequences of policy implementation. As Figure 12.1 shows, this second side of public policy examines whether policy approaches and government programs work. How well government policies achieve broad goals such as stability and narrower goals related to a specific program is a key part of what comparativists label governmental or regime performance. When governments

Comparative Public Policy
A subfield of comparative politics that examines the causes and consequences of policy decisions.

Public Administration
A subfield of political science that studies the inner working of government institutions that produce public policy.

| FIGURE 12.1 | **Understanding the Policy Process and Its Consequences** |

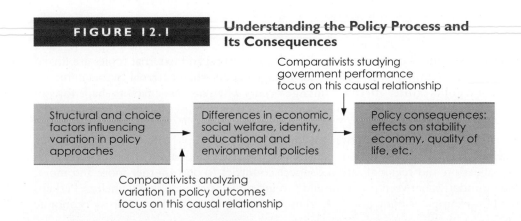

in democratic systems perform badly over time, voters often remove the leader or ruling party at election time. Populations of authoritarian systems do not have that luxury, although ongoing poor performance by an authoritarian government can lead to a popular uprising, which may trigger military action to overthrow the sitting government.

Although this focus on understanding policy effectiveness is a central part of the comparative study of public policy, it is rarely covered in detail in general comparative politics courses. Instead, comparativists highlight the first part of the causal process—the factors that shape important policy outcomes—and consequently this is the focus of the thematic portion of this chapter. This chapter's Topic in Countries (TIC) section also centers on identifying the major policy debates in the TIC cases and the structural and choice factors that influence major policy initiatives in them, while the Spotlight on . . . box addresses the role of external influences on Iraq's judicial training program.

Public Policy

Public Policy An output of a political system designed to alter some aspect of political, economic, or social conditions.

Public policy is a commonly used political science term. Policies are outputs of a decision-making body created with the objective of altering some aspect of behavior. Policies are broader than laws. Laws are specific acts of a government that alter the rules for individual and collective behavior. All laws are part of one or more policies, but not all parts of a particular policy are laws. Policies also include specific government programs and implementation strategies. The *public* modifier indicates that political scientists are generally interested in governmental policies rather than those of other social bodies such as corporations or religious groups.

A policy is a purposive government act, but the term can also refer to a lack of effort to address a problem. Not everything governments fail to do is a policy, but inaction becomes a policy when it occurs over time and in the face of pressure on the government to act.[4] For example, by the start of the twenty-first century, with the American people supporting a federal role in addressing rising health care costs in the United States, the absence of a significant government approach to health care costs had become a policy. The existence of national health insurance or health care programs in other economically developed countries (EDCs) indicated that the lack of such programs in the United States was the result of choices by political leaders not to address to the problem, at least until major health care reform was passed under President Barack Obama.

Foreign, Domestic, and Intermestic Policy

Domestic Policy The set of government approaches designed to improve economic, social, and political conditions within a country.

Foreign Policy The set of approaches to foreign relations, national security, and defense.

Inner-Directed Linkage When external factors influence domestic policy.

Outer-Directed Linkage When domestic factors influence foreign policy.

Political scientists distinguish among three broad categories of policy. The first two, domestic and foreign, likely sound familiar. **Domestic policy** is the set of programs and directives that seek to improve economic, social, and political conditions within a country. **Foreign policy** typically refers to all policies concerning the country's international relations, national security, and defense.

Note that a policy is labeled as foreign or domestic based on its target, not on its causes. Causal factors from outside the country can affect domestic policies, and internal issues may drive foreign policy. Thus, internal and external topics are linked in the study of policy. **Inner-directed linkage** occurs when external factors influence domestic policy; **outer-directed linkage** occurs when domestic factors shape foreign policy.[5] Figure 12.2 captures how internal and external causes intersect with domestic and foreign policy.

Although differences between domestic and foreign policy are clear in principle, placing particular policies in one category or the other is not always easy in practice. As globalization and regionalization connect countries to one another more and more, the boundaries between domestic and foreign policy are increasingly unclear. Perhaps the best example is trade policy. A country's trade policies seek to improve economic

FIGURE 12.2   Types of Policies and Causes

Type of causal factor

	Internal	External
Domestic	Traditional focus of comparative politics	"Inner-directed linkage"
Foreign	"Outer-directed linkage"	Traditional focus of international relations

Type of policy

conditions within that country, but they also affect international relations between that country and others. Immigration policy also has both domestic and international targets. The difficulty of labeling such policies as either domestic or foreign has led to the creation of a new category, **intermestic policy**.

Major Types of Domestic and Intermestic Policy

Within comparative politics, public policy studies span domestic and intermestic policy arenas. The types of policies comparativists examine include economic strategies, regulatory practices, social welfare programs, education programs, and identity-related policies.

Economic Policies

Of the various types of government policies, a large number—and many of the most important ones—fall under the category of economic policy. These include policies concerning government spending; initiatives to alter government revenue through taxation and other means; efforts to reduce budget deficits caused by more spending than revenue; approaches to the supply of money in the economy, including the setting of interest rates; programs aimed at improving economic development; and practices involving foreign trade.

Fiscal policy refers to the set of government decisions affecting taxing and spending. Government programs cost money, and governments spend money on almost every policy decision they make. In federal systems, it is also possible for a government to command lower levels of government to take certain actions without providing the necessary money to those lower levels of government. Such dictates are known as **unfunded mandates**. These policies require spending, but the spending does not take place at the federal level.

In most countries, the national government budget is a source of ideological and partisan conflict. How much and on what programs money is spent is the heart and soul of the "who gets what" nature of politics. Because most national government budgets are passed annually, the budget process is an opportunity to review and adjust policy priorities. As scholars who emphasize incrementalism point out, however, government programs are rarely eliminated and budgets rarely decrease. In most countries, the national government budget has consistently increased in recent decades. In percentage terms, annual increases are often well above both the rate of inflation and the rate of growth in gross domestic product (GDP). For example, Canada's GDP grew significantly from late 1960s to the early 1990s. Yet, spending by Canada's federal and provincial governments as a percentage of GDP doubled over the same period.[6]

The other side of fiscal policy is the collection of revenues through taxation and other sources of income. In most countries, taxes fall into a handful of categories: personal income taxes, corporate income taxes, value added taxes, sales taxes, excise

Intermestic Policy The set of government policies that share the traits of both domestic and foreign policy. Examples include trade and immigration policies.

Fiscal Policy Government decisions affecting taxing and spending.

Unfunded Mandates Commands from higher levels of government to lower levels of government to take certain actions without the money necessary to cover expenses.

Flat Tax A form of income tax in which individuals pay the same percentage of income in tax regardless of their level of income.

Progressive Tax A form of income tax in which the percentage of income paid in taxes increases as one's level of income increases.

Tax Deduction A reduction in the amount of an individual's income subject to tax.

Tax Credit A reduction in the tax an individual owes on income subject to tax.

Budget Surplus The amount that remains when a government takes in more revenue than it spends in a fiscal year.

Budget Deficit The shortfall when a government spends more than it takes in during a given a fiscal year.

Government Debt The sum of annual budget deficits over time; also known as the public debt.

Monetary Policy Government controls over the supply of money circulating in the economy and the interest rates charged when lending that money.

Central Bank A governmental entity that controls the supply of a country's money and affects interest rates in the country through changes to the rate it charges private banks.

Federal Reserve System The central bank of the United States.

Federal Reserve Board The body that sets U.S. monetary policy; also known as the "Fed."

taxes (tariffs), and property taxes. Americans are most familiar with personal income taxes, sales taxes, and property taxes, which generate much of the revenue for the various levels of government in the United States. Sales taxes add a certain percentage to the cost of a product, which a seller must turn over to the government. Property taxes are based on a percentage of the value of personal property—often restricted to the value of one's home and land.

Income taxes extract a portion of money based on an individual's income. In a few countries, the tax rate (the percentage of income paid as tax) is constant across all levels of income. This is known as a **flat tax**. Most countries, including the United States, use some form of **progressive tax**, where the tax rate increases as one's income increases. The top tax rates can be very high, although individuals in the top tax bracket usually still take home a lot of money. Sweden used to have a top tax rate of nearly 90 percent. Over the last few decades, top tax rates have fallen in most advanced industrial countries. Sweden's top tax rate dropped to a little more than 50 percent in the early 1990s before again creeping upward. At the start of 2007, it was nearing 60 percent.

People also pay different amounts of tax based on the number and type of deductions and credits for which they qualify. A **tax deduction** is a reduction, based on some criterion, in the portion of taxable income. For example, if a married couple with three children lives in a country with a $5,000 deduction per child on national income taxes, the deduction for these children would reduce their taxable income by $15,000. A **tax credit** is a reduction in the amount of tax paid, rather than in the amount of taxable income. If the same couple with three children lived in a country with a child tax credit of $1,000 per child, this credit would reduce their tax bill by $3,000. The array of credits and deductions used around the world is immense, partly because they are a way to reward political allies or politically important groups.

Corporate taxes secure a portion of a particular business's revenues. Like personal income taxes, there may be a large number of deductions that reduce the amount of taxable revenue or of credits that reduce the amount of tax owed. Governments employ a vast assortment of deductions designed to protect domestic companies, encourage investment in domestic facilities, and spur job creation. Again, because these deductions can be used to reward political allies or to win political support from powerful economic groups, their number tends to grow over time, and some corporate deductions may be very narrow, benefiting only a single large company.

The final aspect of fiscal policy falls at the intersection of spending and taxing. When a government secures more revenue than it spends in a given year, it runs a **budget surplus** for that year. If it spends more than it takes in—as is often the case—it runs a **budget deficit**. Running deficits over time can lead to a large **government debt** (also known as the public debt). While a deficit is an annual shortfall in revenue compared to spending, the debt is the sum of money owed when governments repeatedly run deficits. Running a deficit forces a government to borrow money, typically by issuing government bonds.

While fiscal policy concerns taxing and spending, **monetary policy** relates to the supply of money circulating in the economy and the interest rates charged when lending that money. In most countries, the government's **central bank** officially controls the money supply and affects interest rates across the country by altering the interest rate on loans it makes to private banks. A central bank's actual independence from the chief executive and legislature varies. In some countries, including the United States and the United Kingdom (UK), decisions regarding money supply and credit conditions are not made by elected officials but rather by a small group of bureaucrats who run the central bank. In the United States, the central bank is known as the **Federal Reserve System**, and the **Federal Reserve Board**, commonly called the "Fed," sets monetary policy. In many other countries, however, top government officials not only have control over fiscal policy but also can put significant pressure on the central bank or even completely control monetary policy decisions.

A country's money supply and prevailing interest rates can have a dramatic impact on its economic performance. Too little money in circulation can make investment difficult and stifle economic growth, while too much money weakens the value of the country's currency and can fuel significant increases in inflation. Effective monetary policy helps achieve the central goals of fiscal policy (maintaining economic growth and reducing unemployment), and it also keeps inflation in check and stabilizes the currency's value.

Much of what government does with its fiscal and monetary policies is meant to foster stable economic growth. Governments also take a large number of additional steps to encourage economic development. These activities are known broadly as **development policy**, but they vary greatly. One type of development policy is the construction of the country's physical and communication infrastructure: its roads, bridges, railway systems, electricity and energy systems, telephone systems, and radio and television broadcasts. Particularly in the early stages of a country's economic development, none of these activities is typically left solely to the private sector. Not only are they too vital to run the risk that they will not be developed, but their almost universal benefit to the population makes them attractive to politicians. As countries develop, some or all of these activities may fall to the private sector, though the government typically keeps a close watch on them through regulation by components of the bureaucracy.

Development policy also involves programs that target particular industrial sectors or businesses. A government may provide a **subsidy**, a tax break, or another incentive to a company that it deems crucial to the country's economy and its future development. Subsidies are payments to a company that allow it to charge less for its product and may encourage it to employ more people. Tax incentives or low-interest loans can enable companies to invest in new technology that they otherwise would not have been able to afford.

In addition to the question of how to target particular companies, broader development questions include how much the government should directly control industries in the name of developing the country's economy. There are two approaches to dramatically altering the presence of the government in economic development. The first is known as **nationalization**, a process in which the government takes over existing private companies and runs them as state-owned enterprises or creates its own companies, often with monopoly status in a major economic sector. Nationalization efforts might target a domestic company, but the target is often a foreign-owned company. The energy sector is a popular venue for nationalization policies, although in the past the practice also included heavy industry in the manufacturing sector. Proponents of nationalization argue that it greatly increases the government's ability to guide economic development not only by controlling a significant source of revenue but also by controlling the production of key goods.

The opposite approach from nationalization is **privatization**. It takes place when government-owned enterprises are sold to the public. Those who support privatization as a development strategy argue that nationalized companies tend to be inefficient and prone to corruption. However, the privatization process is also vulnerable to corrupt practices. As the TIC section on Russia discusses in some detail, the privatization of Russia's economy benefited people with political connections tremendously but did little for ordinary Russian citizens.

Trade is a good example of an intermestic policy. **Trade policy** affects the way products produced outside a country are handled within it, as well as how products produced within the country compete as exports in foreign markets. It is also at the heart of theoretical debates in comparative politics, such as the divergent views of trade contained in dependency theory and modernization theory (see Chapter 2).

Trade policies include the use of tariffs and quotas on imports. A **tariff** is a tax on an imported product. Tariffs serve a dual purpose, providing the government with additional revenue and helping protect domestic businesses by making foreign products more expensive. A **quota** is a more extreme trade policy measure. It sets a limit on the number or value of a certain product that can be imported, either from a particular country or across all imports. As with tariffs, a quota can encourage the

Development Policy The set of programs and activities designed to encourage economic development in a country.

Subsidy A government disbursement to a company that allows the company to sell its products for less, both domestically and abroad.

Nationalization A process in which the government takes over existing private companies or develops its own companies, which are often given monopoly status.

Privatization A process in which government-owned enterprises are sold to the general public or to foreign investors.

Trade Policy Government regulation of the import of products produced outside the country as well as products produced within that country for export.

Tariff A tax on an imported good or service.

Quota A limit on the number or value of a certain product that can be imported.

purchase of a domestic product, but it also tends to increase the cost of that product for consumers. The widespread combination of high tariffs and restrictive quotas can fuel inflation. Thus, politicians considering new trade policy provisions must consider the impact not only on domestic businesses but also on domestic consumers.

Regulatory Policy

Regulatory Policy A set of rules that places restrictions on the activities of individuals or groups.

Regulatory policy places restrictions on the activities of individuals or groups. Although one typically thinks of regulations on businesses, laws defining criminal acts and civil rights rules can also be thought of as regulatory policies.[7] Of those affecting business, some regulatory policies set standards for products, others require certain disclosures, and still others limit certain companies from engaging in practices that give them something close to a monopoly in a particular market.

One of the best examples of regulatory policy is the set of rules governing the physical environment. Environmental policies establish and enforce regulations for individuals and businesses, setting rules against and punishments for polluting the soil, water, and air. Environmental policy is one of the newer areas of public policy. While governments have been involved in matters related to education for centuries, the environment became a widespread concern only after World War II, when states in Europe and North America began to measure "quality of life" with more than economic statistics such as growth, inflation, and unemployment.[8]

This does not mean that approaches to environmental policy are identical across Western countries. Compared with most European countries, environmental regulations in the United States are more detailed, U.S. enforcement of environmental policies is much more confrontational, and the American judicial system is involved in environmental regulation to a much greater extent.[9] If one looks beyond the Western EDCs, variation in environmental policy increases dramatically. As a basic rule, the less developed the country, the less restrictive the environmental regulations.

Social Welfare Policies

One of the most controversial public policy arenas addresses economic hardship, or potential hardship, among a country's general population. These policies include pension and other retirement or disability programs; health programs for the elderly, disabled, and poor; unemployment compensation and job training programs; and antipoverty programs. Social welfare policies differ across countries both in scope (how much the program expects individuals to contribute to their own welfare) and universality (the portion of the population eligible for the program).

Old Age and Retirement Policy Government efforts designed to protect the economic well-being of the elderly.

State Pension Regular payments from the government to individuals after they reach retirement age.

Most governments take some responsibility for caring for the elderly. These efforts are often labeled **old age and retirement policy**. In many cases, this is done through a **state pension**, a payment the government makes, typically monthly, to individuals after they retire. In some countries, workers may also receive pension payments from their employers, as well as income from private retirement funds to which they made payments while employed. Old age and retirement policies vary from country to country according to whether state pension programs are designed to be universal or are targeted at the poorest elderly people and whether individuals are expected to contribute to private funds that supplement the retirement income from the government. The United States, for example, assumes that retired workers will receive some compensation (from employer pension programs or private individual retirement accounts) in addition to their social security payments. Switzerland requires workers to contribute to private retirement funds.

Retirement policies become more difficult to manage as the overall population ages and, in some cases, declines in overall numbers. The combination of longer life expectancy and declining birthrates eventually means a smaller portion of the population in the workforce and a larger portion of the population retired from it. If retirement systems actually collected revenues from individuals and held onto them until those individuals retired, the problem would be less severe. In most countries, however, current funds for retirement programs come from the current workforce. In such cases, an aging population places significant stress on the retirement system, as more and more retirees must be supported by a proportionately smaller number of workers.

Europe is already experiencing this problem, and it will significantly worsen over the next several decades. By 2050, the number of Europeans over age sixty-five will approach 50 percent of the number between twenty and sixty-four, in essence meaning that no more than two workers will be supporting each retired person. In the United States, the problem is on the immediate horizon, as the "baby boomers" are reaching their mid-sixties. The problem is less severe in the United States than in parts of Europe, however, mostly because of the combination of higher birthrates and higher levels of immigration. The contributions of younger immigrant workers are crucial for the longer-term prospects of the American retirement system. China faces its own problem related to its one-child policy. A significant portion of the population—born before the one-child policy was instituted—is over sixty, with a comparatively smaller number of people entering the workforce than in the past.

At earlier times in history, few political leaders considered health care a public policy matter. Today, health care is a public policy issue around the world.[10] **Health care policy** includes the development of national health care systems in which individual medical outlets are run by the central government bureaucracy, or of the government's full or partial coverage of costs of medical care that is largely provided privately. While the United States has neither a nationalized health care system nor universal health insurance coverage, health care still makes up a significant portion of government spending. American federal health care expenses, including Medicare, Medicaid, and medical care for veterans, have risen from $7.5 billion (or less than 1 percent of GDP) in 1967 to well more than one hundred times that level (and approaching 6 percent of GDP) in 2011.[11] Health care policy reforms passed in 2010 are set to increase the U.S. government's role in health care.

Despite the different approaches and levels of spending, certain problems related to health care are shared by all countries. First, the need for health care—and for increasingly expensive care per visit—increases with age. Thus, it is precisely at the time when most individuals are retired and often struggling to make ends meet that health care costs spike. The increased health care needs of the elderly are one of the central justifications for government involvement in the provision and funding of health care. Second, the poor are often in worse health than members of the middle and upper classes, who tend to eat better, exercise more, and see doctors more frequently for preventive care. Finally, doctors tend to be concentrated in large cities. Even in countries without a general shortage of doctors, the rural population may have a difficult time receiving health care services.

Most governments pursue policies to encourage high levels of employment, and most also implement programs designed to protect the unemployed. **Unemployment policy**, which includes programs to provide financial benefits and job training to the unemployed, varies from country to country. In general, such programs are less generous today than they were in the past, particularly in the countries of Western Europe, although many countries continue to provide unemployed workers with a large portion of their original salaries for months while they search for new jobs. Government-funded training provides the unemployed with additional skills, which are sometimes related to their previous jobs and are sometimes in completely different fields of work. Job training programs are not an alternative to unemployment compensation, but they are designed to make it easier for workers to find new jobs and less likely that those workers will be laid off in the near future.

Another major goal of social welfare programs is to redistribute wealth in society to help address poverty. As a result, policies aimed at reducing the portion of the population living in poverty and improving the living conditions of those remaining in poverty are sometimes known as **redistributive policies**. This broad policy category can include progressive tax systems, discussed earlier, since they take money from wealthier individuals for use in government programs that may, but do not always, benefit the poor.

Health Care Policy
Government programs designed to enhance health care coverage, either through a national health care system or full or partial payment of health care costs.

Unemployment Policy
Government programs to assist the unemployed, including economic assistance and job training.

Redistributive Policies
Policies aimed at reducing poverty by making the wealth in a particular society less unequal.

In the United States, antipoverty policies such as aid to families with dependent children (AFDC) came under attack in the 1990s amid concerns about their fairness and effectiveness. Despite the existence of such programs for several decades, a high percentage of single-parent families remained poor. (At the beginning of the 1990s, the figure was over 50 percent.) In addition to not solving single-parent family poverty, critics argued, such programs provided no incentives for single parents to find work and instead made them dependent on government assistance.

Education

Education policy refers the government's management of the education process. Government involvement in education includes running a publicly funded education system, overseeing student performance, and providing partial support for the cost of private schools and institutions of higher learning. Education policy may be incorporated into existing categories, such as economic development policy or social welfare policy. Yet, the issues related to education policy are important enough and evolving to such an extent that education deserves consideration as its own policy category. Education is at the heart of efforts to create greater equality of opportunity.

According to political scientists Arnod Heidenheimer, Hugh Heclo, and Carolyn Teich Adams, education policies vary globally in four basic ways.[12] The first is the extent to which the government maintains something approximating an education monopoly by discouraging private educational institutions. The second is the scale of the educational system's centralization, ranging from systems overseen by a national government to those managed almost entirely by local governments. The third is the way in which educational opportunities are available to the general population. In many European countries, secondary education is specialized and is based on performance in earlier grades or on national exams; in the United States, such distinctions between elite academic institutions and technical schools do not typically appear until postsecondary education. Finally, approaches to higher education differ in expectations of the number of years it should take a student to complete a degree, the types of degrees available, and the extent to which admissions decisions are based solely on applicants' academic abilities.

Identity-Related Policies

Another broad set of policies relate to identity and identity diversity. These policies include citizenship, immigration, integration of minority groups, and other programs designed to address social divisions and cultural diversity. Approaches to identity policies differ around the world as much as any other policy areas.

Chapter 1 introduced the concept of citizenship, a status that designates individuals as a state's "official members" and that is held by a large portion of the population of every internationally recognized state.[13] In addition to being a status, citizenship is a policy. **Citizenship policy** includes the rules for obtaining citizenship automatically at birth and the rules for naturalization—the process through which noncitizens become citizens—as well as the rights and obligations reserved for citizens and whether to allow individuals to be dual citizens. In the case of newly independent states, the government must determine the initial base of citizens to which naturalization will add over time.

Citizenship practices vary significantly around the world. In some countries, it is relatively easy for noncitizens who have been longtime residents to gain citizenship. In other countries, the naturalization rules are exceedingly restrictive. Because citizenship is a form of identity, carries rights and obligations, and presumes a certain degree of loyalty to the state, decisions regarding citizenship policy can be controversial.

Immigration is the process of entering a country with the intention of residing there for a significant period of time. **Immigration policy** is the set of government rules on how individuals can enter a country and how long they are allowed to stay. Immigrants typically seek residence in a new country that they feel offers opportunities for employment, education, and better lives for their families. The new residents may provide a number of benefits to the country to which they

Education Policy Government involvement in education, from running a publicly funded education system to overseeing student performance and providing partial support for the cost of private schools and institutions of higher learning.

Citizenship Policy Rules that establish how to become a citizen, the rights and duties of citizens, and the conditions under which dual citizenship is allowed.

Immigration Policy Government rules governing how individuals can enter a country and how long they are allowed to stay.

immigrate, such as typically working for lower wages than workers who are citizens. Because immigrants pursue employment and sometimes are covered by government-funded social welfare programs, immigration is also a highly controversial policy area around the world. In both the United States and the UK, survey data have indicated that around half of the countries' citizens believe that immigrants "take jobs" and around two-thirds support reducing the number of immigrants.[14]

Countries differ greatly on their rules for official immigration, the extent to which illegal immigrants want to enter, and their responses to illegal immigration. Even within a particular country, different groups may have decidedly different ideas about the proper approach to the topic of immigration. Policy can change significantly depending on which party or coalition controls the government.

Chapter 4 included a discussion of various government options for dealing with significant

SARGENT © 2006 Austin American-Statesman. Reprinted with permission of Universal Uclick. All rights reserved.

racial, ethnic, and cultural divisions. These include efforts to eliminate minority identity groups (genocide, ethnic cleansing, and assimilation); to accept the minority identity (integration); and to cultivate the minority identity (accommodation, ethnofederalism, and recognition of claims for territorial independence). Most countries with sharp identity divisions choose one of the approaches near the middle of the spectrum of policy options—assimilation, integration, and accommodation—though even these middle-ground policies represent very different ideas about the role of government in fostering minority cultures.

Integration policies are perhaps the most interesting policy option because they involve a delicate balancing act. The minority group recognizes that its culture is subordinate to an overarching culture, often largely overlapping with the culture of the majority group. On the other hand, the majority group recognizes that the minority has a right to protect its unique culture. While this seems an appropriate balance in theory, implementing policies consistent with the concept of integration can be difficult in practice.

Degrees of Policy Transformation

In addition to studying different types of policies, many comparativists focus on changes to particular government approaches over time. Both changes in existing policies and the creation of entirely new policies tend to result from vocal demands for change. But the degree of resulting changes can differ significantly. In an article looking at changes to economic policies in the UK, comparativist Peter Hall provides a useful framework for considering policy modifications. Hall distinguishes among first, second, and third order policy changes. A **first order policy change** is one in which the policy's details change, but the "overall goals and instruments of policy remain the same."[15] Examples are small alterations in fiscal and monetary policy, such as changes in marginal tax rates or interest rates.

A **second order policy change** occurs when the goals behind a particular policy remain the same, but the techniques used to achieve these goals change. For example, the switch in environmental policy from punishing companies that exceed pollution limits to allowing companies to sell unused pollution "credits" to each other is a second order change. The goal of reducing pollution remains, but the instrument used to achieve that goal is altered.

First Order Policy Change Policy modification in which the details of the policy change, but the general approach of the policy remains the same.

Second Order Policy Change Policy modification in which a policy's underlying goals are unchanged, but significant changes are implemented in how the goal is pursued.

Third Order Policy Change
Policy modification in which the goals behind a policy are dramatically altered.

A **third order policy change** takes place when the goals behind a policy dramatically shift. Third order changes are rare, generally occurring only when an examination of past experiences indicates that the policy has failed to meet its goals or has created negative consequences that far exceed its intended effects. Welfare reform in the United States in the 1990s was a third order change. A perception that existing approaches had created dependency among welfare recipients led to a change in the goal of the policy, from enhancing the economic standing of single parents in poverty to improving the prospects for such individuals to gain long-term employment.

Understanding Policy Outcomes

Given the range of policy areas studied by comparativists—economic policies, social welfare programs, education programs, and identity-related policies—it may not be surprising to learn that not all policies have the same causes. The same policy may have come about for different reasons in one country than in another, and looking at different policies within the same country can also lead to different causal stories. As discussed in the previous chapter, however, the various possible causal factors can be fairly well organized into four categories: internal structure, external structure, internal choice, and external choice.

As with other aspects of comparative politics, comparativists have typically paid more attention to internal factors than to external ones. Internal choice factors include the role of analysis, calculations, and the ultimate decision about which policy approach to take. Comparativists commonly label internal structural factors the **policy environment**, capturing the fact that the policy-making process occurs within an economic, cultural, identity, and political context. Social and economic structures shape interest group and broader public demands, while political structures privilege some policy approaches and hinder others.

Policy Environment The set of internal structural factors that influence policy outcomes.

Internal Structural Factors

Throughout this book, various types of internal structural features—economic, cultural, identity, and political—have been highlighted. Understanding policy outcomes requires considering these various structural factors.

Economic Structural Factors

A number of underlying economic features can influence policy outcomes. These include the main economic structural conditions, outlined in Chapter 2, which vary from country to country: level of economic development, class structure, degree of economic globalization, and type of economic system.

Comparativists have long argued that economic development affects the amount of money a government spends and the kinds of policies it funds. Development creates a larger pie from which the government is able to extract and redistribute money. In addition, development is associated with other changes—education improvements, urbanization, and, eventually, an aging population—that both give citizens skills to participate in the political process and alter the current situation in ways that can increase anxiety. The emergence of this combination of skills and grievances leads democratic governments to spend money on new programs.[16] As a result, economic development creates conditions that lead governments of countries with different cultural and political backgrounds to take similar policy approaches.[17]

Different class structures can have disparate effects on policy approaches. Leveling the economic playing field is a central goal of many government programs. Since policies are in part a response to demands placed on the political system, the existence of visible poverty in an otherwise wealthy society can cause the poor and the wealthy alike to demand programs targeting such poverty.

How interconnected a country's economy is with other economies can also play a role in shaping that country's public policies, particularly those related to trade, immigration, and welfare state protections. In the 1970s, political scientist David Cameron's landmark study pointed to the important role of economic interdependence in the growth of government spending.[18] Because economic openness makes their economies more vulnerable to external economic shocks and because open trade policies are often opposed by domestic interest groups, governments overseeing economies with high levels of imports and exports develop more elaborate social welfare policies to protect their workers. In addition, globalized economies require changes in policy areas such as education. While much of the focus on education revolves around the idea of making life chances more equal for a country's citizens, globalization also encourages a well-educated, technologically literate population.

Finally, comparativists consider the extent to which the government plays an active role in the economy. As discussed in Chapter 2, scholars focus on three broad types of economic systems: capitalist, socialist, and mixed. Free-market capitalism is based on private ownership and the principle that conditions of economic exchange are set by interactions between suppliers and purchasers. Socialism, also called central planning, is an economic system in which government owns the means of production, employs workers, and makes decisions about production and distribution. A large number of systems in the world fall between free-market capitalism and socialism. These cases are called mixed economies or "varieties of capitalism." Some of them accept general principles of capitalism but allow for conspicuous government intervention and even some government ownership of industry and a large welfare state. Other mixed systems give the state the central role in guiding investment into growing sectors of the economy and encourage protectionist trade policies. In still other mixed systems, the state owns important industries but does little economic planning and does not develop a strong welfare state.

Political Culture and Ideology

Ideas also drive policy outcomes. A society's values and system of meaning shape how much individuals in that society view certain situations as problems and influence the range of alternatives available to policy makers to address them. Social scientist Karl Deutsch argued that people's tendency to look to the past, present, or future plays a major role in differences in broad policy approaches across societies.[19] Ronald Inglehart's postmaterialism theory, discussed in Chapter 3, posits that economic development brings shifts in values away from survival and security and toward quality of life issues like the environment. Western governments began to focus on environmental policy around the same time that the culture shift Inglehart identifies began to emerge. Political culture is, therefore, important to consider when seeking explanations for variation in policies from one type of country to the next, such as differences in environmental policies between Western EDCs and non-Western lesser developed countries (LDCs).

It is also helpful in understanding policy approaches within EDCs. A number of comparative public policy studies have sought to explain why public policies in the United States are less expansive and intrusive than those in Western Europe. In the early 1970s, British political scientist Anthony King proposed that this divergence is largely the result of a different political culture on the two sides of the Atlantic, arguing that government "plays a more limited role in America than elsewhere because Americans, more than other people, want it to a play a limited role."[20] More than thirty years later, scholars who contend that the European social welfare systems have noticeably contracted see them as remaining more encompassing than the American approach, and many of these scholars continue to argue that cultural factors largely shape the difference.[21]

As with other types of political outcomes, there are limitations to using political culture to understand policy outcomes. The degree to which a society's culture is unified can influence that culture's effect on products of the political system. In addition, while cultural differences can explain why two countries take different general approaches to a similar problem, they are less helpful in explaining policy changes, especially dramatic policy changes, within the same country over a short period of time. If political culture is the driving force behind policy selection and political culture is "sticky" (see Chapter 3), policy approaches should be sticky as well.

An existing official ideology also provides policy makers with opportunities and constraints. If the general population accepts this ideology, people will support policies consistent with it, at least initially. Policy alternatives that contradict the ideology are difficult for a government to implement, requiring it to engage in logical gymnastics to justify their adoption.

Identity Structure

Policies regarding identity differ greatly across countries based on policy makers' choices about how best to address identity diversity. These differences are also driven by the extent to which a country has significant ethnic, religious, linguistic, or other cultural minorities. Where minorities exist, the country's identity structure forces the government to consider how best to address the identity diversity. As they make policy decisions designed to address identity diversity, officials must also take into account the extent to which the minorities are self-aware, territorially concentrated, or politically mobilized, or otherwise have the resources to cause problems if they are unhappy.

At the same time, leaders must consider views of the majority of the population. While a minority group may support adopting particular group rights approaches or affirmative action programs, the majority of the population may strongly oppose such policies. The dilemma facing governments of states with deep identity divisions is significant. The deeper the social divisions, the more pressing the need to address the minority group's concerns. Yet, deep identity divisions also mean that the majority is likely to oppose policies it sees as unfairly favoring the minority.

Political Structure

Political structures are the part of the policy environment closest to actual policy decisions. As a result, the political system's design—its regime type and specific institutional arrangements—affects the policies it produces. Political scientist E. E. Schattschneider labels political organization "the mobilization of bias," arguing that "some issues are organized into politics while others are organized out."[22]

Regime type can have great influence over policy approaches to a problem. In some cases, authoritarian systems have a wider range of policy options than do democracies, such as the ability to use coercive force against the population in order to enact a policy that government leaders see as necessary. Democratic leaders, on the other hand, fear voters' ability to remove them from office if their policies produce short-term costs just prior to an election, even if these same policies will ultimately produce long-term benefits. At the same time, electoral mechanisms in democratic systems favor the development of new programs. Candidates make policy promises to secure the support of segments of the population, and successful candidates pursue at least some of these promises after the election.

The form of policies may also vary between countries that share the same general regime type but differ in specific governmental arrangements.[23] As discussed in Chapter 5, the more veto points a political system has, the more difficult it is to adopt substantial policy initiatives, particularly those designed to reallocate economic wealth. The fear that a proposal to greatly alter an existing policy approach will never make it past the numerous veto points means that government officials in such systems are often reluctant to introduce such proposals in the first place.

Within democratic systems, the institutional options discussed in Chapters 5 through 7 affect policy outcomes. Federal systems make certain policy issues the prerogative of lower levels of government. Even in policy areas not reserved for lower levels, federal officials must take into account the potential for regional or local governments to obstruct policy implementation. Presidential systems with checks and balances place a premium on policy compromise. In democracies with strong judicial review provisions, the threat that a policy will be viewed as unconstitutional or in violation of existing statutes constrains policy makers.

Existing approaches to elite-mass linkage also matter. In nearly every country, interest groups are a hugely important part of the story of public policy. Yet, these groups share a common challenge of acquiring members and mobilizing support—the collective action problem discussed in Chapter 8. The environment is a classic collective action problem, in that the costs of improving the environment are targeted while the benefits of ecological improvement are shared collectively across society. The exception is the case of protecting against or cleaning up highly localized environmental damage. Because the benefits of such environmental action are more concentrated, NIMBY ("not in my backyard!") interest groups often deal with environmental matters, and they are typically successful in their endeavors.

While interest groups in different countries have many features in common, how they are brought into the policy process and their ability to shape particular proposals can vary. A corporatist approach to bringing interest groups into the policy process requires compromise up front but generates fewer disputes over the final policy once the major "peak associations" are on board. Systems in which iron triangles are common may produce different policies than systems in which interest groups compete more openly for policy makers' attention. The ability of a group to affect policy can also differ from group to group within the same country based on each group's resources (membership size, financial assets, etc.).

Electoral and party systems matter. Two-party systems produce more moderate policies than multiparty systems, especially if the country's population falls more in the middle of the political spectrum. Having an electoral system that encourages numerous parties—thus necessitating coalition governments—can lead certain policy options to get more attention than they would in a two-party system. Policies regarding agricultural subsidies, for example, can be a central topic for a coalition government that includes a small farmers' party.

External Structural Factors

The discussion of regime change in the previous chapter highlighted three important external factors—demonstration effects, imposition through conquest, and conditionality—that comparativists also emphasize in public policy studies. These three factors influence not only the broad form of the political system but also the specific policies that the system produces. Like other structural factors, they provide political leaders with both opportunities and constraints.

A program adopted in one country can serve as a model for another country. Just as government officials assess the performance of policies in their own country, they evaluate policy results in other countries. Other countries' policies provide them with a menu of policy options complete with evidence about how successful or unsuccessful each may be. Political leaders, seeing the successful implementation of the policy in the first country, may emulate the policy in their own country. Such emulation is a conscious process.[24] Other states' policy approaches and experiences provide leaders with opportunities to learn about the effectiveness of the policies that they would not have had otherwise. As a result, comparativists frequently examine policy trends across countries. Often, these analyses center on a number of states within a distinct global region, such as the EDCs of Western Europe. At other times, the focus is more global, looking at the pervasiveness and rapidity of the spread of general approaches to certain types of policy around the world.

When policy approaches become similar over time globally or regionally, comparativists often label the phenomenon **policy convergence**. Others use the term **policy diffusion**, particularly when tracing the spread of a new policy from an initial country to others. Just as the policy process is complex, involving various stages and practices, convergence can take different forms. It can be indicated by increasingly similar policy goals, instruments, outcomes, and style. In this case, the term *style* applies to broad approaches such as consensual versus conflictual, incremental versus more fully rational, and corporatist versus pluralist.[25] Of interest to comparativists for decades, the topic of policy convergence has become increasingly prominent in recent years because of the growing importance of globalization and regional integration, particularly in Europe, North America, Latin America, and Asia.

Policy Convergence The spread of policies from one country to another over time, with the result that policies become similar globally or in a particular region.

Policy Diffusion Another term for the spread of a policy approach from one country to another over time.

Sometimes, external structures constrain government leaders more than they provide opportunities. The most extreme example occurs when a country is occupied militarily by another country. The occupied country may establish a regime favorable to the occupying power, or the occupying forces may dictate a wide range of policy approaches during the occupation.

External policy constraints need not be so blatant. Leaders of states pursuing membership in an international organization, for example, must meet conditions for membership that include adopting new policies or significantly amending existing ones.

Iraqi Chief Justice Medhat Al-Mahmoud, who made the opening presentation at the launch of the comprehensive legal training program in Erbil, Iraq, January 2011.
REUTERS/Saad Shalash

When their statehood was restored at the end of the Soviet period, for example, Estonia and Latvia needed to decide which people should receive automatic citizenship, which should be required to naturalize, and how difficult naturalization should be. Both countries chose to exclude large portions of their Russian-speaking minority populations from their citizenries. A variety of international organizations put pressure on them to amend these policies, and they made small changes over the next few years. The most dramatic changes took place in the late 1990s and early 2000s, when European Union (EU) membership first became a real possibility. The EU required the two countries to adopt more inclusive citizenship policies and to institute policies to better integrate their Russian-speaking minorities. This pressure was made more effective by the willingness of external intergovernmental organizations (IGOs) and foreign governments to provide funding for Estonian and Latvian integration programs, a theme highlighted in this chapter's "Spotlight on . . ." box on judicial training in Iraq.

Spotlight on...IRAQ

External Influences on Iraq's Judicial Training Program

On March 20, 2003, a United States–led coalition attacked Iraq. Although some analysts predicted a quick victory, many others expected a long-lasting fight on the ground. Both predictions were correct. Within a month, the U.S.-led forces had ousted the Iraqi government of Saddam Hussein, and on May 1, 2003, leaders of the coalition forces declared an end to combat operations. Attention turned to governing postwar Iraq.

The development of a stable postwar Iraqi government has been a long process. While many outside observers have focused on the challenges facing the executive and legislative branches, cultivating an effective Iraqi judicial branch is no less important. In addition to affirming judicial independence, Iraq's constitution lays out a federal judicial branch that includes a Supreme Court (which, like the U.S. Supreme Court, rules on constitutionality and acts as a final court of appeal) and other federal courts. The Iraqi federal judicial branch also has a body called the Higher Judicial Council that oversees the federal courts. At the start of 2011, the Higher Judicial Council, in partnership with the United Nations Development Program (UNDP), launched a new training program for judges in Iraq. The program included more than twenty courses taught at different sites around the country. More than four hundred Iraqi judges and legal officials attended the courses, which were conducted by the Arab Centre for Rule of Law and Integrity, a nongovernmental organization based in Lebanon.[26] Financial support for the training program came from both the EU, and the Spanish government's Iraqi Trust Fund.[27]

What factors drove the development of this judicial training initiative? Internal structure and choice factors were certainly in play. The existence of the Higher Judicial Council within the Iraqi governmental structure provided a useful anchor point for activities concerning judicial practices in Iraq. Iraqi officials were also aware of existing judicial corruption and the need for a commitment to the rule of law.[28] Even when supported from the outside, new domestic programs require at least some buy-in from political leaders inside the country.

Although moving forward with the program required internal choices, external factors were more important than internal ones in many ways. The internal awareness of the challenges facing judicial independence and commitment to the rule of law has been enhanced by the efforts of external actors. The Rule of Law Program of the United States Institute for Peace, for example, helped create the Iraqi Committee on Judicial Independence (ICJI)—a network of government officials, civil society organizations, and representatives of academia and media—and sponsored conferences on the topic in Iraq.[29] In similar fashion, the American Bar Association's Rule of Law Initiative provided advice and assistance to the Iraqi government from 2003 through 2006.[30] In addition to playing a central role in the new judicial training program, the UNDP and the EU worked together on other related initiatives from 2007 through 2011 as part of their Support to the Rule of Law and Justice project.[31] Finally, without the external funding of the judicial training program, it is difficult to imagine that it would have been implemented.

The new Iraqi judicial training program highlights the importance of concepts such as rule of law and judicial independence presented earlier in the book. More important for thinking about influences on major policy outcomes, Iraq's new judicial training program demonstrates the extent to which domestic policies can be largely shaped by external factors. Although Iraqi officials ultimately needed to agree that the new program was necessary, its development and implementation were largely the result of planning and funding from IGOs such as the EU and UNDP and from the government of Spain.

The example of judicial training in Iraq also underscores how IGO or foreign government officials who call for major policy changes in a particular country are more likely to have an effect on policy outcomes when they provide money as well as advice. This is especially true when the target country is a newly independent one—in Iraq's case, one that recently regained its sovereignty—and is still establishing political stability. Given the amount of money that external entities like the United States spent in overthrowing Iraq's previous regime and helping establish its current one, the comparatively small costs of helping to foster a stable and effective judiciary in Iraq are, arguably, money well spent.

Internal Choice Factors

Policy making is a process in which individuals make decisions, and the decisions are often made in public. As a result, like many comparativists who study democratization, those who study public policy emphasize internal choice explanations of differences across countries or across time within the same country. The focus on internal choice includes an examination of leaders and their leadership skills as well as a consideration of how rational their decisions tend to be.

Leadership

While the structure of the political system determines who has the authority to make policy decisions, not all those who hold institutional powers are equally adept at using them. A leader may choose to "go public," making speeches or issuing press releases in support of a policy.[32] The leader may also work behind the scenes, using persuasion, trading support for other policy initiatives, and at times accepting compromises in order to see a proposal pass. The ability of the leader to lead—to influence others to achieve a set of defined goals—can be decisive for the adoption of a policy.

Effective leadership skills are even more important in the case of controversial or unpopular policies that the leader believes are necessary. In such cases, the leader may need to persuade many people who are initially hostile to the proposal. In democracies, efforts to pass such policies typically involve the leader making public statements, since without some increase in support from the general public, the leader is likely to fail to convince skeptical legislators. Early in Bill Clinton's first term as U.S. president, for example, he attempted to win support for a major overhaul of the American health care system. His efforts included a number of speeches on the topic and a series of events involving the First Lady, Hillary Rodham Clinton. These efforts were unsuccessful, and the vision of a third order change in health care policy failed.

The Rationality of the Decision-Making Process

Much research on public policy uses decision-making theories to explain particular initiatives or examines policies to test existing decision-making theories. This research often centers on the question of how rational policy choices are. Do policy makers act rationally by identifying the problem, ordering their goals, weighing the costs and benefits of every policy alternative in light of their goals, and choosing the best policy? Do they take shortcuts but still operate in a broadly rational way? Or, do many policy decisions result from irrationality?

Comparative policy studies tend to reject the idea that policy makers regularly engage in full-blown rational efforts involving ranking goals, identifying all possible alternatives, and considering the costs and benefits of these alternatives. Instead, comparativists point to theoretical perspectives like satisficing and incrementalism, introduced in Chapter 10. When a new policy is introduced, the proposal is likely to be the first one on which all the decision makers involved can agree, rather than the result of an exhaustive effort to produce the best possible policy.[33] Likewise, when old policies are modified, the alterations rarely involve innovative third order changes. Controlling for a variety of other possible explanations, the strongest predictor of expenditures on particular government programs is the previous amount spent on that program—a finding highly consistent with incremental policy making.[34]

Over the last two decades, comparativists have paid increasing attention to the notion of policy making as a form of learning. This idea of learning links together what are sometimes thought of as separate stages of the policy-making process: the creation of a policy and the assessment of whether the policy worked. While political leaders look abroad for policies to possibly emulate, they pay even more attention to past policy experiences in their own country. They evaluate the performance of past and current policies, and they take these evaluations into account when they consider changes to existing policy or entirely new policy approaches. As Peter Hall puts it, "Policy responds less directly to social and economic conditions than it does to the consequences of past policy."[35]

External Choice Factors

The decisions leaders make in one state can affect policy decisions in other states. For diffusion to occur, government leaders somewhere must first decide to adopt the policy. Only then can the existence of the policy and experiences with its adoption in one state affect the policies adopted in another.

Likewise, while the role of international organizations also must be taken into account when examining particular domestic policies, individuals within an international organization decide how the organization should become involved in a country's domestic politics. Funding from international institutions like the World Bank and the International Monetary Fund (IMF) can have a significant impact on a state's economic performance, but a relatively small number of individuals decide how to distribute the funds. The United Nations can have a significant impact on domestic policies in a country. Once again, however, individuals such as the representatives of the UN member states, officials in the UN bureaucracy, and sometimes the UN secretary-general alone decide how and for what purposes the UN interacts with the country.

Sometimes ordinary people from outside a country rise to the occasion and successfully advance a cause they passionately support. Jody Williams, a former teacher of Spanish and English as a second language in the United States, played a crucial role in the creation and success of the International Campaign to Ban Landmines (ICBL). Partly because of her efforts, an international treaty banning such weapons was signed in Ottawa, Canada, in 1997. Williams and the ICBL were awarded the 1997 Nobel Peace Prize.

TOPIC IN COUNTRIES

In democracies and non-democracies alike, government officials struggle to generate effective policies that have broad support across the population. This is due in part to the large number of structural and choice factors that can influence policy outcomes. Countries that on the surface appear different from one another may face similar policy and performance difficulties, while countries that are often placed into the same category focus on different policy challenges. Even the same country at the same point in time may be addressing various important policy issues, with the outcomes driven by different sets of causal factors. Consequently, the Topic in Countries sections cannot cover all the major recent policy discussions in each country or all the causal factors that have shaped them. Instead, they provide brief overviews of the main policy debates and then focus in detail on one policy and the main causal factors that have shaped it. As you read these discussions, look for:

- The historical and contemporary context of major public policy approaches in each of the nine TIC cases.
- Examples of more recent major policy debates.
- The structural and choice factors that have influenced the major policy outcome highlighted in each case.

The United Kingdom

The relatively early development of the British economy had important policy implications. The emergence of a sizable working class, for example, led to the creation of the Labour Party at the start of the twentieth century. Particularly after World War II, the large working class and its Labour Party allies pushed the UK in the direction of a mixed economy, leading to the creation of a large welfare state. Although the UK accepted the postwar settlement—the compromise between a largely capitalist economic system and major social welfare protections—found in much of Western Europe after World War II, the UK did not adopt the more social democratic approach of other European countries.

The Conservative Party accepted the idea of significant social welfare protections prior to Margaret Thatcher's term as prime minister, which began in the late 1970s. Because Thatcher believed that social welfare policies were inefficient and generated dependency on the state, she pursued a third order policy change. Consistent with its label of "New Labour," the Labour Party left in place many of Thatcher's reforms after coming to office in 1997.

Major Policy Debates

Labour did preside over three major domestic or intermestic policy debates—immigration, health care, and devolution and other constitutional reforms—that have continued to the present. As in many of the TIC cases, immigration remains a thorny issue. Terrorist bombings on July 7, 2005, altered the immigration debate. Already a concern for many in the working class, immigration became fused with national security at a previously unseen level. Conservatives made immigration a major campaign issue, and they clearly pulled some support from Labour in recent elections as a result. It was a central campaign issue in 2010, with the Conservatives promising a reduction in immigration. Ironically, given that most British concerned with immigration have in mind Muslim or Eastern European immigrants, economic troubles in Ireland and the resulting immigration into the UK from that country most challenged the Conservatives in trying to follow through on their campaign promise in 2011.[36]

Perhaps no issue arises more frequently in the House of Commons Question Time than health policy. When sitting in opposition, Labour and Conservative MPs alike have attacked the performance of the British National Health Service (NHS). When in power, both parties have simultaneously defended the NHS's general performance and sought to reform it.[37] Since the late 1970s, reforms have emphasized the idea that government services may be more efficiently administered by giving lower-level bureaucrats, as well as regional and local governments, greater autonomy to implement policy.[38] Following the 2010 elections, the new British health secretary, Andrew Lansley, proposed a new round of NHS reforms, arguing that the UK's health care problems justified his proposed changes. Around the same time, an article in *The Guardian* newspaper criticized Lansley's proposals and argued that, although the NHS has been reorganized fifteen times in the past three decades, there was little evidence that the reforms produced positive results.[39]

As touched on earlier in the book, former prime minister Tony Blair's government sought major constitutional reforms, but the reforms ended up being less ambitious in practice. Devolution was begun, but even the record on this reform was mixed, with a particularly bumpy road in Northern Ireland, at least until the middle 2000s. The House of Lords was reformed, but far less than the Labour Party had planned. What could have been one of the most significant changes in the British system, overhauling the British electoral system, became a front burner policy issue after the creation of the Conservative Party-led coalition government following the 2010 elections. Although the coalition partner, the Liberal Democrats, had hoped for a change to a proportional representation (PR) system, they accepted the offer of a national referendum on adopting an alternative vote (AV) system, to replace the UK's long-standing first past the post (FPTP), single-member district approach (see Chapter 9). The proposal to overhaul the electoral system was defeated in the referendum held in May 2011.

Factors Affecting the Alternative Vote System Referendum

A number of causal factors contributed to the outcome of maintaining the existing approach and not changing the electoral system. First, the idea for an overhaul of the electoral system was closely tied to the structure of the existing FPTP electoral system and its effect on electoral outcomes. Historically, British elections had tended to produce two large parties, one of which almost always controlled a majority of the seats in the House of Commons. In recent years, however, the FPTP electoral system had no longer produced the stable two-and-a-half party system. In the 2010 general elections, the Conservative Party defeated the Labour Party but failed to secure a majority of the seats in Parliament. Because the Conservatives were forced to reach out to the Liberal Democrats to form a government and because the Liberal Democrats strongly supported overhauling the electoral system, the outcome of 2010 elections was the most important factor driving the idea of major electoral system reform.

Comparativists often struggle with how far back in a sequence of events to look. In this case, the importance of the 2010 elections begs the question of why the Labour Party failed to maintain control of the government. Here, two factors were in play. One was the combination of the perceived weak leadership of Prime Minister Gordon Brown and the impressive rhetorical and campaign skills of the Conservative Party leader, David Cameron. Second, Brown had become prime minister only because of the declining popularity of his predecessor, Tony Blair. While not the only factor, Blair's weakening support was closely tied to his support for the Iraq War.

Because the policy decision on overhauling the electoral system was ultimately left to the British electorate, the final factor is the calculations of the voters. They were certainly influenced by the effectiveness of the campaigns that supporters and opponents of the electoral system ran. Voters' rational calculations also came into play. The change to an AV electoral system would likely help smaller parties like the Liberal Democrats at the expense of the Labour and Conservative Parties. Supporters of the two largest parties, therefore, had little reason to support the proposed changes, and their leaders did little to change their minds. Although Prime Minister Cameron went along with the idea of a referendum, it was obvious in the weeks leading up to the vote that he was less than enthusiastic about the proposed change.

Germany

Germany's social market economy (SME, see Chapter 2) combines a strong social safety net with an emphasis on traditional social values. As a result, many of the major policy debates in Germany have centered on how to maintain economic protections as the population continues to age and fewer workers are entering the workforce—a problem facing countries across the European continent. There is also an increasing sense that the underlying assumptions about family and work are inconsistent with the realities of twenty-first century economic life.

The political elites who created West Germany's SME in the post–World War II period did so to forge a "third way" between the free-market capitalism that had yielded mass unemployment and insecurity during the Great Depression, and the socialist command economy that thwarted individual freedom in the Soviet Union and East Germany. The approach allows for private property and market-driven economic growth, but also accepts a role for the state in directing the proceeds of economic growth and the compensation of those whom the market leaves behind.

Major Policy Debates

Until the 1980s, the SME delivered economic growth rates that were well above other EDCs in this period (the *Wirtschaftswunder* or economic miracle). It also provided the population with a comprehensive welfare state. Furthermore, the SME's "social partnership" of labor unions and employers delivered high wages and peaceful industrial relations. But the model ran into serious trouble in the 1990s, when persistent high unemployment, exceeding 9 percent of the workforce, became a regular feature of the German economy.

The unsustainability of the current approach sparked serious debate over labor market reform in Germany, but the policy debate has also extended to the viability of the welfare state itself. The heavy reliance on payroll taxes to finance welfare state programs is particularly perilous, given the shrinking number of workers and the burgeoning number of people reliant on welfare state benefits. Moreover, high payroll taxes raise overall labor costs, discouraging job creation and leading to a vicious cycle of "welfare without work."[40] This trend began to be reversed under former chancellor Gerhard Schröder. His reforms encouraged the creation of part-time, low-wage employment by changes in labor market rules and stricter access to less generous unemployment benefits. The Merkel government has, by and large, continued these reforms.[41]

At the same time, the growth in single-parent families and the rising number of women in paid employment have generated new demands for child care and parental leave that the welfare state has had to address.[42] A policy implemented in 2007 provides a parent who stays home with a child for the first year after it is born with 65 percent of his or her income and protects the parent's job. The policy is dramatically different from the American approach of weeks-long, unpaid family leave.

Factors Affecting Debate over Welfare State Reform

Efforts at reforming welfare state programs are not unique to Germany. In the United States, the Clinton Administration pursued a policy to "end welfare as we know it," and other European countries have struggled with how to sustain welfare state protections in the face of demographic changes. Simply put, across the European continent, too few workers contribute payroll taxes to finance the welfare benefits of those who are not working. The low fertility rate and aging population in countries like Germany exacerbate the situation and threaten a severe shortfall in welfare state financing in future decades. Thus, internal economic and demographic structural factors are forcing Germany to consider reforms to its social safety net. Because the problem extends to countries around Germany as well, one would expect welfare reform to be affected by the external structural forces of policy diffusion and participation in international organizations like the EU. Comparative politics research provides support for the effects of both external structural factors.

An additional concern relates to the cultural assumptions on which the conservative corporatist welfare state system is based. To many, the assumptions of a traditional family structure and gender division of labor between a full-time breadwinner husband and a wife who stays home full time to care for children no longer reflect the realities of German society. Thus, while cultural factors may have shaped the development of the welfare state policies over time, the breakdown of these traditional norms has pushed the government to respond. Responses include the government's generous family leave policy, even though it runs counter to broader efforts to constrain spending on social programs.

India

India's efforts to liberalize the economy, especially after 1991, led to numerous debates about the specifics of the economic reform. Topics included what parts of the economy should be privatized, how quickly privatization should occur, and how open India should be to foreign capital. Other debates developed between those championing the rights of farmers whose land was to be acquired during the economic development process and those championing the transition to an industrialized economy. These debates have not undermined India's economic growth, which has been substantial.

Major Policy Debates

The majority of the rural population has not shared in India's economic progress.[43] Partly as a result, debates over how to deal with this problem occur regularly, especially at the federal unit and local levels and as elections approach. The debate centers around issues

Social activist Medha Patkar, right, speaks at a rally in Bangalore, India, in June of 2006. The rally occurred at the end of the three-day convention of the National Alliance of People's Movements (NAPM), a network of over two hundred movements in India, with an ideology against globalization, caste discrimination, and religious fundamentalism. © AP photo/Gautam Singh

such as the provision of water, power, fertilizer, seeds, prices, and subsidies. Maintaining a regular supply of freshwater is one of India's great problems. If the monsoon does not arrive regularly, drought often results. When the monsoon comes, flooding frequently follows. Dams, such as on the Narmada River, have been built to offset both problems, but they produce political tensions, including the displacement of residents and disputes over the use of the water by upriver and downriver communities.[44]

In a country with as much identity diversity as India, policy debates concerning identity are expected to be vigorous. The role of religion in India, that is, whether the government of India should be secular or communal, is a contentious topic. The debate focuses on the appropriateness of using *Hindutva* (Hindu nationalism) to guide the governance of India.[45] Policies aimed at creating a greater sense of inclusion among many groups have also aroused considerable debate. A key policy has been that of "reservations," that is, reserving a certain percentage of places in public educational institutions and public employment for individuals from groups that are deemed to have been excluded.[46] The debates center on which groups should be given reservations and whether reservations should be extended to private sector schools and jobs. Alongside the calls for new reserved positions and categories, opposition to reservations has grown. Opponents often use the argument that only a few people within these groups, referred to as the "creamy layer," seem to benefit.

Factors Affecting Debates over Identity-Related Policies

As Chapter 4 presents in detail, a country's identity structure is a huge factor in its identity-related policies. India's identity structure is complex. India is an incredibly diverse country, with identity divisions often complementing each other at the regional level but crosscutting each other at the national level. The crosscutting nature of India's identity groups makes developing an overarching sense of national identity easier than it would otherwise be, but figuring out on what to base the national identity is still a challenge. Advocates of Hindutva say that it is a set of ideas inclusive of most of the people and religions of India, though it excludes some of the ideas associated with Islam and Christianity. The divisiveness of Hindutva is reflected in its presence as a major point of contention among India's largest political parties. It pits the Bharatiya Janata Party (BJP), which advocates Hindutva, against the Left, which advocates secularism. The Congress Party (INC) leans toward secularism, but sometimes uses communalism in its struggle for power. Even among those who oppose Hindutva, the idea of accommodating India's large Muslim population has been controversial. Particularly intense debate has arisen over whether Muslims should be accorded reservations in universities and employment.

The controversies over identity are also fueled by India's frequent terrorist incidents. Debates over how to deal with terrorism frequently involve the extent to which the policy should allow infringement of civil liberties—a topic of significance to many Indians. Some acts of the terrorism are carried out by militant domestic groups like the Naxalites or Maoists, who assert they are fighting to improve the lives of the rural poor. Others are fomented by communally based groups to stir conflict, especially among Muslims and Hindus, and still others are inspired by pro-Pakistani groups or those associated with Pakistan's Inter-services Intelligence (ISI). In the northeast and northwest, there is secessionist violence and terrorism.

Mexico

Since Mexico became an established democracy, the country's citizens have paid increasing attention to government policies and performance. Well before this, however, a number of significant policy reforms occurred. Economic development has been a central concern of Mexican policy makers since independence, leading to significant state involvement in the economy.

Major Policy Debates

In the latter years of Mexico's party authoritarian system under the Institutional Revolutionary Party (PRI), the government engaged in both significant political reform and major economic initiatives. While the political reforms were largely supported by the population (if not by everyone within the ruling party), economic policies such as participation in NAFTA generated significant opposition. Along with broader economic development policy, the Mexican government's approaches have been criticized for deepening class and regional divides in the country.

Other policy debates have centered on drug violence, education, and health care. The approach of President Felipe Calderón's government to the explosion of drug-related violence in Mexico has led to two major criticisms. The first is that Calderón's tactics early in his presidency exacerbated the problem. Some have argued that his decision to use the Mexican military to fight the drug cartels in the streets backfired, turning what had been a source of instability into a civil war.[47] The second criticism is almost the opposite, charging that Calderón has not done enough to solve the problem, leaving too much autonomy to local officials, many of whom have connections to drug cartels. This example highlights the challenges that governments face in developing policies to address pressing social problems.

Most scholars and policy analysts recognize the importance of education and adequate health care to a country's long-term economic development. While the government has attempted to reform the country's educational system, its efforts have been criticized as haphazard and half-hearted.[48] The most ambitious effort at improving education was the *Progresa* program (now known as *Oportunidades*), a set of reforms launched in 1997 to address rural poverty. By the middle of 2010, one of every four families in Mexico was receiving assistance from Oportunidades.[49] The program included cash incentives for parents who kept their children in school and included financial incentives for receiving preventive health care treatments such as vaccinations. The Progresa-Oportunidades program shows how programs can incorporate several types of policy. The program is not only a redistributive policy, serving to reduce poverty in the short run, but also comprises education and health care policy components.

Beyond the Progresa-Oportunidades health care feature, health care system reform has been notable. Its centerpiece is the national health insurance program launched in 2004. Designed to provide universal coverage by 2010, the program has dramatically increased the portion of the population with access to health care. The national and state governments pay most of the cost of the insurance, and individuals pay the rest. The cost structure is progressive, with wealthier families required to contribute more than poorer ones.[50] Debate continues over the quality of the care that is being provided and the balance between the program's benefits and its significant costs.[51] The universal nature of the program, consistent with both the ideals of the Mexican Revolution and the claim in Mexico's constitution that health care is a human right, has helped it earn support across the political spectrum.[52]

Factors Affecting the Development and Implementation of Progresa-Oportunidades

In addition to the internal economic divisions in Mexico that the Progresa-Oportunidades program was designed to help address, other internal and external factors have affected its development and implementation. One of the most important was an internal choice factor: Progresa was developed through an elite learning–based rational choice process. Its developers looked at what the Mexican government had been doing wrong and weighed possible solutions. They decided that existing approaches, such as subsidizing certain food staples, were inefficient and ineffective, since both the rich and the poor benefited from the subsidies. The Mexican government used the savings from abolishing the subsidy on tortillas to pay much of Progresa's costs.[53] The underlying idea of Progresa-Oportunidades is also based on rational choice assumptions. To achieve the desired outcomes, such as regular medical checkups for poor women, the policy required the behaviors in order for individuals to receive the program's direct financial payments.

It is important to note that while many policies come through the diffusion of policies created in other countries, policy diffusion requires the creation of an innovative policy in the first place. Progresa-Oportunidades has been such a policy. The program's success has made it a model for similar programs in dozens of other countries and major cities such as New York.

In Mexico, one of the most important factors driving any policy outcome is the ongoing challenge of corruption. Corruption feeds into pressing problems like drug violence, and it also limits the ability of the

As part of a visit to Mexico in April of 2007, New York City Mayor Michael Bloomberg, center, walks through the city of Toluca. Bloomberg visited Toluca to see firsthand the implementation of Mexico's *Progresa* Program, now known as *Oportunidades*, on which he modeled the Opportunity NYC initiative.

government to act. Particularly at the regional and local levels, it casts a shadow over the implementation of new government programs. Because the central government administers the Progresa-Oportunidades program, however, its implementation has been less vulnerable to corruption than programs that rely more heavily on local administration. Santiago Levy, one of the architects of the program, argues that this "pioneering" national approach is one of the reasons that "scholarly evaluations of Progresa-Oportunidades have been overwhelmingly positive."[54]

Brazil

The Brazilian government has long focused on economic development as its central policy concern. The result has been a focus on development policy with a heavy role for the state, the technocrat approach to governing discussed in Chapter 2. The development policy emphasizes growth over equality. Even governments on the left of the political spectrum have had a difficult time making progress on their stated goals of an improved quality of life for the large number of people in Brazil living in poverty.

Major Policy Debates

The main problem with rule by technocrats is that someone must decide what the goals of policy should be before the "technically appropriate" policy can be applied. Fiscal and monetary policies, for example, can be designed to favor lending or to encourage savings. In the case of Brazil, the main conflict involves trade-offs between policies designed to maximize macroeconomic growth and policies designed to reduce Brazil's staggering levels of inequality. Much of Brazil's historical political instability can be attributed at least in part to pendulum swings between governments that emphasized equality and redistribution and governments (often the product of military coups) that emphasized economic growth, privileging the property rights of the ruling class in order to stimulate investment.

Factors Influencing Development Policy

A country's existing economic structure typically plays a central role in the development and effectiveness of economic development policies. Countries that begin the development process with more equal incomes, such as South Korea, Taiwan, and Japan, often do better in economic development because they have larger domestic markets and higher average levels of health and education, more evenly spread across the population. Obviously, a sick, malnourished, and uneducated workforce is less productive.

Achieving greater average levels of health, education, and consumption capacity—especially when starting from a highly unequal distribution of resources—typically requires some redistribution of wealth and assets through progressive taxation or land reform. However, high tax rates and redistribution of real property are likely to arouse opposition among the propertied classes and potential investors, which in turn reduces the amount invested in the creation of new jobs. Leftist presidents like Luiz Inácio "Lula" da Silva and Dilma Rousseff have struggled to achieve their campaign promises to the poor, while also spurring economic growth and keeping the economically powerful inside Brazil happy.

In an increasingly globalized world, external factors can also have a significant impact on development policy. The economically powerful also includes policy makers outside the country, such as those at the IMF. For President Rousseff, the challenge of addressing inequality without alienating internal and external economic elites is particularly great. The Brazilian people expect her to oversee the continuation of Brazil's sizable economic growth while also fostering greater equality than the popular Lula was able to do. As one Brazilian resident in his twenties put it after her election in late 2010, "Dilma will be able to continue working for the people, to continue improving many of the things that Lula started and didn't have time to finish."[55]

Nigeria

Tackling corruption remains the central policy issue in Nigeria, as it affects the effectiveness of initiatives in all other policy arenas. Not only does corruption eat away at a new policy's ability to address the problem it was designed to tackle, but corruption also makes reform of existing policies difficult. In other words, it not only affects the performance of new policy initiatives but also significant constrains the kinds of policy changes that are adopted in the first place. Entrenched interests, who benefit from existing policies, use their connections to undermine efforts to engage in second or third order policy change in Nigeria. Until corruption is successfully attacked, Nigeria's great potential is likely to remain unrealized.

Major Policy Debates

Former president Olusegun Obasanjo took a number of steps to address corruption—or at least appeared to be addressing it—during his two terms as president. These included the arrests of high-profile government officials, including regional governors, federal government ministers, and the inspector general of the police.[56] Nigeria's next president, Umaru Yar'Adua, seemed more serious about addressing the corruption problem. He demanded that ministries return unspent funds in 2007 and in March 2008 fired two ministers who defied the order. Yet, local organizations such as the Coalition against Corrupt Leaders criticized the Yar'Adua administration for delays in trials of officials charged with corruption, which have "undermined public confidence in the anticorruption efforts."[57]

Beyond corruption, the government faces other pressing issues. One is how to better distribute and invest oil wealth while addressing fiscal problems. A fiscal responsibility bill with significant economic reforms was stalled in the legislature throughout Obasanjo's second term[58] before it was finally passed and signed into law after Yar'Adua took office. Despite these reform efforts, Nigeria remains heavily dependent on oil revenue.

Another vital problem is the deepening of identity divisions. Nigeria's policy approaches to identity have been uneven. It has tried to emphasize a strong overarching identity and worked to minimize religious and ethnic divisions, but its federal system allows regional governments say over many cultural matters and has fueled disputes over the use of Sharia (Islamic law) in Nigeria's north. A number of regional and local politicians have exploited the power of identity, working hard to inject identity divisions into the political process.

Factors Influencing Anticorruption Efforts

Once corruption has penetrated society and the political system, tackling it is one of the most difficult policy challenges for a government. The reason is that corruption attaches itself to, transforms, and becomes part of all the types of structures discussed in this book. Corrupt economic elites use their wealth to undo reforms designed to attack corruption. Values supportive of corruption become a defining feature of political culture. Corrupt officials and identity group leaders play on, and thus deepen, identity divisions. Finally, corruption shapes the political structure itself, creating incentives for greater corruption and establishing institutional barriers to anticorruption efforts.

With the sets of internal structural factors working against addressing corruption, internal choice factors such as leadership and external structural factors provide the main opportunities for anticorruption policies to be developed. Great leaders can rise above corruption, using their popularity to get the population on their side as difficult steps are taken. But leaders are part of the social and political structures they oversee. Individual leaders may be tainted, limiting their effectiveness and leading observers and the general population to question their commitment to tackling corruption. Whether Yar'Adua's successor, Goodluck Jonathan, is better able to follow through on anticorruption efforts than those before him remains to be seen. There is reason for optimism. As acting president, he fired Justice Minister Michael Aondoakaa, who was seen as an ineffective point person in the fight against corruption. On the other hand, Jonathan and his wife were accused of questionable practices when he was governor of Bayelsa State from 2005 to 2007.

External structural factors include the role of intergovernmental and nongovernmental international organizations. By monitoring corruption, they play the role of "naming and shaming," providing valuable information to others in the international community as well as the Nigerian people. Such external actors can also have an impact by putting their money where their mouths are. Corruption survives in part because of the financial benefits it provides. When foreign governments and international organizations provide economic incentives for reducing corruption, anticorruption efforts are far more likely to succeed.

Russia

The collapse of the Soviet Union in 1991 dramatically altered not only Russia's political landscape but its economic and social landscapes as well. Although reforms under Soviet leader Mikhail Gorbachev had weakened state control of the economy to an extent, full-scale privatization of the economy under Russian president Boris Yeltsin took place during the first few years of the post-Soviet period. The privatization benefited only a small portion of the population, increasing significantly the growing divide between rich and poor. After Vladimir Putin became president at the end of 1999, he oversaw both a reinsertion of the state into the Russian economy and the undoing of Russia's fragile democracy.

Major Policy Debates

The two most important domestic policy debates in Russia since 1991 have been about economics and identity. Major economic policy topics have included how to remove the state from the economy through privatization and the extent to which the state has reentered the domestic economy as a major player. More than Soviet leader Mikhail Gorbachev had done, President Boris Yeltsin introduced elements of capitalism into the Russian economy. The Russian government privatized most state-owned enterprises during the 1990s but maintained some large state-owned companies. After Putin's ascendancy to the presidency, Russia adopted a more obvious state capitalist approach.

Identity policy discussions have centered on, but have not been limited to, the conflict in Chechnya. The Russian government has struggled to forge an overarching identity that would unite ethnic Russians with the sizable number of citizens who are ethnically non-Russian. Policy approaches have varied since 1991. Russia has maintained its ethno-federal system, but the central government has taken steps to weaken the autonomy of ethnic republics. The one consistent position has been opposition to the idea of granting independence to territorially concentrated minority groups. In the case of the Chechens, Presidents Yeltsin and Putin both supported military action to prevent Chechnya from seceding from Russia.

Factors Influencing Economic Policy

Both internal and external factors played a major role in the years of privatization, while internal structural and choice factors have been more central in the development of state capitalism. The international community—from foreign countries like the United States to international organizations like the IMF—pushed Russia to privatize much of its state-run economy. Although their influence was increasingly unpopular in Russia, President Yeltsin largely went along with their general suggestions. Internal structural and choice factors included the extent to which people with political connections benefited from privatization more than the rest of the population. As discussed in Chapter 2, some labeled Russia's economic system in the 1990s "oligarchic capitalism" because of the tendency for a small number of wealthy individuals to have significant influence over the economy and policy decisions during and after the privatization period.

Internal structures and choices heavily influenced the state's reinsertion of itself into the economy. The extent to which the Russian economy was dependent on its energy sector, and the highly profitable nature of that sector, made the sector a desirable target for Russian elites, including political leadership. As the government became a more important economic actor in the state capitalist system, those with connections again benefited. However, political connections in the first decade of the twenty-first century were increasingly about ties to President Vladimir Putin. His political opponents, even very wealthy and powerful ones like Mikhail Khodorkovsky, found themselves targeted in the name of economic development and weeding out corruption from the economy. Khodorkovsky was once the wealthiest person in Russia and one of the twenty wealthiest in the world. He was arrested and imprisoned—and later tried on new charges to keep him in prison longer—after becoming more vocal about Putin and the creeping authoritarianism that he was overseeing. His arrest and imprisonment not only removed one of Putin's major political opponents, but also allowed the assets of Khodorkovsky's giant energy company, Yukos, to be auctioned off. The company's assets were sold for a fraction of their value and purchased by Russian government–controlled energy companies.

China

For decades, China has emphasized a pragmatic approach to economic growth, turning away from its past commitment to a socialist development blueprint. The result has been dramatic economic growth. China's development approach provided a model to other countries, becoming the country most associated with the Asian economic model (see Chapter 2), a combination of protectionism, state-led development, and authoritarian rule. Alongside China's significant economic growth, economic inequality has increased dramatically over the last two decades.

Major Policy Debates

China's approach has been largely successful on the economic front, but citizens have been less happy with perceived incompetence and corruption within the various levels of government. China has been relatively open about corruption and has taken steps to tackle, or at least to appear to tackle, the problem.

Related to the broad arena of economics, one of the most important and controversial policy questions in China concerns the relative autonomy of the regions versus the center. As discussed earlier in the book, China has granted regional and local governments a greater degree of autonomy to administer government policy. Thus, in contrast to Russia—a federal system in which the lower levels of government are less powerful than they had been a decade earlier—China remains a unitary system in which lower levels of government are increasingly assertive and the central government is increasingly acquiescent. At the same time, because of its stated goal of decreasing corruption in the country, the Chinese government tries to keep a watchful eye on regional and local government officials.

The government's concern about growing powers in the regions is also tied to debates over its treatment of minority identity groups. The Chinese government's treatment of minorities has varied, with its most extreme policies directed at the Muslims of the Xinjiang Uighur Autonomous Region and the population of Tibet. Xinjiang Province is a huge region, bordering six countries to China's north and west. The Chinese government has used force against Uighur leaders, labeling the main Uighur political movements terrorist organizations, and it has settled Han Chinese in the region to dilute the Uighur population. In 2008, Chinese authorities put down an uprising in Tibet. Although debate exists over the extent of the crackdown, Chinese leaders (and the regional government in Tibet) acknowledged that riots took place, blaming them on the government in exile of the Dalai Lama.

Factors Influencing China's Identity Policies

China's identity divides are significant, particularly those between the majority Han Chinese population and ethnic minorities who live in China's outlying provinces. As the

In Theory and Practice box in Chapter 4 discussed, the Chinese government has tried to assimilate some groups into Han Chinese identity while also recognizing that the ability to reconstruct new identities is limited in other cases. Because China's minorities include around 100 million people, the potential for minority nationalist movements to destabilize the country is significant. Although the government has been more forceful in its dealings with Xinjiang and Tibet than with other regions, the complementary nature of minority identity and region is a source of constant concern.

Identity policies sometimes have causes beyond identity structure itself. Regions in which minorities are concentrated may have important economic resources. This is certainly the case in Xinjiang, which has valuable raw material deposits including oil, coal, and minerals. China is increasingly dependent on external raw materials for its economic development, and Xinjiang's energy and mineral deposits have significant value to the government. External factors are also in play. In the case of Tibet, the Chinese government has cracked down when it feels necessary, but it is well aware of the extent to which other nations have expressed concern over its treatment of Tibet. Such international pressure has been less noticeable in the case of Xinjiang, partly because of the Chinese government's labeling of Xinjiang nationalists as Muslim terrorists.

Iran

Iranian governments have long stressed the goal of economic development. This trend continued following the 1979 revolution. From 1989 to 2010, the government proposed four successive development plans. These plans have met with mixed success, partly because of internal structural factors that limit the efficiency of Iranian economic production. Sporadic uprisings against the Iranian government, including the Green Revolution of 2009, have reinforced the importance of producing effective economic policies.

Major Policy Debates

The country's economic development plans—with the fifth development plan covering 2010 to 2015—have been overly optimistic about economic prospects. The reality has been mediocre growth and a perception among many ordinary Iranians that they have failed to reap the benefits of the country's oil reserves. Iran's hard-line president, Mahmoud Ahmadinejad, won election and reelection in part because he successfully portrayed himself as an economic populist willing to stand up to those hoarding Iran's oil wealth for themselves.

The other major areas of debate concern social life and identity. Initially, President Ahmadinejad's rhetoric had little impact on most Iranians' daily lives. By the middle of his first term, however, Ahmadinejad's vision for Iranian society had begun to materialize. The changes were most evident in the arena of gender relations, already a touchy subject in Iran. New policies led to the segregation of previously co-ed classes, bans on women smoking in cafés in Tehran, and new restrictions on women's clothing stores and the public performance of music by women.[59] Although some Iranians opposed these changes, the opposition was not strong enough—despite the efforts of the Green Revolution protesters—to prevent Ahmadinejad from winning reelection in 2009.

Other controversial identity policy questions surround the question of Iran's sizable ethnic minority population. Although the government continues to keep an eye on the large Azari population in the north, its main focus has been on its Kurdish population. In November 2010, for example, four Kurds were arrested in western Iran and charged with terrorist activities. The Iranian government linked them to American and British efforts to generate dissent among Iran's ethnic minorities.[60]

Factors Affecting Iran's Economic Development Plans

Thanks to clientelism and the presence of significant corruption in both the public and private sectors, Iran has failed to come through on its promise to distribute oil wealth to the general population. As discussed in previous chapters, the powerful *bonyads*, some of which have a net worth in the billions of dollars, have been allowed to keep a sizable portion of the wealth generated by their economic holdings in exchange for ongoing support of the government. Once again, connections with government officials matter.

The situation changed somewhat following the Green Revolution. In 2010, the government pledged to increase social welfare spending dramatically to counter rising prices. It is too early to know whether these promises will lead to significant changes in government policy. What Iran does demonstrate, however, is that electoral results and resulting protests are not just major political outcomes that comparativists seek to understand. They are also causal factors that shape policy outcomes by changing the internal political structure of a country, or at least by pointing out to the government that it needs to seriously consider major policy changes to address unhappiness in the population.

Think and Discuss

When examining the major policy issues and the factors that influence them in the nine TIC cases, what themes emerge across these otherwise very different countries?

COUNTRY SUMMARY

TIC Country	Historical Context for Policy Development	Examples of Major Policy Debates in Recent Years	Most Important Factors Affecting a Policy Outcome
The United Kingdom	Early economic development; postwar settlement after World War II created a mixed economy; July 7, 2005 terrorist bombings	Immigration; health care policy; constitutional reforms; debate over overhauling the electoral system	Electoral system referendum affected by the decline in popularity of the Labour Party because of the Iraq War, the results of the 2010 elections, and the rational calculations of British voters
Germany	Development of the social market economy; Europe-wide pressures to contract welfare state spending	Maintaining versus contracting the generous system of social welfare protections	Changing demographic and economic structures (aging population, breakdown of traditional family, too few workers to sustain generous welfare programs); policy diffusion and pressures from EU membership
India	Complexities of post-independence Indian society; liberalization of the economy beginning in the early 1990s	How to protect the poor in a market-based system; poverty among the rural population; water issues; identity-related policies	Identity-related policies driven by identity structure complexities, differing conceptions of national identity, and terrorist activities
Mexico	Dominance of the Institutional Revolutionary Party (PRI) for much of the twentieth century; democracy established in 2000	NAFTA and ongoing debates about trade and economic development policy; education; health care policy	Progresa reforms sparked by ongoing poverty and rational assessments of previous programs' failure to address it; corruption has less impact on the Progresa program than other policies due to its administration by the central government rather than local leaders
Brazil	Political instability and military involvement in politics; role of technocrats; significant levels of economic inequality when and after democracy was established	Challenges of balancing increased economic development and addressing economic inequality	Sharp class and regional divisions; external factors supporting economic development such as the IMF
Nigeria	Political instability since independence; oil-dominated economy; identity divisions throughout postindependence period	Efforts to address corruption; use of oil revenue; cultural disputes, including the issue of Sharia (Islamic law) in the north of the country	Anticorruption efforts hindered by deep levels of corruption within existing internal economic, social, and political structures; leadership and external structures can help overcome these challenges

TIC Country	Historical Context for Policy Development	Examples of Major Policy Debates in Recent Years	Most Important Factors Affecting a Policy Outcome
Russia	Collapse of the Soviet Union in 1991; privatization of the economy under President Boris Yeltsin benefited a small portion of the population; creeping authoritarianism under Vladimir Putin	Some opposition to growing state role in economy, but policies largely supported since 2000 because the economy has grown; crackdown against political opponents in the name of fighting corruption; identity issues and treatment of minorities	Privatization driven by internal and external factors; existence of profitable natural resources encouraged government intervention into the energy sector; those with political connections have benefited from economic policies
China	Past commitment to ideology under Mao Zedong replaced by pragmatic approach under Deng Xiaoping and his successors; significant economic growth (and economic inequality) over the last two decades	Questions about the Asian economic model combining state-guided economic development and authoritarian politics; efforts to address corruption; ongoing debates about the appropriate amount of power for the regions versus the central government	Policies aimed at identity group minorities influenced by strong identity divisions, especially in the outlying areas of the country; economic potential of outlying regions also a factor in how the central government approaches ethnic minorities in those regions
Iran	Islamist regime since 1979; mediocre economic development; sporadic uprisings against the government, including the unsuccessful 2009 Green Revolution	Disagreement over the effectiveness of the five-year economic plans; appeal of populist policies aimed at redistributing oil wealth; poor treatment of minority identity groups	Corruption and power of the bonyads places limits on economic policy reform; Green Revolution changed this somewhat, leading the government to consider new welfare spending programs
Spotlight on . . . Country			
France	Importance of the French Revolution and its key principles; establishment of the Fifth Republic, with its strong executive branch	Employment policies, particularly regarding the youth and immigrants; identity policies, particularly regarding religious dress and other forms of public religious expression and minority and regional language rights	Identity divisions, particularly between immigrants and longer-term French citizens; political culture supportive of unconventional forms of participation; political culture's emphasis on secularism
Iraq	Strong dictatorship under Saddam Hussein, U.S.-led invasion and occupation from 2003 to 2011, transition to established democracy and full sovereignty	Economic policies, including government budget delays in 2010 and 2011; debate over diversifying the economy versus expanding the oil sector; relations between the central government and the Kurdish region; efficiency of distribution of promised government services	Improved social stability but lingering poverty, inequality, and dependence on oil revenues; identity divisions, complemented by region; U.S. oversight of policy during occupation; difficulty in forming a government in 2010

Spotlight on . . . Country	Historical Context for Policy Development	Examples of Major Policy Debates in Recent Years	Most Important Factors Affecting Policy Outcomes
South Africa	Apartheid system; liberalization leading to the end of apartheid; postapartheid democracy, dominated by the ANC	Land reform and redistribution; addressing labor unrest and widespread strikes; constitutional review authority of the courts	Major role of key leaders in liberalization period and postapartheid period; design of the postapartheid political system; lingering racial and class divisions

TIC Wrap-Up

Many comparative public policy studies have pointed to themes across European countries, including the adoption of a strong set of welfare state provisions after World War II and the criticism of and attempts to reform those policies since the late 1970s. These themes certainly hold for the UK and Germany. At the same time, important differences exist between the two states, particularly in terms of which policy questions prompt the greatest debate at the present time and which causal factors are most important in directing those debates. This is even more obvious when one compares these European democracies with the other consolidated democracy in the group of TIC cases, India. In the UK, the central policy issues in recent years have been constitutional reforms and attempt to overhaul the electoral system. These were affected most directly by the declining support for former Prime Minister Tony Blair and the Labour Party, a trend that was driven significantly by declining support for participation in the Iraq War. In Germany, changes in social programs have been the defining policy issue of the last decade, driven by demographic and economic changes, as well as lessons from other European countries that share these challenges and the constraints imposed by EU membership. In India, identity-related policy debates have been as central as economic ones. The outcomes of these debates are shaped by India's complex identity structure, its struggles to identify the defining features of its national identity, and that way that particular events such as terrorist acts feed into discussions about identity.

An overview of major policy issues in Mexico, Brazil, and Nigeria highlights challenges of policy making in developing countries. In Mexico, policy debates have centered on economic issues, social welfare, and reducing drug-related violence. Its Progresa program was driven by perceived failures in past poverty reduction efforts, by the need to reduce poverty, and by the use of rational choice to overhaul its existing approach. The history of policy making in Brazil highlights the contrast between making policy and implementing policy. Brazilian domestic policy has become increasingly intermestic—aimed at influencing foreign investors, lending agencies, and domestic economic actors—and increasingly driven by external influences. Nevertheless, its domestic capacity to enforce and implement policy remains a stumbling block to effective public policy. In Nigeria, the economic structure includes high levels of poverty but also oil wealth that could aid in the country's development. The lingering affliction of corruption negatively affects policy initiatives, including those designed to reduce corruption.

Like the other TIC cases, economic concerns have driven policy debates in Russia, China, and Iran. In all three countries, policy challenges have included economic development and identity. In Russia, connections with government officials in large part determined who benefited from economic policy changes. In China, sustained economic growth has allowed the government to focus on other areas of concern, such as how to address the large minority population living in the outlying regions of the country. Policy debates in Iran surround the role of the government in controlling Iranians' daily lives, identity divisions in the country, and how to more effectively distribute Iran's oil-based wealth to the general population. The events of 2009 point out that existing structural impediments to economic reform can be shaken loose by large antigovernment protests.

Research in Context

One of this textbook's central themes is that causal factors that shape major political outcomes can be understood as different types of structures and choices. Comparativists sometimes employ this framework in their own research. One example is comparativist Francesco Stolfi's recent research project on budget reform in Italy.[61] Stolfi sought to understand major changes to the "formulation, approval, and implementation stages of Italy's budget process in the 1990s."[62] He compared structural arguments with those emphasizing the ideas and actions of individual political leaders and concluded that different factors played roles in the reform of the various stages of budgeting. Structural factors were most important in reform of the policy formulation process, while choice factors drove the changes to the approval and implementation stages of the policy-making process.

Reform of the Budget Process in Italy

In the early 1990s, Italy's annual budget deficits and overall public debt reached levels that concerned economists and government officials. Other European countries mounted pressure on Italy to reduce government spending. According to Stolfi, the conventional wisdom about Italy was that reform of the Italian budgeting process would be difficult due to existing institutional arrangements and past efforts at reform that had failed.

Unlike researchers who emphasized structural impediments to change, Stolfi believed that scholars should weigh these structural factors against the "goals, beliefs, and self-understandings"[63] of those making policy decisions. He also pointed out that political structural context in Italy had changed, with a new electoral system that helped stabilized the party system.

Contrary to conventional wisdom-based expectations, significant reforms in the Italian budgeting process took place in the late 1990s and early 2000s. These included merging the Treasury Ministry with the Budget Ministry and simplifying the process of formulating the budget. In the approval and implementation stages of the budget process, the reforms allowed for amendments to the government's proposed budget and more autonomy at lower levels of the bureaucracy. Using theories based in structural and choice-based analysis, Stolfi concluded that structural arguments worked best to explain the changes to the budget formulation process, while choice-based factors had a clearer impact on the new approaches to the approval and implementation stages.

So What?

Stolfi's research points to an important reality in the comparative study of politics: the types of variables that shape one important outcome can differ from those that shape another outcome. In Stolfi's study, structural factors and choice factors drove decisions in different parts of a single set of policy reforms. As the discussion of stages of democratization in the previous chapter indicated, political processes often involve different phases, and each phase can be influenced by different causal factors.

Why might Stolfi's research matter to those not directly affected by Italian politics? His contention that policy reforms are driven (and limited) by a combination of structural and choice factors is important for everyone to keep in mind. Whether it is major political upheaval in North Africa or arguments about reducing the debt in the United States, significant political reforms are difficult and complex. As H. L. Mencken once wrote, "For every problem, there is a solution that is simple, neat, and wrong."[64] Stolfi's research reminds us that, although solutions may not be simple and neat, they are possible to find through an understanding of structures and choices.

CONCLUSION

Policy making is multifaceted. It involves the identification of a problem, the crafting of a policy solution to that problem, and the implementation of that policy. Policy changes are often incremental and occasionally dramatic. The policy approach to a particular problem is affected by socioeconomic factors, governmental institutions, and the leadership and choices of a number of individuals. The constellation of these factors differs from country to country and sometimes from situation to situation within the same country.

Policies are created by individuals who are dispersed across economic, social, and political configurations. These structures provide the socioeconomic and political setting for the decision-making process. As a result, differences in these structures can affect policy outcomes. An examination of policy and government performance demonstrates that, while individuals make political choices, they do not make them in a structureless vacuum.

Consideration of policy and government performance also highlights interconnections between structural and choice factors. In the case of a large number of veto points, incrementalism is not only a rational strategy for reducing information costs during the process of policy creation but also a response to the institutional setting in which such policy creation takes place. Likewise, choices within a country are affected by existing policies in other countries. The existing policies serve as an external structural factor, providing opportunities for political elites to craft policies, in part at least, by learning from other countries' experiences. Thus, while elite learning is typically treated as an internal choice factor, policy diffusion and convergence often occur through political elites searching for external lessons.

Finally, the comparative study of public policy highlights the extent to which the political outcomes of interest to comparativists—in this case, public policies—themselves have consequences, including their ability to shape the structural environment. Economic development affects policy options, but many policy initiatives are designed to stimulate economic development. Cultural factors influence how people perceive pressing problems and potential solutions to them, but policy successes and failures can alter a society's values and system of meaning. The identity structure in a society generates challenges for governments to address and affects the range of policy options, while identity-related policies can alter how individuals view their membership in identity groups. Political institutions, the part of the policy environment closest to the actual policy decisions, create incentives for certain policy approaches and disincentives for others. Yet, many policy initiatives also alter the institutional rules of the game, changing the political structure in which future policy decisions are made. Thus, the comparative study of public policy emphasizes how interconnected structures and choices really are, an idea that has surfaced at times throughout this textbook and is the theme of the book's epilogue.

KEY TERMS

Budget deficit, p. 356
Budget surplus, p. 356
Central bank, p. 356
Citizenship policy, p. 360
Comparative public policy, p. 353
Development policy, p. 357
Domestic policy, p. 354
Education policy, p. 360
Federal Reserve Board, p. 356
Federal Reserve System, p. 356
First order policy change, p. 361
Fiscal policy, p. 355
Flat tax, p. 356
Foreign policy, p. 354
Government debt, p. 356

Health care policy, p. 359
Immigration policy, p. 360
Inner-directed linkage, p. 354
Intermestic policy, p. 355
Monetary policy, p. 356
Nationalization, p. 357
Old age and retirement policy, p. 358
Outer-directed linkage, p. 354
Policy convergence, p. 365
Policy diffusion, p. 365
Policy environment, p. 362
Privatization, p. 357
Progressive tax, p. 356
Public administration, p. 353

Public policy, p. 354
Quota, p. 357
Redistributive policies, p. 359
Regulatory policy, p. 358
Second order policy change, p. 361
State pension, p. 358
Subsidy, p. 357
Tariff, p. 357
Tax credit, p. 356
Tax deduction, p. 356
Third order policy change, p. 362
Trade policy, p. 357
Unemployment policy, p. 359
Unfunded mandates, p. 355

Structured Choices and the Comparative Study of Politics

"People's thoughts and actions—even if haphazard and spontaneous—are the mediating link between structural conditions and social outcomes."
—Eric Selbin[1]

"Politics is more difficult than physics."
—Albert Einstein

In a book called *The Thinking Game*, political scientist Eugene Meehan argues that structures and choices come together in all aspects of life:

> [T]he quality of human life is a function of two major factors: (1) the content of the natural environment; and (2) human capacity for molding or shaping that environment. The natural environment sets limits to what can be accomplished, positive or negative. . . . The channel through which human knowledge is applied to the environment is the choice or action.[2]

Meehan's point is consistent with this textbook's approach to the comparative study of politics. Existing structures provide political decision makers with certain opportunities while also constraining their ability to do whatever they want. These structures have been molded by individuals in the past, and some of them continue to be shaped by other individuals' choices and actions. Though comparativists often see structure and choice as rival perspectives, the reality of domestic politics around the world is that structures and choices are very much intertwined.

Contemplating how structures and choices interact produces explanations of political outcomes that are less tidy than those relying on only one theoretical perspective. But that is not all bad. Politics is complex and not accurately captured with simple, bumper-sticker explanations. As long as the explanations generated by combining theoretical perspectives are more precise, but not so complex that they become impossible to apply, a little complexity can be a good thing.

Examining Structural Factors in Combination

Before thinking about how structures and choices interact, it is useful to consider how different structural features themselves relate to one another. Having a fuller understanding of the impact of economic forces, for example, requires us to consider the way in which these forces both influence and are influenced by political institutions. Chapter 11's topic of regime transition points out how economic structure can shape government institutions, but the pre- and post-transition institutions also make certain economic approaches more or less likely. As Chapter 2 highlighted, the intersection of economic and political structures can also generate important conceptual categories. It is impossible to discuss capitalism, socialism, and mixed economies without taking into account the extent of government penetration into and control of the economic system. Not all economic concepts involve government, but the ideal types of economic systems certainly do.

Likewise, the discussion of political culture is rarely isolated from the ideas of economic development. One of the major comparative politics theories of political culture discussed in Chapter 3, Ronald Inglehart's theory of post-materialism, takes economic development as its starting point. While a number of comparativists have challenged Inglehart's specific formulation of the concept of postmaterialism, few would argue with the idea that economics plays a role in the development of political culture.

Another valuable pairing of structural theories is culture and identity. Most scholars who look at identity understand culture's significance, but it is important not to completely subsume identity within the cultural approach. Culture is part of what makes identity powerful, but not all features of identity can easily be forced into our understanding of culture. As comparativist Marc Ross states, culture "is only one basis" for connecting individual identity and social identity.[3]

Culture and political structures may also be tightly interconnected. New institutionalists, discussed in Chapter 5, like to emphasize the importance of one set of rules compared to another. But without a deep understanding of culture, questions such as why that set of rules, rather than another, was adopted and why the rules, once adopted, are obeyed can be difficult to answer. New institutionalists seeking answers to such questions often turn to rational choice rather than cultural structure, but it is often "beliefs and shared meanings that prevent institutional chaos."[4]

Additional structural intersections could be highlighted. Economic structure can shape and reinforce identity. Identity structure can affect the design of a country's political institutions. The different components of political structure can affect each other. Thus, while putting structural factors into the categories of economics, culture, identity, and political institutions can help us make sense of their possible effects on political outcomes, it is important to remember that in practice they rarely operate in isolation.

Examining Choice Factors in Combination

The two broad sets of causal factors emphasized in the choice approach—leadership and individual decision making—can also interact. Perhaps the best example is found in the concept of charismatic authority, introduced in Chapter 1. Leaders who effectively use their charisma to mobilize the population (and gain the support of other political officials) can greatly shape a country's major political outcomes. But the emotions they whip up in the process decrease the likelihood that other political officials and members of the general population are engaging in rational decision making. Great leaders sometimes encourage people to slow down and think carefully about pressing national problems, but a charismatic leader typically prefers individuals not to think too carefully about their support for the leader and his or her policies.

Effective leaders do sometimes employ rational choice–based arguments. But successful leaders can also alter calculations during the decision-making process, even when a group is attempting to make a rational choice. A persuasive group leader can control how the group's goals are framed and ordered. In directing the discussion, the leader might set the stage for groupthink to emerge if the first couple of comments from other members of the group echo the leader's position. The leader may also challenge any rival ideas that do emerge as contradictory to core beliefs of the group. Playing on people's resistance to cognitive dissonance (discussed in Chapter 10), the leader can get other members of the group to agree to dismiss the rival ideas.

Structures, Choices, and Structured Choices

The final type of interactions involving structures and choices take place when elements of the choice approach are united with particular structural factors. The idea that the decisions of political leaders such as the United Kingdom's David Cameron or Brazil's Dilma Rousseff are important is compatible with an emphasis on economics, culture, identity, and political institutions. Structural conditions such as identity are unlikely to be fully politically salient without some degree of leadership from intellectual, social, or political elites. For example, studies of electoral behavior have shown that people often vote for candidates who share a similar ethnic, linguistic, or religious identity,[5] but political candidates also sometimes go to great lengths to highlight their identity characteristics, particularly when speaking to a crowd of potential supporters who are "their own" people. As a result, understanding electoral behavior requires considering not only the identity traits of the general public but also the actions of candidates that provide the spark that turns the fuel of identity into what can become an inferno of "identity politics."

The structure versus choice framework allows us to separate and make sense of the various factors that affect particular political outcomes. Using these factors to develop a comprehensive understanding of such outcomes, however, requires the willingness to think about how structures and choices combine in various ways. In short, it requires a move from "structures versus choices" to "structured choices."

The structured choices approach recognizes both the importance of individuals and the crucial nature of context. It acknowledges that humans have created a large part of the setting in which they make political decisions. But it also grants that existing structures affect how people make new decisions, that these existing structures may have emerged decades or centuries before, and that they may have been relatively fixed over that period of time.[6] This approach accepts that individuals are often rational political agents, but it also appreciates that their ability to act in a fully rational manner is constrained by limited information, emotion, and the economic, cultural, identity, and political settings of which they are a part.

This is true whether the individuals are part of the elite or of the masses. The idea that a voter in the general population agonizes for months over a voting decision, while collecting all possible information about the candidates and considering all conceivable costs and benefits of the voting decision, is hard to take seriously. You have spoken to enough of your friends and family members about politics to know this is not how most people make decisions. Yet the stereotype that the masses always blindly and irrationally follow the elites also does not hold up to scrutiny. Ordinary citizens are sometimes rational, sometimes not.

The image of members of the political elite as always being fully rational, manipulative, and able to construct mass identity in any way they see fit is likewise flawed. Elites can be both rational actors and true believers. They are able to shape their economic, social, and political environments—usually gradually, occasionally rapidly. But their environment also affects their actions, sometimes hampering them and other times providing them with new opportunities. Elites cannot construct structures out of thin air in any way they want, and they do not make decisions in a structureless vacuum.

A full understanding of comparative politics requires a comprehensive perspective. As a comparative politics student, you need to understand economic development, the importance of economic class, and arguments about economic inequality. You need to consider the importance of underlying values and ways of thinking in various societies, while understanding the diversity of thought within each. You need to recognize the power of identity to both unite and divide people. You need to be aware of the various institutional arrangements in political systems around the world. You need to consider the ways in which all these structural forces interact. And you need to understand how individuals make political decisions—often rationally, but at times far from rationally—within this complex structural context, and how these choices themselves can, at times, alter that structural context.

Think and Discuss

How can you apply the idea of structured choices to other courses you are taking?

Think and Discuss

In addition to using examples from American politics from time to time, the focus in this textbook was largely on the United Kingdom, Germany, India, Mexico, Brazil, Nigeria, Russia, China, and Iran, and to a lesser extent on France, Iraq, and South Africa. If you were asked to propose one additional country that should be covered in detail in this book, which one would you suggest? Why?

Conclusion

There are times when the comparative study of politics is as puzzling as it is invigorating. Realizing that members of the political elite are not always fully rational and that economic, social, and political structures both close and open doors to individuals might make comparative politics seem too complicated, messy, and difficult. Since you have made it to the end of this book, you are apparently not ready to give up on comparative politics so easily. This leaves three possible responses.

The first possibility is to abandon the effort to explain cases across time and place and to instead engage in detailed descriptions of single cases. Such descriptions play a valuable role in our understanding of individual cases and are incorporated into comparative research. Too often, however, they stop at description and have little to say to those interested in broader understandings of politics. In short, although they are studies of politics, they fail to be comparative politics studies.

The second approach is to filter out much of the messiness, engaging in a form of tunnel vision through the exclusive use of a single, narrow approach. This is not uncommon in comparative politics, with individual comparativists clinging to one theoretical or methodological perspective, such as engaging in only comparative studies of the effects of economic structure or conducting solely "large N" research on policy outcomes based on rational choice assumptions.

The final option is the approach of this textbook: to embrace the messiness, while simultaneously finding a way to organize and make sense of it. This book's mixture of concepts, theories, and country-specific details provides a road map for your ongoing journey toward a more complete understanding of politics around the world. As the quotation from Albert Einstein at the beginning of this epilogue claims, politics may indeed be more difficult than physics. By recognizing how different types of structures and choices influence political outcomes, however, understanding politics is not as hard as Einstein's declaration implies.

While you may not believe it at the moment, as a student at the end of an introductory comparative politics course, you are among a privileged few. You know more about other countries than most people, but you also know more than just the background traits of those countries. You know how to make sense of new economic, social, and political information that you will encounter long after this course is done. You know how to place these details into the "boxes" of structure and choice. Most important, you know how to take them back out of those boxes and bring them together to explain new political outcomes you will encounter in the future.

Enjoy the road ahead!

Glossary

accommodation An approach to managing identity diversity that involves a degree of cultural autonomy and extensive rights or privileges for minority group members.

absolute veto The power of one component of the government, such as one of the legislative chambers in a bicameral legislature, to block a particular bill from being adopted.

ad hoc committee A committee that deals with special circumstances that do not fit neatly into the existing committee structure.

advocacy group An interest group that forms around a particular issue or cause its members believe in and that seeks to influence government policy at the national level.

alternative vote (AV) A preference system approach used in single-member districts.

American model of democracy Dahl's term for a democratic system that combines a presidential system with FPTP district voting in legislative elections.

Asian economic model A combination of state-led development measures and authoritarian political practices; commonly found in Asia from the 1970s through the 1990s.

assimilation A government response to identity diversity that forces a minority group to abandon its cultural characteristics and take on those of the majority group.

attentive public The part of the general population that is not part of the political elite but is more involved in politics than the rest of the masses.

authoritarianism A regime type defined by its rule by a single leader or small group of leaders, limited political participation, existent but limited autonomy of society from state control, lack of an overarching ideology, and limited control over the economy.

authority Power exercised through legitimacy rather than through coercion, though some political scientists use the term interchangeably with *power*.

backbenchers MPs who do not hold seats in the government (or the shadow government).

bicameral The label for a legislature that has two houses (chambers).

black market A market in which goods and services are bought and sold illegally.

blat The Russian word for "connections," used to describe the prevalence of clientelism and interpersonal relationships in which favors are exchanged between elites, between elites and masses, and between members of the general population.

bounded rationality The idea that humans are cognitively limited in important ways that restrict their ability to process information in a comprehensively rational manner.

bourgeoisie A term used by political economy scholars such as Karl Marx to refer to the individuals who own the means of production.

breakdown of non-democracy The first stage of the democratization process, in which the existing nondemocratic system erodes or collapses.

breakdown stage The second stage in the process of democratic breakdown, when the democratic system falls apart.

BRICS Acronym for five of the most important emerging market countries: Brazil, Russia, India, China, and South Africa.

budget deficit The shortfall when a government spends more than it takes in during a given a fiscal year.

budget surplus The amount that remains when a government takes in more revenue than it spends in a fiscal year.

bureaucracy The large part of the executive branch dedicated to the implementation of government policy.

bureaucratic authoritarianism A type of authoritarian system that occurs in countries where the economy is modernized enough to require authoritarian leaders to work closely with a large bureaucracy that has expertise on policy matters.

bureaucratic autonomy theory A theory that contends that bureaucrats emphasize their professional civil service expertise and control information in order to make oversight of their activities more difficult and maximize their independence from political control.

cabinet The chief executive and most important government ministers.

cabinet department A U.S. bureaucratic section closely tied to the president.

capitalism An economic system based on private ownership of property with business and economic activity taking place within the market.

case law The concept, found in common law systems, that judicial decisions have the force of law.

case study A research project looking at only one case; also called a single case study.

caste A hereditary identity category, primarily in Hindu society, that divides individuals based on social functions associated with each group.

catch-all parties Political parties that adopt a range of ideologically moderate policies designed to capture broad segments of the population, particularly voters from the middle of the political spectrum.

causality A relationship between two or more variables in which changes in the presence or value of one produces a change in the presence or value of another.

central bank A governmental entity that controls the supply of a country's money and affects interest rates in the country through changes to the rate it charges private banks.

charismatic authority A form of authority based on the general population's personal attachment to a particular leader.

choice approach A broad approach to studying politics and understanding political outcomes that emphasizes individual political leaders, leadership, and the process of individual decision making.

citizenship A designation of official membership that a state confers to most of its permanent population, carrying rights and responsibilities not afforded noncitizens.

citizenship policy Rules that establish how to become a citizen, the rights and duties of citizens, and the conditions under which dual citizenship is allowed.

civic culture theory A theory that each society has a distinctive mix of participatory, deferential, and subject political cultures, and that the mix influences political outcomes such as the likelihood of successful democracy.

civic nation A nation whose members are united by multiethnic cultural features and citizenship in the state rather than by shared ethnic identity.

civil law A legal system based on a strong adherence to existing statutes; judges have little discretion to interpret the law.

civil servant A middle- or lower-level bureaucrat hired for his or her expertise.

civil service The part of the bureaucracy made up of middle- and lower-level bureaucrats.

civil society A term used to refer to the array of groups that are both autonomous from the state and that people join voluntarily.

civil society organizations (CSOs) The voluntary autonomous organizations that make up civil society.

civilian control of the military A situation in which the military is subordinate to nonmilitary government officials.

clan An identity group made up of a number of families who are believed to be related through birth or marriage to a common ancestor.

class A large group of people with similar economic attributes that shape their lifestyles and life chances.

class consciousness The sense of belonging to and solidarity with a particular class, as well as the recognition of this class's relationship with other classes.

class structure The pattern of how the population of a particular country falls into different class categories; relates to level of economic equality.

cleavage structure theory An approach that explains political outcomes, including violence and democratic stability, by the extent to which identities are cross-cutting or complementary.

clientelism Linking elites and masses through patron-client relationships.

coalition A group of political parties that formally agree to work together to pass legislation.

coercive power Getting what one wants by using rewards and punishments.

cognitive dissonance The idea that people do not like to hold obviously contradictory positions, which can lead them to reject additional evidence about a topic if it runs counter to their initial beliefs.

collective action problem The difficulty of getting a rational person to participate in a collective activity if the costs of participating are targeted to those who participate but benefits generated are available to the general public.

collectivistic political cultures Political cultures that support government action aimed at benefiting large numbers of people.

committee A group of members of a legislature that works on particular topics.

common law A legal system that allows judges more room to interpret the law, with their decisions setting precedents for lower courts and future court rulings.

Communism A variant of totalitarianism in which the state owns the means of production and seeks to remake society in the name of the working class.

comparative method A research design that seeks to understand the causes of a dependent variable by examining a small number of carefully selected cases.

comparative politics The field of political science that engages in the systematic study of political outcomes through the comparison of different cases.

comparative public policy A subfield of comparative politics that examines the causes and consequences of policy decisions.

comparativists Scholars who investigate and compare domestic politics of countries around the world.

complementary identity divisions Identity divisions that coincide with one another for large numbers of individuals; also known as complementary or accumulative social cleavages.

conceptualization The way that a researcher thinks about a particular concept, including which aspects are most important to consider when studying it.

conditionality The creation and enforcement of standards for IGO membership.

confederation An affiliation of two or more states involving a relatively weak central governing authority set up to facilitate cooperation between them.

Confucianism A set of beliefs based on the writings of Confucius that emphasize respect for authority, hard work, and an obligation by those in power to rule responsibly and in the interests of society as a whole.

consensus democracy A democratic system that unites proportional representation elections, a multiparty system, and diffusion of power across branches and levels of government.

conservative ideology An ideology that advocates minimal regulation of the economy and decreased emphasis on income redistribution.

consolidation of democracy A condition in which elites and masses alike see no viable alternative to an existing democratic system.

constant dollars Technique that controls for increased value due to inflation.

constituency service Legislators' activities on behalf of particular residents in their electoral districts.

constitution A set of understandings about the functioning of a particular political system, which includes the description of official major government bodies and positions, the powers these positions have, and the process for making new laws.

constitutional judicial review The power to declare a law unconstitutional.

constitutionalism The belief that constitutions should limit government power, that government officials must obey the country's laws, and that a government's legitimacy comes from obeying these limitations and laws.

constructivism A theoretical approach that maintains that identity divisions are not natural but rather are the product of elite efforts to define individuals as falling into different identity groups and to make such divisions politically relevant.

conventional participation Political participation that does not advocate or promote political or social instability, that existing political institutions can effectively channel, and of which the political elite approves.

corporatism An approach to organizing interest groups in which the state officially recognizes certain large interest groups as the representatives of large segments of society and brings the leaders of those groups to the table as policy is being created.

countries in transition (CITs) Another term for the postcommunist states.

coup d'état The act of overthrowing an existing government.

creeping authoritarianism The gradual transition from a democracy into an authoritarian system; it is most typically seen in presidential or semi-presidential systems.

crisis stage The first stage of democratic breakdown, when a crisis emerges that threatens an existing democracy.

critical case study A type of case study in which the case is selected because it provides a tough test of the central hypothesis or hypotheses in the researcher's study.

critical elections Elections that mark the beginning of a realignment.

cross-cutting identity divisions Identity divisions that do not coincide with one another for large numbers of individuals; also known as cross-cutting cleavages.

cultural heterogeneity The case when a wide range of beliefs exists within a group.

cultural homogeneity The case when members of a group are relatively unified in their beliefs and system of meaning.

culture Defined in two distinct but related ways: (1) as a particular group's underlying values, and (2) as a system of meaning that shapes the way members of groups make sense of the people and events they encounter.

defining events One factor that can shape political culture; such events are dramatic, providing a shock to the existing political culture.

democracy A regime type that involves the selection of government officials through free and fair elections, a balance between the principle of majority rule and the protection of minority interests, and constitutional limitations on government actions.

democratic breakdown When a democracy collapses or slowly transforms into a nondemocratic system.

democratization A regime transition that establishes a democracy and, if successful, a consolidated democracy.

democratization wave A period in which the number of democracies around the world increases noticeably.

demonstration effects The process in which a regime transition in one country sparks a parallel regime transition in a neighboring or otherwise similar country; also known as contagion.

dependency theory The view that LDCs have become economically dependent on the EDCs through the system of international capitalism.

dependent variable The outcome that investigators seek to explain.

development policy The set of programs and activities designed to encourage economic development in a country.

deviant case study A project that examines a research question in a case that exhibits characteristics very different from a generally known pattern.

devolution The process of transferring power from a central government to lower governments, which does not necessarily turn the system into a federal one.

disturbance theory A term for the theory developed by David Truman that interest groups form from economic and social changes that create disturbances in society and lead those who share concerns about the problems to form groups to solve them.

divided government When the president's political party is different from the political party that controls the legislative branch.

domestic policy The set of government approaches designed to improve economic, social, and political conditions within a country.

dual citizenship The status of a person who holds official citizenship in more than one state.

Duverger's law The label given to Maurice Duverger's argument that FPTP electoral systems generate two-party systems.

ecological fallacy An error resulting from assuming that general trends or observations of groups correspond to particular events or actions of specific individuals.

economic development Changes over time in an economy that enhance its productive capacity and improve society's prosperity.

economic group An interest group that forms around shared economic interests and represents particular sectors of the economy, including labor unions and business groups.

economic growth One way of thinking about economic development, it looks at annual changes in a country's GDP.

economically developed countries (EDCs) Countries with high levels of per capita GDP, a sizable middle class, and diverse economies.

education policy Government involvement in education, from running a publicly funded education system to overseeing student performance and providing partial support for the cost of private schools and institutions of higher learning.

election A form of conventional mass participation in which the population selects among various individual candidates or political parties seeking political office.

elite learning A theory that political leaders learn from previous successes and failures and adjust their behavior accordingly to maximize the likelihood of future successes.

emerging markets The LDCs and CITs that are most desirable to foreign investors.

emotion An intense short-term response to a specific event.

establishment of democracy The second stage of democratization, in which a new democratic system is developed and put into place.

ethnic cleansing Efforts to remove an entire ethnic group from its territory.

ethnic group A large collective sharing a common history and culture whose members are believed to share a common descent.

ethnic identity The sense of belonging to an ethnic group; also known as ethnicity.

ethnic nation A nation whose national identity is based on its ethnic identity.

ethno-federalism A government response to identity diversity in which a minority receives territorial autonomy in exchange for not pursuing complete independence.

European model of democracy A term used by Robert Dahl to discuss democratic systems that combine parliamentary and PR arrangements.

exports Products and services produced inside the borders of a state that are sent outside for consumption.

external validity The extent to which the findings of a study would hold up if data from cases not examined in the study were analyzed.

falsifiable A trait of a good hypothesis, the term means that the hypothesis is not a statement that is true by definition.

fascism A variant of totalitarianism based on militarism and an emphasis on remaking society along racial, religious, or ethnic lines.

Federal Reserve Board The body that sets U.S. monetary policy; also known as the "Fed."

Federal Reserve System The central bank of the United States.

federal system A political system that provides lower levels of government with designated powers that the central government cannot take away.

feminist theory An approach that focuses on the importance of gender, the actions of men and women in positions of power, and obstacles facing women in achieving economic, social, and political equality.

finished products Goods produced from raw materials, which are much more expensive than the raw materials that go into them.

first order policy change Policy modification in which the details of the policy change, but the general approach of the policy remains the same.

first past the post (FPTP) An electoral system in which voters select a particular candidate for each office, and the candidate receiving a plurality of the vote wins.

fiscal policy Government decisions affecting taxing and spending.

flat tax A form of income tax in which individuals pay the same percentage of income in tax regardless of their level of income.

foreign direct investment (FDI) Investment from outside a country into a particular economic entity that is designed to develop a lasting presence.

foreign policy The set of approaches to foreign relations, national security, and defense.

free-market capitalism Another name for the capitalist ideal, with minimal government regulation of the economy and little social welfare spending.

frontbenchers Members of the government who sit in the front row near the prime minister during parliamentary debates.

GDP per capita The gross domestic product of a state divided by the number of people in that state.

gender A term that refers to social understandings of traits, roles, and behavioral differences between men and women and to differences between them in political attitudes and behavior.

generalist approach An approach to filling positions in the bureaucracy in which individuals are hired for general knowledge or expertise, including advanced legal training.

genocide The attempt to eliminate a large portion or all members of an identity group by killing them.

globalization The process of increasing connections in the areas of economics, communications, technology, and politics.

government In its broad meaning, the set of individuals who produce policy decisions on behalf of the state, including the roles those individuals play and the institutions in which they function; in its narrow meaning, the leading policy-making officials such as a prime minister and cabinet at a given time in a particular country.

government debt The sum of annual budget deficits over time; also known as the public debt.

grand coalition A coalition involving two or more large parties that gives the coalition control over a large majority of seats.

gross domestic product (GDP) The sum value of the goods and services in a country's economy.

groupthink Quietly going along with the apparent decision of the group even if one disagrees with it, due to a desire to "fit in."

guanxi The Chinese term for the system of personal connections that shares some features with the blat system in Russia.

hard-liners Those who oppose reform and prefer to maintain or strengthen the current nondemocratic system; also known as "standpatters."

head of government The chief executive who assembles and directs the cabinet officials or other heads of government ministries, agencies, or departments.

head of state The official representative of a country to other countries, who may or may not also be that country's head of government.

health care policy Government programs designed to enhance health care coverage, either through a national health care system or full or partial payment of health care costs.

horizontal social relations Social relations that highlight equality among members of society to help shape political and social decisions.

human capital The skills and other productive characteristics of workers.

Human Development Index (HDI) A measure of economic development that includes not only GDP but also education and health statistics.

hybrid electoral system An electoral system that combines PR and FPTP methods by dividing the legislature into separate groups of PR and district seats and having voters select both a party and a candidate.

hypothesis A tentative statement by a researcher about the expected relationship between what the researcher is seeking to understand and what the researcher is examining as a potential cause or causes.

ideal type A pure form of a concept that may never be realized in practice.

identity The set of characteristics by which individuals or collectives of individuals are known to themselves and others.

immigration policy Government rules governing how individuals can enter a country and how long they are allowed to stay.

impeachment The process of removing a president in a presidential system, initiated by the legislature or judiciary.

imports Products and services made outside the borders of a state that are brought inside for consumption.

import substitution industrialization (ISI) A development strategy emphasizing subsidies of key domestic industries and other protectionist trade policies; used by countries such as Mexico and Brazil, particularly from World War II through the 1970s.

incomplete democratization A transition in which a democracy is established but does not last for an extended period of time.

incrementalism A theory of decision making that assumes that, other than during a crisis, government officials will make small changes to existing policy rather than start from scratch.

independent variable Something investigators use to explain an outcome, whose value or existence is not affected by the rest of the factors they examine.

individualistic fallacy The assumption that collective concepts like culture can be adequately measured by aggregating individual level data.

individualistic political cultures Political cultures that discourage government involvement in society.

informal economy The portion of a country's economic activity from illegal undertakings as well as unreported legal economic activities.

in-group A group (e.g., an ethnic group) to which a particular individual belongs.

inner-directed linkage When external factors influence domestic policy.

institution A set of formal or informal rules, often taking the form of a purposive organization, that shapes individual behavior.

integration An approach to managing identity diversity that allows minority groups to continue to practice their culture in exchange for accepting that the majority group's culture will be dominant.

interest group An organization whose members share concerns about an issue and work to shape government policies, but do not seek governmental office.

intergovernmental organizations (IGOs) Political organizations whose members are internationally recognized states.

intermestic policy The set of government policies that share the traits of both domestic and foreign policy. Examples include trade and immigration policies.

internal validity The soundness of the researcher's claims based on the data.

international recognition The international community's acceptance of a state's right to sovereignty.

inverse judicial power theory A theory that explains judicial activism as a function of the relative power of the courts compared to other branches of government.

iron triangle A set of three groups with similar interests on a particular topic: government agencies, those responsible for overseeing the agencies, and interest groups pushing for particular policies related to the work of the agency.

Islamic Revolution Guard Corps Military units in Iran that were originally formed as an informal militia but became increasingly important in the maintenance of internal order in the country; known by the acronym IRGC or as the "Revolutionary Guards."

Islamism An ideology advocating Islamic law as the basis of government structure and policies and as a way to immunize Muslim countries from the corrupting cultural influences of Western-led globalization.

Jeito A key component of Brazilian political culture emphasizing and valuing the ability to get around social and political rules.

Jihad versus McWorld Benjamin Barber's term for the tension between the forces of particularism, which draw on ethnic and tribal identity and local attachments, and the forces of globalization.

judicial activism One or a series of rulings in which a court creates new policies rather than basing a ruling on a narrow interpretation of the legal question under review.

judicial independence The extent to which the judiciary is free from influence from the other branches of government.

judicial review The power of the judiciary to rule on whether laws and government policies are consistent with the constitution or existing laws.

junta A collective comprising the heads of the various segments of the armed forces that oversees policy decisions in some military governments.

labor-led capitalism Approach that involves a substantial role for government in the regulation of the economy and the establishment of social welfare programs; also known as a social democratic system.

Latin American model of democracy Dahl's term for a political system that combines presidentialism with a PR electoral system.

leadership The ability to influence a group to achieve goals through the combination of a position of authority, effective argumentation, and charisma.

leadership skills Qualities that can be developed, such as technical expertise and the ability to work with others.

leadership style The approach a leader takes when interacting with those working for him or her, including task-oriented behaviors and relationship-oriented behaviors.

leadership traits Innate personal qualities that make for a successful leader.

least developed of the lesser developed countries (LLDCs) The poorest countries in the world.

legal authority A form of authority based on an established set of rules that govern how leaders are chosen and how they make policy decisions.

legislature A multimember government institution whose key responsibility is making new laws.

legitimacy The belief by those obeying commands that those making the commands have the right to rule.

lesser developed countries (LDCs) Countries with low per capita GDP and a small middle class; economic activity is often concentrated in agriculture and raw materials extraction.

level of analysis A choice from a continuum of options—from the individual to the international system—concerning where a researcher will look for data.

liberalization The process of making a nondemocratic political system more open and less repressive.

libertarian ideology An ideology that seeks even more limited government in all facets of society than that promoted by conservatives.

local issue group An interest group that forms to address a specific short-term issue in a community.

majoritarian democracy A democratic system combining strong executives, few checks on the power of the majority to pass laws and amend the constitution, and conflictual politics between two major political parties.

majority (majoritarian) system Another name for a runoff system, since a candidate needs a majority of the vote in the second round to win.

market A system of economic exchange in which suppliers and purchasers find each other and agree to the terms of the transaction.

market forces Forces, such as supply and demand, that drive the terms of transaction in capitalism.

Marxist ideology An ideology that supports control of the government on behalf of the working class and the elimination of significant income differences.

masses Members of the population who are not involved in day-to-day governing.

means of production The individual businesses, factories, and other entities that produce goods, as well as the machines and other inputs used to produce them.

median income The amount of income above that earned by those in the bottom half of the population and below that earned by those in the upper half of the population.

membership boundary The divide between individuals who belong to a group and those who do not.

mercantilism A form of capitalism that accepts the general principal of free-market economics but allows significant government involvement in the economy in order to protect domestic economic interests; also known as protectionism.

merit system An approach in which members of the bureaucracy earn their initial positions and promotions on the basis of their qualifications and performance.

middle class Includes individuals in a variety of occupations who generate moderate levels of income, including small business owners and service sector employees.

militarism A state's preoccupation with having a strong military force and being prepared to use it aggressively.

military authoritarianism A type of authoritarian system, most common in Latin America and Africa, in which the government leaders are also military leaders.

military-industrial complex (MIC) A hypothesized form of iron triangle in the United States in which the military and Department of Defense, Congress, and defense contractors control and manipulate information to justify increased defense spending.

minimum necessary winning coalition A coalition involving only the parties required to gain control of a majority of the seats in the parliament.

minister The head of a government ministry.

minister without portfolio An individual considered to be a member of the government without heading a ministry.

ministry The term used in many countries for a cabinet-level department.

minority government A situation in which the prime minister comes from a party that does not control a majority of the seats in the parliament, and no official coalition agreement exists that creates such a majority.

mixed economies Economies with elements of capitalist and socialist practices.

mode of production The type of economic system based on methods of production, patterns of property ownership, and relations between workers and owners.

moderate ideology An ideology that advocates positions that fall between progressive and conservative approaches.

moderates Members of the opposition in a nondemocratic system who support cooperating with the government to encourage liberalization and democratization.

modernization theory The view that a country's move from underdevelopment to modernization can be understood from and modeled after development in the West.

monetary policy Government controls over the supply of money circulating in the economy and the interest rates charged when lending that money.

monopoly Control of all or nearly all the market for a given good or service by a single company.

mood Less intense than emotions but deeper and longer lasting feelings, which may not be tied to particular events.

most different approach A form of the comparative method examining cases that are very different from one another, but in which the dependent variable is similar.

most similar approach A form of the comparative method examining cases that are very much alike, but in which the dependent variable varies.

MP The acronym for member of parliament.

multi-member district (MMD) A system in which more than one candidate is selected from a particular electoral district.

multiparty system A party system with several important political parties, none of which generally gains a majority of the seats in the national legislature.

nation A large, self-aware segment of society united by shared cultural features and possessing a belief in the right of political control over a particular territory.

national identity A nation's self-awareness and sense of unity.

nationalism The pursuit of a set of rights for a nation, including the right of political control over a certain territory.

nationalist A leader of a movement based on nationalism.

nationalization A process in which the government takes over existing private companies or develops its own companies, which are often given monopoly status.

nation-state An independent state that exists for a single nation, it is the ultimate goal of most nationalists.

neo-corporatism A label used to refer to societal corporatism.

neoliberalism A pro-market economic approach that emphasizes reductions in the role of government to encourage economic growth.

nepotism Favoring relatives in granting positions or distributing resources.

new middle class Service workers, white-collar managers, and civil servants.

new professionalism theory The theoretical perspective, advanced by comparativist Alfred Stepan, that maintains that whether a professionalized military will intervene in politics depends on whether it sees its mission as primarily defending against external or internal threats.

new social movements Large movements that emerged following World War II to address noneconomic issues, such as women's rights and the environment.

new institutionalism A theoretical perspective emphasizing the importance of political institutional arrangements and the extent to which the political system represents historical changes, shapes individual choices, and reflects underlying values and identities.

newly industrialized countries (NICs) The more economically developed LDCs, found particularly in Asia and Latin America.

NIMBY An acronym for "not in my backyard" used to highlight the positions of many local issue groups.

noblesse oblige The belief among the British social, economic, and political elite that their position implies an obligation to enhance the quality of life for those less fortunate than themselves.

nomenklatura **system** The method of controlling bureaucratic appointments during the Soviet period by selecting individuals from a preexisting list of names (the nomenklatura).

noncoercive power Getting what one wants because of legitimacy.

nongovernmental organizations (NGOs) Political organizations whose members are individuals and/or groups.

norms Unwritten rules or expectations of behavior that help govern society.

North American Free Trade Agreement (NAFTA) A trade agreement involving Canada, Mexico, and the United States launched at the beginning of 1994.

old age and retirement policy Government efforts designed to protect the economic well-being of the elderly.

old middle class Small business owners.

old institutionalism A label for the traditional approach of political science to the study of political institutions, common from the late 1800s into the middle 1900s, which was highly descriptive.

oligarchic capitalism A term used by analysts to describe the Russian economic system of the 1990s, which they believed benefited a small number of economically and politically powerful individuals.

ombuds activities Actions by legislators to address concerns of specific members of the general population in systems where the legislators do not represent particular districts.

one-party dominant system A party system in which one large party directs the political system, but small parties exist and may compete in elections.

one-party system A party system in which one political party controls the government and voters have no option to choose an opposition party; also known as a single-party system.

open list proportional representation (open list PR) An electoral system in which voters cast a vote for a particular party but also play a role in the decision of which candidates receive the seats earned by that party.

operationalization The establishment of a particular measurement scheme for a concept, allowing one to observe and categorize data about it.

outer-directed linkage When domestic factors influence foreign policy.

out-group A group to which a particular individual does not belong but which is the same type of group (e.g., another ethnic group) as the in-group.

overlapping homelands A situation in which two or more nations lay claim to the same territory as part or all of their homeland.

pact A negotiated agreement during democratization that often establishes the institutional arrangements of the new democracy as well as specific policy approaches to be adhered to by the democratic government.

parliamentary supremacy Also known as parliamentary sovereignty, a feature of the Westminster system in which no other part of government can block an act of Parliament.

parliamentary system A political system in which the chief executive is directly responsible to the legislature and elections can be held at irregular intervals.

party authoritarianism A type of authoritarian system that involves the control of an authoritarian system by a single political party.

party corporatism The variant of corporatism in Mexico during the PRI's dominance of the Mexican political system.

party discipline The extent to which members of a legislature follow the direction of their party leaders.

party government theory A theory that contends a legislature's rules about the majority party's control of the institution's actions drives the political outcomes emanating from it.

party identification An individual's attachment to a particular political party.

party organization theory A theory that highlights the similarities and differences between political parties and businesses, interest groups, and government agencies.

party system A label based on the number of prominent political parties in a country.

peak organization A large interest group given official status in a corporatist system.

permanent secretary A senior member of the British civil service, just below the position of minister, who usually continues in this position if the minister is replaced.

physical capital The means of production used in an enterprise.

pluralism An approach to organizing interests in which groups form autonomously, lobby government officials, and compete with other groups engaged in similar activities.

pocketbook calculations Voters' assessments made on the basis of their personal economic well-being.

polar system The arrangement of poles—unipolar, bipolar, tripolar, or multipolar—at a point in time.

pole A dominant state in the international system.

policy An official decision on how to organize people, resolve disputes, or address other collective problems.

policy convergence The spread of policies from one country to another over time, with the result that policies become similar globally or in a particular region.

policy diffusion Another term for the spread of a policy approach from one country to another over time.

policy environment The set of internal structural factors that influence policy outcomes.

political culture A given population's underlying set of values and beliefs about politics and system of meaning for interpreting politics.

political economy The part of political science that focuses on the connections between economics and politics.

political elite Individuals who are far more involved in, and have a far greater impact on, daily politics than the rest of the population.

political ideology A set of beliefs or guiding principles about the proper functioning of politics and society.

political institution A set of rules or a purposive organization created to establish or influence rules that apply across society.

political participation The process of engaging in activities that are intended to influence the selection of officials and the policies that they create.

political party An organization that articulates its stance on a large number of policy positions and runs candidates for political office.

politics The set of activities that organizes individuals, resolves disputes, and maintains order in society through the creation and enforcement of rules and policies. Such decisions involve winners and losers; as a result, politics can also be thought of as the process of deciding "who gets what, when, and how" in a particular society.

portfolio A position in the government associated with a particular ministry.

postmaterialism theory A theory associated with political scientist Ronald Inglehart that emphasizes causes and consequences of differences between those who value freedom and quality of life and those who value order and veconomic prosperity.

postwar settlement The compromise in Western Europe after World War II between those who wanted a socialist system and those who desired one that was more free market.

power Defined by political scientists both as influence—A getting B to do something even if B does not want to do it—and as the capabilities that allow A to get B to do what A wants.

power as capabilities The conceptualization of power focusing on characteristics that would give a person the ability to influence important outcomes.

power as influence The conceptualization of power as the ability of A to get B to do what A wants, even if B does not want to do it.

power elite An elite made up of political, military, and economic leaders working in unison to control the government and produce policies that serve its interests.

praetorianism A political system in which the military is an active participant in politics.

preference system An electoral system that allows voters to rank candidates in a district race and uses the rankings to determine who fills the seat from that district.

presidential system A political system in which the general population votes for the chief executive, there are fixed terms for the chief executive and the legislature, and a separation of powers exists between the executive and legislative branches.

primary election An election for a particular political office in which candidates from the same political party compete against each other for the right to represent the party in a general election.

prime minister The label normally given to the chief executive of the government in a parliamentary system.

primordialism A theoretical approach that maintains that identity divisions are based on deep-rooted features (blood ties, physical appearance, etc.) that have naturally divided people throughout history.

privatization A process in which government-owned enterprises are sold to the general public or to foreign investors.

programmatic representation Linking the general population to the political elite through institutions such as political parties that stress particular political programs.

progressive ideology An ideology that supports an active role for government in income redistribution through use of taxes and government programs.

progressive tax A form of income tax in which the percentage of income paid in taxes increases as one's level of income increases.

proletariat A term used by political economy scholars like Karl Marx to refer to the individuals who use the means of production in their work but do not own them.

proportional representation (PR) An electoral system in which voters cast their votes for political parties and the percentage of the vote that each party receives translates into the percentage of seats that the party receives in the legislature.

prospective calculations Choosing candidates or parties to support on the basis of which politician or political party is expected to perform best in the future.

prosperity The overall wealth and standard of living of a country; it is usually measured by GDP per capita or similar statistics.

public administration A subfield of political science that studies the inner working of government institutions that produce public policy.

public policy An output of a political system designed to alter some aspect of political, economic, or social conditions.

purchasing power parity (PPP) An adjustment to statistics, such as GDP per capita, that takes into account the cost of living in a given country.

qualitative studies Studies that involve a small number of cases and do not allow the researcher to use statistical techniques to analyze the data.

quantitative studies Studies that involve a large number of cases, allowing the researcher to use statistical techniques to analyze the data.

quota A limit on the number or value of a certain product that can be imported.

race A large identity group whose members are perceived to be distinct on the basis of genetically transmitted physical differences.

race to the bottom A component of weak state theories that contends that states lower standards and reduce regulations to attract or maintain the presence of large corporations.

radical middle position A theoretical approach that incorporates elements of constructivism and primordialism, accepting that social and political elites play a central role in creating and triggering identity while highlighting the way in which historical events and existing circumstances constrain such efforts.

radicals Opponents who are unwilling to work with the nondemocratic rulers.

rational choice theory A wide-ranging theoretical perspective based on the assumption that individuals make rational decisions to maximize their interests that is used to explain both individual political behavior and collective actions.

rationality A condition in which people base decisions on reason and logic, leading them to act in ways that they believe will maximize their personal interests.

reactionary ideology An ideology that advocates a return to traditional social arrangements, including those that economically privilege one group over another.

realignment theory A theoretical perspective that contends that the fortunes of major political parties remain stable for long periods, followed by a dramatic change.

redistributive policies Policies aimed at reducing poverty by making the wealth in a particular society less unequal.

reds Bureaucrats in Communist countries who are more committed to Communist ideology than to technical expertise.

reequilibration An overhaul of a democratic system in response to a major crisis.

reformers Members of the nondemocratic political elite committed to liberalization and possibly to democratization; also known as "soft-liners."

regime The political system of a state.

regime transition The process of changing from one type of political system to another.

regulatory policy A set of rules that places restrictions on the activities of individuals or groups.

religion An organized system of beliefs and devotion regarding a spiritual force or forces.

repeated experiences Events that recur or are sustained over time that can shape political culture.

research question A puzzle that does not have an obvious answer and forms the basis for a research project.

reserved powers Powers designated to a particular level of government that another level of government cannot take away.

resource curse The tendency for developing countries with an exportable commodity to focus on the extraction of that resource at the expense of broader economic development; associated with government corruption and failure to develop a middle class.

retrospective calculations Choosing candidates or parties to support on the basis of recent performance by the government.

reverse wave A period with a sizable reduction in the number of democracies globally.

rule of law A condition in which laws are passed according to the constitution, government officials are not above the law, and society respects contracts as legally binding.

runoff An election in which the two candidates who receive the most votes in the first round compete in a second round.

satisficing Choosing the first acceptable solution rather than searching for a best solution.

science A form of systematic study undertaken to better understand nature and human behavior that relies on empirical data, employs a generally accepted methodology to allow others to replicate findings, and focuses on questions about how things are rather than how things ought to be.

second order policy change Policy modification in which a policy's underlying goals are unchanged, but significant changes are implemented in how the goal is pursued.

second past the post (SPTP) An electoral system, also known as the principle of the first minority, that reserves seats in a particular body for the party that finishes second in a district election.

secretary The head of a U.S. cabinet department, who is also a member of the cabinet.

semiauthoritarianism A political system in which elements of democracy are integrated into an otherwise authoritarian system.

semidemocracy A political system that is similar to semiauthoritarianism but has more democratic features.

semi-presidential system A political system that has both a directly elected president with significant powers and a prime minister who is responsible to the parliament (and, in some cases, to the president as well).

shadow government A group of MPs who would replace the current government if the opposition party or parties were to win the next election.

shared powers Powers held by both the central and the lower levels of government.

single case study Another name that is sometimes used for the term case study.

single transferable vote (STV) system An electoral system that combines preference voting with multi-member districts.

single-member district (SMD) An electoral district in which voters choose only one representative, often using the plurality rule to determine the winner.

social cleavages The categories of identity that create us-them divisions in a society.

social democratic ideology An ideology that traditionally supported nationalization of industry but today focuses more on maintaining welfare state protections.

social market economy (SME) The economic approach that developed in Germany, which united corporatism and welfare state protections with traditional social values.

social movement An informal network sharing a common viewpoint; working to promote or resist certain political, economic, or social changes; and engaging in activities such as mass protests.

socialism An economic approach that emphasizes government ownership of the means of production and government control of economic decisions such as the supply and prices of particular products; also known as central planning.

socialization The process of transmitting components of a political culture to the next generation through social institutions, such as families, churches, and schools.

societal corporatism A variant of corporatism in which the main interest groups form independently of state action, force the state to accept them in the policy-making process, and have greater autonomy from state control.

society A large group of people connected through interactions and common traits, such as proximity.

sociological new institutionalism A theoretical perspective that sees institutions as reflecting society's underlying culture rather than as the product of rational choices in the pursuit of increased efficiency.

sociotropic calculations Assessments by voters that take into account the well-being of society as a whole.

sovereignty The legal right of a state to conduct its own affairs within its territory; also the actual ability to control the territory.

specialist approach An approach to filling positions in the bureaucracy in which individuals are hired to fill specific roles in particular government departments.

spoils system An approach in which bureaucrats get their initial jobs and promotions on the basis of connections to top government officials or favors done for such officials.

standing committee A committee that meets on a regular basis.

stare decisis The idea that a previous judicial decision creates a binding precedent.

state The basic unit of political organization in the world, combining a permanent population, a defined territory, governing institutions, sovereignty over its territory, and international recognition.

state capitalism A system in which the government neither engages in economic planning nor oversees an extensive welfare state, but owns certain individual enterprises, typically in lucrative industries such as energy.

state control system An interest group system in which the state creates and controls the main interest groups; groups have no autonomy from the state.

state corporatism A variant of corporatism in which the state recognizes the main interest groups; the groups have little autonomy, and they are "junior partners" during policy making.

state pension Regular payments from the government to individuals after they reach retirement age.

state-led capitalism A system in which the government intervenes in the economy to guide economic activities in an effort to foster economic growth.

stateless A designation for those who lack citizenship in any state.

statutory judicial review The power to judge whether government policies are consistent with existing government statutes.

strong state theories A set of theories that argue that even with increasing globalization, governments have maintained and even enhanced their ability to tax, spend, and regulate.

structural approach A broad approach to studying politics that seeks to explain political outcomes by looking at the effects of the underlying economic, social, or political-institutional setting in a country or set of countries.

subgovernment theory A theoretical perspective that emphasizes the extent to which interest groups concerned about a particular issue create a subgovernment by working closely with interested legislators and bureaucrats.

subsidiarity An idea from Social Catholicism that individuals have a right to make decisions for themselves and that, as much as possible, families and small social organizations should provide economic protection and distribute social goods to individuals.

subsidy A government disbursement to a company that allows the company to sell its products for less, both domestically and abroad.

suspensive veto The power, often given to the upper house of a bicameral legislature, to delay enactment of legislation but not prevent it.

systems theory The name given to the efforts by David Easton to model the political process as a set of inputs (demands and supports) that feed into the political system and outputs (policies) that flow from it.

tariff A tax on an imported good or service.

tautology A statement that is true by definition.

tax credit A reduction in the tax an individual owes on income subject to tax.

tax deduction A reduction in the amount of an individual's income subject to tax.

technocrats Bureaucrats who emphasize technical expertise and often have significant scientific knowledge.

territorial autonomy A group's control of much of what happens in a particular region that is not officially independent.

theocracy A political system in which religious leaders hold the main government positions and religious law is the basis of policy decisions.

theory A set of propositions about how and why phenomena relate to one another in a variety of settings.

theory of "going public" A theoretical perspective that highlights the way that the U.S. president can promote specific policies by using the mass media to change public opinion.

theory of parliamentary superiority Juan Linz's view that presidential systems encourage political conflicts without providing the means to resolve them.

theory of presidential system design Donald Horowitz's argument that certain presidential system features can enhance political stability compared with parliamentary approaches.

third order policy change Policy modification in which the goals behind a policy are dramatically altered.

threshold A rule in PR systems that forces parties to receive a certain percentage of the vote before they receive seats in the legislature.

tort law Judicial action to address disputes involving torts (harms done to an individual), including injury and nuisance.

totalitarianism A regime type defined by an effort to remake society using an official ideology, a single mass political party, a secret police force employing terror against the population, a monopoly over means of communication, a monopoly over weapons in society, and a command economy.

trade policy Government regulation of the import of products produced outside the country as well as products produced within that country for export.

traditional authority A type of authority based the leader's family's claim to the throne and/or the belief that God has granted the leader the right to rule.

transference A concept that highlights the extent to which contact or experiences are filtered through past contacts or relationships with similar individuals or settings.

tribe An identity group that is similar to a clan but larger; sometimes made up of a number of clans.

triggering events Incidents, such as the death of an authoritarian leader or a severe economic crisis, that initiate political transitions.

two-and-a-half party system A party system in which two large parties exist alongside a third party that receives a smaller but notable share of the national vote.

two-party system A party system in which two main parties compete for majority control of the government; small parties may exist but play no role in national electoral outcomes.

unconventional participation The set of political activities not approved by the political elite, including strikes, boycotts, and terrorism.

underclass The poorest individuals in society who have few chances for improving their lives.

unemployment policy Government programs to assist the unemployed, including economic assistance and job training.

unfunded mandates Commands from higher levels of government to lower levels of government to take certain actions without the money necessary to cover expenses.

unicameral The label for a legislature that has only one house (chamber).

unitary system A political system in which the central government has authority over lower levels of government, and lower levels have no powers reserved for them.

upper class The wealthiest and most powerful members of society.

urbanization A dramatic increase in the portion of a country's population that lives in large cities.

variable An item whose existence or value can change.

vertical social relations Social relations in societies that emphasize an authority hierarchy.

veto points Individuals or collective political bodies whose failure to accept a policy change results in the policy's not being adopted.

vote of censure Another name for a vote of no confidence.

vote of confidence A vote called for by the sitting government in a parliamentary system; if this vote fails, the government is forced to resign, and new elections may be held.

vote of no confidence A vote sponsored by the opposition, which results in the formation of a new government or the holding of new parliamentary elections if it passes.

weak state theories A set of theories that argue that globalization limits the ability of governments to tax, spend, and regulate.

Welfare State An approach in which a broad set of government programs guarantees economic and social assistance, such as health care and retirement benefits.

Westminster model of democracy Dahl's term for a democratic system that combines a parliamentary approach with a FPTP (plurality) electoral system.

working class Includes individuals in a variety of occupations, such as manual laborers, who have historically generated relatively low levels of income.

working-class deference The belief by the lower classes, present throughout English and British history, that the British elite have the authority to rule over them.

Notes

Chapter 1

1. "Profile: Egypt's Wael Ghonim," BBC News, February 8, 2011, http://www.bbc.co.uk/news/world-middle-east-12400529 (accessed February 18, 2011).

2. Ibid.

3. "Extra: Revolution 2.0," CBS News/60 Minutes video, http://www.cbsnews.com/video/watch/?id=7349173n (accessed February 18, 2011). Ghonim himself provided the name "Revolution 2.0."

4. Mark I. Lichbach and Alan S. Zuckerman, "Research Traditions and Theory in Comparative Politics: An Introduction," in *Comparative Politics: Rationality, Culture, and Structure*, ed. Lichbach and Zuckerman (Cambridge, UK: Cambridge University Press, 1997), 4.

5. Harold Lasswell, *Politics: Who Gets What, When, and How* (New York: McGraw-Hill, 1936).

6. Max Weber, *From Max Weber: Essays in Sociology*, trans. and ed. H. H. Gerth and C. Wright Mills (New York: Oxford University Press, 1946), 78.

7. See Lowell W. Barrington, "The Making of Citizenship Policy in the Baltic States," *Georgetown Immigration Law Journal* 13, no. 2 (1999): 159–199.

8. Linda Weiss, "Introduction: Bringing Domestic Institutions Back In," in *State in the Global Economy: Bringing Domestic Institutions Back In*, ed. Linda Weiss (Cambridge, UK: Cambridge University Press, 2003), 20.

9. Weber, *From Max Weber*, 78.

10. Ibid, 82.

11. See Anthony Richmond, "Ethnic Nationalism: Social Science Paradigms," *International Social Science Journal* 39, no. 111 (February 1987): 3–18.

12. For a discussion of ethnic boundaries, see Fredrick Barth, ed., *Ethnic Groups and Boundaries: The Social Organization of Cultural Difference* (London: Allen and Unwin, 1969).

13. See Clifford Geertz, *The Interpretation of Cultures* (New York: Basic Books, 1973).

14. Bent Flyvbjerg, "Five Misunderstandings about Case-Study Research," *Qualitative Inquiry* 12, no. 2 (April 2006): 230; italics added. Flyvbjerg adds that it is easier to understand in general how the critical case would work than it is to identify such a case ahead of time, but he gives the example of a classic study by Robert Michels published in 1911. Michels (a student of Max Weber) proposed that all social and political organizations have a tendency to develop an oligarchic leadership structure. According to Flyvbjerg, by choosing a "horizontally structured grassroots organization with strong democratic ideals"—that is, an organization that one would not expect to be ruled by an oligarchy—Michels was able to "test the universality of the oligarchy thesis" through the study of a single case (p. 231).

15. Mark I. Lichbach, "Social Theory and Comparative Politics," in *Comparative Politics: Rationality, Culture, and Structure*, ed. Lichbach and Alan S. Zuckerman (Cambridge, UK: Cambridge University Press, 1997), 243.

Chapter 2

1. Dulue Mbachu, "The Poverty of Oil Wealth in Nigeria's Delta," *ISN Security Watch*, March 2, 2006, http://www.isn.ethz.ch/news/sw/details.cfm?id=14670 (accessed December 21, 2007).

2. Theda Skocpol characterizes Marx's argument: "For Marx, the key to any society is its mode of production or specific combination of socioeconomic forces of production (technology and division of labor) and class relations of property ownership and surplus appropriation." Theda Skocpol, *States and Social Revolutions: A Comparative Analysis of France, Russia, and China* (Cambridge, UK: Cambridge University Press, 1979), 7.

3. This figure is based on a comparison of the percentage of non-Hispanic whites and African Americans in poverty, using the official U.S. government poverty measure. See "Annual Demographic Survey, March Supplement: The Effects of Government Taxes and Transfers on Income and Poverty," U.S. Census Bureau, http://pubdb3.census.gov/macro/032006/altpov/newpov01_000.htm (accessed October 20, 2008).

4. Carmen DeNavas-Walt, Bernadette D. Proctor, and Jessica C. Smith, "Income, Poverty, and Health Insurance Coverage in the United States: 2008," U.S. Census Bureau, http://www.census.gov/prod/2009pubs/p60-236.pdf (accessed February 8, 2010); Alexandra Harris, "U.S. Household Income Falls for 2nd Straight Year, Census Says," Bloomberg.com, September 28, 2010, http://www.bloomberg.com/news/2010-09-28/median-household-income-in-u-s-falls-second-year-to-50-221-census-says.html (accessed March 2, 2011).

5. Sources on class structure and economic equality include the Organization for Economic Cooperation and Development (OECD), http://www.oecd.org/; the United Nations Human Development Index (UNHDI), http://hdr.undp.org/; the World Bank's World Development Index, http://www.worldbank.org/.

6. Karl Marx, *The Eighteenth Brumaire of Louis Napoleon*, in *Karl Marx: Selected Writings*, ed. David McLellan (Oxford, UK: Oxford University Press, 2000), p. 347.

7. Among those who discussed France's "200 families" was Leon Trotsky in his 1938 work, *The Death Agony of Capitalism and the Tasks of the Fourth International*, http://www.marxists.org/archive/trotsky/1938/tp/index.htm (accessed July 24, 2008).

8. Class consciousness is related to the concept of alienation, which was at the center of Marx's early writings. See T. B. Bottomore, trans. and ed., *Karl Marx: Early Writings* (New York, McGraw-Hill, 1964).

9. Russell J. Dalton, *Citizen Politics: Public Opinion and Political Parties in Advanced Western Democracies*, 2nd ed. (Chatham, NJ: Chatham House, 1996), 174.

10. Friedrich Schneider, "Size and Measurement of the Informal Economy in 110 Countries around the World," paper presented at a workshop of Australian National Tax Centre, ANU, Canberra, Australia, July 17, 2002, 3, http://rru.worldbank.org/Documents/PapersLinks/informal_economy.pdf (accessed October 20, 2008).

11. See *The Inequality Predicament: Report on the World Social Situation 2005* (New York: United Nations Department of Economic and Social Affairs, 2005), ch. 2, www.un.org/esa/socdev/rwss/media%2005/cd-docs/fullreport05.htm (accessed July 15, 2008).

12. Ibid., 33.

13. International Monetary Fund World Economic Outlook Database, October 2010, http://www.imf.org/external/pubs/ft/weo/2010/02/weodata/index.aspx (accessed March 2, 2011).

14. Edward N. Wolff, "Recent Trends in Household Wealth in the United States: Rising Debt and the Middle-Class Squeeze—an Update to 2007," Levy Economics Institute Working Paper, No. 589, March 2010, http://www.levyinstitute.org/pubs/wp_589.pdf (accessed March 1, 2011).

15. Jon Gertner, "The Rise and Fall of the G.D.P.," *New York Times Sunday Magazine*, May 16, 2010, MM60.

16. See "Billionaires List: The 20 Richest People in the World," *Forbes*, March 29, 2010, http://www.forbes.com/forbes/2010/0329/billionaires-2010-wealth-richest-people-slim-helu-gates-buffett-top-20.html (accessed May 17, 2010).

17. International Monetary Fund's World Economic Outlook data, April 2010, http://www.imf.org/external/pubs/ft/weo/2010/01/weodata/index.aspx (accessed May 17, 2010). Gross domestic product is measured in U.S. dollars at current prices.

18. This term is borrowed from the title of the best book available on the history of the Soviet Union: Ronald G. Suny, *The Soviet Experiment: Russia, the USSR, and the Successor States* (New York: Oxford University Press, 1998).

19. Lester Thurow, *Head to Head: The Coming Economic Battle among Japan, Europe, and America* (New York: William Morrow, 1992).

20. David Coates, "Models of Capitalism in the New World Order," *Political Studies* 47, no. 4 (1999): 643–661.

21. Ibid.

22. Francis Fukuyama and Sanjay Marwah, "Dimensions of Development," *Journal of Democracy* 11, no. 4 (2000): 80–94.

23. "Globalization Must Work for the Poor, Says New Research Report," press release of the World Bank (no. 2002/132/S), December 5, 2001, http://go.worldbank.org/DQP7G280Y1 (accessed June 12, 2008).

24. The GDP-related statistics in this chapter's Topic in Countries sections come from the International Monetary Fund World Economic Outlook database, October 2010, http://www.imf.org/external/pubs/ft/weo/2010/02/weodata/index.aspx (accessed March 2, 2011).

25. See Norman Flynn, "Modernising British Government," *Parliamentary Affairs* 52, no. 4 (October 1999): 586.

26. The rankings are based on a score from 0 to 100, calculated from a series of 0 to 10 scales on ten indicators. These indicators include concepts such as business freedom, the size of government spending compared to the economy as a whole, and freedom from corruption. The 2010 rankings are available at http://www.heritage.org/index/pdf/2010/index2010_ranking.pdf (accessed February 4, 2010).

27. Herbert Kitschelt and Wolfgang Streeck, "From Stability to Stagnation: Germany at the Beginning of the Twenty-First Century," *West European Politics* 26, no. 4 (2003): 1–34, esp. Table 6.

28. Average unemployment in the east rose from 16.5 percent in 1991 to 18.3 percent in 2004. For both years, eastern unemployment was more than twice as high as in the western states. See Bertrand Benoit, "Growing Apart: 15 Years After the Wall's Fall, Germany's Two Halves Diverge," *Financial Times*, September 23, 2004.

29. Stephen Padgett, "Political Economy: The German Model under Stress," in *Developments in German Politics*, ed. Stephen Padgett, William E. Paterson, and Gordon Smith (Durham, NC: Duke University Press, 2003), 123.

30. Charles S. Maier, *Dissolution: The Crisis of Communism and the End of East Germany* (Princeton, NJ: Princeton University Press, 1997), ch. 2.

31. Herbert Kitschelt and Wolfgang Streeck, "From Stability to Stagnation: Germany at the Beginning of the Twenty-first Century," *West European Politics* 26, no. 4 (2003): 1–34, Table 1.

32. Benoit, "Growing Apart."

33. Anton Hemerijck and Philip Manow, "The Experience of Negotiated Reform in the German and Dutch Welfare State," paper presented at the Varieties of Welfare Capitalism conference, Max Planck Institute for the Study of Societies, Cologne, June 11–13, 1998; Gøsta Esping-Andersen, *The Social Foundations of Post-Industrial Economies* (Oxford, UK: Oxford University Press, 1999); Philip Manow and Eric Seils, "Adjusting Badly: The German Welfare State, Structural Change and the Open Economy," in *Welfare and Work in the Open Economy: Diverse Responses to Common Challenges*, vol. 2, ed. Fritz W. Scharpf and Vivien A. Schmidt (Oxford, UK: Oxford University Press, 2000).

34. Gosta Esping-Andersen, *The Three Worlds of Welfare Capitalism* (Princeton, NJ: Princeton University Press, 1990); Esping-Andersen, *The Social Foundations of Post-Industrial Economies*.

35. On the influence of the Catholic Church in social policy, see Kees van Kersbergen, *Social Capitalism: A Study of Christian Democracy and the Welfare* State (London and New York: Routledge, 1995); Esping-Andersen, *The Three Worlds of Welfare Capitalism*. The Catholic Center Party was a key actor in enacting social welfare legislation in the Bismarckian and Weimar eras. Social Catholicism, as embodied in papal encyclicals of the nineteenth and twentieth centuries, championed social policy as a way to humanize capitalism.

36. Wolfgang Streeck, "German Capitalism: Does It Exist? Can It Survive?" *New Political Economy* 2, no. 2 (1997): 237–256.

37. See Luisa Kroll, Matthew Miller and Tatiana Serafin, "The World's Billionaires," March 11, 2009, http://www.forbes.com/2009/03/11/worlds-richest-people-billionaires-2009-billionaires_land.html (accessed February 9, 2010); Naazneen Karmali, "India's 100 Richest," November 18, 2009, http://www.forbes.com/2009/11/18/india-100-richest-india-billionaires-09-wealth_land.html (accessed February 6, 2010).

38. See "India's Rural Employment Guarantee Act," UNDP Poverty Reduction, http://www.undp.org/poverty/projects_india.shtml (accessed February 8, 2010).

39. P. Sainath, *Everybody Loves a Good Drought: Stories from India's Poorest Districts* (London: Review, 1996).

40. François Bourguignon, "The Poverty-Growth-Inequality Triangle," paper prepared for the Conference on Poverty, Inequality and Growth, Agence Française de Développement / EU Development Network, Paris, November 13, 2003.

41. "World Gas: Mexico—Reform or Bust," *Petroleum Economist*, May 19, 2003, 23–26.

42. See Maria Victoria Murillo, "Political Bias in Policy Convergence: Privatization Choices in Latin America," *World Politics* 54, no. 4 (2002): 464.

43. On the issue of drug violence in Mexico, see Phil Williams, "Drug Trafficking, Violence, and the State in Mexico," *Op-Ed*, April 2009.

44. "Free Trade on Trial: Ten Years after NAFTA," *Economist*, January 3, 2004, 13–16.

45. David Korten, *When Corporations Rule the World*, 2nd ed. (Bloomfield, CT: Kumarian Press, 2001), is a more readable but also more alarmist and less scholarly account of the topic than is Dani Rodrik, *Has Globalization Gone Too Far?* (Washington, DC: Institute of International Economics, 1997).

46. For contrasting views of the race to the bottom idea, see Alan Tonelson, *The Race to the Bottom* (Boulder, CO: Westview Press, 2000); Thomas L. Friedman, *The Lexus and the Olive Tree* (New York: Farrar, Straus, and Giroux, 1999).

47. On corruption, however, a large amount of systematic research—both qualitative and quantitative—has been conducted. One leading source is Transparency International, http://www.transparency.org.

48. Ross Perot, businessman and independent candidate for U.S. president in 1992 and 1996, was especially fond of the "giant sucking sound" phrase when arguing against the launch of NAFTA.

49. It is important to note that this emerging crisis was due only in part to economic issues. Investors were also concerned about political stability after the emergence of the Zapatista National Liberation Army (EZLN, see Chapter 9) and the assassinations of PRI presidential candidate Luis Donaldo Colosio and the PRI's secretary general Ruiz Massieu in 1994.

50. "Free Trade on Trial."

51. "The World Factbook: Brazil," https://www.cia.gov/library/publications/the-world-factbook/geos/br.html, July 15, 2008 (accessed July 31, 2008).

52. Benjamin Senauer and Linda Goetz, "The Growing Middle Class in Developing Countries and the Market for High-Value Food Products," paper prepared for the Workshop on Global Markets for High-Value Food Economic Research Service, USDA, Washington, DC, February 14, 2003, 5.

53. Lloyd Amaghionyeodiwe and Tokunbo Osinubi, "Poverty Reduction Policies and Pro-Poor Growth in Nigeria," *Brazilian Electronic Journal of Economics* 6, no. 1 (2004).

54. See "Country Summary: Nigeria," United States Census Bureau International Data Base (IDB), http://www.census.gov/ipc/www/idb/country.php (accessed January 7, 2010).

55. Mbachu, "The Poverty of Oil Wealth in Nigeria's Delta."

56. For examples of dependency theory, see Raúl Prebisch, "The Economic Development of Latin America and Its Principal Problems," *Economic Bulletin for Latin America* 7, no. 1 (1962): 1–22; Theotonio dos Santos, "The Structure of Dependence," *American Economic Review* 60, no. 2 (May 1970): 231–236; Immanuel Wallerstein, *The Modern World System I: Capitalist Agriculture and the Origins of the European World-Economy in the Sixteenth Century* (New York: Academic Press, 1974). For a critical overview of the theory, see Robert A. Packenham, *The Dependency Movement: Scholarship and Politics in Development Studies* (Cambridge, MA: Harvard University Press, 1992). Reading various works by Brazilian sociologist Fernando Henrique Cardoso (who also served two terms as president of Brazil) is an interesting exercise. Initially one of the leading proponents of dependency theory, by the 1970s Cardoso had become a critic of the perspective.

57. See the table on Nigerian attitudes in "Nigeria: Views of the Free Market," Pew Global Attitudes Project Key Indicators Database, http://pewglobal.org/databse/?indicator=18&country=160&response=Agree (accessed February 4, 2010).

58. David Hoffman, *The Oligarchs: Wealth and Power in the New Russia* (New York: Public Affairs, 2002).

59. Stephen Sestanovich, "Force, Money, and Pluralism," *Journal of Democracy* 15, no. 3 (2004): 36.

60. Minxin Pei, "Contradictory Trends and Confusing Signals," *Journal of Democracy* 14, no. 1 (2003): 75.

61. An Chen, "The New Inequality," *Journal of Democracy* 14, no. 1 (2003): 55.

62. Minxin Pei, "Contradictory Trends and Confusing Signals," *Journal of Democracy* 14, no. 1 (2003): 75. The IMF puts the bad debt figure for China at 40 percent, above most other countries. The U.S. figure is well below 10 percent, while even Mexico is only slightly higher than 10 percent.

63. The work most often associated with post–World War II claims about economic development and democracy is Seymour Martin Lipset, "Some Social Requisites of Democracy: Economic Development and Political Legitimacy," *American Political Science Review* 53, no. 1 (March 1959): 69–105.

64. Jean-Marie Guehenno, "Globalization and the International System," *Journal of Democracy* 10, no. 1 (1999): 31.

65. Ibid., 32.

66. Sanam Vakil, "Iran: The Gridlock between Demography and Democracy," *SAIS Review* 24, no. 2 (Summer–Fall 2004): 45–53.

67. See Judith A. Teichman, "Competing Visions of Democracy and Development in the Era of Neoliberalism in Mexico and Chile," *International Political Science Review* 30, no. 1 (2009): 69.

68. Ibid., 67.

Chapter 3

1. Alexis de Tocqueville, *Democracy in America*, Part II, trans. Henry Reeve (London: Longman, Green, Longman, and Roberts, 1862), 47.

2. Marc Howard Ross, "Culture and Identity in Comparative Political Analysis," in *Comparative Politics: Rationality, Culture, and Structure*, ed. Mark I. Lichbach and Alan S. Zuckerman (Cambridge, UK: Cambridge University Press, 1997), 44.

3. François Furet, "The *Ancien Régime* and the French Revolution," in *Realms of Memory: Rethinking the French Past, Volume 1, Conflicts and Divisions*, ed. Pierre Nora (New York: Columbia University Press, 1996), 79–108.

4. Ibid.

5. Francis Fukuyama, *The End of History and the Last Man* (New York: Free Press, 1992).

6. Leonard Freedman, *Politics and Policy in Britain* (New York: Longman, 1996), 27.

7. Ibid.

8. "Geert Hofstede Cultural Dimensions," http://www.geert-hofstede.com/hofstede_dimensions.php (accessed May 29, 2011).

9. "Geert Hofstede Cultural Dimensions: United Kingdom," http://www.geert-hofstede.com/hofstede_united_kingdom.shtml (accessed May 29, 2011).

10. Ibid., 293.

11. Gabriel A. Almond and Sidney Verba, *The Civic Culture: Political Attitudes and Democracy in Five Nations* (Princeton, NJ: Princeton University Press, 1963).

12. Lyman Tower Sargent, *Contemporary Political Ideologies*, 12th ed. (Belmont, CA: Wadsworth/Thomson, 2003), 63.

13. Most scholars who study nationalism connect the emergence of modern nationalism with the American and French Revolutions. In her well-known book *Nationalism: Five Roads to Modernity* (Cambridge, MA: Harvard University Press, 1992), Leah Greenfeld contends that nationalism had developed in England nearly two centuries earlier.

14. See Jesse Norman and Janan Ganesh, "Compassionate Conservatism: What It Is and Why We Need It," 2006, http://www.jessenorman.com/downloads/Compassionate_Conservatism.pdf, p. 1 (accessed February 22, 2011).

15. David P. Conradt, *The German Polity*, 8th ed. (New York: Pearson/Longman, 2005), 80–89.

16. Charles Maier, *Dissolution: The Crisis of Communism and the End of East Germany* (Princeton, NJ: Princeton University Press, 1997), esp. chs. 1 and 2.

17. Gaston V. Rimlinger, *Welfare Policy and Industrialization in Europe, America and Russia* (New York: John Wiley, 1971), 138–148; Gordon Smith, *Democracy in Western Germany: Parties and Politics in the Federal Republic* (New York: Holmes & Meier, 1986).

18. Pavan K. Varma, *Being Indian: The Truth about Why the 21st Century Will Be India's* (New Delhi: Penguin, 2004), 14.

19. Ibid., 208.

20. Dipankar Gupta, *Mistaken Modernity, India between Worlds* (New Delhi: Harper Collins, 2000), 30.

21. Ibid., 211. According to Gupta, there are so many "mahatmas" in India because "in societies which resist institutionalization, there is always a need for great people" (Ibid., 42).

22. Ibid., 61.

23. See "Geert Hofstede Cultural Dimensions: India," http://www.geert-hofstede.com/hofstede_india.shtml (accessed July 31, 2008).

24. Varma, *Being Indian*, 193.

25. "Geert Hofstede Cultural Dimensions: Mexico," http://www.geert-hofstede.com/hofstede_mexico.shtml (accessed May 28, 2011).

26. Ibid.

27. Stephen D. Morris, "Corruption and Mexican Political Culture," *Journal of the Southwest* 23, no. 3 (2003): 671–708.

28. Alejandro Moreno and Patricia Méndez, "Attitudes toward Democracy: Mexico in Comparative Perspective," working paper, http://www.-worldvaluessurvey.org/Upload/5_ArticleMoreno Mendez.pdf (accessed August 2, 2008).

29. For more on the *jeito*, see Keith Rosenn, "The Jeito: Brazil's Institutional Bypass of the Formal Legal System and Its Developmental Implications," *American Journal of Comparative Law* 19, no. 3 (Summer 1971): 514–549.

30. "Geert Hofstede Cultural Dimensions: Brazil," http://www.geert-hofstede.com/hofstede_brazil.shtml (accessed May 28, 2011).

31. Ibid.

32. Latinobarómetro 2007 Report ("Informe Latinobarómetro 2007: Banco de Datos en Línea"), November 2007, p. 93, http://www.latinobarometro.org/ (accessed July 30, 2008).

33. "Brazil: Statistics," http://www.unicef.org/infobycountry/brazil_statistics.html (accessed July 31, 2008).

34. Latinobarómetro 2007 Report, 75.

35. M. A. O. Aluko, "The Impact of Culture on Organizational Performance in Selected Textile Firms in Nigeria," *Nordic Journal of African Studies* 12, no. 2 (2003): 170.

36. See James T. Gire, "The Varying Effect of Individualism–Collectivism on Preference for Methods of Conflict Resolution," *Canadian Journal of Behavioural Science* 29, no. 1 (January 1997): 38–43.

37. Ronald Inglehart and Daphna Oyserman, "Individualism, Autonomy, and Self-Expression: The Human Development Syndrome," in *Comparing Cultures: Dimensions of Culture in a Comparative Perspective*, ed. Henk Vinken, Joseph Soeters, and Peter Ester (Leiden, Netherlands: Brill, 2004). 74–96, Figure 2.

38. Vladimir Shlapentokh, *A Normal Totalitarian Society: How the Soviet Union Functioned and How It Collapsed* (Armonk, NY: M.E. Sharpe, 2001).

39. See Ronald Inglehart and Christian Welzel, *Modernization, Cultural Change, and Democracy: The Human Development Sequence* (Cambridge, UK: Cambridge University Press, 2005).

40. "Geert Hofstede Cultural Dimensions: China," http://www.geert-hofstede.com/hofstede_china.shtml (accessed May 29, 2011).

41. Ronald Inglehart, *Culture Shift in Advanced Industrial Society* (Princeton, NJ: Princeton University Press, 1989).

42. Lampton made this comment during an interview on PBS's *Frontline* in the fall of 2001. "Interview: David Lampton," *Frontline* interview transcript, http://www.pbs.org/wgbh/pages/frontline/shows/china/-interviews/lampton.html (accessed July 21, 2008).

43. "Geert Hofstede Cultural Dimensions: Iran," http://www.geert-hofstede.com/hofstede_iran.shtml (accessed May 29, 2011).

44. Ibid.

45. Inglehart and Oyserman, "Individualism, Autonomy, and Self-Expression," Figure 2.

46. Ibid.

47. George Ritzer, *The McDonaldization of Society* (London: Sage, 1993).

48. Samuel P. Huntington, *The Clash of Civilizations and the Remaking of World Order* (New York: Simon & Schuster, 1996).

49. Benjamin R. Barber, *Jihad versus McWorld* (New York: Ballantine, 1995), 4.

50. Ibid., 9.

51. Ibid., 221.

52. Japanese business leaders first used the term *glocalization* (the uniting of global trends and local distinctiveness) in the 1980s, and it entered the social science lexicon in the West in the early 1990s.

53. Mahmood Sariolghalam, "Understanding Iran: Getting Past Stereotypes and Mythology," *Washington Quarterly* 26, no. 4 (Autumn 2003): 69–82.

54. Clarisa Pérez-Armendáriz and David Crow, "Do Migrants Remit Democracy? International Migration, Political Beliefs, and Behavior in Mexico," *Comparative Political Studies* 43, no. 1 (January 2010): 120.

55. Ibid., 142.

56. Ibid., 135.

57. Ibid., 126.

Chapter 4

1. "Egyptian Marchers Protest Church Violence," UPI, May 9, 2011, http://www.upi.com/Top_News/World-News/2011/05/09/Egyptian-marchers-protest-church-violence/UPI-90761304940313/ (accessed June 1, 2011).

2. Benedict Anderson, *Imagined Communities: Reflections on the Origin and Spread of Nationalism* (London: Verso, 1991).

3. David Laitin, *Identity in Formation: The Russian-Speaking Populations in the Near Abroad* (Ithaca, NY: Cornell University Press, 1998).

4. Donald L. Horowitz, *Ethnic Groups in Conflict* (Berkeley: University of California Press, 1985), 12.

5. Ibid., 57.

6. Cited in Eric Dickson and Kenneth Scheve, "Social Identity, Political Speech, and Electoral Competition," paper presented at the Eighth Meeting of the Laboratory in Comparative Ethnic Processes, University of Washington at Seattle, October 17, 2003, 1.

7. Peter J. Schraeder, "From Irredentism to Secession: The Decline of Pan-Somali Nationalism," in *After Independence: Making and Protecting the Nation in Postcolonial and Postcommunist States*, ed. Lowell W. Barrington (Ann Arbor: University of Michigan Press, 2006), 107–137.

8. Thomas J. Reese, *Inside the Vatican: The Politics and Organization of the Catholic Church* (Cambridge, MA: Harvard University Press, 1996), 1.

9. Some scholars also treat Sufism as a third key division within Islam. Sufism is a variant of Islam centered on the idea that one can find love and deeper knowledge through a mystical path that links the individual more directly with Allah.

10. See Ronald Inglehart and Pippa Norris, "The Developmental Theory of the Gender Gap: Women's and Men's Voting Behavior in Global Perspective," *International Political Science Review* 21, no. 4 (2000): 441–463.

11. See, for example, Lowell Barrington, "Examining Rival Theories of Demographic Influences on Political Support: The Power of Ethnic, Linguistic, and Regional Divisions in Ukraine," *European Journal of Political Research* 41, no. 4 (June 2002): 455–491.

12. On relations among the Canadian provinces, see Stephen Brooks, *Canadian Democracy: An Introduction*, 4th ed. (New York: Oxford University Press, 2004).

13. The term *bargain* has especially been applied to the integrationist approach taken in Malaysia. See Diane Mauzy, "From Malay Nationalism to a Malaysian Nation?" in *After Independence: Making and Protecting the Nation in Postcolonial and Postcommunist States*, ed. Lowell W. Barrington (Ann Arbor: University of Michigan Press, 2006), 45–70.

14. "No 10 Plays Down 'Ethnic Rebrand,'" BBC News, online edition, August 8, 2005, http://news.bbc.co.uk/2/hi/uk_news/4130594.stm (accessed August 24, 2008).

15. "Population," Facts about Germany, http://www.tatsachen-ueber-deutschland.de/en/inhaltsseiten-home/zahlen-fakten/bevoelkerung.html (accessed August 25, 2008).

16. Carl-Ulrik Schierup, Peo Hansen, and Stephen Castles, "The 'Migration Crisis' and the New European Diversity," in *Migration, Citizenship and the European Welfare State* (Oxford, UK: Oxford University Press, 2006), 30–32.

17. Veysel Oezcan, "Changes to German Law Help Boost Naturalization Numbers," *Migration Information Source*, August 2003, http://www.migrationinformation.org/Feature/display.cfm?id=152 (accessed July 23, 2008).

18. Ludwig Siegele, "Thinning Blood," in "Waiting for a Wunder: A Survey of Germany," *Economist*, February 11, 2006, 12–14.

19. Pradeep K. Chhibber and John R. Petrocik, "The Puzzle of Indian Politics: Social Cleavages and the Indian Party System," *British Journal of Political Science* 19, no. 2 (April 1989), 191.

20. Ernst B. Haas, *Nationalism, Liberalism, and Progress*, vol. 2, *The Dismal Fate of New Nations* (Ithaca, NY: Cornell University Press, 2000), 158.

21. See John Gledhill, "Liberalism, Socio-economic Rights and the Politics of Identity: From Moral Economy to Indigenous Rights," in *Human Rights, Culture and Context: Anthropological Approaches*, ed. Richard Wilson (London: Pluto Press, 1997), 70–110.

22. See Glynn Custred, "North American Borders: Why They Matter," *Backgrounder*, May 2003, http://www.cis.org/articles/2003/back803a.pdf, p. 4 (accessed July 12, 2008).

23. See Ludwig Lauerhass Jr., "A Four-Part Canon for the Analysis of Brazilian National Identity," in *Brazil in the Making: Facets of National Identity*, ed. Carmen Nava and Ludwig Lauerhass Jr. (Rowman & Littlefield, 2006), 1–14.

24. Fernando Henrique Cardoso, with Brian Winter, *The Accidental President of Brazil: A Memoir* (New York: Public Affairs, 2006), 4.

25. Ibid.

26. In one of the more telling examples of this struggle to define Russian national identity, mentioned briefly in Chapter 3, Russian President Boris Yeltsin established a commission to study and report on the Russian National Idea shortly after he won reelection in 1996. The commission sought a set of guiding principles to unite the Russian population, something along the lines of the U.S. concept of the American Dream. After a year, the commission produced a report, "Russia in Search of an Idea," that emphasized the value of thinking about what united Russians, but it produced no definitive Russian national idea. Russia seems no closer today to an answer to the questions of its national identity and its raison d'être as a state than it was in the 1800s.

27. On the question of Muslims in Russia, see Dmitri Glinski, "Russia and Its Muslims: The Politics of Identity at the International-Domestic Frontier," *East European Constitutional Review* 11, nos. 1–2 (Winter/Spring 2002): 71–83.

28. Arend Lijphart, *Democracy in Plural Societies: A Comparative Exploration* (New Haven, CT: Yale University Press, 1977).

29. Horowitz, *Ethnic Groups in Conflict*.

30. Elizabeth Fromberg, "Ethnic Conflict, Secession, and Political Violence in Tatarstan and Chechnya: The Role of the Russian State," paper presented at the IREX Caucasus Regional Policy Symposium, Shepherdstown, WV, March 25–28, 2004), 1–3.

31. Mark Cichock, *Russian and Eurasian Politics: A Comparative Approach* (New York: Longman, 2003), 143.

32. Fromberg, 2–3. Because their birthrates are higher than those of ethnic Russians, Tatars have since become a majority of the republic.

33. Ibid., 2.

34. Dru C. Gladney, "The Chinese Program of Development and Control, 1978–2001," in *Xinjiang: China's Muslim Borderland*, ed. S. Frederick Starr (Armonk, NY: M.E. Sharpe, 2004), 118.

35. At the same time, the Chinese government has refused to address the question of whether certain groups are indigenous to the territories in which they presently reside. See Ibid., 102.

36. Some associate primordialism with Anthony Smith, one of the world's leading scholars on national identity, though he might be better labeled as a proponent of the radical middle position. See the discussion in Soren Rinder Bollerup and Christian Dons Christensen, *Nationalism in Eastern Europe* (New York: St. Martin's Press, 1997), 36–38.

37. John L. Comaroff, "Ethnicity, Nationalism, and the Politics of Difference in an Age of Revolution," in *The Politics of Difference: Ethnic Premises in a World of Power*, ed. Edwin N. Wilmsen and Patrick McAllister (Chicago: University of Chicago Press, 1996), 165.

38. Ronald G. Suny, "Nationalism, Nation Making, and the Post-Colonial States of Asia, Africa, and Eurasia," in *After Independence: Making and Protecting the Nation in Postcolonial and Postcommunist States*, ed. Lowell W. Barrington, (Ann Arbor: University of Michigan Press, 2006), 280. Stephen Cornell and Douglas Hartmann offer the label "constructed primordiality," although their description of this approach is strongly anchored in constructivism's contention that perceptions such as shared blood ties are only powerful because they have been constructed to be powerful. Stephen Cornell and Douglas Hartmann, *Ethnicity and Race: Making Identities in a Changing World* (Thousand Oaks, CA: Pine Forge Press, 1998), 89.

39. Dru C. Gladney, "China's National Insecurity: Old Challenges at the Dawn of the New Millennium," paper presented at the 2000 Pacific Symposium: Asian Perspectives on the Challenges of China conference, Washington, DC, March 7–8, 2000.

40. Dru C. Gladney, "China's Ethnic Divisions Are Showing Up and Could Cause Trouble," *International Herald Tribune*, February 22, 1995, www.iht.com/articles/1995/02/22/eddru.php (accessed August 24, 2008).

41. Alessio Loreti, "More Authentic, or Less?" *The Iranian*, August 27, 2002, http://www.iranian.com/Opinion/2002/August/Identity/index.html (accessed July 15, 2008).

42. For an overview of Azeri identity and the implications for Iran, see Brenda Shaffer, *Borders and Brethren: Iran and the Challenge of Azerbaijani Identity* (Cambridge, MA: MIT Press, 2002).

43. Amy G. Mazur, *Theorizing Feminist Policy* (Oxford, UK: Oxford University Press, 2002).

44. For example, Christina Hoff Sommers has criticized the use of anecdotes in the landmark work of social psychologist Carol Gilligan, including in Gilligan's *In a Different Voice (1982)*. See Amy Benfer, "Battle of the Celebrity Gender Theorists," *Salon*, March 9, 2001, http://archive.salon.com/mwt/feature/2001/03/09/sommers/index.html (accessed July 25, 2008).

45. "Ethnic Minorities Singled Out for Attack in Iran," *Wire* 35, no. 9 (October 2005), http://www.amnesty.org/en/library/asset/NWS21/009/2005/en/dom-NWS210092005en.html (accessed August 24, 2008).

46. Gokhan Bacik, "The Rise of Identity Politics in Turkey," UNISCI Discussion Papers 23 (May 2010), Madrid, Spain.

47. Ibid., 59.

Chapter 5

1. Thomas A. Koelble, "The New Institutionalism in Political Science," *Comparative Politics* 27, no. 2 (1995): 231.

2. Karen Orren and Stephen Skowronek, "Beyond the Iconography of Order: Notes for a 'New Institutionalism,'" in *The Dynamics of American Politics: Approaches and Interpretations*, ed. Larry Dodd and Calvin Wilson (Boulder, CO: Westview Press, 1994), 325.

3. Robert A. Dahl, *Polyarchy: Participation and Opposition* (New Haven, CT: Yale University Press, 1971).

4. Robert A. Dahl, *A Preface to Democratic Theory* (Chicago: University of Chicago Press, 1956), esp. ch. 1.

5. See Arend Lijphart, "Dimensions of Democracies," *European Journal of Political Research* 31, nos. 1–2 (February 1997): 193–204.

6. Robert Dahl, *On Democracy* (New Haven, CT: Yale University Press, 1998).

7. Carl J. Friedrich and Zbigniew K. Brzezinski, *Totalitarian Dictatorship and Autocracy* (Cambridge, MA: Harvard University Press, 1956); Hannah Arendt, *The Origins of Totalitarianism* (New York: Harcourt, Brace, 1951).

8. Linz and O'Donnell are the scholars most associated with developing the core ideas surrounding authoritarianism in comparative politics. See Juan Linz, "An Authoritarian Regime: Spain," in *Mass Politics: Studies in Political Sociology*, ed. Erik Allardt and Stein Rokkan (New York: Free Press, 1970), 252–283; Guillermo O'Donnell, *Modernization and Bureaucratic Authoritarianism: Studies in South American Politics* (Berkeley: University of California Press, 1973).

9. Arend Lijphart, *Patterns of Democracy* (New Haven, CT: Yale University Press, 1999).

10. Stephen Ingle, "Overview: A Wilderness Year," *Parliamentary Affairs* 58, no. 2 (2005): 199.

11. The definitive work on veto points is George Tsebelis, *Veto Players: How Political Institutions Work* (Princeton, NJ: Princeton University Press, 2002).

12. Ibid., ch. 1.

13. Comparativist Duane Swank states that the changes under Thatcher's watch were "notable." Duane Swank, "Withering Welfare? Globalisation, Political Economic Institutions, and Contemporary Welfare States," in *State in the Global Economy: Bringing Domestic Institutions Back In*, ed. Linda Weiss (Cambridge, UK: Cambridge University Press, 2003), 71.

14. Vernon Bogdanor, "Constitutional Reform in Britain: The Quiet Revolution," *Annual Review of Political Science* 8 (2005): 73–98.

15. Matthew Flinders, "Majoritarian Democracy in Britain: New Labour and the Constitution," *West European Politics* 28, no. 1 (January 2005): 61–93.

16. Bogdanor, "Constitutional Reform in Britain."

17. See Flinders, "Majoritarian Democracy in Britain," 64.

18. Ibid., Table 3. Flinders points out, for example, that although the reforms of the House of Lords were supposed to pave the way for a more representative and powerful upper house, the elimination of most of the hereditary peers in the House of Lords has weakened its role as a check on the House of Commons.

19. Ibid., 209.

20. V. R. Berghahn, *Modern Germany: Society, Economy and Politics in the Twentieth Century*, 2nd ed. (Cambridge, UK: Cambridge University Press, 1987), 18–22.

21. Ibid., 93–95.

22. Germany specialist Peter Katzenstein has termed this dispersal of state power as a condition of "semisovereignty" that is realized through coalition governments, federalism, and a corporatist form of interest group consultation. Peter J. Katzenstein, *Policy and Politics in West Germany: The Growth of a Semisovereign State* (Philadelphia: Temple University Press, 1987).

23. Ibid. See also the discussion of German corporatism by Wolfgang Streeck and Philippe C. Schmitter, "Community, Market, State—and Associations? The Prospective Contribution of Interest Governance to Social Order," *European Sociological Review* 1, no. 2 (September 1985): 119–138.

24. Gaston V. Rimlinger, *Welfare Policy and Industrialization in Europe, America and Russia* (New York: John Wiley, 1971), 139.

25. *Basic Law for the Federal Republic of Germany,* Promulgated by the Parliamentary Council on May 23, 1949 (Bonn: Press and Information Office of the Federal Republic, March 1995), 22.

26. Rimlinger, *Welfare Policy and Industrialization,* 138–148, esp. p. 139.

27. Katzenstein, *Policy and Politics in West Germany*, 45–50; Gordon Smith, *Democracy in Western Germany*, 3rd ed. (Aldershot, UK: Gower, 1986), xx.

28. Katzenstein, *Policy and Politics in West Germany,* 16.

29. David P. Conradt, *The German Polity*, 8th ed. (New York: Pearson/Longman, 2005), 199.

30. Hugh Williamson, "Germany to Make Big Changes to Constitution," *Financial Times*, July 1, 2006, 2.

31. Ministry of Law and Justice, Government of India, *Constitution of India (Updated up to 94th Amendment Act)*, http://indiacode.nic.in/coiweb/welcome.html (accessed September 9, 2008).

32. Robert Hardgrave Jr. and Stanley A. Kochanek, *India: Government and Politics in a Developing Nation*, 7th ed. (Boston: Thompson Wadsworth, 2008), 84.

33. In 1992, the Seventy Third Amendment Act was passed with the objective of fostering the development of local governments and standardizing their form around a basic unit called the *gram panchayat*. Similarly, problems with municipal government led to the passage of the Seventy-Fourth Amendment Act (1993), which sought to improve urban governance. Rapidly growing cities have severely challenged municipal governments, which often lack the resources and power to carry out policies to meet these challenges. Although local governing institutions have greater capacities to deal with constituents than they had in the past, the complexities of the problems before them have increased even more. See Hardgrave and Kochanek, *India*, 129–136.

34. Orren and Skowronek, "Beyond the Iconography of Order," 313.

35. These included replacing the presidential system with a parliamentary one. See Chappell Lawson, "Fox's Mexico at Midterm," *Journal of Democracy* 15, no. 1 (January 2004): 149.

36. Freedom House Freedom in the World 2010, http://www.freedomhouse.org/template.cfm?page=22&year=2010&country=7788 (accessed January 6, 2011).

37. Fernando Henrique Cardoso, *The Accidental President of Brazil: A Memoir* (New York: Public Affairs, 2006), 166.

38. See "Title VIII: The Social Order," Federative Republic of Brazil, Constitution of 1988 with 1996 reforms in English, http://pdba.georgetown.edu/Constitutions/Brazil/brtitle8.html (accessed September 3, 2008).

39. R. Andrew Nickson, *Local Government in Latin America* (Boulder, CO: Lynne Rienner Press, 1995), 118.

40. Ibid., 52

41. Ibid., 44.

42. As Andrew Nickson notes, "The outcome of this complex legal arrangement is that there is almost no service uniformly offered by all municipalities, and very few in which the state may not be an alternate provider or regulator." Ibid., 121–122.

43. See Gabriella Montinola, Yingyi Qian, and Barry R. Weingast, "Federalism, Chinese Style: The Political Basis for Economic Success in China," *World Politics* 48, no. 1 (October 1995): 50–81.

44. See Yahong Li, "The Law-Making Law: A Solution to the Problems in the Chinese Legislative System?" *Perspectives* 2, no. 2, http://www.oycf.org/Perspectives/8_103100/lawmakinglaw.htm (accessed September 6, 2008).

45. See Ellen Immergut, "The Theoretical Core of the New Institutionalism," *Politics and Society* 26, no. 1 (March 1998): 7.

46. Adam Przeworski, "Institutions Matter?" *Government and Opposition* 39, no. 4 (2004): 527–540.

47. Peter Hall and Rosemary Taylor, "Political Science and the Three New Institutionalisms," *Political Studies* 44, no. 5 (1996): 936–957.

48. Koelble, "The New Institutionalism in Political Science," 232.

49. Kian Tajbakhsh, "Political Decentralization and the Creation of Local Government in Iran: Consolidation or Transformation of the Theocratic State?" *Social Research* 67, no. 2 (Summer 2000): 377–404.

50. Ibid.

51. Andrea Pozas-Loyo and Julio Rios-Figueroa, "Enacting Constitutionalism: The Origins of Independent Judicial Institutions in Latin America," *Comparative Politics* 42, no. 3 (April 2010): 293–311.

52. Przeworski, "Institutions Matter?" 530.

53. Ibid., 528.

Chapter 6

1. "Dilma Rousseff: Brazil's First Female President," CBC News Profile, October 31, 2010, http://www.cbc.ca/world/story/2010/10/29/f-brazil-dilma-rousseff.html (accessed November 7, 2010).

2. Some have labeled this trend "presidentialization." Thomas Poguntke and Paul Webb, eds., *The Presidentialization of Politics: A Comparative Study of Modern Democracies* (Oxford, UK: Oxford University Press, 2005).

3. The concept of separation of powers is found in the works of John Locke and the *Federalist Papers,* especially those by James Madison. John Locke, *Two Treatises of Government*, ed. Peter Laslett (Cambridge, MA: Harvard University Press, 1960); Clinton Rossiter, ed., *The Federalist Papers* (New York: Mentor Books, 1961).

4. The South African Constitution, ch. 5, sec. 89, http://www.info.gov.za/documents/constitution/1996/index.htm (accessed January 8, 2011).

5. According to the South African constitution, no more than two ministers at any one time can be chosen from outside the membership of the National Assembly. Unlike the president, the ministers do not surrender their legislative seats while serving in the cabinet.

6. "SA's Mbeki Says He Will Step Down," BBC News, September 20, 2008, http://news.bbc.co.uk/2/hi/africa/7626646.stm (accessed January 3, 2011).

7. Clinton Rossiter uses this term in *The American Presidency* (New York: Mentor, 1960).

8. Gary W. Cox and Matthew McCubbins, *Legislative Leviathan: Party Government in the House* (Berkeley: University of California Press, 1993).

9. David P. Conradt, *The German Polity*, 8th ed. (New York: Pearson Longman, 2005), 199.

10. Ibid., 219.

11. This scenario has also been repeated in subsequent elections within the *Länder*. Hugh Williamson, "Defiant Beck Sees Links with Left as SPD's Salvation," *Financial Times*, March 11, 2008, 2.

12. Both the *Lok Sabha* and the *Rajya Sabha* have Web sites with considerable current and historical information: http://loksabha.nic.in/, http://rajyasabha.nic.in, and http://parliamentofindia.nic.in/ls/intro/introls.htm (accessed September 8, 2008).

13. See "117 Hours of Parliament Lost to Frequent Disruptions (To Go with 'Parliament Session Ends with Little Business Conducted')," *The Gaea Times*, May 7, 2010, http://politics.gaeatimes.com/2010/05/07/117-hours-of-parliament-lost-to-frequent-disruptions-to-go-with-parliament-session-ends-with-little-business-conducted-33785/ (accessed March 21, 2011).

14. Carole Spary, "Disrupting Rituals of Debate in the Indian Parliament," *Journal of Legislative Studies* 16, no. 3 (September 2010): 338.

15. Soutik Biswas, "India's Architect of Reforms," BBC News, October 14, 2005, http://news.bbc.co.uk/go/pr/fr/-/1/hi/world/-south_asia/3725357.stm (accessed March 24, 2008).

16. Howard Handelman, *Mexican Politics: The Dynamics of Change* (New York: St. Martin's Press, 1997).

17. Juan J. Linz, "The Perils of Presidentialism," *Journal of Democracy* 1, no. 4 (Winter 1990): 51–69; Donald L. Horowitz, "Comparing Democratic Systems," *Journal of Democracy* 1, no. 4 (Winter 1990): 73–79.

18. Horowitz, "Comparing Democratic Systems."

19. The president also appoints the representatives to the seven federal districts. Mark Chicock, *Russian and Comparative Politics: A Comparative Approach* (New York: Longman, 2003), chs. 5–6.

20. Thomas F. Remington, *Politics in Russia*, 3rd ed. (New York: Pearson Longman, 2004), ch. 3.

21. See, e.g., Claire Bigg, "Does Russia Care What the West Thinks?" Radio Free Europe/Radio Liberty, August 29, 2008, http://www.rferl.org/content/Article/1194876.html (accessed September 9, 2008); "Who Rules Russia: Putin or Medvedev?" *The Daily Telegraph* online edition, September 5, 2008, http://www.telegraph.co.uk/opinion/main.jhtml?xml=/opinion/2008/05/09/dl0902.xml (accessed September 9, 2008).

22. Samuel Kernell, *Going Public: New Strategies of Presidential Leadership* (Washington, DC: CQ Press, 1997).

23. Others, such as George Edwards, challenge the idea that presidential efforts to use the bully pulpit actually change public opinion or lead to policy successes. See George C. Edwards III, *On Deaf Ears: The Limits of the Bully Pulpit* (New Haven, CT: Yale University Press, 2003).

24. Federico Russo and Matti Wiberg, "Parliamentary Questioning in 17 European Parliaments: Some Steps towards Comparison," *Journal of Legislative Studies* 16, no. 2 (June 2010): 215–232.

Chapter 7

1. "'Shame Games' Mar India's Reputation: Analysts," *Himalayan Times*, online edition, September 9, 2010, http://www.thehimalayantimes.com/printNepaliNews.php?id=259660 (accessed November 22, 2010).

2. J. K. Rowling, *Harry Potter and the Deathly Hallows* (New York: Scholastic, Inc., 2007).

3. "Indonesia's Bureaucracy among Worst in Asia: Survey," *Jakarta Globe*, June 2, 2010, http://www.thejakartaglobe.com/home/indonesias-bureaucracy-among-worst-in-asia-survey/378341 (accessed November 22, 2010); "'Shame Games' Mar India's Reputation."

4. Benjamin H. Barton, "Harry Potter and the Half-Crazed Bureaucracy," *Michigan Law Review* 104, no. 6 (2006): 1525.

5. Tom Ginzburg and Tamir Moustafa, eds., *Rule by Law: The Politics of Courts in Authoritarian Regimes* (Cambridge, UK: Cambridge University Press, 2008).

6. C. Neal Tate, "Past, Present, and Future with the 'Comparative Advantage': Part I, 1892–1989," *Law and Courts* 12, no. 2 (Spring 2002): 1, 3–10.

7. Christopher Wolfe, "The Rehnquist Court and 'Conservative Judicial Activism,'" in *That Eminent Tribunal: Judicial Supremacy and the Constitution*, ed. Christopher Wolfe (Princeton, NJ: Princeton University Press, 2004), 199–224.

8. This statement can be found in the section written by Jeremy Waldron in Laurence H. Tribe, Jeremy Waldron, and Mark Tushnet, "On Judicial Review," *Dissent*, Summer 2005, http://www.dissentmagazine.org/article/?article=219 (accessed June 20, 2011).

9. Stephen Brooks, *Canadian Democracy: An Introduction*, 4th ed. (Oxford, UK: Oxford University Press, 2004), 239.

10. John Ferejohn and Charles Shipan, "Congressional Influence on Bureaucracy," *Journal of Law, Economics, and Organization* 6 (1990): 3.

11. Ibid., 2.

12. Scott N. Schools, "An Overview of the General Counsel's Office of the Executive Office for United States Attorneys," *The United States Attorneys' Bulletin* 55, no. 3 (May 2007): 2–3.

13. James Q. Wilson, *Bureaucracy: What Government Agencies Do and Why They Do It* (New York: Basic Books, 1989), 334–335.

14. Ibid., 317–325.

15. Ibid., 326–327.

16. Roger D. Masters, *The Nature of Politics* (New Haven, CT: Yale University Press, 1989), 204.

17. Wilson, *Bureaucracy*, 221.

18. Samuel P. Huntington, "Reforming Civil-Military Relations," *Journal of Democracy* 6, no. 4 (1995): 9–17.

19. See, for example, Dale R. Herspring, "Civil-Military Relations in Post-Communist Eastern Europe: The Potential for Praetorianism," *Studies in Comparative Communism* 25, no. 2 (1992): 99–122.

20. Faleh A Jabar, "Iraq: The Military Response," *Le Monde Diplomatique* (English edition), January 2003, http://mondediplo.com/2003/01/03military (accessed January 2, 2011).

21. Ibid.

22. "Iraqi General Says Planned US Troop Pull-out 'Too Soon'" BBC News, August 12, 2010, http://www.bbc.co.uk/news/world-middle-east-10947918 (accessed January 3, 2011).

23. See, for example, Eric Robinson, "Iraq's Forthcoming Military Coup," YaleJournal.org, October 13, 2010, http://yalejournal.org/2010/10/iraq%e2%80%99s-forthcoming-military-coup/ (accessed January 2, 2011).

24. "Assessment of U.S. Government Efforts to Develop the Logistics Sustainment Capability of the Iraq Security Forces," Department of Defense Inspector General, Report No SPO-2011-001, November 17, 2010, http://www.dodig.mil/SPO/Reports/ISF10Nov10.pdf (accessed January 3, 2011).

25. "Iraq Cobbles Together New Government after Nine-month Power Struggle," The Guardian, online edition, December 21, 2010, http://www.guardian.co.uk/world/2010/dec/21/iraq-new-government-power-struggle (accessed December 29, 2010).

26. Barabar Surk and Qassim Abdul-Zahra, "Iraq Finally Has a New Government," Forbes.com, December 21, 2010, http://www.forbes.com/feeds/ap/2010/12/21/general-ml-iraq_8817725.html (accessed December 29, 2010).

27. Tom Ginsburg, *Judicial Review in New Democracies: Constitutional Courts in Asian Cases* (Cambridge, UK: Cambridge University Press, 2003), 3.

28. Ibid., 4.

29. Leonard Freeman, *Politics and Policy in Britain* (New York: Longman, 1996), 154–155.

30. Terry M. Moe, "The Politics of Structural Choice: Toward a Theory of Public Bureaucracy," in *Organizational Theory: From Chester Barnard to the Present and Beyond*, ed. Oliver E. Williamson (New York: Oxford University Press, 1990) 116–153.

31. Ibid., 145.

32. Freeman, *Politics and Policy in Britain,* 154–156.

33. Ibid.

34. Gaston V. Rimlinger, *Welfare Policy and Industrialization in Europe, America and Russia* (New York: John Wiley and Sons, 1971), 139.

35. David P. Conradt, *The German Polity,* 8th ed. (New York: Pearson Longman, 2005), 251.

36. Ibid., 252.

37. Ibid., 249. See also Douglas Webber, "Die Kassenärztlichen Vereinigungen zwischen Mitgliederinteressen und Gemein-wohl," in *Verbände zwischen Mitgliederinteressen und Gemein-wohl*, ed. Renate Mayntz, (Gütersloh: Verlag Bertelsmann Stiftung, 1992).

38. Alexander Gerschenkron, *Economic Backwardness in Historical Perspective* (Cambridge, MA: Belknap Press, 1962).

39. Conradt, *The German Polity,* 232.

40. Ibid., 229–31; Peter J. Katzenstein, *Politics and Policy in West Germany: The Growth of a Semisovereign State* (Philadelphia: Temple University Presss, 1987), 19–22.

41. Conradt, *The German Polity,* 229; Katzenstein, *Politics and Policy in West Germany*, 19–22.

42. Conradt, *The German Polity,* 207.

43. Ibid., 208.

44. Somnath Chatterjee, "Foreword," in *The Supreme Court versus the Constitution: A Challenge to Federalism*, ed. Pran Chopra (New Delhi: Sage Publications, 2006), 12–13. A former attorney general of India, Soli Sorabjee, identified five fundamental features that characterize the basic structure, stating, "The first is secularism; second, democracy; third, rule of law; fourth, federalism; and the fifth is an independent judiciary with the power of judicial review." Soli Sorabjee, "The Ideal Remedy: A Valediction," in *The Supreme Court versus the Constitution: A Challenge to Federalism*, ed. Pran Chopra (New Delhi: Sage Publications, 2006), 204.

45. "India Has World's Largest Backlog of Court Cases: PM," NDTV, August 16, 2009, http://www.ndtv.com/news/india/india_has_worlds_largest_backlog_of_court_cases_pm.php (accessed January 9, 2011).

46. Robert Hardgrave Jr. and Stanley Kochanek, *India: Government and Politics in a Developing Nation,* 7th ed. (Boston: Thomson Wadsworth, 2008), 108–109.

47. Ibid., 110.

48. Ibid., 109.

49. Bimal Jalan, *Future of India: Politics, Economics and Governance* (New Delhi: Penguin, 2006), 105.

50. Jodi Finkel, "Judicial Reform as Insurance Policy: Mexico in the 1990s," *Latin American Politics and Society* 47, no. 1 (Spring 2005): 87–113.

51. Jose Antonio Caballero Juarez and Hugi A. Concha Cantu, "The Elements of Judicial Reform: A Multidisciplinary Proposal for Studying Mexican State Courts," *Mexican Law Review* 1 (January–June 2004), http://info8.juridicas.unam.mx/cont/1/arc/arc1.htm (accessed September 16, 2008).

52. Kristopher Mendez, "Mexico's New Hope: Vicente Fox and a Vision for Reform," *Harvard International Review* 22 , no. 4 (Winter 2000), http://www.harvardir.org/articles/876/ (accessed September 4, 2008).

53. George W. Grayson, "Mexico Prefers to Export Its Poor, Not Uplift Them," *Christian Science Monitor*, March 30, 2006, http://www.csmonitor.com/2006/0330/p09s02-coop.html (accessed September 3, 2008).

54. Alfred Stepan, "The New Professionalism of Internal Warfare and Military Role Expansion," in *Authoritarian Brazil: Origins, Policies, and Future*, ed. Alfred Stepan (New Haven, CT: Yale University Press, 1973).

55. "Economic Effects of Legal Infrastructure: Effect of Brazilian Restructuring," *Emerging Market Strategies* 3, no. 3 (June 25, 1999), http://www.emergingmarketstrategies.-com/brazil.htm (accessed September 3, 2008).

56. Ibid.

57. "Brazil—Supreme Court," http://www.v-brazil.com/government/judiciary-branch/supreme-court.html (accessed September 6, 2008).

58. See, for example, "Brazil: Investment Climate Assessment, Volume I: Executive Summary and Policy Recommendations," World Bank, December 6, 2005, http://www.enterprisesurveys.org/documents/enterprisesurveys/ICA/Brazil_Volume%20I.pdf (accessed September 12, 2008).

59. "Corruption Perceptions Index 2007," Transparency International, http://www.transparency.org/policy_research/surveys_indices/cpi/2007 (last modified July 10, 2008; accessed September 16, 2008).

60. Kim R. Holmes, Edwin J. Feulner, Mary Anastasia O'Grady, and others, *2008 Index of Economic Freedom* (Washington, DC: The Heritage Foundation, 2008).

61. Data available at http://info.worldbank.org/governance/wbes/questions3.asp (accessed September 17, 2008). Data are not provided for Iran.

62. Ronald E. Ahnen, "The Politics of Police Violence in Democratic Brazil," *Latin American Politics and Society* 49, no. 1(Spring 2007): 141–164.

63. "Brazil: 'They Come in Shooting': Policing Socially Excluded Communities," AI Index: AMR 19/033/2005, December 2, 2005, http://www.amnesty.org/en/library/asset/AMR19/033/2005/en/dom-AMR190332005en.html (accessed August 22, 2008).

64. "Nigeria: Time for Justice and Accountability," *AI Index*, AFR 44/014/2000, December 21, 2000, http://www.amnesty.org/en/library/asset/AFR44/014/2000/en/dom-AFR440142000en.html (accessed August 23, 2008).

65. M. A. O. Aluko and A. A. Adesopo, "An Appraisal of the Two Faces of Bureaucracy in Relation to the Nigerian Society," *Journal of Social Science* 8 no. 1 (2004): 18.

66. Ibid., 19.

67. One such scholar was Claude Welch, who wrote in 1995 that "were the armed forces of Nigeria to disengage, they would, in fact, be equally likely to hasten back." Claude E. Welch Jr., "Civil-Military Agonies in Nigeria: Pains of an Unaccomplished Transition," *Armed Forces and Society* 21, no. 4 (Summer 1995): 593–594.

68. Ibid.

69. "Putin Approves Move of Russia's Constitutional Court to St. Petersburg," *International Herald Tribune*, February 5, 2007, http://www.iht.com/articles/ap/2007/02/05/europe/EU-GEN-Russia-Court-Move.php (accessed March 15, 2008).

70. John Ferejohn, "Judicializing Politics, Politicizing Law," *Law and Contemporary Problems* 65, no. 3 (June 2002): 63.

71. Cornell W. Clayton, "The Supply and Demand Sides of Judicial Policy-Making (or, Why Be So Positive about the Judicialization of Politics?)," *Law and Contemporary Problems* 65, no. 3 (June 2002): 72.

72. Ibid.

73. "Russian Federation, Attacks on Justice 2002," International Commission of Jurists, Geneva, August 27, 2002, http://www.icj.org/news.php3?id_article=2690&lang=en (accessed September 6, 2008).

74. For more on the nomenklatura, see Dmitriy Gershenson and Hershall I. Grossman, "Cooption and Repression in the Soviet Union," *Economics and Politics* 13, no. 1 (March 2001): 31–47.

75. *Anti-Corruption in Transition #3: Who Is Succeeding . . . and Why?* (Washington, DC: World Bank, 2006).

76. Peter Finn, "Tycoon Decries Russia's 'Criminal Bureaucracy' as Trial Ends," *Washington Post*, April 12, 2005, A15.

77. Brian D. Taylor, "The Soviet Military and the Disintegration of the USSR," *Journal of Cold War Studies* 5, no. 1 (Winter 2003): 17–66.

78. Philip P. Pan, "In China, Turning the Law into the People's Protector," *Washington Post*, December 28, 2004, A1.

79. Mei-Ying Gechlik, "Judicial Reform in China: Lessons from Shanghai," *Columbia Journal of Asian Law* 19, no. 1 (Spring-Fall 2005): 98.

80. Ibid. On intellectual property cases, see "Courts Gather 30K New IP Civil Trial Cases in 2009," China IP News, March 8, 2010, http://www.sipo.gov.cn/sipo_English/news/iprspecial/201003/t20100208_503900.html (accessed January 10, 2011).

81. Harlan W. Jencks, "Civil-Military Relations in China: Tiananmen and After," *Problems of Communism* 40 (May-June 1991): 14–29.

82. Statement of Admiral Robert F. Willard, United States Navy Commander, United States Pacific Command, before the United States House of Representatives Armed Services Committee, January 13, 2010.

83. Hootan Shambayati, "A Tale of Two Mayors: Courts and Politics in Iran and Turkey," *International Journal of Middle East Studies* 36, no. 2 (May 2004): 253–275.

84. According to Amnesty International, there were at least ten executions of individuals under the age of eighteen from 1990 to 2005. "Iran: Amnesty International Outraged at Reported Execution of a 16 Year Old Girl," *Amnesty International Public Statement*, AI Index News Service No: 210, August 23, 2004, http://www.amnesty.org/en/library/asset/MDE13/036/2004/en/dom-MDE130362004en.html (accessed September 18, 2003).

85. Ibid.

86. Suzanne Maloney, "Islam and Iran's Postrevolutionary Economy: The Case of the Bonyads," in *Gods, Guns, and Globalization: Religious Radicalism and International Political Economy*, ed. Mary Ann Tetreault and Robert A. Denemark (Boulder, CO: Lynne Rienner Publishers, 2004), 201.

87. Rebecca Cann and Constantine Danopoulos, "The Military and Politics in a Theocratic State: Iran as a Case Study," *Armed Forces and Society* 24, no. 2 (1997): 269–288.

88. Ibid.

89. Ibid., 280–283.

90. Daniel J. Beers, "A Tale of Two Transitions: Exploring the Origins of Post-Communist Judicial Culture in Romania and the Czech Republic," *Demokratizatsiya* 18, no. 1 (Winter 2010): 29.

91. Ibid., especially 30.

92. Ibid.

93. Ibid., 36.

94. Ibid., 34.

Chapter 8

1. "In Libya, Volunteers Flock to Join the Rebels' Drive-in War," *The Guardian*, March 8, 2011, http://www.guardian.co.uk/world/2011/mar/08/libya-volunteers-rebels-drive-in-war (accessed March 26, 2011).

2. Robert A. Dahl, *Who Governs? Democracy and Power in the American City* (New Haven, CT: Yale University Press, 1961).

3. C. Wright Mills, *The Power Elite* (New York: Oxford University Press, 1956).

4. For example, Russell J. Dalton, *Citizen Politics in Western Democracies: Public Opinion and Political Parties in the United States, Great Britain, West Germany, and France* (Chatham, NJ: Chatham House Publishers, 1988).

5. Ibid., 59.

6. Samuel P. Huntington, *Political Order in Changing Societies* (New Haven, CT: Yale University Press, 1968).

7. Herbert Kitschelt, "Linkages between Citizens and Politicians in Democratic Polities," *Comparative Political Studies* 33, no. 6–7 (2000): 845–879.

8. Ibid., 845.

9. Jacek Tarkowski, "Poland: Patrons and Clients in a Planned Economy," in *Political Clientelism, Patronage and Development*, ed. S. N. Eisenstadt and Rene Lemarchand (Beverly Hills, CA: Sage Publications, 1981), 173–188.

10. Kitschelt, "Linkages," 849.

11. Ibid.

12. Rene Lemarchand, "Comparative Political Clientelism: Structure, Process and Optic," in *Political Clientelism, Patronage and Development*, ed. S. N. Eisenstadt and Rene Lemarchand (Beverly Hills, CA: Sage Publications, 1981), 7.

13. Charles Tilly, *From Mobilization to Revolution* (Reading, MA: Addison-Wesley, 1978).

14. Friedhelm Neidhart and Dieter Rucht, "The Analysis of Social Movements: The State of the Art and Some Perspectives for Further Research," in *Research on Social Movements: The State of the Art in Western Europe and the USA*, ed. Dieter Rucht (Boulder, CO: Westview Press, 1991), 451.

15. The SSCS is the subject of the Animal Planet television program *Whale Wars*.

16. Robert A. Dahl, "Pluralism Revisited," *Comparative Politics* 10, no. 2. (January 1978): 191–203.

17. For a classic work on the difference between state and societal corporatism, see Philippe C. Schmitter, "Still the Century of Corporatism?" in *The New Corporatism: Social-Political Structures in the Iberian World*, ed. Fredrick B. Pike and Thomas Stritch (Notre Dame, IN: University of Notre Dame Press, 1974), 85–131.

18. Phillipe Schmitter, "Modes of Interest Intermediation and Models of Societal Change in Western Europe," *Comparative Political Studies* 10, no. 1 (April 1977): 9.

19. Compare this to Phillipe Schmitter's characterization of state corporatism as involving the "imposition of a symbiotic relationship between such 'semivoluntary' associations and the central bureaucracy." Philippe Schmitter, "The Portugalization of Brazil," in *Authoritarian Brazil*, ed. Alfred Stepan (New Haven, CT: Yale University Press, 1973), 16.

20. Habib discusses this idea in terms of an opening within the "political opportunity structure." Adam Habib, "State-Civil Society Relations in Post-Apartheid South Africa," *Social Research* 72, no. 3 (Fall 2005): 671–692.

21. Ibid., 675.

22. Tanja Winkler, "A Donor Agency Scramble for South Africa," *International Planning Studies* 14, no. 1 (February 2009): 7–24; Mark Robinson and Steven Friedman, "Civil Society, Democratization, and Foreign Aid: Civic Engagement and Public Policy in South Africa and Uganda," *Democratization* 14, no. 4 (August 2007): 643–668.

23. Saras Jagwanth, "Democracy, Civil Society, and the South African Constitution: Some Challenges," UNESCO Management of Social Transformations (MOST) Program, Discussion Paper No. 65, 2003, http://unesdoc.unesco.org/images/0012/001295/129557e.pdf (accessed January 4, 2011), 13.

24. Brian Grodsky, "From Neo-corporatism to Delegative Corporatism? Empowerment of NGOs during Early Democratization," *Democratization* 16, no. 5 (October 2009): 898–921; Jagwanth, "Democracy, Civil Society, and the South African Constitution."

25. For a discussion of the examples of these different outcomes for civil society organizations in South Africa, see Grodsky, "From Neo-corporatism to Delegative Corporatism?"; Robinson and Friedman, "Civil Society, Democratization, and Foreign Aid."

26. Unless otherwise specified, turnout rates are based on percentage of registered voters and come from the IFES Election Guide Web site, http://www.electionguide.org (accessed January 2, 2011).

27. Dalton, *Citizen Politics in Western Democracies,* 48.

28. On voluntary association membership in the United Kingdom, see Peter A. Hall, "Social Capital in Britain," *British Journal of Political Science* 29, no. 3 (July 1999): 417–461.

29. David Broughton, "Participation and Voting," in *Developments in West European Politics 2*, ed. Paul Heywood, Erik Jones, and Martin Rhodes (Basingstoke and New York: Palgrave, 2002), 97.

30. David P. Conradt, *The German Polity*, 8th ed. (New York: Pearson Longman, 2005), 5.

31. Otto Kirchheimer, "The Transformation of West European Party Systems," in *Political Parties and Political Development*, ed. Joseph LaPolombara and Myron Weiner (Princeton, NJ: Princeton University Press, 1966).

32. Charles S. Maier, *Dissolution: The Crisis of Communism and the End of East Germany* (Princeton, NJ: Princeton University Press, 1997), 39–40.

33. For an excellent analysis of corporatism, see Peter J. Katzenstein's classic work, *Policy and Politics in West Germany: The Growth of a Semisovereign State* (Philadelphia: Temple University Press, 1987). See also Wolfgang Streeck and Philippe C. Schmitter, "Community, Market, State—and Associations? The Prospective Contribution of Interest Governance to Social Order," *European Sociological Review* 1, no. 2 (1985): 119–138.

34. On the Greens, see Andrei S. Markovits and Philip S. Gorski, *The German Left: Red, Green and Beyond* (Cambridge, UK: Polity Press, 1993).

35. Dean E. McHenry Jr., "The Numeration of Events, Studying Political Protest in India," in *Interpretation and Method, Empirical Research Methods and the Interpretive Turn*, ed. Dvora Yanow and Peregrine Schwartz-Shea (Armonk, NY: M.E. Sharpe, 2006), 187–202.

36. Robert Hardgrave Jr. and Stanley Kochanek, *India: Government and Politics in a Developing Nation,* 7th ed. (Boston: Thomson and Wadsworth, 2008), 196–202.

37. Joseph L. Klesner, "Social Capital and Political Participation in Latin America," paper presented at the XXV International Congress of the Latin American Studies Association, Las Vegas, Nevada, October 7–9, 2004.

38. Jonathan Fox, "The Difficult Transition from Clientelism to Citizenship: Lessons from Mexico," *World Politics* 46, no. 2 (1994): 153.

39. Tina Hilgers, "The Nature of Clientelism in Mexico City," paper presented at the Canadian Political Science Association Annual Conference, London, Ontario, Canada, June 2–4, 2005.

40. For example, Jonathan Rosenberg, "Mexico: The End of Party Corporatism?" in *Political Parties and Interest Groups: Shaping Democratic Governance*, ed. Clive Thomas (Boulder, CO: Lynne Rienner, 2001), 247–268.

41. James G. Samstad, "Corporation and Democratic Transition: State and Labor during the Salinas and Zedillo Administrations," *Latin American Politics and Society* 44, no. 4 (Winter 2002): 1–28.

42. For an excellent discussion of both the student movement and the peasant rebellions, see Dolores Trevizo, "Between Zapata and Che: A Comparison of Social Movement Success and Failure in Mexico," *Social Science History* 30, no. 2 (2006): 197–229.

43. David B. Truman, *The Governmental Process: Political Interests and Public Opinion* (New York: Alfred A. Knopf, 1951).

44. Ronald F. Inglehart et al., eds., *Human Beliefs and Values: A Cross-Cultural Sourcebook based on the 1999–2002 Values Surveys* (Mexico City: Siglo XXI, 2004), Tables E025–E029.

45. On this point, see Barry Ames, *The Deadlock of Democracy in Brazil* (Ann Arbor: University of Michigan Press, 2001).

46. Brian Wampler, "Can Participatory Institutions Promote Pluralism? Mobilizing Low-Income Citizens in Brazil," *Studies in Comparative International Development* 41, no. 4 (Winter 2007): 57–78.

47. See also Rebecca Abers, "From Clientelism to Cooperation: Local Government, Participatory Policy, and Civic Organizing in Porto Alegre, Brazil," *Politics and Society* 26, no. 4 (December 1998): 511–37.

48. Wampler, "Can Participatory Institutions Promote Pluralism?" 74.

49. Omar Encarnación, *The Myth of Civil Society: Social Capital and Democratic Consolidation in Spain and Brazil* (New York: Palgrave Macmillan, 2003), 178.

50. The government did not release official turnout rates for the 2007 elections, so this figure is based on the reported number of votes for the various candidates and the estimated number of registered voters prior to the vote. Many observers believe the reported number of votes cast was greatly inflated.

51. Peter Maass, "Niger Delta Dispatch: Road to Hell," *New Republic*, January 31, 2005, 15–17.

52. See Larry Diamond, "Nigeria: Pluralism, Statism, and the Struggle for Democracy," in *Politics in Developing Countries: Comparing Experiences with Democracy*, ed. Larry Diamond, Juan J. Linz, and Seymour Martin Lipset (Boulder, CO: Lynne Reinner Publishers, 1990), 351–409.

53. Charles Gore and David Pratten, "The Politics of Plunder: The Rhetorics of Order and Disorder in Southern Nigeria," *African Affairs* 102, no. 407 (April 2003): 211–240.

54. Ian McAllister and Stephen White, "Political Participation in Postcommunist Russia: Voting, Activism, and the Potential for Mass Protest," *Political Studies* 42, no. 4 (December 1994): 593–594.

55. "Russia Elects Putin Successor in Tarnished Poll," Agence France-Presse, March 2, 2008, http://news.ph.msn.com/topstories/article.aspx?cp-documentid=1271515 (accessed September 21, 2008).

56. "Ingush Oppositionist Sheds Light on Low Turnout Figure," *RFE/RL Newsline* 12, no. 43, March 4, 2008, http://www.rferl.org/newsline/2008/03/040308.asp (accessed March 26, 2008).

57. William M. Reisinger, Arthur H. Miller, and Vicki L. Hesli, "Public Behavior and Political Change in Post-Soviet States," *Journal of Politics* 57, no. 4 (November 1995): 941–970.

58. Ronald Inglehart and Gabriela Catterberg, "Trends in Political Action: The Developmental Trend and the Post-Honeymoon Decline," *International Journal of Comparative Sociology* 43, no. 3 (2002): 300–316.

59. For an interesting recent work on Russian social movements, see Graeme B. Robertson, "All They Need Is Someone to Organize It: Protest and Politics in Post-Communist Russia" (Ph.D. diss., Columbia University, 2005).

60. Murray Scot Tanner, "China Rethinks Unrest," *Washington Quarterly* 27, no. 3 (2004): 137–156.

61. See, for example, J. C. Oi, "Communism and Clientelism: Rural Politics in China," *World Politics* 38, no. 2 (1985): 238–266.

62. Snejina Michailova and Verner Worm, "Personal Networking in Russia and China: *Blat* and *Guanxi*," *European Management Journal* 21, no. 4 (2003): 509–519, see Table 2.

63. Ibid.

64. Bruce Dickson, "Cooptation and Cooperation in China: The Logic of Party Adaption," *Political Science Quarterly* 115, no. 4 (Winter 2000–2001): 533.

65. James Q. Wilson, *Bureaucracy: What Government Agencies Do and Why They Do It* (New York: Basic Books, 1989), 251.

66. "Weapons Proliferation and the Military-Industrial Complex of the PRC," *Commentary*, a Canadian Security Intelligence Service publication, no. 84, August 23, 2003, http:// www.fas.org/nuke/guide/china/com84.html. (accessed November 12, 2008).

67. Kazem Alamdari, "The Power Structure of the Islamic Republic of Iran: Transition from Populism to Clientelism, and Militarization of the Government," *Third World Quarterly* 26, no. 8 (2005): 1285–1301.

68. Ibid., 1288.

69. Mancur Olson, *The Logic of Collective Action: Public Goods and the Theory of Groups* (Cambridge, MA: Harvard University Press, 1965).

70. Arndt Wonka, Frank Baumgartner, Christine Mahoney, and Joost Berkhout, "Measuring the Size and Scope of the EU Interest Group Population," *European Union Politics* 11, no. 3 (2010): 463–476.

71. Ibid., Table 3.

72. C. Wright Mills, *The Power Elite* (London: Oxford University Press, 1956), 324.

Chapter 9

1. "Khomeini's Grandson Quits Iran Race after Slurs: Report," AFP, March 2, 2008, http://afp.google.com/-article/ALeqM5ijcHx_rywt3GwWI8AiN5cLqJ_t-g (accessed September 22, 2008).

2. Maurice Duverger, *Political Parties: Their Organization and Activity in the Modern State*, 3rd ed., trans. Barbara North and Robert North (London: Methuen, 1967), 17.

3. Richard Gunther and Larry Diamond, "Species of Political Parties: A New Typology," *Party Politics* 9, no. 2 (March 2003): 167–199.

4. Ibid.

5. Giovanni Sartori, *Parties and Party Systems: A Framework for Analysis*, vol. I (Cambridge, UK: Cambridge University Press, 1976), 222.

6. Ibid., 230.

7. Jean Blondel, "Party Systems and Patterns of Government in Western Democracies," *Canadian Journal of Political Science* 1, no. 2 (June 1968): 180–203.

8. Ibid.

9. Ibid.

10. Duverger, *Political Parties*, 228.

11. Adam Przeworski, *Democracy and the Market* (Cambridge, UK: Cambridge University Press, 1991), 10.

12. David M. Farrell, *Comparing Electoral Systems* (London: Prentice Hall, 1997), ch. 6.

13. Ibid., 151.

14. Roger F. S. Kaplan, "Elections and Ideologies in France: 2002," *Society* 40, no. 1 (November/December 2002): 86–91.

15. Sharif Gemie, "Anti-Le Pen Protests: France, April–May 2002," *Journal of Contemporary European Studies* 11, no. 2 (November 2003): 231–251.

16. Duverger, *Political Parties*, 208–210.

17. "Kennedy Hails 'Party of Future,'" BBC News Election 2005 report, May 6, 2005, http://news.bbc.co.uk/1/hi/uk_politics/vote_2005/frontpage/4518803.stm (accessed September 24, 2008).

18. Andre Blais and Louis Massicotte, "Electoral Systems," in *Comparing Democracies: Elections and Voting in Global Perspective*, ed. Lawrence LeDuc, Richard G. Niemi, and Pippa Norris (Thousand Oaks, CA: Sage Publications, 1996), 49–82.

19. See, for example, William H. Riker, "The Two-Party System and Duverger's Law," *American Political Science Review* 76, no. 4 (December 1982): 753–766.

20. Duverger, *Political Parties*, 217.

21. See Andre Krouwel, "Otto Kirchheimer and the Catch-All Party," *West European Politics* 26, no. 2 (April 2003): 23–40. Kirchheimer described such parties as *Volksparteien*, or "people's parties," which are essentially catch-all parties.

22. David P. Conradt, *The German Polity*, 8th ed. (New York: Pearson Longman, 2005), 162–166.

23. German parties often designate a person to lead the party in the *Bundestag* elections and serve as the chancellor candidate. This person may not necessarily be the chairman of the party.

24. Theodore Rosenof, *Realignment: The Theory That Changed the Way We Think about American Politics* (Lanham, MD: Rowman & Littlefield, 2003).

25. Chris Bryant and Gerrit Wiesmann, "Reformers at Helm as SPD Prepares for Poll," *Financial Times*, September 8, 2004, 4; Gerrit Wiesmann, "Merkel Strikes First Blow at Rival," *Financial Times*, September 9, 2008; "Steinmeier at Helm," *Financial Times*, September 10, 2008.

26. A good source of information on political parties in India is Robert Hardgrave Jr. and Stanley Kochanek, *India: Government and Politics in a Developing Nation,* 7th ed. (Boston: Thomson and Wadsworth, 2008), 259–369.

27. The Indian Election Commission supervises the process. It provides a complete report of information about past and present elections in India, including election results, at http://www.eci.gov.in/index.asp.

28. Sartori, *Parties and Party Systems,* 235.

29. On the 2000 election, see Joseph L. Klesner, "The End of Mexico's One-Party Regime," *PS: Political Science and Politics* 34, no. 1 (March 2001): 107–114.

30. "EU Says Disputed Mexico Vote Fair," BBC News report, July 8, 2006, http://news.bbc.co.uk/2/hi/americas/5160188.stm (accessed September 27, 2008).

31. Joseph A. Schlesinger, "On the Theory of Party Organization," *Journal of Politics* 46, no. 2 (May 1984): 369–400.

32. Ibid., 380.

33. Schlesinger borrows this term from Robert Salisbury. See Robert H. Salisbury, "An Exchange Theory of Interest Groups," *Midwest Journal of Political Science* 13, no. 1 (February 1969): 1–32.

34. Schlesinger, "On the Theory of Party Organization," 390.

35. Pita Ogaba Agbese, "Party Registration and the Subversion of Democracy in Nigeria," *Issue: A Journal of Opinion* 27, no. 1 (1999): 63–65.

36. Sat Obiyan, "Political Parties under the Abubakar Transition Program and Democratic Stability in Nigeria," *Issue: A Journal of Opinion* 27, no. 1 (1999): 41–43.

37. The unofficial estimates of the legislative election results vary greatly, depending on the source. In March 2008, an examination of the party affiliations of members of the House of Representatives and the Senate, according to the two bodies' official Web pages, put the total seats for the PDP at 257 in the House and 78 in the Senate.

38. See, for example, Ben Rawlence and Chris Albin-Lackey, "Briefing: Nigeria's 2007 General Elections: Democracy in Retreat," *African Affairs* 106, no. 424 (2007): 497–506.

39. Kevin J. O'Brien and Lianjiang Li, "Accommodating 'Democracy' in a One-Party State: Introducing Village Elections in China," *China Quarterly* 162 (June 2000): 465–489.

40. Ibid.

41. Robert A. Pastor and Qingshan Tan, "The Meaning of China's Village Elections," *China Quarterly* 152 (June 2000): 490–512.

42. "Iran: Country Reports on Human Rights Practices, 2004," Bureau of Democracy, Human Rights, and Labor of the United States Department of State, February 28, 2005, http://www.state.gov/g/drl/rls/hrrpt/2004/41721.htm (accessed September 24, 2008).

43. Kamal Nazer Yasin, "Election Landslide in Iran May Moderate President-Elect's Domestic Policies," *Eurasia Insight*, June 29, 2005, www.eurasianet.org/departments/insight/articles/eav062905.shtml (accessed September 24, 2008).

44. Sunny Tanuwidjaja, "Political Islam and Islamic Parties in Indonesia: Critically Assessing the Evidence of Islam's Political Decline," *Contemporary Southeast Asia* 32, no. 1 (2010): 29–49.

45. Ibid., 31.

Chapter 10

1. Details of Peshev's actions are available at Norbert J. Yasharoff, "Bulgaria's Schindler," www.peshev.org/yashar.htm (accessed March 23, 2008).

2. "Transports from Macedonia and Thrace," Aktion Reinhard Camps project, Deathcamps.org, June 2, 2006, http://www.deathcamps.org/reinhard/macedonia%20thrace%20transports.html (accessed March 23, 2008).

3. Eric Selbin, "Agency and Culture in Revolutions," in *Revolutions: Theoretical, Comparative, and Historical Studies,* ed. Jack A. Goldstone (Belmont, CA: Wadsworth/Thomson Learning, 2003), 79.

4. Of course, this is not true of all political science works. William Riker contends that, above all else, decision making is the subject of political science. William Riker, *The Theory of Political Coalition* (New Haven, CT: Yale University Press, 1962), 10.

5. Writing about revolutions, for example, Jack Goldstone states, "'Agency' implies that not all aspects of a revolution are predetermined by macro-social, structural factors. The decisions of key actors (or 'agents') make a difference in whether a revolution will be successful and how it evolves." Jack A. Goldstone, "Introduction," in *Revolutions: Theoretical, Comparative, and Historical Studies,* ed. Jack A. Goldstone (Belmont, CA: Wadsworth/Thomson Learning, 2003).

6. Howard Gardner, in collaboration with Emma Laskin, *Leading Minds: An Anatomy of Leadership* (New York: Basic Books, 1995).

7. Peter G. Northouse, *Leadership: Theory and Practice* (Thousand Oaks, CA: Sage, 2004), ch. 3.

8. For an overview of Mandela's life and achievements, see "Biography," nelsonmandela.org, http://www.nelsonmandela.org/index.php/memory/views/biography/ (accessed January 22, 2011).

9. "Early Years," Ibid.

10. Nelson Mandela, "An Ideal for Which I Am Prepared to Die," *The Guardian*, April 23, 2007, http://www.guardian.co.uk/world/2007/apr/23/nelsonmandela (accessed January 20, 2011).

11. See, for example, Theodore F. Heckels, "The Rhetoric of Nelson Mandela: A Qualified Success," *Howard Journal of Communications* 12, no. 2 (April-June 2001): 85–99.

12. It is also important to note that, by the end of the 2000s, there had been a backslide in Freedom House scores for African countries. Gary Feuerberg, "Freedom House's Report on Global Erosion of Freedom," *The Epoch Times*, January 16, 2010, http://www.theepochtimes.com/n2/content/view/28044/ (accessed January 22, 2011).

13. The previous chapter discussed one of the classic works that takes an economic approach to understanding voting, Anthony Downs's *An Economic Theory of Democracy* (New York: Harper, 1957).

14. For an overview of Simon's arguments, see Bryan D. Jones, "Bounded Rationality," *Annual Review of Political Science* 2 (1999): 297–321; Bryan D. Jones, "Herbert A. Simon: Political Scientist," *Annual Review of Political Science* 6 (2003): 433–471.

15. Bruce Bower, "Past Impressions: Prior Relationships Cast a Long Shadow over Our Social Lives," *Science News* 171, no. 23 (June 9, 2007): 364.

16. Sarah Lyall, "Cameron Faces Challenges beyond His Coalition," *New York Times*, May 11, 2010 (accessed January 18, 2011).

17. Ibid.

18. See, for example, the discussion by Alastair Campbell, former British Prime Minister Tony Blair's press secretary: "Insight into Cameron's Style of Leadership," AlastairCampbell. org, November 18, 2010, http://www.alastaircampbell.org/ blog/2010/11/18/insight-into-camerons-style-of-leadership/ (accessed May 2, 2011).

19. Daniel L. Byman and Kenneth M. Pollack, "Let Us Now Praise Great Men (and Women): Restoring the First Image," *International Security* 25, no. 4 (Spring 2001): 107–146.

20. Bertrand Benoit, "New Kid from the Bloc," *Financial Times*, September 10–11, 2005, W1–W2.

21. Ibid.; Bertrand Benoit, "Waiting for a Wunder," Survey on Germany, *Economist*, February 11, 2006, 5–6.

22. Henry A. Kissinger, "Angela Merkel," *Time* magazine ("The Time 100"), May 3, 2007, http://www.time.com/time/specials/2007/ time100/article/0,28804,1595326_1615513_1616468,00.html (accessed May 1, 2011).

23. Gerrit Wiesmann, "Merkel Strikes First Blow at Rival," *Financial Times*, September 9, 2008, 4.

24. Cameron Abadi, "Frau Germania: How Angela Merkel's Selfishness Is Killing Europe," *Foreign Policy*, May 24, 2010, http://www.foreignpolicy.com/articles/2010/05/24/frau_ germania (accessed January 15, 2011).

25. Charles S. Maier, *Dissolution: The Crisis of Communism and the End of East Germany* (Princeton, NJ: Princeton University Press, 1997), 227.

26. Ibid., 228.

27. Ibid., 227–44.

28. "A Conversation with Prime Minister Dr. Manmohan Singh," Council of Foreign Relations, http://www.cfr.org/ publication/20840/conversation_with_prime_minister_ dr_manmohan_singh.html (accessed January 15, 2011).

29. In late 2006, the U.S. Congress passed the Hyde Act that was interpreted by the Left as undermining India's sovereignty and requiring coordination of foreign policies. The Bush administration's international behavior also produced deep concerns among parties on the left.

30. Venkitesh Ramakrishnan, "On the Brink," *Frontline* 25, no. 14 (July 5–18, 2008), http://www.hinduonnet.com/fline/fl2514/ stories/20080718251400400.htm (accessed September 27, 2008).

31. Charles Lindblom, "The Science of 'Muddling Though,'" *Public Administration Review* 19 (Spring 1959): 79–88; David Braybrooke and Charles Lindblom, *A Strategy of Decision* (New York: Free Press, 1963). Incrementalism is also associated with Aaron Wildavsky, especially in the arena of government budgeting.

32. Kevin G. Hall, "Calderón's Views Rooted in Devotion to the Church," *Miami Herald*, July 22, 2006, http://www.miami .com/mld/miamiherald/news/world/americas/15096651.htm (accessed March 14, 2008).

33. "Profile: Felipe Calderon," *BBC News,* September 5, 2006, http://news.bbc.co.uk/2/hi/americas/5318434.stm (accessed September 29, 2008).

34. "A Positive Spin on Mexico Violence," *Grassroots Press,* January 17, 2011, http://www.grass-roots-press.com/2011/01/17/ a-positive-spin-on-mexico-violence/ (accessed January 22, 2011).

35. For more on what Zedillo set out to do, see Stephen Fidler, "Mexico: What Kind of Transition?" *International Affairs* 72, no. 4 (1996): 713–725.

36. Salinas had taken a trip to Europe early in his presidency in which his efforts to expand economic connections with Western European countries garnered only a lukewarm reception.

37. Rogério L. F. Werneck, "Meeting the Challenge of Setting up a Modern Macroeconomic Policy Framework: Brazil, 1993–2004," Commission on Growth and Development Workshop on Country Case Studies, Washington, DC, April 12–14, 2007, http://www.growthcommission.org/storage/cgdev/documents/- CaseStudies/Presentation%20Werneck%20on%20Brazil.pdf (accessed October 1, 2008).

38. This section is based on Cardoso's recollections of these events in Fernando Henrique Cardoso, with Brian Winter, *The Accidental President of Brazil: A Memoir* (New York: Public Affairs/Perseus Books, 2006), esp. ch. 9.

39. Ibid.

40. Ibid.

41. Ibid.

42. Nicholas Sambanis develops this point in "Using Case Studies to Expand the Theory of Civil War," CPR Working Paper no. 5, Social Development Department, Environmentally and Socially Sustainable Development Network, May 2003, http://www.forecastingprinciples.com/ Conflicts/PDF%20files/Using_Case_Studies.pdf (accessed September 29, 2008).

43. Ariel Cohen, "Russian Succession: Putin Prime Minister, Medvedev President," *Web Memo*, Heritage Foundation, no. 1731 (December 11, 2007): 1.

44. Ibid., 1–2.

45. Joshua Eisenman, "A Shift in China's Leadership Style?" *Straits Times*, May 8, 2003, http://www.nixoncenter.org/ EISENMAN%20PUBLICATIONS/Straits%20Times%20 May%208,%202003.htm (accessed September 29, 2008).

46. "President Hu Sets Forth Guidelines on Taiwan (03/04/05)," Press release of the Chinese Embassy in Hungary, March 5, 2005, http://www.chinaembassy.hu/hu/xwdt/t185890.htm (accessed July 9, 2011).

47. Jerrold D. Green, "Countermobilization in the Iranian Revolution," in *Revolutions: Theoretical, Comparative, and Historical Studies*, ed. Jack A. Goldstone (Belmont, CA: Wadsworth/Thomson Learning, 2003), 238.

48. Stephen Evans, "'Mother's Boy': David Cameron and Margaret Thatcher," *British Journal of Politics and International Relations* 12 (2010): 325–343.

49. David Cameron, "Conference Speech 2008," October 1, 2008, http://www.conservatives.com/News/Speeches/2008/10/ David_Cameron_Conference_Speech_2008.aspx; cited in Evans, "'Mother's Boy.'"

50. Jack Goldstone, Introduction to Eric Selbin, "Agency and Culture in Revolutions," in *Revolutions: Theoretical, Comparative, and Historical Studies*, ed. Jack A. Goldstone (Belmont, CA: Wadsworth/Thomson Learning, 2003), 76.

51. See, for example, James Mahoney and Richard Snyder, "Rethinking Agency and Structure in the Study of Regime Change," *Studies in Comparative International Development* 34, no. 2 (1999): 3–32; Katherine Adeney and Andrew Wyatt, "Democracy in South Asia: Getting beyond the Structure-Agency Dichotomy," *Political Studies* 52, no. 1 (2004): 1–18.

Chapter 11

1. See, for example, Elizabeth Dickinson, "The First WikiLeaks Revolution?" *Foreign Policy*, January 13, 2011, http://wikileaks .foreignpolicy.com/posts/2011/01/13/wikileaks_and_the_ tunisia_protests (accessed January 28, 2011).

2. On the question of stability and political openness, see Ian Bremmer, *The J-Curve* (New York: Simon & Schuster, 2006). For an overview of the body of literature in international relations about what is called the "democratic peace" theory, see James Lee Ray, "The Democratic Path to Peace," *Journal of Democracy* 8, no. 2 (April 1997): 49–64.

3. Ian Bremmer argues that consolidated democracies are more stable than consolidated non-democracies, but also points out that consolidated non-democracies are more stable than the transitional periods of increasing political openness. See Bremmer, *The J-Curve*.

4. Jack Snyder, *From Voting to Violence: Democratization and Nationalist Conflict* (New York: W. W. Norton and Co., 2000); Edward D. Mansfield and Jack Snyder, *Electing to Fight: Why Emerging Democracies Go to War* (Cambridge, MA: MIT Press, 2005).

5. Samuel Huntington, *The Third Wave: Democratization in the Late Twentieth Century* (Norman: University of Oklahoma Press, 1991).

6. Ibid.

7. Dankwart A. Rustow, "Transitions to Democracy: Toward a Dynamic Model," *Comparative Politics* 2, no. 3 (April 1970): 337–365.

8. Terry Lynn Karl, "Dilemmas of Democratization in Latin America," *Comparative Politics* 23, no. 1 (October 1990): 1–21.

9. Scott Mainwaring, "Transitions to Democracy and Democratic Consolidation: Theoretical and Comparative Issues," in Mainwaring, Guillermo O'Donnell, and J. Samuel Valenzuela, eds., *Issues in Democratic Consolidation: The New South American Democracies in Comparative Perspective* (Notre Dame, IN: University of Notre Dame Press, 1992).

10. Rustow, "Transitions to Democracy."

11. See, for example, Juan Linz, "Transitions to Democracy," *Washington Monthly* 13 (Summer 1990): 143–164.

12. A number of democratization scholars have used the phrase "only game in town" to describe consolidation. See, for example, Adam Przeworski, *Democracy and the Market: Political and Economic Reforms in Eastern Europe and Latin America* (Cambridge, UK: Cambridge University Press, 1991), 26.

13. Ibid., 10.

14. Huntington, *The Third Wave*.

15. On the Latin American cases, see Karen Remmer, "The Political Impact of Economic Crisis in Latin America in the 1980s," *American Political Science Review* 85, no. 3 (September 1991): 777–800.

16. Lawrence Whitehead, *Democratization: Theory and Practice* (Oxford, UK: Oxford University Press, 2002), 28.

17. Doh Chull Shin is one scholar who emphasizes the maturation stage. Doh Chull Shin, "On the Third Wave of Democratization: A Synthesis and Evaluation of Recent Theory and Research," *World Politics* 47, no. 1 (October 1994): 143.

18. Juan J. Linz and Alfred Stepan, eds., *The Breakdown of Democratic Regimes* (Baltimore: Johns Hopkins University Press, 1978).

19. Juan J. Linz, "The Process of Reequilibration," in *The Breakdown of Democratic Regimes*, ed. Juan J. Linz and Alfred Stepan (Baltimore: Johns Hopkins University Press, 1978), 87–97.

20. Shin, "On the Third Wave of Democratization," 139.

21. S. M. Lipset, "Some Social Requisites of Democracy: Economic Development and Political Legitimacy," *American Political Science Review* 53 (1959): 69–104.

22. See Gabriel A. Almond and Sidney Verba, *The Civic Culture: Political Attitudes and Democracy in Five Nations* (Princeton, NJ: Princeton University Press, 1963).

23. Rustow, "Transitions to Democracy."

24. Nancy Bermeo, "The Import of Institutions," *Journal of Democracy* 13, no. 2 (April 2002): 96–110.

25. Donald L. Horowitz, *Ethnic Groups in Conflict* (Berkeley: University of California Press, 1985).

26. Juan J. Linz, "The Perils of Presidentialism," *Journal of Democracy* 1, no. 4 (Winter 1990): 51–69; Donald L. Horowitz, "Comparing Democratic Systems," *Journal of Democracy* 1, no. 4 (Winter 1990): 73–79.

27. Robert D. Putnam (with Robert Leonardi and Raffaella Y. Nanetti), *Making Democracy Work: Civic Traditions in Modern Italy* (Princeton, NJ: Princeton University Press, 1993).

28. M. Foley and B. Edwards, "The Paradox of Civil Society," *Journal of Democracy* 7, no. 4 (1996): 38–52.

29. Sheri Berman, "Civil Society and the Collapse of the Weimar Republic," *World Politics* 49, no. 3 (April 1997): 401–429.

30. Kenneth Waltz, *Theory of International Politics* (New York: McGraw-Hill, 1979).

31. For a chronology of the invasion as well as interviews with decision makers on the U.S. side, see "Operation Iraqi Freedom," Frontline, http://www.pbs.org/wgbh/pages/frontline/shows/ invasion/cron/ (accessed January 26, 2011).

32. They included a refugee crisis in the aftermath of the invasion and the inability of the post-invasion Iraqi leadership to resolve the crisis, significant corruption, the revival of the question of territorial autonomy for the Kurds in Iraq (and, by extension, Kurdish populations in neighboring states), and other unresolved issues of general security. "Iraqi Refugees and Internally Displaced Persons: A Deepening Humanitarian Crisis," Congressional Research Service, February 13, 2009, http://www.fas.org/sgp/ crs/mideast/RL33936.pdf (accessed January 29, 2011); Ali Allawi, "Iraq's Past, Present, and Future," *Brown Journal of World Affairs* 14, no. 2 (May 1, 2008): 265–271; Saad Naji Jawad, "The Kurdish Question in Iraq: Historical Background and Future Settlement," *Contemporary Arab Affairs* 1, no. 1 (January 2008): 25–41; Alice Hills, "The Unavoidable Ghettoization of Security in Iraq," *Security Dialogue* 41, no. 3 (2010): 301–321; Anthony H. Cordesman, "The Uncertain Security Situation in Iraq: Trends in Violence, Casualties and Iraqi Perceptions," Center for Strategic and International Studies, February 17, 2010, http:// csis.org/files/publication/100217_iraq_security_study.pdf (accessed January 25, 2011).

33. See p. 408 of Hans Peter Schmitz, "Domestic and Transnational Perspectives on Democratization," *International Studies Review*, vol. 6 (2004): 403–426.

34. Samuel Huntington uses the term "snowballing" in *The Third Wave*.

35. Michael McFaul, "The Fourth Wave of Democracy and Dictatorship: Noncooperative Transitions in the Postcommunist World," *World Politics* 54, no. 2 (January 2002): 214.

36. Shale Horowitz, "Sources of Post-Communist Democratization: Economic Structure, Political Culture, War, and Political Institutions," *Nationalities Papers* 31, no. 2 (June 2003): 119–137.

37. Daniel H. Levine, "Venezuela since 1958: The Consolidation of Democratic Politics," in *The Breakdown of Democratic Regimes: Latin America*, ed. J. Linz and A. Stepan (Baltimore: Johns Hopkins University Press, 1978), 82–109.

38. See Joseph S. Nye, "Mikhail Gorbachev and the End of the Cold War," *Project Syndicate*, http://www.project-syndicate.org/commentary/nye31/English (accessed October 1, 2008); Andrew E. Busch and Elizabeth Edwards Spalding, "1983: Awakening from Orwell's Nightmare," *Policy Review* 66 (Fall 1993): 71–75; Jonathan Kwitny, *Man of the Century: The Life and Times of Pope John Paul II* (New York: Henry Holt, 1997), 592.

39. Juan J. Linz, "The Process of Breakdown," in Juan J. Linz and Alfred Stepan, eds., *The Breakdown of Democratic Regimes* (Baltimore: Johns Hopkins University Press, 1978), 54.

40. Ibid., 66–69.

41. Terry Lynn Karl, "Petroleum and Political Pacts: The Transition to Democracy in Venezuela," *Latin American Research Review* 22, no. 1 (1987): 63–94.

42. Vernon Bogdanor, "Constitutional Reform in Britain: The Quiet Revolution," *Annual Review of Political Science* 8 (2005): 73.

43. John R. Freeman and Duncan Snidal, "Diffusion, Development, and Democratization: Enfranchisement in Western Europe," *Canadian Review of Political Science* 15, no. 2 (June 1982): 300.

44. John Garrard makes the point that the British transition was more ad hoc than a conscious effort aimed at total enfranchisement of the population from the start. John Garrard, "Democratization in Britain," in John Garrard, Vera Tolz, and Ralph White, eds., *European Democratization Since 1800* (New York and Basingstoke: Palgrave Macmillan, 1999), 29.

45. Barrington Moore Jr, *Social Origins of Dictatorship and Democracy* (Boston: Beacon Press, 1966), 437.

46. Gordon Smith, *Democracy in Western Germany*, 3rd ed. (Aldershot, UK: Gower, 1986), 16–20.

47. The Nazi government blamed the fire on Communists in Germany and arrested a number of leading Communist Party officials. Many historians believe that the Nazis had a hand in the fire in order to use it to justify granting Hitler emergency powers.

48. Peter J. Katzenstein, *Policy and Politics in West Germany: The Growth of a Semisovereign State* (Philadelphia: Temple University Press, 1987), esp. ch. 3. In the early years of the Federal Republic, business elites were discredited by their prior collaboration with the Nazi regime, and labor leaders found legitimacy in their resistance to Hitler. As a result, labor made gains in the industrial relations arena.

49. Gaston V. Rimlinger, *Welfare Policy and Industrialization in Europe, America and Russia* (New York: John Wiley, 1971), 138–148; Ibid., chs. 2 and 4.

50. Ashutosh Varshney, "Why Democracy Survives," *Journal of Democracy* 9, no. 3 (1998): 36–50.

51. In his book *The Great Indian Middle Class* (New Delhi: Penguin Books, 1998 p. xiii), Pavan Varma refuses to define the size of the middle class. On the other hand, he argues that "disproportionate to its size, [it] has played a pivotal role in the making of modern India."

52. Varshney, "Why Democracy Survives," 42.

53. Ibid.

54. José Woldenberg Karakowsky, "Lessons from Mexico," *Journal of Democracy* 12, no. 2 (April 2001): 151–156.

55. Ibid.

56. Terry Lynn Karl, "Dilemmas of Democratization in Latin America."

57. Nigeria's Third Republic never got off the ground, as its founding elections were immediately invalidated by the ruling military government.

58. Carol Skalnik Leff, "Democratization and Disintegration in Multinational States: The Breakup of the Communist Federations," *World Politics* 51, no. 2 (January 1999): 205–235.

59. On the role of the design of the Russian system in its democratic breakdown, see M. Steven Fish, *Democracy Derailed in Russia* (Cambridge, UK: Cambridge University Press, 2005).

60. On the way in which the views of the more conservative masses toward democracy constrained Russia's liberal elites and thus gave opportunities to the conservative elites, see Judith S. Kullberg, "Liberal Elites, Socialist Masses, and the Problems of Russian Democracy," *World Politics* 51, no. 3 (April 1999): 323–358.

61. "Russia's Weakened Democratic Embrace," Pew Global Attitudes Project Report, 2006, http://pewglobal.org/reports/display.php?ReportID=250 (accessed October 2, 2008).

62. Bruce Gilley, "Should We Try to Predict Transitions to Democracy: Lessons for China," *Whitehead Journal of Diplomacy and International Relations* 6, no. 1: 113–128.

63. Ibid., 124.

64. Junhan Lee, "Primary Causes of Asian Democratization: Dispelling Conventional Myths," *Asian Survey* 42, no. 6 (November/December 2002): 821.

65. Bruce Bueno de Mesquita and George W. Downs, "Development and Democracy," *Foreign Affairs* 84, no. 5 (September/October 2005): 77–86.

66. Sanm Vakil, "Iran: The Gridlock between Demography and Democracy," *SAIS Review* 24, no. 2 (Summer-Fall 2004): 45–53.

67. Ibid., 49.

68. Ko Maeda, "Two Modes of Democratic Breakdown: A Competing Risks Analysis of Democratic Durability," *Journal of Politics* 72, no. 4 (October 2010): 1129–1143.

69. Ibid., 1130.

70. Ibid., 1141.

71. Larry Diamond, "Universal Democracy?" *Policy Review* 119 (June 2003), http://www.hoover.org/publications/policyreview/3448571.html (accessed October 1, 2008).

72. Sheri E. Berman, "Modernization in Historical Perspective: The Case of Imperial Germany," *World Politics* 52 (2001): 459.

Chapter 12

1. Martin McKee, "Alcohol in Russia," *Alcohol and Alcoholism* 34, no. 6 (1999): 824–829.

2. John Moody, "Soviet Union Fighting the Battle of the Bottle," *Time magazine*, October 21, 1985, http://www.time.com/time/magazine/article/0,9171,960191,00.html (accessed March 28, 2008).

3. Arnod J. Heidenheimer, Hugh Heclo, and Carolyn Teich Adams, *Comparative Public Policy: The Politics of Social Choice in America, Europe, and Japan,* 3rd ed. (New York: St. Martin's Press, 1990), 3.

4. Ibid., 5–6.

5. Geoffrey Pridham, "The International Dimension of Democratization: Theory, Practice, and Inter-regional Comparisons," in *Building Democracy? The International Dimension of Democratization in Eastern Europe*, ed. Geoffrey

Pridham, Eric Herring, and George Sanford (New York: St. Martin's Press 1994), 7–29.

6. "Making Sense Out of Dollars 2002–2003: Trend in Government Spending by Level," March 16, 2005, Canadian Department of National Defence, http://www.admfincs.forces .gc.ca/financial_docs/Msood/2002-2003/intro_e.asp (accessed March 28, 2008).

7. James E. Anderson, *Public Policymaking: An Introduction* (Boston: Houghton Mifflin, 1990), 12.

8. Heidenheimer, Heclo, and Adams, *Comparative Public Policy,* 308–309.

9. Ibid., 323.

10. Ibid., 13.

11. Estimates for 2011 are based on 2010 figures reported in *CBO's 2011 Long-Term Budget Outlook*, Chapter 3, "The Long-Term Outlook for Mandatory Spending on Health Care," http:// www.cbo.gov/ftpdocs/122xx/doc12212/06-21-Long-Term_ Budget_Outlook.pdf (accessed July 20, 2011).

12. Heidenheimer, Heclo, and Adams, *Comparative Public Policy,* ch. 2.

13. Lowell W. Barrington, "The Making of Citizenship Policy in the Baltic States," *Georgetown Immigration Law Journal* 13, no. 2 (1999): 159–199.

14. Russell J. Dalton, *Citizen Politics: Public Opinion and Political Parties in Advanced Industrial Democracies*, 3rd ed. (New York: Chatham House Publishers, 2002), Table 6.4.

15. Peter A. Hall, "Policy Paradigms, Social Learning, and the State: The Case of Economic Policymaking in Britain," *Comparative Politics* 25, no. 3 (April 1993): 278.

16. On the issue of industrialization fostering an aging population that demands more government programs, see Harold L. Wilensky, *The Welfare State and Equality: Structural and Ideological Roots of Public Expenditures* (Berkeley: University of California Press, 1975).

17. Ibid.

18. David Cameron, "The Expansion of the Public Economy: A Comparative Analysis," *American Political Science Review* 72 (1978): 1243–1261.

19. Karl W. Deutsch, *Politics and Government* (Boston: Houghton Mifflin, 1970).

20. Anthony King, "Ideas, Institutions and the Policies of Governments: A Comparative Analysis, Part III," *British Journal of Political Science* 3, no. 4 (October 1973): 418. The text of this quotation is in italics in the original article.

21. See, for example, Wim Van Oorschot, Birgit Pfau—Effinger, and Michael Opielka, eds., *Culture and Welfare State: Values and Social Policy in Comparative Perspective* (Northampton, MA: Edward Elgar Publishing, Inc., 2008).

22. E. E. Schattschneider, *The Semi-Sovereign People* (New York: Holt, Rinehart, and Winston, 1960), 71.

23. See, for example, Giuliano Boloni, "Political Institutions, Veto Points, and the Process of Welfare State Adaptation," in *The New Politics of the Welfare State*, ed. Paul Pierson (Oxford, UK: Oxford University Press, 2001), 238–264.

24. Colin J. Bennett, "What Is Policy Convergence and What Causes It?" *British Journal of Political Science* 21, no. 2 (April 1991): 220.

25. Ibid., 218.

26. "Enforcing the Rule of Law in Iraq: Training for Judges and Legal Officials," Rule of Law Unit, Executive Office of the Secretary-General of the United Nations, http://unrol.org/ article.aspx?article_id=155 (accessed July 20, 2011).

27. "Promoting Justice and the Rule of Law in Iraq," *Footprint* (UNDP-Iraq E-Magazine), no. 7 (January 2011): 3.

28. Ibid. See, for example, the comments by Iraqi chief justice Medhat al-Mahmoud.

29. "Judicial Independence in Iraq," USIP Rule of Law Program— Strengthening the Rule of Law in Iraq, http://www.usip.org/ programs/projects/judicial-independence-in-iraq (accessed July 19, 2011).

30. "Background," ABA Rule of Law Initiative Home—Middle East and North Africa-Iraq, http://apps.americanbar.org/rol/ mena/iraq.shtml (accessed July 19, 2011).

31. "Enforcing the Rule of Law in Iraq."

32. See, for example, Andrew W. Barrett, "Gone Public: The Impact of Going Public on Presidential Legislative Success," *American Politics Research* 32, no. 3 (2004): 338–370.

33. While such policy is usually the result of satisficing, Breena Coates argues that in the case of certain policies, such as the USA Patriot Act (2001), the result may not even be one of satisficing but rather a policy that is "sufferable." Breena E. Coates, "'Sufferable' or Satisficing? Hard Policy Choices within the USA Patriot Act of 2001," *Public Administration and Management: An Interactive Journal* 7, no. 3 (2002): 211–228.

34. Roger Friendland, Frances Fox Piven, and Robert R. Alford, "Political Conflict, Urban Structure, and the Fiscal Crisis," in *Comparing Public Policies: New Concepts and Methods*, ed. Douglas E. Ashford (Thousand Oaks, CA: Sage, 1978), 216.

35. Hall, "Policy Paradigms, Social Learning, and the State," 277.

36. "Irish Influx to Thwart Conservative Election Pledge on Migration," *The Guardian*, December 30, 2010, http://www.guardian.co.uk/ world/2010/dec/30/irish-influx-conservative-migration-pledge (accessed February 4, 2011).

37. Gwyn Bevan and Ray Robinson, "The Interplay between Economic and Political Logics: Path Dependency in Health Care in England," *Journal of Health Politics, Policy and Law* 30, nos. 1–2 (February-April 2005): 53–78.

38. For an interesting discussion on this topic, see Mike Marinetto, "Governing beyond the Centre: A Critique of the Anglo-Governance School," *Political Studies* 51, no. 3 (October 2003): 592–608.

39. "Evidence Supporting Your NHS Reforms? What Evidence, Mr Lansley?," *The Guardian*, February 5, 2011, http://www .guardian.co.uk/commentisfree/2011/feb/05/lansley-use-word-evidence (accessed February 5, 2011).

40. Gosta Esping-Andersen, *The Social Foundations of Post-Industrial Economies* (Oxford, UK: Oxford University Press, 2000); Philip Manow and Eric Seils, "Adjusting Badly: The German Welfare State, Structural Change, and the Open Economy," in *Diverse Responses to Common Challenges*, vol. 2, *Welfare and Work in the Open Economy*, ed. Fritz W. Scharpf and Vivien A. Schmidt (Oxford, UK: Oxford University Press, 2000), 264–307.

41. Achim Kemmerling and Liver Bruttel, "'New Politics' in German Labour Market Policy? The Implications of the Recent Hartz Reforms for the German Welfare State," *West European Politics* 29, no. 1 (January 2006): 90–112; Bertrand Benoit, "A Temporary Solution? Germany's Labour Market Develops a Second Tier," *Financial Times*, October 27, 2006.

42. Esping-Andersen, *The Social Foundations of Post-Industrial Economies*; Gerrit Wiesmann, "Germany's Career Women Look for a Lifeline from First Female Chancellor," *Financial Times*, October 13, 2005; Wolfgang Streeck, *Endgame? The*

Fiscal Crisis of the German State, MPiFG Discussion Paper 07/7 (Cologne: Max Planck Institute for the Study of Societies, 2007).

43. P. Sainath, *Everybody Loves a Good Drought, Stories from India's Poorest Districts* (Delhi: Penguin Books India Ltd., 1996).

44. M. V. V. Ramana, *Inter State River Water Disputes in India* (Madras: Orient Longman Ltd., 1992); S. N. Sadasivan, *River Disputes in India: Kerala Rivers under Siege* (New Delhi: Mittal Publications, 2003).

45. Thomas Blom Hansen, *The Saffron Wave: Democracy and Hindu Nationalism in Modern India* (Princeton, NJ: Princeton University Press, 1999).

46. Ashghar Ali Engineer, ed., *Mandal Commission Controversy* (Delhi: Ajanta Publications, 1991); Anirudh Prasad, *Reservation Policy and Practice in India: A Means to an End* (New Delhi: Deep and Deep Publications, 1991); Sagar Preet Hooda, *Contesting Reservations* (Jaipur: Rawat Publications, 2001); A. K. Lal, *Protective Discrimination: Ideology and Praxis* (New Delhi: Concept Publications, 2002).

47. William Booth and Steve Fainaru, "New Strategy Urged in Mexico: Calderón's U.S.-Backed War against Drug Cartels Losing Political Support," *Washington Post*, July 28, 2009, http://www.washingtonpost.com/wp-dyn/content/story/2009/07/27/ST2009072703105.html?sid=ST2009072703105 (accessed July 11, 2011).

48. Germán Álvarez-Mendolia, "Lifelong Learning Policies in Mexico: Context, Challenges, and Comparisons," *Compare: A Journal of Comparative Education* 36, no. 3 (September 2006): 379–399.

49. Miguel Niño-Zarazúa, "Mexico's Progresa-Oportunidades and the Emergence of Social Assistance in Latin America," Brooks World Poverty Institute, BWPI Working Paper, no. 142 (March 2010): 10, http://www.bwpi.manchester.ac.uk/resources/Working-Papers/bwpi-wp-14211.pdf (accessed July 28, 2011).

50. Harvey V. Fineberg, "Health Reform in Mexico: A Work in Progress," *Lancet* 368 (November 18, 2006): 1755–1756. See also Felicia Marie Knaul, Héctor Arreola-Ornelas, Oscar Méndez-Carniado, et al., "Evidence Is Good for Your Health System: Policy Reform to Remedy Catastrophic and Impoverishing Health Spending in Mexico," *Lancet* 368 (November 18, 2006): 1828–1841.

51. Elisabeth Malkin, "Mexico's Universal Health Care Is Work in Progress," *New York Times*, January 29, 2011, http://www.nytimes.com/2011/01/30/world/americas/30mexico.html?_r=1 (accessed July 28, 2011).

52. Fineberg, "Health Reform in Mexico."

53. John Egan, "Mexico's Welfare Revolution," BBC News, October 15, 1999, http://news.bbc.co.uk/2/hi/programmes/crossing_continents/412802.stm (accessed July 10, 2011).

54. "Progress against Poverty: Sustaining Mexico's Progresa-Oportunidades Program," Brookings Institution Press, http://www.brookings.edu/press/Books/2006/progressagainstpoverty.aspx (accessed July 11, 2011).

55. Bradley Brooks, "Big Task Ahead for Brazil New Leader Rousseff," *USA Today*, November 1, 2011, http://www.usatoday.com/news/topstories/2010-10-31-1021272528_x.htm (accessed February 8, 2011).

56. Ike Oguine, "War on Corruption," *New Internationalist*, December 2005, 29.

57. Gilbert da Costa, "Top Nigerian Officials Fired for Alleged Graft," VOA News, March 26, 2008, http://www.voanews.com/english/2008-03-26-voa36.cfm?rss=africa (accessed March 29, 2008).

58. "The Lady Was for Moving," *Economist*, July 6, 2006.

59. Azadeh Moaveni, "Iran's Hard Line Begins at Home," *Time magazine*, September 4, 2006, http://www.time.com/time/magazine/article/0,9171,1376212,00.html (accessed October 5, 2008).

60. Ladane Nasseri, "Iran Arrests Four Kurds with British Links on Charges Related to Terrorism," Bloomberg, http://www.bloomberg.com/news/2010-11-04/iran-says-it-has-arrested-four-kurdish-terrorists-with-links-to-britain.html, November 4, 2010 (accessed February 8, 2011).

61. Francesco Stolfi, "Testing Structuralist and Interpretative Explanations of Policy Change: The Case of Italy's Budget Reform," *Governance: An International Journal of Policy, Administration, and Institutions* 23, no. 1 (January 2010) 109–132.

62. Ibid., 109.

63. Alexander Wendt, "The Agent-Structure Problem in International Relations Theory," *International Organization* 41, no. 3 (1987), 340, cited in Ibid., 109.

64. H. L. Mencken, *Mencken on Religion*, ed. S. T. Joshi, (Amherst, NY: Prometheus Books, 2002).

General Index

Country Index

identity divisions in, xxxvi
interest groups in, xxxvi
judiciary in, xxxvi
leadership in, xxxvi
legislature in, xxxvi
political culture in, xxxvi
political parties in, xxxvi
political system in, xxxvi
South Korea, 35, 39, 208
Spain, 135, 324, 331, 335
Sudan, 108
Syria, 12, 333

Tunisia, 319, 334
Turkey, 12, 125–126

Ukraine, 16, 108, 136
United Kingdom, xxv, 58, 91, 123, 155,
    191, 223, 253, 285, 314, 346, 378
  bureaucracy in, 210
  class in, 40–41
  constitution of, xxv, 141
  economic development in, xxv, 41
  elections in, 271
  executive in, xxv, 179
  Falkland Islands, territorial dispute
    between Argentina and, 297–298

globalization in, 41–42
government role in, 41
identity divisions in, xxv, 111
ideology in, 75
interest groups in, xxv, 240–241
judiciary in, xxv, 209–210
leadership in, xxv, 297–298
legislature in, xxv, 177–178
levels of government in, 141–142
military in, 210–211
Northern Ireland, as region of, 74,
    111, 142, 211
policy debates in, 369–371
political culture in, xxv, 73
political participation in, 240
political parties in, xxv, 270–271
political system in, xxv, 140–141
programmatic *vs.* clientelistic linkage
    in, 240
regime transitions in, 336
Scotland, as region of, 74, 139, 142
  socialization in, 75
  Wales, as region of, 74, 111, 142
United States
  and accommodation, 109
  bureaucracy in, 201–203
  and capitalism, 37

constitution of, 137
economic development in, 31, 34
elections in, 266–267
executive in, 175–176
invasion of Iraq, 10, 329, 330
interest groups in, 235, 237
judiciary in, 197–199
legislature in, 173–175
levels of government in, 138–139
and NAFTA, 47–48
model of democracy, 131–133
national identity, 12
party identification, 20
political culture in, 64, 68–69,
    71–72
political parties in, 262–263
presidential system, 166–168
and public policy, 354, 356, 358–363,
    368
and socialism, 37–38
and sovereignty, 9
state, definition of, 7

Venezuela, 82, 332–333, 335
Vietnam, 34

Yugoslavia, 10, 109–110